January 2012-

First and foremost, thank you for choosing Berkeley Review to help you on your path to becoming a physician. We take your trust seriously and it is our deepest hope that we can make your MCAT experience a little easier. To do this, we have created books that are designed with both the exam and the typical student in mind. The books may seem long at first glance, but that's because there are so many questions and explanations. We write our books for the student who starts around a 7 to 9 and plans to grow into an 11 or 12. Before starting this book, please take time to assess your goals, needs, and time available for studying. That will help you to get the most out of this book and your preparation.

It's probably best to start by addressing the elephant in the room. On average, organic chemistry makes up a quarter to a third of the biological sciences section of the MCAT. Just to toss an arbitrary number out there, let's say you get sixteen organic chemistry questions on your actual MCAT. That leaves 36 questions for biology. At first thought you may think organic chemistry is not that important. However, because of the nature of students taking the MCAT and their inherent strength in biologically related material, organic chemistry plays a bigger role in distributing the curve than pure statistics would indicate. Don't underestimate the impact of organic chemistry on your Biological Sciences score.

Our goal is to provide you with a resource that will help you to get all of your organic chemistry questions correct on your exam as well as provide insights that will help you with the other sciences. Of all the required classes for medical school, organic chemistry demands the greatest amount of conceptual reasoning rather than mathematics or memorization. If you review organic chemistry in the right mindset, then you'll be developing conceptual logic that will benefit you on all sections of the MCAT.

To achieve this, our book offers a balance between fundamental definitions, general information, and typical questions. Roughly two-thirds of our book will work towards that target. The other third will combine organic chemistry with other sciences to help you review that material as well. All the topics from AAMC's official list for organic chemistry are covered, and nothing else. That is a substantial amount of information, which will make these books look daunting at first appearance. But much of what we do is focus on questions and their detailed explanations. That is where you will do most of your learning.

This book is the latest edition of a project that started in 1989. It has undergone six previous revisions. This latest revision introduces additional passages, consolidates similar subjects, and emphasizes more biological examples. This book is the work of a primary author who has taught MCAT preparation for over 11,000 hours to students just like you. As is the case with all of our books, we write the book in the voice a teacher would use to explain the subject matter one-on-one to a student. Only a teacher with that much experience can foresee where students generally have trouble in their review.

For instance, enantiomers and diastereomers are defined in this book in a simple fashion that you won't find anywhere else but Berkeley Review materials. Our definition makes distinguishing how two stereoisomers relate to one another easier than you ever imagined and perfect for quickly solving questions. If you had trouble recalling sugars and linkages before, that will never be an issue again. Topics such as NMR might have caused stress in the past, but we address it from a multiple-choice exam perspective that makes it surprisingly simple. Basically we teach you how to pick a *best answer* based on simple logic built from basic information.

To get the most out of these books, you should do every practice question and thoroughly review the answers to see if you could solve the question more efficiently next time you see something like it. After taking the chapter exams, quiz yourself on the topics you just studied and how they can be mixed into other subjects. Repeat any questions you miss until you get them right, and then read and review the answer explanations.

Each chapter has an average of 26 multiple-choice questions intertwined in the text followed by a 25-question review exam, a 52-question practice test, and a 5-passage final phase review. Take as much time as you need on the text questions and the 25-question review exams and 5-passage summaries, but do your best to finish the 52-question practice tests within the 70-minute limit. Developing speed is critical in your preparation.

We wish you the best of luck and sincerely hope you enjoy your preparation experience. Once again, thank you for sharing this stage of your pathway to medical school with us.

Sincerely and with great respect,

The Berkeley Review

Table of Contents

3. Stereochemistry

4. Hydrocarbons

Molecular Structure

Organic Chemistry Chapter 1

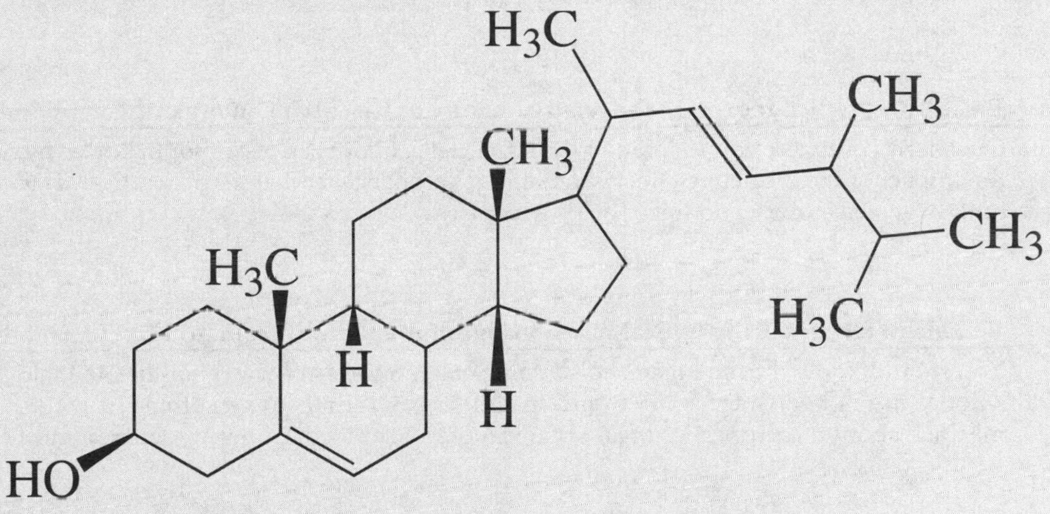

Ergosterol (Provitamin D$_2$)

by Todd Bennett of

the Berkeley Review

Molecular Structure

Key objectives of this section

Be able to translate between molecular starcture, IUPAC name, and Common name.

While it is unlikely that the test writers will ask you to directly translate a name into a structure or vise versa on a question, questions and passages will present organic molecules to you in different ways and you'll need to translate between name and structure to answer their question.

Be able to draw resonance structures and determine how they impact chemical reactivity.

Questions could involve determining the relative strength of reactants based of the electron withdrawing or electron donating aspects of the substituent through resonance. Questions could also emphasize the impact of resonance on structural stability or acidity and basicity.

Be able to predict or explain the relative acidity or basicity of an organic compound.

Questions could ask you to identify the strongest acid or base out of four choices by comparing the impact of the inductive effect, aromaticity, resonance, and atom properties. This extends to both Brønsted-Lowry and Lewis acids and bases.

Be able to recognize the typical functional groups and know common facts about them.

You should know that small alcohols and primary amines are water soluble, that aldehydes and ketones are not so water soluble, and that ethers and lipids are insoluble in water. Questions may ask about the properties of an organic molecule or its behavior under biological conditions.

Be able to recall basic facts about certain molecules and predict their behavior in solution.

You need to know that the pK_a for a carboxylic acid falls between roughly 3 and 5, and that protonated amines, phenols, and thiols have a pK_a between roughly 9 and 11. Questions may ask about separating various compounds using acid-base extraction with water of varying pH.

Be able to predict the relative melting points and boiling points of organic molecules.

Questions may ask you to explain the melting points of hydrocarbons or the cell fluidity dependence on the alkyl group in a lipid membrane. Questions may ask about the boiling points of compounds or the impact of intermolecular forces such as hydrogen bonding on volatility.

Molecular Structure

The perfect place to start any review of organic chemistry is the basics of molecular structure, which traditionally include bonding, hybridization, and electronic distribution. We shall consider a chemical bond to be the result of atomic orbitals overlapping to form molecular orbitals. We shall consider all bonds involving carbon to be covalent in nature. A covalent bond is thought to involve the sharing of electrons between two adjacent nuclei. According to the rules of electrostatics, the region between two nuclei offers a highly favorable environment for electrons, where they can be shared by neighboring atoms.

However, there are several other factors to consider in bonding. If bonding were purely a matter of electrostatics, then all of the electrons would be found between two neighboring nuclei, not just the bonding electrons. The sharing of electrons may be either symmetric (when the two atoms of the bond are of equal electronegativity) or asymmetric (when the two atoms of the bond are of unequal electronegativity). Sharing of electrons occurs when the atoms of a bond lack a complete valence electron shell. By sharing electrons, each atom moves closer to completing its shell. This is the driving force behind the formation of stable covalent bonds.

Having looked briefly at electron distribution, we can introduce the idea of electronic orbitals, which are three-dimensional probability maps of the location of an electron. They represent the region in space where an electron is found 95% of the time. We shall consider the orbitals and the overlap of orbitals to describe the electronic distribution within a molecule. Once one has established a foundation in bonding, the classification of molecules can be made based on similarities in their bonding of particular atoms, known as *functional groups*. Each functional group shall be considered in terms of its unique electron distribution, hybridization, and nomenclature. Nomenclature, both that of the International Union of Pure and Applied Chemists (IUPAC) and more general methods describing the substitution of carbon within a functional group, shall be used to describe a particular organic molecule. The review of nomenclature is continuous throughout all sections of this book.

Then, we shall consider the factors that affect the distribution of electron density within a molecule, including resonance, the inductive effect, steric hindrance, aromaticity, and hybridization. The distribution of electron density can be used to explain and predict chemical behavior. The simplest rule of reactivity in organic chemistry is that regions of high electron density act as nucleophiles by sharing their electron cloud with regions of low electron density, which act as electrophiles. If you can correctly label a molecule in terms of the region that carries a partially negative charge (the electron-rich environment) and the region that carries a partially positive charge (the electron-poor environment), you can understand chemical reactions better.

And so begins your review of organic chemistry. Fortunately, much of organic chemistry is taught from the perspective of logic, which makes preparing for organic chemistry on the MCAT easier. In organic chemistry courses you are required to process information and reach conclusions based on observations, which is also required on the MCAT. Reviewing and relearning this material will help you develop critical thinking skills, which will carry over into your review for other portions of the exam. Despite what you may have perceived was a girth of information when you initially studied organic chemistry, you don't need to review that much material to prepare successfully for the MCAT.

Nomenclature

IUPAC Nomenclature (Systematic Proper Naming)

IUPAC Nomenclature is an internationally used system for naming molecules. Molecular names reflect the structural features (functional groups) and the number of carbons in a molecule. In IUPAC nomenclature, the name is based on the carbon chain length and the functional groups. The suffix indicates which primary functional group is attached to the carbon chain. Table 1-1 lists prefixes for carbon chains between one and twelve carbons in length. Table 1-2 lists the suffices for various functional groups. Be aware that "R" stands for any generic alkyl group. When R is used, it indicates that the carbon chain size is irrelevant to the reaction. Table 1-3 summarizes the nomenclature process by listing several four-carbon compounds.

Carbons	Prefix		Carbons	Prefix		Carbons	Prefix
1	meth-		5	pent-		9	non-
2	eth-		6	hex-		10	dec-
3	prop-		7	hept-		11	undec-
4	but-		8	oct-		12	dodec-

Table 1-1

Functionality	Compound Name	Bonding
R-CH$_3$	Alkane	C—C & C—H
R-O-R	Ether	C—O—C
R-CO-H	Aldehyde	$\overset{\displaystyle O}{\overset{\|}{C}}$—$\overset{\displaystyle O}{\overset{\|}{C}}$—H
R-CH$_2$-OH	Alcohol	C—O—H
R-CO-R	Ketone	$\overset{\displaystyle O}{\overset{\|}{C}}$—$\overset{\displaystyle O}{\overset{\|}{C}}$—C
R-CO-OH	Carboxylic acid	$\overset{\displaystyle O}{\overset{\|}{C}}$—$\overset{\displaystyle O}{\overset{\|}{C}}$—OH

Table 1-2

Formula	IUPAC Name	Structural Class
H$_3$CCH$_2$CH$_2$CH$_3$	Butane	Alkane
H$_3$CCH=CHCH$_3$	Butene	Alkene
H$_3$CCH$_2$CH$_2$CHO	Butanal	Aldehyde
H$_3$CCH$_2$COCH$_3$	Butanone	Ketone
H$_3$CCH$_2$CH$_2$CH$_2$OH	Butanol	Alcohol
H$_3$CCH$_2$CH(OH)CH$_3$	2-butanol	Alcohol
H$_3$CCH$_2$CH$_2$CH$_2$NH$_2$	Butanamine	Amine
H$_3$CCH$_2$CH$_2$CO$_2$H	Butanoic acid	Carboxylic acid

Table 1-3

Figure 1-1 shows examples of IUPAC nomenclature for four organic compounds with variable functional groups:

①

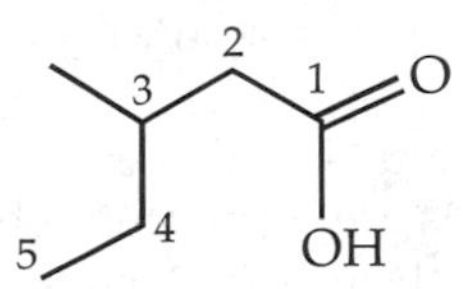

3-methylpentanoic acid
Longest chain: 5 carbons
Carboxylic acid group
Methyl substituent at C-3

②

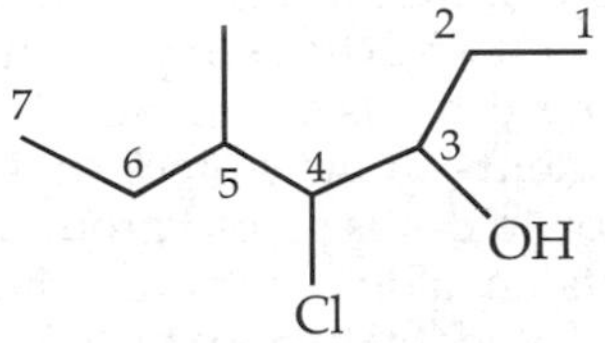

4-chloro-5-methyl-3-heptanol
Longest chain: 7 carbons
Alcohol group at C-3
Chloro substituent at C-4
Methyl substituent at C-5

③

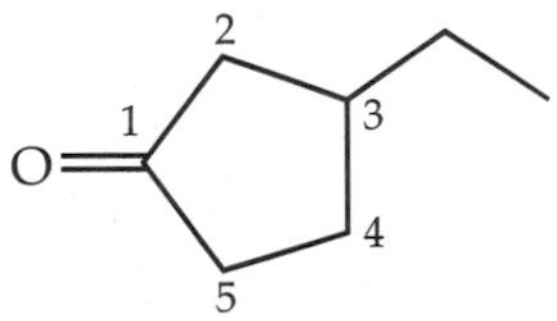

3-ethylcyclopentanone
Ring of 5 carbons
Ketone group
Ethyl substituent at C-3

④

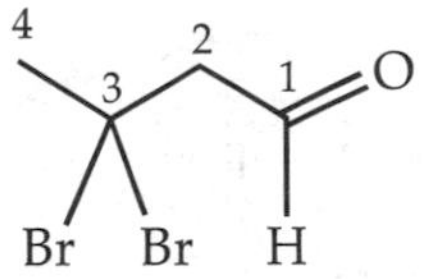

3,3-dibromobutanal
Longest chain: 4 carbons
Aldehyde group
2 Bromo substituents at C-3

Figure 1-1

General Nomenclature (Common Naming Based on Substitution)

In addition to the IUPAC naming system, there is a less rigorous method of naming compounds by functional group and carbon type (based on carbon substitution). Carbon type refers to the number of carbon atoms attached to the central carbon atom (carbon atom of interest). A carbon with one other carbon attached is referred to as a primary (1°) carbon. A carbon with two other carbons attached is secondary (2°). A carbon with three other carbons attached is tertiary (3°). Figure 1-2 shows some sample structures.

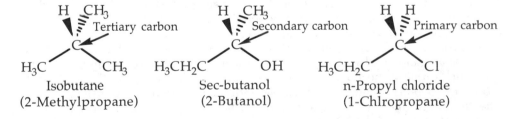

Isobutane
(2-Methylpropane)

Sec-butanol
(2-Butanol)

n-Propyl chloride
(1-Chloropropane)

Figure 1-2

Nomenclature is an area of organic chemistry best learned through practice and experience. We will deal with nomenclature throughout the course, as we introduce each new functional group. Understanding nomenclature is especially important in MCAT passages where names rather than structures are given. Be sure to know the Greek prefixes for carbon chain lengths up to twelve carbons.

Bonding and Molecular Orbitals

Lewis Dot Structures (Two-Dimensional Depiction of Molecules)
Lewis dot structures represent the electrons in the valence shell of an atom or bonding orbitals of a molecule. Typically, we consider the Lewis dot structures of elements in the s-block and p-block of the periodic table. For every valence electron, a dot is placed around the atom. Single bonds are represented by a pair of dots in a line between the atoms, or by a line itself. A double bond is represented by a double line (implying that four electrons are being shared.) Likewise, a triple bond is represented by a triple line (implying that six electrons are being shared.) Lewis dot structures are familiar to most chemistry students, so recognize the exceptions to the rules, as they make good test questions.

Example 1.1
What is the Lewis dot structure for H_2BF?

A.

$$:H—\overset{..}{B}—\overset{..}{\underset{..}{F}}:$$
$$|$$
$$\underset{..}{H}$$

B.

$$:H—B—\overset{..}{\underset{..}{F}}:$$
$$|$$
$$\underset{..}{H}$$

C.

$$H—\overset{..}{B}—\overset{..}{\underset{..}{F}}:$$
$$|$$
$$H$$

D.

$$H—B—\overset{..}{\underset{..}{F}}:$$
$$|$$
$$H$$

Solution
Boron has only three valence electrons, hence it can make only three bonds. There is no lone pair on the boron atom, eliminating choices A and C. Hydrogen has only one electron, which is in the bond to boron, so there is never a lone pair on a bonded hydrogen. This eliminates choices A (already eliminated) and B. Fluorine has a completed octet, so it makes one bond and has three lone pairs, as depicted in choice **D**, the best answer.

Bonding Model
Bonding is defined as the sharing of electron pairs between two atoms in either an equal or unequal manner. As a general rule, a bond is the sharing of two electrons between two adjacent nuclei. The region between two nuclei is the most probable location for an electron. In most cases, with the exception of *ligand bonds* (known also as *Lewis acid-base bonds*), one electron from each atom goes into forming the bond. When electrons are shared evenly between two atoms, the bond is said to be a *covalent bond*. When electrons are transferred from one atom to another, the bond is said to be an *ionic bond*. The difference between a covalent and ionic bond is measured in the degree of sharing of the electrons, which can be determined from the dipole. The more evenly that the electrons are shared, the less the polarity of the bond. The relative electronegativity of two atoms can be determined by measuring the dipole of the bond they form. When the difference in electronegativity between two atoms is less than 1.5, then the bond is said to be covalent. When the difference in electronegativity between two atoms is greater than 2.0, then the bond is said to be ionic. When the difference in electronegativity between two atoms is greater than 1.5 but less than 2.0, then the bond is said to be polar-covalent (or partially ionic).

Example 1.2
Which of the following bonds is MOST likely to be ionic?

A. C—O
B. N—F
C. Li—H
D. Li—F

Solution
A bond is ionic when the difference in electronegativity between the two atoms exceeds 2.0. This means that the bond that is most likely to be ionic is the one between the two atoms with the greatest difference in electronegativity. Lithium is a metal and fluorine is a halide, so they exhibit the greatest electronegativity difference of the choices listed. The best answer is therefore choice **D**.

Covalent Bonds
Bonds can be classified in one of three ways: ionic, polar-covalent, and covalent. A covalent bond occurs when electrons are shared between two atoms having little to no difference in electronegativity. As the difference in electronegativity decreases, the covalent nature of the bond increases. There are two types of covalent bonds: *sigma* bonds (σ), defined as having electron density shared between the nuclei of the two atoms; and *pi* bonds (π), defined as having no electron density shared between the nuclei of the two atoms, but instead only above and below the internuclear region. Sigma bonds are made from many types of atomic orbitals (including hybrids), while pi bonds are made exclusively of parallel *p*-orbitals. In almost all cases, the sigma bond is stronger than the pi bond, with molecular fluorine (F_2) being a notable exception. Figure 1-3 shows a generic sigma bond. You may notice that within a sigma bond, only about eighty to ninety percent of the electron density lies between the nuclei, not all of it.

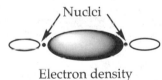

Electron density

Figure 1-3

Example 1.3
Which drawing depicts the electron density associated with a carbon-carbon sigma bond?

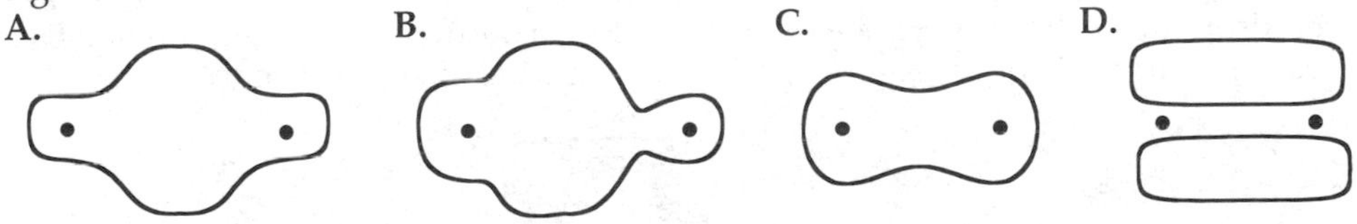

A.    B.    C.   D.

Solution
A sigma bond has its electron density between the two nuclei, which eliminates choice D. The two atoms in the bond are identical, so the electron density should be symmetrically displaced between the two nuclei. This eliminates choice B. Most of electron density is between the nuclei, so choice **A** is a better answer than choice C. These drawings are ugly, so focus on the concept, not the pictures.

Figure 1-4 shows a generic π-bond. Within a π-bond, there is no electron density between the two nuclei. The electron density in a π-bond results from electrons being shared between the adjacent lobes of parallel p-orbitals.

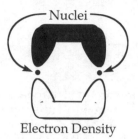

Figure 1-4

In organic chemistry, covalent bonds are viewed in great detail, taking into account hybridization and overlap. In alkanes, carbons have sp^3-hybridization and all of the bonds are sigma bonds. In alkanes, there are two types of bonds: C— H ($\sigma_{sp^3\text{-}s}$ bonds) and C— C ($\sigma_{sp^3\text{-}sp^3}$ bonds). In alkenes, there are sigma and pi bonds present. The π-bond consists of p-orbitals side by side, and its carbons have sp^2-hybridization. The C=C bond is made up of a $\sigma_{sp^2\text{-}sp^2}$ bond and a $\pi_{2p\text{-}2p}$ bond. Bond length varies with the size of the orbitals in the bond. For instance, a sigma bond composed of an sp^2-hybridized carbon and an sp^3-hybridized carbon is shorter than a sigma bond comprised of two sp^3-hybridized carbons. Hydrogens use s-orbitals to form bonds. Figure 1-5 shows three sigma bonds with their relative bond lengths. The longer bond is associated with the larger orbitals (bond radii: $d_z > d_y > d_x$).

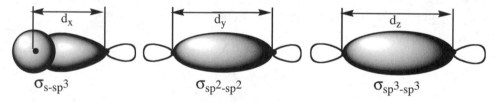

Figure 1-5

Figure 1-5 confirms that most of the electron density lies between the two nuclei in sigma bonds, no matter what the orbitals are from which the sigma bond originates. In pi bonds, electron density does not lie between the two nuclei. The length of a bond is defined as the distance between the nuclei of the two atoms making the bond. Figure 1-6 shows an example of a π-bond between two $2p_z$-orbitals, which is typical for nearly all π-bonds encountered in organic chemistry, because carbon, nitrogen, and oxygen have $2p$-orbitals in their valence shells.

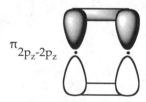

Figure 1-6

Pi bonds are found as the second bond present in double bonds and the second and third bonds present in triple bonds. The first type of bond to form between atoms is usually the sigma bond. Once a sigma bond exists between two carbon atoms, then pi bonds can form between the atoms. Fluorine gas is an exception to the "sigma bond first" rule. Molecular fluorine (F_2) has only one π-bond, with no σ-bond present. This is attributed to the small size of fluorine and the inter-nuclear repulsion associated with a typical single bond. This is why the bond dissociation energy of F_2 is less than the bond dissociation energy of Cl_2, even though chlorine is below fluorine in the periodic table.

Molecular Orbitals

Molecular orbital is a fancy way of describing a bond or anti-bond that exists between two atoms. An anti-bond is a molecular orbital that results in bond-breaking when coupled with a bonding orbital. It is important to recognize the shape and location of electron density in molecular orbitals. Figure 1-7 shows the common bonding and anti-bonding orbitals associated with organic chemistry.

Sigma bonding molecular orbital

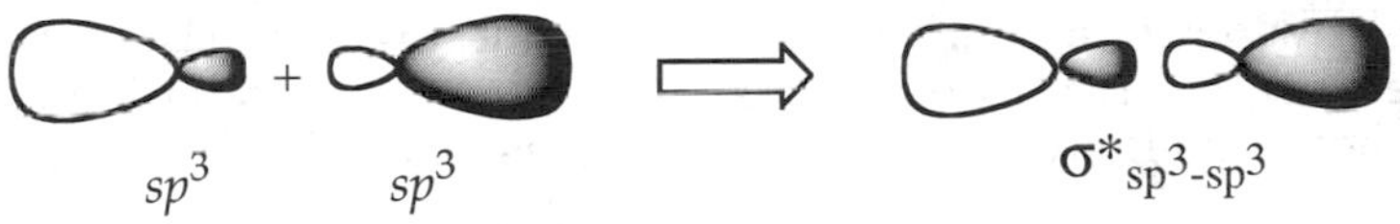

Sigma anti-bonding molecular orbital

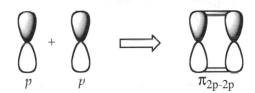

Pi bonding molecular orbital

Pi anti-bonding molecular orbital

Figure 1-7

The shading of the lobes in each orbital represents the direction of spin for the electron. In order for electron density to overlap, the electrons must have the same spin. This is analogous to driving on the freeway. If you join a freeway in the same direction as traffic is flowing, you can easily blend into traffic. This is a favorable interaction. If you join a freeway in the opposite direction as traffic is flowing, you cannot easily blend into traffic. This is an unfavorable interaction.

Molecular Bonds

Of greater interest than the sigma-bonds and pi-bonds are the single, double, and triple bonds present between atoms. Single, double, and triple bond nature is discussed more so than the sigma and pi nature of bonds. In organic molecules, there are only single, double, and triple bonds. Between like atoms, the descending order of relative strengths of bonds is triple bond > double bond > single bond. Another rule to consider is that for bonds between like atoms, the longer the bond, the less the electron density overlaps between nuclei, and thus the weaker the bond. This is summarized as: *longer bonds are weaker bonds.*

Single Bonds: Single bonds are composed of only one sigma bond between the two atoms. Single bonds are longer than double and triple bonds between two atoms, even though fewer electrons are present. Ethane has sigma bonds only and is shown in Figure 1-8 in both stick figures and with the relevant orbitals.

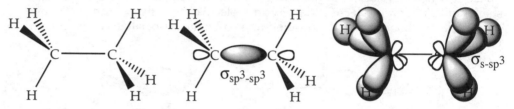

Figure 1-8

Double Bonds: Double bonds are composed of one sigma bond and one pi bond between two adjacent atoms. Ethene (C_2H_4) has four sigma bonds between carbon and hydrogen, a sigma bond between the two carbons, and a pi bond present between the two carbons to complete the carbon-carbon double bond. Ethene is shown in Figure 1-9 in both stick figures and with the relevant orbitals.

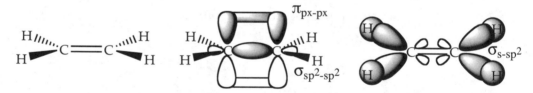

Figure 1-9

Triple Bonds: Triple bonds are composed of a sigma bond and two pi bonds between two adjacent atoms. Triple bonds are shorter than either single or double bonds. Ethyne (C_2H_2) has two sigma bonds between carbon and hydrogen, a sigma bond between the two carbons, and two pi bonds between the two carbons to complete the carbon-carbon triple bond. Ethyne is shown in Figure 1-10 in both stick figures and with the relevant orbitals.

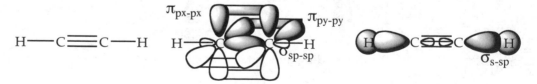

Figure 1-10

Example 1.4
What is the relative bond strength of carbon-carbon bonds in the molecule shown below?

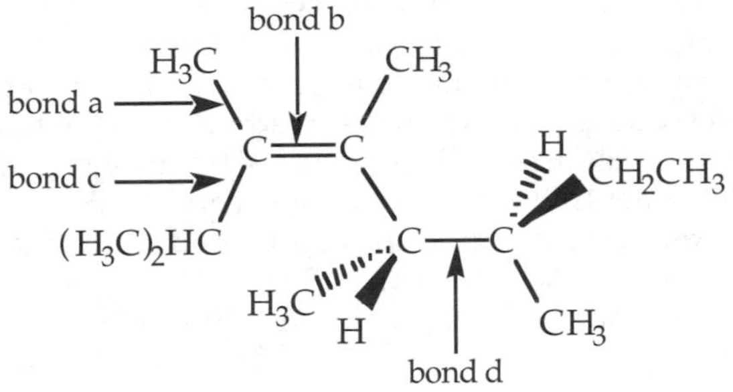

A. Bond a > Bond b > Bond c > Bond d
B. Bond b > Bond a > Bond c > Bond d
C. Bond d > Bond a > Bond c > Bond b
D. Bond b > Bond c > Bond a > Bond d

Solution
There strongest C-C bond is a double bond, bond b, so choices A and C are eliminated. Bond d is the weakest, because it is between two sp^3-hybridized carbons. Bond a is stronger than bond c, despite both sharing an sp^2-hybridized and an sp^3-hybridized carbon, because bond c contains the more highly substituted carbon. Choice **B** is the best answer.

Molecular Structures
We shall continue from the fundamental concept that a valence electron can be shared between two nuclei rather than being isolated to just one nucleus, because the attractive force of two positive sites is greater than the attractive force of one. This is the basic, perhaps oversimplified, perspective of a chemical bond. The sharing of electrons is what characterizes a covalent bond. One of the first rules of organic chemistry that you must understand is the octet rule. It is valid for carbon, nitrogen, and oxygen atoms. To understand organic chemistry, it is important that you recall VSEPR theory, which applies to bonding (in particular, to the subgroups of covalent bonding like single, double, and triple bonds and their component σ-bonds and π-bonds). Table 1-4 shows the skeletal structures of molecules that contain carbon, nitrogen, oxygen, and hydrogen.

Atom	Valence Electrons	To Complete Shell	Number of Bonds in Neutral Compounds		
Carbon (C)	4 $\cdot\ddot{C}\cdot$	4 e⁻ needed	4 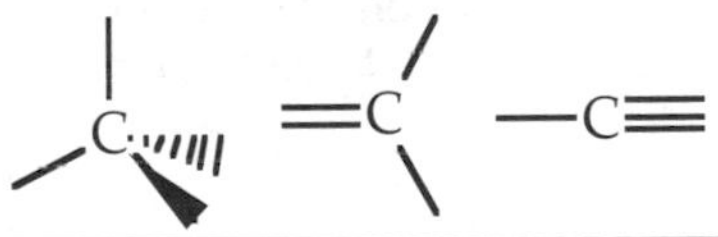		
Nitrogen (N)	5 $\cdot\ddot{N}\cdot$	3 e⁻ needed	3 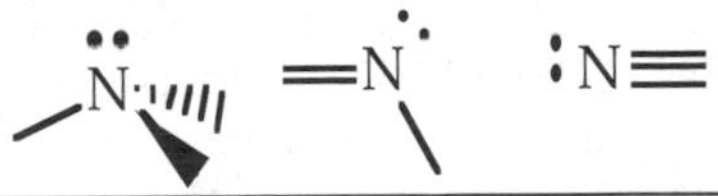		
Oxygen (O)	6 $\cdot\ddot{O}\cdot$	2 e⁻ needed	2 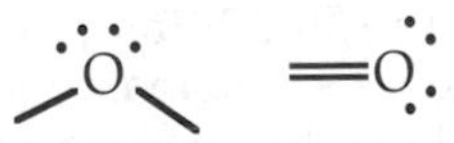		
Hydrogen (H)	1 H·	1 e⁻ needed	1 H —		

Table 1-4

Octet Rule and the HONC Shortcut:

Every molecular structure should have atoms that obey the octet rule (eight valence electrons for C, N, and O). The numbers of electrons needed to complete the shell in the Table 1-4 are derived from the electrons needed to obey the octet rule. All neutral structures have atomic arrangements as described in Table 1.4. To complete the octet valance shell, carbon requires four electron pairs in the form of bonds, nitrogen requires one lone pair in addition to the three bonds it makes, and oxygen requires two lone pairs in addition to the two bonds it makes. You must be able to recognize valid structures by applying the bonding rules (HONC-1234). In a neutral compound, **h**ydrogen makes *one* bond, **o**xygen makes *two* bonds, **n**itrogen makes *three* bonds, and **c**arbon makes *four* bonds. Neutral structures always obey this rule. Figure 1-11 shows examples of valid and invalid structures and a brief description of the bonding to the component atoms.

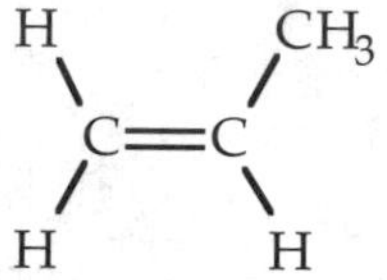

All carbons have 4 bonds.
All hydrogens have 1 bond.

Good Structure

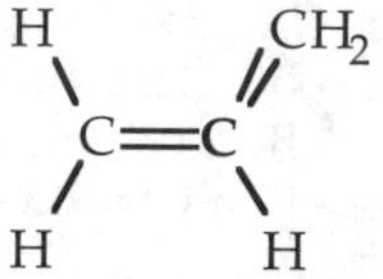

Most carbons have 4 bonds,
but one carbon has 5 bonds.
All hydrogens have 1 bond.
Bad Structure

$H_3C—C≡C—CH_2CH_2CH_3$

All carbons have 4 bonds.
All hydrogens have 1 bond.

Good Structure

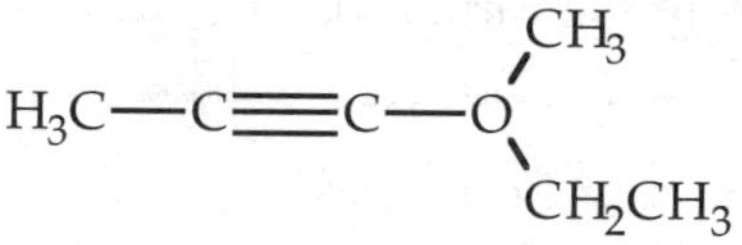

All carbons have 4 bonds.
All hydrogens have 1 bond,
but oxygen has 3 bonds.
Bad Structure

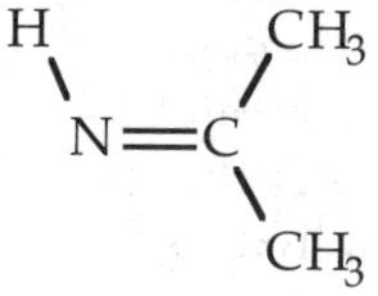

All carbons have 4 bonds.
All hydrogens have 1 bond.
Nitrogen has 3 bonds.
Good Structure

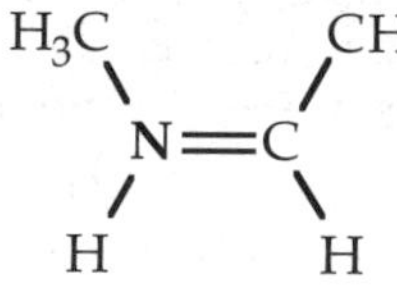

All carbons have 4 bonds.
All hydrogens have 1 bond,
but nitrogen has 4 bonds.
Bad Structure

Figure 1-11

You can validate molecular structures by seeing whether they satisfy bonding rules (HONC-1234) and conventions with regard to the number of bonds and lone pairs. If a structure does not satisfy the rules, then there must be a charge present. Generally, having too many bonds in a molecule results in a cation and too few bonds results in an anion, except with carbon. For instance, if oxygen makes three bonds and has one lone pair, it carries a positive charge. When nitrogen makes two bonds and has two lone pairs, it carries a negative charge. When carbon makes three bonds, the charge depends on the presence or absence of a lone pair (presence yields an anion, while absence yields a cation).

Charged Structures

Formal charges (charged sites on a molecule) occur when there is an excess, or shortage of electrons on an atom. For instance, an oxygen atom typically has six valence electrons and wishes to have eight. This means that oxygen makes two bonds to complete its valence shell (and thus satisfy the octet rule). However, if an oxygen atom had only five valence electrons, it would be short one electron from its original six and would consequently carry a positive charge. Having only five valence electrons, the positively charged oxygen would need to make three bonds (one more than its standard two) to complete its octet. We can conclude that oxygen with three bonds carries a positive charge. Table 1-5 shows some common organic ions to commit to memory:

Number of Bonds to **Neutral** Atom	Number of Bonds to **Cationic** Atom	Number of Bonds to **Anionic** Atom
Carbon (C) 4 $\cdot\overset{\cdot}{C}\cdot$	3 $\diagup\!\!\overset{\mid}{C^+}\!\!\diagdown$ $=C^+-$	3 $\overset{\cdot\cdot}{C}$ $=\overset{\cdot\cdot}{C}\diagdown$ $\equiv C:$
Nitrogen (N) 3 $\cdot\overset{\cdot\cdot}{\underset{\cdot}{N}}\cdot$	4 $\diagup\!\!\overset{\mid}{N^+}\!\!\diagdown$ $=N^+\diagdown$ $-N^+\equiv$	2 $\diagup\!\!\overset{\cdot\cdot}{N}\!\!\diagdown$ $=\overset{\cdot\cdot}{N}:$
Oxygen (O) 2 $\cdot\overset{\cdot\cdot}{\underset{\cdot\cdot}{O}}\cdot$	3 $\diagup\!\!\overset{\cdot\cdot}{O^+}\!\!\diagdown$ $=\overset{\cdot\cdot}{O^+}\diagdown$ $:O^+\equiv$	1 $-\overset{\cdot\cdot}{\underset{\cdot\cdot}{O}}:$

Table 1-5

Drawing Molecular Structures

Drawing molecular structures from a given formula requires following the octet rule for all atoms except hydrogen. On occasion, there will be charged atoms within the compound, but the number of charged atoms within the structure should be minimized. Figure 1-12 shows some sample structures for a few common molecules.

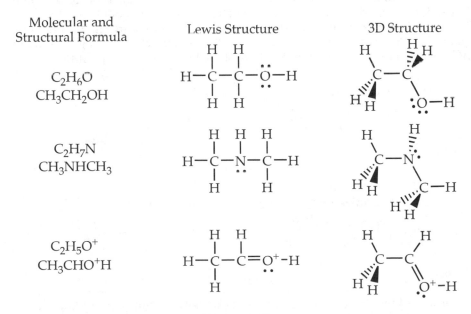

Molecular and Structural Formula	Lewis Structure	3D Structure
C_2H_6O CH_3CH_2OH		
C_2H_7N CH_3NHCH_3		
$C_2H_5O^+$ CH_3CHO^+H		

Figure 1-12

         Exclusive MCAT Preparation

Hybridization

Hybridization of Atomic Orbitals

Hybridization entails theoretically relocating electron density in atomic orbitals prior to bonding, in order to minimize the repulsion between electron pairs and thereby allow for bonding between atoms. There are three main types of hybrid orbitals to consider in organic chemistry: sp, sp^2, and sp^3 *hybrids*. Hybrid orbitals are atomic orbitals that are involved in making bonds between atoms. Listed in Table 1-6 are some pertinent facts and structural features for each of the three types of hybridization. Table 1-6 represents general trends that are observed in nearly all molecules with hybridized orbitals involved in their molecular orbitals.

Hybrid	sp	sp^2	sp^3
Atomic Orbitals	$s + p$	$s + p + p$	$s + p + p + p$
Angle	180°	120°	109.5°
Shape	linear	trigonal planar	tetrahedral
σ-bonds and e⁻ pairs	2	3	4
π-bonds	2	1	0

Table 1-6

The number of π-bonds in Table 1-6 is for typical molecules that obey the octet rule. Boranes, such as BH_3, BF_3, and BR_3, are exceptions to the features in Table 1-6. In a borane, neutral boron has only three valence electrons. The result is that boron has sp^2-hybridization for its three sigma bonds, but no pi bond.

Structures with Orbitals

Lewis structures are used as shorthand representations of molecules. However, in organic chemistry, molecules should be visualized in three dimensions, which hybridization helps to facilitate. Determining the three-dimensional shape of a molecule requires first assuming a shape based on hybridization of the central atoms, then applying valence shell electron pair repulsion (VSEPR) theory. Figure 1-13 shows molecular structures with orbitals and three-dimensional orientation. Structures should be drawn with and correct bond lengths and bond angles should be based on hybridization, steric hindrance, and VSEPR rules.

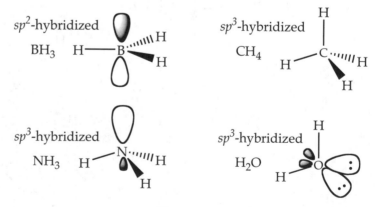

Figure 1-13

The orbital shown for BH_3 in Figure 1-13 is actually an empty p-orbital, while the other orbitals depicted in Figure 1-13 are hybrid orbitals. The p_z-orbital of BH_3 is devoid of electrons, so the hybridization is sp^2. While an empty p-orbital does not actually exist, we consider the region where an electron pair could be accepted. The three hybrid orbitals are detailed in Figures 1-14, 1-15, and 1-16.

sp-Hybridization: *sp*-hybridization is the result of the mixing of the *s*-orbital and the p_x-orbital.

Figure 1-14

sp²-Hybridization: *sp²*-hybridization is the result of the mixing of the *s*-orbital, the p_x-orbital, and the p_y orbital.

Figure 1-15

sp³-Hybridization: *sp³*-hybridization is the result of the mixing of the s-orbital, the p_x-orbital, the p_y-orbital, and the p_z-orbital.

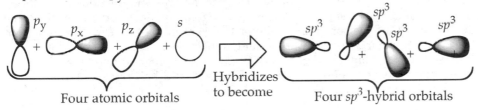

Figure 1-16

Example 1.5
What is the hybridization of each carbon in propene ($H_2C=CH-CH_3$)?

A. *sp*, *sp*, and *sp³*
B. *sp²*, *sp*, and *sp³*
C. *sp²*, *sp²*, and *sp³*
D. *sp³*, *sp³*, and *sp³*

Solution
There are three carbons in propene. The first two carbons are involved in a π-bond, so they are each *sp²*-hybridized. This makes the best answer choice **C**. The last carbon is not involved in any π-bonds, so it has *sp³*-hybridization.

Common Three Dimensional Shapes
Hybridization theory supports the notion that there are recurring molecular shapes (tetrahedral, trigonal planar, and linear) that can be seen within different molecules. This means that there is a electronic explanation for the structures that are observed within various molecules. Hybridization is a theoretical explanation to rationalize why electron pairs in the valence shells of bonding atoms assume orientations as far from one another as possible. Hybridization is used to explain bond lengths and bond angles. Figures 1-17, 1-18, and 1-19 show structures with their corresponding geometry and structural features.

Tetrahedral and sp³-Hybridization
A central atom with four electron pairs (any combination of sigma bonds and lone pairs) has tetrahedral orientation of the electron pairs about the central atom. This does not mean that the shape is tetrahedral, but that the orientation of electron pairs about the central atom (geometry) is tetrahedral. Figure 1-17 shows three structures with tetrahedral geometry about the central atom.

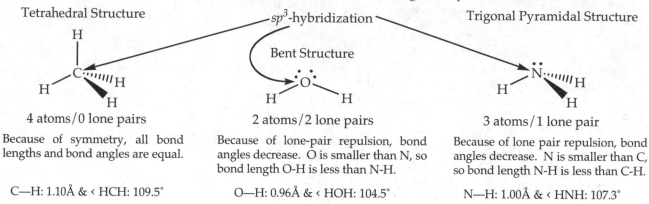

Tetrahedral Structure — sp³-hybridization — Trigonal Pyramidal Structure

Bent Structure

4 atoms/0 lone pairs

Because of symmetry, all bond lengths and bond angles are equal.

C—H: 1.10Å & ‹ HCH: 109.5°

2 atoms/2 lone pairs

Because of lone-pair repulsion, bond angles decrease. O is smaller than N, so bond length O-H is less than N-H.

O—H: 0.96Å & ‹ HOH: 104.5°

3 atoms/1 lone pair

Because of lone pair repulsion, bond angles decrease. N is smaller than C, so bond length N-H is less than C-H.

N—H: 1.00Å & ‹ HNH: 107.3°

Figure 1-17

Trigonal Planar and sp²-Hybridization
A central atom with three other atoms, two other atoms and one lone pair, or one other atom and two lone pairs attached has trigonal planar geometry of the three substituents (or electron pairs) about the central atom. The shape is not necessarily trigonal planar, but the orientation of electron pairs about the central atom is trigonal planar. Figure 1-18 shows the planar structure and spatial representation of the bonds in ethene. The stick and ball representation shows the three-dimensional perspective for ethene.

3 atoms/0 lone pairs

Each carbon in ethene has sp²-hybridization.

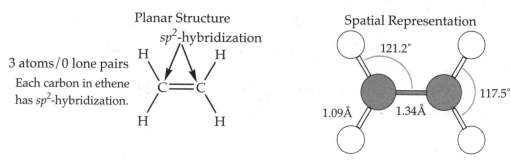

Planar Structure
sp²-hybridization

Spatial Representation

121.2°

117.5°

1.09Å   1.34Å

Figure 1-18

Linear and sp-Hybridization
A central atom with two other atoms or one other atom and one lone pair attached has linear geometry of the two substituents (or electron pairs) about the central atom. This does not mean that the shape is linear (although in most cases it is), but that the orientation about the central atom is linear. Figure 1-19 shows the linear structure and spatial representation of the bonds in ethyne. The stick and ball representation shows the three-dimensional perspective for ethyne.

2 atoms/0 lone pairs

Each carbon in ethyne has sp-hybridization.

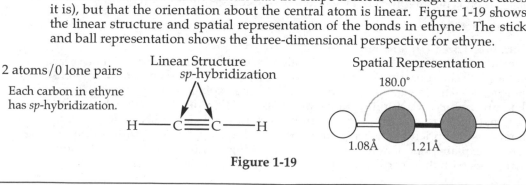

Linear Structure
sp-hybridization

Spatial Representation

180.0°

1.08Å   1.21Å

Figure 1-19

Hybridization can influence the reactivity and acidity of a compound. The hybridization of an atom affects the bond length and the distribution of electron density within a bond, so the hybridization of an atom directly bonded to the acidic proton affects the acidity of the compound. The relationship is not obvious in that it is *not* true that longer bonds lead to stronger acids, as is the case with most other acids. In fact, the relationship between length and acid strength is exactly the opposite. As the hybrid orbital gets smaller, the electrons are held closer to the nucleus of the atom bonded to hydrogen, so the bond can be cleaved in a heterolytic fashion more easily.

> The result is that **the more s-character in the hybrid orbital** of the atom bonded to hydrogen, **the stronger the acid**.

This results in the relative acidity being $sp > sp^2 > sp^3$. It is most commonly observed with carbon acidity, but can also be observed with nitrogen and oxygen. Figure 1-20 shows the comparison of acids where hybridization explains the difference in acid strength.

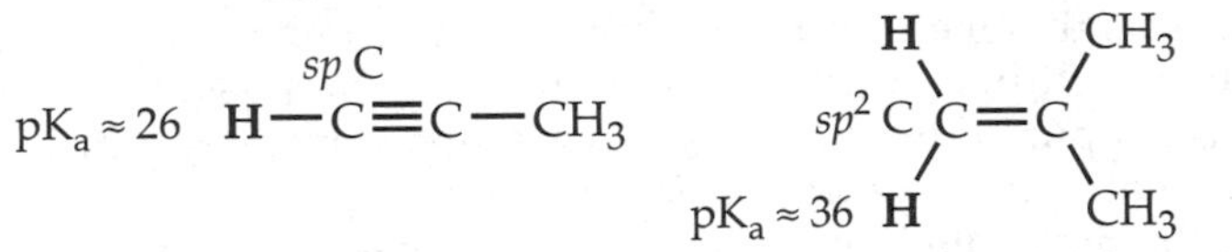

$$pK_a \approx 26 \quad \overset{sp\ C}{H-C\equiv C-CH_3}$$

Stronger Acid

$$pK_a \approx 36$$

Weaker Acid

An H on an *sp* carbon is more acidic than an H on an sp^2 carbon

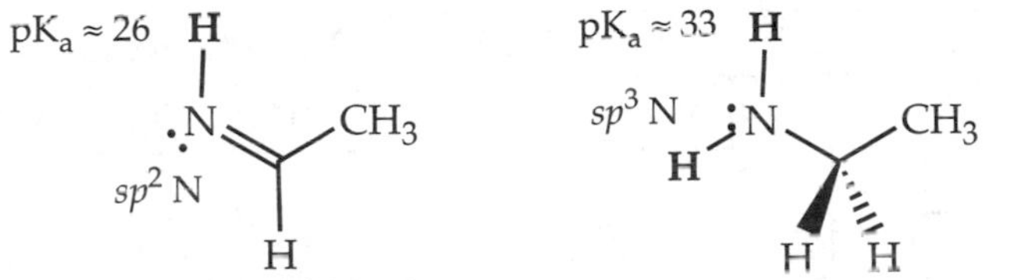

$$pK_a \approx 26$$

Stronger Acid

$$pK_a \approx 33$$

Weaker Acid

An H on an sp^2 nitrogen is more acidic than an H on an sp^3 nitrogen

Figure 1-20

Example 1.6

The hydrogen-carbon-hydrogen bond angle in formaldehyde (H_2CO) is BEST approximated by which of the following values?

A. 108.3°
B. 111.7°
C. 118.5°
D. 121.5°

Solution

The first feature to look at is the hybridization of carbon. Carbon is involved in one π-bond, so the hybridization is sp^2. The bond angle about an sp^2-hybridized carbon is predicted to be 120°. The question here is whether the angle is slightly greater or slightly less than 120°. Because there are two pairs of electrons on the oxygen, the electron density repels the electrons in the two carbon-hydrogen bonds. This forces the two bonds closer together, which compresses the hydrogen-carbon-hydrogen bond angle. According to valence shell electron pair repulsion (VSEPR) theory, the angle should be slightly less than 120°. The best answer is thus choice **C**.

Bond Energy

Bond Dissociation Energy

In organic chemistry, the energy required to cleave a bond in a homolytic fashion is commonly used to compare relative bond strengths. Homolytic cleavage refers to the breaking of a chemical bond into two free radical fragments. This is typically viewed in the gas phase or an aprotic, nonpolar solvent, where ions are too unstable to exist. It is important that you recall that energy is released when a bond is formed and that energy must be absorbed by the molecule to break a bond. By subtracting the energy released upon forming new bonds from the energy required to break bonds, the enthalpy of a reaction can be determined. This is shown in Equation 1.1.

$$\Delta H_{\text{Reaction}} = \sum \text{Energy}_{\text{(bonds broken)}} - \text{Energy}_{\text{(bonds formed)}} \qquad \textbf{(1.1)}$$

If the enthalpy of a reaction is known, then the bond dissociation energies for bonds that are formed and broken during the course of a reaction can be determined. It is this method that allows for the comparison of bonds between identical atoms within different molecules. For instance, the theory of aromaticity is supported by the excess energy that is released upon the formation of a π-bond that completes the aromatic ring. The release of excess energy implies that the molecule is more stable than expected from the standard bond dissociation energies, so some other factor must be involved. Table 1-7 lists some bond dissociation energies for typical bonds in some common organic molecules. By no means try to memorize any of these numbers, but instead learn to apply the data to estimate the energy of specific bonds.

Bond Dissociation Energies for A—B Bonds (Kcal/mole)								
A	B = H	Me	Et	*i*-Pr	*t*-Bu	Ph	OH	NH$_2$
Methyl	105	90	89	86	84	102	93	85
Ethyl	101	89	88	87	85	101	95	85
n-Propyl	101	89	88	86	85	101	95	85
Isopropyl	98	89	87	85	82	99	96	85
t-Butyl	96	87	95	82	77	99	96	85
Phenyl	111	102	100	99	96	115	111	102
Benzyl	88	76	75	74	73	90	81	71
Allyl	86	74	70	70	67	N/A	78	69
Acetyl	86	81	79	77	75	93.5	107	96
Ethoxy	104	83	85	N/A	N/A	101	44	N/A
Vinyl	112	102	101	100	95	105	N/A	N/A
H	104.2	105	101	98	96	111	119	107

Table 1-7

A greater value in Table 1-7 implies that the bond is stronger. You may note that the weakest bond listed in Table 1-7 is an O—O single bond within a peroxide molecule (EtO-OH). Because this bond is so weak, peroxides are highly reactive species, often used to oxidize other compounds. The data in Table 1-7 also reveal that the substitution of the carbon and the position of the bond within the molecule affect the bond energy. The effect of hybridization can also be extracted when comparing bond energies between vinyl and methyl substituents.

Example 1.7
According to the data in Table 1-7, which of the following carbon-carbon single bonds is the MOST stable?

A.   An sp^2-carbon to a primary sp^3-carbon
B.   An sp^2-carbon to a secondary sp^3-carbon
C.   A secondary sp^3-carbon to a primary sp^3-carbon
D.   A secondary sp^3-carbon to a secondary sp^3-carbon

Solution
The most stable bond is the strongest bond. The strongest bond has the greatest bond dissociation energy, so to solve this question, the bond energies from Table 1-7 must be referenced. An sp^2-hybridized carbon is found in the double bond of an alkene. This is described as a vinylic carbon, so the vinyl entry in Table 1-7 is necessary for choices A and B. Considering that we are looking at carbon-carbon bonds, a primary carbon (with only one bond to a carbon) would have to come from a methyl group. This value is necessary for choices A and C. Likewise, a secondary carbon would come from a group such as ethyl or *n*-propyl. Considering only Et is listed as a substituent in Table 1-7, the value for Et is necessary in choices B, C, and D.

Choice A is found by looking at the entry for Vinyl—Me, which is 102 kcal/mole. Choice B is found by looking at the entry for Vinyl—Et, which is 101 kcal/mole. Choice C is found by looking at the entry for Et-Me, which is 89 kcal/mole. Choice D is found by looking at the entry for Et-Et, which is 88 kcal/mole. The most stable bond is the one that requires the greatest energy to break. The greatest bond dissociation energy among these choices is 102 kcal/mole, so choice **A** is the best answer.

Ionic Bonds
Ionic bonds are bonds formed between two oppositely charged ions. They are common between metals and nonmetals. The strength of an ionic bond can be determined using Coulomb's law, Equation 1.2. Coulomb's law states that the force between two charged species is equal to a constant k times the charge on each ion, divided by the square of distance between the two charges, which are treated as point charges:

$$F = k\frac{q_1 q_2}{r^2} = \frac{1}{4\pi\varepsilon_0}\frac{q_1 q_2}{r^2} \qquad (1.2)$$

where F = force, q = charge, r = distance, and $\varepsilon_0 = 8.85 \times 10^{-12}\ \dfrac{C^2}{N \cdot m^2}$.

The greater the charge on the ion, the stronger the bond; and the closer the ions are to one another, the stronger the bond. Ionic bonds are typically stronger than covalent bonds. However, because ions can be solvated in a polar, protic solvent, ionic bonds are often cleaved more readily than covalent bonds in a protic environment. In other words, despite the strength of ionic bonds, they are broken easily by adding water to the ionic lattice. This implies that the Coulombic attraction of the ions to water is comparable to the attraction of the ions to one another.

Intramolecular Features

Intramolecular Features

Intramolecular features encompass anything that affects the stability of a molecule and the sharing of electron density beyond the localized region between two neighboring, bonding atoms. There are various factors that dictate the chemical reactivity of a compound and explain the distribution of electron density within a molecule. I like to call them the "five excuses" to explain organic chemistry. They are *resonance*, the *inductive effect, steric interactions, aromaticity*, and *hybridization*. We have already examined hybridization and seen the effect it has on the structure of a molecule in terms of bond angles. Besides considering the three-dimensional position of the atoms within a molecule, we will consider electron density and thus establish reactive sites within a molecule. We shall start by considering the ever-so-loved resonance theory.

Resonance

Resonance is an intramolecular phenomenon whereby electron density is shifted through regions of the molecule via π-bonds. Resonance is defined as the delocalization of electrons through a continuous array of overlapping p-orbitals (π-bonds and adjacent lone pairs). Resonance theory can be used to determine the stability of a structure. There are three rules to follow to determine the stability of a resonance form prioritized according to importance from most to least:

1. The resonance structure should contain atoms with filled octets (excluding hydrogen).

2. The best structure minimizes the number of formal charges throughout the molecule.

3a. If the molecule contains a negative charge, it is best placed on the most electronegative atom.

3b. If the molecule contains a positive charge, it is best placed on the least electronegative atom.

Figure 1-21 shows two resonance forms for an amide compound that obey the octet rule, and a resonance hybrid that shows the composite effect. The resonance hybrid is an average of all the major resonance contributors.

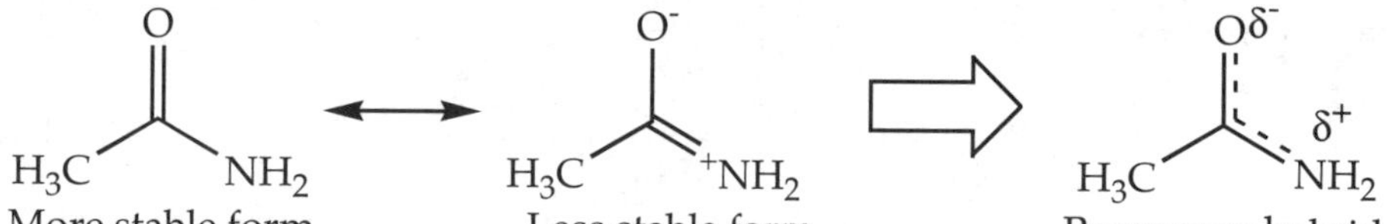

More stable form   Less stable form   Resonance hybrid

Figure 1-21

The resonance structure farthest to the left in Figure 1-21 is more stable than the middle structure, because there is no separation of charge. You must be able to rank the stability of resonance structures and decide whether it is a major contributor. Typical questions based on resonance include determining where certain molecules are most reactive. You should be able to apply resonance theory to other features of chemical structure and reactivity. For instance, when viewing an amide, the electron-rich oxygen is the most nucleophilic site on the molecule. When protonating an amide, it is the oxygen that gets protonated. When amides form hydrogen bonds, the oxygen is the electron-donating site. This has a significant impact on molecular structure in protein folding.

Figure 1-22 shows four examples of resonance structures and the arrow pushing necessary to convert between resonance forms. To draw resonance structures that are stable, it is often helpful to start with a lone pair and push those electrons into a π-bond. The electrons from the adjacent π-bond turn into a new lone pair.

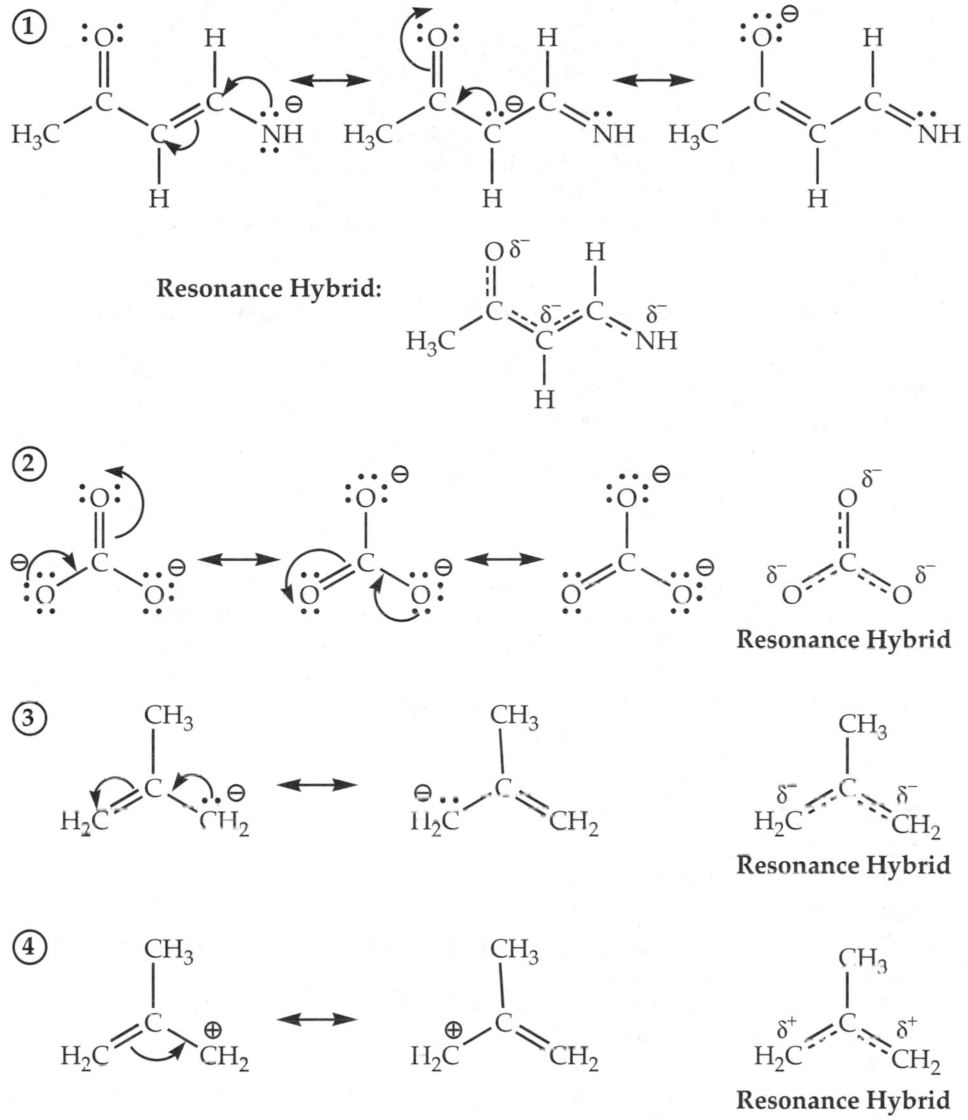

Figure 1-22

In Examples 1, 2, and 3, shown in Figure 1-22, the negative charge moves every other atom between resonance forms. The lone pair becomes a π-bond, and the π-bond becomes a lone pair two atoms away. This is true when the number of total charged sites remains constant. In Example 1, there is only one charged atom in each of the resonance forms. You must look for the all-octet resonance structures. All of the resonance forms except the carbocations in Example 4 are all-octet resonance forms. This satisfies Rule 1 on the list of resonance rules. Neither structure in Example 4 satisfies the octet rule. The resonance hybrid is a composite of the individual resonance contributors. The most stable resonance structures (*major resonance contributors* as they are called) have the greatest effect on reactivity and structure for a compound exhibiting resonance.

Example 1.8

The C-O bond length is LONGEST in the compound on the:

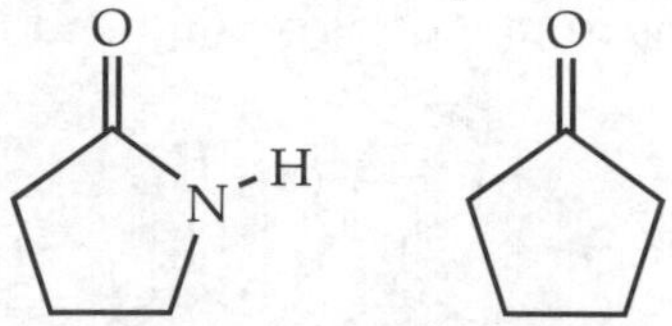

A. left, because nitrogen donates electrons through resonance.
B. right, because nitrogen donates electrons through resonance.
C. left, because nitrogen withdraws electrons through resonance.
D. right, because nitrogen withdraws electrons through resonance.

Solution

For this question, the resonance forms of the lactam should be drawn first:

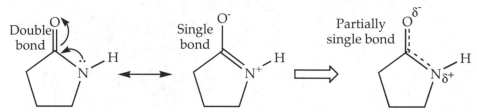

The all-octet resonance form on the right has the carbonyl bond in single bond form. The single-bond resonance is caused by the donation of a lone pair of electrons by nitrogen. This means that the C-O bond is longer in the compound on the left, because nitrogen donates electrons through resonance. The correct answer is thus choice **A**. The effect of resonance outweighs the inductive effect. The inductive effect predicts that the nitrogen would be electron-withdrawing, because it is more electronegative than carbon.

Example 1.9

Which of the following statements BEST explains why amides are protonated at oxygen rather than nitrogen?

A. Oxygen is less electronegative than nitrogen, so it donates electrons more readily.
B. Oxygen is larger than nitrogen, so it binds protons more readily.
C. Oxygen carries a partial positive charge due to resonance withdrawal from the nitrogen.
D. Oxygen carries a partial negative charge due to resonance donation from the nitrogen.

Solution

As shown below, the nitrogen of the amide donates electron density to the carbonyl oxygen through resonance. This places a partial negative charge on oxygen (increasing its basicity), and a partial positive charge on nitrogen (decreasing its basicity). Choice A is eliminated, because oxygen is more electronegative than nitrogen. Choice B is eliminated, because oxygen is smaller than nitrogen, not larger. Because of resonance, oxygen carries a partial negative charge, while nitrogen carries a partial positive charge. This means that choice C is false and choice **D** is true. This explains the basicity of amides.

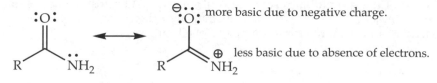

Example 1.10
Which of the following statements is true as it pertains to pK_a values?

A. A functional group that is electron-withdrawing by resonance lowers the pK_a value, while a functional group that is electron-withdrawing by the inductive effect raises the pK_a value.

B. A functional group that is electron-withdrawing by resonance lowers the pK_a value, while a functional group that is electron-donating by the inductive effect raises the pK_a value.

C. A functional group that is electron-donating by resonance lowers the pK_a value, while a functional group that is electron-withdrawing by the inductive effect raises the pK_a value.

D. A functional group that is electron-donating by resonance lowers the pK_a value, while a functional group that is electron-donating by the inductive effect raises the pK_a value.

Solution
Regardless of the effect (whether it is resonance or the inductive effect), electron-withdrawing groups increase acidity and lower the pK_a while electron-donating groups decrease acidity and raise the pK_a. This eliminates choices A, C, and D and leaves choice **B** as the best answer. The effect of an electron-withdrawing group can be seen in the following trend: H_3CCO_2H ($pK_a = 4.74$) is less acid than H_2ClCCO_2H ($pK_a = 2.85$), which is less acidic than HCl_2CCO_2H ($pK_a = 1.26$), which in turn is less acidic than Cl_3CCO_2H ($pK_a = 0.64$). As the amount of electron-withdrawal increases, the acidity increases.

Example 1.11
Which nitrogen atom in the following molecule is the MOST basic?

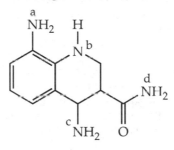

A. Nitrogen a
B. Nitrogen b
C. Nitrogen c
D. Nitrogen d

Solution
The most basic nitrogen atom is the one most capable of sharing its lone pair with a proton or electrophile, which means that the nitrogen where the lone pair is least shared within the molecule is the most basic. Nitrogens a and b have reduced basicity, because the electron pair on nitrogen is being donated to the aromatic ring through resonance. Nitrogen d has reduced basicity, because the electron pair is being donated to the carbonyl group through resonance. Only Nitrogen c is free to share its electrons (which are not being delocalized anywhere within the molecule.) The best answer is choice **C**.

Inductive Effect

The inductive effect induces charge separation in a molecule because of the delocalization of electrons induced by electronegative atoms. The inductive effect involves the transfer of electron density through the sigma bonds. A highly electronegative atom pulls electron density from its neighbor, which in turn pulls electron density from its neighbor. The effect dissipates over distance, but it can affect bonds between atoms up to three or four atoms away.

The inductive effect increases with the electronegativity of the atom. Fluorine is the most electronegative atom found in organic molecules, so it pulls electrons from the carbon to which it is bonded in a strong manner. This makes that carbon electron-poor, so it in turn pulls electrons from its neighbor. Ultimately, as we see with polarity, the electron density in the molecule is pulled towards the most electronegative atom in the compound. An electronegative atom therefore withdraws electron density and thus can increase a compound's acidity, increase its electrophilicity, decrease its basicity, or decrease its nucleophilicity.

For the relative electronegativity of common atoms in organic chemistry, the following relationship holds: $F > O > N > Cl > Br > I > S > C > H$. Just recall "Fonclbrisch" and you'll be fine. Alkyl groups are electron-donating by the inductive effect, because hydrogen is less electronegative than carbon. Figure 1-23 shows how the inductive effect applies to the nucleophilicity of amines.

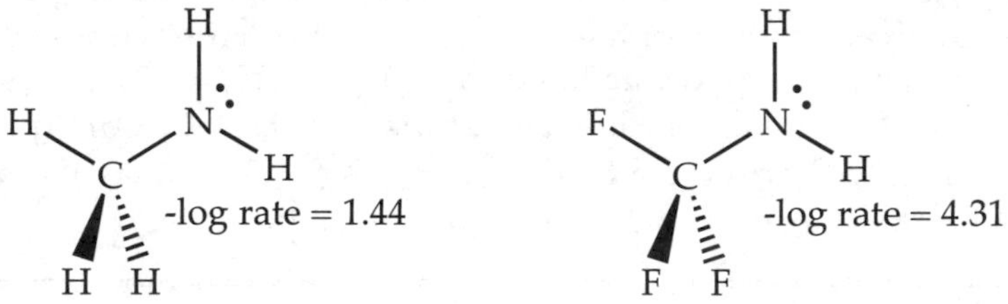

Methylamine -log rate = 1.44 Trifluoromethylamine -log rate = 4.31

Rate for H_3CNH_2 > rate for F_3CNH_2
Less nucleophilic due to the electronegative fluorine atoms

Figure 1-23

The withdrawal of electron density by fluorine atoms reduces the nucleophilicity of the amine compound by pulling electrons away from the nitrogen atom. As electron density is removed, the compound becomes electron-poor and thus a worse electron donor. This is verified by the reaction rate in a substitution reaction, where a higher negative log of the rate indicates a slower reaction.

Example 1.12
Which of the following compounds is the STRONGEST acid?

A. H_3CCH_2OH

B. H_3CCO_2H

C. F_3CCH_2OH

D. F_3CCO_2H

Solution
Carboxylic acids are stronger acids than alcohols, due to the withdrawing of electron density by the carbonyl oxygen through resonance. This eliminates choices A and C. Fluorine is highly electronegative, so it withdraws electrons from the acidic hydrogen via the inductive effect, thus increasing the acidity. The strongest acid is the carboxylic acid with fluorine atoms attached, choice **D**.

Example 1.13
Which of the following compounds undergoes a nucleophilic substitution reaction with ethyl chloride at the GREATEST rate?

A. $H_3CCHFNH_2$
B. $FH_2CCH_2NH_2$
C. $H_3CCHClNH_2$
D. $ClH_2CCH_2NH_2$

Solution
The greatest reaction rate (the fastest reaction) is observed with the best nucleophile. Each answer choice has one halogen, so all the choices have slower rates than ethyl amine. The question asks which experiences the least inductive withdrawal. Chlorine is less electronegative than fluorine (Fonclbrisch), so choices A and B are eliminated. The inductive effect diminishes with distance, so the least electron withdrawal is observed with choice **D**. You must consider both proximity and electronegativity when looking at the inductive effect.

Although not applicable in Example 1.13, you must also consider whether the inductive effect involves electron donation or electron withdrawal. For instance, methyl amine is more nucleophilic than ammonia (NH_3), because the methyl group is electron-donating. Varying the R-group changes the inductive effect. It also changes the size of the molecule, so steric hindrance can affect the reaction. For instance, trimethyl amine (($H_3C)_3N$) is less nucleophilic than dimethyl amine (($H_3C)_2NH$), because the electron donation by the additional methyl group does not compensate for the increase in molecular size.

Example 1.14
How can the difference in acidity between trifluoroacetic acid and trichloroacetic acid be explained?

A. Fluorine is larger than chlorine, so trifluoroacetic acid is a stronger acid.
B. Chlorine is larger than fluorine, so trichloroacetic acid is a stronger acid.
C. Trichloroacetic acid is a stronger acid, because chlorine is more electronegative than fluorine.
D. Trifluoroacetic acid is a stronger acid, because fluorine is more electronegative than chlorine.

Solution
Fluorine is smaller than chlorine, so choice A is eliminated. The acidic proton is not bonded to the halogen, so atomic size does not dictate the acid strength. This eliminates choice B. Fluorine is more electronegative than chlorine, so F withdraws electron density more than Cl, making trifluoroacetic acid more electron poor and a stronger acid (better electron pair acceptor). The pK_a of trifluoroacetic acid (F_3CCO_2H) is 0.18, while the pK_a of trichloroacetic acid (Cl_3CCO_2H) is 0.64. A lower pK_a value confirms that trifluoroacetic acid (F_3CCO_2H) is the stronger of the two acids. Choice **D** is the best answer.

Steric Hindrance
Steric hindrance occurs any time two atoms attempt to be in the same place at the same time. It is repulsive in nature and increases as the atoms draw closer. No one is certain about the nature of the force, but it is believed to be electron cloud repulsion. The effects are similar to what is observed in general chemistry with VSEPR (valence shell electron pair repulsion) theory, except that it is considered only when two separate atoms or functional groups interact. Electrons move to be as far apart as possible, so lone pairs and bonds spread out to accommodate the geometry that spaces the greatest distance between electrons. Figure 1-24 demonstrates the effects of steric hindrance on a couple of organic molecules. Because the alkene is planar, the substituents on the alkene carbons have a tendency to collide with one another.

Larger C-C-C bond angle   Smaller C-C-C bond angle

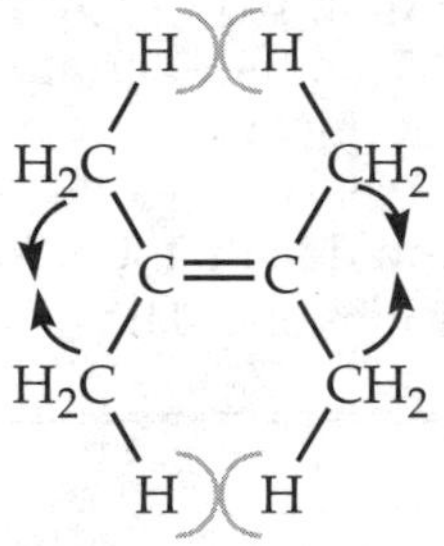

Reduced bond angle in dimethylbutene, because the methyl group hydrogens repel.

Figure 1-24

Example 1.15
Which of the following functional groups is MOST likely to be found in the equatorial position on cyclohexane?
A. —OCH$_3$
B. —OCH$_2$CH$_2$CH$_2$CH$_3$
C. —OCH(CH$_3$)CH$_2$CH$_3$
D. —OC(CH$_3$)$_3$

Solution
On cyclohexane, substituents with axial orientation experience greater steric hindrance than substituents with equatorial orientation. Because of steric hindrance, the substituent most likely to assume the equatorial orientation is the bulkiest. The tert-butoxide substituent, choice **D**, has the most crowded alkyl groups, resulting in the greatest steric hindrance. This makes the best answer choice **D**.

Aromaticity

Aromaticity is stability generated from having $4n + 2$ π electrons in a continuous, overlapping ring of p-orbitals, where n is any integer including 0. This is known as the *Hückel rule*. The stability is rooted in the molecular orbital model, where an energy level is completely filled when there are $4n + 2$ π-electrons in the cyclic π-network. Figure 1-25 lists experimental values for the enthalpy of hydrogenation of a series of cyclic alkenes including benzene. The large deviation associated with benzene is attributed to its aromatic stability.

$$\Delta H = -28 \; {}^{kcal}/_{mole}$$

$$\Delta H = -56 \; {}^{kcal}/_{mole}$$

$$\Delta H = -54 \; {}^{kcal}/_{mole}$$

$$\Delta H = -49 \; {}^{kcal}/_{mole}$$

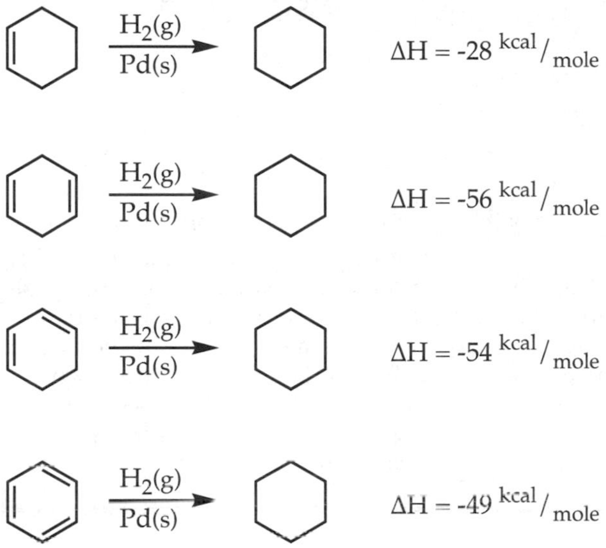

Despite the presence of three π-bonds, the 1,3,5-cyclohexatriene (benzene) yields far less heat from hydrogenation than expected due to its aromatic stability.

Figure 1-25

The first two entries show that the enthalpy of hydrogenation of an alkene is -28 kcal/mole per π-bond. The third entry shows that conjugation results in stability, reducing the amount of heat released upon hydrogenation, but only by about 2 kcals/mole. Based on -28 kcal/mole for each π-bond, benzene should be expected to have a ΔH of approximately -84 kcal/mole. The difference of 35 kcal/mole (84 - 49) cannot be attributed to conjugation alone, hence it is said to be due to aromatic stability.

Not all cyclic, conjugated polyenes show such a large deviation from the expected value for the enthalpy of reaction. 1,3,5,7-Cyclooctatetraene (C_8H_8) shows a deviation of only 8 kcal/mole from its expected value of -112 kcal/mole. This implies that conjugation is useful for only a small fraction of the 35 kcal/mole difference observed with benzene between its expected and actual values. Because benzene has 6 π-electrons in a continuous π-cycle, it obeys the Hückel rule (it has $4n + 2$ π-electrons where $n = 1$), while 1,3,5,7-cyclooctatetraene (C_8H_8) has 8 π-electrons in a continuous π-cycle and does not obey the Hückel rule. This lack of aromaticity results in a less stable reactant, so more heat is generated in the hydrogenation reaction.

Example 1.16

The hydrogen-carbon-hydrogen bond angle about the terminal carbon in the following alkene is BEST approximated by which of the following values?

$$H_3CH_2C \diagdown \qquad \diagup H$$
$$C = C$$
$$H_3C \diagup \qquad \diagdown H$$

A. 108.3°
B. 111.7°
C. 118.5°
D. 121.5°

Solution

First we must consider the hybridization of carbon. It is involved in one π-bond, so the hybridization is sp^2. The bond angle about an sp^2-hybridized carbon is predicted to be 120°. The question here is whether the angle is slightly greater or slightly less than 120°. Because there are two alkyl groups on the other carbon of the alkene, the electron density repels the electrons in the two carbon-hydrogen bonds. This forces the two C—H bonds closer together, which compresses the hydrogen-carbon-hydrogen bond angle. According to steric repulsion theory, the angle should be slightly less than 120°. The best answer is thus choice **C**. Choices A and B are too much less than 120°.

Example 1.17

Which of the following explanations accounts for the pK$_a$ of 1,3-cyclopentadiene being only 15, while the pK$_a$ for hydrogen on other sp^3-carbons is around 49?

A. The strain of the five-membered ring forces the proton off.
B. The proton is involved in resonance.
C. The conjugate base is aromatic.
D. The steric hindrance of the sp^3-carbon weakens the C-H bond on that carbon.

Solution

The acidity of a compound capable of losing a proton (H$^+$) can be determined by the stability of its conjugate base. When an ordinary sp^3-hybridized carbon (one that is not stabilized by resonance or the inductive effect) is deprotonated, the carbanion that is formed is unstable. Carbon is not electropositive, so it does not readily lose a proton. With 1,3-cyclopentadiene, however, the carbanion that is formed upon deprotonation has both resonance and aromatic stabilization once it loses the proton. The cyclopentadienyl anion that is formed is aromatic. This makes choice **C** the best choice. The reaction is drawn below:

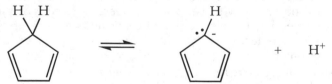

Six conjugated π-electrons in a continuous planar arrangement of p-orbitals is aromatic.

Because it includes the word *resonance*, choice B may at first seem appealing. But a proton, having no electron pair, cannot be involved in resonance. Be careful of wording like this, because it is easy to pick resonance without thinking about it.

Example 1.18

What is observed when histidine is protonated on its side chain?

A. The imine nitrogen gets protonated, because it is more electronegative than the amine nitrogen.

B. The imine nitrogen gets protonated, because it is less electronegative than the amine nitrogen.

C. The amine nitrogen gets protonated, because the imine nitrogen shares its lone pair of electrons with the π-bonds in the ring through resonance, thus it cannot be protonated.

D. The imine nitrogen gets protonated, because the amine nitrogen shares its lone pair of electrons with the π-bonds in the ring through resonance, so it cannot be protonated.

Solution

Both nitrogen atoms are equally electronegative, because neither carries a charge. This eliminates choices A and B.   One could argue that having different hybridization makes the electronegativity different, but the goal here is to find the best answer, and if it is necessary to stretch the definition of terms, you're better off finding a better answer choice.   The histidine is protonated on the imine nitrogen, because the lone pair on the amine nitrogen is being shared with the cyclic π-system through resonance.   This makes the ring aromatic, so the lone pair on the amine nitrogen is not available to be donated as a base.   The best answer is choice D, as shown below.

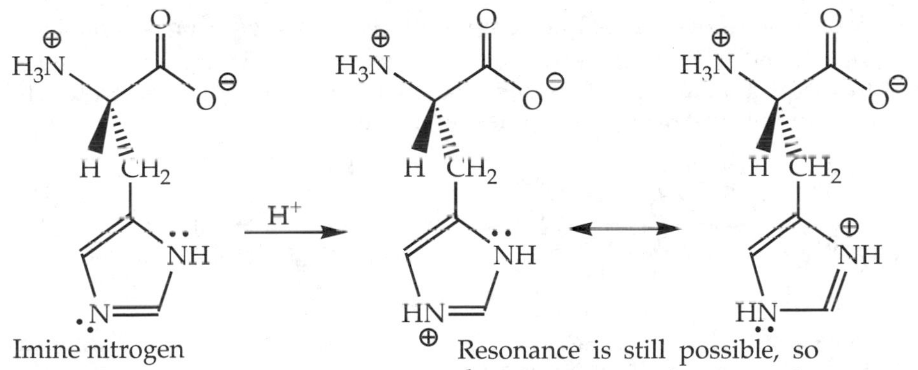

Imine nitrogen

Resonance is still possible, so the π-system remains aromatic.

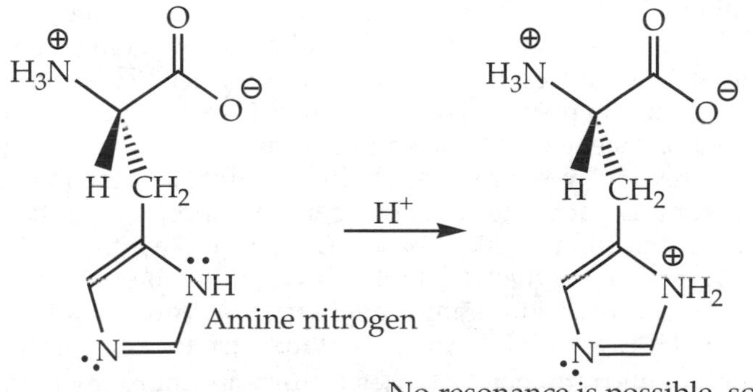

Amine nitrogen

No resonance is possible, so the π-system is no longer aromatic.

Fundamentals of Reactivity

Fundamental Reactions in Organic Chemistry
In organic chemistry, perhaps the most common class of reaction is nucleophilic attack. In the simplest sense, a nucleophilic compound (one with an electron-rich site) attacks an electrophilic compound (one with an electron-poor site) to form a new bond. In some instances a leaving group is discarded, while in others a π-bond is broken. No matter what the result, the reaction has the same fundamental drive and mechanics. The reactions can be viewed as Lewis acid-base reactions, so organic chemistry starts with a thorough look at Lewis acids and bases. Prior to that, we shall review Brønsted-Lowry acid-base chemistry.

Proton Transfer Reactions (Brønsted-Lowry Acid-Base Reactions)
Brønsted-Lowry acid-base reactions involve the transfer of a proton (H^+) from the acid (defined as the proton-donor) to the base (defined as the proton-acceptor). This means that to be a Brønsted-Lowry acid, the compound must have a hydrogen that can be lost as H^+. A hydrogen like this is often referred to as a *protic hydrogen* or *proton*. Throughout this section, we will be using the term *protonation* to describe the gain of an H^+. A hydrogen atom has one proton in its nucleus and one orbiting electron (in a 1s-orbital). When hydrogen loses an electron to become H^+, all that remains is a proton. This is to say that H^+ is a proton, and thus the gain of H^+ can be referred to as *protonation*. *Deprotonation* is the loss of H^+.

To be a Brønsted-Lowry base, the compound must have electrons available that can form a bond to H^+. Because a lone pair of electrons is necessary to form a bond to the proton, all Brønsted-Lowry bases are also Lewis bases. Figure 1-26 shows a proton-transfer reaction, a one-step reaction.

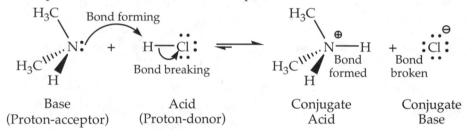

Base	Acid	Conjugate	Conjugate
(Proton-acceptor)	(Proton-donor)	Acid	Base

Figure 1-26

In the reaction in Figure 1-26, you should note that an arrow going from a lone pair to an atom becomes a bond in the product, and an arrow going from a bond to an atom becomes a lone pair on that atom in the product. This is a standard convention in drawing mechanisms. The reaction shown in Figure 1-26 is very favorable, as indicated by the asymmetric equilibrium arrow. The favorability is attributed to the fact that HCl is a strong acid. Proton-transfer reactions proceed favorably ($\Delta G < 0$) from the side with the stronger acid and stronger base to the side with the weaker acid and weaker base. This is to say that a favorable chemical reaction proceeds from the less stable species to the more stable species. There are five strong acids used in organic chemistry that you should recognize: H_2SO_4, HNO_3, HCl, HBr, and HI. An important fact to know is that as a Brønsted-Lowry acid gets stronger, it loses a proton more readily, so its conjugate base is less willing to gain a proton. The result is:

> When comparing two conjugate pairs, the pair with the **stronger acid** has the **weaker conjugate base**.

Lewis Acid-Base Reactions

Lewis acid-base reactions involve the transfer of an electron pair from the base (defined as the electron-pair donor) to the acid (defined as the electron-pair acceptor). This means that for a compound to be a Lewis base, it must have electrons available that can form a bond to an electron deficient atom (such as, but not exclusively, H^+). A Lewis acid can have a protic hydrogen, but a Lewis acid may have an empty valence shell capable of accepting electrons. Typical Lewis acids include BF_3, $AlCl_3$, $FeBr_3$, and $SOCl_2$. Figure 1-27 shows a Lewis acid-base reaction, where ammonia is the Lewis base and BF_3 is the Lewis acid.

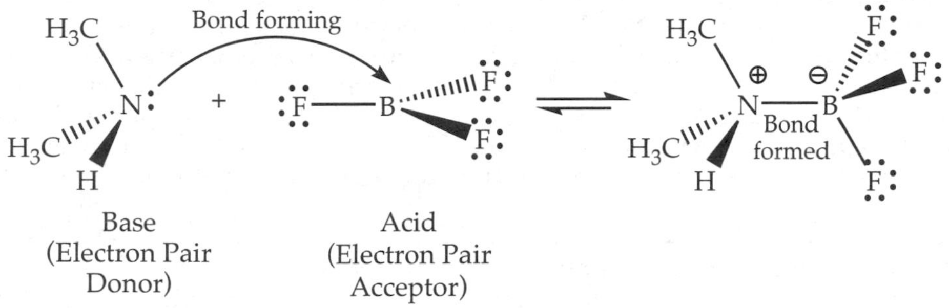

Figure 1-27

The role of a base is essentially the same in both the Lewis and Brønsted-Lowry definitions. A base donates a lone pair of electrons to form a bond to an acid, whether the acid is a Brønsted-Lowry acid or a Lewis acid. In organic chemistry, the terminology varies, and Lewis bases are frequently referred to as *nucleophiles*. Nucleophile means "nucleus loving", which implies that nucleophiles seek out positively charged sites (referred to as electrophiles). The simple guide to organic chemistry is that negative charges seek out and bond to positive charges.

Acidity

Acidity is defined by three definitions: the Arrhenius definition, the Brønsted-Lowry definition, and the Lewis definition. The Arrhenius definition is that an acid yields H_3O^+ when added to water. The Brønsted-Lowry definition is that an acid is a proton (H^+) donor. The Lewis definition is that an acid is an electron pair acceptor. The strength of an acid depends on the effects of intramolecular forces on the bond to the acidic proton. These are the electronic forces *within a* molecule. They are responsible for the distribution of valance electrons, which accounts for the chemical behavior (such as acidity) of the molecule. An acid is stronger when an electron-withdrawing group is attached to the backbone of the acid, because the molecule is electron-poor, and thus a better electron-pair acceptor. An acid is weaker when an electron-donating group is attached to its backbone, because the molecule is electron-rich, and thus a worse electron-pair acceptor. The primary task associated with evaluating organic acid strength is to decide which groups are electron-donating and which are electron-withdrawing. Figure 1-28 shows some common organic acids and their pK_a values.

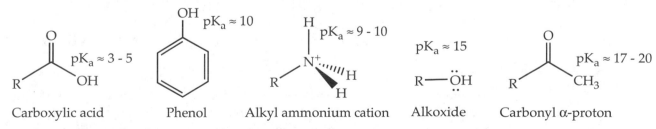

Figure 1-28

Acid Strength Factors
Factors affecting the strength of an acid or base can be broken down into primary effects and secondary effects. *Primary effects* depend on the bond directly to the acidic proton. The weaker the bond to the acidic proton, the more readily it breaks, and consequently more acidic the acid. With acids, the bond breaks in a heterolytic fashion, forming ions. Primary effects include size, electronegativity, and hybridization of the atom directly attached to the acidic proton. *Secondary effects* depend on the effect of the molecule on the atom bonded to the acidic proton. The more electron-rich that atom, the less acidic the proton. The more electron-poor that atom, the more acidic the proton. Secondary effects include resonance, and electron cloud repulsion (deformations of a molecule and elongation of bonds within the molecule). There is also aromaticity to consider, but that is treated as a special case. Secondary effects involve intramolecular forces, which dictate where the electron density within a molecule lies, and thus they dictate the reactivity of a compound. Table 1-8 shows common acids and bases in organic chemistry, listed according to relative strength (in both the acids and the bases).

Strong Acids	$H_2SO_4 > HI > HBr > HCl > HNO_3$
Weak Acids	$HF > HCO_2H > H_3CCO_2H > H_2CO_3 > H_3CSH > H_3CNH_3Cl > H_5C_6OH > H_3COH$
Strong Bases	$CH_3(CH_2)_3Li > NaNH_2 > KH > NaOCH_2CH_3 > NaOH \approx KOH$
Weak Bases	$H_3CNH_2 > NaHCO_3 > H_3CCO_2Na > HCO_2Na > H_3COH$

Table 1-8

Basicity
Basicity is most easily thought of as the opposite of acidity. Basicity is also defined by three definitions: the Arrhenius definition, the Brønsted-Lowry definition, and the Lewis definition. The Arrhenius definition is that a base yields OH^- when added to water. The Brønsted-Lowry definition is that a base is a proton (H^+) acceptor. The Lewis definition is that a base is an electron-pair donor. The rules that you use for acidity can be applied to basicity, but with the opposite effect. Electron-donating groups increase basicity (while they decrease acidity) and electron-withdrawing groups decrease the basicity. As a result, the strength of a base or acid can be determined from the stability of its conjugate. The more stable the conjugate, the weaker the conjugate and the stronger the respective compound (either acid or base). Figure 1-29 shows some common organic bases.

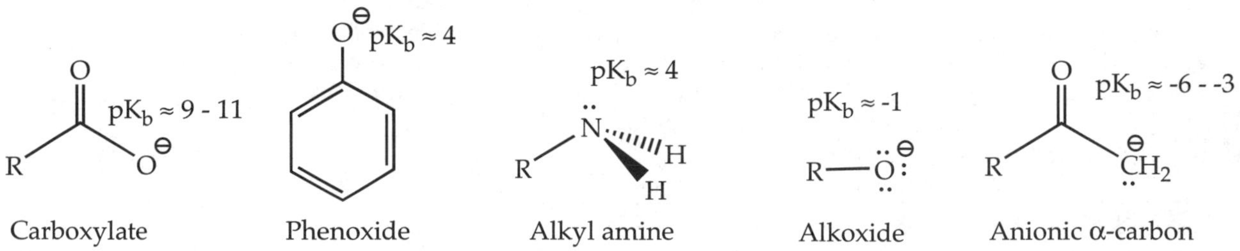

Carboxylate   Phenoxide   Alkyl amine   Alkoxide   Anionic α-carbon

Figure 1-29

Although you are not required to memorize exact pK_a values, it is a good idea to know the "-5-10-15-20 general rule" for organic acids. The pK_a for a carboxylic acid is about 5, for a phenol it's about 10, for an alcohol it's about 15, and for a proton alpha to a carbonyl it's about 20. These are close enough to guess well.

Effect of Temperature on Reaction Rate

The rate of a reaction increases as temperature increases, because there is more free energy available in solution for reaction. Temperature is part the rate constant, k_{rx}, mathematically expressed Equation 1.3.

$$k_{rx} = A\, e^{-Eact/RT} \tag{1.3}$$

where A is the Arrhenius constant and E_{act} is the activation energy.

The energy diagrams in Figure 1-30 show the change in energy level as the reaction proceeds and Figure 1-31 shows the molecular energy distribution throughout the entire system at two different temperatures (T_1 and T_2).

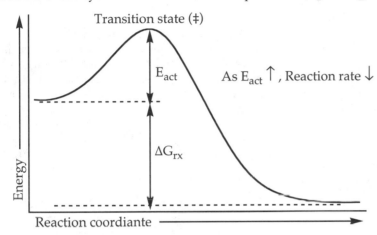

Figure 1-30

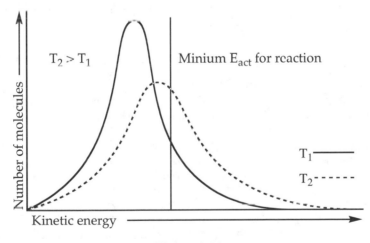

Figure 1-31

At T_2, the average kinetic energy of the molecules is greater than it is at T_1. Thus, at T_2, a greater number of molecules have enough energy to overcome the activation energy barrier of the reaction. This results in more reactants going to products at the higher temperature, meaning that the reaction is faster at the higher temperature.

Physical Properties

Physical Properties and Intermolecular Forces
It is important to have an understanding of how molecules interact with one another. By understanding these interactions, it is easier to predict what will take place in a chemical reaction or physical change. Common MCAT questions involving intermolecular forces include determining the boiling points of two related compounds, as well as a compound's solubility properties or melting point. The rule is simple: the greater the forces, the higher the boiling point. We will use relative boiling points to verify the relative intermolecular forces between compounds. The following are intermolecular forces that affect the boiling points, listed in descending order of strength.

Hydrogen bonding
Hydrogen bonding is a weak bond (approximately 4 to 8 kcals/mole) that exists between a lone pair of electrons and a hydrogen that carries a substantial partial positive charge. A hydrogen has a substantial partial positive charge when it is bonded to a small electronegative atom such as **nitrogen, oxygen, or fluorine**. There are no hydrogen bonds involving hydrogens that are covalently bonded to carbon! You should be aware that not all hydrogen-bonds have the same strength. For instance, an amine lone pair binds the protic hydrogen of an alcohol more tightly than an alcohol lone pair binds the protic hydrogen of an amine. The strength of a hydrogen bond can be estimated from the base properties of the lone pair donor and the acid properties of the hydrogen donor.

Polar Interactions
Polar interactions are the Coulombic interaction between partially charged particles (approximately 1 to 3 kcals/mole). Negatively charged sites attract positively charged sites. The greater the partial charge on the site of the molecule, the stronger the force between opposite charges. The strength of the force also increases as the distance between oppositely charged sites decreases. A typical example of a polar interaction is the dissolving of ions and polar species into water.

Van der Waals
Van der Waals forces exist between all compounds. Van der Waals forces are considered only when no other forces exist to any extent. They are the result of the attraction between temporary dipoles (a very weak force). They are the weakest of the three intermolecular forces between molecules that we shall consider. They are considered to be less than 1 kcal/mole.

The intermolecular forces are the primary consideration when approximating physical properties. When forces are not enough to determine the physical properties such as boiling and melting point, then structural features such as molecular mass and molecular rigidity become the determining factors. The heavier the compound, the harder it is to remove it from a lower energy phase and place it into a higher energy phase (i.e., liquid to gas). What is meant by "molecular flexibility" is the ability to twist and conform to allow for more surface area, and thus more intermolecular interactions. Van der Waals forces are rarely used to explain anything except why there is not a complete absence of intermolecular force. Figure 1-32 shows the different forces.

Hydrogen-bonding:

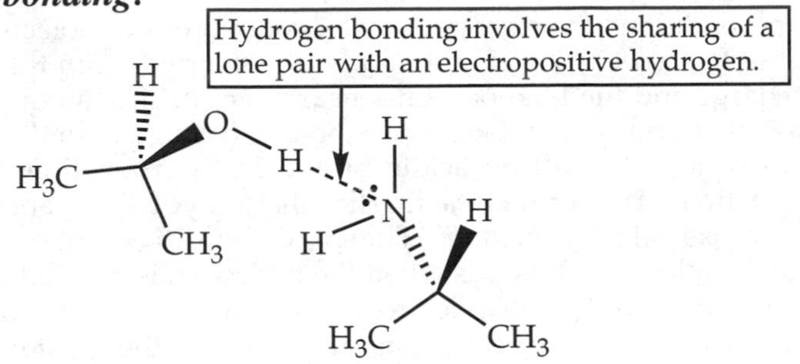

Hydrogen bonding involves the sharing of a lone pair with an electropositive hydrogen.

Dipole-Dipole Interaction:

Coulombic attraction exists here. The larger the charge, the greater the force.

$$F = k \frac{q_1 q_2}{r^2}$$

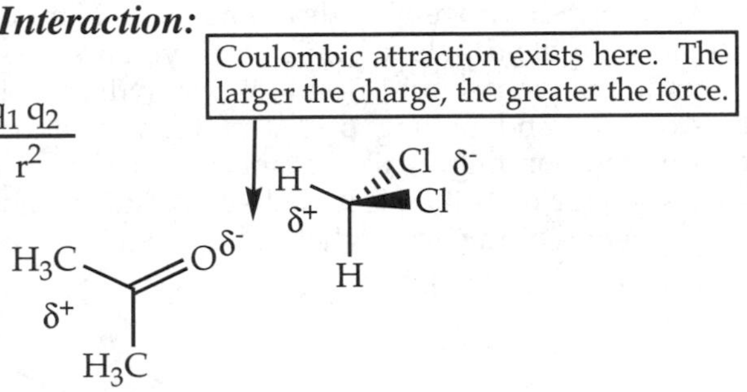

Van der Waals interactions:

Coulombic attraction exists here temporarily. Charges are momentary dipoles.

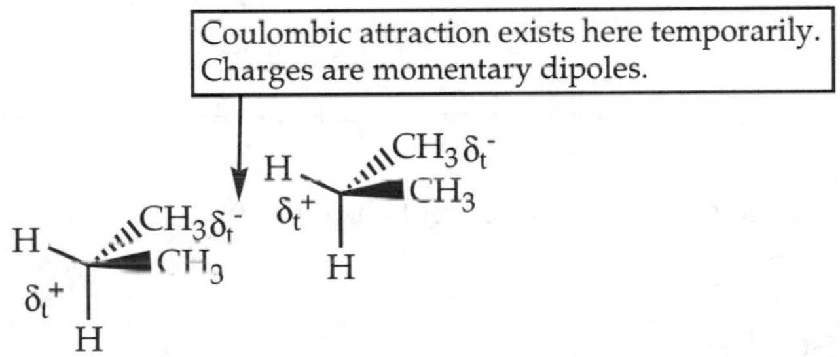

Figure 1-32

Example 1.19
Why is methanol (CH_3OH) a liquid at room temperature, while ethane (CH_3CH_3) is a gas?

A. Ethane is more polar than methanol.
B. Methanol is significantly heavier than ethane.
C. Methanol has stronger van der Waals interactions than ethane.
D. Methanol has hydrogen-bonding, while ethane does not.

Solution
Methanol (CH_3OH) is a liquid at room temperature, while ethane (CH_3CH_3) is a gas, so methanol has the greater boiling point. Ethane is a nonpolar molecule, so choice A is eliminated. Methanol has a molecular mass of 32 grams/mole, while ethane has a molecular mass of 30 grams/mole, so methanol is only slightly (not significantly) heavier than ethane, so choice B is eliminated. The van der Waals interactions are roughly equal for all molecules, so choice C is eliminated. Methanol has hydrogen-bonding, while ethane has no protic hydrogen and therefore no hydrogen-bonding. The higher boiling point is due to the hydrogen-bonding of CH_3OH, so choice **D** is all yours!

Hydrogen-Bonding

Hydrogen-bonding is the strongest of the common intermolecular forces. It can be thought of as a weak covalent bond between a hydrogen that carries a partial positive charge and the lone pair on a nearby atom. The strength of a hydrogen bond varies between 4 and 8 kcals per mole. Hydrogen bonds are similar to the interaction of a base with an acidic proton in the transition state of a proton transfer reaction. The term *protic* implies that a hydrogen capable of hydrogen-bonding is also slightly acidic. The partial positive on hydrogen is strong enough to form hydrogen bonds when the hydrogen is bonded to either fluorine, oxygen, or nitrogen (highly electronegative atoms). Hydrogen bonding in alcohols is stronger than in amines, as supported by the greater boiling points of alcohols relative to amines with comparable mass.

Compounds that form hydrogen bonds are polar, so compounds with hydrogen-bonding also have dipole-dipole interactions. If you are asked to compare boiling points of compounds, you should first look for hydrogen-bonding. Figure 1-33 shows the structures and boiling points of butanol and butanal. Butanol is capable of hydrogen-bonding, while butanal is not. The forces between butanol molecules are stronger than the forces between butanal molecules. The result is that butanol molecules bind one another tightly, causing a higher boiling point.

Butanol (b.p. = 117.4°C)   Butanal (b.p. = 76.1°C)

Figure 1-33

Example 1.20

Which of the following compounds has the HIGHEST boiling point?

A. $(H_3C)_3N$
B. $(H_3C)_2NH$
C. $(H_3C)_3CH$
D. H_3COCH_3

Solution

This question centers on intermolecular forces, particularly hydrogen-bonding. As a rule, the compound with the greatest intermolecular forces has the highest boiling point. Hydrogen-bonding is the strongest of the intermolecular forces, and if a compound has hydrogen-bonding, it also has dipole-dipole interactions, so the compound with hydrogen-bonding has the greatest intermolecular forces. To form a hydrogen bond, both a lone pair of electrons and a hydrogen on a highly electronegative atom (N, O, or F) are required. Choice C does not contain a lone pair, so it is eliminated. Choices A and D have all of their hydrogens on carbon, so they are both eliminated. This leaves choice **B** as the only molecule that forms hydrogen bonds.

Polarity

Polarity is defined as an asymmetric distribution of electron density within a molecule. The more electronegative atoms pull the electrons more tightly. If the molecule has more of one atom on one side of the molecule than another--that is, if it is asymmetric about a central point-- then it is polar. A polar compound has a dipole, which for all intents and purposes is a net vector drawn form the positive side of the molecule to the negative side of the molecule in a way that sums up the polarity vectors of each bond in the molecule. Figure 1-34 shows the molecules with their dipoles.

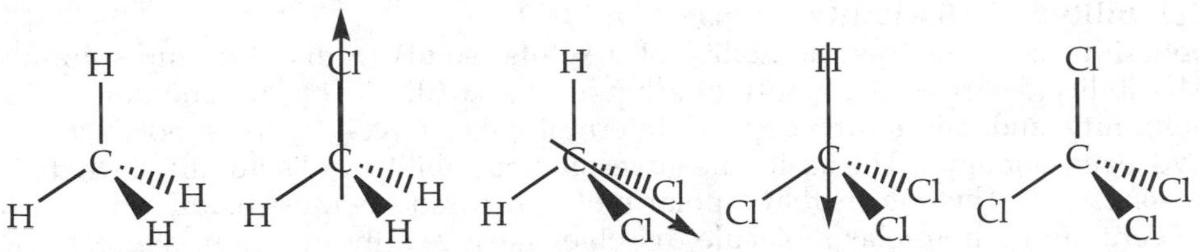

Figure 1-34

Example 1.21
Which of the following molecules has a dipole moment of zero?

A. Carbon monoxide
B. Dichloromethane
C. 2,2-Dichloropropane
D. Trans-1,4-dichlorocyclohexane

Solution
To have a dipole moment of zero, the molecule must be symmetric. Carbon monoxide (CO), dichloromethane, and 2,2-dichloropropane are all asymmetric and thus polar. The two carbon-chlorine bonds of trans-1,4-dichlorocyclohexane are on opposite sides of the molecule, symmetrically displaced about a central point in the molecule, so their dipoles cancel out. Choice **D** is the best answer.

Van der Waals Interactions
Van der Waals forces are weak intermolecular forces that exist between all molecules. These weak attractive forces account for the minimal attraction between hydrocarbons. In biochemical discussions of hydrophobic interactions, it is in fact van der Waals forces that are being considered.

Lard (a saturated fatty chain) has a higher melting point than vegetable oil (an unsaturated fatty chain). The molecules in lard are more flexible, so they are better able to interact with another molecule than is vegetable oil. Perhaps it is easier to picture lard as a pile of strings that can intertwine, while vegetable oil is like a pile of straws that cannot intertwine. If you were to build a pile of strings and a pile of straws, then it would be far easier to remove a straw from the straw pile, because the straws are not tangled up. This is why saturated fats (whose molecules are flexible) are solid at room temperature, while unsaturated fats (whose molecules are rigid) are liquid at room temperature. The greater the number of π-bonds in a compound, the lower its melting point. More π-bonds in the fatty acids in a phospholipid bilayer increases the fluidity of a cell membrane.

Example 1.22
Cell membranes are composed of many molecules, including phospholipids. A phospholipid has two fatty acids and a phosphate attached to the oxygen atoms of glycerol. A cell membrane would be most rigid if both of its fatty acids were:

A. completely saturated and short molecules.
B. completely saturated and long molecules.
C. unsaturated and short molecules.
D. unsaturated and long molecules.

Solution
For the membrane to be rigid, there must be many interactions between the lipid chains. Interactions are greatest with long, saturated fatty acids. Pick **B** to smile.

Solubility and Miscibility

Solubility is defined as the ability of a solute (solid) to dissolve into solution. Miscibility describes the ability of a liquid to mix (dissolve) into another liquid. Solubility and miscibility depend intermolecular forces such as polarity and hydrogen-bonding. The basic rule governing miscibility and solubility is that *like dissolves like*. This means that a polar molecule dissolves most readily in a polar solvent, and a nonpolar molecule dissolves most readily in a nonpolar solvent. There are three combinations of properties that a solvent may have. It may be polar and protic (capable of hydrogen-bonding), polar and aprotic (no hydrogen-bonding, but has dipole-dipole interactions), and nonpolar and aprotic (weak intermolecular forces), as described in the Table 1-9.

Type	Intermolecular Forces	Examples
Polar, Protic	H-bonding, dipole-dipole, and van der Waals	Water, Alcohols, Amines
Polar, Aprotic	Dipole-dipole and van der Waals	Ketones, Ethers, Alkyl halides
Nonpolar, Aprotic	van der Waals	Oils, Lipids, Petroleum

Table 1-9

Simple solubility rules can explain common observations. For instance, salts dissociate into water, because ions are stabilized by water's protic nature. Sugar dissolves into alcohol, because of the hydrogen-bonding between the alcohol solvent and the hydroxyl groups of the sugar. Wax dissolves into oil, because it is entropically favorable to do so and like dissolves like. Although individual van der Waals interactions are weak, over a long molecule they become significant.

Solvent properties impact chromatography and extraction. In chromatography, solutes with high solubility in a solvent have a high affinity for the mobile phase, so they travel farther and faster. In extraction, solutes are separated from one another by their relative solubility in two solvents. Micelles can be employed to increase the apparent solubility of a solute in a solvent in which it is insoluble. This is how a nonpolar particle can dissolve into water. A soap (surfactant) must be both hydrophilic and hydrophobic simultaneously. Such molecules contain a polar (or charged) end (referred to as the *head*) and an alkyl chain (referred to as the *tail*). Soap molecules form micelles when placed into water. Micelles are little pockets (roughly spherical in shape) with an organic core and polar heads sticking out from the core to interact with the water.

Example 1.23

Which of the following compounds would make the BEST micelle?

A. $H_3C(CH_2)_3CO_2H$

B. $H_3C(CH_2)_3CO_2^-$

C. $H_3C(CH_2)_{14}CO_2H$

D. $H_3C(CH_2)_{14}CO_2^-$

Solution

The best micelle has an ionic (charged) head and a long carbon chain for the organic tail. Choices A and C are eliminated, because they have uncharged heads. Although a carboxylic acid group is polar and protic, a charged site is better, because it is more hydrophilic when charged. Choice **D** is better than choice B, because it has a longer organic tail. Pick **D** to score big on this question.

Key Points for Molecular Structure (Section 1)

Nomenclature

1. IUPAC Nomenclature (Names are assigned systematically based on functional groups and carbon chain length)
   a) Name Root (Assigned according to the longest chain)
   b) Suffices (Assigned according to functional group--generally, the most oxidized functional group gets top priority)
   c) Prefixes (Assigned to note stereochemistry; i.e., R or S, E or Z, and α or ß)
   d) Common Nomenclature (Prefixes based on substitution and relative positions of functional groups; i.e., geminal diol and secondary alcohol)

Bonding and Orbitals

1. Bonding (An attractive interaction between neighboring atoms)
   a) Covalent Bond (The sharing of electrons between atoms; carbon makes covalent bonds)
      i. Single bonds are made of a sigma-bond; they are weaker than both double and triple bonds.
      ii. Double bonds are made of one sigma-bond and one π-bond; they are weaker than triple bonds, but stringer than single bonds.
      iii. Triple bonds are made of one sigma-bond and two π-bonds; they are stronger than both single and double bonds.
      iv. Sigma-bonds share electron density between nuclei while π-bonds share electron density in the plane above and below the nuclei.
   b) Molecular Orbitals
      i. Like atoms, bonds have electrons in regions of high probability, so there are sigma and pi orbitals to describe molecular bonds.
      ii. Sigma bonding orbitals are more stable than pi bonding orbitals, while sigma anti-bonding orbitals are less stable than pi anti-bonding orbitals. They fill $\sigma^2 \pi^4 \pi^{*4} \sigma^{*2}$
      iii. Anti-bonding orbitals have no overlap between atoms
   c) Structural Rules (Atoms obey predictable behavior when making bonds)
      i. Octet Rule (Atoms in the second row of the periodic table seek to complete their valence shell by obtaining eight electrons.)
      ii. HONC Rule (In neutral molecules, H makes one bond, O makes two bonds, N makes three bonds, and C makes four bonds. If an atom deviates from these values, it carries a charge.)

Hybridization

1. The mixing of atomic orbitals (s and p in organic chemistry) to form hybrid orbitals capable of combining to make molecular orbitals.
   a) sp-hybridization results in linear compounds, often with two π-bonds, a 180° bond angle, and the shortest of all hybrid orbitals.
   b) sp^2-hybridization results in trigonal planar compounds, often with one π-bond, a 120° bond angle, and a medium sized hybrid orbital.
   c) sp^3-hybridization results in tetrahedral compounds, with no π-bonds, a 109.5° bond angle, and the longest of all hybrid orbitals.

Bond Dissociation Energy

1. The energy required to break a bond in a homolytic fashion (into free radicals) is the bond dissociation energy. Higher BE refers to a stronger bond.
   a) BDE depends on the atoms, the substitution, and electron distribution
   b) Ionic bonds, rare in organic chemistry, break in a heterolytic fashion.

Intramolecular Features

1. Forces Affecting Electron Distribution within a Molecule
   a) Resonance (Sharing of π-electrons through an array of p-orbitals)
      i. Most stable resonance structure has an octet for all atoms but hydrogen, minimal charged sites, and if there must be a charge, it sits on an atom of appropriate electronegativity.
      ii. Also know as conjugation when dealing with just π-bonds
      iii. Atoms with lone pairs are generally electron-donating while atoms with a π-bond and no lone pair are generally electron-withdrawing.
   b) Inductive Effect (The pull of electron density through sigma bonds)
      i. Depends on electronegativity of atoms
      ii. Diminishes over distance, becoming negligible after four carbons.
   c) Steric Hindrance (Repulsion of two atoms at the same location)
   d) Aromaticity (Stability for cyclic systems with a set number of π-electrons)
      i. Must contain a continuous cycle of overlapping p-orbitals
      ii. Must have $4n + 2$ π-electrons, where n is 0, 1, 2, etc... (Hückel's Rule)

Fundamental Reactivity

1. Organic Chemistry at it foundation is Lewis Acid-Base Chemistry
   a) Acid-Base Chemistry
      i. Brønsted-Lowry deals with proton transfer while Lewis deals with the accepting and donating of electron pairs.
      ii. Electron pair donors are Lewis bases and nucleophiles, while electron pair acceptors are Lewis acids and electrophiles.
   b) Determining Acid Strength (stronger acids have lower pK_a values)
      i. Primary factors affecting acid strength are the size, hybridization and electronegativity of the atom to which H is bonded.
      ii. Secondary factors affecting acid strength are resonance and induction.
      iii. Base strength goes in the opposite fashion as an acid.
   c) Acid and Base Terminology and Facts
      i. Acids: $pH = -\log[H_3O^+]$, $[H_3O^+] = 10^{-pH}$, $pK_a = -\log K_a$, $K_a = 10^{-pK_a}$
      ii. As acid strength increases: 1) acid dissociation increases, 2) K_a increases, 3) pK_a decreases, 4) pH in an aqueous solution decreases, and 5) conjugate base strength decreases and stability increases
      iii. Bases: $pOH = -\log[OH^-]$, $[OH^-] = 10^{-pOH}$, $pK_b = -\log K_b$, $K_b = 10^{-pK_b}$
      iv. As base strength increases: 1) base hydrolysis increases, 2) K_b increases, 3) pK_b decreases, 4) pH in aqueous solution increases, and 5) conjugate acid strength decreases and stability increases

Physical Properties

1. The physical properties of a compound are affected by intermolecular forces
   a) Hydrogen Bonding (Occurs between H on N, O, or F and a lone pair)
      i. Increases boiling point and melting point by increasing attraction.
   b) Polarity (Interaction between dipoles of adjacent compounds
      i. Polar interactions are weaker than a hydrogen bonds
   c) Van der Waals Forces (Weak interaction between temporary dipoles)
      i. Small impact on physical properties
   d) Solubility and Miscibility (Ability to dissolve into a solvent)
      i. Based on the idea that "Like dissolves like."
      ii. Solid into solvent is solubility while liquid into solvent is miscibility

25 Molecular Structure Review Questions

The main purpose of this 25-question set is to serve as a review of the material presented in the chapter. Do not worry about the timing for these questions. Focus on learning. Once you complete these questions, grade them using the answer key. For any question you missed, repeat it and write down your thought process. Then grade the questions you repeated and thoroughly read the answer explanation. Compare your thought process to the answer explanation and assess whether you missed the question because of a careless error (such as misreading the question), because of an error in reasoning, or because you were lacking information. Your goal is to fill in any informational gaps and solidify your reasoning before you begin your practice exam for this section. Preparing for the MCAT is best done in stages. This first stage is meant to help you evaluate how well you know this subject matter.

The enthalpy of reaction can be determined from bond energies. This assumes that a bond between two atoms has a fixed value for its bond dissociation energy, regardless of the substituents on the molecule. This is to say that one assumes a covalent bond between carbon and iodine always has the same bond energy, whether the carbon is a tertiary or primary carbon. This assumption is inaccurate but close enough for first approximations. Table 1 lists a series of energies for common bonds in a wide range of organic molecules.

Bond	BE ($\frac{kcal}{mole}$)	Bond	BE ($\frac{kcal}{mole}$)
H_3C-I	56	H_3C-CH_3	88
H_3C-Cl	84	$H_5C_2-CH_3$	85
H_3C-OH	91	$(H_3C)_2CH-CH_3$	84
H_5C_2-I	53	$(H_3C)_3C-CH_3$	81
H_5C_2-Cl	81	$H_2C=CH-CH_3$	97
H_5C_2-OH	91	H_3C-H	104
$(H_3C)_2CH-I$	52	H_5C_2-H	98
$(H_3C)_2CH-Cl$	80	$(H_3C)_2CH-H$	95
$(H_3C)_2CH-OH$	90	$(H_3C)_3C-H$	91
$(H_3C)_3C-I$	50	$H_2C=CH-H$	108
$(H_3C)_3C-Cl$	79	H_3CO-H	102
$(H_3C)_3C-OH$	89	H_5C_2O-H	103

Table 1

The values in Table 1 demonstrate the effect of alkyl groups on neighboring atoms and the bonds that they form. There are correlations between carbon substitution and bond strength and between atomic size and bond strength. There is also a correlation between hybridization and bond strength, but it cannot be inferred from the data in Table 1. There are too few examples of varying degrees of hybridization to reach a solid conclusion about the effect of hybridization on bond strength. The effect of substitution on an alkene on bond strength can also be evaluated using bond energetics. Table 2 lists the enthalpy of reaction for the hydrogenation reactions of various alkenes that vary due to the effect of alkyl groups on the strength of a π-bond.

Alkene	ΔH ($\frac{kcal}{mole}$)
$H_2C=CH_2$	-32.6
$RHC=CH_2$	-30.2
cis-$RHC=CHR$	-28.5
$R_2C=CH_2$	-28.3
trans-$RHC=CHR$	-27.4
$R_2C=CHR$	-26.7
$R_2C=CR_2$	-26.4

Table 2

The presence of an alkyl group on an alkene strengthens its π-bond. Alkyl groups on vinylic carbons are considered to be electron donating, so π-bonds must be electron acceptors.

1. What bond dissociation energy would you expect for the bond between carbon-1 and hydrogen and the only carbon-carbon single bond in $H-C\equiv C-CH_3$?

   A. C_1-H 92 kcal/mole; C_2-C_3 86 kcal/mole
   B. C_1-H 116 kcal/mole; C_2-C_3 86 kcal/mole
   C. C_1-H 92 kcal/mole; C_2-C_3 110 kcal/mole
   D. C_1-H 116 kcal/mole; C_2-C_3 110 kcal/mole

2. Bromine would make the STRONGEST bond with which type of carbon?

   A. Methyl
   B. Primary
   C. Secondary
   D. Tertiary

3. What can be concluded about the relationship between atomic size and bonding?

   A. Smaller atoms form longer, stronger bonds than larger atoms.
   B. Smaller atoms form longer, weaker bonds than larger atoms.
   C. Smaller atoms form shorter, stronger bonds than larger atoms.
   D. Smaller atoms form shorter, weaker bonds than larger atoms.

4. The GREATEST amount of energy is released by the oxidative cleavage of an alkene that is:

   A. unsubstituted.
   B. monosubstituted.
   C. disubstituted.
   D. trisubstituted.

5. The difference in enthalpy of hydrogenation between the cis and trans alkenes can be attributed to a difference in:

   A. resonance.
   B. hybridization.
   C. the electronegativity of carbon.
   D. steric hindrance.

6. The hybridization of the carbons in $H_2C=CH-CH_3$ can best be described as:

A. sp, sp, and sp^2.
B. sp, sp, and sp^3.
C. sp^3, sp^3, and sp^2.
D. sp^2, sp^2, and sp^3.

7. Which of the following carbon-halogen single bonds is the strongest?

A. H_3C-I
B. H_3C-Cl
C. $(H_3C)_2CH-I$
D. $(H_3C)_2CH-Cl$

8. The GREATEST amount of energy is required to break which of the following carbon-carbon bonds?

A. H_3C-CH_3
B. $(H_3C)_3C-C(CH_3)_3$
C. $H_2C=CH_2$
D. $(H_3C)_2C=C(CH_3)_2$

Passage II (Questions 9 - 15)

For years, chemists pondered whether amides were protonated on the nitrogen or oxygen atom. The amide is an analog to peptide linkages, so the root of this question is founded in the chemistry of proteins. By determining the site of protonation, conclusions about hydrogen-bonding in the secondary structure of proteins can be made. Before the advent and advancement of x-ray crystallography, protein structure could only be hypothesized. Due to the importance of hydrogen-bonding in protein structure, determination of the protonation site was critical. Figure 1 shows the structural effects of protonation on the oxygen atom of the amide.

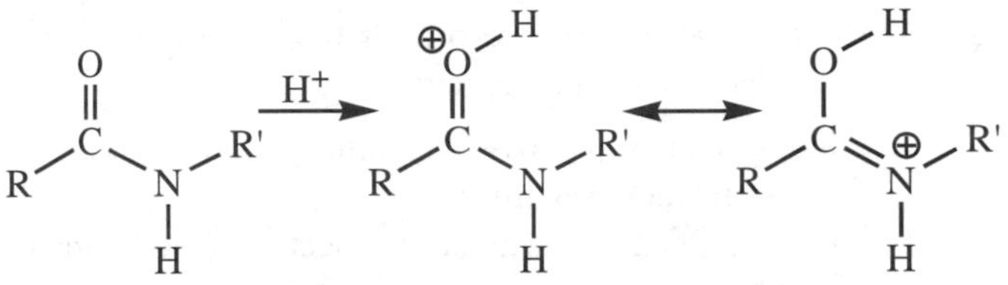

Figure 1 Protonation of amide on oxygen

Figure 2 shows the structural effects of protonation on the nitrogen atom of the amide.

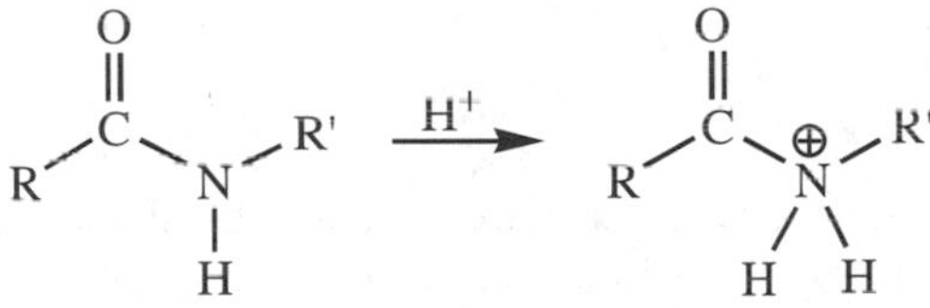

Figure 2 Protonation of amide on nitrogen

Protonation at the oxygen site is favored because of the resonance stabilization of the protonated product, similar to what is observed when protonating esters. Despite the greater basicity of nitrogen relative to oxygen (oxygen is less basic, because it is more electronegative), the resonance stability is great enough to favor O-protonation. This manifests itself in protein structure through the formation of hydrogen-bonds from the carbonyl oxygen (lone-pair donor) to the nitrogen proton (partially positive proton). Support for this conclusion is found in the planar ß-pleated sheets and helices observed in the secondary structure of proteins.

Because of the resonance structures with O-protonation, the six atoms of the amide are all coplanar. This is due to the sp^2-hybridization of carbon, oxygen, and nitrogen.

9. Which arrangement accurately relates the boiling points of acetamide (H_3CCONH_2), acetone (H_3CCOCH_3), and propane to each other in descending order?

A. $BP_{acetamide} > BP_{acetone} > BP_{propane}$
B. $BP_{acetone} > BP_{acetamide} > BP_{propane}$
C. $BP_{propane} > BP_{acetamide} > BP_{acetone}$
D. $BP_{propane} > BP_{acetone} > BP_{acetamide}$

10. Which of the following statements CANNOT be true?

   I.   The C=O bond of an amide is shorter than the C=O bond of a ketone.

   II. The C-N bond of an amide is shorter than the C-N bond of a primary amine.

   III. Amides are more basic that aldehydes.

   A. I only

   B. III only

   C. I and II only

   D. I and III only

11. We know that amides are protonated at oxygen rather than nitrogen, because oxygen:

   A. is less electronegative than nitrogen, so it donates electrons more readily.

   B. is larger than nitrogen, so it's electron cloud attracts protons more readily.

   C. carries a partial positive charge due to resonance withdrawal of π-electrons by the nitrogen.

   D. carries a partial negative charge due to resonance donation of π-electrons from the nitrogen.

12. Which of the following statements correctly describes the geometry of the molecule shown below?

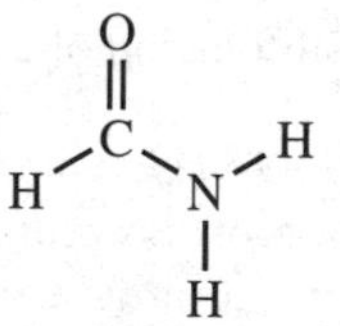

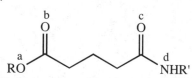

   A. The nitrogen has trigonal pyramidal geometry, so the two hydrogens are outside of the plane created by the other four atoms.

   B. The nitrogen has tetrahedral geometry, so the two hydrogens are outside of the plane created by the other four atoms.

   C. The carbon has tetrahedral geometry, so the carbon hydrogen is outside of the plane created by the other five atoms.

   D. The six atoms are coplanar.

13. The MOST stable hydrogen-bond between amides extends from the:

   A. carbonyl oxygen to the H on nitrogen.

   B. the carbonyl oxygen to the H on carbon.

   C. amide nitrogen to the H on another nitrogen.

   D. amide nitrogen to the H on carbon.

14. Which of the following is NOT a resonance structure of an amide?

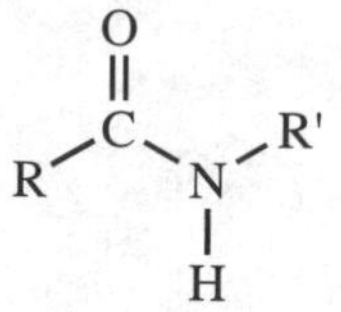

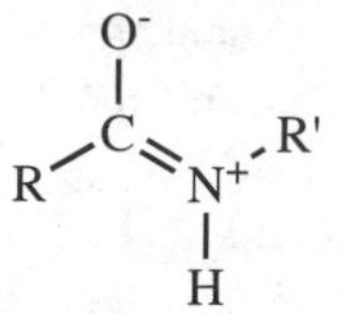

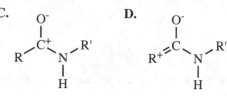

15. What is the MOST basic site on the following molecule?

   A. Site a

   B. Site b

   C. Site c

   D. Site d

Passage III (Questions 16 - 22)

A hydrogen bond is formed between an atom able to donate a lone pair of electrons and an electropositive hydrogen (an H covalently bonded to nitrogen, oxygen, or fluorine). Any hydrogen capable of forming a hydrogen bond is said to be *protic*. A protic hydrogen can form one covalent bond and one hydrogen bond. As the hydrogen bond becomes stronger, the covalent bond becomes weaker. This is to say that as a lone pair is donated to a protic hydrogen, the original covalent bond to hydrogen weakens.

Covalent bonds can be studied using infrared spectroscopy. Different bonds have different characteristic absorbances based on their bond strength and atomic masses. Because the degree of hydrogen-bonding affects the strength of the covalent bond, a hydrogen bond can be seen indirectly in the IR stretch of the hydroxyl peak. Figure 1 shows the IR absorbances associated with four different hydroxyl groups.

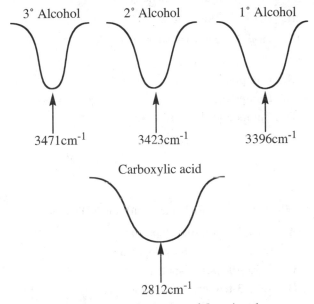

Figure 1 IR signals for hydroxyl functional groups

Because hydrogen-bonding weakens the covalent bond, the IR signal of a covalent bond between atoms involved in hydrogen-bonding broadens as the degree of hydrogen-bonding increases. Not all hydrogen bonds are equivalent, so the signal becomes a range of absorbances that appear as one broad band. The wave number of the absorbance lowers, because the energy decreases. The absorbances in Figure 1 show that as hydrogen-bonding increases, the IR signal broadens and the maximum absorbance occurs at a lower wave number.

16. According to the IR absorbances in Figure 1, which of the following compounds exhibits the GREATEST amount of hydrogen-bonding?

   A. The tertiary alcohol
   B. The secondary alcohol
   C. The primary alcohol
   D. The carboxylic acid

17. Which of the following amine compounds should show the BROADEST signal above 3000 cm^{-1}?

   A. Ammonia
   B. Propylamine
   C. Dipropylamine
   D. Tripropylamine

18. How is the absorbance value in the IR for a covalent bond between oxygen and hydrogen affected by the bond length and hydrogen-bonding to other atoms?

   A. As the bond length increases, the wave number (cm^{-1}) of the absorbance decreases; so as the degree of hydrogen-bonding increases, the bond length increases and the wave number (cm^{-1}) of the absorbance decreases.

   B. As the bond length increases, the wave number (cm^{-1}) of the absorbance increases; so as the degree of hydrogen-bonding increases, the bond length increases and the wave number (cm^{-1}) of the absorbance increases.

   C. As the bond length increases, the wave number (cm^{-1}) of the absorbance decreases; so as the degree of hydrogen-bonding increases, the bond length decreases and the wave number (cm^{-1}) of the absorbance increases.

   D. As the bond length increases, the wave number (cm^{-1}) of the absorbance increases; so as the degree of hydrogen-bonding increases, the bond length decreases and the wave number (cm^{-1}) of the absorbance decreases.

19. Hydrogen-bonding occurs within which of the following compounds?

   A. Aldehydes
   B. Esters
   C. Ketones
   D. Primary amines

20. The STRONGEST hydrogen bond is formed between:

   A. the lone pair of O and a hydrogen bonded to O.
   B. the lone pair of N and a hydrogen bonded to O.
   C. the lone pair of O and a hydrogen bonded to N.
   D. the lone pair of N and a hydrogen bonded to N.

GO ON TO THE NEXT PAGE

21. As dimethyl sulfide is mixed into a pure sample of an alcohol, the O-H absorbance:

   A. broadens and shifts to a lower value on the wave number scale.

   B. broadens and shifts to a higher value on the wave number scale.

   C. sharpens and shifts to a lower value on the wave number scale.

   D. sharpens and shifts to a higher value on the wave number scale.

22. Which of the following statements CANNOT be true?

   I. The IR absorbance of a covalent bond involving an atom engaged in hydrogen-bonding is not affected by the hydrogen-bonding.

   II. The bond length of the covalent bond to the protic hydrogen increases with hydrogen-bonding.

   III. The acidity of a proton is increased by hydrogen-bonding.

   A. I only
   B. II only
   C. I and II only
   D. II and III only

Questions 23 through 25 are **NOT** based on a descriptive passage.

23. Which of the following compounds has the HIGHEST boiling point?

   A. 2-pentene
   B. Diethyl ether
   C. Heptanal
   D. Cyclohexanol

24. Which of the following molecules would have a dipole moment NOT equal to zero?

   I. Z-1,4-dichloro-2-butene
   II. E-1,4-dichloro-2-butene
   III. cis-1,2-dichlorocyclopentane

   A. Compound I only
   B. Compound II only
   C. Compound III only
   D. Compounds I and III only

25. Which of the following molecules is NOT polar?

   A. cis-1,3-dichlorocyclopentane
   B. trans-1,3-dichlorocyclopentane
   C. E-1,4-dichloro-2-butene
   D. 1,2,2,3-tetrabromopropane

1. D	2. A	3. C	4. A	5. D
6. D	7. B	8. D	9. A	10. A
11. D	12. D	13. A	14. D	15. C
16. D	17. A	18. A	19. D	20. B
21. D	22. A	23. D	24. D	25. C

YOU ARE DONE.

Answers to 25-Question Molecular Structure Review

1. **Choice D is the best answer.** Table 1 does not include any alkynes, so the bond energies for bonds involving sp-hybridized carbons must be estimated from trends in the data. According to data in Table 1, a bond between two sp^3-hybridized carbons has a bond dissociation energy, BDE, between 81 and 88 kcals/mole. A bond between an sp^2-hybridized carbon and an sp^3-hybridized carbon has a BDE of 97 kcals/mole. This means that the bond between C_2 and C_3, a bond between an sp-hybridized carbon and an sp^3-hybridized carbon, should have a BDE greater than 97 kcals/mole. This eliminates choices A and B. A bond between a hydrogen and an sp^3-hybridized carbon has a BDE between 91 and 104 kcals/mole. A bond between a hydrogen and an sp^2-hybridized carbon has a BDE of 108 kcals/mole. This means that the bond between hydrogen and an sp-hybridized carbon should have a BDE greater than 108 kcals/mole. This eliminates choice C and leaves choice **D** as the only remaining answer choice. This question is good in that it asks you to use the trends in the table to make a logical choice.

2. **Choice A is the best answer.** According to the bond dissociation energies listed in Table 1, iodine and chlorine both make their strongest bonds to methyl carbons (followed by primary, then secondary, and finally tertiary carbons). It thus can be assumed that bromine would exhibit the same behavior as these other two halides, resulting in the strongest bond to bromine being formed by a methyl carbon. Choice **A** is the best answer.

3. **Choice C is the best answer.** Table 1 shows an increase in bond strength for bonds formed between equivalent carbons and atoms of decreasing size (I, Cl, and O). From this, it can be concluded that shorter bonds are generally stronger than longer bonds, and that as atomic size decreases, the bond length to a neighboring atom decreases. No bond-length data are provided in the table, but this can be inferred from the passage. Choice **C** describes this relationship best, with smaller atoms forming shorter and stronger bonds.

4. **Choice A is the best answer.** The hydrogenation of an unsubstituted alkene yields the greatest energy according to the heats of hydrogenation listed in Table 2. In general, a less stable reactant yields a greater amount of heat upon reaction, so the π-bond must be weakest in an unsubstituted alkene (making it the least stable of the alkenes). The energy generated from oxidative cleavage, or any reaction that breaks the π-bond, is greatest when the alkene is unsubstituted. The best answer is choice **A**. If you didn't reach this conclusion from the data, you should have eliminated choices B and C at the minimum, because they are *middle* choices. For questions asking for the most or the least, the best answer is nearly always one of the extreme answers.

5. **Choice D is the best answer.** The difference in reactivity between the cis and trans geometrical isomers of an alkene is attributed to greater intramolecular steric hindrance in the cis compound than the trans compound, because the substituents are on the same side of the molecule where they can interact. The resonance, hybridization, and electronegativity of carbon are the same in both geometrical isomers of the alkene. This eliminates choices A, B, and C and leaves choice **D** as the best answer.

6. **Choice D is the best answer.** This question should be a welcome freebie, relative to other questions in this passage. In the interest of generating a bell curve for any standardized exam (such as the MCAT), there needs to be some straight-forward questions. You must not make careless errors on such questions. Alkene carbons have sp^2-hybridization, and alkane carbons have sp^3-hybridization. Two of the three carbons in the compound are alkene carbons, while the other carbon is an alkane carbon. The best answer is choice **D**, two sp^2-hybridized carbons and one sp^3-hybridized carbon. Pick choice **D** to get your point for correctness.

7. **Choice B is the best answer.** Table 1 lists the bond dissociation energy for several bonds. The energy listed is the energy required to break the bond in a homolytic fashion. This in essence means that Table 1 lists the bond strength. The strongest bond, according to that data listed in Table 1, is the bond with the highest bond energy. This questions requires we read straight form the table. The highest value among the answer choices is the bond between the methyl carbon and chlorine (84 kcals/mole). The best answer is choice **B**.

8. **Choice D is the best answer.** From background information, you must know that double bonds are stronger than single bonds, meaning that more energy is required to break a double bond than a single bond. Choices A and B are thus eliminated. A lower heat of hydrogenation in Table 2 implies that the reactant alkene molecule is more stable. The more stable the alkene compound, the stronger its π-bond. This means that the double bond in the tetrasubstituted alkene is stronger than the double bond in the unsubstituted alkene. The best answer is choice **D**.

9.   **Choice A is the best answer.** Given that the molecular masses of the three compounds are roughly equal (59 g/mol, 58 g/mol, and 44 g/mol), the top consideration for determining their boiling points is the intermolecular forces. An amide has hydrogen-bonding, while a ketone and a hydrocarbon do not. At room temperature, most amides are solids, acetone is a volatile liquid, and propane is a gas. Based strictly on the phases, the best answer (and the only answer that lists acetamide as the highest) is choice **A**, $BP_{acetamide} > BP_{acetone} > BP_{propane}$. Acetone has a higher boiling point than propane, because it is polar and more massive.

10.   **Choice A is the best answer.** Because of the resonance donation from nitrogen, the carbonyl bond (C=O) of an amide has some single-bond character. Since a single bond is longer than a double bond, the single-bond character of the amide carbonyl bond results in a longer carbonyl bond than the unconjugated carbonyl (as observed with the ketone). This makes statement I a false (*not* true) statement. Because of the previously mentioned resonance, the carbon-nitrogen bond has some double-bond character, making it shorter than a standard carbon-nitrogen single bond (as seen with a primary amine). This makes statement II a true statement. Because of the resonance, the carbonyl oxygen carries a partial negative charge. This makes the oxygen more basic than typical carbonyl oxygens (such as the one in an aldehyde). Statement III is also a true statement. Only statement I is *not* true, so choice **A** is the best answer.

11.   **Choice D is the best answer.** As emphasized in the passage, nitrogen donates electron density to oxygen through resonance. This places a partial negative charge on oxygen (increasing its basicity) and a partial positive charge on nitrogen (decreasing its basicity). Choice C is thus eliminated, and choice **D** is correct. Choice A should be eliminated, because oxygen is more electronegative than nitrogen. Choice B should be eliminated, because oxygen is smaller than nitrogen. Picking choice **D** is the only thing to do in a situation like this.

12.   **Choice D is the best answer.** Because of the resonance donation from nitrogen, the nitrogen has sp^2-hybridization. Having sp^2-hybridization results in trigonal planar geometry. The carbonyl carbon also has trigonal planar geometry, so the central two atoms force the three hydrogens and one oxygen to assume a coplanar orientation. Choices A, B, and C therefore all must be eliminated as incorrect geometric descriptions, making choice **D** the best answer. The two resonance forms and the resonance hybrid are drawn below:

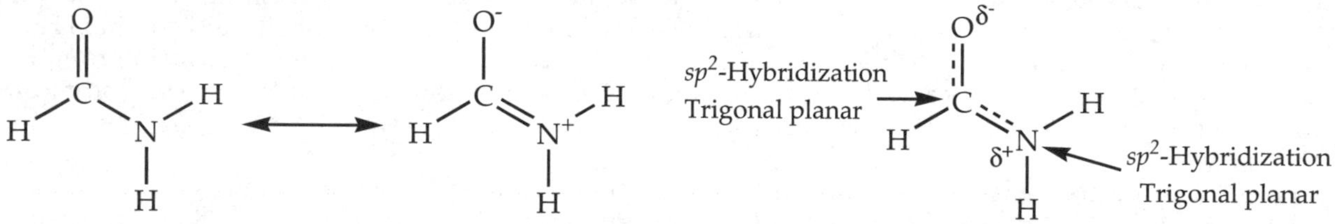

13.   **Choice A is the best answer.** The most stable hydrogen bond forms between the best lone-pair donor (most basic site) and the hydrogen with the greatest partial positive charge. Because amides are protonated at the carbonyl oxygen (as stated and drawn in the passage), the carbonyl oxygen is most basic and thus donates one lone pair of electrons. This eliminates both choice C and choice D. Of the answer choices remaining, the hydrogen on nitrogen carries the partial positive charge, not the hydrogen on carbon. This means that the hydrogen bond forms between the carbonyl oxygen and the hydrogen bonded to nitrogen, thus the best answer is choice **A**. If you are unsure, think of the hydrogen-bonding in ß-pleated sheets.

14.   **Choice D is the best answer.** Choice A is the most stable resonance structure of the amide (all octet and no formal charges are present). When nitrogen donates electron density to oxygen, choice B becomes the resonance structure. This is a minor contributor due to the formation of charges on the molecule. The fact that it is an all-octet resonance structure is favorable. If the nitrogen were to pull its π-electrons back from the carbon in answer choice B, the resonance structure represented by answer choice C would be formed. Because carbon does not have a complete octet in this resonance structure, it is a very minor contributor, but it is none-the-less a resonance structure of the amide. It is not possible to form a double bond to the R-group, because that would require five bonds to carbon. In order for carbon to donate in that manner (and have only four bonds), it must have had a lone pair (and thus a negative charge) in the original structure. R was not drawn as having a lone pair, so it is assumed that the R represents a standard alkyl group. The best answer is therefore choice **D**.

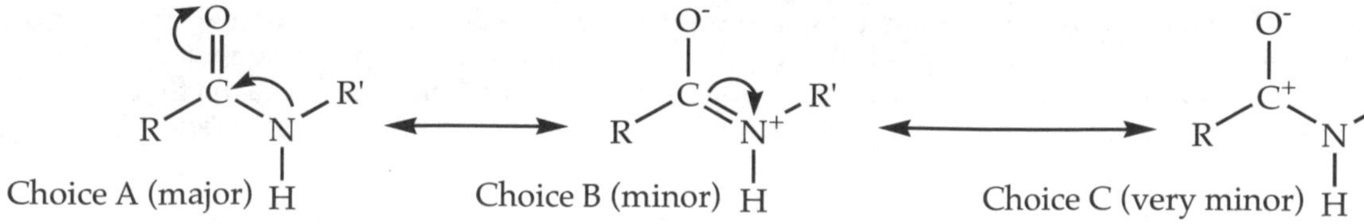

15. **Choice C is the best answer.** From the passage, we know that amides are protonated at the carbonyl oxygen, so choice D is eliminated. Because nitrogen is less electronegative than oxygen, it donates more electron density to the carbonyl oxygen (through resonance) than the ester oxygen donates to the ester carbonyl oxygen. This places a larger partial negative charge on the amide carbonyl oxygen than on the ester carbonyl oxygen. The larger negative charge makes Site c the most basic site. Choice **C** is therefore the best answer.

Passage III   (Questions 16 - 22)   **IR Determination of 1°, 2°, and 3° Alcohols**

16. **Choice D is the best answer.** Hydrogen-bonding weakens the covalent bond to hydrogen and thus makes the bond easier to vibrate (stretch and compress). This means that as the degree of hydrogen-bonding to a protic hydrogen increases, the IR absorbance for the covalent bond decreases in energy (as well as in terms of wave numbers) and the peak broadens (showing a range of various strengths associated with the hydrogen-oxygen covalent bond). The smallest wave number and broadest absorbance in the IR in Figure 1 is associated with the carboxylic acid, so the greatest amount of hydrogen-bonding is found with the carboxylic acid and not any of the alcohols. This fact is supported by the greater acidity associated with a carboxylic acid than an alcohol, implying that the O—H bond is weaker in a carboxylic acid than an alcohol. The best answer is choice **D**.

17. **Choice A is the best answer.** The broadest peak is associated with the compound having the greatest amount of hydrogen-bonding. As is observed in alcohols (where primary alcohols exhibit greater hydrogen-bonding than their secondary and tertiary counterparts), the amine with the least steric hindrance exhibits the greatest amount of hydrogen-bonding. The least steric hindrance of the four choices is found in ammonia. The best answer is choice **A**. As a point of interest, the tertiary amine has no N-H covalent bonds, so it has no hydrogen-bonding as well as no peak above 3000 cm^{-1}.

18. **Choice A is the best answer.** The relationship between bond strength and IR absorbance is that the lower the absorbance value in the IR (as measured in cm^{-1}), the lower the energy associated with the stretching vibration of the bond. The lower the energy necessary to stretch a bond, the lower the energy necessary to break the bond, and thus the weaker that bond. Longer bonds are usually weaker bonds. Thus, as bond length increases, the wave number for the bond's IR absorbance decreases. This eliminates choices B and D. An increase in the degree of hydrogen-bonding weakens and thus lengthens the bond. This eliminates choice C and makes choice **A** the best answer. If you want to do what you should do, pick **A** and gain incredible satisfaction doing what you should do.

19. **Choice D is the best answer.** Hydrogen bonding requires the presence of an atom with lone pairs to share and a protic hydrogen (found bonded to either r N, O, or F). Of the four choices, only primary amines have a protic hydrogen, which means that only primary amines exhibit hydrogen-bonding. All of the Hs in an aldehyde, ketone, and ester are bonded to carbons, so they cannot form hydrogen-bonds. The best answer is choice **D**.

20. **Choice B is the best answer.** The strongest hydrogen bond comes from the more basic lone-pair donor (found on the nitrogen atom, which is less electronegative than oxygen) being donated to the most protic hydrogen (found covalently bonded to the oxygen). This makes choice **B** the best answer.

21. **Choice D is the best answer.** The addition of dimethyl sulfide to solution reduces the degree of hydrogen bonding exhibited by the alcohol, because fewer alcohols will be adjacent to one another to form hydrogen bonds. The absorbance associated with a hydroxyl peak sharpens with the reduced hydrogen bonding. Associated with reduced hydrogen-bonding is a stronger average covalent bond and thus an IR absorbance with a higher wave number. Pick choice **D** for optimum correctness satisfaction.

22. **Choice A is the best answer.** The IR absorbance of a covalent bond is affected by hydrogen-bonding as stated in the passage, so Statement I is *not* true. As hydrogen-bonding increases, the covalent bond lengthens, so Statement II is true. The acidity of a proton increases with hydrogen-bonding, because the covalent bond to hydrogen is weakened. This is why acidity is higher in water than in other solvents. This makes Statement III true. The only *not* true statement is Statement I. The best answer is thus choice **A**.

Questions 23 - 25   **Not Based on a Descriptive Passage**

23. **Choice D is the best answer.** Alcohols exhibit hydrogen-bonding, which increases their intermolecular forces. The stronger forces make it harder to move a molecule from the liquid phase into the gas phase. This raises the boiling point of an alcohol compared to a molecule of comparable size, so choice **D** has the highest boiling point. Molecular mass is of concern as well, but choice **D** is also the heaviest of the choices.

24. **Choice D is the best answer.** Saying that a compound has a dipole that is not equal to zero is equivalent to saying that the compound is polar. Cis compounds (both alkenes and cyclic structures) are always polar, because they always have substituents on the same side as one another. This makes both Compound I and Compound III polar. You need not even examine Compound II, because no answer choice includes all three compounds. Pick choice **D** to score more MCAT points.

25. **Choice C is the best answer.** For a compound not to be polar, it must be symmetric. Cis compounds are asymmetric about a point (although they may have mirror-plane symmetry, rather than point symmetry), and thus are always polar, so choice A is eliminated. This leaves choices B, C and D as possible answers. An odd-numbered ring must be polar when it has two substituents, so choice B is polar and thus ruled out. In choice D, the middle carbon has varying substituents attached (not all four groups are identical), so it cannot be symmetric, thus it is polar, too. By eliminating three choices, choice **C** must be the best answer. Drawing choice **C** out shows that the individual dipoles for the bonds cancel each other out, making the compound overall nonpolar.

E-1,4-dichloro-2-butene

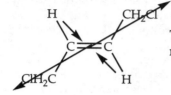

The individual vectors cancel out, so there is no net vector. The compound is nonpolar.

52-Question Molecular Structure Practice Exam

Molecular Structure Exam Scoring Scale

Raw Score	MCAT Score
42 - 52	13 - 15
34 - 41	10 - 12
24 - 33	7 - 9
17 - 23	4 - 6
1 - 16	1 - 3

Passage I (Questions 1 - 6)

Pheromones are chemicals secreted by animals (most commonly insects) that elicit a specific behavioral reaction in other members of the same species. They are effective in low concentration in sending signals between members of the same species for such things as reproduction, danger warnings, and aggregation (in the case of a food supply.) The structures of four pheromones are shown in Figure 1.

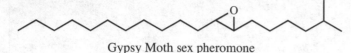

Gypsy Moth sex pheromone

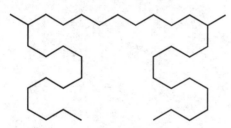

Grape Berry Moth sex pheromone

Green Peach Aphid defense pheromone

Female Tsetse Fly sex pheromone

Figure 1 Selected pheromones

For sex pheromones, a female in the species will release the pheromone when she is ready to mate so that another member of species can detect the pheromone from far away.

1. The Gypsy Moth sex pheromone has all of the following structural features EXCEPT:

   A. two stereogenic centers.
   B. one unit of unsaturation.
   C. three tertiary carbons.
   D. ring strain.

2. What functional groups are found in the sex pheromone for the Grape Berry Moth?

   A. An alkene and an ester
   B. An alkene and an ether
   C. An alkene and an anhydride
   D. An alkyne and an ester

3. Which of the following statements accurately relates the four structures shown in Figure 1?

   I. The Gypsy Moth sex pheromone has a shorter wavelength absorbance in UV-visible spectroscopy than the Grape Berry Moth sex pheromone.
   II. The female Tsetse fly sex pheromone has the least structural flexibility.
   III. The Green Peach Aphid defense pheromone has the most sp^2-hybridized carbons of the four structures in Figure 1.

   A. I only
   B. III only
   C. I and II only
   D. I and III only

4. Which of the pheromones exhibits conjugation?

   A. The Grape Berry Moth sex pheromone
   B. The Green Peach Aphid defense pheromone
   C. The Gypsy Moth sex pheromones
   D. The Tsetse Fly sex pheromone

5. Which spectroscopic observation does NOT correlate with the corresponding compound?

   A. The Grape Berry Moth sex pheromone: an IR absorbance at 1741 cm^{-1}
   B. The Green Peach Aphid defense pheromone: a UV-visible absorbance at 227 nm
   C. The Gypsy Moth sex pheromones: two signals above 2.00 ppm in its ^{1}H NMR
   D. The Tsetse Fly sex pheromone: 23 unique carbons in its ^{13}C NMR spectrum

6. When treated with aqueous hydrochloric acid, the Grape Berry Moth sex pheromone in Figure 1 would yield:

   A. a diene.
   B. an ester and an alcohol.
   C. a carboxylic acid and an alcohol.
   D. a carboxylic acid and an ether.

Two of the more common applications of fatty acids in biological systems are as part of a phospholipid within cell membranes and as part of a triglyceride in energy storage. The fluidity and permeability of a cell membrane depends greatly on the nature of the fatty acids in the phospholipid bilayer. In general, as the units of unsaturation within the fatty acids increase, the fluidity of the cell membrane increases. Because of their utility in biological systems, a researcher opted to study the physical properties of several naturally occurring fatty acids. Figure 1 shows the structures for three of those compounds.

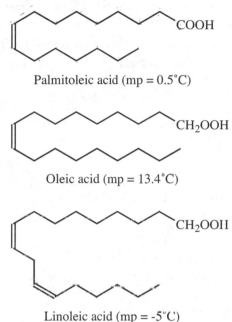

Palmitoleic acid (mp = 0.5°C)

Oleic acid (mp = 13.4°C)

Linoleic acid (mp = -5°C)

Figure 1 Three common fatty acids in biological systems

Shorthand notation for fatty acids involves naming the carbon count followed by the number of π-bonds. For instance, linoleic acid would be referred to as an 18:2 fatty acid. Listed below are the shorthand representations of some common fatty acids.

Compound	Shorthand	M.P.
Lauric acid	12:0	45°C
Myristic acid	14:0	55°C
Palmitic acid	16:0	
Stearic acid	18:0	
Palmitoleic acid	16:1 cis Δ^9	0.5°C
Oleic acid	18:1 cis Δ^9	13.4°C
Palmitolenic acid	16:2 cis Δ^9, Δ^{12}	-11°C
Linoleic acid	18:2 cis Δ^9, Δ^{12}	-5°C
Linolenic acid	18:3 cis $\Delta^9, \Delta^{12}, \Delta^{15}$	-34°C
Eleostearic acid	18:3 cis $\Delta^9, \Delta^{11}, \Delta^{13}$	-37°C
Arachidonic acid	20:4 cis $\Delta^5, \Delta^8, \Delta^{11}, \Delta^{14}$	-49°C

Table 1

7. What are the melting points for palmitic acid ($C_{15}H_{31}COOH$) and stearic acid ($C_{17}H_{35}COOH$)?
   - **A.** Palmitic acid mp = 62°C; stearic acid mp = 68°C
   - **B.** Palmitic acid mp = 71°C; stearic acid mp = 58°C
   - **C.** Palmitic acid mp = -12°C; stearic acid mp = 4°C
   - **D.** Palmitic acid mp = -8°C; stearic acid mp = -14°C

8. What is the IUPAC name for palmitoleic acid?
   - **A.** (E)-8-hexadecanoic acid
   - **B.** (E)-9-hexadecanoic acid
   - **C.** (Z)-9-hexadecanoic acid
   - **D.** (Z)-10-hexadecanoic acid

9. Which of the following statements accurately describes the impact of unsaturation on the properties of a fatty acid?
   - I. A fatty acid has at least one unit of unsaturation.
   - II. As units of unsaturation increase, the melting point of a fatty acid will increase.
   - III. As units of unsaturation increase, the fluidity of a cell membrane containing that acid increases.
   - **A.** I only
   - **B.** III only
   - **C.** I and III only
   - **D.** I, II, and III

10. Between oleate and stearate, which is more likely to be found in the cell membrane of a bone cell?
   - **A.** Oleate, because it has greater flexibility than stearate due to its carbon-carbon π-bond.
   - **B.** Stearate, because it has greater flexibility than oleate due to its lack of a carbon-carbon π-bond.
   - **C.** Oleate, because it has greater rigidity than stearate due to its carbon-carbon π-bond.
   - **D.** Stearate, because it has greater rigidity than oleate due to its lack of a carbon-carbon π-bond.

11. Assuming that a fatty acid is synthesized from acetyl CoA, it requires one mole of $FADH_2$ for every two carbons beyond the first two, if it is fully saturated. Synthesis of which fatty acid consumes the most $FADH_2$?
   - **A.** Fatty acid 16:1 cis Δ^9
   - **B.** Fatty acid 18:1 cis Δ^9
   - **C.** Fatty acid 16:2 cis Δ^9, Δ^{12}
   - **D.** Fatty acid 18:2 cis Δ^9, Δ^{12}

Many common household items are the products of basic organic chemistry. Dissolving one or more colored dyes into a volatile organic solvent, such as isopropanol, for instance, makes ink. Paint, like ink, is the combination of a dye and a solvent. When ink is applied to a porous surface such as paper, the pores of the material absorb the solution. Then as the volatile organic solvent evaporates away, the solid dye is left bound to the pores of the material. This is why ink can smear when initially applied, but once it has dried (once the solvent has evaporated away), the ink does not smear.

It is possible to remove dried ink from paper by treating it with organic solvent. A problem with this method is that the solvent diffuses radially across the paper, taking the dissolved dye with it as it travels. This is commonly referred to as *running* and is the basis of paper chromatography. Inks that run when water is spilled onto the paper to which they are bound are made out of water-soluble dyes. The eraser capable of removing erasable ink has a surface to which the dye in the ink adheres more tightly than it adheres to the paper.

Another common household product derived from organic compounds is soap. Each soap molecule has a *hydrophilic* (water-loving) end and a *hydrophobic* (water-fearing) end. In water, the hydrophobic portions of several soap molecules form an aggregate pore in which nonpolar, hydrophobic species (dirt and oil) can gather. This pore or *micelle* (the spherical cell formed by several aligned and coagulated soap molecules) is water-soluble, because the hydrophilic end of each molecule composing it solvates in the water. A micelle is removed by continuous exposure to running water, into which it dissolves and migrates.

One of the most common industrial soaps is sodium dodecyl sulfate (SDS), found in many commercial shampoos and hand soaps. Soaps can be made by treating animal lard (fatty-acid triglycerides) with a strong base (such as NaOH). This forms glycerol $(HOCH_2CH(OH)CH_2OH)$ and carboxylate anions (fatty-acid carboxylates) by a reaction referred to as *saponification*. Carboxylic acids once deprotonated form carboxylates (the conjugate base of the acid). The organic chain of a soap molecule is most useful when it contains at least eight carbons. Longer carbon chains are common in soaps that are used to remove oils having longer carbon chains.

12. All of the following would be ideal properties for a solvent used to dissolve a dye within an ink EXCEPT:

    A. exerting a high vapor pressure at room temperature.

    B. containing functional groups similar to the dye.

    C. being highly reactive with cellulose.

    D. having a boiling point slightly above room temperature.

13. Which of the following would be the BEST solvent to remove an ink dye that has hydroxyl (OH) groups attached to a carbon backbone?

    A. Propanone

    B. Propanol

    C. Propanal

    D. Propanoic acid

14. Some kinds if ink run when water is spilled on the paper to which they adhere. Which of the following reasons best explains this observation?

    A. The organic solvent of the ink is miscible in water.

    B. The organic solvent of the ink is immiscible in water.

    C. The dye of the ink is soluble in water.

    D. The dye of the ink is insoluble in water.

15. Which of the following would be the BEST soap?

    A. $CH_3CH_2CO_2H$

    B. $CH_3CH_2CO_2Na$

    C. $CH_3CH_2CH_2CH_2CH_2CH_2CH_2CO_2H$

    D. $CH_3CH_2CH_2CH_2CH_2CH_2CH_2CO_2Na$

16. Which of the following compounds is MOST soluble in water?

    A. $CH_3CH_2CO_2H$

    B. $CH_3CH_2CO_2K$

    C. $CH_3CH_2CH_2CH_2CH_2CO_2H$

    D. $CH_3CH_2CH_2CH_2CH_2CO_2K$

17. Which of the following reactions forms CH_3CO_2Na?

    A. Acetic acid + CH_3MgCl

    B. Formic acid + CH_3MgCl

    C. Ethanoic acid + NaOH

    D. Propanoic acid + NaOH

Questions 18 through 21 are **NOT** based on a descriptive passage.

18. Which of the following compounds exhibits conjugation?

I. 1,4-cyclohexadiene

II. 3-ethylcyclohexene

III. 2-methyl-1,3-cyclopentadiene

A. I only

B. II only

C. III only

D. I and III only

19. Which of the following isomers has the HIGHEST boiling point?

A. $H_3CCH_2OCH_2CH_3$

B. $H_3CCH_2CH_2OCH_3$

C. $(H_3C)_2CHOCH_3$

D. $H_3CCH_2CH_2CH_2OH$

20. Which of the following compounds releases the GREATEST amount of heat energy upon combustion?

A.

B.

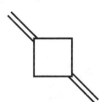

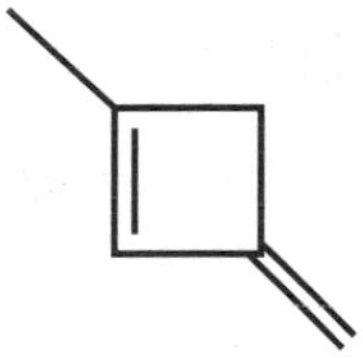

C.

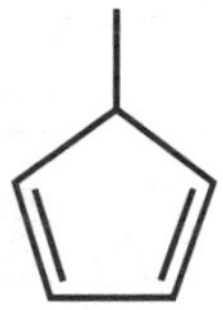

D.

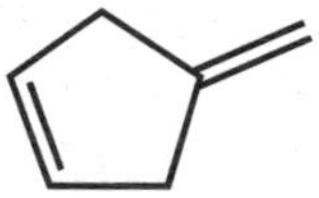

21. Which of the following functional groups is found in $C_2H_5CH(OCH_3)C(O)CH(CH_3)_2$?

A. Aldehyde

B. Ester

C. Ketone

D. Oxirane

The dipole of a bond can be found by considering the distribution of charge within the bond and the length of the bond. As the difference in electronegativity between the two atoms forming the bond increases, the magnitude of the partial charges on each atom increases, which results in a larger overall dipole. The dipole of a molecule is the sum of all of the bond dipoles in the molecule. When considering the dipole associated with molecules, the electron density of the entire structure is determined by the symmetry of the structure. Each bond is treated individually, and the sum of the component vectors is the approximate dipole. The estimated dipole is good enough to predict chemical behavior. Figure 1 shows examples of a polar and a nonpolar cyclohexane derivative.

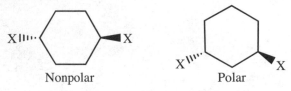

Nonpolar   Polar

Figure 1. Polar and nonpolar disubstituted cyclohexanes

The magnitude of a dipole can be measured by placing the compound between the two charged plates and observing the drop in voltage. A large voltage drop in the capacitor implies that the dielectric constant for the compound is large, so the molecule has a large dipole. This technique works because of the ability of a neutral polar compound when added to an electric field to align with the field. If there is a net charge on the molecule, it migrates toward the capacitor plate with the opposite charge. One downfall to this technique is that it can induce a dipole in the compound being measured.

22. In which of the following reactions is it possible to form a nonpolar organic product?

   A. Hydrolysis of an alkene
   B. Halogenation of an alkane
   C. Hydrogenation of an alkene
   D. Reduction of an amide

23. Which change does NOT result in an increased dipole moment?

   A. Replacing iodine with bromine on an alkyl halide
   B. Oxidizing a primary alcohol into a carboxylic acid
   C. Replacing fluorine with chlorine on an alkyl halide
   D. Adding HBr anti-Markovnikov to an alkene

24. Which is the BEST description of the nonpolar structure of $Fe(NH_3)_4Cl_2$?

   A. Octahedral shape with the two Cl ligands cis
   B. Octahedral shape with the two Cl ligands trans
   C. Tetrahedral shape with the two Cl ligands cis
   D. Tetrahedral shape with the two Cl ligands trans

25. Which of the following compounds shows a dielectric constant of zero when placed in a capacitor?

   A. 1,1-dichloroethane
   B. cis-1,2-dichloroethene
   C. trans-1,2-dichloroethene
   D. E-1-chloro-2-fluoroethene

26. Which compound has the LARGEST dipole moment?

   A. 1,1,2,2-tetrafluoroethane
   B. 1,1,2,2-tetrafluoropropane
   C. 1,1-difluoro-2,2-dichloroethane
   D. 1,1-difluoro-2,2-dichloropropane

27. Which of the following statements CANNOT be true?

   I. For a tetrahedral structure, if any of the four ligands are not equivalent to the others, the molecule is polar.
   II. All 1,4-disubstituted cyclohexane molecules are polar.
   III. All optically active molecules are polar.

   A. I only
   B. II only
   C. I and II only
   D. II and III only

GO ON TO THE NEXT PAGE

The acidity, bond strengths, and bond lengths of hydrocarbons depend on the hybridization of the carbons within the compound. Hybridization is defined as the mixing of atomic orbitals to form new hybrid orbitals that are aligned to make up the covalent bonds. Hybrid orbitals are oriented to minimize electronic repulsion within a structure. The orientation of electrons allows the molecule to form structures with a central carbon that has either tetrahedral (sp^3-hybridized), trigonal planar (sp^2-hybridized), or linear (sp-hybridized) geometry. Although the geometry dictates the hybridization, the hybridization of a carbon within a molecule can be used to predict the structure of the molecule.

The more p-character there is in the hybrid, the longer the hybrid orbital is, and thus the further away the electrons are from the nucleus. This variation in length can be used to explain differences in chemical reactivity and physical properties. When estimating properties of a bond, one must consider that acidity results from heterolytic cleavage, while bond energies are determined from homolytic cleavage. Figure 1 shows both heterolytic and homolytic cleavage for the C—H bond of a terminal alkyne.

Hetreolytic Cleavage (into ions)

R—C≡C—H ⇌ R—C≡C:⊖ + H⊕

Homolytic Cleavage (into free radicals)

R—C≡C—H ⇌ R—C≡C· + H·

Figure 1. Heterolytic and homolytic cleavage of a C-H bond

Acidity is explained in terms of heterolytic cleavage. The closer the electrons of a carbon-hydrogen bond are to the carbon nucleus, the more acidic the hydrogen on that carbon. As the electrons in a bond get closer to the carbon nucleus, it gets easier to break the bond heterolytically, and thus the acidity of the hydrogen increases. Electrons get closer to the nucleus of carbon when the bond is shorter. However, as the bond gets shorter, it becomes more difficult to break the bond in a homolytic fashion. It is more difficult for hydrogen to remove one bonding electron from the bond to carbon. This means that as the hydrogen becomes more acidic, the homolytic bond energy increases.

Less s-character within a hybrid results in a longer bond between carbon and the atom to which it is bonded. As a bond becomes longer, it gets weaker in a homolytic sense.

28. The MOST acidic hydrogen on 3-methyl-1-pentyne is on which carbon?

A. Carbon-1
B. Carbon-2
C. Carbon-3
D. Carbon-4

29. Which of the following compounds has the WEAKEST carbon-carbon single bond?

A. H—C≡C—H
B. H_3C—C≡C—CH_3
C.
D.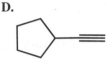

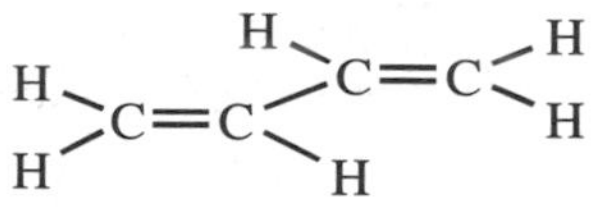

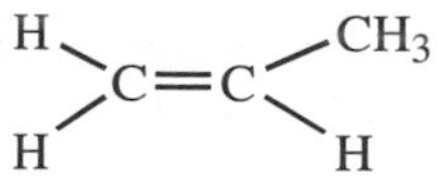

30. The LARGEST K_a is associated with which of the following compounds?

A. | B.

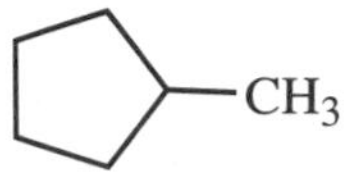

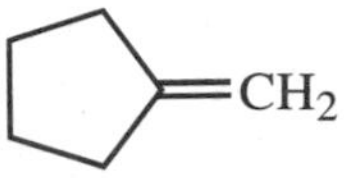

C.  | D.

31. Which of the following organic compounds is the STRONGEST base?

A. $CH_3CH_2CH_2CH_2Na$
B. $CH_3CH_2CH=CHNa$
C. $CH_3CH_2CNa=CH_2$
D. $CH_3CH_2C≡CNa$

32. $NaNH_2$ is a base strong enough to deprotonate the first hydrogen on a terminal alkyne. Which of the following hydrogens could it also deprotonate?

A. H on carbon-1 of 2-methyl-1-butene
B. H on carbon-2 of 2-methyl 1-butene
C. H on carbon-1 of 2-methyl-1-butanol
D. H on oxygen of 2-methyl-1-butanol

33. The LOWEST pK_b is associated with which of the following nitrogen containing compounds?

A.
B.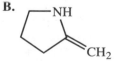

C. 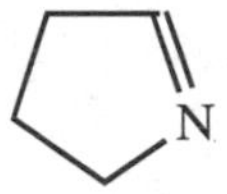 | D.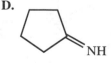

Questions 34 through 37 are **NOT** based on a descriptive passage.

34. Which of the following compounds, when added to the gap between the two plates of a capacitor, produces the GREATEST reduction in voltage?

A. ArHF

B. C_6H_6

C. N_2

D. CO_2

35. Infrared spectroscopy involves radiating a compound with electromagnetic radiation of a known wavelength and observing any changes in the lengths of bonds within that molecule as they stretch. When the bonds are stretched, the dipole moment changes and thus can be detected. Which of the following would show the LEAST change in dipole moment?

A. Stretching a carbonyl bond in an asymmetric molecule

B. Bending a carbonyl bond in an asymmetric molecule

C. Stretching a carbonyl bond in a symmetric molecule

D. Bending a carbonyl bond in a symmetric molecule

36. The LONGEST carbon-carbon bond can be found in which of the following compounds?

A. $H-C\equiv C-CH_3$

B. $H-C\equiv C-H$

C.

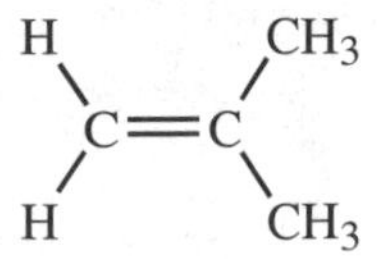

$$\begin{array}{c} H \quad\quad CH_3 \\ \diagdown\quad\diagup \\ C=C \\ \diagup\quad\diagdown \\ H \quad\quad CH_3 \end{array}$$

D.

$$\begin{array}{c} H \quad\quad H \\ \diagdown\quad\diagup \\ C=C \\ \diagup\quad\diagdown \\ H \quad\quad H \end{array}$$

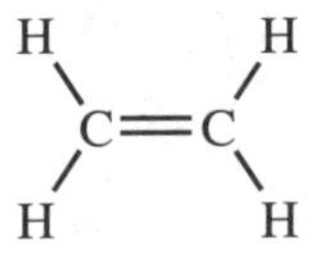

37. The difference between succinic acid and aspartic acid is that Carbon 2 of aspartic acid has a primary amine. What is the impact of the ammonium group in water?

A. pK_{a1} and pK_{a2} are lower in succinic acid than in aspartic acid.

B. pK_{a1} is lower in succinic acid than in aspartic acid, while pK_{a2} is lower in aspartic acid than in succinic acid.

C. pK_{a1} is lower in aspartic acid than in succinic acid, but pK_{a2} is lower in succinic acid than in aspartic acid.

D. pK_{a1} and pK_{a2} are higher in succinic acid than in aspartic acid.

GO ON TO THE NEXT PAGE

Passage VI (Questions 38 - 43)

Biologically active molecules have a vast array of functional groups such as amines, ketones, carboxylic acids and so on. For that reason, it is rather difficult to predict the biological activity of a compound, despite being able to explain the chemical behavior of biological processes. This is often explained by noting that chemical behavior changes with the functional group's microenvironment.

Bioorganic chemistry research thus involves isolating biologically active molecules and making analogs of them, according to their chemical properties and molecular size. Figure 1 shows three common biological molecules-- histidine (a common amino acid), guanine (one of the four bases found in DNA), and succinic acid (found in certain biochemical pathways):

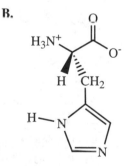

Histidine (at pH = 7.4)   Guanine (DNA base)

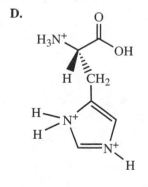

Succinic Acid (at pH = 3)

Figure 1 Three common biologically active molecules

38. Which of the following structures represents histidine at pH = 1.0?

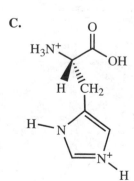

A.

B.

C.

D.

39. The side-chain of histidine can BEST be described as:

   A. planar, and exhibiting aromaticity.
   B. planar, with conjugation, but no aromaticity.
   C. bent, and exhibiting aromaticity.
   D. bent, with conjugation, but no aromaticity.

40. What can be said of the C=O bond in guanine?

   I. It is longer than the C=O bond of acetone.
   II. It is more likely to be protonated on the carbonyl oxygen than on the alpha nitrogen.
   III. It can be observed in the IR spectrum of guanine.

   A. I only
   B. I and II only
   C. I and III only
   D. I, II, and III

41. In which configuration does succinic acid exist at physiological pH?

   A. $^-O_2CCH_2CH_2CO_2^-$
   B. $HO_2CCH_2CH_2CO_2^-$
   C. $HO_2CCH_2CH_2CO_2H$
   D. $HO_2CCH=CHCO_2H$

42. How many chiral centers and units of saturation are present in guanine?

   A. 0 chiral centers and 2 units of unsaturation
   B. 0 chiral centers and 6 units of unsaturation
   C. 1 chiral center and 2 units of unsaturation
   D. 1 chiral center and 6 units of unsaturation

43. What is TRUE of the hybridization of the imine nitrogen in histidine's side-chain, before and after protonation?

   A. It starts with sp^2-hybridization and becomes sp^3.
   B. It starts with sp^3-hybridization and becomes sp^2.
   C. It is sp^2-hybridized before and after protonation.
   D. It is sp^3-hybridized before and after protonation.

Esters are semi-reactive carbonyl compounds that undergo substitution chemistry at the carbonyl carbon. Several biological reactions (including transesterification and transamination) proceed through standard carbonyl chemistry. The reactivity of the carbonyl depends on both the nucleophile and the leaving group. A researcher set out to determine the reactivity of three different nucleophiles in a standard substitution reaction using an ester electrophile. For the reaction in Figure 1, three different compounds (Compound A, Compound B, and Compound C) were used.

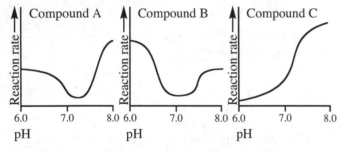

Figure 1. Deacylation of an ester

Compound A has the formula $C_{13}H_{24}S$, Compound B has the formula $C_9H_{18}O$, and Compound C has the formula C_7H_9N. Figure 2 shows three graphs depicting the change in reaction rate of the deacylation reaction as a function of the solution pH for each of the three separate compounds.

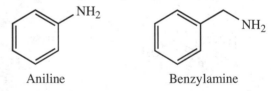

Figure 2. Reaction rate as a function of solution pH

Each reaction obeys standard mechanistic behavior for carbonyl substitution. They are believed to proceed through a mechanism where the nucleophile attacks the carbonyl carbon, breaking the C=O π-bond and forming a tetrahedral intermediate. A lone pair of electrons on oxygen then reforms the π-bond, ejecting the leaving group. Although the nucleophilicity of the different compounds is not equal, the similar mechanisms make the reactions comparable. At low pH, the carbonyl compound can be protonated, making it a better electrophile. This negates the effect of decreasing nucleophilicity of alcohols and thiols, because they remain uncharged at low pH values.

44. The nucleophilicity of each reagent in aqueous solution:

   A. decreases as the pH is increased.
   B. is best when the species is a cation.
   C. is best when the species is neutral.
   D. depends only on the size of the nucleophile.

45. Which of the following compounds would be the MOST reactive nucleophile at pH = 9.0?

   A. $H_3CCH_2CH_2OCH_3$
   B. $H_3CCH_2CCO_2CH_3$
   C. $H_3CCH_2CH_2CONH_2$
   D. $H_3CCH_2CH_2CH_2NH_2$

46. If the pK_a for $H_3CNH_3^+$ is 10.3, which of the following is the BEST approximation for the pK_a for $Cl_3CNH_3^+$?

   A. 17.3
   B. 12.3
   C. 8.3
   D. 1.0

47. How does the hybridization of the carbonyl carbon change during the reaction?

   A. It changes from sp^2 to sp^3 and back to sp^2.
   B. It changes from sp^3 to sp^2 and back to sp^3.
   C. It remains sp^2 throughout the reaction.
   D. It remains sp^3 throughout the reaction.

48. Aniline and benzylamine, drawn below, are both:

   Aniline   Benzylamine

   A. primary amines.
   B. aromatic amines.
   C. conjugated amines.
   D. nonalkyl amines.

         GO ON TO THE NEXT PAGE

Questions 49 through 52 are **NOT** based on a descriptive passage.

49. The compound 1,1-difluoro-2,3-diphenylcyclopropane is highly reactive, because the:

A. phenyl groups provide resonance stability.
B. phenyl and fluoro groups repel via steric hindrance.
C. three-membered ring is strained.
D. overall system is aromatic.

50. Which of the following types of compounds is the MOST basic?

A. Primary alcohols
B. Esters
C. Secondary amines
D. Tertiary thiols

51. The correct IUPAC name for the following molecule is:

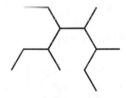

A. 2,4-diethyl-3,5-dimethylheptane
B. 4-ethyl-3,5,6-trimethyloctane
C. 3-ethyl-5,6-dimethylnonane
D. 3,5,6-trimethyldecane

52. Which of the following compounds is MOST stable?

A. 2-methyl-1,4-pentadiene
B. 3-methyl-1,4-pentadiene
C. 2-methyl-1,3-pentadiene
D. 1,5-hexadiene

1. C	2. A	3. D	4. B	5. D	6. C
7. A	8. C	9. C	10. B	11. B	12. C
13. B	14. C	15. D	16. B	17. C	18. C
19. D	20. B	21. C	22. C	23. C	24. B
25. C	26. D	27. B	28. A	29. C	30. D
31. A	32. D	33. A	34. A	35. C	36. C
37. D	38. C	39. A	40. D	41. A	42. B
43. C	44. C	45. D	46. C	47. A	48. A
49. C	50. C	51. B	52. C		

YOU ARE DONE.

Answers to 52-Question Molecular Structure Practice Exam

1. **Choice C is the best answer.** The Gypsy Moth sex pheromone has a three-membered ring, so it definitely has ring strain. This eliminates choice D. Both of the carbons in the epoxide have four unique substituents and sp^3-hybridization, so they are both stereogenic centers. All of the other carbons have at least two identical substituents, so there are only two stereogenic centers. This eliminates choice A. The compound has one ring and no π-bonds, so it has only one unit of unsaturation. This eliminates choice B. The structure has only one tertiary carbon, so choice **C** is the best answer.

2. **Choice A is the best answer.** The Grape Berry Moth sex pheromone has a double bond between carbons 9 and 10, so it contains an alkene. This eliminates choice D. There is an acetoyl group on carbon one, which makes the compound an ester. The best answer is choice **A**.

3. **Choice D is the best answer.** Ultraviolet-visible spectroscopy is used to detect π-bonds. The Grape Berry sex pheromone has π-bonds, while the Gypsy Moth sex pheromone does not. This means that the Grape Berry Moth sex pheromone has a UV-visible absorbance around 180 nm. The Gypsy Moth sex pheromone has no π-bond, so it has no peak above 180 nm, making Statement I a valid statement. This eliminates choice B. The female Tsetse fly sex hormone is an aliphatic alkane, so it has high flexibility. All of the other structures have at least one unit of unsaturation, so each has at least one site about which there is reduced flexibility. This makes Statement II an invalid statement. This eliminates choice C. The Green Peach Aphid defense pheromone has the most π-bonds of any of the compounds (four), so it also has the most sp^2-hybridized carbons of all four structures. This makes Statement III valid and makes the choice **D** the best answer.

4. **Choice B is the best answer.** Conjugation occurs when you have alternating double bonds and single bonds. This is only seen in the structure of the Green Peach Aphid defense pheromone, so choice **B** is the best answer. Having no π-bonds, choices C and D should have been eliminated immediately.

5. **Choice D is the best answer.** The Grape Berry Moth sex pheromone has an ester group. A carbonyl has an IR absorbance above 1700 cm^{-1}, so an ester is likely to account for the IR absorbance at 1741 cm^{-1}. Choice A is a valid correlation of structure to spectroscopic observation, so it is eliminated. The Green Peach Aphid defense pheromone has several π-bonds, including two in a conjugated network. The presence of π-bonds in a structure results in an absorbance in the ultraviolet-visible range of the EM spectrum, so an absorbance of 227 nm seems viable. Choice B is a valid correlation of structure to spectroscopic observation, so it is eliminated. The Gypsy Moth sex pheromone has two carbons bonded to heteroatoms (oxygen), each of which have hydrogens attached. This means that the hydrogens on those carbons will be found downfield, resulting in two signals with values greater than 2.00 ppm in ^{1}H NMR. Choice C is a valid correlation of structure to spectroscopic observation, so it is eliminated. The Tsetse Fly sex pheromone has thirty-seven carbons and a plane of symmetry. Because of this plane of symmetry, the compound has two equal halves. By symmetry, there are nineteen unique carbons, so the ^{13}C NMR would at best show only nineteen signals. The reality is that many of the signals would overlap, so it would likely show less. It will definitely not show twenty-three signals in its ^{13}C NMR spectrum, so choice **D** is an invalid correlation of structure to spectroscopic observation, making it the best answer.

6. **Choice C is the best answer.** When an ester is treated with acidic water, it undergoes hydrolysis. The products after adding water are an alcohol and a carboxylic acid. The best answer is choice **C**. The reaction is shown below.

7. **Choice A is the best answer.** From the data in Table 1, we see that the melting point increases with the length of the alkyl chain. A twelve-carbon, fully-saturated fatty acid has a melting point of 45°C, A fourteen-carbon, fully-saturated fatty acid has a melting point of 55°C. The sixteen-carbon, fully-saturated fatty acid should have a melting point greater than 55°C, and the eighteen-carbon, fully-saturated fatty acid should have a melting point greater than the sixteen-carbon, fully-saturated fatty acid. Because both melting points are greater than 55°C, choices C and D are eliminated. Because stearic acid (18-carbon) is longer than palmitic acid (16-carbon), stearic acid has the greater melting point. This makes choice **A** the best answer and eliminates choice B.

8. **Choice C is the best answer**. Figure 1 shows us that palmitoleic acid has cis orientation about its double bond. Cis orientation of the two highest priority groups on the double bond corresponds to a Z designation in IUPAC nomenclature, so choices A and B are eliminated. Referencing the carboxylic acid carbon as number one, we see that the π-bond lies between carbons 9 and 10. IUPAC conventions dictate that double bonds use the lower number, so the formal name is (Z)-9-hexadecanoic acid. Choice D is eliminated and choice **C** is the best answer.

9. **Choice C is the best answer**. Because a fatty acid contains a carboxyl group (as part of the acid moiety), it has at least one unit of unsaturation. This makes Statement I a valid statement, which eliminates choice B. We see from the data in Table 1 that for fatty acids of identical carbon count (16 and 18 for example), as the number of π-bonds increases, the melting point decreases. This makes Statement II an invalid statement, which eliminates choice D. The decrease in melting point can be explained by decrease in packing efficiency as the molecules become more rigid in their conformation. This increase in structural rigidity makes it hard for the molecules to pack together, which ultimately reduces the intermolecular interactions. The result is a lower melting point and more fluidity. This means that as the units of unsaturation in a fat increase, the fluidity of cell membranes containing phospholipids made from those fats will increase. This makes Statement III a valid statement, which eliminates choice A and makes choice **C** the best answer.

10. **Choice B is the best answer**. Bone cells are used for structural support, so their cell membranes should be fairly rigid. Fluidity decreases with saturation, so bone cells are apt to have phospholipids containing saturated fats in their cell membranes. Stearate is more saturated than oleate, so choices A and C are eliminated. Stearate lacks the π-bond in its backbone that oleate has, so it has a greater ability to rotate into different conformations. This is to say that stearate is more flexible than oleate, making choice **B** the best answer.

11. **Choice B is the best answer**. From either the question or a strong knowledge of fatty acid synthesis from biochemistry, we know that for every two carbons added to the chain of a fat, one molecule of $FADH_2$ gets consumed (if it is a fully saturated fat). This means that the most $FADH_2$ molecules will be consumed in the synthesis of the longest chain having the least π-bonds. Of the choices, 18 carbons is longer than 16 carbons, so choices A and C are eliminated. Choice **B** has one π-bond while choice D has two π-bonds, so more $FADH_2$ would be consumed in the synthesis of choice **B** than choice D. The location and geometry of the π-bonds is irrelevant minutiae for this question.

Passage III (Questions 12 - 17)   **Solubility of Dyes and Soaps**

12. **Choice C is the best answer**. A good solvent for dissolving a dye to form an ink is one that is a liquid at room temperature, evaporates quickly, and exhibits a high degree of dye solubility. Having a high vapor pressure implies that it evaporates readily, so choice A is eliminated. If it has functional groups that are similar to the dye, then the dye is likely to be highly soluble in the solvent, so choice B is eliminated. If the boiling point is slightly above room temperature, then it is a volatile liquid, so choice D is eliminated. The solvent should not react with paper (cellulose), so the correct answer is choice **C**.

13. **Choice B is the best answer**. Because like dissolves like, the best solvent for dissolving the dye should also have hydroxyl groups attached to it, just as the dye does. The best choice is therefore the alcohol. The carboxylic acid is not a good choice, because carboxylic acids are not as volatile as alcohols. If you have melting points memorized, then you may be aware that carboxylic acids that are three carbons or greater in length are solids at room temperature. If you don't have them memorized, like 99.999% of us, that's okay too. Aldehydes and ketones may work, but not as well as the alcohol. The best choice is **B**.

14. **Choice C is the best answer**. When water is spilled on paper, it diffuses across the surface of the paper. If the ink bound to the paper is soluble in water, it dissolves into the water and spreads out, or runs. So if an ink runs, it must be soluble in water. The colored portion of the ink is the dye, not the solvent. Running ink means that the ink dye is water soluble. Pick choice **C** for best results.

15. **Choice D is the best answer**. As stated in the last paragraph of the passage, a compound must contain at least eight carbons in its chain to be a good soap. The best soap has a polar and nonpolar end associated with the molecule. The negatively charged carboxylate is at one end and an organic tail is at the other end. Molecules with charged and organic ends are optimal for making a soap. Choice **D** has both eight carbons and a charged end.

16. **Choice B is the best answer**. To be soluble in water, a compound must be either charged or polar. Because choices **B** and D are ionic, they are better in this regard than choices A or C. The organic tail is smaller in choice **B**, so it dissolves into water more readily than choice D. Pick choice **B**, and feel the sensation of correctness.

---

17. **Choice C is the best answer.** Carboxylates are formed when a carboxylic acid is deprotonated. The Grignard reagent in choice A deprotonates the carboxylic acid (acetic acid is a two-carbon carboxylic acid) to form the carboxylate, but the cation is not sodium, so choice A is eliminated. Choice B is invalid, because the Grignard reagent deprotonates the carboxylic acid (formic acid), and the carboxylic acid does not have enough carbons to make sodium acetate. Choice D is invalid, because it has too many carbons (propanoic acid has three carbons). The H_3CCO_2Na molecule results from the deprotonation of acetic acid by a base with a counterion of Na^+. The best choice is therefore choice **C**.

Questions 18 - 21   **Not Based on a Descriptive Passage**

18. **Choice C is the best answer.** Conjugation is defined as consecutive, alternating π-bonds. The structures are drawn below. Only Compound III has conjugation, so choice **C** is the best answer.

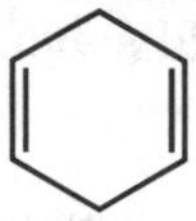

       1,4-cyclohexadiene 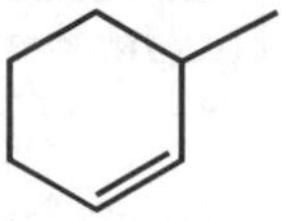   3-methylcyclohexene 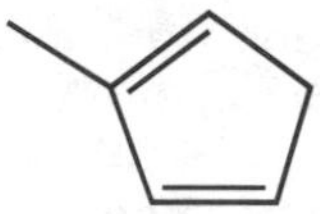   2-methyl-1,3-cyclopentadiene

19. **Choice D is the best answer.** All alcohols have hydrogen-bonding, which increases their intermolecular forces and thus increases their boiling points, so choice **D** has the highest boiling point. Note that all of the compounds have exactly the same formula (and thus the same molecular mass). This eliminates the need to account for any differences in molecular mass (which would also affect the boiling point). Because of the linear nature of choice B and its asymmetry (which makes it more polar than the two remaining choices), it should have the second-highest boiling point.

20. **Choice B is the best answer.** The most heat energy is generated by the least stable compound; thus finding the least stable compound is the task at hand. All of the choices have the same formula (C_6H_8) so it comes down to structural features. The four-membered ring is unstable, so choices A and **B** are good. Choice **B** has no conjugation, while choice A does (conjugation is a stabilizing feature), so this makes **B** the least stable compound among the answer choices. The bond angles are not the optimal 109.5°, whether the π-bond is in the ring or not.

21. **Choice C is the best answer.** Translating from the chemical formula into the structure yields the compound below:

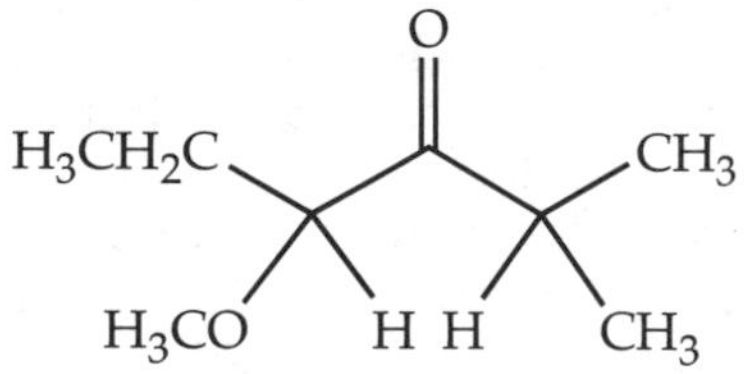

$$H_3CH_2C \quad \overset{\displaystyle O}{\underset{H_3CO \quad H \; H \quad CH_3}{\diagdown \; C \; \diagup}} \quad CH_3$$

There is no aldehyde group (which would have been represented as CHO), so choice A is eliminated. There is no ester group (which would have been represented as CO_2R), so choice B is eliminated. There is a carbonyl adjacent to two alkyl groups, so the compound has a ketone functionality. This eliminates choice D and makes choice **C** the best answer.

Passage IV   (Questions 22 - 27)   **Molecular Structure and Polarity**

22. **Choice C is the best answer.** The hydrolysis of an alkene forms an alcohol. An alcohol is polar, so choice A is eliminated. The halogenation of an alkane forms an alkyl halide. An alkyl halide is polar, so choice B is eliminated. The hydrogenation of an alkene forms an alkane. An alkane is most often nonpolar, so the best answer is choice **C**. Reduction of an amide forms a primary amine. An amine is polar, so choice D is eliminated.

23. **Choice C is the best answer.** Assuming that an alkyl iodide is polar to begin with, then replacing iodine with bromine results in a more polar compound, because bromine is more electronegative than iodine, so that the difference in electronegativity between the halogen and carbon has increased. A carboxylic acid is more polar than a primary alcohol (or any alcohol, for that matter), so choice B results in a more polar compound. Alkenes are typically nonpolar, so the addition of HBr forms an alkyl bromide, which increases the polarity, so choice D is eliminated. Because fluorine is more electronegative than chlorine, replacing a fluorine substituent with a chlorine substituent results in a compound that is less polar, making choice **C** the choice that does *not* result in increased polarity. Pick choice **C** to be a star of chemistry.

24. **Choice B is the best answer.** To be nonpolar, all of the ligands must pull in such a way that the vectors of each individual bond cancel out. Tetrahedral structures are not possible with six ligands, so choices C and D are eliminated. It is only when the two chlorine ligands are trans to one another that they cancel out one another in terms of polarity. The best answer is therefore choice **B**.

25. **Choice C is the best answer.** A dielectric constant of zero results from a nonpolar molecule. The only nonpolar molecule among the answer choices is trans dichloroethene. Cis alkenes are polar, so choice B is eliminated. Choice D is trans, but there are different substituents on each carbon, so it is polar. The best answer is choice **C**.

26. **Choice D is the best answer.** Choice A is nonpolar, because the vectors expressing the electron withdrawal of the fluorines cancel out, so choice A is eliminated. Fluorine is more electronegative than chlorine, so the asymmetric electron distribution is found with choices C and **D**, which rules out choice B. In choices C and **D**, the fluorine atoms withdraw the electron density, making the molecule asymmetric. In the propane molecule (choice **D**), the methyl substituent donates electron density to the electron-poor central carbon, placing a partial positive charge on the methyl group; therefore, it increases the dipole moment. This makes the propane molecule more polar than the ethane molecule. The structures are shown below:

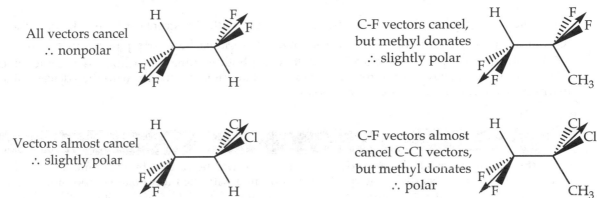

27. **Choice B is the best answer.** For a tetrahedral structure, if the four ligands are not all equivalent, then the structure is asymmetric. If the compound is asymmetric, then it must be polar (have an asymmetric distribution of electron density). This makes statement I true. Figure 1 shows an example of a 1,4-disubstituted cyclohexane molecule that is *not* polar, which means that statement II is *not* true. All optically active compounds must be asymmetric in order to be optically active, so they must be at least slightly polar. This makes statement III true. Only statement II is *not* true, so choice **B** is the best answer.

28. **Choice A is the best answer.** The start of the third paragraph states that the closer the electrons within a carbon-hydrogen bond are to the carbon nucleus, the more acidic the compound is. To determine the relative acidity, you must make a decision about how close the electrons are to the nucleus. The passage also states that the more p-character there is in the hybrid, the longer the bond is. Connecting the two concepts, you should reach the conclusion that the shorter the bond, the closer the electrons are to the nucleus. This means that the less p-character there is in the hybrid, the more acidic the hydrogen. The most acidic hydrogen is thus found on an *sp*-carbon. In 3-methyl-1-pentyne, carbons 1 and 2 are *sp*-hybridized, but only carbon 1 has a hydrogen attached. Pick choice **A** for optimal results. Make a note from the conclusions that $sp > sp^2 > sp^3$ for acidity.

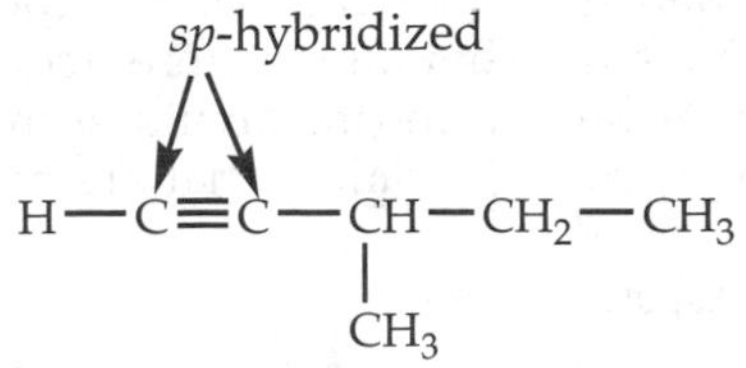

$$sp\text{-hybridized}$$
$$H-C\equiv C-CH-CH_2-CH_3$$
$$\underset{|}{CH_3}$$

29. **Choice C is the best answer.** The weakest carbon-carbon bond is associated with the longest carbon-carbon bond. Choice A is eliminated, because the C-C bond is a triple bond, and triple bonds are the shortest of carbon-carbon bonds. Choice B is between an *sp*-hybridized carbon and an sp^3-hybridized carbon, choice **C** is between an sp^2-hybridized carbon and an sp^3-hybridized carbon, and choice D is between an sp^2-hybridized carbon and an sp^2-hybridized carbon. Choice **C** is the longest, so it would terrific if you would pick choice **C**.

30. **Choice D is the best answer.** The largest K_a is associated with the strongest acid. All of the choices are hydrocarbons, so the most acidic proton is the one on an *sp*-hybridized carbon, as opposed to either an *sp²*-hybridized or *sp³*-hybridized carbon. Of the four answer choices, only choice **D** has a hydrogen bonded to an *sp*-hybridized carbon, so choice **D** is the best answer.

31. **Choice A is the best answer.** All of the compounds are deprotonated hydrocarbons (with a lone pair on carbon), so the strongest base is the one with the lone pair on an *sp³*-hybridized carbon. The only choice with a lone pair of electrons on an *sp³*-hybridized carbon is choice **A**. The cation is irrelevant to the problem, because it is sodium in each answer choice.

32. **Choice D is the best answer.** $NaNH_2$ is a base strong enough to deprotonate a hydrogen on an *sp*-hybridized carbon. Although this is true, it is not critical information in solving this question. Only one answer choice can be correct, so the correct choice must be the compound with the most acidic hydrogen. This means that this question is reduced to asking "Which compound, of the choices listed, has the most acidic proton?" The most acidic hydrogen is attached to the oxygen, so you had better pick **D**.

33. **Choice A is the best answer.** The lowest pK_b is associated with the strongest base. Because the most acidic proton is found on an *sp*-hybridized atom, the strongest base must be a lone pair on an *sp³*-hybridized atom. Choices C and D are *sp²*-hybridized nitrogens, so they are both eliminated. Choice **A** is better than choice B, because the lone pair of electrons on nitrogen in choice B is tied into resonance with the adjacent alkene π-bond. Electron-withdrawing resonance reduces a compound's basicity.

Questions 34 - 37   **Not Based on a Descriptive Passage**

34. **Choice A is the best answer.** The largest decrease in voltage will be caused by the compound with the greatest dielectric constant. The greatest dielectric constant is associated with the most polar compound. Choices B, C, and D are all symmetric, so they are all nonpolar. This eliminates choices B, C, and D. Only ArHF (choice A) is polar, meaning that ArHF has the greatest dielectric constant. Choice **A** is a fine choice in a situation like this.

35. **Choice C is the best answer.** The dipole moment changes only when a compound's bonds are either stretched or bent, if the compound is asymmetric. This makes choices A and B less likely to exhibit the *least* change in dipole moment. The dipole moment does not change drastically (if at all), when the chemical bonds of a symmetric compound are either bent or stretched. Therefore, the *least* change in dipole is observed in a symmetric molecule. Stretching a symmetric molecule often balances out, meaning that the electron density is shifted uniformly in opposing directions. The result is that the dipole of the molecule does not change. The best answer is choice **C**. Bending a symmetric molecule can make it asymmetric, so choice D is not as good as choice **C**.

36. **Choice C is the best answer.** The longest carbon-carbon bond is a single bond between the two largest orbitals. The largest of the three possible hybrid orbitals is *sp³*, so the longest carbon-carbon bond is formed between an *sp³*-hybridized carbon and an *sp³*-hybridized carbon. Choices B and D are eliminated immediately, because they contain no C-C single bond. Choice A is a bond between an *sp*-hybridized carbon and an *sp³*-hybridized carbon, while choice **C** is between an *sp²*-hybridized carbon and an *sp³*-hybridized carbon. An *sp²*-hybrid orbital is longer than an *sp*-hybrid orbital, so choice **C** is the best answer.

37. **Choice D is the best answer.** The ammonium group is positively charged and electron-withdrawing. An electron-withdrawing group pulls electron density away from the carboxyl group (through induction), making the carboxyl site electron-poor. This makes the compound more acidic (a better electron-pair acceptor) and means that the ammonium group present in aspartic acid (the amino terminal) makes the two carboxylic acid functional groups more acidic. The result is pK_{a1} and pK_{a2} values that are both lower in aspartic acid than in succinic acid. The best answer is choice **D**.

Aspartic Acid   Succinic Acid

The —NH_3^+ group is electron-withdrawing

38. **Choice C is the best answer.** At a low pH, the histidine molecule is fully protonated (protonated at all sites). This means that the amino terminal and carboxyl terminal are both protonated, so eliminate choice B. The side-chain can be only singly protonated, so choice D is eliminated. The imine nitrogen (lower right) has available electrons, so the side-chain is protonated on that nitrogen. This makes choice **C** the correct structure. Choice A is not possible, because the lone pair on the amine nitrogen (upper left) is tied up in the resonance associated with the aromaticity.

39. **Choice A is the best answer.** All of the atoms that constitute the side-chain of histidine have sp^2-hybridization, either because they are involved in the π-bond shown, or, in the case of nitrogen, because the lone pair can resonate into the ring system. The hybridization makes the side-chain ring system planar. There are two π-bonds, accounting for four electrons, and there is one lone pair, accounting for two more electrons. That gives a total of six π-electrons, making the compound aromatic. Choice **A** is the best answer choice.

40. **Choice D is the best answer.** The carbonyl bond in guanine has some single-bond character, due to the resonance donation of the nearby nitrogen lone pairs. A single bond is longer than a double bond, so the guanine carbonyl bond is longer than the acetone carbonyl bond. This makes statement I true. Because of resonance, the oxygen in the amide carries a slightly negative charge, while the nitrogen carries a slightly positive charge. This means that a proton is more attracted to the oxygen (due to resonance). The fact that oxygen is the better electron-pair donor can be verified by looking at hydrogen bonding in proteins, where the hydrogen bonding is from the oxygen lone pair, in the ß-pleated sheets. This makes statement II true. The carbonyl bond of guanine is found at around 1700 cm^{-1} in the IR spectrum, meaning statement III is also true. Because all three statements are true, the best answer is choice **D**.

41. **Choice A is the best answer.** The pK_a value for carboxylic acids is between 4 and 5, except for amino acids where the pK_a value can be as low as 2.0 for the carboxyl terminal. At physiological pH, said to be 7.4, the pH of the solution is greater than the pK_a for both acidic sites. When the pH is greater than the pK_a, then the structure exists in its deprotonated state. The best answer, the one where both sites are depicted as deprotonated, is choice **A**.

42. **Choice B is the best answer.** All of the carbons in guanine are sp^2-hybridized, so they cannot be chiral. We will not consider nitrogens for chirality, because they all have no more than three bonds, and their lone pairs are not fixed. This means that there are no chiral centers, eliminating choices C and D. Guanine has two rings and four π-bonds, so there are six units of unsaturation. The correct answer is choice **B**.

43. **Choice C is the best answer.** Before protonation, the imine nitrogen has two σ-bonds, one π-bond, and a lone pair. The lone pair is not involved in resonance into the ring, so it has sp^2-hybridization. Once protonated, those electrons are shared with the hydrogen; but the hybridization does not change, because the proton is orthogonal to the ring system. The result is that the hybridization, both before and after the protonation, is sp^2. Choice **C** is the best answer.

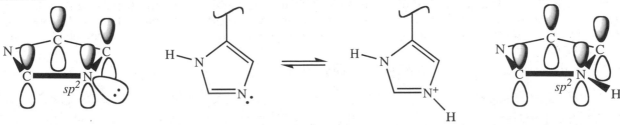

44. **Choice C is the best answer.** The rate referred to in Figure 2 is for a nucleophilic substitution reaction at a carbonyl site. There is a direct correlation between nucleophilicity and the rate of reaction. The graphs show that above a pH of 7, as the pH increases, so does the reaction rate. This means that the nucleophilicity increases. As pH increases, compounds are no longer cationic. This eliminates choices A and B. Size is not applicable here, so choice D is eliminated. After eliminating the wrong choices, you should settle for choice **C** as the best answer.

45. **Choice D is the best answer.** At pH = 9.0, all of the compounds should be neutral (although the amine in choice D may have a small fraction that remains protonated). The most reactive compound is the best nucleophile. For nucleophilicity, an amine is better than an ether, an ester, or an amide. For this reason, pick **D**.

46. **Choice C is the best answer.** The chlorine atoms are electron-withdrawing by the inductive effect (chlorine is more electronegative than carbon). Electron-withdrawing groups make the compound more acidic and thus lower its pK_a value. Both choice **C** and choice D are lower than 10.3. Choice **C** is the better choice, because the inductive effect is not so substantial that it will make the ammonium cation that acidic. For the pK_a to drop down to 1.0 would mean that the three chlorine atoms on the methyl group increased the acidity by a factor of $10^{9.3} = 2 \times 10^9 = 2,000,000,000$ times. That is too much. Be conservative and pick **C**.

47. **Choice A is the best answer.** The hybridization of carbon in a carbonyl compound, such as an ester (which contains one π-bond), must be sp^2 (the π-bond requires one p-orbital, so only two p-orbitals remain for hybridization). This can also be deduced from the trigonal planar structure of the carbonyl compound. The hybridization of carbon in the tetrahedral intermediate (which contains no π-bonds) is sp^3. The final product again has the carbonyl functionality, only now with the nucleophile attached. The carbonyl product still has trigonal planar geometry. The hybridization therefore changes from sp^2 to sp^3 and back to sp^2 in the overall reaction, making choice **A** your choice. Make that choice today!

48. **Choice A is the best answer.** In each case, there is a nitrogen with one alkyl group and two hydrogens. This defines a primary amine , so both compounds are primary amines. It just so happens that the R-groups are aromatic rings, but they are not aromatic amines *per se*, because the nitrogen atom is not a part of the aromatic system. The best answer is choice **A**. Of the two amines, only one is conjugated (aniline), so choice C does not describe both structures.

Questions 49 - 52   **Not Based on a Descriptive Passage**

---

49. **Choice C is the best answer.** "High reactivity" is equivalent to "low stability" or "highly unstable." This eliminates choice A, because the stability provided by resonance decreases the reactivity of the compound and makes it unreactive. The fluoro group is small, so the likelihood of steric hindrance playing a role is minimal. This eliminates choice B. A three-membered ring is highly reactive, because the ring is strained to form the small angles between the ring bonds. This makes choice **C** the best answer. Where the compound has phenyl rings, and thus aromatic groups, the overall system does not have a continuous array of cyclic *p*-orbitals. This eliminates choice D.

50. **Choice C is the best answer.** The most basic species is the compound containing nitrogen. In general, nitrogen compounds are more basic than oxygen- and sulfur-containing compounds of equal hybridization. This eliminates choices A and D. The degree of substitution is irrelevant. Esters have no lone pair of electrons that can be readily donated to a proton, so choice B is not correct. The best answer is an amine, independent of whether it is primary, secondary, or tertiary. This means that you really should pick **C** for the sensation of correctness.

51. **Choice B is the best answer.** The longest chain is eight carbons, so based on that alone, you know that the best answer is choice **B** (octane). All you need to do is find the longest chain to decipher the correct answer choice.

52. **Choice C is the best answer.** The diene in choice **C** is the most stable compound, because it is the only diene of the choices that has conjugation. Note that the structures are straight chains and not rings. It is easy to insert the word "cyclo" inadvertently into the name. Avoid careless mistakes and choose **C**. Drawn below are the structures of all four choices:

    2-methyl-1,4-pentadiene   3-methyl-1,4-pentadiene   2-methyl-1,3-pentadiene   1,5-hexadiene

Phase III Homework for Molecular Structure

Molecular Structure Phase III Scoring Scale

Raw Score	MCAT Score
30 - 33	13 - 15
22 - 29	10 - 12
15 - 22	7 - 9
11 - 14	4 - 6
1 - 10	1 - 3

Passage I (Questions 1 - 6)

The boiling point of a compound is defined as the temperature at which the vapor pressure of the compound equals the atmospheric pressure. It is also thought of as the highest temperature at which a compound may still be observed in a liquid state. Boiling points vary with atmospheric pressure, so when comparing the boiling points of different compounds, a standard pressure is referenced. Under standard pressure, a compound's boiling point correlates with the heat energy required to vaporize a molecule of it from solution. As the heat energy of vaporization ($\Delta H_{vaporization}$) increases, the boiling point for the compound increases.

Two chemists speculate about the reasons for the differences they observe in the boiling points of various organic compounds.

Chemist 1

Chemist 1 proposes that the difference in boiling points for two similar organic compounds is related to the differences in their molecular masses. The heavier the molecule, the more energy that must be required to liberate the compound into the gas phase from the liquid phase. To liberate the molecules into the gas phase, heat energy must be added to the solution, which increases the temperature of the solution. Chemist 1 concludes that heavier molecules have higher boiling points than lighter molecules.

Chemist 2

Chemist 2 proposes that the boiling point of a compound depends primarily on the strength of the attractive intermolecular forces between molecules in solution. The stronger the attractive intermolecular forces between molecules, the harder it must be to remove a molecule from the solution to the gas phase. As it becomes more difficult to liberate a molecule from its liquid phase into its gas phase, more heat energy is required to carry the process out. The result is that the boiling point of a compound increases as the molecules bind to each other more tightly in solution. When the intermolecular forces are greater, fewer molecules vaporize, so the boiling point of the compound increases, and the vapor pressure of the compound decreases.

The hierarchy in attractive intermolecular forces is hydrogen-bonding first, polarity is second, and van der Waals forces rank third in strengths. Hydrogen bonds contain the greatest amount of energy of these three forces, but not all hydrogen-bonds are equal in strength. For instance, alcohols have stronger hydrogen bonds than amines, because the hydrogen of the alcohol is more acidic than the hydrogen of the amine. The greater acidity allows the hydrogen to accept electron density more readily. Any compound capable of forming hydrogen bonds is also polar. Polar attractions are stronger than van der Waals forces, the weakest of the intermolecular forces.

1. All of the following observations support Chemist 1's theory EXCEPT:

    A. $(H_3C)_2CHOH$ has a higher boiling point than H_3CCH_2OH.

    B. H_3CCH_2OH has a higher vapor pressure than H_3CCO_2H.

    C. $H_3CCH_2CH_2OH$ has a higher boiling point than $H_3CCH_2OCH_2CH_3$.

    D. H_3COH has a higher vapor pressure than $H_3C(CH_2)_6CH_3$.

2. How would Chemist 2 rank the following compounds according to their boiling points?

    I. H_3CCH_2OH

    II. H_3COCH_3

    III. $H_3CCH_2NH_2$

    A. $H_3CCH_2OH > H_3CCH_2NH_2 > H_3COCH_3$

    B. $H_3CCH_2OH > H_3COCH_3 > H_3CCH_2NH_2$

    C. $H_3CCH_2NH_2 > H_3CCH_2OH > H_3COCH_3$

    D. $H_3CCH_2NH_2 > H_3COCH_3 > H_3CCH_2OH$

3. As you climb higher in the mountains, the amount of gases in the atmosphere decreases. This affects the boiling point of propanol such that it:

    A. decreases, because the amount of hydrogen-bonding decreases.

    B. decreases, because the amount of hydrogen-bonding increases.

    C. decreases, because the atmospheric pressure increases.

    D. decreases, because the atmospheric pressure decreases.

4. The hydrogenation of an eight-carbon diene has which of the following effects on the physical properties of the compound?

    A. Both the molecular mass and the melting point increase.

    B. The molecular mass increases, while the melting point decreases.

    C. The molecular mass decreases, while the melting point increases.

    D. Both the molecular mass and the melting point decrease.

GO ON TO THE NEXT PAGE

5. According to Chemist 2, as intermolecular hydrogen-bonding increases, which of the following trends should be observed?

A. Both the boiling point and the vapor pressure increase.

B. The boiling point increases, while the vapor pressure decreases.

C. The boiling point decreases, while the vapor pressure increases.

D. Both the boiling point and the vapor pressure decrease.

6. How do the boiling points of the following three chlorohydrocarbons compare with each other?

I.

H$_3$C   CH$_3$

    Cl   Cl

II.

Cl   CH$_3$

H$_3$C   Cl

III.

H$_3$C   CH$_3$

H   H

   Cl   Cl

A. Compound I > Compound III > Compound II

B. Compound I > Compound II > Compound III

C. Compound II > Compound I > Compound III

D. Compound III > Compound I > Compound II

Passage II (Questions 7 - 13)

A common problem facing pharmacists is developing drugs in a form that can be easily ingested by human beings, particularly the problem of getting organic compounds to dissolve in water. As a general rule, organic compounds are not water-soluble, so it is difficult for them to migrate through the bloodstream. Because most organic compounds exhibit little to no hydrogen-bonding, they are referred to as *hydrophobic* (Greek for "water fearing"). To overcome the hydrophobic nature of organic compounds, one of two techniques can be employed.

Technique 1

Technique 1 involves the use of micelles, three-dimensional bulbs composed of compounds that are partly ionic and partly hydrophobic (organic). A prime example of a compound that forms a micelle in water is the conjugate base of a fatty acid (H$_3$C(CH$_2$)$_n$CO$_2^-$ Na$^+$). The micelle is a roughly spherical membrane that forms when the organic tails aggregate as shown in Figure 1.

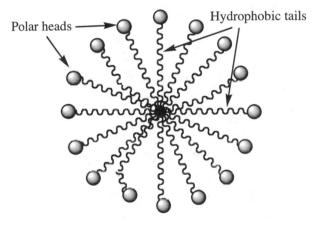

Figure 1. Aqueous arrangement of molecules in a micelle

An organic compound (such as an antibiotic) prefers the core of the micelle over the aqueous solution. Overall, the micelle is water-soluble due to the polar heads of the individual fatty-acid carboxylate anions. After migrating from an aqueous environment to a hydrophobic environment (lipid), a micelle turns itself inside out and releases the organic compound in its core. This mechanism is what enables water-insoluble drugs to be transported through the bloodstream (an aqueous environment) to hydrophobic target regions of the body (such as lipid membranes).

Technique 1

Technique 1 involves the use of micelles, three-dimensional bulbs composed of compounds that are partly ionic and partly hydrophobic (organic). A prime example of a compound that forms a micelle in water is the conjugate base of a fatty acid (H$_3$C(CH$_2$)$_n$CO$_2^-$ Na$^+$). The micelle is a spherical membrane that forms when the organic tails aggregate as shown in Figure 1.

7. How would a micelle appear in an organic solvent?

A.

B.

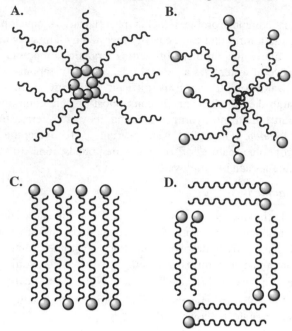

C.

D.

8. Which of the following compounds should be used in order to make a dication more soluble in an organic solvent?

A. $H_3C(CH_2)_nCO_2H$

B. $H_3C(CH_2)_nCO_2^-$

C. $H_3C(CH_2)_nNH_2$

D. $H_3C(CH_2)_nNH_3^+$

9. Which of the following compounds could MOST likely be taken into the body through respiration?

A. $(H_3C)_2CHOCH_3$

B. $(H_3C)_2CHCH_2OH$

C. $(H_3C)_2CHNHCH_3$

D. $(H_3C)_2CHCH_2NH_2$

10. Which of the following compounds would require a micelle to make it water-soluble?

A. An alcohol (RCH_2OH)

B. A carboxylic acid (RCO_2H)

C. An amine (RCH_2NH_2)

D. An alkene ($R_2C=CR_2$)

11. Which of the following compounds would be MOST soluble in water?

A.

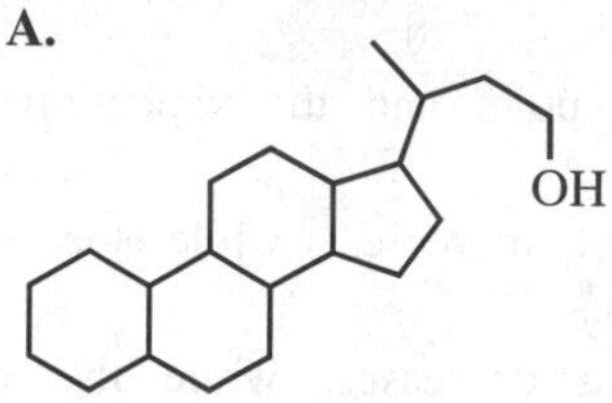

B.

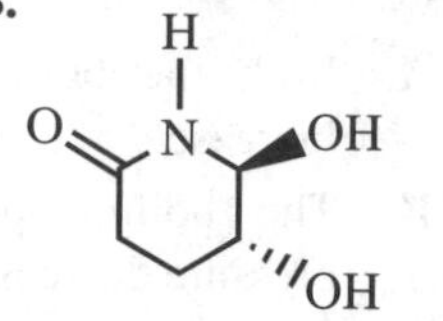

C.

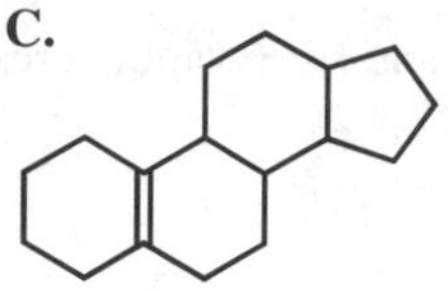

D.

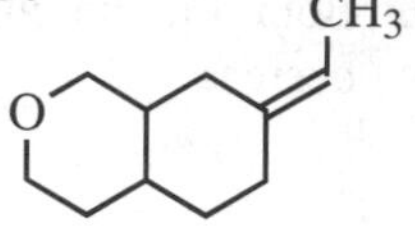

12. What force holds the organic tails of a micelle together?

A. Van der Waals forces

B. Polar attractions

C. Hydrogen-bonding

D. Covalent bonding

13. Which of the following compounds would make the BEST micelle?

A. $H_3C(CH_2)_3CO_2H$

B. $H_3C(CH_2)_3CO_2^-$

C. $H_3C(CH_2)_{13}CO_2H$

D. $H_3C(CH_2)_{13}CO_2^-$

         GO ON TO THE NEXT PAGE

The petroleum industry provides roughly forty percent of the annual energy needs of the United States. Crude oil is a mixture of hydrocarbons that is refined to produce fuels, including heating oil and petroleum. Many lightweight, alkene by-products from the refinement of crude oil are used as raw materials in making polymers. The industrial process for refining crude oil into useful components is referred to as *cracking* and is similar to fractional distillation. Figure 1 shows a schematic representation of the cracking column used to refine crude oil and the fragments collected at different levels of refinement.

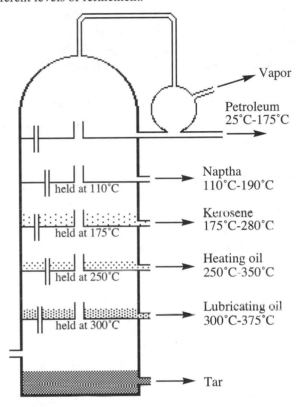

Figure 1. Cracking column used to refine crude oil

Petroleum distillate is sold as gasoline, the fuel most commonly used in internal combustion engines. The best air-petroleum mixture for such engines is the one that produces the most uniform distribution of heat over the period of time that the piston is doing work. This allows for an even expansion of the gas in the piston, which results in more useful work. The result is a smooth lifting of the piston, rather than an explosive jerk. Engine efficiency depends on the uniformity of heat distribution within it, so the choice of fuel influences engine efficiency.

Gasoline is given an octane rating that is based on its combustion rate. An octane rating is a measure of a fuel's tendency to cause *knocking* (non-uniform combustion.) The scale is set using 2,2,4-trimethylpentane, which is assigned an octane rating of 100, and n-heptane, which is assigned an octane rating of zero. A higher octane rating implies a better fuel. Table 1 lists the octane ratings and boiling points for some components of petroleum distillate.

Hydrocarbon	Octane Rating	Boiling Point
2-Methylbutane	93	28°C
Benzene	106	80°C
n-Hexane	25	69°C
Toluene	120	104°C
n-Heptane	0	98°C
2-Methylhexane	42	88°C
2,2,3-Trimethylbutane	125	82°C
2,2,4-Trimethylpentane	100	104°C

Table 1

14. Which is NOT an effect of branching in a hydrocarbon chain?

   A. An increase in octane rating
   B. A decrease in boiling point
   C. A increase in density
   D. An increase in hydrogen-bonding

15. The cracking (refining) column operates according to the principle that:

   A. more dense hydrocarbons rise higher than less dense hydrocarbons.
   B. hydrocarbons with lower boiling points rise higher than hydrocarbons with higher boiling points.
   C. hydrocarbons with higher boiling points rise higher than hydrocarbons with lower boiling points.
   D. aromatic hydrocarbons rise higher than non-aromatic hydrocarbons.

16. Which of the following eight-carbon hydrocarbons has the GREATEST octane rating?

   A. 2-Methylheptane
   B. n-Octane
   C. 2,2-Dimethylhexane
   D. 2,2,4-Trimethylpentane

17. Which of the following components is MOST likely a component of kerosene?

   A. n-Octane
   B. n-Decane
   C. 2,2-Dimethyloctane
   D. 2,2,4,4-Tetramethyloctane

   GO ON TO THE NEXT PAGE

18. The efficiency (octane rating) of a fuel depends on the:

    A. enthalpy of combustion.

    B. entropy of combustion.

    C. ratio of CO_2 to water in the exhaust.

    D. rate of combustion.

19. Which of the following statements must be true?

    I. Aromaticity increases octane rating.

    II. Ethylbenzene has an octane rating of less than 100.

    III. 2,2,3-Trimethylbutane is a good fuel additive to increase fuel efficiency.

    A. I only

    B. III only

    C. I and II only

    D. I and III only

20. The hybridization of carbon in the aerobic combustion of 2,2,4-trimethylpentane changes from:

    A. sp^3 to sp^2.

    B. sp^2 to sp^3.

    C. sp to sp^3.

    D. sp^3 to sp.

Passage IV (Questions 21 - 27)

Most reactions using organic reagents require a solvent other than water, so acid-base chemistry is best viewed from either the Brønsted-Lowry definition or the Lewis definition. Brønsted-Lowry defines an acid as a compound that acts as a proton donor, while the Lewis definition of an acid is a compound that accepts electron pairs. For acid-base reactions that involve the transfer of a proton from one reactant to another, the equilibrium constant associated with this process can be predicted from the pK_a values of the two acids in the reaction (the reactant acid and the product acid).

To determine the K_a value for organic acids, an organic acid is added quantitatively to an organic base. The equilibrium constant (K_{eq}) is determined from the concentration of each species, once equilibrium is reached. Reaction 1 is a generic reaction between an organic acid (HA) and the conjugate base (B^-) of a second organic acid

$$HA + B^- \rightleftharpoons A^- + HB$$

Reaction 1

Equation 1 can be used to determine the equilibrium constant for Reaction 1.

$$K_{eq} = \frac{[A^-][HB]}{[HA][B^-]} = \frac{K_{a \text{ (acid HA)}}}{K_{a \text{ (acid HB)}}} = 10^{(pK_a \text{ (HB)} - pK_a \text{ (HA)})}$$

Equation 1

A series of six different organic acids are treated with 1,3-cyclopentadienyl anion ($C_5H_5^-$), which react as shown in Reaction 2.

Reaction 2

Table 1 lists the theoretical equilibrium constants for the six acid-base reactions patterned after Reaction 2.

Organic Acid (HA)	Equilibrium Constant (K_{eq})
H_3CCOCH_3	2.0×10^{-4}
$H_3CCOCH_2COCH_3$	1.2×10^{6}
H_3COH	3.9×10^{-1}
H_3CCH_2SH	5.2×10^{4}
Cl_3CH	8.0×10^{-9}
H_3CNO_2	8.2×10^{4}

Table 1

The concentration of each organic species at equilibrium is determined using UV-visible spectroscopy whenever possible. In cases where no π-bond is present in both the reactant acid and the product acid, the concentrations are determined using gas chromatography. The conjugate base and reactant base concentrations are determined by the difference between initial acid concentration and equilibrium acid concentration. The concentrations are used to determine equilibrium constants. The calculated values are compared to values found using pK_a numbers in Equation 1. It is found that the error is greatest when K_{eq} is greater than 10^4.

21. Which of the following compounds can deprotonate C_5H_6?

   A. H_3CCOCH_3

   B. H_3CCH_2SH

   C. H_3CO^-

   D. $H_2CNO_2^-$

22. For the following reaction: *pKa 16*

$$H_3CCH_2SH + H_3CO^- \rightleftharpoons H_3CCH_2S^- + H_3COH$$

what is true about the relative concentrations of each species at equilibrium, if the reactants are mixed in equal molar portions?

   A. $[H_3CO^-] > [H_3CCH_2S^-]$; $[H_3CO^-] > [H_3COH]$; $[H_3CCH_2SH] > [H_3CO^-]$

   B. $[H_3CCH_2S^-] > [H_3CO^-]$; $[H_3COH] > [H_3CO^-]$; $[H_3CCH_2SH] > [H_3CO^-]$

   C. $[H_3CO^-] > [H_3CCH_2S^-]$; $[H_3CO^-] > [H_3COH]$; $[H_3CCH_2SH] = [H_3CO^-]$

   D. $[H_3CCH_2S^-] > [H_3CO^-]$; $[H_3COH] > [H_3CO^-]$; $[H_3CCH_2SH] = [H_3CO^-]$

23. Which of the following reactions has an equilibrium constant greater than 1?

   A. $Cl_3CH + H_3CCH_2S^- \rightleftharpoons Cl_3C^- + H_3CCH_2SH$

   B. $H_3COH + H_2CNO_2^- \rightleftharpoons H_3CO^- + H_3CNO_2$

   C. $H_3CCOCH_3 + H_3CO^- \rightleftharpoons$
                    $H_3CCOCH_2^- + H_3COH$

   D. $H_3CCOCH_2COCH_3 + Cl_3C^- \rightleftharpoons$
                 $H_3CCOCHCOCH_3^- + Cl_3CH$

24. Which of the following acids has a pK_a value close to 10.0, given that the pK_a for C_5H_6 is 15.0?

   A. H_3CCOCH_3

   B. Cl_3CH

   C. H_3COH

   D. H_3CNO_2

25. Which of the following relationships accurately shows the relative pK_a values for the given acids?

   A. $pK_{a(Cl_3CH)} > pK_{a(CH_3OH)} > pK_{a(H_3CNO_2)}$

   B. $pK_{a(H_3CNO_2)} > pK_{a(CH_3OH)} > pK_{a(Cl_3CH)}$

   C. $pK_{a(CH_3OH)} > pK_{a(Cl_3CH)} > pK_{a(H_3CNO_2)}$

   D. $pK_{a(CH_3OH)} > pK_{a(H_3CNO_2)} > pK_{a(Cl_3CH)}$

26. Which of the following compounds is NOT an example of a Lewis acid?

   A. Cl_3CH

   B. H_3CNO_2

   C. $NaCH_3$

   D. BF_3

27. The acidity of the C_5H_6 is abnormally high for hydrocarbons, because:

   A. it is aromatic.

   B. it has an aromatic conjugate base.

   C. its hydrogens withdraw electron density through the inductive effect.

   D. in the conjugate base, the hydrogens withdraw electron density through the inductive effect.

A typical laboratory experiment that first-quarter organic chemistry students encounter involves measuring physical properties of organic compounds. In this experiment, a team of six students measures the boiling points and densities of eighteen organic compounds. The boiling point is measured by heating a small sample of the compound in a thin, glass capillary tube. The density is measured using a balance and a 10.0-mL volumetric pipette. The students compare these values with those given in scientific literature. Table 1 is a collection of experimental values.

Compound	B.P. (°C)	M.P. (°C)	ρ^{20} (g/mL)
CH_3OH	65	-97	0.793
CH_3CH_2OH	79	-115	0.789
$CH_3CH_2CH_2OH$	97	-126	0.804
$CH_3CH(OH)CH_3$	82	-86	0.789
CH_3OCH_3	-24	-140	1.617 g/L
$CH_3CH_2OCH_2CH_3$	35	-116	0.713
CH_3CHO	20	-121	0.788
CH_3CH_2CHO	49	-81	0.807
$CH_3CH_2CH_2CHO$	75	-99	0.802
H_3CCOCH_3	56	-94	0.788
$H_3CCOCH_2CH_3$	80	-86	0.805
HCO_2H	101	8	1.220
H_3CCO_2H	118	17	1.049
$H_3CCH_2CO_2H$	141	-21	0.993
$HCO_2CH_2CH_3$	54	-80	0.917
$H_3CCO_2CH_2CH_3$	77	-83	0.902
$HCONH_2$	210d	3	1.113
H_3CCONH_2	222	81	1.159

Table 1. Physical properties of eighteen organic compounds

28. Which of the following is MOST likely to be a solid at room temperature?

    A. 1-Butanol
    B. Dipropyl ether
    C. Pentanal
    D. Octanoic acid

29. How is the significant difference in boiling points between 1-propanol and 2-propanol BEST explained?

    A. 1-Propanol has greater intermolecular steric hindrance, so it forms weaker hydrogen bonds.
    B. 1-Propanol has less intermolecular steric hindrance, so it forms weaker hydrogen bonds.
    C. 2-Propanol has greater intermolecular steric hindrance, so it forms weaker hydrogen bonds.
    D. 2-Propanol has less intermolecular steric hindrance, so it forms weaker hydrogen bonds.

30. Which factor(s) influence(s) boiling point?

    I. Molecular mass
    II. Intermolecular forces
    III. Chirality

    A. I only
    B. I and II only
    C. II and III only
    D. I, II, and III

31. Why do ethyl esters have lower melting points than the corresponding carboxylic acid derivatives?

    A. Greater molecular mass results in a greater melting point.
    B. Greater chain-length results in a reduced melting point.
    C. Hydrogen bonding exists only in the acids, not the esters.
    D. Van der Waals forces are more significant in short-chain compounds.

32. Which distillation sequence is possible?

    A. Distillation of 1-propanol from tetrahydrofuran
    B. Distillation of ethyl formate from acetone
    C. Distillation of ethanol from diethyl ether
    D. Distillation of tetrahydrofuran from acetic acid

33. Why do the boiling point and melting point of acetamide exceed those of acetic acid?

    A. Acetamide has greater hydrogen bonding.
    B. Acetamide has weaker hydrogen bonding.
    C. Acetamide has substantially greater molecular mass.
    D. Acetamide has substantially smaller molecular mass.

YOU ARE DONE.

Answers to Molecular Structure Phase III Homework

1. C	2. A	3. D	4. A	5. B	6. A	7. A	8. B	9. A	10. D
11. B	12. A	13. D	14. D	15. B	16. D	17. D	18. D	19. D	20. D
21. C	22. D	23. D	24. D	25. A	26. C	27. B	28. D	29. C	30. B
31. C	32. D	33. A							

Passage I (Questions 1 - 6)   **Physical Properties and Intermolecular Forces**

1. **Choice C is the best answer.** We must start questions like this by having a firm grasp on the two theories presented in the passage. Chemist 1 considers molecular mass to determine the relative boiling points of compounds. We are looking for the exception, so the correct answer is the choice where the lighter compound has the higher boiling point (or lower vapor pressure). A higher vapor pressure at room temperature corresponds to a lower boiling point. In choice A, the heavier compound of the two has the higher boiling point, so choice A is not an exception to Chemist 1's general rule. In choice B, the heavier compound of the two has the lower vapor pressure (and thus higher boiling point), so choice B also follows Chemist 1's rule. In choice D, the heavier compound of the two has the lower vapor pressure (and thus higher boiling point), so choice D follows Chemist 1's rule too. In choice C, the heavier compound of the two has the lower boiling point, so choice C contradicts Chemist 1's theory. The best answer is choice C.

2. **Choice A is the best answer.** Chemist 2 considers intermolecular forces to determine the boiling point of a compound. The strongest intermolecular forces correspond to the highest boiling point. The passage states that alcohols have stronger hydrogen-bonding than amines. This means that ethanol (Compound I) has the strongest H-bonds of the three compounds, so it has the highest boiling point (and thus should be listed first). Dimethyl ether (Compound II) has the lowest boiling point of the three compounds, because it cannot form hydrogen bonds with itself (it lacks an electropositive hydrogen). The order of the boiling points is therefore: I > III > II, making choice A the best answer.

3. **Choice D is the best answer.** At higher elevations there are fewer molecules of gas per volume of air, and thus a lower atmospheric pressure. This eliminates choice C. The elevation and atmospheric pressure have no effect on the intermolecular forces between molecules in solution, so choices A and B are not feasible. A lower atmospheric pressure means that less energy (heat) is required to reach a temperature at which the vapor pressure (P_{vapor}) equals the atmospheric pressure ($P_{atmospheric}$), which is defined as the boiling point. The boiling point is therefore lowered as elevation increases. This makes choice D the best answer.

4. **Choice A is the best answer.** Hydrogenation is the addition of hydrogen atoms to the π-bond carbons of an alkene and the subsequent reduction the compound to an alkane. This is what is observed when an unsaturated fat is treated with $FADH_2$. For every π-bond that is lost by the alkene molecule, two hydrogens are gained. This increases the molecular weight of the compound (a minor factor) and drastically increases the molecular flexibility of the compound (the product is slightly more massive and significantly more flexible than the reactant). Both of these effects increase the melting point of the compound, making the melting point of the product greater than the melting point of the reactant. This makes choice A the best answer. Pick A and you'll be an MCAT supernova.

5. **Choice B is the best answer.** According to Chemist 2 (and as a general rule in organic chemistry), the stronger the intermolecular forces, the greater the boiling point for a compound. The greater the boiling point for a compound, the less of it there is that evaporates, thus the lower its vapor pressure. Pick choice B, to soundly apply the logic of Chemist 2.

6. **Choice A is the best answer.** The boiling points of Compounds I and II are directly comparable, because they are geometrical isomers. Compound I (the cis isomer) is polar, while Compound II (the trans isomer) is nonpolar. This means that the boiling point of Compound I is greater than the boiling point of Compound II, which eliminates choice C. Because Compound III is an alkane, it is flexible (whereas Compounds I and II are unable to rotate freely, due to the π-bond), so Compound III is able to rotate between conformers. The most stable conformation of Compound III is nonpolar, but because it can assume polar conformations on occasion, the compound is considered to be slightly polar. The molecular masses for all three compounds are roughly equal, so the relative boiling points will come down to their relative polarities. The boiling point of Compound III is less than the boiling point of Compound I. Compound III should have the second highest boiling point, because it is slightly polar, while Compound II is nonpolar. Thus, the correct order for their relative boiling points is I > III > II, making choice A the best answer.

7. **Choice A is the best answer.** A micelle assumes a shape where its exterior matches the environment (solvent) and its interior is repelled by the environment. This means that a micelle will turn inside out from its aqueous form when it is added to an organic solvent (as stated in the passage). Figure 1 shows a micelle as it appears in water, where the polar heads are exposed to the surrounding liquid, and the organic tails are isolated in the core. In a hydrophobic (organic) solvent, the organic tails would be exposed, and the polar heads form the isolated core. This is best illustrated in choice **A**. Choice B is out, because that is how the micelle would form in water. Choice C may look familiar, in that cell membranes arrange themselves in such a manner, but it's not the best answer to this question. Choice D is a "throw-away" answer, because the tail and the head of the compound exhibit no attractive forces, so they would not arrange in a fashion where they are so close.

8. **Choice B is the best answer.** A dication carries a +2 charge, so in order to pull it into an organic solvent (hydrophobic environment), it must be coupled with an anion that is organically soluble. The only organic anion among the answer choices is choice **B**. The carboxylate heads would aggregate around the cation and the organic tails would form the surrounding micelle.

9. **Choice A is the best answer.** For a compound to be absorbed through respiration, it must be a gas or a vapor, because only gases are absorbed through respiration. This means that any compound intended to be taken into the lung must be either a gas or a liquid with a low boiling point (one with a high vapor pressure). There is hydrogen-bonding in choices B, C, and D, but not in choice **A**. Hydrogen-bonding increases the boiling point of a compound and thus lowers its vapor pressure. All of the compounds have roughly comparable masses (either 73 or 74 grams per mole), so mass won't help to differentiate between the boiling points of the four compounds. The only factor to consider in approximating the relative boiling points is hydrogen-bonding. The best answer is the ether, choice **A**. As a point of trivia, it is estimated that the average human adult takes in approximately 3500 gallons of air a day. Just thought you might like to know.

10. **Choice D is the best answer.** A micelle enhances the water solubility of a compound that is normally insoluble in water. This question therefore is asking for the *least* water-soluble compound. An alcohol, a carboxylic acid, and an amine all exhibit hydrogen-bonding (although within a tertiary amine, there is no protic hydrogen for hydrogen-bonding), so they should all be water-soluble to some extent. How soluble in water will depend on the length of the alkyl chain, but in the context of this question we need to focus on the functional group. Because an alkene has no hydrogen-bonding (it has neither a lone pair of electrons to donate nor an electropositive hydrogen), it is unlikely that it would be water-soluble at all. In order to get it to go into water, a micelle must be employed. The best answer of the given choices is therefore choice **D**.

11. **Choice B is the best answer.** To be water-soluble, the compound should be able to form hydrogen bonds or at the very least be polar with a minimal number of carbons. Choices C and D are eliminated immediately, because they are hydrophobic and have no protic hydrogens to form hydrogen bonds. Although choice A has an alcohol group, the steroid ring system makes it primarily organic (hydrophobic). Choice A will not be very water-soluble, so it is eliminated. Choice **B** has two hydroxyl groups and an amide group as well as the least number of carbon atoms of the four answer choices. Both amides and hydroxyl groups readily form hydrogen bonds, so choice **B** exhibits the greatest amount of hydrogen-bonding of the choices. The best answer is choice **B**.

12. **Choice A is the best answer.** The organic tails of micelles are held together by the weak attraction associated with van der Waals forces (choice **A**). The organic tails are alkyl-based, so they are nonpolar. This eliminates choice B. The alkyl tails contain only carbon and hydrogen and not any nitrogen, oxygen, or fluorine. This means that the alkyl tails cannot form hydrogen bonds, so choice C is eliminated. You must recall that to form hydrogen bonds, a compound must have an electropositive hydrogen bonded to either nitrogen, oxygen, or fluorine. Choice D is eliminated, because covalent bonds are formed in chemical reactions, and the organic tails in micelles exhibit only attractive forces, nothing as strong as covalent bonding. No electrons are shared within a molecular orbital between the two alkyl groups, so there is no covalent bond holding alkyl groups together. The best answer, and thus choice to make, is choice **A**.

13. **Choice D is the best answer.** We are looking for the compound with the most water-soluble end on one side and the most lipid-soluble end on the other side. The best micelle should have an ionic (charged) head for enhanced water-solubility and a long carbon chain as its organic tail for enhanced lipid-solubility. Choices A and C are eliminated, because they have uncharged heads, which won't be as water-soluble as the charged heads in choices B and D. Choice **D** is a better answer than choice B, because it has a longer organic tail, which will increase its lipid-solubility and make a better hydrophobic pocket with the micelle. Choice **D** is the best answer.

This is an extremely useful passage in that it is based on simple organic chemistry and at the same time asks about something that is unfamiliar to most of us. MCAT passages will require that you interpret new information and apply it to questions. The point of this passage is not to teach you about octane rating and petroleum processing, but to expose you to a passage on a topic you haven't studied that can be understood quickly using fundamental organic chemistry principles.

14. **Choice D is the best answer.** From the data in Table 1, it can be seen that branching increases the octane rating of a hydrocarbon. For example, as branching increases, so does octane rating for the seven-carbon aliphatic hydrocarbons: 2,2,3-trimethylbutane > 2-methylhexane > n-heptane. This makes choice A a valid statement, thus eliminating choice A. From the data in Table 1, it can be seen that as branching increases, the boiling point decreases (for hydrocarbons of comparable mass). This can also be seen with the boiling points of the seven carbon aliphatic hydrocarbons, which have relative boiling points of n-heptane > 2-methylhexane > 2,2,3-trimethylbutane. Choice B is a valid statement, so it is also eliminated. Due to branching, the hydrocarbon with the greatest number of alkyl substituents has the greatest mass of compound occupying the smallest volume. This results in an increase in density with branching. Choice C is a valid statement, so it is also eliminated. Hydrocarbons have no hydrogen-bonding, so regardless of the amount of branching, hydrogen-bonding neither increases nor decreases from hydrocarbon to hydrocarbon. This makes choice **D** an invalid statement as to the effect of branching. You should smile brightly when you pick choice **D**.

15. **Choice B is the best answer.** As density increases for a hydrocarbon (or any gas), it does not rise as easily. This means that as density decreases, the ability of the vapor to rise (ascend the cracking column) increases. This eliminates choice A. Choice D is eliminated, because as shown in the apparatus in Figure 1, the aromatic hydrocarbons are not collected in the highest chamber of the cracking column. You could have immediately deduced that the correct answer is either choice **B** or C, because they are opposites of one another and the boiling point is listed in the diagram. As indicated by the picture in Figure 1, the hydrocarbons with the lower boiling points are collected towards the top of the cracking column, which makes choice **B** the best answer. Compounds with higher boiling points do not rise higher, so choice C is incorrect. You'd be sad if you were to choose anything besides choice **B**.

16. **Choice D is the best answer.** From the trend in the data in Table 1, it can be concluded that branching in a hydrocarbon increases its octane rating. This is due to the fact that branching causes steric hindrance, which slows the oxidation reaction so that the fuel burns more slowly and efficiently. In the four choices, the greatest amount of branching is observed with 2,2,4-trimethylpentane, choice **D**, making it the best answer. It can be inferred from the passage that 2,2,4-trimethylpentane has an octane rating of 100, higher than the straight-chain hydrocarbons. Don't be a dodo, pick **D**.

17. **Choice D is the best answer.** According to Figure 1, kerosene has a boiling-point range of 175°C to 280°C, so the component most likely to be found in kerosene should have a boiling point in that range. The four answer choices are saturated hydrocarbons of eight, ten, ten, and twelve carbons. To make an estimate of the boiling points for both n-octane and n-decane, you can use the trend in Table 1 for the other straight-chain hydrocarbons. We see that n-hexane has a boiling point of 69°C and n-heptane has a boiling point of 98°C, for a difference of 29°C. Following this trend predicts that n-octane has an approximate boiling point of 127°C (in the 125°C - 130°C range) and n-decane an approximate boiling point of 185°C (in the180°C - 185°C range). Choice C is also ten carbons (like n-decane), but it has branching, which reduces the boiling point relative to the straight-chain structure. The branching of 2,2-dimethyloctane reduces the boiling point from that of n-decane (the straight-chain, ten-carbon alkane) to somewhere around 165°C to 170°C. The eight-carbon compound should be found in the petroleum range, so choice A is eliminated. The ten-carbon compounds are probably found in the petroleum-to-naphtha range. You should use test-taking logic to eliminate choices B and C, because their boiling points are similar, given that their molecular masses are identical and their structures are similar. The best answer is choice **D**, the compound with the highest molecular mass (and thus the higher boiling point) of the choices. Being a 12-carbon species, 2,2,4,4-tetramethyloctane is most likely to have a boiling point in the 225°C to 230°C range, which lies in the kerosene boiling point range of 175°C to 280°C. Your job, should you accept it, is to pick choice **D**.

18. **Choice D is the best answer.** Octane rating is based on the ability of a compound to distribute heat uniformly as it combusts. This ability is found in compounds that are capable of releasing their heat energy steadily over an extended period of time. This is to say that a hydrocarbon that burns slowly and uniformly will have the greatest octane rating. The best answer is therefore choice **D**. The octane rating does not depend on the enthalpy or entropy of combustion, although the favorability of the combustion reaction does on these. Choices A and B are eliminated. The ratio of carbon dioxide to water depends only on the number of carbons and hydrogens in the fuel and has no influence whatsoever on the octane rating. Choice C is eliminated.

19. **Choice D is the best answer.** Because toluene and benzene have octane ratings higher than the other six- and seven-carbon saturated hydrocarbons, it can be inferred that aromaticity increases octane rating. Statement I is therefore a true statement. Because benzene has an octane rating of 106 and toluene (methylbenzene) has an octane rating of 120, the trend tells us that ethylbenzene should have an octane rating around 134, which is in excess of 100. Statement II is therefore a false statement. Because of the branching associated with 2,2,3-trimethylbutane, it has a high octane rating. A high octane rating is a quality associated with a good fuel additive, so a branched hydrocarbon such as 2,2,3-trimethylbutane is a good fuel additive. Statement III is therefore a true statement. Because Statements I and III are both true statements, the best answer is choice **D**. Do what is best, and pick choice **D**.

20. **Choice D is the best answer.** Because 2,2,4-trimethylpentane is a fully saturated hydrocarbon, all of its carbons have a hybridization of sp^3. In the final product, the carbons are all present in the form of carbon dioxide. The hybridization of carbon in carbon dioxide (CO_2) is sp. This means that in this reaction, the hybridization of carbon changes from sp^3 to sp. The best answer, and one we highly recommend to all parties interested in MCAT success, is choice **D**.

Passage IV   (Questions 21 - 27) K_{eq} **and Acidity**

21. **Choice C is the best answer.** Reaction 2, the experimental reaction from the passage, involves the protonation of $C_5H_5^-$ to form C_5H_6. This question asks for the reverse reaction. This means that any acid that shows an equilibrium constant less than 1.0 has a conjugate base that is strong enough to deprotonate C_5H_6. Choices A and B are eliminated, because they are acids, not bases. Because only methanol (CH_3OH) shows an equilibrium constant less than 1.0, only methoxide anion (CH_3O^-) is strong enough to deprotonate C_5H_6. The best answer is choice **C**.

22. **Choice D is the best answer.** The reaction as drawn proceeds from the stronger acid to the weaker acid, therefore the equilibrium constant for the reaction is greater than 1.0. When the equilibrium constant is greater than 1.0 for a reaction with equal number of products as reactants, the products are in higher concentration at equilibrium than the reactants. This means that $H_3CCH_2S^-$ is in higher concentration than H_3CO^- ($[H_3CCH_2S^-] > [H_3CO^-]$). This eliminates choices A and C. To distinguish choice B from choice **D**, the initial concentrations must be known. Because H_3CCH_2SH and H_3CO^- are mixed equally initially, they must be equally concentrated at equilibrium ($[H_3CCH_2SH] = [H_3CO^-]$). The best answer therefore is choice **D**.

23. **Choice D is the best answer.** For a reaction to have an equilibrium constant greater than 1.0, the reaction must be favorable in the forward direction as written. A favorable acid-base reaction proceeds from stronger acid to weaker acid in the forward direction as written. The larger the equilibrium constant, the more favorable the reaction, so the strength of each acid can be inferred from the K_{eq} values in Table 1. In choice A, the reaction proceeds from the weaker acid (Cl_3CH with K_{eq} of 8.0×10^{-9}) to the stronger acid (H_3CCH_2SH with K_{eq} of 5.2×10^4). This means that this reaction is unfavorable as written and thus has a $K_{eq} < 1$. Choice A is therefore eliminated. In choice B, the reaction proceeds from the weaker acid (H_3COH with K_{eq} of 3.9×10^{-1}) to the stronger acid (H_3CNO_2 with K_{eq} of 8.2×10^4). This means that this reaction is unfavorable as written and thus has a $K_{eq} < 1$. Choice B is therefore eliminated. In choice C, the reaction proceeds from the weaker acid (H_3CCOCH_3 with K_{eq} of 2.0×10^{-4}) to the stronger acid (H_3COH with K_{eq} of 3.9×10^{-1}). This means that this reaction is unfavorable as written and thus has a $K_{eq} < 1$. Choice C is therefore eliminated. It is only in choice **D** that the reaction proceeds from a stronger acid ($H_3CCOCH_2COCH_3$ with $K_{eq} = 1.2 \times 10^6$) to a weaker acid (Cl_3CH with $K_{eq} = 8.0 \times 10^{-9}$). This means that this reaction is favorable as written and thus has a $K_{eq} > 1$, so the best answer is choice **D**.

24. **Choice D is the best answer.** Using Equation 1 from the passage, the K_{eq} for a reaction is found by taking 10 to the power of the product acid pK_a minus the reactant acid pK_a. In the standard reaction, C_5H_6 is the product acid and its pK_a value is given as 15.0. If the pK_a of the reactant acid is 10.0, then the equilibrium constant would be $10^{(15.0 - 10.0)} = 10^5$. The question can therefore be thought of as: "Which acid in Table 1 has an equilibrium constant of roughly 10^5?" The best answer is choice **D**, CH_3NO_2, with an equilibrium constant of $8.2. \times 10^4$ when it reacts with $C_5H_5^-$.

25. **Choice A is the best answer.** The weaker of the two acids has the larger of the two pK_a values. This question is asking for the weakest acid relative to the strongest acid. As the acid gets weaker, the reaction with $C_5H_5^-$ becomes less favorable, so the equilibrium constant for the reaction gets smaller. Cl_3CH shows the lowest equilibrium constant of the answer choices, so it is the weakest acid and thus has the highest pK_a value. It is only in choice **A** that Cl_3CH is listed as having the highest pK_a value, which makes choice **A** correct.

26. **Choice C is the best answer.** A Lewis acid is an electron-pair acceptor. The classic example of a Lewis acid is choice **D**, BF_3, with highly electronegative fluorine atoms on a boron atom with an empty p-orbital that can readily accept electrons. This makes the boron severely electron-deficient. Both CH_3Cl and CH_3NO_2 are listed as acids in Table a, so choices **A** and **B** are not good choices. $NaCH_3$ is a carbanion that cannot accept a lone pair, but instead readily donates a lone pair. This means that choice **C** is not a Lewis acid, and in fact is a Lewis base. Pick choice **C** to be terrific.

27. **Choice B is the best answer.** The conjugate base of the 1,3-cyclopentadiene species has six π-electrons in a continuous cyclic planar array of p-orbitals. These conditions result in aromatic stability. The best explanation for the relative ease with which the 1,3-cyclopentadiene loses its proton is the aromaticity associated with the conjugate base (1,3-cyclopentadienyl anion). The more stable that the conjugate base is, the stronger the acid is. Pick choice **B** and be satisfied.

Passage V (Questions 28 - 33) | **More Physical Properties**

28. **Choice D is the best answer.** From the table, the trend observed in the alcohols leads us to the conclusion that 1-butanol would have a melting point around -125°C and a boiling point around 115°C. The actual values (for those of you who are data mongers) are -90°C and 117° to 118°C, which would imply that at 25°C, the compound exists as a liquid. This eliminates choice A. Following the same trend for the ethers would lead us to the conclusion that for dipropyl ether, the melting point is -90°C and the boiling point is 95°C. The actual values are -122°C and 89° to 91°C, which would imply that at 25°C, the compound exists as a liquid. This eliminates choice B. Following the same trend for the aldehydes would lead us to the conclusion that for pentanal, the melting point is -80°C and the boiling point is 98°C. The actual values are -87°C and 102° to 103°C, which would imply that at 25°C, the compound exists as a liquid. This eliminates choice C. Choice **D** remains, the only compound among the choices to exhibit hydrogen bonding. Octanoic acid, because it has the greatest molecular mass of the choices and has hydrogen bonding, is the most likely to be a solid at room temperature. In actuality, octanoic acid is an oily liquid at room temperature, with a melting point of 16.7°C. The trends are not perfect for carboxylic acids, as acetic acid (with only two carbons) has a higher melting point than the aliphatic acids of three to eight carbons. Nevertheless, the question asks for the most likely candidate, so go with choice **D**.

29. **Choice C is the best answer.** Both 1-propanol and 2-propanol have the same molecular mass and one hydroxyl group, so they have the same number of functional groups that form hydrogen bonds. The difference between having the hydroxyl group on a terminal carbon versus an interior carbon is that the terminal carbon is less sterically hindered. This means that 1-propanol can form stronger hydrogen bonds than 2-propanol, so it has stronger intermolecular forces. The consequence is that 1-propanol has a higher boiling point than 2-propanol. Choice **C** explains this best. This difference in hydrogen bonding can be observed in the infrared spectra of different alcohols, where primary alcohols have the broadest peaks, due to the high degree of hydrogen-bonding. Tertiary alcohols show the sharpest peak of any alcohol.

30. **Choice B is the best answer.** Intermolecular forces and the mass of the molecule affect the boiling point of a compound. The greater the mass, the more energy required to put the molecule into motion in the gas phase (it takes energy to "lift" the molecules from the liquid phase into the gas phase.) Intermolecular forces must be overcome for the compound to go from the liquid to the gas phase. Thus, intermolecular forces definitely affect the boiling point. Chirality has no influence on the boiling point, but it does affect how molecules pack in the solid phase. As such, chirality affects the melting and sublimation points. Because chirality does not affect the boiling point, the best answer is choice **B**.

31. **Choice C is the best answer.** Melting point depends on the intermolecular forces, the molecular mass, and the ability of the molecule to be packed into a lattice structure. The ester of a carboxylic acid has a greater molecular mass; so based strictly on mass, we would assume that the ester has the higher melting point. Because the carboxylic acids have the higher melting points than corresponding esters, we know that the acids must have stronger intermolecular forces and are able to be packed more tightly than esters. These properties can be attributed to the fact that carboxylic acids form hydrogen bonds, while esters have no hydrogens that are protic (capable of accepting electron density). This makes choice **C** the best answer.

32. **Choice D is the best answer.** During distillation, the compound with the lower boiling point must be removed from the mixture, leaving behind the compound with the greater boiling point. Tetrahydrofuran is a four-carbon ether, so it has a lower boiling point than 1-propanol. That means choice A is wrong. The boiling point of ethyl formate is 54°C; for acetone it is 56°C. Thus, they cannot easily be separated using distillation. Choice B is eliminated. Choice C cannot work for the same reasons that choice A cannot work: An ether has a lower boiling point than an alcohol, so the distillation removes diethyl ether (b.p. = 35°C) from ethanol (b.p. = 79°C), not ethanol from diethyl ether. In the last choice, the ether (tetrahydrofuran) has a lower boiling point than acetic acid, meaning it can be removed from the acetic acid by boiling. The best answer is choice **D**.

33. **Choice A is the best answer.** The molecular masses of acetic acid (H_3CCO_2H) and acetamide (H_3CCONH_2) differ by only one gram per mole, so choices C and D should be eliminated immediately. Because boiling point increases with hydrogen-bonding, the acetamide having the greater boiling point is the acetamide with stronger hydrogen-bonding than acetic acid. Because of resonance, the oxygen in the amide carries a slightly negative charge, while the nitrogen carries a slightly positive charge. This means that a hydrogen-bonding proton is more attracted to the oxygen in an amide than in a carboxylic acid, which can be verified by observing the high degree of hydrogen-bonding within proteins.

Structure Elucidation

Organic Chemistry Chapter 2

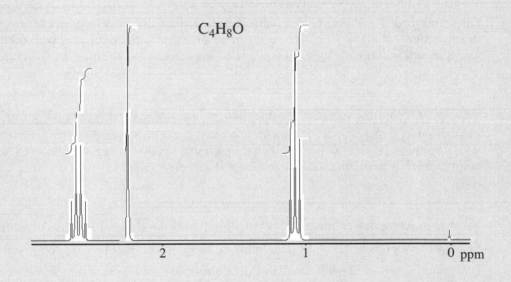

C_4H_8O

by Todd Bennett of

the Berkeley Review

Structure Elucidation

Key objectives of this section

Be able to identify different types of isomers and distinguish how two compounds relate.

Questions may present two or more molecules and then ask you to determine how they relate to one another. You must be able to assess quickly whether they are isomers of one another, and if so, what type of isomers.

Be able to identify the most stable conformation for a given structure like chlorocyclohexane.

Questions may present a two-dimensional representation of a structure and then ask you to identify its most favorable conformation in a traditional drawing such as the chair conformation for cyclohexane or a Newmann projection for a linear hydrocarbon.

Be able to determine the units of unsaturation from a formula and what groups it could have.

Questions could ask you to eliminate structures that do not fit a formula based on units of unsaturation. In all likelihood the units of unsaturation will be coupled with other information about an unknown molecule that you'll need to combine to determine its structure.

Be able to recognize common IR absorbances and know what functional group caused them.

Passages may present spectral data for some unknown compounds. Using the IR data they give you, you must be able to ascertain what functional groups are present on each of the unknown compounds, in particular alcohol groups and carbonyl groups.

Be able to recognize common ^{1}H NMR signals and the skeletal features causing them.

Passages will present ^{1}H NMR data followed by questions that require you to either identify the compound associated with the ^{1}H NMR data or ask you to distinguish between compounds based on a specific feature in the ^{1}H NMR data. Multiple-choice NMR is easier than regular.

Be able to distinguish pertinent spectral data from extraneous information.

Passages may overload you with all sorts of UV absorbances, IR absorbances, mass spectrometry data, and ^{1}H NMR signals. Questions will require you to only use some of the data they present and to not get overwhelmed by the excessive information.

Structure Elucidation

Structure elucidation involves applying all available information, from spectroscopic data to chemical reactivity, to ascertain the three-dimensional shape of a molecule. It entails determining the atoms within the molecule, the functional groups present on the molecule, and in advanced cases, the three-dimensional folding of the structure. Structure elucidation requires determining the number of isomers that fits a molecular formula, and then systematically eliminating ones that do not fit the data until only one structure remains.

In this section, we shall address the concept of isomerism and the many classes of isomers. Isomers have the same atoms within the molecule, but they differ in some manner, so that the molecules are not superimposable on one another. The difference could result from different bonding within the molecules, similar bonding but different three-dimensional distribution about a stereogenic center, or the same bonds and stereogenic symmetry with different conformational orientation. A significant part of structure elucidation is determining the exact isomers that are formed in a chemical reaction.

Other structure elucidation tools shall be discussed. Questions that involve structure elucidation are often made easier by first determining the units of unsaturation from the molecular formula of a compound. This information provides hints as to the presence of π-bonds and/or rings within the structure. Chemical tests can be carried out to determine the number of π-bonds, which when combined with the units of unsaturation, can specify the exact number of rings and π-bonds within a molecule.

In this section we shall also address spectroscopy and the information about structure it can provide. Infrared (IR) spectroscopy is typically used to determine the functional groups within a compound. It can also give some information about the symmetry of the molecule, the hybridization of carbon, and the presence of groups capable of forming hydrogen bonds. Ultraviolet-visible (UV-vis) spectroscopy tells us information about the π-bonds and conjugation within a molecule. Although all molecules absorb ultraviolet radiation, for practical purposes, we use it only to detect π-bonds. Nuclear magnetic resonance (NMR) spectroscopy describes the connectivity of a molecule and its specific structural features. In its simplest application, NMR can show the carbon skeleton of a molecule. In its more sophisticated application, NMR can show the presence of stereoisomers and the exact positions of functional groups. Finally, we shall consider mass spectrometry. Combining ^{1}H NMR data with UV-vis spectroscopy data, IR spectroscopy data, and mass spectrometry data, allows for precise determination of three-dimensional molecular structure.

It is best to consider ^{1}H NMR with symmetry as your primary focus. The question "How can you distinguish compounds by ^{1}H NMR?" can be reduced to "How many different types of hydrogens are there in each compound?" Multiple-choice ^{1}H NMR questions can be answered easily by predicting the spectra from possible structures. For instance, if you can narrow down the potential structures to ketones, then it's just a matter of systematically eliminating ketones that do not fit the spectral data. This is the perspective from which we will approach ^{1}H NMR. The ability to predict spectra from structures is best attained through practice. As you do the multiple-choice questions in the spectroscopy sections, predict the spectra for the structures in this same manner. The difference between the spectra in each answer choice (A, B, C, or D) is what often answers the question.

Isomerism

Isomers

Isomers are structures with the same formula, meaning they are made of the exact same atoms, but they differ in the location of each atom. The difference in position can be the result of different connectivity (bonds), different spatial arrangement because of asymmetry in the structure, or different orientation about a bond. The result is that there are several different types of isomers. Figure 2-1 shows a flow chart for determining the type of isomers.

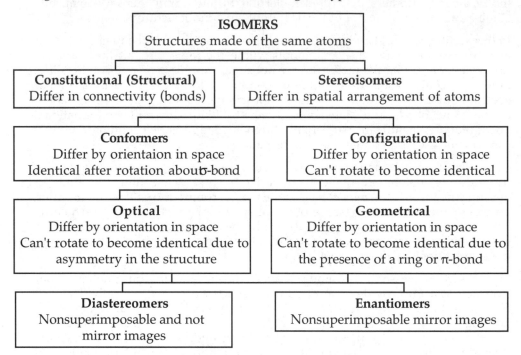

Figure 2-1

Constitutional isomers, which have different bonding, are more commonly referred to as *structural isomers*. Structural isomers are most easily recognized by their difference in IUPAC name. The difference may arise from the functional groups (like an alcohol versus an ether, or a ketone versus an aldehyde) or it may arise from the connectivity of the carbon backbone (like 2-methylhexane versus 3-methylhexane). Structural isomers can be further divided into *functional group isomers*, *positional isomers*, and *skeletal isomers*.

Stereoisomers have exactly the same bonds (and therefore the same connectivity), but they differ in the spatial arrangement of their atoms. On a more general note, stereoisomers can be categorized as either *configurational isomers* (which differ in spatial arrangement and cannot be converted into the other isomer without breaking a bond) or *conformational isomers* (which differ in spatial arrangement but can be converted into the other isomer by rotation without breaking a bond.) Within configurational isomers, there are *optical isomers* (isomers that rotate plane-polarized light differently), *geometrical isomers* (isomers that vary in orientation about a π-bond), *enantiomers* (nonsuperimposable mirror images), and *diastereomers* (nonsuperimposable and not mirror images). Configurational isomers are most easily distinguished by their IUPAC prefix. The IUPAC prefix contains either R or S, if the isomers differ in chirality at a stereocenter, or E and Z, if the isomers differ in their arrangement about a π-bond. We shall address stereoisomers in detail in later sections.

Example 2.1
What types of isomers are 2-methyl-3-pentanol and 3-methyl-2-pentanol?

A. Conformational isomers
B. Geometrical isomers
C. Structural isomers
D. Stereoisomers

Solution
The two compounds have different IUPAC names, so they are structural isomers. The two structures vary in the position of their alcohol and side chain methyl, so they are also positional isomers. The question was not that specific, so the best answer is choice **C**. The two structures are drawn below:

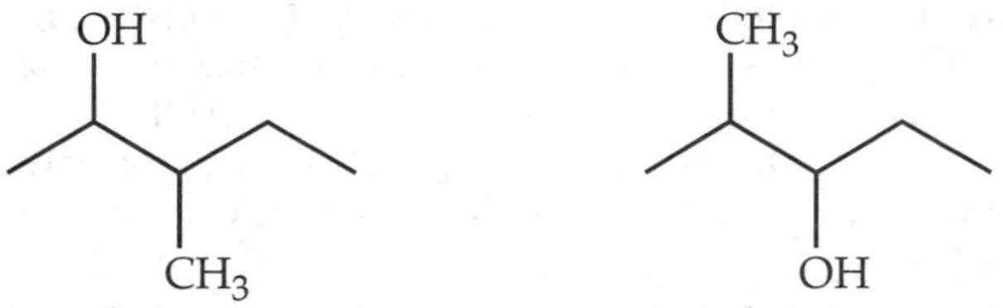

3-methyl-2-pentanol   2-methyl-3-pentanol

Constitutional Isomers
Constitutional isomers (also referred to as *structural isomers*) are unique molecules that have the same formula, but different connectivity. In other words, they have the same atoms, but the atoms have different bonding. For instance, 3-methylhexanal and 3-methyl-2-hexanone are constitutional isomers. They each have the formula $C_7H_{14}O$, but they have a different sequence of bonds. They can also be referred to as positional isomers. Using nomenclature helps to determine whether two structures are constitutional isomers, because constitutional isomers must have different IUPAC names. Figure 2-2 shows three pairs of structural isomers, one set of functional group isomers, one set of positional isomers, and one set of skeletal isomers.

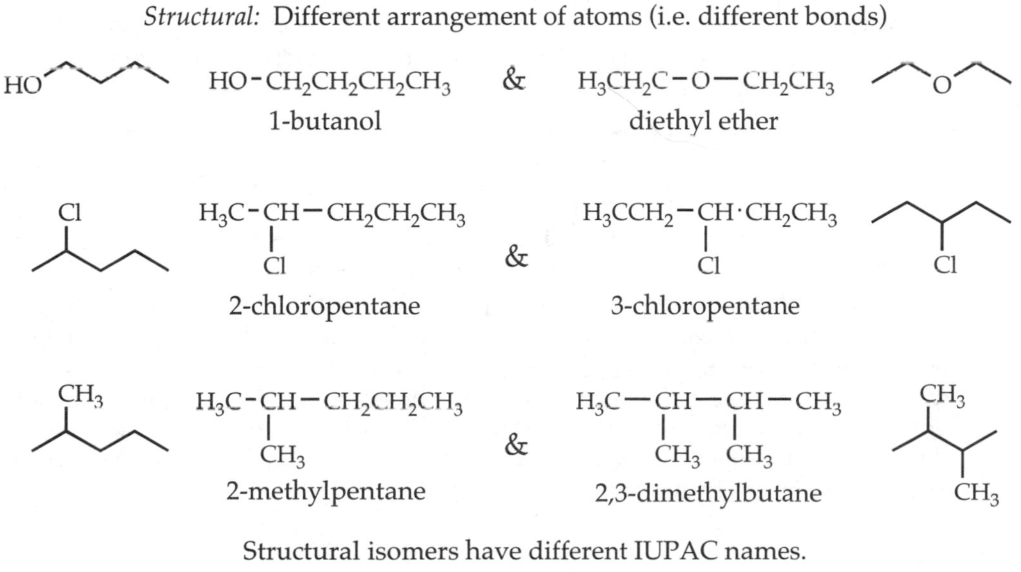

Structural: Different arrangement of atoms (i.e. different bonds)

HO–$CH_2CH_2CH_2CH_3$ & H_3CH_2C–O–CH_2CH_3
1-butanol   diethyl ether

H_3C–CH–$CH_2CH_2CH_3$ & H_3CCH_2–CH·CH_2CH_3
          | |
          Cl   Cl
2-chloropentane   3-chloropentane

H_3C–CH–$CH_2CH_2CH_3$ & H_3C–CH–CH–CH_3
          | | |
         CH_3 CH_3 CH_3
2-methylpentane   2,3-dimethylbutane

Structural isomers have different IUPAC names.

Figure 2-2

Example 2.2
How many possible constitutional isomers exist for a molecule with the molecular formula C_4H_{10}?

A. 1
B. 2
C. 3
D. 4

Solution
The maximum number of hydrogen atoms possible on a four-carbon alkane is ten, so there are no units of unsaturation in C_4H_{10}. This means that there are no π-bonds or rings in the molecule. To solve this question, chains of varying carbon connectivity (skeletons) must be considered. There is always one longest chain structure (C—C—C—C). There is also the possibility of a three-carbon chain with a methyl group off of the second carbon (if the methyl were on the first carbon, it is still butane). This means that there are two constitutional isomers for C_4H_{10}, butane and 2-methylpropane. Pick choice **B** for the smile that a correct answer brings.

Example 2.3
Which of the following pairs of molecules is NOT a set of constitutional isomers?

A. 2-Methylpentane and 3-methylpentane
B. Cyclobutanol and tetrahydrofuran
C. 1-Chlorobutane and 2-chlorobutane
D. 4-Ethylchlorocyclohexane and 3-methylchlorocyclopentane

Solution
In choice A, both compounds have the formula C_6H_{14} and different IUPAC names, so they are constitutional isomers. In choice B, both compounds have the formula C_4H_8O and different IUPAC names, so they are constitutional isomers. In choice C, both compounds have the formula C_4H_9Cl and different IUPAC names, so they are constitutional isomers. In choice D, the first compound has the formula $C_8H_{15}Cl$, while the second compound has the formula $C_6H_{11}Cl$, so they are not even isomers, let alone constitutional isomers. This makes choice **D** the correct answer.

For a given formula, there are a finite number of possible structural isomers. The number of possible structural isomers depends on the molecular formula. Saturated aliphatic compounds (linear alkanes) are the simplest case. For each extra carbon, the number of structural isomers increases. For instance, C_3H_8 has only one structural isomer, while C_6H_{14} has five different structural isomers. It is important to realize that both formulae (C_3H_8 and C_6H_{14}) are for structures that are fully saturated (have no units of unsaturation). There is no easy formula for determining the number of structural isomers possible for a given formula, but there is a systematic way to determine the number. Figure 2-3 shows all of the structural isomers for C_3H_8, C_4H_{10}, C_5H_{12}, and C_6H_{14}, and lists them in terms of chain length and substituent location.

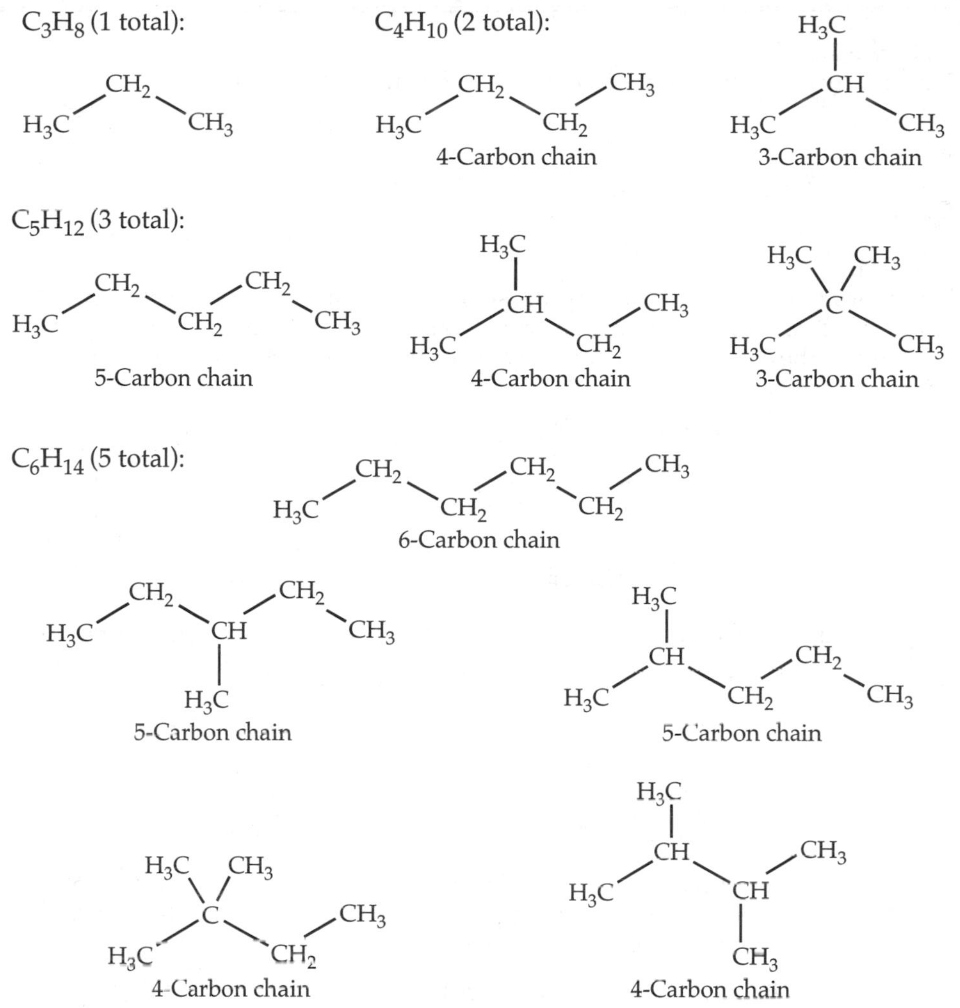

C₃H₈ (1 total):

C₄H₁₀ (2 total):

4-Carbon chain

3-Carbon chain

C₅H₁₂ (3 total):

5-Carbon chain

4-Carbon chain

3-Carbon chain

C₆H₁₄ (5 total):

6-Carbon chain

5-Carbon chain

5-Carbon chain

4-Carbon chain

4-Carbon chain

Figure 2-3

This procedure of determining the number of structural isomers is systematic. First, start with the longest continuous chain of carbons (equal to the total number of carbons in the formula). In the case of C₆H₁₄, the longest possible chain is six carbons. After drawing the longest chain, draw a carbon chain of one less carbon (five carbons) and systematically deduce all of the possible isomers by moving the methyl group across the chain one carbon at a time. In the case of C₆H₁₄, the next smallest chain after six carbons is five carbons and the extra (sixth) carbon is attached to one of the interior carbons in the chain. If the extra carbon were attached to a terminal carbon, then the longest chain would be six carbons in length, not five. In the case of C₆H₁₄, it is not possible to have 1-methylpentane, because that is really n-hexane. A guideline to follow as you deduce isomers is that structural isomers must have different IUPAC names. If you are ever in doubt about whether or not two compounds are structural isomers of one another, name them using IUPAC conventions. To complete the process of determining the isomers, systematically count isomers for each possible chain length, reducing the length by one carbon each time. When you are finished with each possible chain length, sum all of the structures and that's your answer. For alkanes with functional groups attached, the procedure is the same except once all of the skeletal structures are determined; there is an additional step of systematically placing the functional group at all unique carbons. Example 2.4 demonstrates this procedure.

Example 2.4
How many structural isomers are possible for the formula C_4H_9Cl?

A. 3
B. 4
C. 5
D. 6

Solution
For a problem of this type, the possibilities for the carbon skeleton must be determined first. The four carbons can either be aligned four in a row or three in a row with the fourth carbon coming off of the second carbon of the three-carbon chain.

STEP 1: 2 possible carbon skeletons

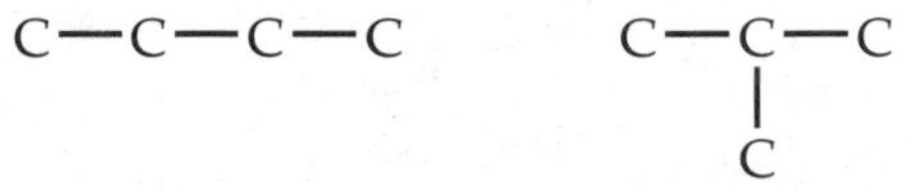

$$C-C-C-C \qquad \begin{array}{c} C-C-C \\ | \\ C \end{array}$$

4-Carbon chain   3-Carbon chain

The second step is to determine how many unique carbons each chain contains.

STEP 2: Each skeleton has two unique carbons

2 Unique carbons   2 Unique carbons

The last step requires placing a chlorine atom on each unique carbon one structure at a time and then verifying each structure as distinct by checking to see if each one has a unique IUPAC name.

STEP 3: 4 structural isomers total

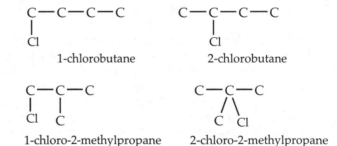

1-chlorobutane   2-chlorobutane

1-chloro-2-methylpropane   2-chloro-2-methylpropane

The best choice is answer **B**, because there are four possible structural isomers. This systematic procedure works every time. It is assumed that isomer problems much beyond this example in terms of difficulty will be avoided on the MCAT because of time constraints. The skills employed when deducing the number of structural isomers can also be used when deducing structure from spectral data, such as IR and ^1H NMR information.

Example 2.5

How many possible constitutional isomers have the molecular formula C_4H_8?

A. 4
B. 5
C. 6
D. 7

Solution

These questions are time-consuming, but unfortunately, there is not a convenient way around it. To start, you must determine the units of unsaturation (also known as degrees of unsaturation).

$$\text{Degrees of Unsaturation} = \frac{2(4)+2-(8)}{2} = \frac{8+2-8}{2} = \frac{10-8}{2} = \frac{2}{2} = 1$$

With one unit of unsaturation, the structure must contain either a π-bond or a ring. To get the correct answer, you must systematically consider each linear connectivity and each cyclic connectivity. Be sure not to count stereoisomers (including geometrical isomers). The alkenes are listed first, followed by the cyclic structures.

Possible alkene structures:

4-carbon chain (2 total)   3-carbon chain (1 total)

$H_2C{=}CHCH_2CH_3$ $H_3CHC{=}CHCH_3$

1-Butene   2-Butene

Note that there are two possible geometrical isomers for 2-butene.

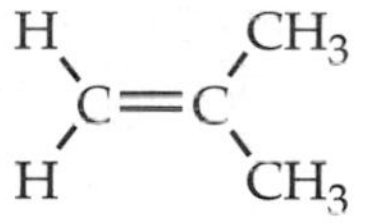

Methylpropene

Possible cyclic alkane structures:

4-carbon ring (1 total)   3-carbon ring (1 total)

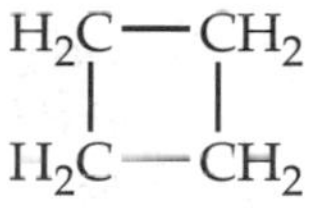

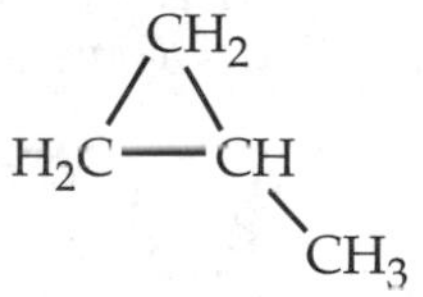

Cyclobutane   Methylcyclopropane

Because there are five total constitutional isomers in all, each with a unique IUPAC name, the best answer is choice **B**.

Stereoisomers

Stereoisomers are molecules of the same formula that have the same bonds (connectivity), but a different spatial arrangement of the atoms. Included in stereoisomers are configurational isomers (molecules that cannot be converted into one another through rotation about a σ-bond) and conformational isomers (caused by rotation and ring-flipping). Configurational isomers can be broken down further into either *geometrical isomers* (associated with nonrotating structures, such as rings and alkenes) and *optical isomers* (isomers that rotate plane-polarized light differently). Not all configurational isomers rotate plane-polarized light, as you have seen with meso compounds, but optical isomers differ in the magnitude and possible direction in which they rotate incident plane-polarized light. Stereoisomers of all types are not superimposable (they cannot be superposed onto one another.) Figure 2-4 shows the types of stereoisomers. Rotamers are conformational isomers that vary in orientation in space because of rotation about a sigma bond.

Stereoisomers: Same bonds, but a different spatial arrangement of the atoms

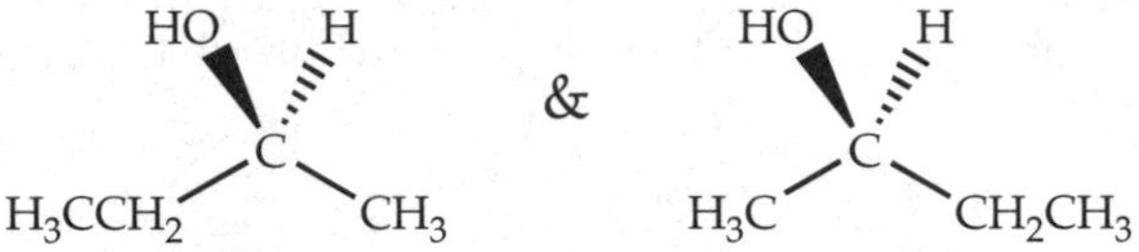

(S)-2-butanol   (R)-2-butanol

Configurational isomers
(Optical isomers)

(cis)-4-methylcyclohexanol   (trans)-4-methylcyclohexanol

Configurational isomers
(Geometrical isomers)

Note: Configurational isomers have different prefixes in their IUPAC names

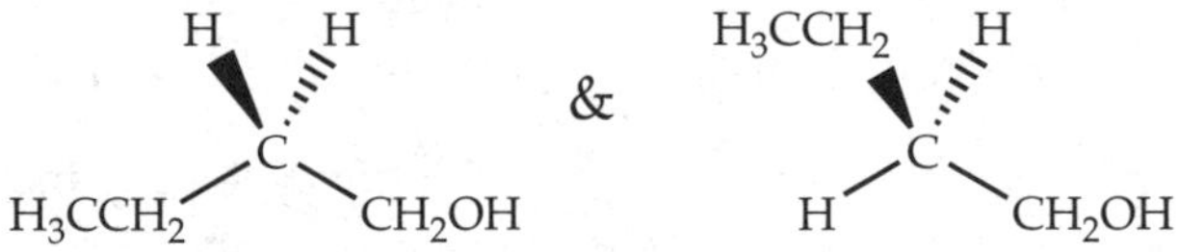

1-butanol   1-butanol

Conformational isomers
(Rotamers)

Figure 2-4

Configurational Isomers

Configurational isomers are a subgroup of stereoisomers that have the same bonds, but a different arrangement of their atoms in space, no matter how the structures are twisted and rotated. Common examples with which you are familiar include optical isomers and geometrical isomers.

Optical Isomers

Optical isomers are molecules of the same formula and the exact same bonds (connectivity), but a different spatial arrangement of the atoms due to asymmetry within the structure. An optical isomer cannot be rotated or manipulated to assume the structure of another isomer. They cannot be converted into another optical isomer without breaking a bond. Optical isomers rotate plane-polarized light differently from one another. Figure 2-5 shows an example of a pair of optical isomers.

Optical Isomers: Identical bonds with a different spatial arrangement about an asymmetric carbon that rotate plane-polarized light differently.

(R)-2-chloropentane   (S)-2-chloropentane

Optical Isomers

Figure 2-5

Optical isomers are a class of configurational isomers. Configurational isomers can also be classified as enantiomers and diastereomers, so some optical isomers can also be referred to as enantiomers or diastereomers.

Example 2.6

How can the relationship between the following two molecular structures BEST be described?

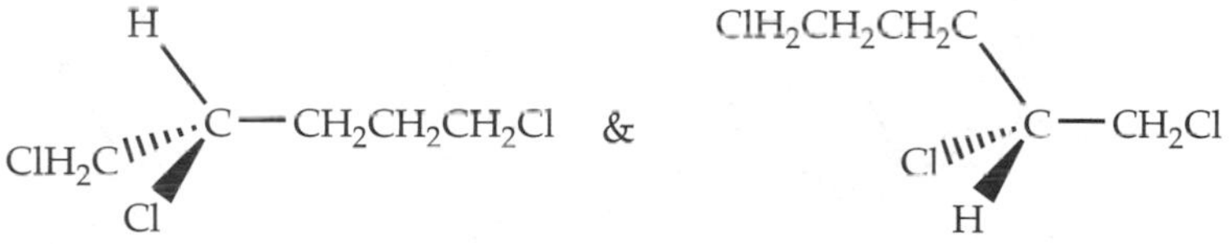

A. Identical molecules
B. Optical isomers
C. Skeletal isomers
D. Structural isomers

Solution

We can start by naming each of the structures. Both have three chlorine atoms on a five-carbon chain. The chlorine atoms are on carbons 1, 2, and 5, so each molecule has the IUPAC name 1,2,5-trichloropentane. To be skeletal or structural isomers requires that the two compounds have different IUPAC names, so choices C and D are eliminated. No matter how you rotate the first structure, it cannot be superposed onto the second structure. This implies that they are not identical molecules, so choice A is eliminated. The left structure has S-stereochemistry at the second carbon, while the right structure has R-stereochemistry at the second carbon. This confirms that the two structures are optical isomers, so the best answer is choice **B**.

Geometrical Isomers

Geometrical isomers, simply put, are the cis and trans forms of a rigid compound (where rigid implies that the molecule is not free to rotate or contort between conformations). They are sometimes referred to as *cis/trans* isomers, which applies to both rings and alkenes. They are nonsuperimposable, because they are locked into an orientation by the cyclic structure or π-bond. If two substituents on a cyclic compound are on the same side of the plane or if two substituents on alkene are on the same side of the carbon-carbon π-bond, then they are said to be *cis* to one another. If two substituents on a cyclic compound are on opposite sides of the plane or if two substituents on alkene are on opposite sides of the carbon-carbon π-bond, then they are said to be *trans* to one another. IUPAC convention does not use cis or trans in the naming of alkenes; instead, the letters E and Z are employed. In general nomenclature, the terms cis and trans are common. For *geometrical isomers*, which have different spatial arrangement about a π-bond, the prefix of E is given for trans orientation of the two highest priority groups, while Z is given for cis orientation of the two highest priority groups. Figure 2-6 shows several examples of pairs of geometrical isomers, both alkenes and cyclic structures.

Geometrical Isomers: Identical bonds with a different spatial arrangement (found with double bonds and rings).

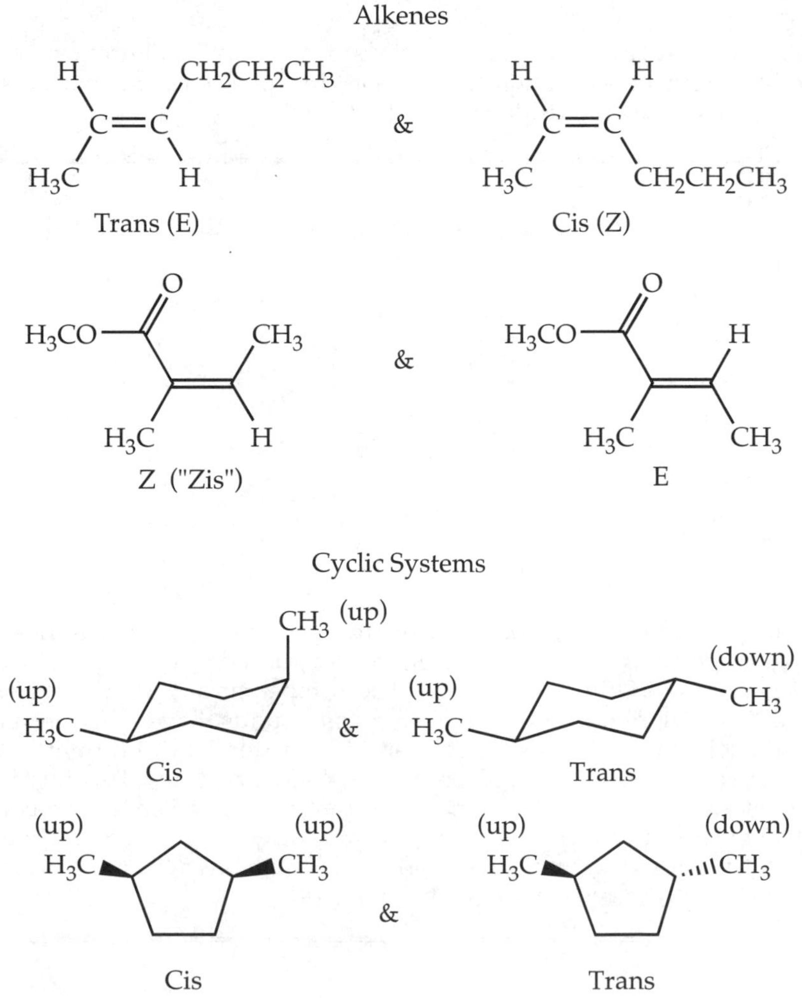

Alkenes

Cyclic Systems

Figure 2-6

The term E is derived from the German word *entgegen* meaning "across from" and refers to a compound where the two highest priority groups on each respective alkene carbon are trans to one another. The term Z is derived from the German word *zusammen* meaning "together" and refers to a compound where the two highest priority groups on each respective alkene carbon are cis to one another. Think of cis as "Zis", and you can always remember which is which.

Example 2.7
All of the following are true about geometrical isomers EXCEPT that:

A. the E designation for an alkene refers to the highest priority groups on each alkene carbon in trans orientation.
B. in both the E and Z isomers of an alkene, the atoms directly bonded to the alkene carbons are all coplanar.
C. molecules capable of forming geometrical isomers have greater entropy than linear alkanes of equal carbon chain length
D. geometrical isomers have relatively static structural features, such as polarity and solubility.

Solution
To determine the geometry of an alkene, first locate the two carbons that constitute the alkene. Determine the highest priority substituent on each of the two alkene carbons, using the Cahn-Ingold-Prelog rules for assigning priorities to substituents by sequentially looking at the atoms attached to the site of interest. If the two highest priority groups are across from one another with respect to the double bond, then the compound is trans and thus is assigned the letter E. If the two highest priority groups are both on the same side of the double bond, then the compound is cis and thus is assigned the letter Z. This makes choice A a true statement, so it is eliminated. Because the two p-orbitals of the π-bond are coplanar with an orientation perpendicular to the substituents on the alkene carbons, the four atoms bonded to the two carbons of the alkene must be coplanar. It is not possible to rotate around the double bond, because the p-orbitals would no longer be coplanar, breaking the π-bond. This makes choice B a true statement, which eliminates it. There are only two geometrical isomers possible for an alkene. Because it is not possible to rotate about a double bond (the π-bond would have to be broken), it is not possible to convert between the cis and trans geometrical isomers without adding a great deal of energy. The consequence is that alkenes are rigid and thus have less entropy than alkanes of a comparable carbon chain length. This makes choice C a false statement, and thus the best answer. The structures of both an alkene and cyclic molecule are relatively static and do not change drastically. The ring may flip-flop a little, but rotation is observed only for the substituents on the ring, and not observed for the bonds in the ring. Because the structure is static, the molecular features are constant. This makes choice D a true statement, eliminating it.

We shall discuss stereoisomers only at this superficial level for the time being. In the stereochemistry and carbohydrate sections, stereoisomers will be discussed in greater detail.

Conformational Isomers

Conformational isomers, or *conformers*, are molecules with identical connectivity (bonds) that are nonsuperimposable because of rotation about a bond or contortion (often referred to as *ring-flipping*) of the molecular structure. The most stable conformation of the compound is predictable based on hybridization, steric repulsion, and VSEPR (Valence Shell Electron Pair Repulsion) theory. Figure 2-7 shows two pairs of conformational isomers.

> *Conformational Isomers:* Identical bonds with different spatial orientations caused by either rotation about sigma bonds or contortion of ring structures.

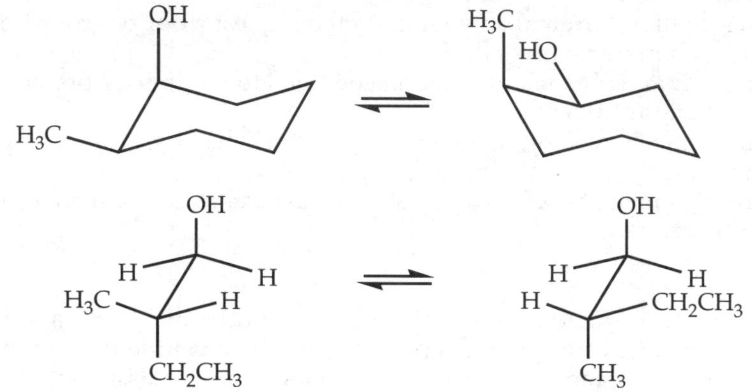

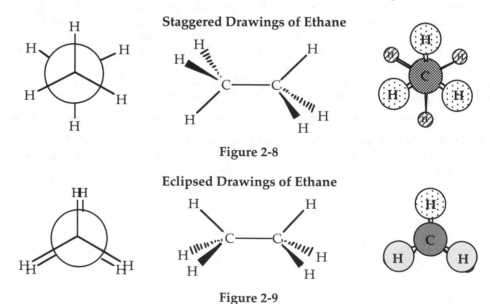

Figure 2-7

Rotation About Sigma Bonds

One way to achieve a different conformation is to rotate about a sigma bond in the interior of the molecule. Conformational isomers are in dynamic equilibrium at room temperature, because rotation about sigma bonds is possible with the energy available. Because molecules are constantly rotating, the structure does not remain in just one of the conformations, but rather assumes all confirmations at one time or another. It assumes the most stable conformation most frequently. The two extreme overall structures are known as *staggered* (where substituents on the first atom do not block the substituents on the back atom of the sigma bond in question) and *eclipsed* (where substituents on the first atom do block the substituents on the back atom of the sigma bond in question). Figure 2-8 shows the staggered conformer of ethane while Figure 2-9 shows its eclipsed structure.

Staggered Drawings of Ethane

Figure 2-8

Eclipsed Drawings of Ethane

Figure 2-9

Within staggered conformation, the terms *gauche* and *anti* describe the relative position of substituents on adjacent atoms. These terms refer to the position of a substituent on one atom relative to the position of a substituent on an adjacent atom. Butane, having a methyl group on both carbon-2 and carbon-3, is ideal for demonstrating gauche and anti orientations. A 120° rotation about the C_2—C_3 bond of butane can convert the staggered and anti conformation into the staggered and gauche conformation, shown in Figures 2-10 and 2-11 respectively.

Staggered Conformation of Butane with CH_3 groups Gauche

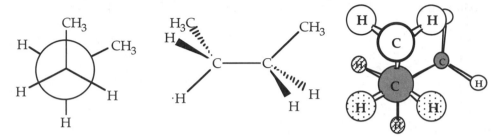

Figure 2-10

Staggered Conformation of Butane with CH_3 groups Anti

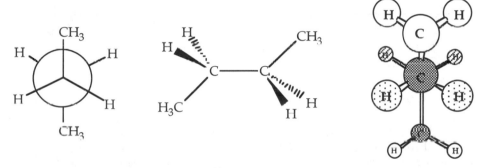

Figure 2-11

In gauche, the two groups of interest (often the largest groups) have a dihedral angle of 60°. Three different perspectives of the staggered conformation of butane, with carbons 1 and 4 gauche to one another, are shown in Figure 2-10. In anti, the two groups of interest have a dihedral angle of 180°. This is the most stable structure! Three different perspectives of the staggered conformation of butane, with carbons 1 and 4 anti to one another, are shown in Figure 2-11.

Of the conformers of butane, Eclipsed and syn (Figure 2-11) is the least stable, due to steric hindrance between the two methyl substituents (the largest groups). Hydrogens on carbon 1 and carbon 4 collide with one another. Staggered and anti is the most stable, because repulsion is minimized. To maximize stability, the largest groups on each carbon (CH_3, in this case) need to be as far apart from one another as possible (in *anti* orientation), if they repel. Figure 2-12 shows a side-view of steric repulsion for the fully eclipsed butane molecule.

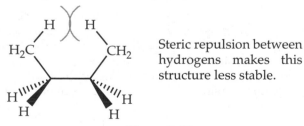

Steric repulsion between hydrogens makes this structure less stable.

Figure 2-12

Because atoms within a molecule are in constant rotational motion, a structure does not exist in one fixed conformation. Figure 2-13 shows the energy diagram that corresponds to a complete 360° rotation about the C_2-C_3 carbon-carbon bond of butane, starting and finishing with the most stable conformation, the anti conformation. The energy diagram starts with the lowest energy structure at 0° (which is the conformation with carbons 1 and 4 anti to one another) and rotates 360° about the C_2-C_3 bond to return to the same orientation. Note that the highest energy structure is exactly 180° apart from the lowest energy structure, and that a 60° dihedral rotation takes you from an apex (a localized energy maximum) to a nadir (a localized energy minimum) on the energy diagram.

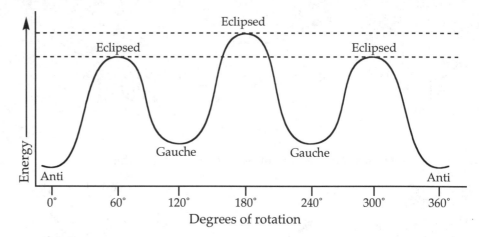

Figure 2-13

The energy diagram for butane is symmetrical, because butane is a symmetrical molecule. When the compound is chiral (contains stereogenic centers), the energy diagram is not symmetric. The energy axis of the diagram is not quantified in Figure 2-13, so it demonstrates only a conceptual relationship. If any calculations are required on the MCAT, values will be provided for the energy of the eclipsed and staggered conformations, and for the gauche and anti interactions of various substituents. Do not memorize specific data, but instead focus on drawing conclusions and seeing trends when you are given data.

Example 2.8
How does the energy diagram for the complete rotation about a central bond of an asymmetric (chiral) compound compare to the energy diagram for its complete rotation about the C_2—C_3 bond of butane?

A. The energy diagram is symmetric like butane, but with higher energy values.
B. The energy diagram is symmetric like butane, but with lower energy values.
C. The energy diagram is asymmetric like butane, but with greater differences in energy values.
D. The energy diagram is asymmetric, with different energy values than butane.

Solution
Because the structure is asymmetric, the energy diagram depicting the rotation associated with the molecule must also be asymmetric, eliminating choices A and B. The energy diagram for the complete rotation about the C_2—C_3 bond of butane is symmetric, so choice C is eliminated. Choice **D** must be the best answer. The three staggered conformations are of unequal energy. Let's consider the staggered conformational isomers of R-2,3-dimethylpentane:

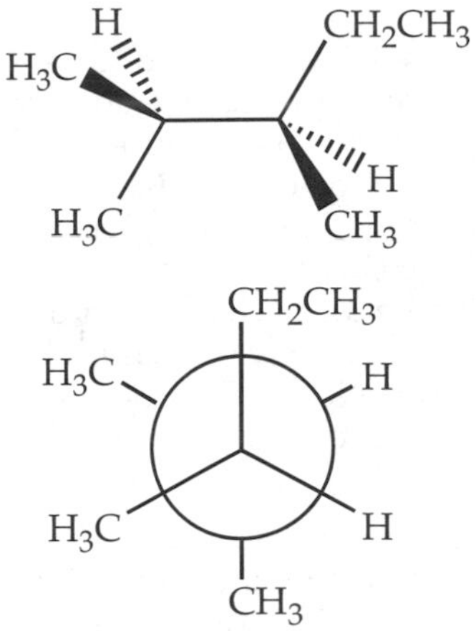

H₃C H CH₂CH₃ ... CH₃ H₃C CH₃

H₃C H CH₂CH₃ ... CH₃ H₃C CH₃

H₃C H₃C CH₂CH₃ ... CH₃ H CH₃

CH₂CH₃
H₃C — H
H₃C — H
CH₃

2 methyl/methyl and 1 ethyl/methyl interactions

CH₂CH₃
H — CH₃
H₃C — H
CH₃

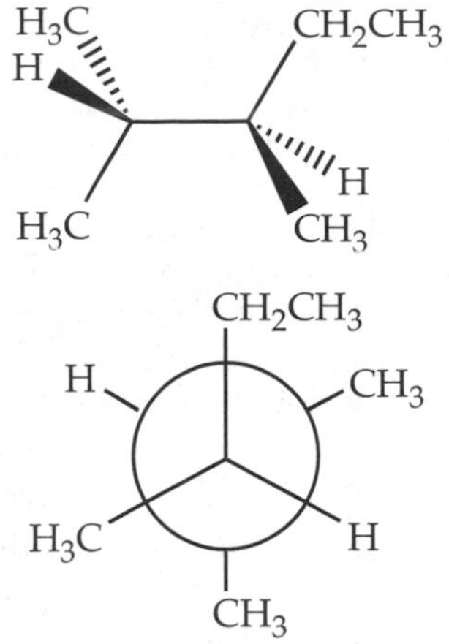

1 methyl/methyl and 1 ethyl/methyl interactions
Lowest Energy Conformation

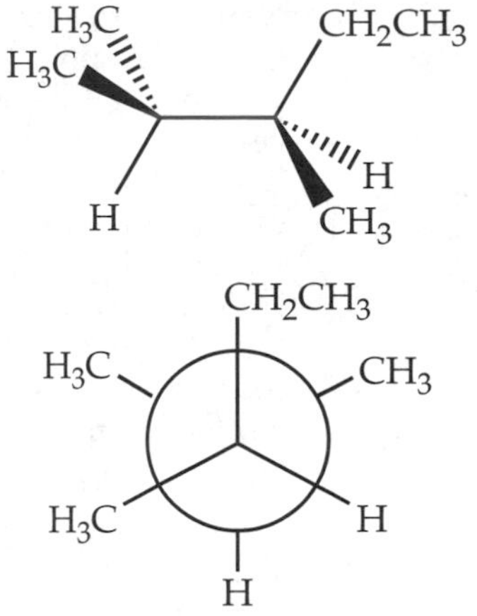

CH₂CH₃
H₃C — CH₃
H₃C — H
H

1 methyl/methyl and 2 ethyl/methyl interactions

Example 2.9

How can it be explained that the most stable orientation about the C_2-C_3 bond in 3-aminopropanoic acid has the NH_2 group and the COOH group gauche?

A. Gauche is the most stable, because it minimizes the steric hindrance between the amino group and the carboxylic acid group.
B. The gauche conformation is always stabler than the eclipsed conformation.
C. The carboxylic acid and amino groups form a hydrogen bond best from gauche orientation.
D. The carboxylic acid and amino groups form a hydrogen bond best from anti orientation.

Solution

Staggered conformation is inherently more stable than eclipsed, so questions like these come down to gauche versus anti. If the substituents attract one another, then the most stable conformation has the two attracting groups gauche with respect to one another. The best choice is **C**, because gauche has the amino and hydroxyl groups close enough to form a hydrogen bond. A hydrogen-bond cannot form when the two groups are anti to one another.

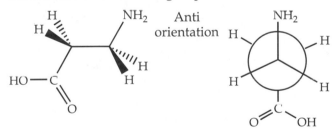

Anti orientation

Hydrogen-bonding is not possible when the two groups are 180° apart.

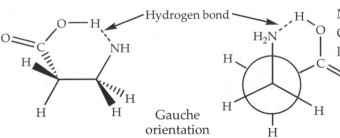

Hydrogen bond

Gauche orientation

Note: N is a better lone pair donor than O and the COOH hydrogen carries a larger δ^+ than the NH_2 hydrogen.

Newman Projections

Understanding the nuances of conformational isomers requires good three-dimensional viewing skills, so you may wish to dig out your molecular models if you still have them. Be able to recognize structures from the stick figure view (with dashed and bold wedges), as well as from Newman projections. Newman projections are front views of a molecule. In drafting, three views are given to see the whole. It is no different in organic chemistry. The side view is a dashed-and-bold wedge representation, the front view is a Newman projection, and a top view is a Fischer projection. Figure 2-14 shows a pictorial explanation of the conversion from a dashed-and-bold wedge drawing to a Newman projection, while Figure 2-15 shows a pictorial explanation of the conversion from a Newman projection to a dashed-and-bold wedge drawing.

When viewed from the right, substituents pointing out of the plane in a dashed-and-bold wedge drawing are on the left side in a Newman projection. Substituents behind the plane in a dashed-and-bold wedge drawing are on the right side in a Newman projection. Substituents on the left side in the Newman projection end up pointing out of the plane in the dashed-and-bold wedge drawing. Substituents on the right side in the Newman projection end up behind the plane in the dashed-and-bold wedge drawing.

Conversion from dashed-and-bold wedge drawing to Newman projection:

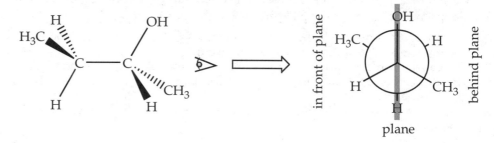

Figure 2-14

Conversion from Newman projection to dashed-and-bold wedge drawing:

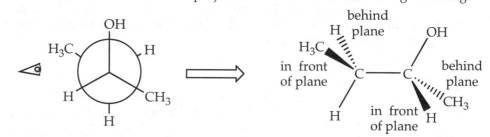

Figure 2-15

Cycloalkanes

Cyclic alkanes that contain only one ring have the chemical formula C_nH_{2n} and contain no π-bonds. The stability of a given cycloalkane is rooted in its ability to form bond angles of approximately 109.5°, the norm for sp^3-hybridized carbons. The farther from 109.5° the angle is, the greater the reactivity of the cycloalkane. For this reason, three- and four-membered rings are reactive, while five- and six-membered rings are stable. When treated with hydrogen gas (H_2), cyclopropane and cyclobutane readily form straight chain alkanes (propane and butane). Cyclopentane and cyclohexane do not undergo hydrogenation.

The reactivity of three- and four-membered rings is attributed to *ring strain*. Ring strain is defined as the energy difference between the linear and cyclic alkanes of equal carbon length. Because the bond angle in cyclopropane is 60°, vastly different than 109.5° associated with a normal sp^3-hybridized carbon, there is a great deal of ring strain. To relieve this angle problem, cyclopropane forms what are referred to as *bent bonds* (sigma bonds in which the electron density does not lie between the two nuclei). Because the electron density is not between the two nuclei, the bond is much weaker and thus easier to break. Figure 2-16 shows the orbital and bonding pictures for various cyclic alkanes.

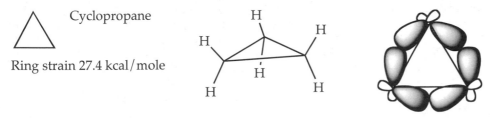

Cyclopropane

Ring strain 27.4 kcal/mole

The carbon-carbon bonds are bent (not collinear), making them weaker than standard carbon-carbon single bonds.

Cyclobutane

Ring strain 26.2 kcal/mole

Cyclopentane

Ring strain 6.8 kcal/mole

Cyclohexane

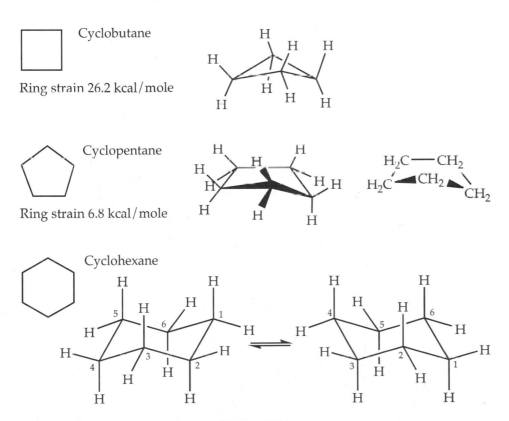

Figure 2-16

Because of their stability, most cyclic organic and bio-organic molecules are either five-membered or six-membered rings, with more examples being six-membered rings because they are slightly more stable than five-membered rings. Given their frequent presence in biological molecules, five-membered and six-membered rings have a high probability of appearing on the MCAT.

Cyclopentane

Cyclopentane does not require much distortion of its bonds and shape to accommodate the 109.5° angle for the sp^3-hybrid. A perfect pentagon has angles of 108°, so there is only a small discrepancy from 109.5°. This angle difference does not account for the small ring strain of 6.8 kcals per mole. To achieve the correct angle and alleviate this torsional strain, cyclopentane forms what is referred to as an *envelope shape*, where one of the carbons is not coplanar with the other four. The major problem with cyclopentane is not the ring bond angles, but the substituents on the ring that are in an eclipsed conformation as a result of the near-planar ring structure. This eclipsing of hydrogen atoms causes further contortion of the structure, which accounts for the ring strain energy. Still, cyclopentane structures are relatively stable. Their stability makes them common in such biological structures as ribose, deoxyribose and the purine ring of the DNA bases adenine and guanine. Figure 2-17 shows a few other common five-membered rings frequently encountered in the biological sciences.

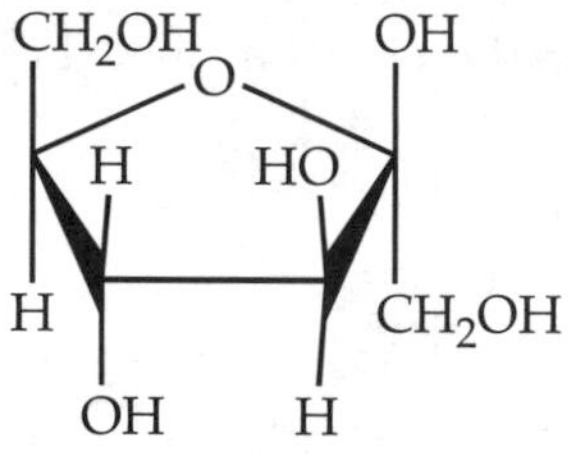

ß-D-Fructofuranose

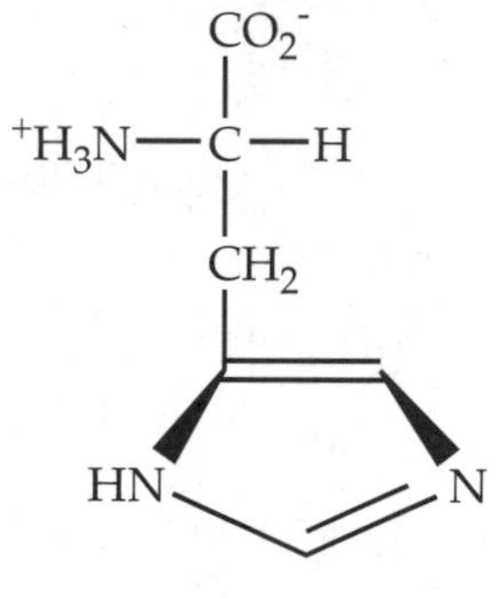

L-Histidine

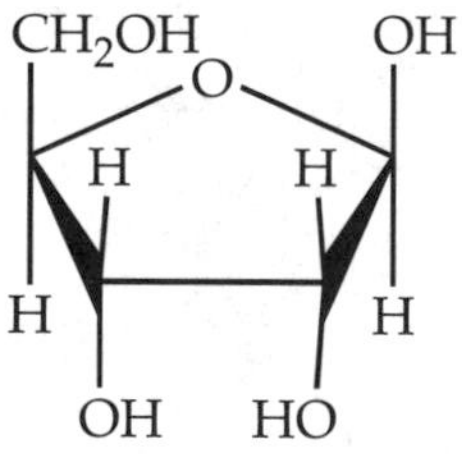

ß-D-Ribofuranose

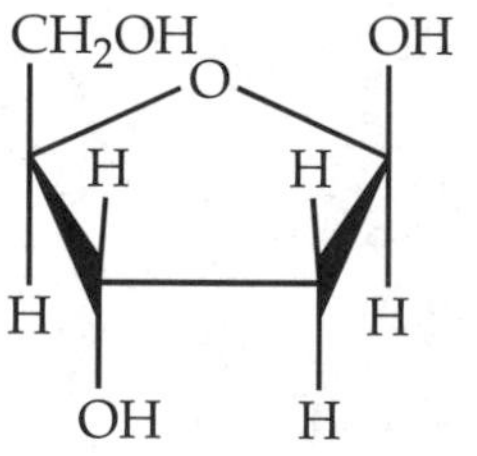

2-Deoxy-ß-D-ribofuranose

Figure 2-17

Cyclohexane
Cyclohexane has the most stable ring structure of all of the cycloalkanes. This is evident in biological molecules, which have multiple rings of six atoms. The most stable form of cyclohexane is the *chair* conformation. There are two different chair conformations for cyclohexane. The two conformational isomers can interconvert through a process referred to as *ring-flipping*. In interconverting, the structure passes through the *boat* conformation. Because the two chair conformations are equally stable, $\Delta G_{rx} = 0$. The interconversion between the two chair conformations of cyclohexane requires 10.8 kcals/mole in activation energy. The chair conformation offers two substituent positions: *equatorial* (named for its orientation around the equatorial plane of the ring) and *axial* (named for its vertical alignment like an axis). Equatorial is more stable than axial, so the most stable conformation of a cyclohexane compound has the largest substituents in the equatorial positions. Figure 2-18 shows chair conformations of cyclohexane with detailed positions.

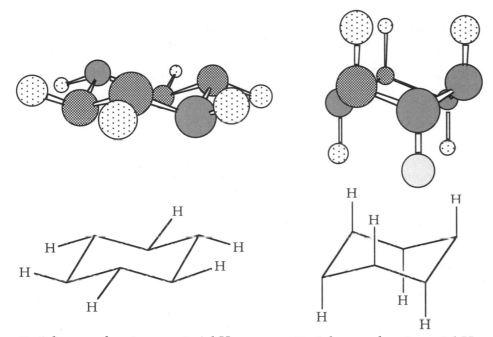

Cyclohexane showing equatorial Hs   Cyclohexane showing axial Hs

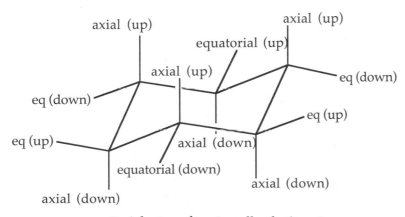

Cyclohexane showing all substituents

Figure 2-18

Monosubstituted Cyclohexane
The ring-flip process is the same when there is a substituent on the cyclohexane ring as it is for cyclohexane, but the energetics are different. When a substituent is present, the activation energy for interconversion is greater, and the two chair conformations differ in stability. Because the two chair conformations are no longer of equal energy, the two twist forms (intermediates in the ring-flipping process) are also no longer of equal energy. The most stable chair conformation is the structure with the least steric repulsion. Substituents with axial orientation on the same side of the ring are close enough to repel (known as *1,3-diaxial interactions*), so axial orientation is less favorable than equatorial orientation. This is indicated in Figure 2-19, where the two chair conformations of both methylcyclohexane and cyclohexanol are shown. The two chair conformations of methylcyclohexane differ in stability by 1.69 kcals/mole. Because a hydroxyl group is smaller than a methyl group, the difference in energy for the two chair conformations of cyclohexanol is only 1.04 kcals/mole.

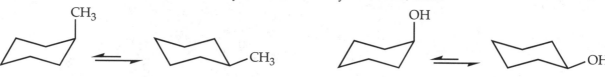

Methylcyclohexane
Equatorial > Axial by 1.69 kcals/mole

Cyclohexanol
Equatorial > Axial by 1.04 kcals/mole

Figure 2-19

Disubstituted Cyclohexane
Disubstituted cyclohexane exhibits different dynamics than monosubstituted cyclohexane. The greatest energy difference is observed when comparing 1,3-diaxial to 1,3-diequatorial, because the steric repulsion of 1,3-diaxial substituents is the strongest repulsion encountered in cyclohexane. When comparing 1,2-diaxial to 1,2-diequatorial, there are no diaxial interactions between the bulkiest substituents, because the two bulky substituents are trans to one another. This makes the energy difference between chair conformations less than what is observed with the 1,3-cyclohexane. The energy difference between the 1,2-diaxial and 1,2-diequatorial orientations is also less than the energy difference between 1,4-diaxial and 1,4-diequatorial (which is another compound where the two bulkiest substituents are trans to one another), because the 1,2-diequatorialcyclohexane species has gauche interactions between the bulkiest substituents. Figure 2-20 shows the energetics of the conformational isomers of all three possible structural isomers of dimethylcyclohexane.

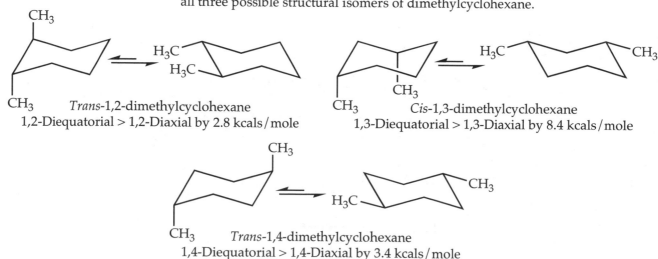

Trans-1,2-dimethylcyclohexane
1,2-Diequatorial > 1,2-Diaxial by 2.8 kcals/mole

Cis-1,3-dimethylcyclohexane
1,3-Diequatorial > 1,3-Diaxial by 8.4 kcals/mole

Trans-1,4-dimethylcyclohexane
1,4-Diequatorial > 1,4-Diaxial by 3.4 kcals/mole

Figure 2-20

It is essential that you be able to translate from nomenclature to the most stable conformation. For instance, *trans*-3-methylethylcyclohexane is a 1,3-*trans* compound. A compound with 1,3-*trans* orientation has both an axial and an equatorial substituent. The ethyl group is larger than the methyl group, so the ethyl group occupies the equatorial orientation in the most stable conformation of *trans*-3-methylethylcyclohexane. This is shown in Figure 2-21.

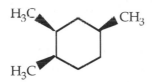

Figure 2-21

You should take note that when you convert from one chair conformer to the other, the axial substituents become equatorial (as seen with the ethyl group), and the equatorial substituents become axial (as seen with the methyl group). The most stable conformation has the least steric repulsion.

Example 2.10
The most stable conformation of *cis*-1,2,4-trimethylcyclohexane has which of the following orientations for the three methyl groups?

A. The chair conformation with 3 equatorial methyls and 0 axial methyls
B. The chair conformation with 2 equatorial methyls and 1 axial methyl
C. The chair conformation with 1 equatorial methyl and 2 axial methyls
D. The chair conformation with 0 equatorial methyls and 3 axial methyls

Solution
The most stable conformation maximized the equatorial methyls. 1,2-*cis* has one axial substituent and one equatorial substituent, so there must be at least one axial substituent. Two equatorials is the maximum. The two chair conformations of *cis*-1,2,4-trimethylcyclohexane show that choice **B** is the best answer.

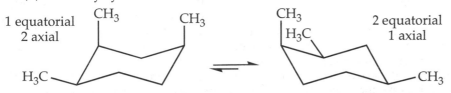

This covers the topics associated with isomerism. You have many passages to solidify these concepts. From the beginning, you want to emphasize the logic behind your answers. The MCAT may not have passages that are verbatim duplicates of what you see in here, but if you answer these questions using logic and fundamental concepts, then you will get acclimated to the MCAT way of thinking. Passages present information that you must incorporate into your background knowledge, and then using all the information you have, you must answer a series of questions. Right now, passage-based questions may seem unfamiliar, but hopefully you will take a liking to the style. Multiple-choice tests require that you find the best, most reasonable answer. You must find the best answer, as fast as you can.

Structural Insights

Structural Symmetry

When deducing the molecular structure for an organic molecule, it helps to know something about the symmetry of the compound and its units of unsaturation. Symmetry can be broken into plane symmetry and point symmetry. In plane symmetry, the compound has two halves that are evenly displaced about an imaginary mirror in the middle of the molecule. In a structure with point symmetry, there is an inversion point at the center of the molecule such that if two lines are drawn in opposite directions along the same axis, then both line segments intercept identical atoms at the same distance from the inversion point. This may not seem clear in words, but looking at a structure helps illustrate the concept. Figure 2-22 shows one compound with mirror plane symmetry and another with inversion symmetry. Molecules with inversion points are nonpolar, because all of the individual bond dipole vectors cancel each other out.

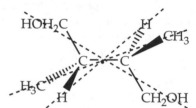

Molecule with mirror symmetry   Molecule with an inversion point

Figure 2-22

Symmetry within a molecule affects its NMR and IR spectra. As symmetry increases, the number of signals in a spectroscopic study decreases. Coupling symmetry information with units of unsaturation helps to deduce the structural features and connectivity of a molecule.

Units of Unsaturation (Index of Hydrogen Deficiency)

Units of unsaturation, sometimes called the degrees of unsaturation, are calculated from the molecular formula. The units of unsaturation give us information about the number of rings and/or π-bonds present within a molecule. There is some minimum number of bonds needed to hold the atoms in a molecule together, and any additional bonds beyond the minimum are the units of unsaturation. To hold two atoms together, it takes one bond ($Atom_1$—$Atom_2$). To hold three atoms together, it takes two bonds ($Atom_1$—$Atom_2$—$Atom_3$). The minimum number of bonds required to hold a molecule together is always one less than the number of atoms. The minimum number of bonding electrons is two times the minimum number of bonds. Any electrons beyond the bare minimum needed to hold the molecule together can be used to form additional bonds. For every extra pair of electrons, there is a unit of unsaturation. To determine the units of unsaturation, the strategy is to determine the number of excess bonding electrons. There are a few different methods for doing this.

1) C_3H_8 contains eleven atoms, which requires at minimum ten bonds (and thus twenty bonding electrons). There are three carbons with four bonding electrons each. There are eight hydrogens with one bonding electron each. This means that propane (C_3H_8) has exactly the twenty bonding electrons needed. There are no extra bonding electrons, so propane has a linear structure with no π-bonds. This is to say that propane has no units of unsaturation.

2) The units of unsaturation for hydrocarbons and carbohydrates can be derived from the formula for aliphatic alkanes, C_nH_{2n+2}. "Aliphatic" refers to a structure that has no rings or π-bonds. An aliphatic alkane has the bare minimum number of bonds, so there are no units of unsaturation. For every unit of unsaturation, there are two fewer hydrogen atoms than the maximum. Thus, the units of unsaturation can be obtained by comparing the actual formula to the fully saturated formula. For instance, C_5H_8 has four hydrogens less than the fully saturated formula for five carbons, C_5H_{12}. Because it has four fewer hydrogens, it has two units of unsaturation.

3) The units of unsaturation depend on the surplus of bonding electrons. To keep any chain propagated, every member of it must make two connections. In a molecule, each atom must make two bonds to keep it intact. This means that every atom needs a minimum of two bonding electrons. Using this perspective, we can determine the number of excess electrons per atom. Hydrogen makes just one bond, so you subtract one for each hydrogen in the molecule. Oxygen atoms are ignored, because they make the minimum two bonds that are needed. Carbons are multiplied by two, because carbons make four bonds, two beyond the minimum to propagate the chain. There are two ends to every chain, so two is added to the total. The units of unsaturation refer to bonds, rather than bonding electrons, so the sum of excess electrons must be divided by two. This is summarized in Equation 2.1.

$$\text{Units of unsaturation} - \frac{2(\#C) + 2 - (\#H)}{2} \qquad (2.1)$$

Method 3 works with other atoms, too. Nitrogen makes three bonds, which is one more than the minimum needed, so you add 1 per nitrogen atom. Halogens make one bond, which is one less than the minimum, so you subtract 1 per halide. Equation 2.2 includes nitrogen and halogens.

$$\text{Units of unsaturation} = \frac{2(\#C) + (\#N) - (\#H) - (\#X) + 2}{2} \qquad (2.2)$$

Example 2.11
How many units of unsaturation are present in a compound with the molecular formula $C_7H_9N_3O_2Cl_2$?

A. 1
B. 2
C. 3
D. 4

Solution
This question is solved by applying Equation 2.2.

$$\frac{2(7) + (3) - (9) - (2) + 2}{2} = \frac{14 + 3 - 9 - 2 + 2}{2} = \frac{17 - 9}{2} = \frac{8}{2} = 4 \text{ Units of unsaturation}$$

Because there are four units of unsaturation, choice **D** is the best answer. With four units of unsaturation, the compound could contain three π-bonds and one ring, meaning it is potentially a benzene derivative. When there are four units of unsaturation, you should immediately consider the possibility that the compound contains an aromatic ring. While there are other combinations of four units of unsaturation, there is a high probability of having an aromatic ring.

Exclusive MCAT Preparation

Spectroscopy and Analysis

Spectroscopy

The MCAT topics include infrared absorption spectroscopy, ultraviolet-visible spectroscopy, [1]H (proton) nuclear magnetic resonance spectroscopy, and mass spectroscopy. While some of these topics may have caused anxiety in your past, there is less to stress over when they are presented in a multiple-choice setting. At just over one minute per problem, if you have to deduce a structure from spectroscopic information, then it will likely be easy or symmetric. For example, a proton NMR of ethanol is an easy example that has made the rounds before. Besides just having to determine the structure of an unknown, you may also have to assign signals and peaks to an existing compound. The spectra should be interpreted using the typical features you have learned. To date, the test has emphasized only a few features that have been stressed in course work. We shall start by reviewing the basic operations of the IR and its applications to structure elucidation. From there we shall consider ultraviolet/visible spectroscopy, proton NMR, and mass spectroscopy.

Infrared Spectroscopy

Every molecule produces a unique IR spectrum. Infrared spectroscopy starts by adding a monochromatic beam of IR photons to either a thin oil suspension (if the compound is a solid) or a neat solution (if the compound is a liquid) between salt plates. The molecule absorbs electromagnetic radiation that causes transitions between vibrational energy levels within it, so that the molecule vibrates more frequently as energy is absorbed or less frequently as energy is emitted. When a molecule soaks up the EM radiation, it vibrates at a higher energy. This change in stretching (vibrating) between atoms within the molecule causes a change in the dipole moment, which can then be monitored. An infrared spectrometer uses light of wavelength 2,500 nanometers to 17,000 nanometers (recorded as 4000 cm^{-1} to 600 cm^{-1} on the graph). What we record is the change in the intensity of the EM radiation from when it enters the molecule to when it exits the molecule. This is compared to a reference beam that traverses a path of identical length but does not pass through the compound itself. If the compound absorbs a given wavelength of light (corresponding to some transition), then we observe an absence of light exiting the sample tube. This is known as *absorption spectroscopy*. The graph records transmittance as a function of wave number (cm^{-1}), so absorbances are represented by drops in intensity.

The frequency at which light is absorbed is specific for each type of bond. As you may have learned in physics, the frequency of light is directly proportional to the masses of the two atoms in the bond and the bond strength. This is to say that the potential energy in a resonating system (such as a spring that obeys Hooke's law) is described by Equation 2.3

$$P.E. = \frac{1}{2} kx^2 \qquad\qquad (2.3)$$

The k-term is the spring constant, which we can say describes the bond strength. The x-term describes the distance from equilibrium that the bond has stretched. The absorbance can be thought of as increasing the potential energy of the bond, so the absorbance is proportional to the energy of the bond. As a result, the bond dissociation is directly proportional to the energy that is absorbed. This is not exactly true, but close enough to help approximate spectra. Because a wave number is measured in cm^{-1}, it is an inverse of the wavelength. The inverse of the wavelength is directly proportional to the energy of the photon. This means that the higher the wave number is, the greater its energy.

For instance, a C=O bond absorbs around 1700 cm $^{-1}$, while a C-O bond absorbs around 1300 cm $^{-1}$. This is because a C=O bond is stronger than a C-O bond. Carbonyl functional groups are common, so you should know the absorbance value for a C=O bond. An sp^3-C-to-H bond absorbs just below 3000 cm^{-1}, while an sp^2-C-to-H bond absorbs just above 3000 cm^{-1}, because an sp^2-C-to-H bond is stronger than an sp^3-C-to-H bond. This is because the sp^2-hybrid, having more s-character, is smaller than the sp^3-hybrid. The result is that an sp^2-C-to-H bond is shorter and thus stronger than an sp^3-C-to-H bond. The stronger bond, having a higher bond dissociation energy, has a higher energy absorbance.

Although the molecule as a whole absorbs the EM radiation, we can use the absorbances we measure to fingerprint particular functional groups and bonds within the molecule. The skill needed to make IR useful is an active process. Scientists use IR not only to confirm the presence of certain functional groups, but to also to help decide which functional groups are not there. IR is most useful as a supplement to the molecular formula and the NMR spectra for molecules. Table 2-1 lists several useful IR absorbances. The values are listed in terms of wave numbers. Note that the absorbance of a given bond varies with the compound in which the bond exists.

Bond type	Stretching (cm^{-1})	Bending (cm^{-1})
O—H alcohol (no H-bonding)	3640 - 3580 (v)	
O—H alcohol (H-bonding)	3600 - 3200 (s, broad)	1620 - 1590 (v)
N—H amides	3500 - 3350 (m)	
N—H amines	3450 - 3200 (m)	
C—H alkynes	3300 - 3220 (s)	
C—H aromatic	3100 - 3000 (v)	880 - 660 (v)
C—H alkenes	3060 - 3020 (m)	1000 - 700 (s)
C—H alkanes	2980 - 2860 (s)	1470 - 1320 (s)
C—H aldehyde	2900+, 2700+ (m, 2 bands)	
O—H acids (H-bonding)	3000 - 2500 (s, broad)	1655 - 1510 (s)
C≡C alkynes	2260 - 2120 (v)	
C≡N nitrile	2260 - 2220 (v)	
C=O ester	1750 - 1735 (s)	
C=O aldehyde	1740 - 1720 (s)	
C=O ketone	1725 - 1705 (s)	
C=O acid	1725 - 1700 (s)	
C=O aryl ketone	1700 - 1680 (s)	
C=O amide	1690 - 1650 (s)	
C=O α,ß-unsaturated ketone	1685 - 1665 (s)	
C=C alkene	1680 - 1620 (v)	
C=C aromatic	1600 - 1450 (v)	
C—O alcohols, ethers, esters	1300 - 1000 (s)	
C—N amines, alkyl	1220 - 1020 (w)	
s = strong absorption m = medium absorption	w = weak absorption v = variable absorption	

Table 2-1

Table 2-1 provides an overwhelming amount of data, as do many tables in our books. You don't need to memorize all this, but you do need to work with tables.

Using Table 2-1, you can evaluate IR data given in spectrum form to identify structures. As for memorizing peaks, according to the *AAMC Guide to the MCAT* you are required to "know the important ones," which is open to interpretation. You don't necessarily have to memorize hundreds of values, but if you do enough problems, the values you repeatedly see should become second nature.

As a diagnostic tool, IR is used to detect certain functional groups. You have reached the pinnacle of utility when you use it to determine which functionalities are not present as well as which functional groups are present. Just as peaks confirm the presence of a certain bond, the absence of a peak supports the absence of that bond. Here is an example of how IR spectroscopy is used:

An unknown compound with formula C_4H_8O is analyzed by IR spectroscopy. An intense band is detected at 1710 cm^{-1} (IR absorbances are listed by energy according to the wave number as measured in cm^{-1}). By comparing the value to a chart of IR absorbances, this peak can be attributed to a C=O. The compound has one degree of unsaturation attributable to a C=O, which makes it possible to narrow it down to a small number of isomers. The structure cannot be cyclic and has a carbonyl. Given that the longest chain is four carbons, the carbonyl can be only on carbon 1 or carbon 2. This narrows it down to only two butane derivatives. The longest chain could be only three carbons, with a methyl substituent on carbon 2. In that particular structure, the carbonyl group has to be on carbon one. This leaves only three possibilities, and they are:

1. $H_3CCOCH_2CH_3$ (butanone)

2. $H_3CCH_2CH_2CHO$ (butanal)

3. $H_3CCH(CH_3)CHO$ (2-methylpropanal)

Thus, we can reduce the choices from many types of compounds having one unit of unsaturation and one oxygen (a cyclic ether, for example) to a few. Ketones and aldehydes have different chemical reactivity and physical properties, so when we combine IR information with chemical tests and the melting point of the compound, we can eliminate two of the three structures. This is a structure elucidation technique you have done many times in the past. Through examples and practice, you can familiarize yourself with the peaks and become talented at solving the problems using deductive reasoning.

Example 2.12
Which of the following compounds with the formula $C_5H_{10}O$ cannot have an IR absorbance peak between 1700 cm^{-1} and 1750 cm^{-1}?
A. An aldehyde
B. A ketone
C. A cyclic ether
D. All of the above have an IR absorbance between 1700 cm^{-1} and 1750 cm^{-1}.

Solution
An IR absorbance between 1700 cm^{-1} and 1750 cm^{-1} implies that the compound has a C=O in its structure. Because it has no absorbance between 1700 cm^{-1} and 1750 cm^{-1}, it does not have a C=O bond. Choices A and B have a C=O in their structure, so they can be eliminated. The best answer is choice **C**. The one degree of unsaturation associated with the formula is used in the ring. The one oxygen in the formula is in the ether, which contains carbon-oxygen single bonds. Choice D is also eliminated, because choices A and B are eliminated.

Example 2.13
How many structural isomers of $C_4H_8O_2$ are possible that have an IR absorbance peak between 1735 cm^{-1} and 1750 cm^{-1}, a peak around 1200 cm^{-1} and no broad peaks above 2500 cm^{-1}?

A. 2
B. 3
C. 4
D. 5

Solution
The absence of a broad peak above 2500 cm^{-1} indicates that the compound does not have an O-H bond, which eliminates the possibility of it being an alcohol or carboxylic acid. It is most likely an ester, although it could have both a carbonyl and ether functionality. According to Table 2-1, the peak between 1735 cm^{-1} and 1750 cm^{-1} indicates that there is a C=O bond of an ester and not a ketone or aldehyde. The compound must be an ester, so the question now becomes, "How many esters are there that contain only four carbons in their structure?" There are only four four-carbon esters, as drawn below, so the best answer is choice **C**.

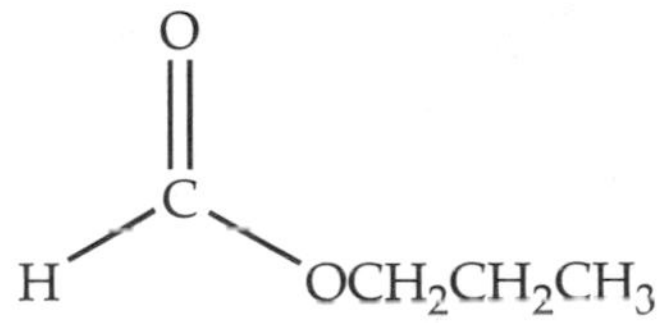

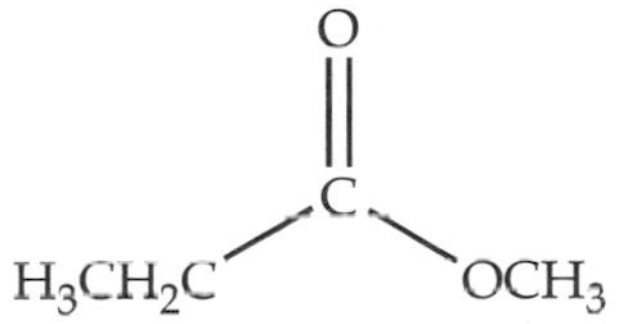

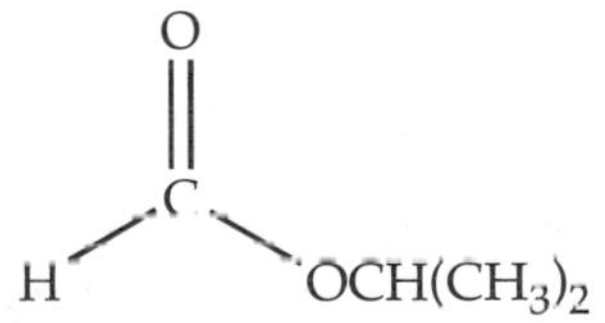

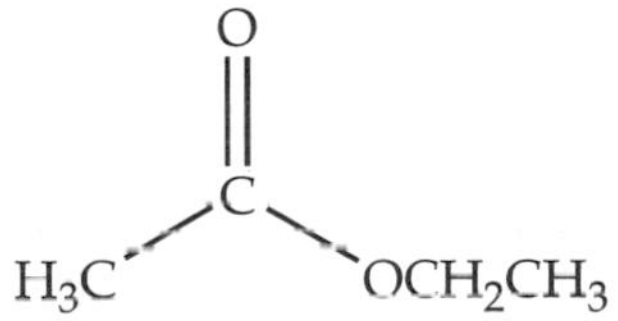

The two aldehyde structures (1 and 3) could be confirmed or eliminated by the presence or absence of two peaks at 2900 cm^{-1} and 2700 cm^{-1}. If this were a real laboratory scenario, it would be far easier at this point to use proton NMR to deduce the structure of the unknown compound. Structure 1 has four types of hydrogen in a 1 : 2 : 2 : 3 ratio. Structure 2 has three types of hydrogen in a 3 : 2 : 3 ratio. Structure 3 has three types of hydrogen in a 1 : 1 : 6 ratio. Structure 4 has three types of hydrogen in a 3 : 2 : 3 ratio. The integration would be enough to distinguish anything except Structure 2 from Structure 4. To distinguish these two structures requires identifying the ppm shift value of each type of hydrogen. We shall address NMR spectroscopy later in this chapter. IR spectroscopy should be applied to identify functional groups.

Hydrogen-Bonding in Infrared Spectroscopy
Because the formation of hydrogen bonds affects the covalent bond between an atom and a partially positive hydrogen involved in hydrogen-bonding, any spectroscopy techniques focusing on the covalent bond to hydrogen, or the hydrogen itself, is affected by hydrogen-bonding. The effect is a broadened peak (observed in both the IR and NMR techniques). In the case of IR, the broadening of the hydroxyl absorbance associated with hydrogen-bonding is caused by the weakening of the covalent bond between the hydrogen and the atom (nitrogen, oxygen, or fluorine) to which it is bonded. This lowers the energy of the covalent bond and thus lowers the energy of absorption for the bond. As the hydrogen bond increases in strength, the covalent bond weakens. Because not all of the hydrogens have the same degree of hydrogen-bonding, their covalent bonds exhibit many different absorptions, ranging from unaffected and therefore standard covalent bonds to covalent bonds that are highly weakened by the hydrogen bond. This range of covalent bonds gets grouped together into the one broad peak. The same alcohol exhibiting two different degrees of hydrogen-bonding is shown in Figure 2-23.

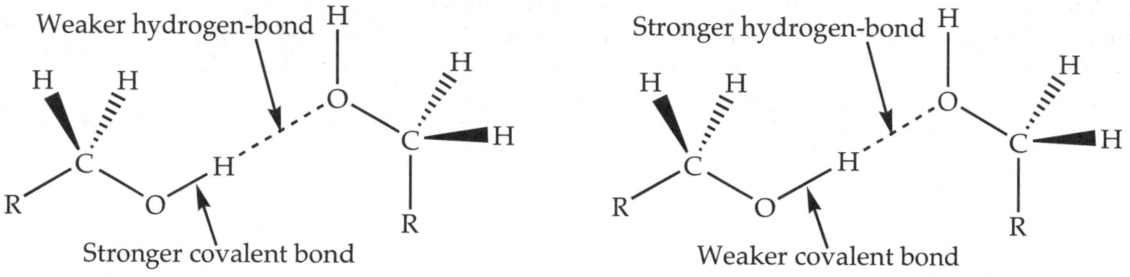

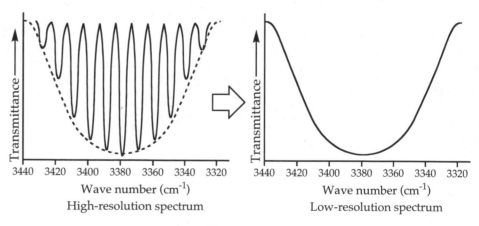

Figure 2-23

Given that molecules are in continuous random motion within a liquid, some alcohols have strong hydrogen bonds, while others have no hydrogen-bonding. This means that the solution has a random distribution of hydrogen bonds and therefore a random distribution of covalent bonds. The result is a distribution of signals in infrared spectroscopy. To see each individual peak for each different covalent bond requires a high resolution IR spectrophotometer. It is unlikely you used such an instrument, so the signal with which your are familiar is a broad composite signal covering the range of the individual signals. Figure 2-24 shows a high-resolution IR signal and the standard-resolution equivalent.

Figure 2-24

Example 2.14
What is true for the compound associated with the following IR spectra?

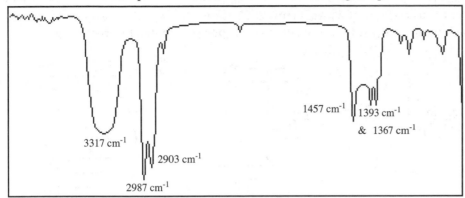

A. It exhibits no hydrogen-bonding.
B. It has a carbonyl group.
C. It has a hydroxyl group.
D. It has a molecular mass that is less than 30 grams per mole.

Solution
The compound represented by the IR spectrum above in the question has a broad peak around 3300 cm^{-1} and no peak near 1700 cm^{-1}. These are the first areas to consider when looking at IR spectra. The compound has a hydroxyl group, but no carbonyl group. This makes choice B incorrect and choice **C** correct. Because it has the hydroxyl group, it can exhibit hydrogen-bonding. This eliminates choice A. Because of the peaks in the 1300-1400 cm^{-1} range, we know the compound has a carbon-carbon bond, so it must have at least two carbons. The lightest compound with two carbons is ethyne (HC≡CH), which has a molecular mass of 26 grams per mole. However, because there is an oxygen present, the compound must have a molecular mass greater than 30 grams per mole. Choice D is eliminated.

Ultraviolet/Visible Spectroscopy
In addition to infrared spectroscopy, there is also ultraviolet/visible spectroscopy. While infrared photons (in the 3-to-10 kcals/mole region) affect the vibrational energies of a molecule, ultraviolet (in the 70-to-300 kcals/mole region) and visible (in the 40-to-70 kcals/mole region) photons affect the electronic energy levels. When UV or visible photons are absorbed by a molecule, an electron is said to be excited from the ground state to an excited state. Because σ-bonds are so much stronger than π-bonds, the lowest energy absorbance for alkanes is significantly higher than the lowest energy absorbance for alkenes. To excite an electron from the σ-level (sigma bonding orbital) to the σ*-level (sigma anti bonding orbital), photons of approximately 140 nm to 170 nm are necessary. However, because molecules in the air readily absorb energy in this region, the spectra must be obtained in a vacuum. Because this constraint is rather impractical, UV-visible spectra typically range from 200 to 800 nm, where air does not interfere. As a result, we typically use only UV-visible spectroscopy to analyze molecules with π-bonds, especially conjugated systems. UV-visible spectroscopy in organic chemistry focuses on transitions between the π and π* energy levels. For systems with conjugation, there are several π-levels, but we care about only the lowest energy transition.

The transition of interest is from π to π^*. The wavelength of highest absorbance, known as *lambda max* (λ_{max}), changes with the amount of conjugation. The value of λ_{max} depends on the amount of conjugation. *As the conjugation increases, so does the wavelength of λ_{max}.* Figure 2-25 shows the λ_{max} values associated with the lowest energy π-to-π^* transition of various conjugated hydrocarbons.

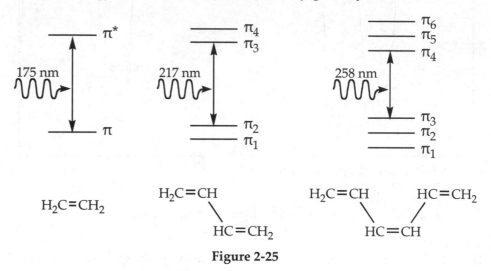

Figure 2-25

Because the energy gap between π and π^* decreases as the conjugation increases, the wavelength of maximum absorbance increases. 1,3,5,7-octatetraene has a λ_{max} of 304 nm and 1,3,5,7,9-decaquintene has a λ_{max} of 353 nm. When more conjugation is added, the absorbance shifts into the visible range. Color results from excessive conjugation within a molecule. For instance, ß-carotene (with 11 π-bonds) has absorbances at 483 nm and 453 nm. Substituted benzenes have a number of peaks. Conjugated aldehydes and ketones have about the same π-π^* absorbances as conjugated alkenes of the same number of π-bonds. However, conjugated aldehydes and ketones have other, more intense absorbances ($\varepsilon >$ 10,000) that are of longer wavelength than their hydrocarbon counterparts. This is attributed to the n-to-π^* transition associated with aldehydes and ketones, possible because of the lone pair of electrons on the carbonyl oxygen. Figure 2-26 shows the λ_{max} values associated with the lowest energy n-to-π^* and π-to-π^* transitions of various ketones.

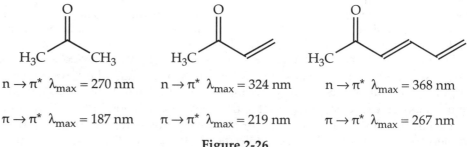

Figure 2-26

Unlike infrared spectroscopy, ultraviolet/visible spectroscopy can also be applied in a quantitative fashion. Ultraviolet/visible spectroscopy can be used to determine the yield of a reaction, if it involves a UV-visible active compound. In organic chemistry, a compound must have a π-bond to be UV-visible active.

Nuclear Magnetic Resonance

The fundamental principle behind nuclear magnetic resonance, NMR, is the same as for other forms of spectroscopy. Energy, in the form of electromagnetic radiation in the radio frequency band, is added to the system and analyzed in terms of what is absorbed. The energy levels that are affected are for the spin of a nucleus in the presence of an external magnetic field. Normally all of the nuclei have spins of the same energy. However, when an external magnetic field is applied, spins can either align with the field or align against the field, so multiple energy states are possible. In the case of ^1H, there are two energy levels: α (the one aligned with the external magnetic field), and ß (the one aligned against the external magnetic field.) The ß energy level is defined as higher than the α energy level. The energies of the two levels depend on the strength of the external magnetic field and the magnetogyric ratio of a particular nucleus. This means that the energy gap between the two levels also depends on the strength of the external magnetic field. As the external magnetic field increases, the frequency of the EM radiation needed to flip the spin increases proportionally.

Any nucleus with an odd number of protons (Z number) or an odd number of nucleons (A number) has a net spin. What is meant by "spin" is that as the nucleus precesses, it generates a weak magnetic field (just as spinning electrons do). Just as a charged particle in linear motion generates a radial magnetic field, a charged particle in rotational motion generates a linear magnetic field. When the atomic nucleus has an odd number of protons (or nucleons), the spins cannot pair up to cancel one another out. The result is that the nucleus has a net spin. In the cases of ^1H, ^{13}C, and ^{19}F, it happens that there are only two energy levels associated with the spins, so they can be analyzed without complication. A nucleus such as ^{14}N has spin, but there are more than two energy states, so its NMR spectrum is too complicated to analyze conveniently.

In the absence of any surrounding electrons, all identical nuclei exhibit the same spin and therefore require the same energy for excitation in an external magnetic field. Within a molecule, two identical nuclei may be in different electronic environments. As a result of the difference in their local magnetic fields, caused by the moving electrons, they do not require exactly the same amount of energy to excite the nucleus to a higher-energy spin state. This can also be viewed as local magnetic fields altering the strength of the applied external magnetic field needed to get excitation (spin-flip) at a set frequency for the EM radiation. NMR machines can be designed to vary the frequency of the radiation or vary the strength of the external magnetic field. The NMR graph we observe typically records changes in the magnetic field strength along the x-axis, so we think of NMR in terms of varying external magnetic field strength.

Proton NMR (which uses the ^1H nucleus) is the most common form of NMR and takes advantage of the magnetic spin associated with the hydrogen nucleus. The MCAT test-writers focus on analyzing the graphs produced by ^1H NMR. Any ^{13}C NMR that appears on the MCAT would simply be giving us a clue as to the symmetry of the molecule (by telling us how many unique carbons there are). You don't need to study ^{13}C NMR. The scale for ^1H NMR is set from 0 to 10 parts per million (ppm) of the total magnetic field of the machine. Just as an inch is an inch because someone made it a unit of measurement, NMR is measured in ppm of the external magnetic field, because that is the arbitrary standard. ^1H NMR shift values are listed relative to a standard compound, tetramethylsilane $((H_3C)_4Si)$. All twelve hydrogen atoms on tetramethylsilane are equivalent, so they absorb at the same value. This value is arbitrarily assigned to be 0 ppm, and all shift values are referenced against it. Rather than go into other intricacies of NMR, we shall concentrate on how to read the graphs.

Symmetry and NMR Signals

The best place to begin NMR for the MCAT is with molecular symmetry. Based on the symmetry of a molecule, you can determine the number of equivalent hydrogens that it contains. We will consider symmetry within different groups of molecules, starting with the four six-carbon esters shown in Figure 2-27.

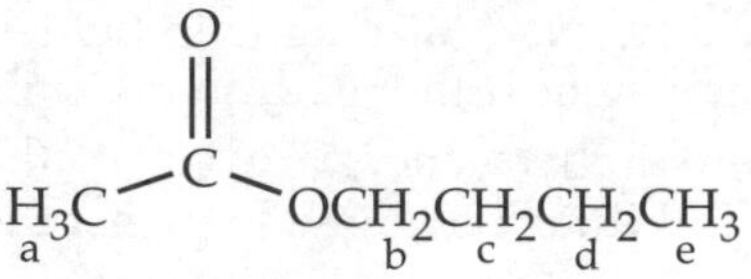

n-Butyl acetate
Five unique hydrogens labeled
a-e in a 3 : 2 : 2 : 2 : 3 ratio.

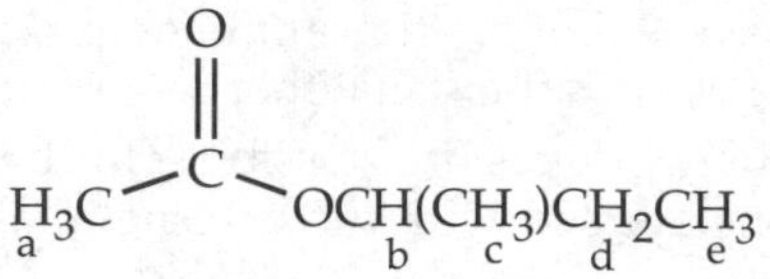

sec-Butyl acetate
Five unique hydrogens labeled
a-e in a 3 : 1 : 3 : 2 : 3 ratio.

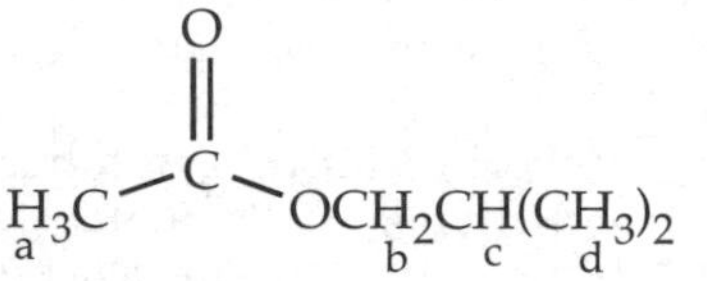

Isobutyl acetate
Four unique hydrogens labeled
a-d in a 3 : 2 : 1 : 6 ratio.

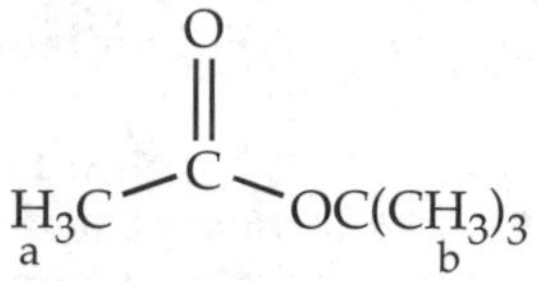

Tertbutyl acetate
Two unique hydrogens labeled
a and b in a 1 : 3 ratio.

Figure 2-27

The first two esters, n-butyl acetate and sec-butyl acetate, each have six unique carbons, of which five have hydrogens. Each exhibits five signals in its ^{1}H NMR spectrum. Isobutyl acetate has five unique carbons, but only four contain hydrogens. This means that isobutyl acetate exhibits four signals in its ^{1}H NMR spectrum. Tertbutyl acetate has four unique carbons, but only two contain hydrogens. This means that tertbutyl acetate exhibits only two signals in its ^{1}HNMR spectrum. The presence of only two signals in an NMR spectrum makes it easy to identify tertbutyl acetate.

The comparison of symmetry between isomers is highly useful, particularly with benzene derivatives. Figure 2-28 shows three structural isomers of methyl anisole (para, meta, and ortho), each of which has different symmetry.

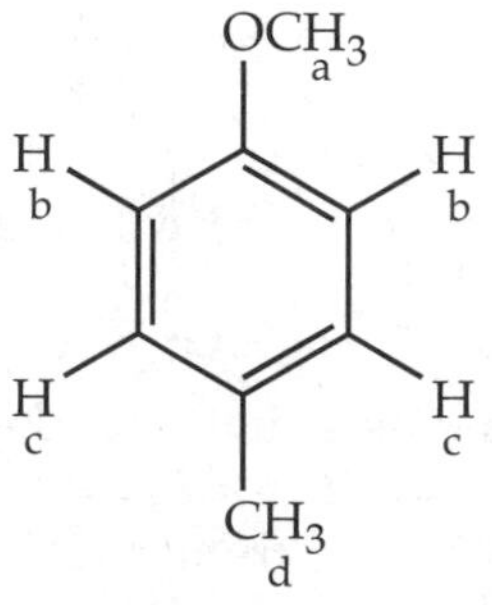

Para-methylanisole
Four unique hydrogens
labeled a-d
in a 3 : 2 : 2 : 3 ratio.

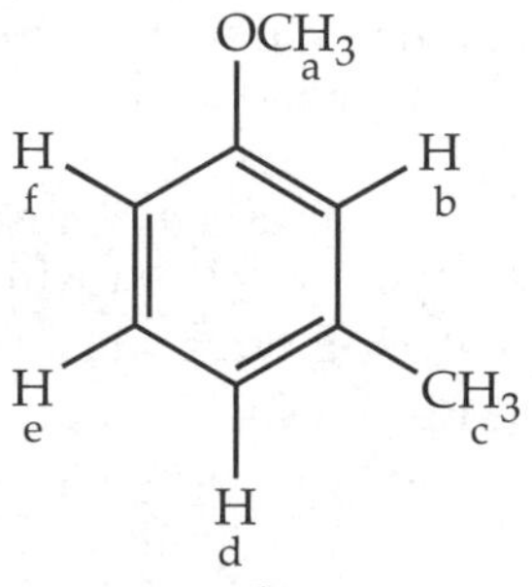

Meta-methylanisole
Six unique hydrogens
labeled a-f
in a 3 : 1 : 3 : 1 : 1 : 1 ratio.

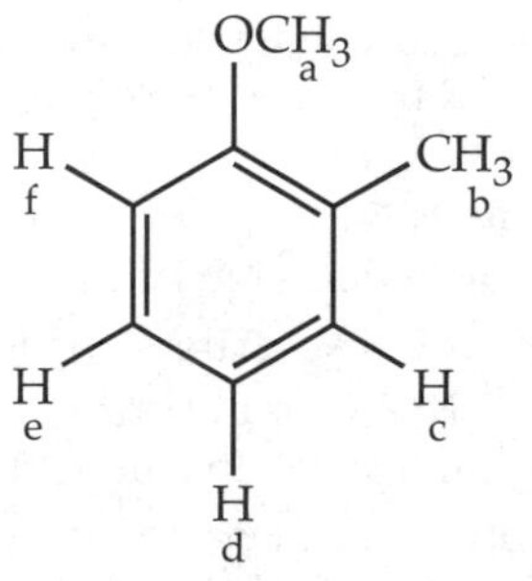

Ortho-methylanisole
Six unique hydrogens
labeled a-f
in a 3 : 3 : 1 : 1 : 1 : 1 ratio.

Figure 2-28

Para-methylanisole has six unique carbons, of which only four contain hydrogens. This means that para-methylanisole has four types of hydrogens and therefore four signals in its proton NMR. Meta-methylanisole has eight unique carbons, of which six contain hydrogens. This means that meta-methylanisole has six types of hydrogens and therefore six signals in its proton NMR. Ortho-methylanisole also has eight unique carbons, of which six contain hydrogens. This means that ortho-methylanisole also has six types of hydrogens and therefore six signals in its proton NMR.

You may have noticed that many problems are often just variations on a single theme. In Figure 2-29, compounds with comparable NMR readings are shown side by side to demonstrate similarities in the distribution of their unique hydrogens. Figure 2-29 shows two sets of three isomers that can be distinguished from one another using ^{1}H NMR by simply looking at the number of signals. Butanol and pentanal each have five unique types of hydrogens. The hydrogens are in the same ratio on both compounds, so their ^{1}H NMR spectra exhibit strong similarities. Each has five signals in its ^{1}H NMR spectrum, although they have a different number of unique carbons. The ^{1}H NMR spectra of the two compounds can be distinguished from one another by the shift values of the respective signals (the aldehyde proton is a dead giveaway around 9-10 ppm). Methylpropyl ether and 2-pentanone each have four unique types of hydrogens in exactly the same ratio on both compounds, so their ^{1}H NMR spectra exhibit strong similarities. Each shows four signals with the same relative area in their ^{1}H NMR spectra, but at different shift values. Diethyl ether and 3-pentanone each have mirror symmetry and thus have similar carbons and similar hydrogens due to this symmetry. There are two unique types of hydrogens in both diethyl ether and 3-pentanone. This means that diethyl ether and 3-pentanone have only two signals in their ^{1}H NMR.

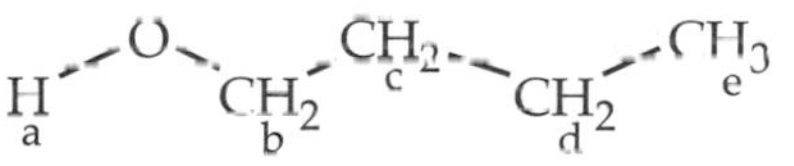

Butanol

Five unique hydrogens labeled
a-e in a 1 : 2 : 2 : 2 : 3 ratio.

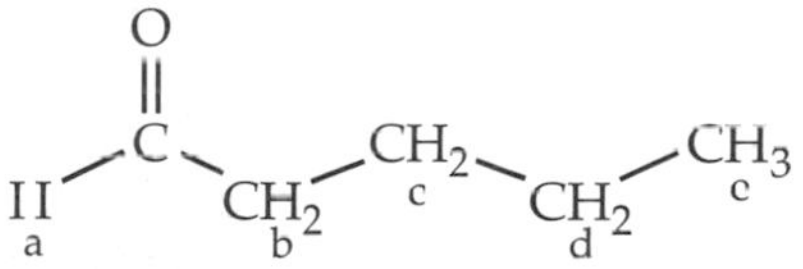

Pentanal

Five unique hydrogens labeled
a-e in a 1 : 2 : 2 : 2 : 3 ratio.

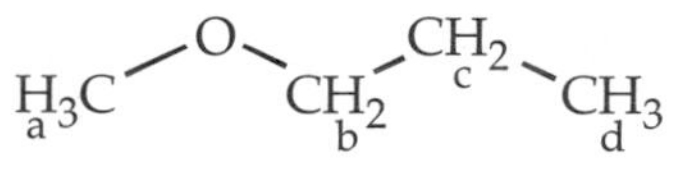

Methylpropyl ether

Four unique hydrogens labeled
a-d in a 3 : 2 : 2 : 3 ratio.

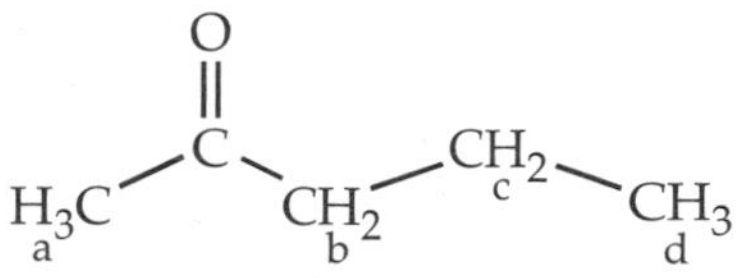

2-Pentanone

Four unique hydrogens labeled
a-d in a 3 : 2 : 2 : 3 ratio.

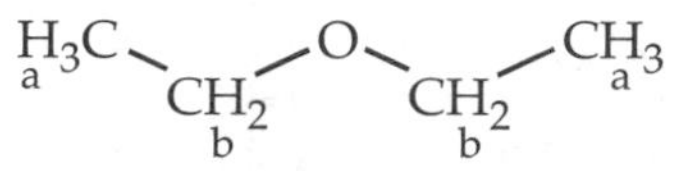

Diethyl ether

Two unique hydrogens labeled
a and b in a 3 : 2 ratio.

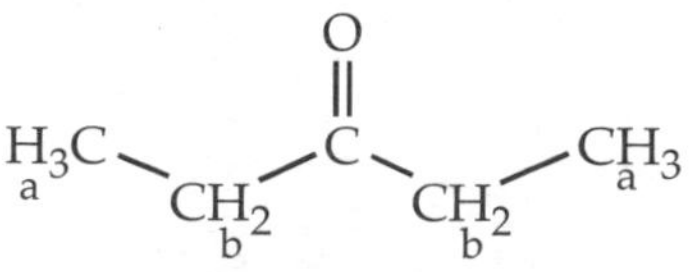

3-Pentanone

Two unique hydrogens labeled
a and b in a 3 : 2 ratio.

Figure 2-29

The comparison of butanol to methylpropyl ether and diethyl ether is similar to the comparison of pentanal to 2-pentanone and 3-pentanone. For instance, the presence of only two signals in the ^{1}H NMR spectrum makes it easy to distinguish 3-pentanone from 2-pentanone and pentanal in the same way it is easy to distinguish diethyl ether from methylpropyl ether and 1-butanol. You may see this theme repeated several times, so it is better to know basic trends rather than specific examples.

In the case of alcohols, such as butanol, the protic hydrogen can be distinguished from other signals by its broadness. Broadening results from hydrogen-bonding in solution. Hence, alcohols are easily distinguished from ethers by the presence of a broad peak in their ^{1}H NMR spectrum. In the case of NMR, the local environment of equivalent hydrogens undergoing hydrogen-bonding is not equal, so they appear at slightly different shift values. The degree of hydrogen-bonding varies, so the effect is also varied, causing the signal to be a broadened. Hydrogen-bonding causes the broadening of peaks in all types of spectroscopy. Broad peaks are a dead give-away for protic hydrogens.

These examples were designed to look at symmetry within a molecule. You will do this over and over throughout the spectroscopy section. The key to predicting an NMR pattern for a compound is to understand the symmetry of the molecule. You must be able to identify unique hydrogens and then determine their respective features. This is where we shall start our analysis. The features we shall focus on primarily are the integration of the peak, the splitting pattern (shape) of the peak, and the shift value (measured in ppm) of the peak. Be sure that you understand the importance of each of these features and the factors that can produce changes in them.

^{1}H Nuclear Magnetic Resonance

Because 3-pentanone has two unique types of hydrogens in a 3:2 ratio, its ^{1}H NMR spectrum has two signals with relative areas of 3:2. Figure 2-30 shows the signals from the ^{1}H NMR spectrum of 3-pentanone. Each peak is explained in terms of its splitting, integral, and shift value. The unique hydrogens are labeled in the same fashion as they were in Figure 2-29.

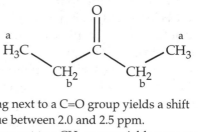

Being next to a C=O group yields a shift value between 2.0 and 2.5 ppm.
Being next to a CH$_3$ group yields a quartet.

Being next to a CH$_2$ group yields a shift value between 0.9 and 1.5 ppm.
Being next to a CH$_2$ group yields a triplet.

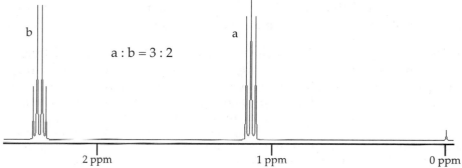

a : b = 3 : 2

Figure 2-30

The zero reference is ignored for analytical purposes, because it is there just to set the scale correctly. The integral is not drawn on the spectrum in this example. In most cases, you will be provided with the relative areas of the peaks, or you will be given a summation line to evaluate the relative areas. Either way, you must be able to apply the relative areas of the peaks to the quantity of hydrogens that each peak represents. This is the start of NMR analysis.

Spectrum Analysis

We shall start off with how to analyze the three basic components of the graph: *integral* (determined by the number of hydrogens making up a signal), *splitting pattern* (derived from the coupling between hydrogen neighbors), and *shift value* (determined by the local magnetic field caused by either lone pair electrons in motion or the electronic density associated with electronegative atoms). Each piece is equally important. At times, one piece of information may be a little more enlightening than the rest, but on the whole, every bit of data counts.

Integral

The peaks for a signal can be integrated, meaning that the area under the curve can be summed up, and set directly proportional to the number of hydrogens that the signal represents. For instance, a CH$_3$ group has a signal with a relative area of 3 compared to a CH$_2$ group with a signal of relative area 2. Working backwards from the integration to the structure, it is possible to deduce the group from the integration. For instance, a relative area of 6 can be attributed to either 2 equivalent CH$_3$ groups or 3 equivalent CH$_2$ groups. Further inspection should reveal which of the two scenarios is responsible for the six equivalent hydrogens.

Splitting Pattern

The splitting pattern, also referred to as *coupling*, corresponds to the number of hydrogens on a neighboring atom. Like electrons, nuclear particles have spin that can be classified as either up or down. The magnetic field resulting from the nuclear spin of hydrogen can be felt by the hydrogens on a neighboring atom. Because the spin can be either of two ways, the magnetic field may be additive or subtractive. The random distribution of spins is used to determine the number of hydrogen neighbors a group has. For instance, the CH_3 group in 3-pentanone (labeled with an *a* in Figure 2-30) is next to a CH_2 (labeled with a *b* in Figure 2-30). The two hydrogens of the CH_2 have one of four possible spin combinations: up/up, up/down, down/up, or down/down. Every CH_3 group next to an up/up CH_2 group has a slightly higher signal, while every CH_3 group next to a down/down CH_2 group has a slightly lower signal. Every CH_3 group next to an up/down or down/up CH_2 group has a normal signal, because the opposite spins cancel each other. The result is that one out of every four times, the CH_3 signal is slightly higher, two out of every four times the signal is unaffected, and one out of every four times the signal is slightly lower. This is why the CH_3 signal in 3-pentanone occurs as a triplet (in a 1 : 2 : 1 ratio).

Likewise, the CH_2 group of 3-pentanone is next to a CH_3. The three hydrogens of the CH_3 have eight possible spin combinations: up/up/up, down/down/up, down/up/down, up/down/down, up/up/down, up/down/up, down/up/up, or down/down/down. If all three spins are up (up/up/up), then the net spin is +3/2. If only two spins are up, then the net spin is +1/2. There are three combinations where two spins are up and one is down (up/up/down, up/down/up, down/up/up), so this is three times as frequent as the all spin up combination. The same thing can be done for the one spin up combinations (down/down/up, down/up/down, up/down/down) and the all spin down combination. The result is that a quartet is found to be in a 1 : 3 : 3 : 1 ratio.

This is why the CH_2 signal in 3-pentanone occurs as a quartet (1 : 3 : 3 : 1). There are eight outcomes, but three of them share one value and three of them share another value, so we see only four different outcomes. Working from a spectrum to a structure, it is possible to say that a 1 : 3 : 3 : 1 quartet is the result of the hydrogens on a carbon being next to three equivalent hydrogens, often due to the presence of a CH_3 group as the neighbor. To determine the ratio of the peaks within an overall signal (like the 1 : 3 : 3 : 1 value for the quartet), you can use Pascal's triangle for binomial expansion to get the relative area of each peak within the signal. Table 2-2 shows Pascal's triangle along with a brief explanation of what the relative numbers are expressing about the shape of the peak and the abundance of the signal. As the relative amount gets smaller, it is harder to distinguish a peak from noise in the baseline signal.

Neighbors	Signal Shape	Pascal's Triangle	Ratio of Peaks in Signal
0 Hs	Singlet	1	1 peak
1 H	Doublet	1 1	2 peaks: 1 : 1 ratio
2 Hs	Triplet	1 2 1	3 peaks: 1 : 2 : 1 ratio
3 Hs	Quartet	1 3 3 1	4 peaks: 1 : 3 : 3 : 1 ratio
4 Hs	Quintet	1 4 6 4 1	5 peaks: 1 : 4 : 6 : 4 : 1 ratio
5 Hs	Sextet	1 5 10 10 5 1	6 peaks: 1 : 5 : 10 : 10 : 5 : 1 ratio
6 Hs	Septet	1 6 15 20 15 6 1	7 peaks: 1 : 6 : 15 : 20 : 15 : 6 : 1 ratio

Table 2-2

Shift Value

The shift value is used to assess the local electronic environment around a hydrogen. It is measured in parts per million (ppm) relative to the magnetic field necessary to detect Hs on a standard compound, tetramethylsilane ($(H_3C)_4Si$).

Shift values tell us what functional groups are present. Consider 3-pentanone, where the CH_2 group adjacent to the carbonyl group is *deshielded* by the magnetic field on the neighboring oxygen and thus requires a stronger external magnetic field to energize the spin levels than a CH_2 group that is next to an alkyl chain. The CH_2 group is said to be *downfield* (at a higher ppm shift value in the spectrum). Table 2-3 lists some ^1H NMR shift values that can be used to analyze spectra. The bold hydrogen in each compound in Table 2-3 is the one to which the shift value corresponds, and all shift values are shown in units of ppm.

Hydrogen Atom	∂ (ppm)	Hydrogen Atom	∂ (ppm)
R**CH₃**	0.8 - 1.0	R**CH**=CR₂	5.2 - 6.4
R**CH₂**R	1.3 - 1.8	R**NH₂**	1 - 3
RCO**CH₃** (ketone)	2.1 - 2.5	RN**H**CH₃	2.0 - 3.2
RC≡C**H**	2.5 - 2.6	RO**H** (alcohol)	1 - 5 (broad)
RO**CH₃** (ether)	3.5 - 4.0	Ar**H** (benzene)	7.0 - 7.4
R**CH₂**X (X = Cl, Br, I)	3.0 - 3.8	RCO**H** (aldehyde)	9.0 - 9.8
RCO₂**CH₃** (ester)	3.5 - 4.0	RCO₂**H** (acid)	10 - 12 (broad)

Table 2-3

Example 2.15

What ^1H NMR feature can distinguish pentanal from 2-pentanone?

A. A 3H triplet at 1.5 ppm
B. A 2H multiplet at 1.8 ppm
C. A 2H triplet at 2.3 ppm
D. A 1H triplet at 9.7 ppm

Solution

Pentanal has an aldehyde hydrogen, while 2-pentanone does not. An aldehyde hydrogen is found between 9.0 and 9.8 ppm. Its peak shape in pentanal is a triplet, because there are two equivalent hydrogens on carbon 2. The two hydrogen neighbors couple with the aldehyde hydrogen to split it into a triplet. This makes choice **D** the best answer. 2-Pentanone could be distinguished by the singlet of relative integration 3 due to the isolated methyl group adjacent to the carbonyl. A ketone carbon has no Hs attached, so the methyl group of carbon one has no neighbor Hs, which makes it a singlet in the ^1H NMR spectrum. The two structures are drawn below, along with their proton NMR features.

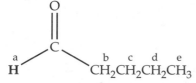

Aldehyde hydrogens show signals around 9.7 ppm in the ^1H NMR.

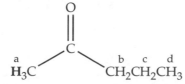

Because there are no hydrogens on the neighboring carbon, the methyl group is a singlet in the ^1H NMR.

Example 2.16

What signals are present in the ^{1}H NMR spectrum of chloroethane?

A. A downfield doublet and an upfield triplet
B. A downfield triplet and an upfield doublet
C. A downfield triplet and an upfield quartet
D. A downfield quartet and an upfield triplet

Solution

Chloroethane has two unique types of hydrogens. This results in two signals in its ^{1}H NMR spectrum. The two hydrogens on carbon 1 are split into a quartet by the three hydrogens on carbon 2. Equally, the three hydrogens on carbon 2 are split into a triplet by the two hydrogens on carbon 1. The lines split according to the neighboring hydrogens and project down to the spectra. The quartet is farther downfield than an ordinary alkyl group due to the electron density on the chlorine atom. This means that the triplet is upfield, making choice **D** the best answer.

There are two types of H, so there are two ^{1}H NMR signals.

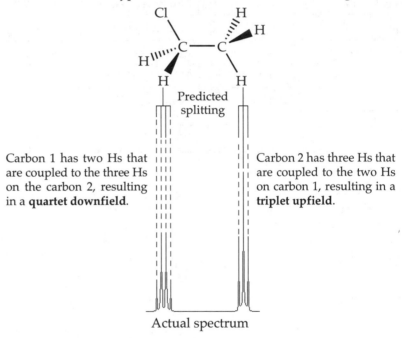

Carbon 1 has two Hs that are coupled to the three Hs on the carbon 2, resulting in a **quartet downfield**.

Carbon 2 has three Hs that are coupled to the two Hs on carbon 1, resulting in a **triplet upfield**.

Actual spectrum

Example 2.17

Pentanol can best be distinguished from ethyl propyl ether by which of the following features in its ^{1}H NMR spectrum?

A. A 3H triplet at 1.2 ppm
B. A 2H triplet at 3.5 ppm
C. A broad 1H peak between 1.0 ppm. and 5.0 ppm
D. The total number of signals in the ether is substantially less

Solution

In general, an alcohol is distinguishable from an ether by its broad peak between 1.0 ppm. and 5.0 ppm due to its hydroxyl proton. Pick choice **C** quickly for best results. The hydroxyl proton peak is broad due to the hydrogen-bonding within the alcohol. The broadening of the peak makes it difficult to evaluate the integration of the alcohol hydrogen peak, but often the integration information is unnecessary. Both pentanol and ethyl propyl ether contain a 3H triplet at 1.2 ppm, so choice A is eliminated. Both structures contain a 2H triplet at 3.5 ppm, so choice B is eliminated. Choice D is eliminated, because the difference in the number of signals between the two compounds is one (six compared to five), so there is a small difference in the number of signals between the two compounds.

Example 2.18

Which of the following is a common feature in the ^{1}H NMR spectra of all methyl ketones?

A. A triplet at 1.5 ppm (3H)
B. A quartet at 2.3 ppm (2H)
C. A doublet at 2.3 ppm (3H)
D. A singlet at 2.1 ppm (3H)

Solution

A methyl ketone has an isolated methyl group neighboring the carbonyl carbon (which has no hydrogens). Having no neighboring hydrogens results in no splitting, which makes the peak a singlet. The protons on a carbon alpha to a carbonyl are found between 2.0 and 2.5 ppm. The signal has a relative integration of 3 hydrogens. Only choice **D** shows a feature common to all methyl ketones, a 3H singlet between 2.0 and 2.5 ppm (at 2.1 ppm is in the range, but is not always the exact value observed(. The best choice is choice **D**.

Example 2.19

A monosubstituted benzene has which of the following in its ^{1}H NMR spectrum?

A. A peak at 1.2 ppm (5H)
B. A peak at 5.3 ppm (5H)
C. A peak at 7.2 ppm (5H)
D. A peak at 8.1 ppm (5H)

Solution

Monosubstituted benzenes have a single peak around 7.0 ppm. The aromatic hydrogens appear as one singlet, despite the fact that they are not all equivalent by symmetry. The key to this question is not the integration or the peak shape, but the shift value. Choice D is just a little too high, so it is eliminated along with choices A and B, which are far too low. To answer this problem quickly, you should be familiar with some of the common ^{1}H NMR peaks. Choice **C** is the best answer.

Be aware of certain peaks and features that occur over and over. For instance, whenever you see a triplet and quartet in a 3 : 2 ratio, you should conclude that there is an isolated ethyl group (H_3CCH_2-) in the molecule somewhere. Whenever you see a doublet and a septet in a 6 : 1 ratio, you should conclude that there is an isolated isopropyl group (($H_3C)_2CH$-) somewhere in the molecule. Rather than looking at molecules to determine the spectra (going from structure to spectrum), it is important to work problems from the spectrum to the structure. By recognizing the combination of peaks, you will save time in determining the unknown structure. This is very common in NMR spectroscopy.

We will use symmetric structures at first and then move on to more difficult examples. The MCAT has traditionally asked simple questions about this topic, but it's better to be safe than sorry, so we will present examples that are harder than the questions they have given on previous exams. In the following few questions are sample spectra from which you must determine the corresponding structures. It helps to solve for the units of unsaturation first. Once these are known, deduce possible functional groups that fit both the heteroatoms in the formula and the calculated units of unsaturation. For instance, zero units of unsaturation and one oxygen can be an aliphatic ether or an aliphatic alcohol. Take advantage of the multiple-choice format by eliminating wrong answers as you come across them. In the case of a compound with zero units of unsaturation and one oxygen, an answer choice of a ketone is eliminated immediately. Any structures with rings or π-bonds should be eliminated. This ability to eliminate wrong answers can be very useful in the multiple-choice format. To gain both insight and experience, try the following spectral problems:

Example 2.20

What is the name of the compound that has the following ^1H NMR spectrum, and whose formula is $C_7H_{14}O$?

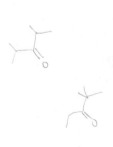

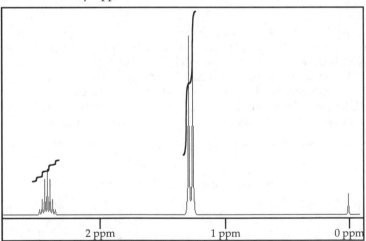

A. 2,4-dimethyl-3-pentanone
B. 2,2,4,4-tetramethyl-3-pentanone
C. 1,1,3,3-tetramethyl-2-propanone
D. 2,2-dimethyl-3-pentanone

Solution

The septet and doublet in a 1 : 6 ratio are a dead give-away for an isopropyl group. Choice D is eliminated, because it does not have an isopropyl group. Choice B is eliminated, because it contains too many carbons (nine instead of seven). Choice C is eliminated, because the structure is misnamed. The best answer, as well as the only remaining choice, is choice **A**.

Example 2.21

The shape of the signal at 2.3 ppm in the ^{1}H NMR spectrum in Example 2.20 is:

A. best described as a quartet.
B. best described as a sextet.
C. best described as a septet.
D. not defined, because of the unusual coupling.

Solution

We count seven apexes within the signal at 2.3 ppm, and seven apexes (peaks) is referred to as a septet. This is supported by the H ratio of 1 : 6 :15 : 20 : 15 : 6 : 1. The best answer is choice **C**. The septet results from six equivalent hydrogen neighbors on the methyl groups neighboring the alpha carbon.

Example 2.22

The ratio of the areas under the peaks within a quartet is:

A. 1 : 2 : 2 : 1.
B. 1 : 3 : 3 : 1.
C. 2 : 5 : 5 : 2.
D. 1 : 4 : 4 : 1.

Solution

By using Pascal's triangle, you can easily determine the ratio. It is a good idea to know the ratios of the more common peaks such as a doublet, a triplet, and in this case a quartet. A quartet has a ratio of 1 : 3 : 3 : 1. Choice **B** is correct.

Example 2.23

What is the IUPAC name of the compound represented by the following ^{1}H NMR spectrum, whose molecular formula is C_4H_8O?

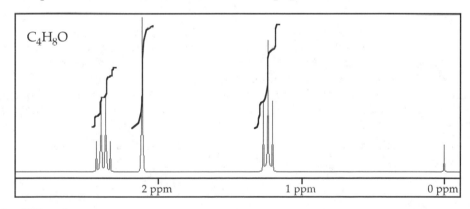

A. Butanal
B. Butanone
C. Ethyl ethanoate
D. Methyl propanoate

Solution

The formula has only one oxygen, so esters (choices C and D) are eliminated. The remaining choices are an aldehyde and a ketone. An aldehyde would have an NMR peak in between 9.0 and 9.8 ppm. There is no peak in that range, so choice A is eliminated. Butanone ($CH_3COCH_2CH_3$) has three types of hydrogens and thus three peaks in its proton NMR spectrum. The peaks are a singlet (3H), a quartet (2H), and a triplet (3H). The spectrum matches, so choice **B** is correct.

Example 2.24

What is the IUPAC name of the compound represented by the following ^{1}H NMR spectrum, whose molecular formula is $C_4H_8O_2$?

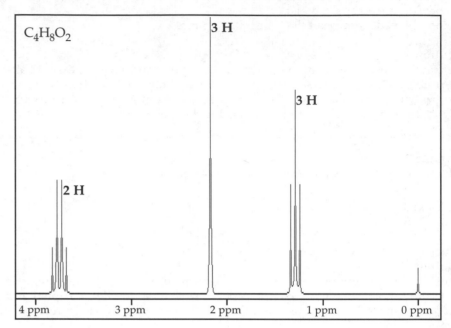

A. Butanal
B. Butanone
C. Ethyl ethanoate
D. Methyl propanoate

Solution

This question is similar to the previous question, except now the ketone and aldehyde are eliminated immediately, because there are two oxygen atoms in the molecular formula. Choices C and D show identical peak shapes and integrals in their ^{1}H NMR spectra. The distinguishing feature is the shift value of each signal. The ethyl ethanoate (structure shown on the left below) exhibits a quartet near 4.0 ppm, making choice **C** correct. The structure of methyl propanoate is shown on the right below.

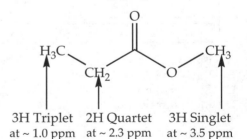

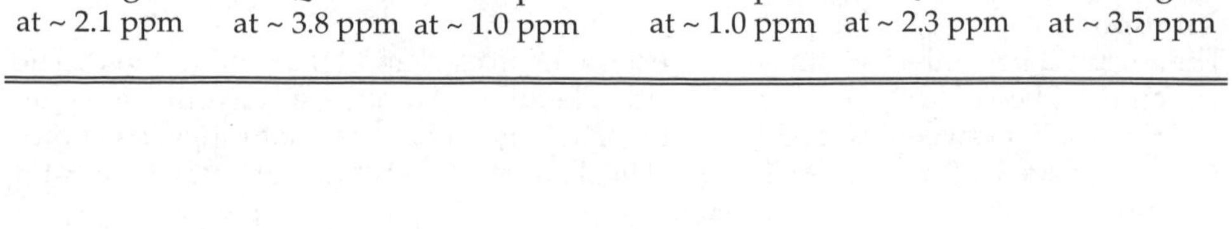

Example 2.25

Hydrogens on a carbon adjacent to two equivalent CH_2 groups show which type of signal in a ^1H NMR spectrum?

A. A $1 : 3 : 3 : 1$ quartet
B. A $1 : 4 : 4 : 1$ quartet
C. A $1 : 3 : 5 : 3 : 1$ quintet
D. A $1 : 4 : 6 : 4 : 1$ quintet

Solution

Having two equivalent CH_2 groups adjacent to the site of interest results in a total of four equivalent hydrogen neighbors. Four equivalent hydrogens split a signal into a total of five (4 + 1) peaks. This makes the signal a quintet, which according to Pascal's triangle (or binomial expansion of any sort) has a ratio of 1 : 4 : 6 : 4 : 1. The best answer is choice **D**.

Example 2.26

What is the common name of the compound represented by the following ^1H NMR spectrum, whose molecular formula is $C_8H_{10}O_2$?

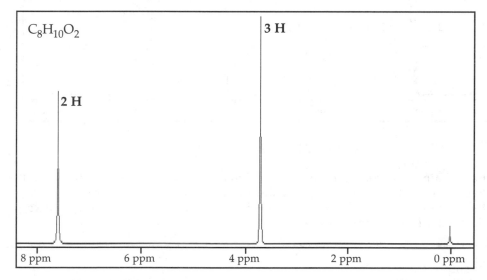

A. Para-ethoxy phenol ($H_3CH_2COC_6H_4OH$)
B. Ortho-ethoxy phenol ($H_3CH_2COC_6H_4OH$)
C. Para-methoxy anisole ($H_3COC_6H_4OCH_3$)
D. Ortho-methoxy anisole ($H_3COC_6H_4OCH_3$)

Solution

The symmetry in the ^1H NMR spectrum is associated with a structure that is also symmetric. The only way to get two types of hydrogens on a disubstituted benzene is to have two equal substituents on benzene para to one another. This eliminates choices B and D. Based on the formula, this molecule has two methoxy groups para to one another on the benzene. All of the benzene hydrogens are equivalent, which explains why only a singlet is observed. The best choice is thus answer **C**. Choice A would exhibit more than two peaks, so it is eliminated.

Recognizing Special Structural Features
Recognizing special structural features requires knowing some general shift values (δ-values) from memory. You should know that a carboxylic acid hydrogen falls in the δ = 10 - 12 ppm range and that the signal is broad. An aldehyde hydrogen falls in the δ = 9 - 10 ppm range, aromatic hydrogens fall in the δ = 7 - 8 ppm range, vinylic hydrogens fall in the δ = 5 - 6 ppm range, alkoxy hydrogens fall in the δ = 3.5 - 4 ppm range, and alpha hydrogens fall in the δ = 2 - 2.5 ppm range. Figure 2-34 shows a molecular structure and its corresponding ^{1}HNMR spectrum that includes many of these key peaks.

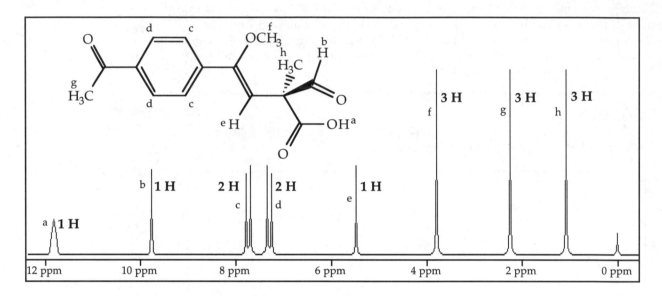

Figure 2-31

Be certain that you can match the signals (peaks) in the spectrum to the hydrogens in the structure drawn above it in Figure 2-31. This can be done on the exam using a chart of values if one is given, but it is not a bad idea to know the values from memory.

Example 2.27
What is the IUPAC name of an unknown compound with the molecular formula C_3H_6O, an IR absorption at 1722 cm[-1], and three ^{1}H NMR peak; one at 9.7 ppm (1H), one at 2.3 ppm (2H), and one at 1.4 ppm (3H)?

A. Propanoic acid
B. Propanal
C. Propanone
D. Methyloxyrane

Solution
There is an excess of information in this question beyond what is needed to answer it. You could choose a best answer based solely on the peak at 9.7 ppm, which makes the compound an aldehyde. This would allow you to pick choice **B** and move on quickly. You could also have solved this by eliminating choice A, which would have been quickly identified by a broad signal above 10 ppm. Propanone could have been eliminated, because it does not have a single hydrogen. Finally, methyloxyrane could have been eliminated, because it has no carbonyl group and thus would have an IR absorption at 1722 cm[-1].

Distinguishing Disubstituted Benzenes

Integrals tell us the number of equivalent hydrogens in a signal and are often employed to determine the position of substituents on disubstituted benzene rings. Structures that are highly symmetrical have more equivalent hydrogens than asymmetrical structures. A 1,4-disubstituted benzene ring (referred to as "para") shows the fewest peaks in the aromatic region of the spectrum of all disubstituted benzenes, due to its mirror symmetry. Both a 1,2-disubstituted and a 1,3-disubstituted benzene ring (referred to as "ortho" and "meta" respectively) have four unique hydrogens in the aromatic region of the spectrum. Figure 2-32 shows two sets of disubstituted benzenes, one set of three with identical groups and another set of three with two different groups on the benzene.

Case 1: The two substituents on benzene are equal:

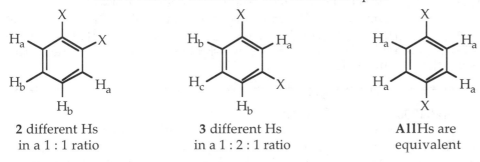

2 different Hs
in a 1 : 1 ratio

3 different Hs
in a 1 : 2 : 1 ratio

All Hs are
equivalent

Case 2: The two substituents on benzene are not equal:

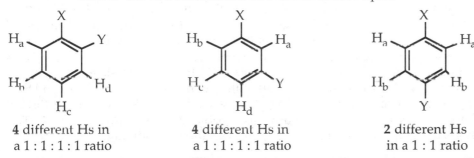

4 different Hs in
a 1 : 1 : 1 : 1 ratio

4 different Hs in
a 1 : 1 : 1 : 1 ratio

2 different Hs
in a 1 : 1 ratio

Figure 2-32

Para substitution is the easiest arrangement to distinguish of the three possible structural isomers, because it has a doublet of doublets. The dissimilar heights of its peaks can be attributed to a mathematical phenomenon whereby peaks, as they near one another, begin to coalesce. Figure 2-33 shows the aromatic region of a ^{1}H NMR spectrum of a para substituted benzene ring, where the two substituents are nonequivalent. Para coupling is a highly recognizable feature.

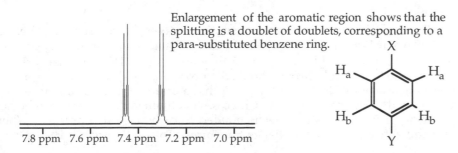

Enlargement of the aromatic region shows that the splitting is a doublet of doublets, corresponding to a para-substituted benzene ring.

Figure 2-33

Example 2.28

What is the common name of the compound that has the formula C_8H_8O, an IR absorption at 1722 cm^{-1}, and three notable ^{1}H NMR peaks at 9.7 ppm (1H, s), 7.3 ppm (4H, dd), and 2.2 ppm (3H, s)?

A. Ortho-methylbenzoic acid
B. Para-hydroxyacetophenone
C. Ortho-methylbenzaldehyde
D. Para-methylbenzaldehyde

Solution

The compound has only one oxygen, so neither a carboxylic acid (methylbenzoic acid) nor a hydroxy ketone (hydroxy acetophenone) is possible. Choices A and B are eliminated. We know that the compound must be an aldehyde from the choices that remain, so the ^{1}H NMR peak at 9.7 ppm and the IR absorption at 1722 cm^{-1} do not help our efforts to identify the compound. The ^{1}H NMR signal at 7.3 ppm is a doublet of doublet (dd), which indicates para-substitution. This makes choice **D** the best answer.

Deuterated Solvents for ^{1}H NMR

Because the solvent is in substantially higher concentration than the solute, it is imperative that the solvent not have any hydrogens. If the solvent has ^{1}H nuclei, then it would produce the largest signal in the spectrum, eliminating integration and causing the other peaks to disappear into the baseline. To avoid this problem, solvents are chosen that have deuterium (^{2}H) instead of the standard isotope of hydrogen (^{1}H). One potential problem occurs when protic compounds are dissolved into deuterated protic solvents, such as D_2O. Protic hydrogens can undergo exchange with the protons of the solvent, if the solvent is protic. Although the dissociation constant (K_a) may be small for compounds such as alcohols, over enough time all of the hydrogens can be released and then are able to reform their bonds. If D_2O is present in the solution, then deuterium will gradually replace protic hydrogens capable of undergoing exchange. This causes the signal for the protic hydrogen to disappear gradually.

Example 2.29

Which of the following compounds does NOT lose a ^{1}H NMR signal after D_2O has been added to a solution containing it?

A. Carboxylic acid
B. Cyclic ether
C. Primary amine
D. Secondary alcohol

Solution

If a compound contains a protic hydrogen, then it loses a peak from its ^{1}H NMR spectrum when D_2O is added to the solution. Primary and secondary amines have a hydrogen bonded to nitrogen, so they are protic. This eliminates choice C. All alcohols have a hydrogen bonded to oxygen, so all alcohols are protic. This eliminates choice D. A carboxylic acid has a dissociable proton, so it readily exchanges with deuterated water. Choice A is eliminated. An ether, whether cyclic or not, has all of its hydrogens bonded to carbon, so it is aprotic. When D_2O is added to an ether, no exchange transpires. The best answer is choice **B**.

Mass Spectrometry

Mass spectrometry, as the name implies, is used to determine the mass of organic molecules. For the most part, it is a quick way to determine the molecular mass of an organic molecule and to identify if the molecule contains either chlorine or bromine. Historically, it was used to determine the cationic fragments generated by the decomposition of unstable cationic free radicals molecules. Knowing the mass of common fragments allowed a chemist to reassemble the pieces and determine the original structure. In recent years, that process became obsolete due to advances in many more useful identification techniques in spectroscopy. Nevertheless, because the MCAT test writers may still consider fragmentation, we will briefly address the highlights in a sample question.

The mechanics behind the machine are addressed in the electromagnetism section in the physics book, so we shall focus on the information. In terms of organic chemistry, the molecule is first converted into a cation following the addition of some input energy (via either high speed collision or incident EM radiation). The cation is then accelerated through an electric field after which it is deflected along a circular path by a perpendicular magnetic field. The radius of the circular path correlates to the particle's mass-to-charge ratio. By comparing to various known standards, masses can be determined rather precisely. Figure 2-34 shows the mass spectroscopy graph for butanone.

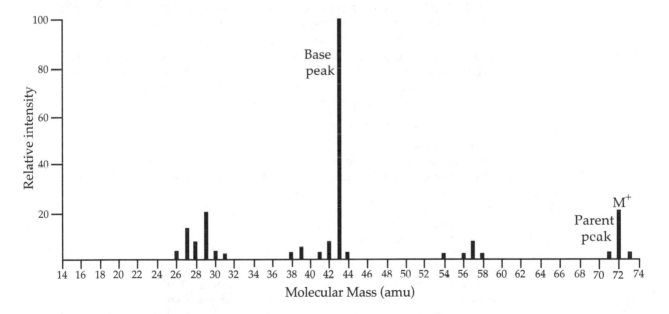

Figure 2-34

The mass of the most abundant molecule of butanone is 72.0575 g/mole, so the peak at 72 is due to the radical cation formed when a nonbonding (lone pair) electron was ionized from oxygen. When ionizing a hydrocarbon, a bonding electron is lost from a carbon-hydrogen bond. Because cations and free radicals are unstable, the species rearranges and fragments, sheering off pieces of the molecule. The mass spectrophotometer detects any charged fragments that splinter off, so the peaks that are observed correspond to stable cationic species that result from rearrangement and fragmentation. The peaks themselves represent charged fragments and the difference between two peaks corresponds to fragments that sheered off. In Figure 8-12, the peaks of interest are found at 72, 57, 43, and 29. The peak at 72 is the parent peak, so it is attributed to the cationic compound. The peaks at 57 and 43 correspond to the acylium ions formed when the parent compound loses a methyl group and ethyl group respectively. The peak at 29 is possibly due to an ethyl cation.

Example 2.30

In mass spectroscopy, the material being analyzed should be:

A. at low pressure and in the gas phase.
B. at high pressure and in the gas phase.
C. at low concentration and in the liquid phase.
D. at high concentration and in the liquid phase.

Solution

Because the particles must travel independently of one another in the apparatus, they must be in the gas phase. This eliminates choices C and D. In order to minimize the number of peaks, the material is at low pressure, so that the highly reactive free radical and cationic particles do not collide and undergo reactions. If there are too many molecules, they can combine, which would lead to more complicated data. The pressure should be low, so choice **A** is the best answer.

Detection of Bromine and Chlorine

For both chlorine and bromine, there are two predominant isotopes in a high concentration. This ratio is easily recognized when viewing the results from mass spectrometry. Elemental bromine is 50.7% ^{79}Br and 49.3% ^{81}Br, so mass spectrometer results for compounds with bromine show two peaks of roughly equal size separated by 2 atomic mass units (amu). This is a telltale feature of a compound that contains a single bromine atom. Elemental chlorine is 75.7% ^{35}Cl and 24.3% ^{37}Cl, so mass spectrometer results for compounds with a single chlorine show two peaks with a 3 : 1 size ratio separated by 2 atomic mass units. No other elements common in organic molecules have isotopes separated by two amu with such large population percentages.

Example 2.31

If a mass spectrometer reading indicates a signal at 80 amu and a signal roughly three times larger at 78 amu, then that the organic molecule likely contains:

A. a bromine atom.
B. a chlorine atom.
C. an amine group.
D. an ester group.

Solution

The key feature is the 3 : 1 ratio of the two values. Chlorine-35 and chlorine-37 isotopes comes in a 3 : 1 ratio, so the most probable explanation for the 3 : 1 ratio is the presence of a chlorine atom. This makes choice **B** the best answer. The answer could not be a bromine atom, because the isotopes are in a 1 : 1 ratio and the total mass of the molecule is less than the bromine isotopes by themselves. Choice A should have been eliminated immediately, if you chose to answer this question using *process of elimination*. Neither an amine group nor an ester group would cause two signals two amu apart from one another, let alone signals in a 3 : 1 ratio. Choices C and D should also have been eliminated immediately. Detecting the presence of a bromine or chlorine in a molecule is easily done using mass spectrometry.

Key Points for Structure Elucidation (Section 2)

Isomerism

1. Isomers (compounds with the same type and number of atoms but different spatial arrangement due to bonding, connectivity, or molecular contortion)
    a) Structural isomers (isomers with different connectivity because of different bonding)
       i. Have different IUPAC names
       ii. Can be classified as skeletal isomers, positional isomers, or functional isomers
       iii. Their number can be determined by evaluating possible chain lengths and connectivity
    b) Stereoisomers (compounds with the same bonding, but different spatial arrangement)
       i. Can be classified as configurational isomers (geometrical and optical) or conformational isomers
       ii. Have same IUPAC root, but a different prefix
       iii. Conformational isomers are formed by rotating or contorting a structure (leading to eclipsed and staggered conformations, with groups gauche and anti to one another)
       iv. Maximum number of possible optical isomers is 2^n, where n is the number of chiral centers in the compound
    c) Newman projections (front view of molecule)
    d) Cyclic molecules
       i. Three- and four-membered rings have ring strain that makes them highly reactive
       ii. Five- and six-membered rings are stable, with six being the more stable of the two
       iii. Cyclohexane (and six-membered rings in general) assume chair conformation, with groups equatorial (more stable position) and axial

Structural Insights

1. Structural symmetry
    a) Plane symmetry (mirror plane in molecule splits molecule into equal halves)
    b) Point symmetry (molecule has an inversion point at its center of mass)
    c) Units of unsaturation
       i. Determined from excess bonding electrons divided by 2
       ii. Units of unsaturation $= \dfrac{2(\#C) + (\#N) - (\#H) - (\#X) + 2}{2}$
       iii. Describes the number of π-bonds and rings in a molecule

Spectroscopy

1. IR spectroscopy (used for vibrational excitation)
    a) Ranges from $1000 \ cm^{-1}$ to $4000 \ cm^{-1}$ (about 3 kcal/mole to 10 kcal/mole)
    b) Correlates bond-stretching and bond-bending to absorbance
    c) Used to identify functional groups
    d) Key peaks: C=O around $1700 \ cm^{-1}$, O–H around $3400 \ cm^{-1}$ (broad), and C–H around $3000 \pm \ cm^{-1}$ (varies with hybridization-- $sp > sp^2 > sp^3$)
    e) Spectrophotometer uses salt plates to hold sample, because salt plates have ionic bonds and therefore do not interfere with the sample molecule's absorbances

---

                   Exclusive MCAT Preparation

2. Ultraviolet-visible (UV-vis) spectroscopy (used for electronic excitation)
   a) Ranges from 200 nm to 800 nm, increasing in wavelength as conjugation increases
   b) Typically used for analyzing compounds with π-bonds, especially conjugated systems
   c) Peak intensity and wavelength increase as the amount of conjugation increases

3. NMR spectroscopy (the basics of ^{1}H NMR analysis)
   a) ^{1}H NMR Integration (Quantitative analysis using relative area under the curves)
      i. Area under the curve for each signal is proportional to the number of hydrogens responsible for the signal
      ii. Connectivity can often be deduced from the integration ratio
   b) ^{1}H NMR peak shape (coupling and J-values)
      i. The number of peaks within a signal equals the number of neighboring hydrogens plus 1
      ii. Hydrogens coupled to one another have the same J-values
      iii. The ratio of the area of the peaks within a signal can be determined using Pascal's triangle
   c) ^{1}H NMR shift value (electron-rich environments affect shift values by exerting a magnetic field)
      i. Common signals include 9-10 ppm for an aldehyde and around 7 ppm for hydrogens on benzene
      ii. "Upfield" refers to shifts at lower ppm values
      iii. All shifts are referenced against $Si(CH_3)_4$, which is assigned a value of 0 ppm
   d) ^{1}H NMR special features (effects of deuterium and structural symmetry)
      i. Exchanging of deuterium for protons (peak disappearance)
      ii. Para substitution pattern (symmetric benzenes have unique spectra)
      iii. Solvent choice (solvent must be invisible)

4. Mass Spectrometry (determines the mass-to-charge ratio for an organic molecule)
   a) Isotopic abundance for bromine and chlorine comes in a unique ratio
      i. Bromine shows two signals separated by two amu in a 1 : 1 intensity ratio
      ii. Chlorine shows two signals separated by two amu in a 3 : 1 intensity ratio
   b) Molecular ion peak has the same mass as the neutral compound.
      i. Cations are detected by the machine, and the loss of an electron from the molecule does not change its mass by a detectable amount.
      ii. Fragmentation occurs when the unstable species formed upon ionization undergoes chemical processes in an effort to form a more stable species.

25 Structure Elucidation Review Questions

The main purpose of this 25-question set is to serve as a review of the material presented in the chapter. Do not worry about the timing for these questions. Focus on learning. Once you complete these questions, grade them using the answer key. For any question you missed, repeat it and write down your thought process. Then grade the questions you repeated and thoroughly read the answer explanation. Compare your thought process to the answer explanation and assess whether you missed the question because of a careless error (such as misreading the question), because of an error in reasoning, or because you were lacking information. Your goal is to fill in any informational gaps and solidify your reasoning before you begin your practice exam for this section. Preparing for the MCAT is best done in stages. This first stage is meant to help you evaluate how well you know this subject matter.

A researcher wishes to determine the relative stability of axial orientation versus equatorial orientation for deuterium and hydrogen on cyclohexane. To do so, she treats benzene (C_6H_6) with D_2SO_4/D_2O at 100°C for thirty minutes to synthesize monodeuterobenzene (C_6H_5D), which is then treated with H_2 gas and palladium metal under 90 psi of pressure to yield monodeuterocyclohexane ($C_6H_{11}D$). For monodeuterocyclohexane ($C_6H_{11}D$), there are two possible chair conformations, one with the deuterium having axial orientation and the other with the deuterium having equatorial orientation. At room temperature, the conversion between the two chair conformations is too rapid to study and all eleven hydrogens appear equivalent, as a singlet 1.38 ppm in the ^1H NMR. However, at low temperatures, the ring-flip from one chair conformation to the other is slow enough that axial and equatorial hydrogens generate different signals in the ^1H NMR. As a result, the ring-flip process can be monitored using ^1H NMR spectroscopy at low temperature.

A ^1H NMR was recorded at -89°C in deuterochloroform solvent. A hydrogen with axial orientation shows a ^1H NMR shift of $\delta = 1.51$ ppm, while a hydrogen with equatorial orientation shows a ^1H NMR shift of $\delta = 1.25$ ppm. Integration shows that the relative area of ^1H NMR signals is 1.12 : 1 in favor of the $\delta = 1.25$ ppm signal. Because the integration shows that a larger amount of equatorial hydrogen is observed than axial hydrogen, the deuterium must have axial orientation in the more favorable chair conformation.

The researcher proposes that a difference in bond length between the C-H bond and the C-D bond, rather than a difference in atomic size between hydrogen and deuterium, accounts for the equatorial preference of hydrogen over deuterium. The difference in bond length is attributed to the greater relative mass of deuterium compared to carbon versus the lesser relative mass of hydrogen compared to carbon. Because the center of mass remains constant when a bond is stretched, the greater difference in mass between hydrogen and carbon than deuterium and carbon makes the carbon-hydrogen bond stretch more asymmetrically than a carbon-deuterium bond. A carbon-hydrogen bond stretches more than a carbon-deuterium bond, and thus occupies a greater amount of space. Deuterium does not affect the bond angles in cyclohexane, which remain between 107.5° and 111°.

1. The addition of H_2 gas and platinum metal to chlorobenzene (C_6H_5Cl) leads to a product whose most stable conformation is:

   A. boat with chlorine anti.
   B. boat with chlorine gauche.
   C. chair with chlorine axial.
   D. chair with chlorine equatorial.

2. The researcher reached the ultimate conclusion that a bond between carbon and deuterium is shorter than a bond between carbon and hydrogen, based on the fact that:

   A. the deuterium favors the equatorial orientation.
   B. the deuterium favors the axial orientation.
   C. the conversion between the two possible chair conformations of the deuterocyclohexane molecule through ring flip is rapid at room temperature.
   D. the ^1H NMR shift at $\delta = 1.25$ ppm is farther upfield than the ^1H NMR shift at $\delta = 1.51$ ppm.

3. Addition of D_2 gas and palladium metal instead of H_2 gas and palladium metal to deuterobenzene would have shown what ratio of equatorial hydrogens to axial hydrogens in its most stable chair conformation?

   A. 6 : 5
   B. 5 : 2
   C. 3 : 2
   D. 2 : 3

4. The reason that the diaxial orientation for cis-3-hydroxycyclohexanol (a cis-1,3-diol) is preferred over the diequatorial orientation is that the hydroxyl groups:

   A. are smaller than hydrogens, so they exhibit no preference for the less hindered equatorial orientation.
   B. are larger than hydrogens, so they exhibit a preference for the less hindered axial orientation.
   C. are larger than hydrogens, so they exhibit a preference for the more hindered equatorial orientation.
   D. can form an intramolecular hydrogen bond from a 1,3-diaxial orientation, while they cannot form an intramolecular hydrogen bond from the 1,3-diequatorial orientation.

5. The D-C-H bond angle about the deuterated carbon is closest to which of the following values?

   A. 90°
   B. 109.5°
   C. 120°
   D. 180°

6. The most stable form of *cis*-1,3,5-trimethylcyclohexane has the chair conformation with:

CH₃

H₃C   CH₃

A. three methyl groups in the equatorial position and no methyl groups in the axial position.

B. two methyl groups in the equatorial position and one methyl group in the axial position.

C. one methyl group in the equatorial position and two methyl groups in the axial position.

D. no methyl groups in the equatorial position and three methyl groups in the axial position.

7. How many units of unsaturation are there in C_6H_5D?

A. 3

B. 4

C. 5

D. 6

8. Which structure represents the MOST stable form of cis-1,4-ethylmethylcyclohexane?

A.
CH₃
CH₂CH₃

B.
H₃C   CH₂CH₃

C.
CH₃
CH₂CH₃

D.
CH₂CH₃
CH₃

Passage II (Questions 9 - 15)

In most research laboratories, Fourier transform infrared (FTIR) spectrophotographers are used to obtain infrared spectra. The FTIR spectrophotographer works by passing an electromagnetic pulse of multiple frequencies through a sample and then collecting and analyzing outgoing radiation. The difference between the output signal and a reference signal is digitized by computer and broken down into a set of component sine waves (this is the Fourier transform process). The signals are processed and recorded to yield the same spectra as those obtained using outdated variable frequency IR spectrophotometers.

One advantage of the FTIR machine is that the wave number for each signal is given precisely. A disadvantage is that it is not possible to focus on one absorbance by using a monochromatic light pulse. Focusing on one absorbance with a monochromatic beam can be done in rate studies, although the rapid shutter speed of IR, (faster than any reaction including reactions that are diffusion controlled) can cause difficulties.

The IR information is most useful if certain common absorbances are understood. For instance, an O-H bond in a compound can be recognized by the broad absorbance it displays around 3300 cm⁻¹, although the exact value varies with the degree of hydrogen-bonding. A carbonyl bond is found around of 1700 cm⁻¹. If a carbon has sp^3-hybridization, the bonds it forms to hydrogen are found just below 3000 cm⁻¹. All of this information combines into a nice packet of data used to deduce the structure of a compound. Figure 1 shows the IR spectrum for 2-heptanone:

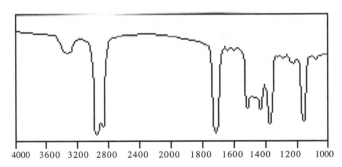

Figure 1 Infrared Spectra for 2-heptanone

The information extrapolated from the IR spectra can be coupled with NMR (nuclear magnetic resonance) data to form a powerful combination in structure elucidation. For instance, aromatic hydrogens are found in the 7 to 8 ppm range in an ¹H NMR spectrum and can be verified by an absorbance in the 3000 cm⁻¹ to 3100 cm⁻¹ range in IR spectroscopy. The IR spectra for 2-heptanone shows no absorbance in this region, which implies that the molecule has no aromatic rings. IR spectroscopy is useful in both the identification of functional groups present on a molecule as well as the support for the absence of a given functional group.

---

139   **GO ON TO THE NEXT PAGE**

9. To distinguish a tertiary alcohol from a primary alcohol (the tertiary alcohol exhibits more steric hindrance to hydrogen-bonding than the primary alcohol does), it would be best to focus on which of the following IR features?

   A. The width of the peaks near 3300 cm^{-1}
   B. The length of the peaks near 3300 cm^{-1}
   C. The width of the peaks near 1700 cm^{-1}
   D. The length of the peaks near 1700 cm^{-1}

10. Which of the following isomers of $C_3H_6O_2$ exhibits a broad IR signal around 2850 cm^{-1}?

    A.
    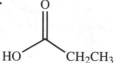

    B.

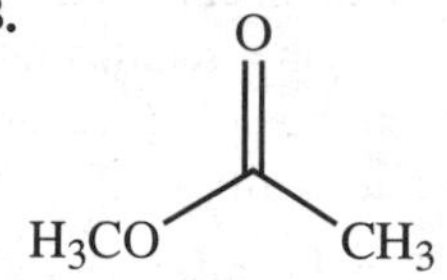

    C.
    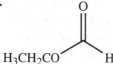

    D.

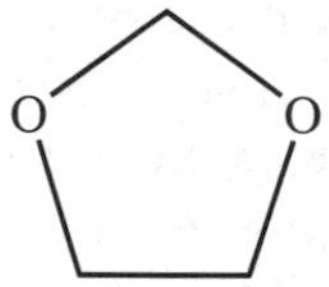

11. The IR spectrum for a straight chain monosaccharide has all of the following absorbance values EXCEPT:

    A. 3300 cm^{-1}.
    B. 2980 cm^{-1}.
    C. 2300 cm^{-1}.
    D. 1715 cm^{-1}.

12. Which of the following pairs of compounds could be distinguished by their splitting patterns in the proton NMR region between 7 and 8 ppm?

    A. Methylpropanoate from ethylethanoate
    B. 3-methyl-2-hexanone from 2-methyl-3-hexanone
    C. 1,4-methylphenol from 1,4-ethylphenol
    D. 1,4-methylphenol from 1,3-methylphenol

13. An absorbance between 1700 cm^{-1} and 1740 cm^{-1} would NOT be present in:

    A. ethyl propanoate.
    B. butanal.
    C. 2-pentanone.
    D. diethyl ether.

14. Which of the following isomers of C_4H_8O would NOT have an IR signal at 1715 cm^{-1}?

    A. 2-methylpropanal
    B. Butanal
    C. Butanone
    D. Tetrahydrofuran

15. Which of these IR spectroscopic observations over the course of the reaction could support that the hydrolysis of an ester occurred?

    A. The appearance of a signal around 1700 cm^{-1}
    B. The disappearance of a signal around 1700 cm^{-1}
    C. The appearance of a signal around 3300 cm^{-1}
    D. The disappearance of a signal around 3300 cm^{-1}

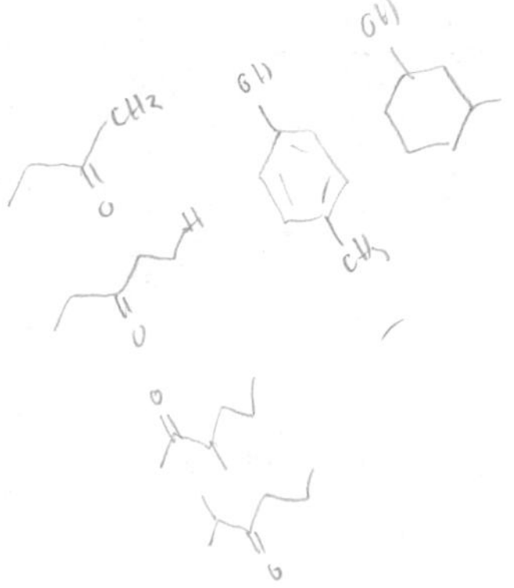

Passage III (Questions 16 - 22)

Compound I, an unknown alkyne with a molecular mass of 122.2 g/mole, is treated with H_2/Pd and $BaSO_4$ to convert it into Compound II, a cis-alkene, as shown in Figure 1.

R1—C≡C—R2
H2(g)/Pd
BaSO4
H
H
C=C
R1
R2

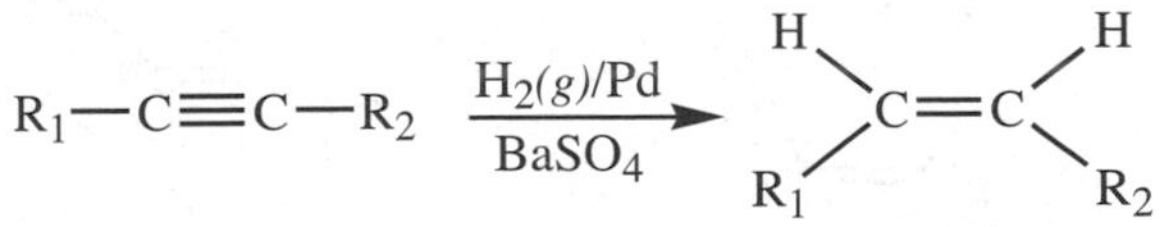

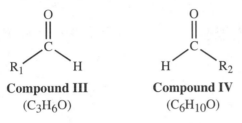

Compound I **Compound II**

Figure 1 Hydrogenation of Unknown Alkene

Compound II is isolated in high purity and then treated with high-pressure ozone (O_3) gas and zinc metal in acetic acid solvent to convert both of the alkene sp^2-hybridized carbons into carbonyl carbons. This results in the formation of two aldehydes, Compounds III and IV, shown in Figure 2.

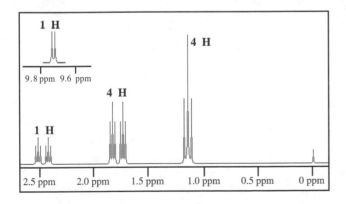

O
C
R1
H
O
C
H
R2

Compound III (C_3H_6O) **Compound IV** ($C_6H_{10}O$)

Figure 2 Aldehyde Products from Second Reaction

The two unknown aldehyde products are analyzed by mass spectrometry and it is found that Compound III has a molecular mass of 58.1 g/mole, leading to the conclusion that its molecular formula is C_3H_6O. Compound IV has a molecular mass of 98.1 g/mole, leading to the conclusion that its molecular formula is $C_6H_{10}O$. An ^{1}H NMR spectrum is obtained for Compound IV and is shown in Figure 3 below. The ^{1}H NMR is carried out using $CDCl_3$ as the solvent.

1 H
9.8 ppm 9.6 ppm
4 H
4 H
1 H
2.5 ppm
2.0 ppm
1.5 ppm
1.0 ppm
0.5 ppm
0 ppm

Figure 3 ^{1}H NMR spectrum of Compound IV

For Compound III, spectral data were obtained from an IR spectrum using pure Compound III in liquid form between cylindrical potassium bromide plates. Table 1 lists the key IR absorbances observed in the IR analysis of Compound III. Any other absorbances were considered to be insignificant and were not considered.

Shift (cm^{-1})	Intensity
2962	strong
2912	medium
2706	medium
1726	strong
1212	strong
all other peaks are irrelevant	

Table 1 IR absorbances of Compound III

The structures of Compounds III and IV can be deduced with great accuracy from the spectral data in the passage. When engaging in structure elucidation, some information is more useful than others. As a general rule, NMR data are applied last, as they are the best information for subtle distinctions in structure.

16. A compound with one degree of unsaturation and two oxygens CANNOT be:

A. a cyclic ketone.
B. a cyclic ether.
C. a carboxylic acid.
D. an ester.

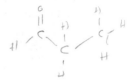

17. Which of the following ^{1}H NMR shifts would be observed for Compound III?

A. 12.0 ppm
B. 9.7 ppm
C. 7.5 ppm
D. 5.5 ppm

18. Which of the following IR absorbances would be observed for Compound IV?

A. 1725 cm^{-1}
B. 2200 cm^{-1}
C. 1620 cm^{-1}
D. 3550 cm^{-1}

19. What spectral observation would NOT be observed for Compound I?

A. An IR absorbance around 2200 cm^{-1}
B. A UV absorbance around 194 nm
C. A ^{1}H NMR singlet at 2.56 ppm.
D. A small abundance peak in mass spectrometry at 123 amu.

GO ON TO THE NEXT PAGE

20. Which of the following IR absorbance values is indicative of an alkene?

A. 3550 cm^{-1}
B. 2200 cm^{-1}
C. 1725 cm^{-1}
D. 1620 cm^{-1}

21. Which of the following sets of ^{1}H NMR signals would be associated with Compound III?

A. A 1H triplet at 9.73 ppm, a 2H multiplet at 2.41 ppm, and a 3H triplet at 1.04 ppm.
B. A 1H singlet at 3.53 ppm, a 2H quartet at 2.33 ppm, and a 3H triplet at 1.07 ppm.
C. A 1H singlet at 9.77 ppm, a 2H doublet at 2.37 ppm, and a 3H triplet at 1.02 ppm.
D. A 1H triplet at 9.71 ppm, a 2H singlet at 2.45 ppm, and a 3H triplet at 1.06 ppm.

22. Which of the following structures corresponds to Compound IV?

A.

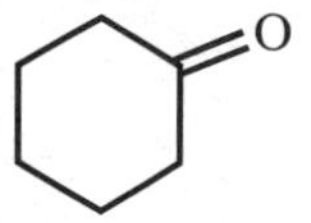

B.

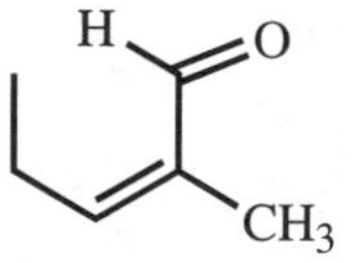

C.

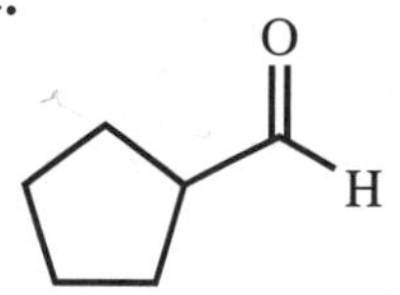

D.

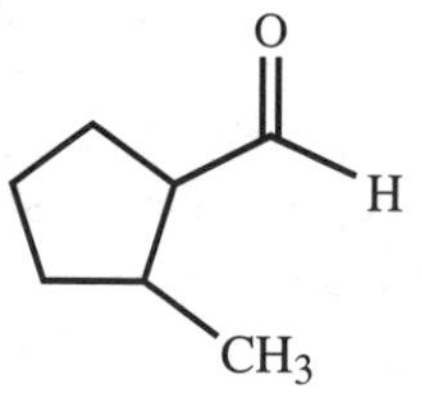

Questions 23 through 25 are **NOT** based on a descriptive passage.

23. The following two molecules are best described as:

A. structural isomers.
B. geometrical isomers.
C. optical isomers.
D. the same molecule with altered spatial orientation.

24. How many structural isomers of C_5H_{12} are possible?

A. 3
B. 4
C. 5
D. 6

25. If a compound had an ethyl group on benzene rather than a methyl group, then which of the following would be observed in the proton NMR?

A. Doublet (2H) and triplet (3H)
B. Doublet (3H) and triplet (2H)
C. Triplet (2H) and quartet (3H)
D. Triplet (3H) and quartet (2H)

1. D	2. B	3. C	4. D	5. B
6. A	7. B	8. D	9. A	10. A
11. C	12. D	13. D	14. D	15. C
16. A	17. B	18. A	19. C	20. D
21. A	22. C	23. B	24. A	25. D

Answers to 25-Question Structure Elucidation Review

1. **Choice D is the best answer.** The addition of H_2 gas to chlorobenzene results in the hydrogenation of the benzene ring and the formation of $CH_{11}Cl$ (chlorocyclohexane). For chlorocyclohexane, there are two possible stable conformational isomers, one having a ring structure in a chair conformation with the chlorine equatorial (choice **D**) and one having a ring structure in a chair conformation with the chlorine axial (choice C). Chlorine is larger than hydrogen, so it prefers to be in the equatorial orientation. Choice **D** is more stable so choose it.

2. **Choice B is the best answer.** The most stable form of cyclohexane is the chair conformation (as opposed to the boat conformation), with the smallest substituents (determined by bond length) in the axial position. The integral from the proton NMR shows that the ratio of peaks for ^1H is 1.12 : 1 in favor of the $\delta = 1.25$ ppm shift, the shift due to the equatorial hydrogen. This indicates that more hydrogens are located in the equatorial position ($\delta = 1.25$ ppm) than the axial orientation ($\delta = 1.51$ ppm). Consequently, the preferred conformation has deuterium in the axial position. For this reason, choose **B**. Drawn below are the two chair structures and their equilibrium.

6 axial H : 5 equatorial H (^1H NMR integral 1.2 : 1)   5 axial H : 6 equatorial H (^1H NMR integral 1 : 1.2)

Actual ratio is 1.12 : 1, which shows H prefers the equatorial position, so the right structure is more stable.

3. **Choice C is the best answer.** Using D_2 gas rather than H_2 gas would have produced $C_6H_5D_7$. The addition of the D_2 is in syn addition for all 6 deuteriums that are added, producing two possible conformational isomers, one having three hydrogens equatorial and two hydrogens axial (choice **C**) and the other having two hydrogens equatorial and three hydrogens axial (choice D). Choice **C** is more stable, because hydrogens prefer the equatorial orientation. Choose **C** if you want to be a star. The structure is drawn below:

3 axial H : 2 equatorial H   2 axial H : 3 equatorial H

H prefers the equatorial position, confirming that the structure on the right is more stable. The K_{eq} for this ring flip is > 1. The ratio is 2 axial : 3 equatorial.

This question could have also been answered without knowing the exact chemistry. The passage infers that hydrogen prefers the equatorial position over deuterium. This means that in the most stable orientation, there are more hydrogens with equatorial orientation than axial orientation. This eliminates choice D. Because there are only five hydrogens present (you start with five on deuterobenzene), the sum of the two numbers must be five. This eliminates choices A and B and makes choice **C** the best answer. Learn to answer questions as quickly as you can, whether you use organic chemistry knowledge or common sense.

4. **Choice D is the best answer.** A hydroxyl group, OH, is larger than a hydrogen, so choice A should be eliminated. The axial orientation is more hindered in terms of sterics, so choice B is invalid. Choice C is a good explanation for why the two hydroxyl groups would be found in a diequatorial orientation, but the question is looking for an explanation for why diaxial, rather than diequatorial, is the preferred conformation. This eliminates choice C. When the two hydroxyl groups are both in axial orientation, they can exhibit 1,3-diaxial interactions. This is normally considered to be steric repulsion; but in the case of two hydroxyl groups, there exists the ability to form hydrogen bonds. This makes choice **D** the best answer.

5. **Choice B is the best answer.** The hybridization of carbon remains sp^3, whether it is bonded to deuterium or to hydrogen. The angle therefore should be around 109.5°. It is stated in the passage that the bond angles are between 107.5° and 111°, which are both nearest to 109.5° of all the choices. Pick **B** for best results on this question.

6. **Choice A is the best answer.** The cis form of 1,3,5-trimethylcyclohexane allows for all three methyl groups to assume identical orientation in terms of axial or equatorial. This means either choice **A** or choice D is the best answer. Equatorial orientation is more stable than axial orientation, so choice **A** is the best answer. The conformation is shown below:

7. **Choice B is the best answer.** Like benzene, C_6H_5D has three π-bonds and one ring. The best answer is choice **B**. If you recall the formula for units of unsaturation, $(2(\#C) - (\#H) + 2)/2$, you can calculate the units of unsaturation, knowing that D behaves the same as H. This would also yield a total of 4.

8. **Choice D is the best answer.** Only in choice C and choice **D** do the rings have their substituents with cis orientation. Choices A and B are eliminated, because the substituents are trans to one another. The more stable conformer has the larger substituent (the ethyl group) in the equatorial position. This describes choice **D**.

Passage II   (Questions 9 - 15)   **Infrared Spectroscopy**

9. **Choice A is the best answer.** First off, we can look at the absorbance values and start to eliminate wrong answers. The alcohol peak is found above 3000 cm^{-1}, while absorbances around 1700 cm^{-1} are indicative of a carbonyl group and not a hydroxyl group. Choices C and D are eliminated. Because the broadness of hydroxyl peaks is associated with hydrogen-bonding, the decreased hydrogen-bonding of a tertiary alcohol is reflected as a narrower absorbance in the IR spectrum as compared to a primary alcohol. Broadness of the absorbance indicates the degree of hydrogen-bonding, nut the length of the absorbance, which makes choice **A** the best answer.

10. **Choice A is the best answer.** A broad signal near 2850 cm^{-1} indicates the hydroxyl group of a carboxylic acid (O-H with hydrogen-bonding). A hydroxyl group exhibits hydrogen-bonding, so the signal for it is broad. Because the O—H bond of a carboxylic acid is weaker that alcohol O—H bonds, its absorbance is lower than that of standard hydroxyl groups. Of the answer choices, only choice **A** has a carboxylic acid functionality, let alone a hydroxyl group. Pick **A** for happiness.

11. **Choice C is the best answer.** A straight-chain monosaccharide has O-H groups, a C=O functionality and C-H bonds. These groups have IR absorbances for bond stretching of 3300 cm^{-1}, 1715 cm^{-1}, and 2980 cm^{-1} respectively. This makes choice **C** the absorbance that doesn't belong, which makes it the best choice. You are required to know common values for the IR absorbances. No common-value peak is found around 2300 cm^{-1}, so that should lead you to answer choice **C**.

12. **Choice D is the best answer.** The region between 7.0 and 8.0 ppm in the proton NMR can be attributed to hydrogens on an aromatic ring. This immediately eliminates choices A and B, which have no aromatic rings associated with them. The difference between ethylphenol and methylphenol can be demonstrated by either the total number of hydrogens (as shown in the integration) or by the coupling of the alkyl portion of the compounds. The ethyl group exhibits a 2H quarter and a 3H triplet, while the methyl group exhibits a 3H singlet. The extra CH_2 group associated with the ethylphenol compared to methylphenol is found in the 2.0 to 2.5 ppm region, not the aromatic region. This eliminates choice C. To decide between the two compounds in choice **D**, one can look at the coupling of the hydrogens on the benzene ring, found in the range between 7.0 ppm and 8.0 ppm. The splitting for the hydrogens on a benzene ring with para-substitution is symmetric, while the splitting for the hydrogens on a benzene ring with meta-substitution is asymmetric. This is the distinguishing factor between the para-substituted and meta-substituted phenols in choice **D**. The best choice is answer **D**.

13. **Choice D is the best answer.** An IR absorbance between 1700 cm^{-1} and 1740 cm^{-1} is the result of a carbonyl (C=O) group, as stated in the passage. Choice A is an ester, choice B is an aldehyde, choice C is a ketone, and choice D is an ether. Of the choices, only the ether doesn't contain a carbonyl group, so it is the ether that does not have an IR absorbance between 1700 cm^{-1} and 1740 cm^{-1}. Pick **D** for best results.

14. **Choice D is the best answer.** An IR absorbance at 1715 cm^{-1} is indicative of a carbonyl group (the stretching of a C=O bond). Aldehydes and ketones contain a carbonyl group, so choices A, B, and C are eliminated. Only the ether (tetrahydrofuran) does not have a carbonyl functionality. Pick **D** and bask in the glow of correctness.

15. **Choice C is the best answer.** The hydrolysis of an ester results in the formation of a carboxylic acid and an alcohol. Both the ester and the carboxylic acid have carbonyl groups, so each has an IR absorbance around 1700 cm^{-1}. This means that both before and after hydrolysis, there is a signal around 1700 cm^{-1}, eliminating choices A and B. An ester has no hydroxyl group, so initially there is no signal around 3300 cm^{-1}. Following hydrolysis, both an alcohol and carboxylic acid are formed, so a signal for the hydroxyl group appears. In particular, the hydroxyl group of an alcohol shows an absorbance around 3300 cm^{-1}. This means that during the course of the hydrolysis of an ester, an IR signal appears around 3300 cm^{-1}, making the best answer choice **C**.

Passage III   (Questions 16 - 22)   **Spectroscopic Product Analysis**

16. **Choice A is the best answer.** Because a ring takes one degree of unsaturation and a carbonyl takes one degree of unsaturation, a cyclic ketone has two degrees of unsaturation. The compound has only one degree of unsaturation, so it cannot be a cyclic ketone. The best answer is choice **A**. A cyclic ether has one ring and no π-bonds, so it has one degree of unsaturation (for the ring). Choice B meets the restriction, so it is eliminated. A carboxylic acid has no rings and one π-bond, so it has one degree of unsaturation (for the π-bond). Choice C meets the restriction, so it is eliminated. An ester has no rings and one π-bond, so it has one degree of unsaturation (for the π-bond). Choice D meets the restriction, so it is eliminated.

17. **Choice B is the best answer.** Compound III, as shown in Figure 2, is a three-carbon aldehyde. Aldehydes can most easily be identified by their peak around 9.7 ppm in the ^{1}H NMR. Knowing this, you could immediately pick choice **B** and move on. A signal around 12.0 ppm is extremely high and could only be a carboxylic acid proton, so choice A cannot be correct. A signal around 7.5 ppm is in the range for hydrogens on benzene, so choice C cannot be correct. A signal around 5.5 ppm is in the range for hydrogens on an alkene, so choice D cannot be correct.

18. **Choice A is the best answer.** The passage shows us that Compound IV is an aldehyde. Like Compound III, it shows an IR absorbance near 1725 cm^{-1} for the stretching mode of the C=O bond. This makes choice **A** the best answer. A signal around 2200 cm^{-1} would indicate the presence of a carbon-carbon triple bond, which is not present in an aldehyde with only two units of unsaturation. Choice B cannot be correct. A signal around 1620 cm^{-1} would indicate the presence of a carbon-carbon double bond, which although it would fit with the restriction of two units of unsaturation, cannot be present because the reaction with ozone would have broken that double bond like it did the one in Compound II. Choice C cannot be correct. A signal around 3550 cm^{-1} would indicate the presence of a hydroxyl group, which is not present in an aldehyde with only one oxygen atom. Choice D cannot be correct.

19. **Choice C is the best answer.** Compound I is an alkyne with two R groups attached. An absorbance at 2200 cm^{-1} may not be top-of-the-head knowledge, but knowing that triple bonds are stronger than double bonds and that double bonds are around 1600 to 1700 cm^{-1} (C=C are in the low 1600s and C–O are around 1700), it should seem feasible that an alkyne triple bond would be of higher energy and that 2200 cm^{-1} is in the realm of feasibility. Even if you don't know the absorbance, there is no reason to choose it without evaluating the other choices. UV absorbances occur with π-bonds, and an alkyne qualifies. Again, it may not be top-of-the head knowledge, but it is feasible and can't be our choice yet. A singlet in the ^{1}H NMR would imply that there is an isolated proton on the molecule, and that would imply that one of the triple bond carbons had an H. Figure 1 shows us that there is no proton on either alkyne carbon, so choice **C** is not possible. The best answer is choice **C**. The passage tells us that the molecular mass of Compound I is 122.1 g/mole, so in a mass spectrometer, we should observe a large parent peak at 122 amu. However, because there are isotopes of carbon (1% could be ^{13}C) and hydrogen 0.8% could be ^{2}H), there is the good chance that one of the Hs or Cs could be a heavier isotope, resulting in a small peak at 123 amu. Choice D is possible, so it is eliminated. This question required a great deal of analysis, so if it was difficult, don't fret about it. Learn from the logic and don't worry as much about the random facts.

20. **Choice D is the best answer.** An alkene is distinguishable by an IR absorbance between 1620 cm^{-1} and 1660 cm^{-1} for the stretching of the C=C bond. You should know that a carbonyl C=O bond absorbs at around 1700 cm^{-1}, and being that a C=C bond is slightly weaker than a C=O bond (they are both double bonds, but a carbonyl bond is slightly shorter), it takes slightly less energy to stretch the C=C bond than the C=O bond. This means that a C=C bond has an absorbance slightly less than 1700 cm^{-1}. Only choice **D** is less than 1700 cm^{-1}, so choice **D** is the best answer. The test requires that you have some IR peaks in your memory; but for ones you don't recall, estimate them by comparison to the values you know. Choose **D** in this question for the feeling of correctitude.

21. **Choice A is the best answer.** Compound III is a three-carbon aldehyde, for which there is only one possible structure: H$_3$C-CH$_2$-CHO. The aldehyde proton comes between 9 and 10 ppm, so we can start by eliminating choice B. The aldehyde proton is on the first carbon, which is bonded to a CH$_2$ group (carbon 2), splitting the aldehyde proton into a triplet. This eliminates choice C. Because many of us picture the carbonyl as separating two sides of the molecule (like it does with a ketone), we sometimes forget that the aldehyde proton is not isolated and will be split by its neighboring hydrogens. The methylene group (CH$_2$ group) will not be a singlet, so choice D is eliminated. Choice **A** is the only choice remaining, so it must be correct. The aldehyde proton is a triplet in the 9-10 ppm range, the alpha protons are split by the aldehyde proton on one side and the CH$_3$ group on the other, so they'll show as a multiplet between 2 and 2.5 ppm. Lastly, the CH$_3$ group will be split into a triplet by the neighboring CH$_2$ group, and will fall just above 1.0 ppm. Choice **A** fits with those ppm ranges and splitting pattern.

22. **Choice C is the best answer.** As shown in the passage, Compound IV is an aldehyde, which eliminates choice A. The compound cannot contain a double bond, because its ^{1}H NMR spectrum shown in Figure 3 does not show a ^{1}H signal in the 5-6 ppm range. Choice B is eliminated. The ^{1}H NMR integration shows a peak ratio of 1:1:4:4, which indicates that there are no methyl groups in the compound. A methyl group would have shown a relative ratio in the integral of 3. This eliminates choice D. Choice D can also be eliminated, because it contains too many carbons. This narrows it down to choice **C**, which does in fact show four nonequivalent hydrogens in a ratio of 1:1:4:4. It is vital that you solve this question by a multiple-choice elimination process rather than structural deduction, because in a multiple-choice format, eliminating invalid structures is faster than elucidating the correct one.

Questions 23 - 25　　　　　　　　　　　　　　　　　　　**Not Based on a Descriptive Passage**

23. **Choice B is the best answer.** Because the compound on the left has cis orientation about the internal double bond, while the compound on the right has trans orientation about the internal double bond, the two compounds must be geometrical isomers of one another. Pick choice **B**, and you won't be sorry. In case you were considering choice C, the two compounds have the same absolute configuration, so they cannot be optical isomers.

24. **Choice A is the best answer.** The best way to do this problem is the systematic counting of carbon backbones, starting with the longest carbon chain possible (five carbons). The tally for each possible carbon backbone is drawn below. There are only three possible structures: pentane, 2-methylbutane, and 2,2-dimethylpropane. Two structures that are in fact structural isomers must have different IUPAC names. Pick **A** to be a correct answer picker person.

25. **Choice D is the best answer.** An ethyl group on benzene is composed of a CH$_3$ group next to two equivalent hydrogens (making it a 3H triplet) and a CH$_2$ group next to three equivalent hydrogens (making it a 2H quartet). The ethyl group is isolated, so there is no other splitting. The mention of a methyl group was useless, extraneous information. If you analyze the AAMC practice material, you'll see that they often put useless information in passages and questions. It is important that you learn to recognize quickly whether a random fact is helpful in solving the question or not.

$$C-C-C-C-C \qquad C-C-C-C \qquad C-C-C$$

52-Question Structure Elucidation Practice Exam

Structure Elucidation Exam Scoring Scale

Raw Score	MCAT Score
42 - 52	13 - 15
34 - 41	10 - 12
24 - 33	7 - 9
17 - 23	4 - 6
1 - 16	1 - 3

Passage I (Questions 1 - 6)

An unknown substance is isolated from the surface of the leaves of an Althnorkat tree. The substance is collected and found to contain three compounds of significance. The compounds are isolated using recrystallization techniques, with a solvent combination of water and ether. Compound L is collected in the highest yield and is subject to a battery of spectroscopic studies. The melting point of the substance is found to be 46.0°C to 47.5°C. The substance is recrystallized from diethyl ether to yield needle-like crystals with a melting point range of 46.5°C to 47.5°C. The following NMR, UV-visible, and IR data are obtained:

^{1}H NMR:	2H doublet at 2.47 ppm; J = 4.5 Hz
	1H triplet at 1.59 ppm; J = 4.5 Hz
	2H singlet at 1.30 ppm
	6H singlet at 0.98 ppm
UV-Vis:	1 major absorbance at 172 nm
	1 minor absorbance at 405 nm
IR:	2 significant peaks total
	1732 cm^{-1}, 1346 cm^{-1}, no peak above 3000 cm^{-1}
Mass Spec:	Parent Peak at 157 amu

Figure 1 Selected spectral data for Compound L

The NMR spectra are obtained using deuterated chloroform as a solvent. The IR is obtained as a nujol mull between sodium chloride salt plates.

1. Which of the following compounds would NOT exhibit an IR peak above 3000 cm^{-1}?

A. 3-Hexanol
B. 3-Aminocyclopentanone
C. Ethyl butanoate
D. 4-Hydroxy-2-octanone

2. Which of the following compounds would exhibit a 6H singlet in its proton NMR spectrum?

A. 2-Chloropentane
B. 2-Chloropropane
C. 2-Butanone
D. 2-Methyl-2-nitropentane

3. How many units of unsaturation are present in the molecule 3-chlorocyclohex-2-enone?

A. 0
B. 1
C. 2
D. 3

4. How can the following compounds be distinguished from one another, using ^{1}H NMR techniques?

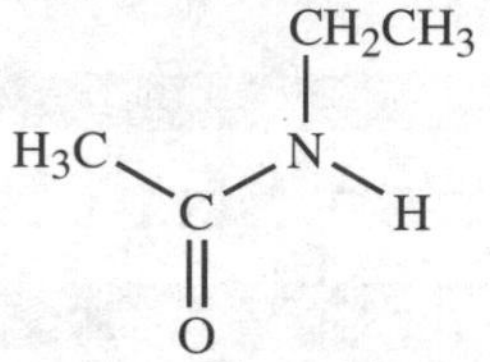

from

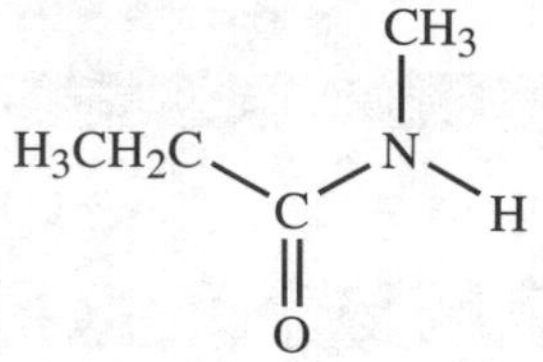

A. From the shape of the CH_3 peak (of the ethyl group) in ^{1}H NMR
B. From the shift value of H on nitrogen in ^{1}H NMR
C. From the integration of the CH_3 peak in ^{1}H NMR
D. From the shift value of the methylene hydrogens (CH_2) of the ethyl group in ^{1}H NMR

5. Which of the following structures fits the spectral data listed for Compound L in Figure 1?

A.

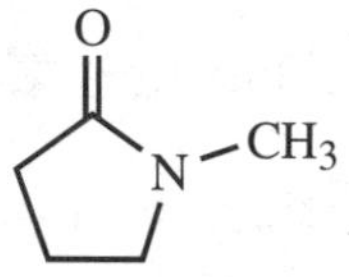

B.

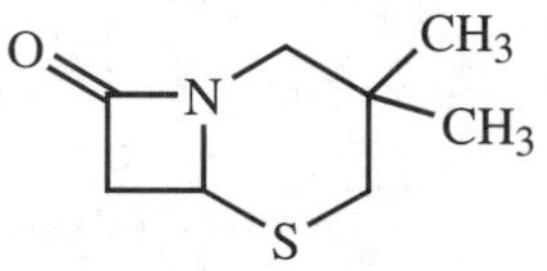

C.

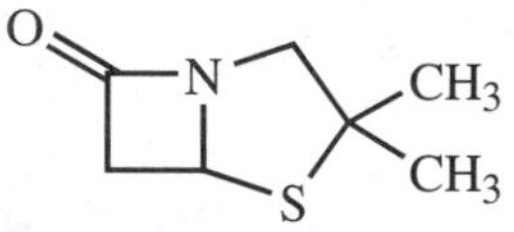

D.

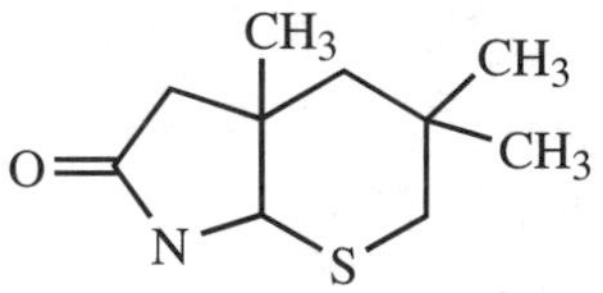

6. Why is there no J-value listed for the 2H singlet at 1.30 ppm in the proton NMR spectrum?

A. The J-value for a singlet is always 3.0 Hz.
B. The J-value for a singlet varies with the solvent.
C. There is no J-value possible for a singlet, because the signal contains only one peak, and no distance can be measured, without at least two peaks.
D. There is no J-value observed for a singlet, because all singlets are decoupled at the frequency of the NMR.

GO ON TO THE NEXT PAGE

Passage II (Questions 7 - 12)

A student is given a project in which he can use any laboratory equipment available to identify an unknown liquid. The unknown liquid has a slight yellowish color and a sweet smell. The following eight facts are the results of eight separate tests that the student conducts:

Experimental Observations

1. The compound has a boiling point of 154°C - 155°C and a freezing point of -27.5°C.

2. The compound is not very soluble in water.

3. The compound shows five signals in the ^1H NMR: Quartet (2H) at 3.61 ppm, Quintet (1H) at 2.41 ppm, Triplet (3H) at 1.23 ppm, Multiplet (4H) at 1.11 ppm, and a Triplet (6H) at 0.95 ppm.

4. No peaks are present above 3000 cm^{-1} in the IR.

5. A sharp absorbance at 1731 cm^{-1} is observed in the IR.

6. Addition of NH_3 to the unknown produces a product that shows four signals in the ^1H NMR.

7. The compound has a molecular mass between 142 and 147 grams per mole.

8. The compound does not convert the oxidizing agent CrO_3 from orange to green.

These results from the battery of tests can be used to determine the structure of the compound accurately. All of the information is valid, but not all of the data are useful.

7. Which of the following compounds would show a change in the number of signals in the ^1H NMR when D_2O is added to the NMR tube?

    A. A ketone
    B. An ester
    C. A secondary alcohol
    D. A lactone

8. Which compound would show five ^1H NMR signals and convert CrO_3 from orange to green?

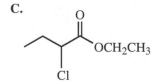

9. Based solely on Observations 2 and 4, what can be concluded?

    I.   The compound forms no hydrogen bonds.
    II. The compound is less acidic than water.
    III. The compound contains oxygen.

    A. I only
    B. I and II only
    C. I and III only
    D. I, II, and III only

10. Which of the following compounds yields an IR absorbance above 3000 cm^{-1}?

    A. N,N-dimethylpropamide
    B. Ethylbutanoate
    C. 4-Oxo-2-heptanone
    D. 3-Amino-3-methyl-4-octanone

11. What structure BEST fits Observations 4, 5, 7, and 8?

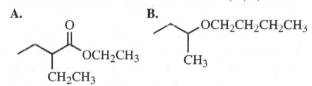

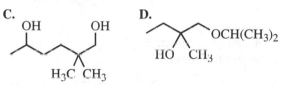

12. How would the ^1H NMR spectrum and the IR spectrum change when 2-pentanol is treated with CrO_3 in $H_2SO_{4(aq)}$?

    A. The number of ^1H NMR signals would decrease by 1; the IR spectrum will lose a peak between 1700 and 1800 cm^{-1}.

    B. The number of ^1H NMR signals would decrease by 1; the IR spectrum will lose all existing peaks above 3000 cm^{-1}.

    C. The number of ^1H NMR signals would decrease by 2; the IR spectrum will lose a peak between 1700 and 1800 cm^{-1}.

    D. The number of ^1H NMR signals would decrease by 2; the IR spectrum will lose all existing peaks above 3000 cm^{-1}.

To determine the structure of an unknown compound or to support the existence of a given structure, spectroscopy is often employed. The types of spectroscopy most commonly used are proton nuclear magnetic resonance (^{1}H NMR) and infrared (IR). Some structure elucidation facts about each technique are listed below:

^{1}**H NMR**: Detects the magnetic environment of hydrogens.

1. It is used to determine the symmetry of a structure.

2. It is quantitative. The area of the peak is proportional to the number of hydrogens in the compound.

3. The shift value is affected by the magnetic field associated with nearby electron-rich environments.

4. Nearby protons can couple with one another, causing splitting of signals into distinct bands.

IR: Detects changes in the dipole caused by vibration.

1. It is used to detect specific bonds within a structure.

2. It is not quantitative. Peak intensity is the result of transition favorability, not population.

3. The shutter speed of infrared spectroscopy is one of the fastest among spectroscopy techniques.

NMR signals are measured in terms of ppm, while IR peaks are measured in terms of cm^{-1} (wave numbers). Both spectroscopy techniques are appropriate in distinguishing structural features, but NMR is generally viewed as being more credible.

13. How can an aldehyde be distinguished from a ketone using spectroscopy?

    A. Ketones have no ^{1}H NMR peaks with an integration of 1H.

    B. Aldehydes exhibit at least one singlet in their ^{1}H NMR spectrum.

    C. Ketones have an IR absorbance above 1700 cm^{-1}, while aldehydes have an IR absorbance just below 1700 cm^{-1}.

    D. Aldehydes exhibit a 1H signal in their ^{1}H NMR spectrum that is far downfield.

14. Which of the following lab techniques CANNOT be employed to determine the equilibrium constant for a chemical reaction?

    A. Infrared spectroscopy

    B. Gas chromatography

    C. ^{1}H NMR spectroscopy

    D. Ultraviolet spectroscopy

15. Which compound shows a 2H quartet in its ^{1}H NMR spectrum?

    A. 2-Chloropentane

    B. 3-Chloropentane

    C. 2,2-Dichloropentane

    D. 3,3-Dichloropentane

16. What is TRUE for the proton NMR spectrum of the compound 2,2-dimethyl-4-chloropentane?

    A. It contains three signals in a 3 : 1 : 1 ratio.

    B. It contains four signals in a 9 : 3 : 2 : 1 ratio.

    C. It contains five signals in a 9 : 3 : 1 : 1 : 1 ratio.

    D. It contains five signals in a 6 : 3 : 3 : 2 : 1 ratio.

17. Which of the following structural distinctions is made better using IR spectroscopy than using ^{1}H NMR?

    A. Determining the chirality of an alpha carbon.

    B. Distinguishing benzene from cyclohexane.

    C. Distinguishing an alkyne from an alkene.

    D. Distinguishing the carbon to which a halogen is bonded in a haloalkane.

18. What is NOT true about the spectroscopy technique?

    A. ^{1}H NMR can be used to identify an aldehyde.

    B. IR can be used to observe hydrogen bonding.

    C. ^{1}H NMR can be used to identify the alkyl chain.

    D. IR can be used to determine the number of alpha hydrogens.

19. The following two molecules are best described as:

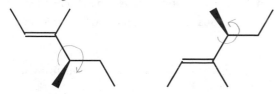

- **A.** structural isomers.
- **B.** geometrical isomers.
- **C.** optical isomers.
- **D.** the same molecule with altered spatial orientation.

20. Why are salt plates used to obtain IR spectra?

- **A.** Because salt plates have an IR absorbance between 3000 cm^{-1} and 4000 cm^{-1}.
- **B.** Because salt plates have an IR absorbance between 2000 cm^{-1} and 3000 cm^{-1}.
- **C.** Because salt plates have no IR absorbance between 1000 cm^{-1} and 4000 cm^{-1}.
- **D.** Because salt plates have no IR absorbance greater than 4000 cm^{-1}.

21. Relative to the Grape Berry Moth sex pheromone, Compound K is its:

Grape Berry Moth sex pheromone

Compound K

- **A.** conformational isomer.
- **B.** geometrical isomer.
- **C.** optical isomer.
- **D.** structural isomer.

22. Which three-dimensional conformation corresponds to the 3-hydroxy-*cis*-decalin, shown below?

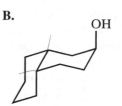

A.

B.

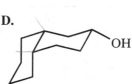

C.

D.

Nuclear magnetic resonance (NMR) spectroscopy and infrared (IR) spectroscopy can be used to identify organic compounds within reaction mixtures. By comparing shift values (measured in ppm), coupling constants (J-values), and the integration of peaks (the area under the curve), it is possible to deduce a structure with great accuracy using ^{1}H NMR. Coupling constants help to deduce what hydrogens are present on neighboring carbons. A hydrogen on a carbon adjacent to a carbon with two equivalent hydrogens generates a signal that is shaped like a triplet. The integration is the area under each peak and it is directly proportional to the number of hydrogens within that peak. Table 1 gives some general absorbance values (shift values) for ^{1}H NMR.

Proton	Shift (ppm)	Proton	Shift (ppm)
-RCH$_3$	0.8	RCH$_2$R´	0.9
-COCH$_3$	2.1	-COCH$_2$R	2.3
-OCH$_3$	3.5	-OCH$_2$R	3.8
-ArH	7-8	-CH$_2$CH=CH$_2$	2.3
-CH=O	9-10	-CH=CH$_2$	5.3
-CO$_2$H	10-12	-CH=CH$_2$	5.5

Table 1

When using ^{1}H NMR information with IR absorbance values, it is possible to quickly deduce the identity of the structure. Important IR absorbances are 3500 cm^{-1} (O-H), 1700 cm^{-1} (C=O), and 1600 cm^{-1} (C=C). There are other absorbances, but other values can be estimated from these values. As a general rule, stronger bonds have higher absorbances in IR spectroscopy than weaker bonds. For instance, the IR absorbance of a C-C bond is less than 1600 cm^{-1}, because a C-C bond is weaker than a C=C bond.

23. Which of the following spectral data BEST distinguishes butanal from 2-butanone?

A. A peak above 1700 cm^{-1} in the IR

B. A peak between 2.0 to 2.3 ppm in the ^{1}H NMR

C. A peak near 3.5 ppm in the ^{1}H NMR

D. A peak near 9.7 ppm in the ^{1}H NMR

24. What is the compound with formula C$_6$H$_{12}$O, a broad IR absorbance at 3450 cm^{-1}, and four ^{1}H NMR peaks at 4.3 ppm (broad, 1H), 1.3 ppm (4H), 1.1 ppm (3H), and 1.0 ppm (4H)?

A. Cyclohexanol

B. 1-methylcyclopentanol

C. 2-methylcyclopentanol

D. Hexanal

25. What signals in the proton NMR are indicative of an ethyl ketone?

A. 2H triplet at 2.17 ppm and 3H doublet at 1.07 ppm

B. 2H quartet at 2.21 ppm and 3H triplet at 1.09 ppm

C. 2H triplet at 2.30 ppm and 3H quartet at 1.13 ppm

D. 2H quartet at 1.11 ppm and 3H triplet at 2.26 ppm

26. A compound with two oxygens in its formula, two units of unsaturation, and no broad IR absorbance between 2500 cm^{-1} and 3000 cm^{-1}, CANNOT be which of the following?

A. A lactone

B. An ester

C. An alkene ether

D. A carboxylic acid

27. The following ^{1}H NMR is associated with which compound?

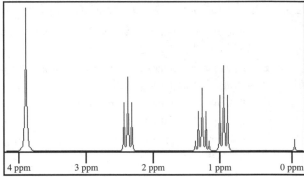

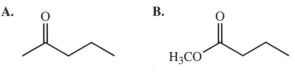

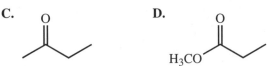

28. To confirm the presence of a secondary amide functionality, it would be best to:

A. add D$_2$O with NaOD and observe whether a broad peak grows in the proton NMR.

B. add D$_2$O with NaOD and observe whether the broad peak disappears from the proton NMR.

C. add H$_2$O with HCl and observe whether a broad peak grows in the proton NMR.

D. add H$_2$O with HCl and observe whether the broad peak disappears from the proton NMR.

A chemist set out to convert 4-hydroxycyclohexanone into 1-ethyl-4-cycanocyclohexanol in a stereospecific fashion. To do so, the chemistry proposed the following synthesis;

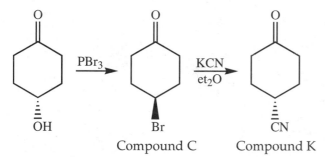

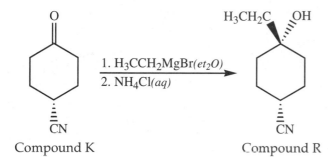

Figure 1. Proposed synthesis

A senior chemist in the lab pointed out that the synthesis as proposed did not require stereospecific reactions to form Compound C and Compound K. As an alternative to using PBr₃, the senior chemist suggested using tosyl chloride. The younger chemist opted to use the original method and carried out the synthesis, isolating Compounds C, K, and R along the way. At each step, the chemist ran an IR and ^{1}H NMR of each product.

29. How are the functional groups in the MOST stable chair confirmation of Compound R aligned?

   A. H₃CCH₂- is equatorial, HO- is axial, and NC- is equatorial.

   B. H₃CCH₂- is equatorial, HO- is axial, and NC- is axial.

   C. H₃CCH₂- is equatorial, HO- is equatorial, and NC- is equatorial.

   D. H₃CCH₂- is axial, HO- is equatorial, and NC- is equatorial.

30. How many ^{1}H NMR signals are expected for the starting reagent at 50°C?

   A. 2
   B. 3
   C. 4
   D. 5

31. How does the ^{1}H NMR change following the Grignard step?

   A. It gains two signals
   B. It gains three signals
   C. It loses a broad signal
   D. It gains two broad signals

32. How many UV-visible absorbances above 180 nm would be observed in the spectra of Compound K?

   A. 0
   B. 1
   C. 2
   D. 3

33. The best way to verify the addition of the cyano group in Compound K would be:

   A. the gain of a triplet signal in the ^{1}H NMR at 2.51 ppm.

   B. the gain of a quartet signal in the ^{1}H NMR at 3.72 ppm.

   C. the gain of an IR absorbance at 1719 cm⁻¹.

   D. the gain of an IR absorbance at 2245 cm⁻¹.

Questions 34 through 37 are **NOT** based on a descriptive passage.

34. Which of the following statements BEST explains why the MOST stable conformation of 2-amino-1-ethanol is gauche and not anti?

A. Hydrogen bonds are strongest when the two substituents have gauche orientation.

B. Hydrogen bonds are weakest when the two substituents have gauche orientation.

C. H is bulkier than NH_2, due to the inductive effect.

D. H is bulkier than NH_2, due to resonance.

35. A methyl group on benzene appears in the ^1H NMR at:

A. 7.25 ppm.

B. 5.37 ppm.

C. 3.76 ppm.

D. 2.25 ppm.

36. Why is deuterated chloroform used as the NMR solvent, rather than standard chloroform?

A. The deuterochloroform is invisible in ^1H NMR.

B. The deuterochloroform is invisible in ^{13}C NMR.

C. The deuterochloroform enhances magnetization.

D. The deuterochloroform depolarizes the magnetic fields.

37. How many signals would be seen in the proton NMR of para-methoxy benzaldehyde?

A. Four

B. Five

C. Six

D. Eight

Coupling in ^{1}H NMR is used to determine the relative positioning of hydrogens within a compound. Hydrogens are considered to be coupled when they are on neighboring carbons. Their respective magnetic fields influence the signals for one another. The effect is mutual, so the coupling interaction is equal in magnitude for all coupled hydrogens. This manifests itself as identical J-values for coupled Hs. A J-value is known as the *coupling constant* and is the distance between adjacent peaks within a ^{1}H NMR signal.

The ^{1}H NMR spectrum for two structural isomers of $C_4H_8O_2$ are collected under identical conditions using the same NMR machine. Figure 1 shows the spectrum for Isomer I, while Figure 2 shows the spectrum for Isomer II.

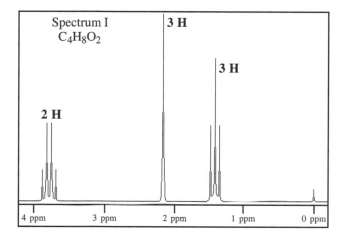

Figure 1 ^{1}H NMR spectrum of Isomer I

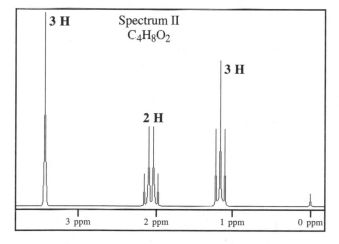

Figure 2 ^{1}H NMR spectrum of Isomer II

Both of the isomers are esters. The exact connectivity of the esters can be deduced from the shift values of the singlet and quartet. ^{1}H NMR signals around 3.5 to 4.0 ppm are due to alkyl groups bonded to an oxygen while alpha hydrogens typically show shift values between 2.0 and 2.5 ppm. The integration information verifies the substitution of each carbon in the ester.

38. Which of the following is the common name for the compound represented by Spectrum I?

   A. Ethyl acetate
   B. Acetone
   C. Methyl acetate
   D. Isopropyl formate

39. A triplet in the proton NMR is associated with the hydrogens:

   A. of a CH_2 group.
   B. on a carbon next to a CH_2 group.
   C. of a CH_3 group.
   D. on a carbon next to a CH_3 group.

40. What type of compound is represented by Spectrum II?

   A. An ethyl ester
   B. A methyl ester
   C. An ethyl ketone
   D. A methyl ketone

41. Which of the following features in the proton NMR spectrum CANNOT be used to distinguish an ester form of a carboxylic acid when the two compounds have the same molecular formula?

   A. A sharp peak between 2.0 and 2.5 ppm
   B. A sharp peak between 3.5 and 4.0 ppm
   C. A sharp peak between 10.0 and 12.0 ppm
   D. The observation that no peak integrates to a relative ratio of 1.

42. A ^{1}H NMR signal in the range between 6 and 8 ppm indicates the presence of which of the following?

   A. a hydroxyl proton.
   B. an aldehyde hydrogen.
   C. a benzene hydrogen.
   D. a carboxylic acid proton.

43. How many unique proton NMR signals are expected for 4-heptanone?

   A. Two
   B. Three
   C. Four
   D. Five

 GO ON TO THE NEXT PAGE

An unlabeled bottle containing an unknown compound is found in a lab storage locker. The compound is an odorless liquid that does not evaporate rapidly when the bottle is left uncapped. A lab technician labels the bottle Compound T. Compound T exhibits three signals in its proton nuclear magnetic resonance spectrum. The three signals are listed in Table 1.

Shift	Integration	Shape	J-Value
δ = 2.5 ppm (broad)	1 H	triplet	3 Hz
δ = 3.1 ppm	1 H	singlet	NA
δ = 4.3 ppm	2 H	doublet	3 Hz

Table 1 ^{1}H NMR signals of Compound T

Shorthand for describing nuclear magnetic resonance spectra describes the chemical shift value (δ), the number of hydrogen atoms (relative area under each signal), and the coupling along with the respective coupling constant, J. Signal shapes can sometimes be described by single letters, such as s = singlet, d = doublet, m = multiplet, q = quartet, and t = triplet.

The significant absorbances in the infrared spectrum of Compound T are found at 3350 cm^{-1} (broad), 2988 cm^{-1}, 2116 cm^{-1}, and 1033 cm^{-1}. The spectral data can be applied to determine the symmetry of a compound as well as the functional groups of the compound. The IR peak at 2116 cm^{-1} is indicative of a triple bond, indicating the presence of either an alkyne or a nitrile in Compound T. There is no spectral evidence to suggest that a nitrogen atom is present in the molecule.

From the spectral data, the lab technician concludes that the compound contains no carbonyl functionality. However, the compound contains a functional group that is involved in hydrogen-bonding, which correlates with the relatively slow evaporation of Compound T when exposed to the environment. Using chemical tests for functional groups and a standard polarimeter (to measure optical rotation of plane-polarized light), the lab technician determines that there is no mirror symmetry within the molecule. The mass spectrometry results show a parent ion peak at 56 and no other abundant peak.

44. The shift at 1033 cm^{-1} in the IR is caused by the C-O bond of:

A. an ether.

B. an ester.

C. a carboxylic acid.

D. an alcohol.

45. The absorbance at 2116 cm^{-1} in the IR implies that the compound is an:

A. alkane.

B. alkene.

C. alkyne.

D. alcohol.

46. Given that Compound T contains one oxygen, how many units of unsaturation does it have?

A. 0

B. 1

C. 2

D. 3

47. Hydrogens that are coupled to one another have the same:

A. shift value in their ^{1}H NMR spectrum.

B. peak integration in their ^{1}H NMR spectrum.

C. area under their peaks in their ^{1}H NMR spectrum.

D. same J-value in their ^{1}H NMR spectrum.

48. Compound T is which of the following compounds?

A.

$$H-C\equiv C-CH_2{\diagdown}_{OH}$$

B.

$$H-C\equiv C-CH_2{\diagdown}_{C}{\diagup}^{H}$$
$$\underset{O}{\overset{\parallel}{}}$$

C.

$$HO-C\equiv C-CH{\diagdown}_{CH_2}$$

D.

$$H-C\equiv C-CH{\diagdown}_{CH_2}$$

49. When using ^{1}H NMR spectra to distinguish between three different compounds, it important that each sample use the same solvent in order to:

   A. ensure the same reactivity in the magnetic field.

   B. increase the pH of the compounds in solution.

   C. view any common impurities between samples.

   D. allow for extraction of protic compounds.

50. Which of the following compounds contains a single bond about which complete rotation is NOT possible?

   A. Dipropyl ether

   B. 2-Butanone

   C. 2,3-butanediol

   D. Methylcyclopentane

51. Where do vinylic hydrogens appear in ^{1}H NMR?

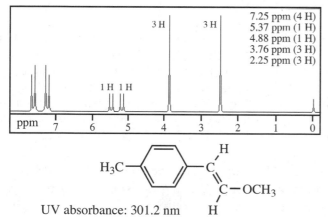

UV absorbance: 301.2 nm

   A. Above 7.0 ppm

   B. Between 4.5 ppm and 5.5 ppm

   C. Between 2.0 ppm and 3.0 ppm

   D. Between 0.5 ppm and 1.5 ppm

52. Following dehydration of 4-hydoxylpentanoic acid, the resulting lactam would have all of the following structural features EXCEPT:

   A. a UV absorbance around 256 nm.

   B. a 3H doublet around 3.49 ppm.

   C. an IR absorbance around 1682 cm^{-1}.

   D. a parent peak in mass spectroscopy at 100 amu.

1. C	2. D	3. D	4. D	5. C	6. C
7. C	8. D	9. B	10. D	11. A	12. D
13. D	14. A	15. D	16. B	17. C	18. D
19. C	20. C	21. B	22. B	23. D	24. B
25. B	26. D	27. B	28. B	29. A	30. C
31. B	32. C	33. D	34. A	35. D	36. A
37. C	38. A	39. B	40. B	41. A	42. C
43. B	44. D	45. C	46. C	47. D	48. A
49. C	50. D	51. B	52. C		

Answers to 52-Question Structure Elucidation Practice Exam

1. **Choice C is the best answer.** An IR peak above 3000 cm⁻¹ is due to either a hydrogen bonded to oxygen in an alcohol, a hydrogen bonded to a nitrogen in an amine, or a hydrogen bonded to an *sp*-hybridized carbon in a terminal alkyne. Choices A and D both contain O—H bonds, so choices A and D are eliminated. Choice B is amine, so it too can be eliminated. The best answer is the ester, which has no N—H or O—H bonds. The correct answer is choice **C**.

2. **Choice D is the best answer.** A 6H singlet in the proton NMR spectrum result from six equivalent hydrogens that have a neighboring atom with no hydrogens. This occurs with either two equivalent methyl groups or three equivalent methylene (CH_2) groups. In the compounds 2-chloropentane and 2-chloropropane, every carbon has at least one hydrogen attached, so no peak is a singlet. The spectrum for 2-chloropentane would have five peaks, a 3H doublet, a 1H multiplet, a 2H quintet, a 2H sextet, and a 3H triplet. This eliminates choice A. The spectrum for 2-chloropropane would have two peaks, a 6H doublet and a 1H septet. This eliminates choice B. Butanone would have a singlet, but it integrates as 3H. This eliminates choice C. The second carbon in 2-methyl-2-nitropentane has no hydrogen attached and two methyl substituents. The methyl groups are equivalent by symmetry, and the peak is a singlet, due to the absence of a hydrogen neighbor. The best answer is choice **D**.

3. **Choice D is the best answer.** The compound has a ring for the "cyclo," a π-bond between carbons for the "en," and a carbonyl π-bond for the "one." Overall, there are two π-bonds and one ring, resulting in three units of unsaturation total. The best answer is choice **D**. If you missed this question, try it again by drawing the structure out and see if that helps. If often does.

4. **Choice D is the best answer.** The CH_3 group of the ethyl substituent is a triplet in both structures, because it neighbors a CH_2 group. This does not distinguish the two structures, so choice A is eliminated. In both structures, the hydrogen is bonded to an amide nitrogen, so the shift values are essentially equal. Because the shift value of the hydrogen on nitrogen does not help to distinguish the two structures, choice B is eliminated. The integration of any CH_3 peak (without symmetry) is going to be 3H. This means that the integration in both structures is equal, so choice C is eliminated. The CH_2 group in the first structure is bonded to nitrogen, while the CH_2 group is alpha to a carbonyl group in the second structure. The environments are different, so the shift values are different. This means that the shift value of the CH_2 group (or isolated CH_3 group, although it is not an answer choice), can be used to distinguish the two structures. This makes the best (and only correct answer) choice **D**.

5. **Choice C is the best answer.** This question is best solved by process of elimination using the various pieces of spectral data provided in the passage. IR and UV data tells us that there is a carbonyl group, but that doesn't help at all. The absence of a peak above 3000 cm⁻¹ in the IR is helpful in that there are no O—H bonds and no N—H bonds in the compound. This eliminates choice D, which has a secondary nitrogen and would exhibit an IR absorbance above 3000 cm⁻¹. Choice A is eliminated, because it would not show a ¹H NMR signal with an integration of 6H That would be due to equivalent methyl groups. Choice B is eliminated because it contains too many hydrogens, and would exhibit three singlets rather than just two. Only choice **C** remains standing. In choice C, there are four unique hydrogens resulting in four signals in the ¹H NMR. The hydrogens in the proton NMR break down as follows:

H_c is 2H in integration, adjacent to no hydrogen-containing groups, making it a singlet, and they are near a nitrogen, making their shift value near 1.5 ppm.

H_d is 6H in integration, adjacent to no hydrogen-containing groups, making it a singlet, and they are near a sulfur, making their shift value near 1.0 ppm.

H_a is 2H in integration, adjacent to a CH-group, making it a doublet, and they are alpha protons, making their shift value between 2.0 and 2.5 ppm.

H_b is 1H in integration, adjacent to a CH_2-group, making it a triplet, and it is on a carbon near nitrogen and sulfur, making the shift value near 1.5 ppm.

6. **Choice C is the best answer.** A J-value is a measure of the distance (energy) between the apices within an NMR peak. It is used to match coupling. For instance, an isolated ethyl group yields a 3H triplet (due to the CH_3) and a 2H quartet (due to the CH_2). The distance between the adjacent spikes in the triplet is equal to the distance between the spikes in the quartet. The distance is given the name "J value." Because a singlet has only one apex, there is no distance between peaks and thus no J-value. This makes choice **C** the correct answer. Choice B is tempting, but it is the shift value that varies with the solvent. Decoupling is a technique that is rarely used in proton NMR, unless it is selective decoupling where one peak is radiated more than the others so that it does not couple with its neighbors. This is beyond the scope of the MCAT, however.

7. **Choice C is the best answer.** A change in the number of signals in the ^1H NMR when D_2O is added to solution is the result of a hydrogen exchanging with a deuterium. Only protic (acidic) hydrogens exchange, so this question is really asking, "Which structure has an acidic proton?" An alcohol has a protic hydrogen, while for a ketone, ester, and lactone, all of the hydrogens are bonded to carbon. This means that only in an alcohol does the proton exchange with deuterium. The result is that the ROH is converted into ROD, losing the alcohol peak in the spectrum. The best answer is choice **C**.

8. **Choice D is the best answer.** To convert CrO_3 from orange to green, the organic compound must be capable of being oxidized. This eliminates choices A and C, because they are both ethers, and ethers cannot be oxidized. Choice B has five unique carbons, each with at least one hydrogen, so on the carbons there are five unique hydrogens. Because of the hydroxyl hydrogen, choice B has six unique protons, so it exhibits six peaks in the ^1H NMR. Choice **D** shows a 3H singlet at 2.20 ppm for the methyl group adjacent to the ketone carbonyl, a 1H multiplet at 2.40 ppm for the other alpha hydrogen, a 3H doublet for hydrogens on the methyl carbon off of the chain, a 2H doublet at 3.60 ppm for the CH_2 group of the primary alcohol, and a broad peak for the alcohol hydrogen. That is five peaks, making choice **D** the best answer.

c: 3H doublet around 1.00 ppm

b: 1H multiplet around 2.40 ppm

d: 2H doublet around 3.60 ppm

a: 3H singlet around 2.20 ppm

e: 1H broad signal in the 1-4 ppm range

9. **Choice B is the best answer.** Observation 2 is that the compound is not very soluble in water, so it is likely that the compound forms no hydrogen bonds. This makes statement I true, which judging from the answer choices alone is obvious. Observation 4 is that the IR of the species shows no peaks above 3000 cm^{-1}. Because no peaks are found above 3000 cm^{-1}, the structure does not contain an O-H or N-H bond, which can be inferred from the lack of hydrogen bonding. This means that the compound is in fact less acidic than water, making statement II valid. This eliminates choices A and C. The compound may or may not contain oxygen according to Observations 2 and 4. Nothing conclusive can be drawn from the information, so statement III cannot be validated. This makes the best answer choice **B**.

10. **Choice D is the best answer.** Absorbances above 3000 cm^{-1} in the IR are the result of hydrogens bonded to highly electronegative atoms, (which include oxygen, nitrogen, and sp-hybridized carbons). In choice A, all of the hydrogens are bonded to sp^3-hybridized carbons, resulting in IR peaks below 3000 cm^{-1}. As a result, choice A can be eliminated. In choice B, an ester, all of the hydrogens are bonded to sp^3-hybridized carbons, resulting in IR peaks below 3000 cm^{-1}, so choice B can be eliminated. In choice C, all of the hydrogens are bonded to sp^3-hybridized carbons, resulting in IR peaks below 3000 cm^{-1}, meaning that choice C can be eliminated. It is only in choice **D**, with the amino substituent, that there are hydrogens bonded to a highly electronegative atom (in this case, nitrogen). This makes choice **D** the best answer.

11. **Choice A is the best answer.** From Observation 4, we learn there is no O-H or N-H bond present, so choices C and D are eliminated. Observation 5 tells us the compound must contain a carbonyl stretch (in the form of an ester, as you know, if you are well versed in IR peaks). Regardless, choice B can be eliminated, and only choice **A** remains. Observation 7 is that the compound has a molecular mass between 142 and 147. With a formula of $C_8H_{16}O_2$, the molecular mass is 144, so choice **A** still agrees with the observations. The ester compound is not oxidized by chromic oxide, so Observation 8 supports choice **A**. Choice **A** must be the correct choice.

12. **Choice D is the best answer.** The 2-pentanol molecule when treated with CrO_3 and $H_2SO_{4(aq)}$ can be oxidized from a secondary alcohol into a ketone, 2-pentanone. The loss of the alcohol and the formation of a ketone results in the loss of a broad absorbance around 3300 cm^{-1} (due to the O—H bond) and the formation of a sharp absorbance in the vicinity of 1700 cm^{-1} (due to the C=O bond). This eliminates choices A and C. Because the hydroxyl proton is lost, and the hydrogen on the secondary alcohol carbon is lost, two peaks are lost from the proton NMR. This makes choice **D** the best answer.

13. **Choice D is the best answer.** Choice A may be tempting at first if you consider that an aldehyde has a lone H where a ketone has an R-group. But ketones may have a peak with integration of 1H, if there is a tertiary carbon present in the structure. This means that an aldehyde is not necessarily distinguished from a ketone by a 1H signal in the ^{1}H NMR. Choice A can be put into limbo until we read the other answer chocies. An aldehyde may exhibit no singlets in its ^{1}H NMR, if the structure is a straight-chain aldehyde, where the aldehyde hydrogen is adjacent to a methylene group (CH$_2$). Choice B can be eliminated. Both ketones and aldehydes have IR absorbances above 1700 cm^{-1}, so choice C can be eliminated. Aldehydes exhibit a signal around 9.3 ppm (due to the aldehyde hydrogen) that is not observed in a ketone. This means that the 1H peak far downfield (at 9.3 ppm) can be used to distinguish an aldehyde from a ketone. This makes choice **D** a better answer than choice A, and thus the best answer.

14. **Choice A is the best answer.** An equilibrium constant is determined by dividing the amount of products by the amount of reactants, in terms of concentration. This means that for a spectroscopy technique to be employed in determining an equilibrium constant, it must be quantitative in nature. In the IR, the presence of a bond can be attributed to a peak, but the intensity of the peak does not depend on concentration. This means that IR spectroscopy is not quantitative. IR spectroscopy cannot be used to obtain numerical values, such as the equilibrium constant, so choice **A** is the best answer. Gas chromatography is quantitative, where the area under each peak is proportional to the amount of compound. The area under the peaks in ^{1}H NMR is proportional to the number of hydrogens, meaning that ^{1}H NMR can be employed in quantitative studies. UV and visible spectroscopy have absorbances where the concentration is directly proportional to the intensity. This means that UV spectroscopy is quantitative. Because GC, ^{1}H NMR, and UV are all quantitative, choices B, C, and D are eliminated, further supporting choice **A**.

15. **Choice D is the best answer.** A 2H quartet results from a CH$_2$ group adjacent to a CH$_3$ group on one side and a carbon with no hydrogens on the other. In 2-chloropentane, there is no isolated CH$_2$ group, so choice A is eliminated. In 3-chloropentane, there are two CH$_2$ groups adjacent to CH$_3$ groups, but each is adjacent to a secondary carbon, bonded to an H. Choice B is eliminated. In 2,2-dichloropentane, there is an isolated CH$_3$ group, but there is no isolated CH$_2$ group, so choice C is eliminated. In 3,3-dichloropentane, there are two CH$_2$ groups adjacent to CH$_3$ groups, and each is adjacent to a CCl$_2$ group (which has no hydrogens). The result is that the CH$_2$ groups are isolated quartets, making choice **D** the correct answer.

16. **Choice B is the best answer.** The compound 2,2-dimethyl-4-chloropentane has a molecular formula of $C_7H_{15}Cl$. This means that the proton NMR must show a total of fifteen hydrogens. The structure is given below:

4 ^{1}H NMR peaks:
a (9H), b (2H), c (1H), and d (3H)
The ratio of the peaks is 9 : 3 : 2 : 1

There are nine equivalent protons, which eliminates choices A and D. The fact that the ratio is 9 : 3 : 2 : 1 makes choice **B** the best answer.

17. **Choice C is the best answer.** Chirality is observed during optical rotation, using a polarimeter. Chirality of an alpha carbon cannot be evaluated using either NMR or IR, so choice A is eliminated. Benzene hydrogens show a distinctive signal around 7.0 ppm in the ^{1}H NMR, so benzene can readily be distinguished from cyclohexane using ^{1}H NMR. This eliminates choice B. The carbon containing the halogen can be identified by looking for the proton with a shift further downfield than typical protons on sp^3-hybridized carbons. This means that information about the carbon bonded to chlorine is most easily gathered using NMR spectroscopy. IR leads to a better, and quicker, result in distinguishing between an alkene (with an IR absorbance between 1620 cm^{-1} and 1680 cm^{-1}) and an alkyne (with an IR absorbance around 2200 cm^{-1}). The NMR distinguishes hydrogens on sp-carbons from hydrogens on sp^2-carbons, but the IR works more cleanly and more quickly. The best answer is choice **C**.

18. **Choice D is the best answer.** Proton NMR can be used to detect an aldehyde by looking for the 1H signal of the aldehyde hydrogen (typically found around 9.3 ppm). Choice A can be eliminated. IR can be used to identify hydrogen bonding, by looking for a broad peak above 3000 cm^{-1}. The broadness is indicative of hydrogen bonding. Choice B can be eliminated. Proton NMR can be used to identify an alkyl chain by looking at the coupling, the number of peaks, and the integration. This eliminates choice C. IR cannot be used for any quantitative measurements, so IR cannot tell us anything about the number of alpha hydrogens. This means that choice **D** is invalid, and thus the best answer is choice **D**.

Questions 19 - 22   **Not Based on a Descriptive Passage**

19. **Choice C is the best answer.** Both double bonds are trans, so they are not geometrical isomers, eliminating choice B immediately. Both have the same connectivity, so they are not structural isomers, which eliminates choice A. The last thing to check is the chiral centers, and each has just one chiral center. The compound on the left has R chirality, while the compound on the right has S chirality. This makes the two structures optical isomers, choice **C**. If you mentally flip the structure on the right by 180° out of the plane of the paper and then back into the plane of the paper but upside-down to align with the structure on the left, then you can see that the chiral center has changed. A change in a chiral center results in an optical isomer, confirming that choice **C** is the best answer.

20. **Choice C is the best answer.** This you may or may not recall from your organic chemistry lab days, but salt plates are chosen because ionic bonds do not absorb in the IR frequency and therefore do not interfere with the IR spectrum of organic compounds, which have an absorbance range between 1000 cm^{-1} and 4000 cm^{-1}. Given that organic compounds have covalent bonds, it should make sense that you'd use a material with no interfering covalent bonds in the range of the spectrum used to analyze organic molecules. Choice **C** is the best answer.

21. **Choice B is the best answer.** The Grape Berry Moth sex pheromone differs from Compound K at the double bond. Compound K has trans geometry, while the pheromone has cis geometry. This makes geometrical isomers the most likely answer. The connectivity is the same, so the structures are not structural isomers. This eliminates choice D. The two structures are not interchangeable by a rotation about a bond, so they are not conformational isomers. This eliminates choice A. There is no stereogenic carbon present, so the two structures cannot be optical isomers. This eliminates choice C. The two structures are geometrical isomers, making choice **B** the best answer. By the way, in the event you ever end up on a game show centered around reproductive pheromones for small insects, you may wish to know that Compound K is a sex pheromone for the European Pine Shoot Moth.

22. **Choice B is the best answer.** The key to this problem is drawing the two hydrogen atoms on the bridging carbons cis to one another. These hydrogens are cis to one another, so one hydrogen assumes axial orientation, while the other assumes equatorial orientation. As a consequence, the carbon-carbon bonds to the left ring must also be axial for one and equatorial for the other. The structure is drawn below. Choice **B** is the best answer.

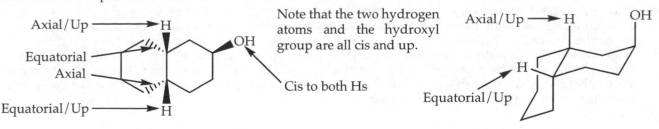

23.   **Choice D is the best answer.** The fundamental difference between the two compounds is that butanal is an aldehyde while 2-butanone is a ketone. An aldehyde is best distinguished from a ketone in ^{1}H NMR by a peak near 9.7 ppm. Choices A and B are eliminated, because both compounds (the aldehyde and the ketone) have a carbonyl absorbance in the IR just above 1700 cm^{-1} and a peak in the proton NMR between 2.0 and 2.3 ppm (for the alpha hydrogens). Only choice **D** is for a signal that is unique to the one of the compounds (the aldehyde).

24.   **Choice B is the best answer.** The broad IR absorbance at 3450 cm^{-1} indicates that the compound contains an alcohol functional group. This eliminates choice D. Cyclohexanol would have five unique hydrogens with a ratio of $1 : 1 : 4 : 4 : 2$. This ratio eliminates choice A. The compound 2-methylcyclopentanol would have seven unique hydrogens with a ratio of $3 : 2 : 2 : 1 : 1 : 1 : 2$. This eliminates choice C. Only choice **B** has four unique hydrogens in its ^{1}H NMR spectrum. The structure and corresponding peaks are shown below.

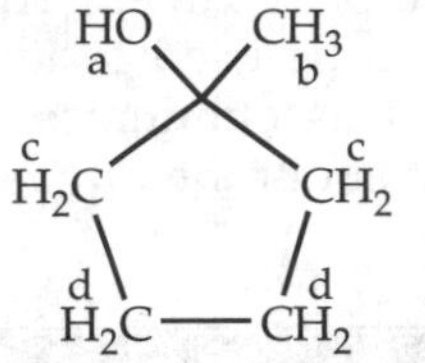

a: 4.3 ppm 1H broad
b: 1.1 ppm 3H (singlet)
c: 1.3 ppm 4H (triplet)
d: 1.0 ppm 4H (triplet)

25.   **Choice B is the best answer.** An ethyl ketone has an isolated CH_2CH_3 group adjacent to the carbonyl. The CH_2 group manifests itself as a 2H quartet between 2.0 and 2.5 ppm and the CH_3 group manifests itself as a 3H triplet between 1.0 and 1.3 ppm. Answer choice **B** corresponds to this combination for the isolated ethyl group.

26.   **Choice D is the best answer.** No broad IR absorbance between 2500 cm^{-1} and 3000 cm^{-1} indicates that the compound does not contain a carboxylic acid O-H bond in its structure. This eliminates choices A, B, and C, and makes choice **D** the best answer. A lactone is a cyclic ester which has a ring and a carbonyl C=O. This would result in two oxygens and two units of unsaturation, so choice A is valid. An ester has two oxygens and at least one unit of unsaturation. The other unit of unsaturation can be used as a ring or π-bond, so choice B is possible. An alkene ether contains at least one oxygen and one unit of unsaturation. This is possible, because the alkene structure has not exceeded the number of oxygens and units of unsaturation.

27.   **Choice B is the best answer.** Choices C and D only have three unique hydrogens and the spectrum shows four signals. Choices C and D are eliminated. The key difference between the remaining choices is the presence of a methoxy group. The methoxy protons of an ester show an absorbance in the ^{1}H NMR around 3.5 to 4.0 ppm. This makes choice **B** the best answer.

28.   **Choice B is the best answer.** An amide hydrogen is mildly acidic due to resonance of nitrogen with the carbonyl oxygen. When a strong base is added to an amide, the H on nitrogen can be removed. If the anion is placed in deuterated water, then it can remove deuterium from *heavy* water to form a deuterium-labeled amide. Deuterium (^{2}H) does not appear in the ^{1}H NMR, so the peak for the H on nitrogen will disappear, making choice **B** the best answer.

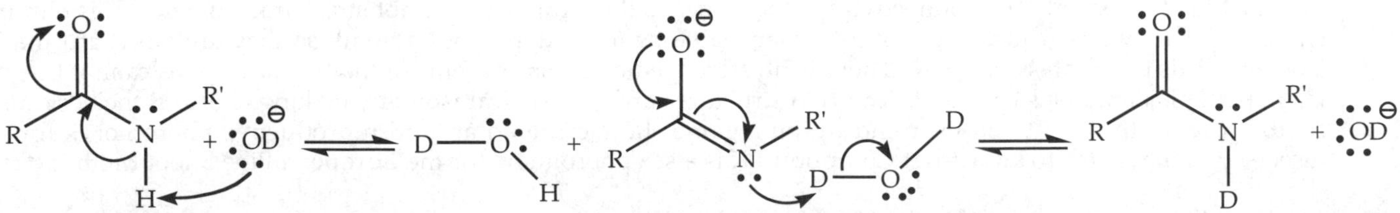

29.   **Choice A is the best answer.** The bulkiest of the three groups is the ethyl group, so the molecule will assume a chair confirmation with the ethyl group in an equatorial alignment in its most stable conformation. This eliminates choice D. This forces the hydroxyl group (which is on the same carbon as the ethyl group) to align in axial orientation. This eliminates choice C. The cyano group is on carbon four and is trans to the ethyl group, so its orientation will be by default relative to the ethyl group. Groups that are trans to one another on carbons 1 and 4 are either both axial or both equatorial. Because the ethyl aligns in an equatorial fashion, the cyano group must do so as well, making choice **A** the best answer.

30. **Choice C is the best answer.** At 50°C, The cyclohexane ring system has enough ambient energy to undergo rapid ring flipping. This results in Hs on the same carbon being equivalent to one another. This means that there are four unique types of hydrogens. The best answer is choice **C**. You may have thought that there are six unique hydrogens, which if the ring flip is slow enough would have been the case, but luckily it wasn't an answer choice. The four unique hydrogens are shown below.

31. **Choice B is the best answer.** The Grignard reaction converts the ketone into an alcohol by adding an ethyl group. The new H of the hydroxyl group will add a broad signal to the ^{1}H NMR spectrum. In addition to the hydroxyl group, there is now a CH_2CH_3 group, which introduces two more unique hydrogens onto the molecule. In all, there will be three new types of hydrogens, so there will be three new signals in the 1H NMR following the reaction. The best answer is choice **B**.

32. **Choice C is the best answer.** In organic chemistry, we use UV-visible spectroscopy to identify the presence of π-bonds within a molecule. Isolated π-bonds are found around 180 nm, depending on the substitution and surrounding groups. Carbonyls have a small secondary absorbance around 270 nm for the transition between the non-bonding energy level and the anti-bonding energy level, but we generally consider just one absorbance for the carbonyl group. Compound K has a ketone functionality (which will have a UV absorbance) as well as a cyano group (triple bond between C and N) which will also have a UV absorbance. The compound has two functional groups that absorb light in the UV range, so choice **C** is the best answer.

33. **Choice D is the best answer.** Cyano groups have no hydrogens, so there will be no gain of signals in the ^{1}H NMR spectra of any kind. This eliminates choices A and B. An IR absorbance around 1719 cm^{-1} indicates the presence of a carbonyl group, not a cyano group, which eliminates choice C. By default, choice **D** is the best answer. A triple bond is stronger than a double bond, so it requires more energy to stretch it. This results in a higher energy absorbance for a triple bond than a double bond. Given that carbon-based double bonds fall in the range of 1600-1740 cm^{-1} for compounds from alkenes to carbonyls, it should seem feasible that a triple bond could be in the neighborhood of 2200 cm^{-1}.

Questions 34 - 37 **Not Based on a Descriptive Passage**

34. **Choice A is the best answer.** Conditioning may cause you to respond automatically that the best orientation is the one with the fewest repulsive interactions. This is often true, but it does not tell the entire story in this case. This can lead to a *repetition error*, so be careful not to blindly pick an answer because of repetition from previous questions. The most stable orientation can also be the result of the strongest attractive interactions. Hydrogen-bonding between the hydroxyl and amine groups occurs only from gauche orientation, where the two groups are close enough to bond. Hydrogen-bonding cannot occur between substituents with anti orientation. This makes choice **A** the best answer.

35. **Choice D is the best answer.** The methyl group has three hydrogens, so the signal for the methyl group on benzene must have a relative integration of 3. The signal for the methyl group on benzene cannot be either the signal at 7.25 ppm or the signal at 5.37 ppm, because neither of those peaks contains three hydrogens. This eliminates choices A and B. The alkoxy methyl group, bonded to an oxygen, is found farther downfield than the methyl group on benzene. Thus from the values on the spectra, the methyl on benzene (3H singlet) comes at 2.25 ppm., which is choice **D**.

36. **Choice A is the best answer.** Deuterium is "heavy hydrogen," where the nucleus has an extra neutron compared to standard hydrogen. This affects the nuclear spin in such a manner that a different energy (and thus a different frequency) is required to excite the deuterium nucleus to detectable levels than to excite the standard hydrogen nucleus. As a result, solvents that have been deuterated (solvents where ^{2}H has replaced ^{1}H) are not detected by the ^{1}H NMR. This makes choice **A** the best answer. Replacing hydrogens with deuteriums in the solvent will have no impact on the external magnetic field, so choices C and D should be eliminated. Nothing has been done to change carbon, so choice B is also one that should be eliminated quickly.

37. **Choice C is the best answer.** Para-methoxybenzaldehyde has a total of eight carbons in its structure, six of which have hydrogens. But the molecule contains a mirror plane that reflects two pairs of equivalent carbons that have equivalent hydrogens. Using symmetry, this means that there are only four unique hydrogens, so the best answer is four signals in the proton NMR, choice C. The structure is shown below:

38. **Choice A is the best answer.** Acetone contains one oxygen and three carbons, so choice B cannot be correct. The three remaining choices are four-carbon esters, so we need to delve into the NMR signals to determine the structure. Spectrum I contains a quartet (2H), a triplet (3H) (this combination is a dead give-away for an isolated ethyl group), and a singlet (3H) (a dead give-away for an isolated methyl group). This eliminates choice D. The big question here is whether the ethyl group or methyl group is singly bonded directly to the oxygen of the ester group (ethyl acetate has the ethyl group bonded to the oxygen.) Because the 2H quartet is so far downfield (at a higher shift value), the ethyl group must be attached to the oxygen and the methyl group to the carbonyl carbon. This makes the best choice an ethyl group on the two-carbon ester, whose common name is ethyl acetate. Choose A for best results. Methyl acetate (H_3CO-CO-CH_3) could have been eliminated, because it has no CH_2 group.

39. **Choice B is the best answer.** Splitting of an NMR signal is the result of coupling to the neighboring hydrogens, and there are two equivalent hydrogens on the adjacent carbon in the case of a triplet. The integral (quantity of hydrogens for the signal) has no effect on the shape of the signal, meaning that the peak shape does not tell you any information about the hydrogens of the signal, only about the neighboring hydrogens. This eliminates choices A and C. A triplet is therefore the result of neighboring a CH_2 group. This eliminates choice D and makes choice B the best answer. Choose B for a grade A, genuine, altogether correct, best answer.

40. **Choice B is the best answer.** Spectrum II contains a quartet (2H), a triplet (3H) (this combination is a dead give-away for an isolated ethyl group), and a singlet (3H) (a dead give-away for an isolated methyl group). Because the 3H singlet is found around 4.0 ppm, the methyl group is bonded to the oxygen. This makes the best choice a methyl group on a three-carbon ester. Choose B for the happiness of another correct answer. The drawing below lists how the name and structure are determined for the compound.

Nomenclature rules state that the alkyl group on oxygen is named first, followed by the ester chain. This makes this compound methyl propanoate.

41. **Choice A is the best answer.** A carboxylic acid has one proton that forms a broad peak between 10 ppm and 12 ppm in the ^{1}H NMR. The hydrogen in question is the acidic proton of the carboxylic acid. Because there is only one proton, the peak between 10 ppm and 12 ppm has an integration value of one hydrogen, so choices C and D are eliminated. An ester has an alkyl group attached to the noncarbonyl oxygen of the ester. Protons on the first carbon from the oxygen have a peak between 3.5 ppm and 4.0 ppm. This eliminates choice B, leaving only choice A as the possible answer. The peak between 2.0 ppm and 2.5 ppm is the result of alpha hydrogens, which are present in both an ester and a carboxylic acid. This means that a peak between 2.0 ppm and 2.5 ppm cannot be used to distinguish an ester from a carboxylic acid. The best answer is choice A.

42. **Choice C is the best answer.** This is one of the NMR values that you should know. A signal (or peak) in the neighborhood of 7 ppm in ^{1}H NMR is indicative of hydrogens on an aromatic ring. This means that benzene hydrogens are observed around 7 ppm. Pick choice C, to score big!

43. **Choice B is the best answer.** 4-Heptanone is a seven-carbon ketone with the carbonyl directly in the middle. The structure is symmetric, so there are many equivalent carbons and hydrogens. There are four unique carbons, of which three contain hydrogens. This results in three signals in the ^{1}H NMR for 4-heptanone. The best answer is choice **B**.

---

44. **Choice D is the best answer.** The question here is not what type of bond is causing the shift, because all four of the answer choices contain a C-O bond, which is responsible for causing the absorbance at 1033 cm^{-1}. The question is: "What type of molecule is Compound T?" Because of the broad IR absorbance at 3350 cm^{-1}, the compound has an O-H bond that undergoes H-bonding, so Compound T must be an alcohol. The only possible answer is therefore choice **D**. Choices B and C should be eliminated, because the passage states there is no carbonyl present in Compound T. Choice A can be eliminated, because ethers exhibit no hydrogen-bonding with themselves, although they have lone pairs to share.

45. **Choice C is the best answer.** The passage tells us that an absorbance at 2116 cm^{-1} is indicative of a triple bond, which implies that the compound is either an alkyne or a nitrile. The passage tells us that there is not a nitrogen atom in the compound, so by default the compound must be an alkyne. If they didn't tell you the absorbance was associated with a carbon-carbon triple bond, the question would have been harder. You could deduce the IR absorbance value for an alkyne knowing that a C-C bond has an IR absorbance between 1100 cm^{-1} and 1300 cm^{-1}, and that a C=C bond has an IR absorbance between 1620 cm^{-1} and 1680 cm^{-1}. As the bond strength increases (or bond length decreases), the IR shift value increases. Choice **C** is the best answer.

46. **Choice C is the best answer.** This question requires several pieces of spectral data. From the broad IR absorbance at 3350 cm^{-1}, we know that there is an alcohol functional group present in Compound T. From the ^{1}H NMR data, we know that Compound T has four hydrogen atoms. From the parent ion peak in the mass spectrometry data, we know the compound has a molecular mass of 56 amu, of which 20 amu is due to the one oxygen and four hydrogens. This leaves 36 amu to be due to carbon, so the structure must contain only three carbons. The molecular formula is C_3H_4O. The formula involves multiplying the number of carbons by two, subtracting the number of hydrogens, adding 2, and then dividing that sum by two. As a result we get two units of unsaturation, making choice **C** the best answer. You might also know that for three carbons, the maximum number of hydrogens is eight, so in C_3H_4O there are four less hydrogens than maximum, which equates to two units of unsaturation.

47. **Choice D is the best answer.** Two nonequivalent hydrogen groups have different shift values, so choice A is eliminated. Choices B and C are the same answer, so they should both be eliminated. This leaves only choice **D** as the best answer. When hydrogens are coupled to one another, they have the same coupling constants (J-values). This makes choice **D** the best answer.

48. **Choice A is the best answer.** From the ^{1}H NMR data, we know that Compound T has four hydrogen atoms. All of the choices have four hydrogens, so that information didn't help. From the broad IR absorbance at 3350 cm^{-1}, we know that there is an alcohol functional group. This eliminates choices B and D. From the parent ion peak in the mass spectrometry data, we know the compound has a molecular mass of 56 grams/mole. Choice **A** has a molecular formula of C_3H_4O while choice C has a molecular formula of C_4H_4O. Choice C has a molecular mass of 68 grams/mole, so it is eliminated. The only choice that fits the molecular mass and contains a hydroxyl group is choice **A**. Once this question is resolved, it can help to solve some of the other questions. This happens often on the MCAT.

---

49. **Choice C is the best answer.** When using ^{1}H NMR spectra to distinguish between three different compounds, you want only the signals from the compound to vary between the spectra. The three separate ^{1}H NMR spectra are to be compared to determine the compounds in solution. It is important that nothing varies between samples, so the same solvent should be used in each case. Any impurity peak would be common to all of the spectra and thus could be eliminated. This makes choice **C** the best answer. A common solvent has no effect on the pH or the behavior of a protic species in the ^{1}H NMR. Although ^{1}H NMR invokes an external magnetic field, the solvent has no bearing on that field, so choice A is a poor answer.

50. **Choice D is the best answer.** The only single bond about which rotation is not possible is a single bond between two atoms in a cyclic compound. The only cyclic compound of the answer choices is methylcyclopentane, choice **D**. The best answer is therefore choice **D**. One item of notable interest is that both π-bonds and rings lower the entropy of a compound by lowering its degrees of freedom (i.e., its ability to rotate freely).

51. **Choice B is the best answer.** The compound in the question has two nonequivalent vinylic Hs. The 1H peaks (the vinylic hydrogens) in the spectrum fall between 4.88 and 5.37 ppm, implying that the hydrogens on an alkene are found in this range. Hydrogens on an alkene are referred to as vinylic hydrogens. This means that vinylic hydrogens are found in the range of 4.5 ppm to 5.5 ppm. This makes choice **B** the best answer.

52. **Choice C is the best answer.** Following dehydration of an alcohol group and a carboxylic acid, an ester is formed. In this case, it's a cyclic ester, which is known as a *lactam*. The structure of the resulting lactam is shown below.

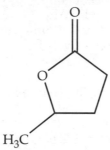

The compound has a carbonyl group, so it will be UV active. A peak around 260 nm is feasible for the nb-to-π* transition in a carbonyl group, so choice A is eliminated. The methyl group is next to a CH group, so there will be a 3H doublet in the ^{1}H NMR spectrum, but because the methyl group is on a carbon, it will be around 1ppm, not 3.5 ppm. A signal around 3.5 ppm would be attributed to an alkoxy group. A 3H doublet around 3.49 ppm is not observed, which makes choice **B** the best answer. An IR absorbance around 1682 cm^{-1} indicates a carbonyl group with some conjugation, which fits with an ester. Choice C is eliminated. The molecular formula of the compound is $C_5H_8O_2$, which results in a molecular mass of 100 grams/mole. A parent ion peak at 100 amu is expected, eliminating choice D. Choice **B** is the only choice that does not fit the structure.

Phase III Homework for Structure Elucidation

Structure Elucidation Phase III Scoring Scale

Raw Score	MCAT Score
25 - 28	13 - 15
19 - 24	10 - 12
14 - 18	7 - 9
10 - 13	4 - 6
1 - 9	1 - 3

Cyclohexane is not a planar molecule, but in its most stable conformation, four of the six carbons that make up the ring are coplanar. Studies using ^1H NMR and X-ray crystallography demonstrate that the most stable conformation of the molecule has carbon-carbon-carbon bond angles of approximately 107.5° and 111° in the ring and that there are two types of hydrogens present, *axial* and *equatorial*. The axial hydrogens are bonded directly above and directly below the ring carbons. The equatorial hydrogens lie away from the cyclohexane ring.

A low-temperature ^1H NMR study was conducted to determine the equilibrium constant for the conversion from diaxial conformation to the diequatorial conformation for 1,2-dimethyl-cyclohexane by way of a ring-flip process ($K_{eq-1,2}$). This value is comparable to the equilibrium constant for conversion from the diaxial to the diequatorial conformations of 1,4-dimethylcyclohexane by way of a ring-flip process ($K_{eq-1,4}$), given that they are both *trans*-substituted cyclohexanes. The difference between their equilibrium constants is attributed to the gauche and anti orientations possible with the methyl substituents at the 1,2 positions. Studies have shown that larger substituents prefer the equatorial orientation of the so-called *chair* conformation. Figure 1 summarizes the findings of the study.

CH$_3$ ⇌ H$_3$C

$K_{eq} = 4.31$

CH$_3$

$K_{eq} \neq 4.31$

Figure 1. Ring-flipping of *trans*-dimethylcyclohexane

The values for the equilibrium constants can be applied to determine the relative steric hindrance of one substituent compared to another. A bulkier group exhibits greater steric hindrance, so the equilibrium lies more towards the more stable of the two possible chair confirmations. Hence, a greater equilibrium constant implies that there is a greater degree of steric hindrance in the less stable conformation.

1. Which of the following is the most stable orientation of a substituent on a cyclohexane molecule?

   A. Axial orientation of a chair conformation
   B. Equatorial orientation of a chair conformation
   C. Bridge orientation of a boat conformation
   D. Oar orientation of a boat conformation

2. A carbon-deuterium bond is shorter than a carbon-hydrogen bond. Using this idea, how many deuterium atoms assume axial orientation in the most stable conformation of the following molecule?

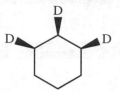

   A. 0
   B. 1
   C. 2
   D. 3

3. What is the value of $K_{eq-1,4}$ for the conversion of *trans*-1,4-dimethylcyclohexane from its diaxial conformation to its diequatorial conformation?

   A. 0.0029
   B. 2.16
   C. 4.31
   D. 345

4. *Cis*-1,4-dimethylcyclohexane, in its most stable chair conformation, CANNOT have which of these interactions?

   A. CH$_3$/H gauche
   B. CH$_3$/H anti
   C. CH$_3$/CH$_3$ gauche
   D. H/H anti

5. Which of the following accurately describes the value of K_{eq} for the conversion from one chair conformation to the other chair conformation for the compound *cis*-1,2-dimethylcyclohexane?

   A. Less than or equal to 0
   B. Greater than 0 and less than 1
   C. Equal to 1
   D. Greater than 1

6. The value of K_{eq} for the conversion of *cis*-1,3-dimethylcyclohexane from its diaxial conformation to its diequatorial conformation is:

   A. less than 0.22.
   B. between 0.22 and 1.
   C. between 1 and 4.31.
   D. greater than 4.31.

 GO ON TO THE NEXT PAGE

Passage II (Questions 7 - 11)

Alkanes are hydrocarbons that contain all sigma bonds. Sigma bonds have linear electron density (electron density that is localized between the two nuclei of the bonding atoms). This allows for free rotation about a sigma bond. Rotation about sigma bonds is continually occurring at temperatures above absolute zero, although the rate of the rotation varies. However, the rotation does not necessarily complete a full 360° cycle about the sigma bond.

Some conformations encountered during rotation are of high energy (due to steric repulsion) and others are of low energy (due to minimal steric interactions). The most stable conformation occurs when the largest groups are as far apart as possible. When two groups are as far apart as possible, the conformation is referred to as *staggered*, and the bulkiest substituents are said to be *anti* to one another. The least stable conformation occurs when the largest groups interfere with one another. This is known as *fully eclipsed*. Drawn in Figure 1 is an energy diagram for the counterclockwise rotation about the C_2-C_3 bond for R-2-methyl-1-butanol.

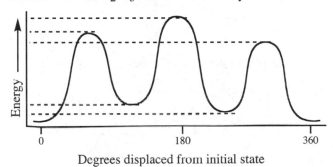

Degrees displaced from initial state

Figure 1. Energy during rotation about the C_2-C_3 bond

The three apexes occurring at 60°, 180° and 300° on the graph are not of equal energy. In 2-methyl-1-butanol, carbon 2 is a stereocenter. Because of this asymmetry, none of the eclipsed or staggered conformations are equal in energy. All visual projections show asymmetric steric interactions. Although the molecule is constantly rotating about its bonds, it assumes its most stable conformation most of the time.

7. Which of the following structures represents the molecule at the 240° point on the graph in Figure 1?

A.

H₃C, CH₃
H‖‖‖ ‖‖‖H
H CH₂OH

B.

H₃C, CH₃
H‖‖‖ ‖‖‖CH₂OH
H H

C.

H₃C, CH₂OH
H‖‖‖ ‖H
H CH₃

D.

H₃C, H
H‖‖‖ ‖‖CH₂OH
H CH₃

8. Which of the following structures represents the molecule at the 330° point on the graph in Figure 1?

A.

H₃C CH₃
H—
H H
CH₂OH

B.

H₃C CH₃
—H
H H
HOH₂C

C.

H₃C CH₂OH
H—
H H
CH₃

D.

HOH₂C CH₃
—H
H H
H₃C

9. The 60° point on the graph in Figure 1 represents the structure when it is:

A. eclipsed and the methyl substituent on carbon-2 interferes with carbon-4.

B. eclipsed and carbon-1 interferes with carbon-4.

C. staggered and the methyl substituent on carbon-2 interferes with carbon-4.

D. staggered and carbon-1 interferes with carbon-4.

10. The strongest hydrogen bond occurs between which of the following?

A. A lone pair on nitrogen bonded to an H on nitrogen

B. A lone pair on oxygen bonded to an H on nitrogen

C. A lone pair on oxygen bonded to an H on oxygen

D. A lone pair on nitrogen bonded to an H on oxygen

11. The reason there is no rotation diagram for *trans*-2-butene is that:

A. gauche is not favorable for alkenes.

B. anti is not favorable for alkenes.

C. steric hindrance does not affect alkenes.

D. rotation about a π-bond requires energy in excess of room temperature.

 GO ON TO THE NEXT PAGE

An unknown compound, labeled Compound B, has only two singlets in its proton magnetic resonance spectrum. One shows a shift of δ 1.42 ppm and the other shows a shift of δ 1.96 ppm, with relative intensities (from the integration of the ^{1}H NMR spectrum) of 3 : 1. Figure 1 shows the ^{1}H NMR spectrum of Compound B.

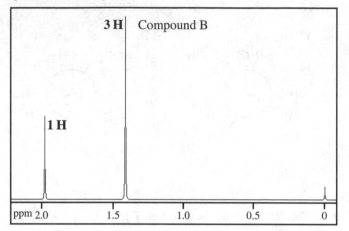

Figure 1. ^{1}H NMR spectrum of Compound B

There are four nonequivalent carbons in the compound, one of which is a quaternary carbon according to ^{13}C NMR data. The important bands in the infrared spectrum of Compound B are found at 1738 cm^{-1}, 1256 cm^{-1}, and 1173 cm^{-1}. The band at 1738 cm^{-1} is attributed to the stretching of a carbonyl bond. Elemental analysis of Compound B shows that it contains two oxygen atoms. The spectral data, in conjunction with mass percent values from elemental analysis, can be combined to determine the structure of Compound B. Overlapping spectral data, such as an IR absorbance at 1738 cm^{-1} and a UV absorbance at 271 nm can be used to verify aspects of the structure.

12. The shift at 1738 cm^{-1} in the IR can be attributed to the C=O of:

  A. an aldehyde.
  B. a carboxylic acid.
  C. an ester.
  D. a ketone.

13. The *molecular* ratio of hydrogens in the structure is which of the following?

  A. 3 : 1
  B. 6 : 2
  C. 9 : 3
  D. 12 : 4

14. The ^{1}H NMR peak at 1.96 ppm can be attributed to a hydrogen bonded to a carbon:

  A. adjacent to a C=O bond.
  B. adjacent to a C-O bond.
  C. of a C-O bond.
  D. of a C=O bond.

15. In ^{1}H NMR, a singlet is explained as the evidence of hydrogens of the signal being coupled to:

  A. equivalent hydrogens on all adjacent carbons.
  B. non-equivalent hydrogens on all adjacent carbons.
  C. only one hydrogen on an adjacent carbon.
  D. no hydrogens, because there are no hydrogens on any of the adjacent carbons.

16. Which of the following structures is Compound B?

  A.

  B.

  C.

  D.

A chemist sets out to determine the structural identity for three structural isomers with a molecular formula of $C_5H_{10}O$. Using data from infrared spectroscopy, ^1H NMR spectroscopy, ultraviolet-visible spectroscopy, and mass spectroscopy, she sets out to identify each compound. The following spectral data are observed for three separate compounds, labeled Compound I, Compound II and Compound III.

Compound I:

IR:	1714 cm^{-1}
^1H NMR:	2.32 ppm (triplet, 2H), 2.08 ppm (singlet, 3H), 1.12 ppm (multiplet, 2H), 0.96 ppm (triplet, 3H)
UV-Visible:	268 nm and 189 nm

Compound II:

IR:	3428 cm^{-1} (broad)
^1H NMR:	3.71 ppm (multiplet, 1H), 1.88 ppm (broad, 1H), 1.33 ppm (multiplet, 4H), 1.14 ppm (triplet, 4H)
UV-Visible:	No intense peaks above 180 nm

Compound III:

IR:	1282 cm^{-1}
^1H NMR:	3.58 ppm (triplet, 4H), 1.28 ppm (multiplet, 4H), 0.92 ppm (multiplet, 2H)
UV-Visible:	No intense peaks above 180 nm

All ^1H NMR spectra are obtained using deuterated chloroform as solvent. The mass spectrometer shows an intense peak at 86 amu for all three isomers, confirming their molecular formula. Compound I fragmented more than Compounds II and III in mass spectrometry. Elemental analysis confirms that carbon and hydrogen are not the only atoms present.

17. Compound II is what type of compound?

- **A.** An alcohol
- **B.** An ether
- **C.** A ketone
- **D.** An alkene

18. The integration of a signal in a proton NMR is useful for determining the:

- **A.** local magnetic field experienced by a hydrogen.
- **B.** neighboring hydrogen atoms.
- **C.** presence of an atom other than hydrogen or carbon.
- **D.** relative quantities of unique hydrogens in the compound.

19. What is the IUPAC name for Compound I?

- **A.** Pentanal
- **B.** 2-Pentanone
- **C.** 3-Pentanone
- **D.** 3-Methylbutanone

20. Which of the following is NOT a valid conclusion from the spectral data for Compound III?

- **A.** The absence of a broad signal in the ^1H NMR means the compound cannot be an alcohol.
- **B.** The absorbance around 1700 cm^{-1} in IR spectroscopy means the compound cannot be a carbonyl.
- **C.** The absence of an absorbance above 180 nm confirms that the structure must contain a ring for its unit of unsaturation.
- **D.** The large number of signals, with none of them being broad, in the ^1H NMR means the compound is an ether with little symmetry.

21. What can be concluded about the three compounds using only the data obtained from UV-visible spectroscopy?

- **A.** Compound I is a conjugated diene.
- **B.** Compounds II and III are carbonyl compounds.
- **C.** Compound I is a ketone.
- **D.** There is no π-bond present in Compounds I and II.

NMR is a valuable tool used to deduce the structure of unknown organic compounds. It helps one distinguish between structural features of two similar compounds. The three useful components of the spectral data for extracting structural information are the shift value (δ, measured in ppm), the coupling and coupling constants (peak shape), and the integral (the area under the curve of a signal).

From the shift value, information about the electronegativity of adjacent atoms may be obtained. Coupling is used to determine the number of neighboring hydrogens on any atoms bonded to the atom bound to the hydrogens producing the signal. The integral is directly proportional to the number of hydrogens in the compound, so it cs used to find the ratios of hydrogens in the compound. Figure 1 and Figure 2 show the ^{1}H NMR spectra for two simple organic structures, Compound A and Compound B.

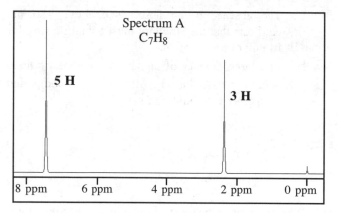

Figure 1 ^{1}H NMR spectrum of Compound A

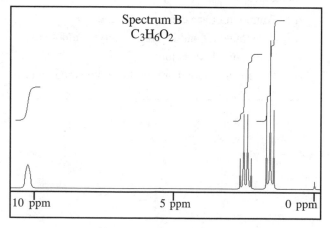

Figure 2 ^{1}H NMR spectrum of Compound B

Structures can often be deduced using only some of the ^{1}H NMR information, such as the coupling information and the integration. Often, the coupling information is the most helpful of all the data. The coupling constants can give information about the connectivity of the structure, as well as hints about the three-dimensional orientation of atoms within the molecule.

22. Which of the following is the IUPAC name for the compound represented by Spectrum A?

A. Phenylmethane

B. Toluene

C. Methylbenzene

D. Orthoxylene

23. In Spectrum B, what is the ratio of the areas under the three signals?

A. 3 : 2 : 3

B. 1 : 1 : 4

C. 2 : 3 : 5

D. 1 : 2 : 3

24. What signals are expected for the ^{1}H NMR spectrum of 2-bromopropane?

A. A 6H sextet and a 1H singlet

B. A 1H sextet and a 6H singlet

C. A 6H septet and a 1H doublet

D. A 1H septet and a 6H doublet

25. Which of the following compounds would NOT have a quartet in its proton NMR spectrum?

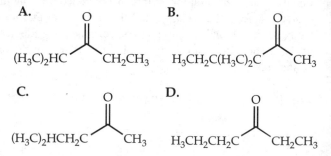

26. Which of the following compounds would NOT have a doublet in its proton NMR spectrum?

A. 2-methyl-1-pentanol

B. 3-methyl-1-pentanol

C. 4-methyl-1-pentanol

D. All isomers of methyl-1-pentanol have doublets in their proton NMR spectrum.

27. The iodoform test involves the addition of hydroxide anion and iodine to a carbonyl compound. If a carbon contains three alpha hydrogens, then the iodine will react with the carbonyl compound to yield a yellow precipitate. A compound with a positive iodoform test would likely have which of the following signals in its proton NMR?

   A. Singlet at 2.0 - 2.5 ppm
   B. Doublet at 3.5 - 4.0 ppm
   C. Triplet at 2.0 - 2.5 ppm
   D. Septet at 3.5 - 4.0 ppm

28. The broadness of the signal around 10 ppm in Spectrum B is explained as a signal caused by hydrogens:

   A. on a carbon involved in resonance.
   B. coupled to more than eight hydrogens.
   C. on a carbon involved in hydrogen bonding.
   D. involved in hydrogen bonding.

YOU ARE DONE.

Answers to Structure Elucidation Phase III Homework

1.	B	2.	C	3.	D	4.	C	5.	C	6.	D	7.	C	8.	A	9.	A	10.	D
11.	D	12.	C	13.	C	14.	A	15.	D	16.	D	17.	A	18.	D	19.	B	20.	D
21.	C	22.	C	23.	D	24.	D	25.	C	26.	D	27.	A	28.	D				

Passage I (Questions 1 - 6)   **Chair Conformation**

1. **Choice B is the best answer.** The most stable form of the cyclohexane ring is the chair conformation. The most stable position on the chair form is referred to as *equatorial*. Combine these two facts and the result is choice **B**. The boat conformation is an unstable transition state structure for cyclohexane that exists for a fleeting moment as the structure flips from one chair conformation into the other. There is no such thing as the oar orientation for a substituent.

2. **Choice C is the best answer.** Because the three deuterium atoms are cis with respect to one another, they cannot all be axial nor all be equatorial. The most stable orientation (most stable chair confirmation) has as many deuterium atoms with axial orientation as possible. However, because the deuterium atoms are all mutually cis to one another, the structure must have at least one deuterium with equatorial orientation. The best choice (and consequently your choice) is **C**, which is drawn below.

2 axial deuteriums and 1 equatorial deuterium   1 axial deuterium and 2 equatorial deuteriums

3. **Choice D is the best answer.** As the reaction is written, the value of $K_{eq-1,4}$ must be greater than 1, because the product is more stable than the reactant. The reaction is favorable in the forward direction as written. This eliminates choice A, a value less than 1.

    The question now focuses on whether the conformational change with $K_{eq-1,4}$ is more favorable than the conformational change with $K_{eq-1,2}$, because the value of $K_{eq-1,2}$ is 4.31. In the case of the 1,2-disubstituted compound, there are both diequatorial versus diaxial interactions as well as gauche versus anti interactions to consider. The diequatorial orientation is better than the diaxial orientation, because with diaxial there are eclipsed interactions with the axial hydrogens. However, the anti orientation of the methyl groups is better than the gauche orientation.

    Overall, diequatorial preference over diaxial is a more important factor than a preference for gauche over anti, so the value of $K_{eq-1,2}$ is greater than 1. The 1,4-disubstituted compound has no gauche-versus-anti interactions between the methyl groups to consider, because the carbons are far apart. Thus, the conformational preference is purely an effect of the diequatorial orientation being preferred over the diaxial orientation. This makes the value of $K_{eq-1,4}$ greater than the value of $K_{eq-1,2}$, making choice **D** the best answer. Drawn below is one picture's worth (approximately equal to 1000 words worth) of explanation.

Methyl groups are apart from one another when diaxial.   Methyl groups are close to one another when diequatorial.   Methyl groups collide with axial Hs when diaxial.   Methyl groups do not collide with one another when diequatorial.

1,2-diaxial orientation results in anti orientation, while 1,2-dieqatorial orientation results in gauche orientation. The equilibrium still favors product (the right), but not as much as the 1,4-equilibrium does.

1,4-diaxial orientation results in steric hindrance from diaxial interactions with hydrogens, while 1,4-diequatorial has no eclipsing steric hindrance. Equilibrium favors the products more than with 1,2.

4. **Choice C is the best answer.** In order for substituents to be gauche or anti to one another, they must be bonded to carbons that are connected to one another. In the case of 1-4-dimethylcyclohexane, the methyl groups are not bonded to adjacent carbons, so the two methyl groups cannot be gauche or anti to one another. This makes choice **C** correct. There are hydrogens on every carbon, so H can be gauche to methyl. For the H to be anti to a methyl, the methyl group must assume axial orientation. The only possible chair conformation of cis-1,4-dimethylcyclohexane has one methyl group axial and the other in an equatorial orientation. This makes choices A, B, and D valid.

5. **Choice C is the best answer.** Both of the chair conformations possible for cis-1,2-dimethylcyclohexane are equivalent in energy. In both of the chair conformations, one methyl substituent assumes axial orientation and the other methyl substituent assumes equatorial orientation. The equilibrium constant for the ring-flip process is equal to 1, because the energy level of the product is equal to the energy level of the reactant. This makes choice **C** correct. Do the correct thing and pick **C**. As a point of interest, the value of K_{eq} can never be less than or equal to 0 (products and reactants always have some positive quantity), so choice A is an absurd answer.

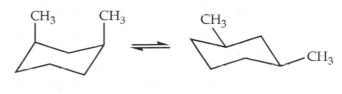

Both structures have one methyl equatorial and the other methyl axial

6. **Choice D is the best answer.** With cis-1,3-dimethylcyclohexane, the cis-1,3-diaxial interactions (steric repulsion) between the two methyl groups makes the diaxial orientation less stable than the trans-1,2-diaxial orientation. This decrease in stability in the conformation drawn on the reactant side results in a greater value for K_{eq} as written. This means that $K_{eq-1,3} > K_{eq-1,2}$, which is choice **D**.

| Methyl groups are apart from one another when diaxial. | Methyl groups are close to one another when diequatorial. | Methyl groups collide with one another when diaxial. | Methyl groups do not collide with one another when diequatorial. |

1,2-diaxial orientation results in anti orientation, while 1,2-dieqatorial orientation results in gauche orientation. The equilibrium still favors product (the right), but not as much as the 1,3-diaxial-to-diequatorial equilibrium does.

1,3-diaxial orientation results in increased steric hindrance. This has an effect on the equilibrium by shifting it heavily to the right. 1,3-diequatorial has no eclipsing steric hindrance between the methyls.

Passage II (Questions 7 - 11)   Rotational Energy Diagrams

7. **Choice C is the best answer.** Because 240° is at the nadir (low point) of the graph in Figure 1, it correlates with the staggered structure (given that the staggered structure is more stable than the eclipsed structure. This eliminates choices A and B, which are in the eclipsed conformation. Choosing between the remaining structures depnds on the stereochemistry and no the structural stability of the molecule. The compound has R stereochemistry at carbon two which makes the correct answer choice **C** and eliminates choice D, which has S stereochemistry.

8. **Choice A is the best answer.** The 330° point on the graph is near (30° away from) the most stable conformation (which has anti orientation of the CH_2OH group and the CH_3 group of carbon 4). This eliminates choices C and D. Because of R stereochemistry, the correct choice is **A**. Stereochemistry is difficult to see in the Newman projection and can be seen more easily in other projections. Drawn below is a way to convert the Newman projection back to the stick-wedge drawing and a subsequent evaluation of stereochemistry.

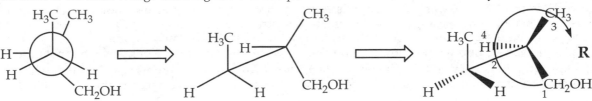

9. **Choice A is the best answer.** Because 60° is at a local apex (high point) of the graph in Figure 1, it correlates with an eclipsed structure. This eliminates choices C and D, which have the compound in its staggered confirmation. The 60° point is not the highest point on the energy diagram, so it does not involve the largest groups (carbon 1 and carbon 4) interfering with one another. This eliminates choice B. The best answer is choice **A**, with the two methyl groups eclipsing one another.

10. **Choice D is the best answer.** Hydrogen bonds have some acid-base character to them, so the most favorable proton transfer reaction is a good indicator of the strongest hydrogen bond. Because the amine is more basic than the hydroxyl group, the nitrogen is the lone pair donor. Likewise, the hydroxyl is more acidic than the amine, so the hydroxyl is the hydrogen donor. This makes choice **D** correct.

11. **Choice D is the best answer.** Because of the planar nature of electron density in a π-bond, rotation about a double bond requires that the π-bond be broken. This is not observed under thermal conditions. To convert a cis π-bond into a trans π-bond, UV light is needed. Pick **D** to tally big points. The drawing below shows that a 90° rotation about the C—C breaks the π-bond. It requires substantial energy to break a π-bond.

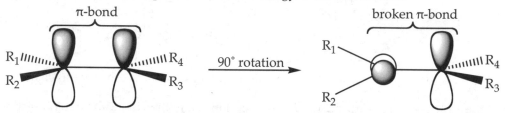

12. **Choice C is the best answer.** Because the compound contains two oxygen atoms, choice A (an aldehyde) and choice D (a ketone) are both eliminated. There is no absorbance in the IR spectrum that is indicative of an O-H bond, so the compound is not a carboxylic acid. This eliminates choice B. The only choice left is an ester, choice **C**. You don't need to memorize exact IR values, but you should know that C=O bonds are around 1700 cm^{-1}.

13. **Choice C is the best answer.** The compound has four equivalent carbons, one of which is a carbonyl, one of which is quaternary, and two of which have Hs attached. This tells us that the structure cannot simply have a CH group and CH$_3$ group, because the connectivity won't work. In order for there to be only one hydrogen on a carbon, there must be other groups attached to that carbon, which can't be the case with so few equivalent carbons in the compound. The molecular ratio of hydrogens cannot be 3:1, so choice A is eliminated. The key feature in the ^{1}H NMR spectrum are the singlets, implying that the hydrogens are all isolated with no coupling to neighbors. If the ratio were 6:2, then the structure would need to have a CH$_2$ group and two equivalent CH$_3$ groups, which again would not work out in terms of connectivity with a quaternary carbon and a carbonyl carbon as the only remaining groups. This eliminates choice B. A 9:3 ratio would likely be an isolated CH$_3$ group and three equivalent CH$_3$ groups, which is possible if the three equivalent CH$_3$ groups are all bonded to the quaternary carbon, which is in turn bonded to the carbonyl carbon. That would lead to a 3H singlet and a 9H singlet, which reduces to a 3:1 ratio in the ^{1}H NMR. Choice **C** looks to be the only possible choice. Choice D can't work, because getting 12 equivalent Hs would not be possible with so few equivalent carbons. Choose **C** for best results.

14. **Choice A is the best answer.** The shift value for hydrogens on an alpha carbon (the carbon adjacent to a carbonyl) is found to be between 2.0 ppm. and 2.5 ppm. The alpha hydrogens are described in the answer choices as hydrogens on a carbon adjacent to a carbonyl (C=O) bond. This is choice **A**; your choice for a question like this.

15. **Choice D is the best answer.** A singlet in a ^{1}H NMR spectrum occurs when there is an isolated hydrogen (or group of equivalent hydrogens), with no hydrogens on the neighboring atoms. This eliminates choices A, B, and C (which all described a scenario with neighboring Hs), and makes choice **D** the best answer.

16. **Choice D is the best answer.** Compounds A and C are eliminated, because they do not contain two oxygen atoms, as is stated in the passage. The remaining two structures, choices B and **D**, both would yield two singlets in a 9:3 ratio, so the best answer can only be deduced using the shift values. Choice B is eliminated, because the CH$_3$ of a methoxy group would show a shift value between 3.5 ppm and 4.0 ppm, which is not observed in the 1H NMR spectrum of Compound B. The peak for the lone methyl group is found near 2.0 ppm, which indicates that the methyl group is adjacent to the carbonyl (on the alpha carbon). The correct structure is choice **D**.

17. **Choice A is the best answer.** For Compound II, the absence of an IR absorbance between 1650 cm^{-1} and 1750 cm^{-1} supports the idea that it has no C=O group. This eliminates choice C. No IR absorbance between 1600 cm^{-1} and 1650 cm^{-1} confirms that there is no C=C double bond present. This eliminates choice D. The broad IR absorbance at 3428 cm^{-1} supports the idea that there is an O—H group present. This means that the compound is an alcohol, which makes choice **A** the best answer. There is one unit of unsaturation in the compound, which without having a π-bond present means that it must be the result of a ring. The presence of a broad peak in the ^{1}H NMR spectrum supports the idea that the compound is an alcohol, further eliminating choice B and confirming that choice **A** is the best answer. The ^{1}H NMR spectrum shows that there is great symmetry in the structure. The choices are either cyclopentanol or 2,3-dimethylcyclopropanol. The integral of the proton NMR says that there are mostly CH$_2$ groups present, which favors cyclopentanol over 2,3-dimethylcyclopropanol. Cyclopentanol is drawn below:

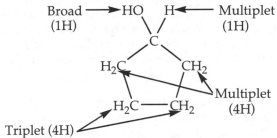

18. **Choice D is the best answer.** Integration is used to determine the relative quantity of hydrogens within a signal by looking at the area of the signal. Integration does not change with magnetic environment, so choice A is eliminated. The neighboring hydrogen atoms affect the splitting, not the integral, so choice B is eliminated. Integration does nothing to determine the presence of atoms other than hydrogen, so choice C is eliminated. The best answer is choice **D**.

19. **Choice B is the best answer.** Key features from each spectrum must be extracted. From the molecular formula, we know there is one unit of unsaturation and one oxygen. This means that the compound must contain either a ring, a C=C bond, or a C=O bond. All of the answer choices have a C=O bond with no ring in their structures, so we must use the spectroscopic data. The IR data show an absorbance at 1714 cm^{-1}. This means that the compound is a carbonyl, which does nothing to eliminate any choices. The ^{1}H NMR data shows no peak between 9 and 10 ppm, which means that the compound cannot be an aldehyde, thereby eliminating choice A. The ^{1}H NMR data shows a 3H singlet at 2.08 ppm, which means that the compound has an isolated methyl next to the carbonyl group, thereby eliminating choice C. The ratio of the hydrogen signals in the ^{1}H NMR (3 : 2 : 2 : 3) supports choice **B** and does not fit with choice D. The structure is shown below:

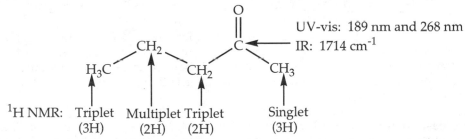

There can be no branching in the structure, because the proton NMR shows that the integral values are 3, 2, 2, 3. This implies that the structure is linear. Choice D would show Hs in a 3 : 1 : 6 ratio, because the methyl group and carbon 4 are equivalent. You'd get a 3H singlet around 2-2.5 ppm for the Hs on carbon-1, a septet around 2-2.5 ppm for the H on carbon-3, and a 6H doublet for the two equivalent methyl groups.

20. **Choice D is the best answer.** For Compound III, the absence of a broad peak in its ^{1}H NMR spectrum confirms that there is no alcohol in the compound. This makes choice A a valid statement, and thus the incorrect choice. The absence of an IR absorbance between 1650 cm^{-1} and 1750 cm^{-1} confirms there is no C=O present. This makes choice B a valid statement, which eliminates it. The absence of an absorbance above 180 nm in the UV-visible spectrum implies that there is no π-bond in the compound, confirming that the structure must be cyclic to account for the one unit of unsaturation. This makes choice C a valid statement, which eliminates it. The ^{1}H NMR shows very few signals (only three), which implies that there is great symmetry in the structure. It must be a symmetric, cyclic ether. This makes choice **D** an invalid statement, making it the best answer.

21. **Choice C is the best answer.** According to the data, only Compound I has a UV absorbance above 175 nm. This means that only Compound I has a π-bond. There is only one unit of unsaturation, so Compound I can have, at most, one π-bond. This means that Compound I cannot be a conjugated diene, which eliminates choice A. If it were a conjugated diene, there would be a UV absorbance above 200 nm for the π to π* transition. Compounds II and III cannot be carbonyl compounds, according to their UV data. A carbonyl group on the molecule would lead to a π-to-π* transition around 190 nm and an n-to-π* transition around 260 nm. This eliminates choice B. Because Compound I has two UV absorbances and only one π-bond, it must be a carbonyl species of some sort. While it is not possible to decide between an aldehyde and ketone based on this information, choice **C** is a solid answer. Because Compounds II and III show no UV absorbance above 175 nm, there is no π-bond present. However, choice D refers to Compounds I and II, not II and III, so choice D is eliminated. Choice **C** is the best answer.

---

22. **Choice C is the best answer.** Five hydrogens constituting a singlet with a shift value between 6.0 and 8.0 ppm indicates that the compound is a monosubstituted benzene. The three remaining hydrogens make up a methyl group. This now becomes a nomenclature question, rather than a spectroscopy question. The correct name for a methyl group attached to benzene is methylbenzene. The common name for methylbenzene is toluene. Choose **C** for optimal results.

23. **Choice D is the best answer.** The formula contains six hydrogens in all, so the sum of the ratio values must equal 6. The first peak is shortest, the middle peak is the second tallest, and the last peak is the tallest. This means that the values must be ascending. The only combination of ascending values adding to 6 is 1:2:3. Choice **D** is the best answer.

24. **Choice D is the best answer.** The compound 2-bromopropane has two unique types of hydrogens, so it has two peaks in its ^1H NMR spectrum. The two terminal methyl groups are equivalent, so they are seen as one signal with an integration of 6. The middle carbon (carbon 2) has one hydrogen, so it has a signal with an integration of 1. The peak shape is determined by adding 1 to the number of hydrogens on the adjacent carbons. The six equivalent hydrogens have one hydrogen neighbor, so there is a doublet of integration 6. The one hydrogen has six hydrogen neighbors, so there is a septet of integration 1. Choice **D** is the best answer.

25. **Choice C is the best answer.** A quartet is the result of the observed hydrogens being coupled to three equivalent hydrogens. This is often the result of hydrogens that are adjacent to a methyl group on one side and no other protons on the other. The quartet hydrogens are in bold face, and the neighboring three hydrogens are boxed in the drawing below. Choice **C** is the only structure that shows no quartet in its proton NMR spectrum.

A.   (H₃C)₂HC—C(=O)—CH₂CH₃   B.   H₃CH₂C(H₃C)₂C—C(=O)—CH₃   C.   (H₃C)₂HCH₂C—C(=O)—CH₃   D.   H₃CH₂CH₂C—C(=O)—CH₂CH₃

26. **Choice D is the best answer.** A doublet is the result of hydrogens on a carbon that neighbors a carbon with only one hydrogen attached (most easily recognized as a tertiary carbon). In each of the first three answer choices, the methyl group attached to the interior of the carbon chain is bonded to a carbon with only one hydrogen (a tertiary carbon), which results in every compound having a doublet with an integration of three hydrogens. This leaves choice **D** as the best answer.

27. **Choice A is the best answer.** A positive iodoform test, as stated in the question, is caused by a compound with three alpha hydrogens on one carbon. This means that the iodoform test is positive for a methyl ketone, which would have a CH₃ group adjacent to a carbonyl (there are no hydrogens on a carbonyl). With no hydrogens on the neighboring carbon (carbonyl), there is no coupling and thus a the peak is a singlet. Pick **A** for the pleasure of correctness. The iodoform test works by removing an alpha hydrogen to form an anion. The anion subsequently attacks iodine, adding an iodide to the alpha carbon. This is repeated two more times, until there are three iodides bonded to the alpha carbon. The CI₃ group is a great leaving group, and it forms a yellow, oily compound when protonated.

28. **Choice D is the best answer.** The hydrogen responsible for the broadness is the carboxylic acid proton. It is bonded to an oxygen, making choice A an incorrect answer. The coupling to eight or more other hydrogens would result in a multiplet made of many sharp peaks, not a broadened signal, which eliminates choice B. Choice C can be eliminated, because hydrogens on carbon do not form hydrogen bonds. The hydrogen forming the hydrogen bond in this molecule is bonded to oxygen. This makes choice **D** the best answer.

Stereochemistry

Organic Chemistry Chapter 3

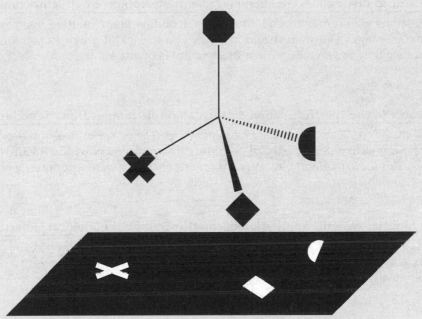

Fits the Template While its Enantiomer will not fit.

by Todd Bennett of

the Berkeley Review

Stereochemistry

Key objectives of this section

Be able to identify the absolute configuration of stereocenters within chiral molecules.

Questions will ask that you determine whether a stereogenic center is R (Latin, *rectus*) or S (Latin, *sinister*). Questions may present you with optical rotation data for a specific stereocenter and then ask you to make an educated guess about the optical rotation of a stereoisomer.

Be able to distinguish enantiomers from diastereomers by structure or physical properties.

Questions may center around differences in boiling point, melting point, or density between two stereoisomers. Questions could also ask you to look at a pair of stereoisomers and determine whether they are enantiomers or diastereomers of one another.

Be able to use specific rotation data to determine composition of a product mixture.

Questions could give you the enantiomeric excess or net optical rotation of a product mixture and ask you to determine the distribution of stereoisomers within the mixture. Questions could also ask you to explain why an enantiomeric excess or stereo-preference occurred in a reaction.

Be familiar with the application of chirality in typical biological molecules.

Passages often present biological molecules and discuss aspects of their chemistry. Questions may ask you to identify the specific chirality or generally describe why a certain stereoisomer is biologically active while its enantiomer is not active.

Be able to identify the favored type of nucleophilic substitution reaction for given conditions.

Passages may present multiple nucleophilic substitution reactions and have you distinguish the mechanism based on either the reaction conditions or the product distribution. Questions may ask about inversion of chirality versus the formation of a racemic product mixture.

Be able to recognize typical nucleophiles and leaving groups.

Passages on nucleophilic substitution could require that you be familiar with common examples of good nucleophiles and good leaving groups. You may be asked to determine the favorability of a substitution reaction or to explain why a leaving group must first be protonated to react.

Stereochemistry

Stereochemistry involves the asymmetry of a molecule. We can consider the asymmetry as a whole or the asymmetry about specific atoms in the molecule, most often carbon. If there is asymmetry within a molecular structure, the compound's reactivity, physical properties, and stability are all impacted. The study of stereochemistry has direct implications in the biological applications of molecules.

In this particular section we shall address the concept of configurational isomerism and the many different classifications of configurational isomers. As with all isomers, configurational isomers have the same atoms within the molecule, but they differ in some manner so that the molecules are not superimposable on one another. No matter how a compound is rotated or contorted, it is not superimposable on its configurational isomer. As a consequence of their different configurations, one configurational isomer may have the correct arrangement of atoms to offer minimal steric hindrance in a chemical reaction with another asymmetric molecule, while another configurational isomer proves to be too sterically hindered on one side to undergo reaction. This is frequently seen with enzymatic chemistry, where enzymes have several stereogenic centers and are highly specific about which configurational isomer can bind and undergo a reaction.

Configurational isomers can be categorized as either optical isomers or geometrical isomers. Optical isomers rotate plane-polarized light while geometrical isomers are structures with limited rotation. In addition to that categorization, configurational isomers can also be categorized as either enantiomers or diastereomers. Enantiomers are nonsuperimposable mirror images while diastereomers are nonsuperimposable structures that are not mirror images. The two categorizations are not mutually exclusive; meaning a pair of configurational isomers could be enantiomeric optical isomers, diastereomeric optical isomers, enantiomeric geometrical isomers, or diastereomeric geometrical isomers.

In this section we shall also address nucleophilic substitution. We will consider the two mechanisms for nucleophilic substitution: the S_N1-mechanism and the S_N2-mechanism. In a nucleophilic substitution reaction that proceeds by an S_N1-mechanism, the leaving group leaves to form a carbocation intermediate before the nucleophile attacks. An S_N1-reaction has a unimolecular rate-determining step. In a nucleophilic substitution reaction that proceeds by an S_N2-mechanism, the nucleophile attacks the electrophile from the opposite side of the leaving group and forces the leaving group off of the electrophile. An S_N2-reaction has only one step, a bimolecular step. We will compare and contrast the conditions and features of an S_N1-reaction with that of an S_N2-reaction to establish a set of criteria you can use when deciding which mechanism (S_N1 or S_N2) is applicable for a given nucleophilic substitution reaction.

We will consider the impact of stereochemistry on reactant interactions, transition state formation, and product distribution. We will present the basic tenant that if the reactants are optically active, then the product mixture is likely optically active, and at the very least enantiomerically rich in one configurational isomer (possibly a geometrical isomer, which is optically inactive.) We will also consider enantiomeric distribution in a product mixture and discuss ways to increase the optical purity.

Configurational Isomers

Stereochemistry
Stereochemistry centers around the formation, orientation, and reactivity of molecules with stereogenic centers, referred to as stereoisomers. The molecules we shall consider in this section are configurational isomers.

Configurational Isomers
Configurational isomers have identical bonds, but they have a different spatial arrangement of their atoms, no matter how the structures are contorted. Common examples, with which you are familiar, are optical isomers. Optical isomers, due to their asymmetry, rotate plane-polarized light. This is used as a diagnostic test to identify a specific configurational isomer. We shall first look at asymmetry and chirality, as configurational isomers are based on chirality.

Asymmetry
A molecule with asymmetry has a site about which there is uneven distribution of the bonded atoms. At least one of two stereoisomers must be asymmetric in some manner if the two structures are not superimposable. To understand stereoisomers, it helps to be familiar with mirror plane symmetry and chirality (molecular asymmetry). Figure 3-1 shows the asymmetry of carvone and the symmetry of 2,2-dichloropropane.

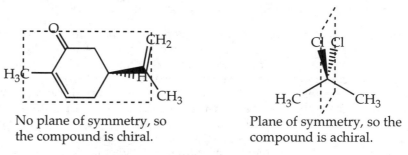

No plane of symmetry, so the compound is chiral.

Plane of symmetry, so the compound is achiral.

Figure 3-1

Chirality
Chiral is the term assigned to a molecule with no plane of symmetry, therefore a chiral molecule has an asymmetric structure. Simply put, chirality is the "left and right handedness" of a molecule. From our perspective (keeping at the level of this test), a chiral molecule has at least one stereogenic center present. A stereogenic center is an atom within the chiral compound that has asymmetry about it. For our needs, chiral (asymmetric) carbons are sp^3-hybridized carbons with four unique substituents attached. Within 2-chloropentane there is one stereocenter (chiral carbon), as emphasized in Figure 3-2 below. Figure 3-2 shows the two configurational isomers (enantiomers) of 2-chloropentane in such a manner that the two structures are mirror images of one another. The plane mirror reflects a configurational isomer as its image.

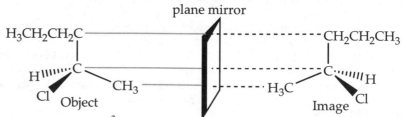

Each structure has sp^3-hybridization with four different groups attached.

Figure 3-2

What makes this important is that an atom with four unique substituents attached has two possible ways that the substituents may be connected (which are mirror images of one another). The two structures with identical bonds may exhibit different chemical properties despite identical physical properties as one another. This is observed frequently in biological systems. For instance, humans digest only D-sugars (D refers to one of the two possible stereogenic orientations associated with the penultimate carbon within a sugar backbone), because enzymes bind and react only with D-sugars.

Example 3.1 shows some examples of pairs of substituted butane molecules that have four unique substituents on carbon two. The goal of this question is for you to master the skills necessary for quickly recognizing when two structures represent conformational isomers (discussed in section II) versus when they represent configurational isomers.

Example 3.1
Which of the following structural pairs represents the same molecule and not a pair of configurational isomers?

A.

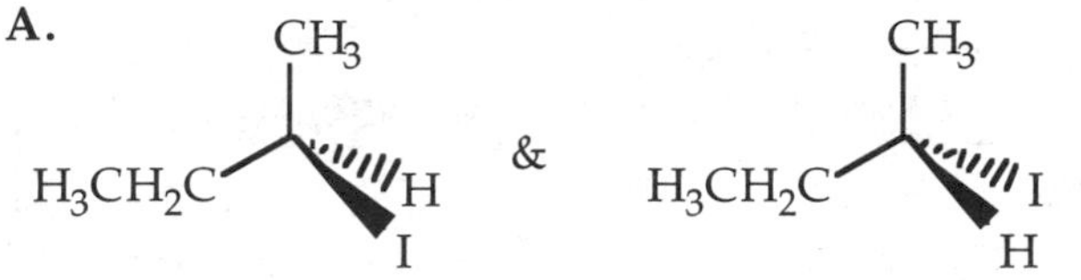

B.

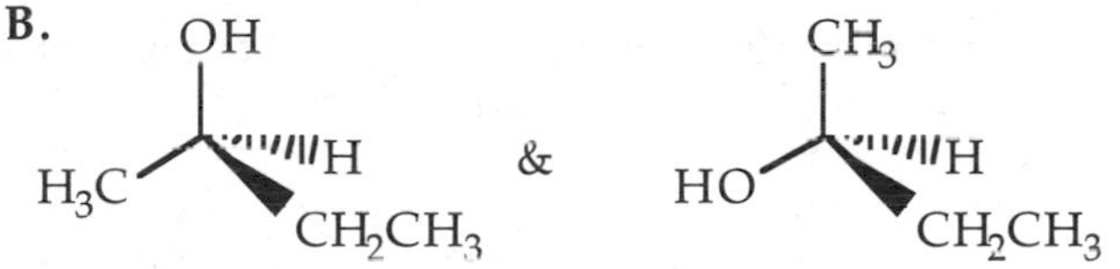

C.

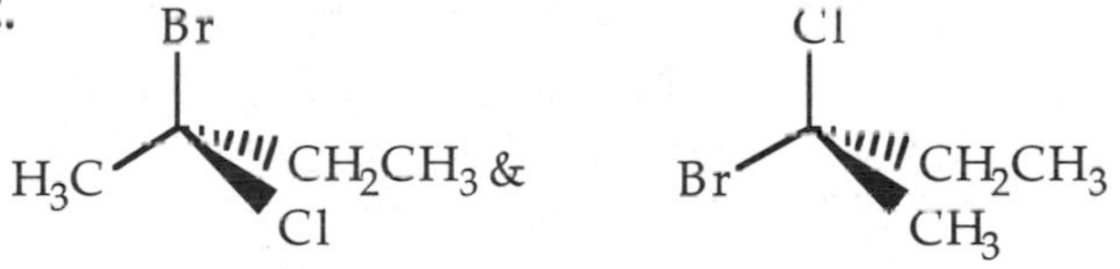

D.

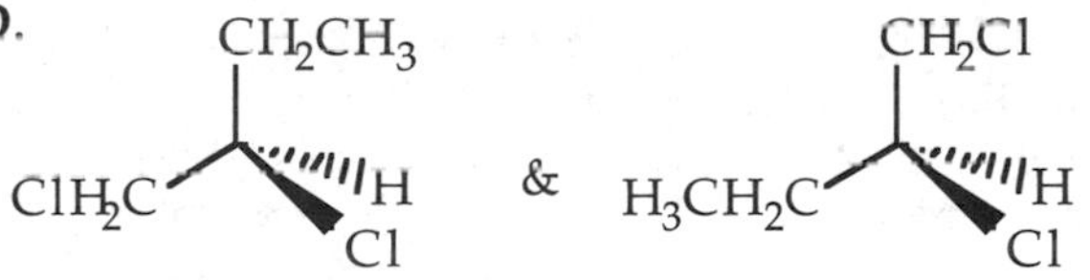

Solution
You must decide whether the compounds are either enantiomers or the identical compound with different spatial orientation. Rotate the molecules in your mind to see if the atoms overlay. If you do this successfully, then you will see that they are identical only in choice **C**. However, if this is hard for you to visualize, there is an alternative method. A shortcut you may recognize is that when two of the substituents are interchanged, the chirality of that stereocenter changes. In choice A, the H and I substituents are interchanged, making the two structures an enantiomeric pair (configurational isomers). In choice B, the CH_3 and OH substituents are interchanged, making the two structures an enantiomeric pair (configurational isomers). In choice D, the CH_2CH_3 and CH_2Cl substituents are interchanged, making the two structures an enantiomeric pair (configurational isomers). Choices A, B, and D are eliminated, and only choice **C** remains. In choice **C**, three substituents have interchanged, making the two structures conformational isomers. Choice **C** is the best answer.

We could have solved Example 3.1 many different ways, including determining whether each structure was R or S. We chose to solve it using visualization of symmetry, noting that the pairs of molecules in choices A, B, and D are mirror images of one another, because according to our shortcut, when two of the substituents interchange their locations on a molecule with only one chiral center, the two molecules are mirror images of one another. Mirror images that are non-superimposable are defined as enantiomers. You can also see this if you rotate either structure by the correct amount about the correct axis, to show that the structures are not superimposable.

The two molecules in choice C in Example 3.1 are identical. If the leftside structure is rotated counterclockwise by 120° about the carbon 2 - carbon 3 bond (as shown in Figure 3-3), the structure and orientation of the rightside molecule is formed. You should note that when a structure is rotated by 120° about a bond, the three other substituents interchange their locations on the molecule. The conclusion from this is that when three substituents are different from one structure to another, those two structures represent different conformational isomers (orientations) of the same compound.

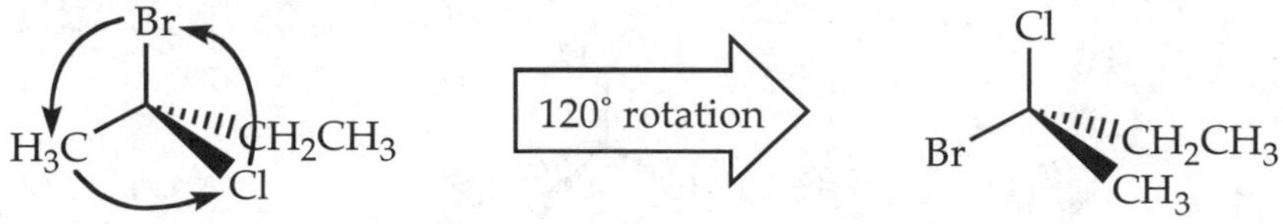

Figure 3-3

Rotating molecules in your mind becomes easier with practice, although if the skill is never fully developed, you can still answer stereochemistry questions by following a few simple rules. If two groups are interchanged and the rest of the molecule remains in place, then the two structures are configurational isomers. If there is a mirror plane between two molecules and no mirror plane within the molecule, then the two structures are configurational isomers.

Another method we could have employed would be to have determined the absolute configuration of the stereogenic centers in each structure to see which pairs involved different configurational isomers.

Determining Absolute Configuration
The identification and naming of a chiral center is based on nomenclature convention. There is a set of guidelines, the Cahn-Ingold-Prelog rules, to follow for determining R and S for a stereocenter (chiral carbon). The Cahn-Ingold-Prelog rules to determine the stereochemical orientation (R or S) are as follows:

1) First, you must prioritize the substituents that are attached to the carbon of the stereocenter according to the atomic mass of the atom directly bonded to the chiral carbon (from heaviest atom to lightest atom). You may need to consult the periodic table.

2) Second, orient the molecule in such a way that the substituent with the lowest priority (number four) points behind the plane of the molecule.

3) Third, you must draw a semicircular arc from substituent 1 through substituent 2 and on to substituent 3. If the arc is clockwise, then the stereocenter is referred to as R. If the arc is counterclockwise, then the stereocenter is referred to as S.

R is from the word *rectus*, which is *right* in Latin, while S is from the word *sinister* which is *left* in Latin. If you point your thumb in the direction of substituent number four on a compound with R-stereochemistry, the fingers of your right hand will curl from one to two and on to three. Thus, R-chirality can be thought of as right handedness. The same holds true for your left hand with an S-center.

Any carbon with four unique substituents has two different orientations that it can assume (the *R* and *S* configurations). What is meant by "unique substituents" is not four different atoms, but four unique groups including any atoms bonded to the four atoms attached directly to the chiral carbon. For example, carbon two of 2-chloropentane (see Figure 3-2) is chiral, because it has a chlorine (priority 1), a propyl group (priority 2), a methyl group (priority 3), and a hydrogen (priority 4) bonded to it. These four substituents are unique substituents.

Figure 3-4 shows a generic *R* structure and a generic *S* structure as oriented according to convention. The steps of rotation presented, take the structure from a standard view to a view with the fourth priority substituent eclipsed, to the Newman projection from which the stereochemical identity is derived.

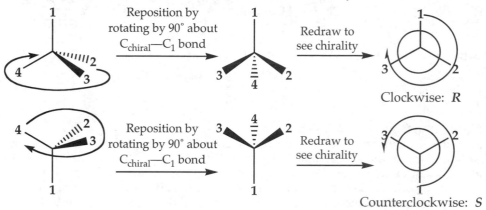

Figure 3-4

Knowing the terminology is key; it is recognition, not recall, that is emphasized on a multiple-choice exam. Here are some *modified* definitions of common terms.

S-center:
A carbon center that when you look down the bond from the chiral carbon to the fourth priority substituent (usually a C—H bond) in a way that you can't see the fourth priority substituent, the remaining substituents form a **counterclockwise** arc when moving from priority one to priority two and on to priority three according to the priority rules. This can be thought of as a **left-handed** molecule when placing your thumb in the direction you're looking and curling your fingers to match your left hand to the structure.

R-center:
A carbon center that when you look down the bond from the chiral carbon to the fourth priority substituent (usually a C—H bond) in a way that you can't see the fourth priority substituent, the remaining substituents form a **clockwise** arc when moving from priority one to priority two and on to priority three according to the priority rules. This can be thought of as a **right-handed** molecule when placing your thumb in the direction you're looking and curling your fingers to match your right hand to the structure.

Figure 3-5 shows a convenient shortcut that involves placing your thumb in the direction of substituent #4 and then curling your fingers. *R*-stereocenters correlate with right hands and *S*-stereocenters correlate with left hands.

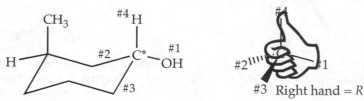

Test Tip
R/S **Thumb Trick**

Figure 3-5

Prioritizing Substituents to Determine *R* and *S*

To prioritize, first you must look at the four atoms directly bonded to the asymmetric carbon. You then rank those atoms according to their atomic mass with the heaviest atom taking the highest priority. If two atoms are equal (as is often the case with carbon) you must continue down the molecule following the bonds outward from the chiral center. Figure 3-6 shown below presents four examples with the priorities labeled on the molecules.

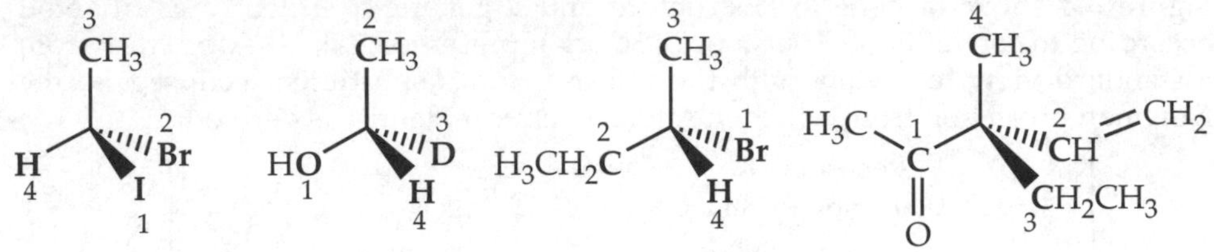

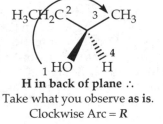

$$I > Br > C > H \quad O > C > D > H \qquad \begin{array}{c} Br > C = C > H \\ CH_2CH_3 > CH_3 \end{array} \qquad \begin{array}{c} C = C = C = C \\ C=O > C=C > C-C > C-H \end{array}$$

Figure 3-6

Shortcut to Determine *R* and *S*

As with so many other topics in organic chemistry, *R* and *S* questions become easy and redundant with time. There are useful quick tricks to help you to identify chiral centers as being either *R* or *S*. For instance, when the fourth-priority substituent is sticking out from the molecule, it is easiest to first solve for the arc using the structure as it is, and then take the opposite chirality for the stereocenter. Thinking about it in a pragmatic sense, substituent number four can either be **behind** the plane, **in front of** the plane or **in the plane**. In each of these three cases, there is a *best* technique to apply to arrive at the chiral center easily. Figure 3-7a shows how to get the chirality easily when the structure is drawn in the conventional manner and #4 is in front or in back.

H in back of plane ∴
Take what you observe **as is**.
Clockwise Arc = *R*

H in front of plane ∴
Reverse what you observe.
Clockwise Arc reverses to *S*

Figure 3-7a

When the #4 substituent is in the plane, it's a little more challenging. If it's in the plane but drawn in a way that it's right next to the group pointing back (as is the case in the right structure in Figure 3-7b), then you take the opposite of that the arc shows you. This is because switching that group with the one in back would cause an inversion of the stereocenter. If it's in the plane but drawn in a way that it's right next to the group pointing in front (as is the case in the left structure in Figure 3-7b), then you take the same as what the arc shows you.

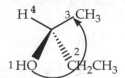

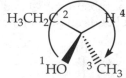

H in plane close to front group ∴
Take what you observe **as is**.
Counterclockwise Arc = *S*

H in plane close to back group ∴
Reverse what you observe.
Clockwise Arc reverses to *S*

Figure 3-7b

Example 3.2
The following molecule has what type of chiral orientation?

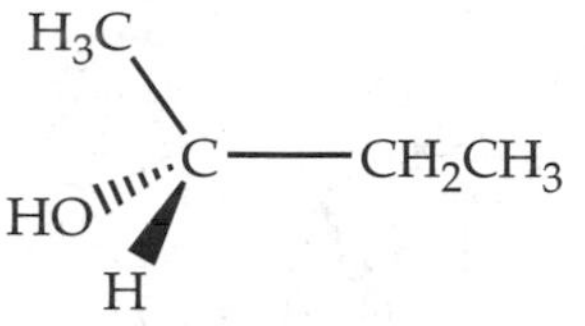

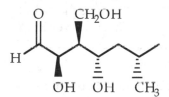

A. *R*
B. *S*
C. The molecule has no chiral center.
D. The compound is meso.

Solution
The compound has one stereocenter, so it cannot be meso (to be meso requires an even number of chiral centers). The compound is chiral, because carbon two has four unique substituents attached it. The molecule must therefore be either *R* or *S*, eliminating choices C and D. The priorities are OH > CH_2CH_3 > CH_3 > H. Correct alignment of the substituents shows that the compound has an *R* chiral center. A counterclockwise arc connects priorities 1, 2 and 3. Because the H (priority 4) is in front, the arc should be reversed. Pick **A** for best results.

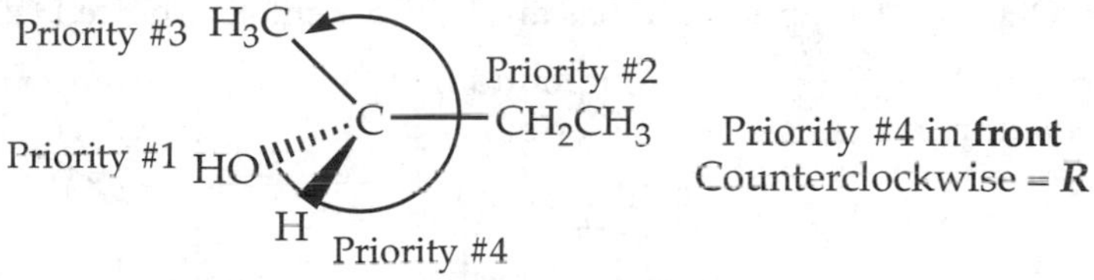

Priority #3 H_3C
Priority #1 HO
Priority #2 CH_2CH_3
Priority #4 H

Priority #4 in **front**
Counterclockwise = *R*

Example 3.3
What is the chirality of the triol below according to the Cahn-Ingold-Prelog rules?

O CH_2OH
H
OH OH CH_3

A. 2*R*,3*S*,4*S*,6*R*
B. 2*R*,3*R*,4*R*
C. 2*R*,3*R*,4*S*
D. 2*R*,3*S*,4*S*

Solution
Carbon six is not a chiral center, because there are two equivalent methyl groups present. This eliminates choice A. To get the correct answer, we must consider each stereocenter, although carbon 2 must be R according to the answer choices. The chiral centers are 2*R*,3*S*,4*S* (as shown below), which makes choice **D** correct.

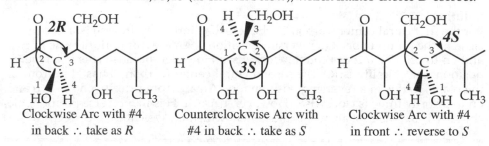

Clockwise Arc with #4 in back ∴ take as *R*   Counterclockwise Arc with #4 in back ∴ take as *S*   Clockwise Arc with #4 in front ∴ reverse to *S*

Example 3.4
Which of the following compounds have *R* orientation?

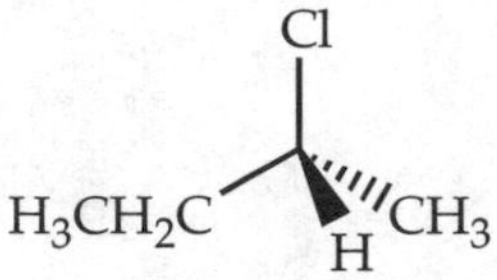

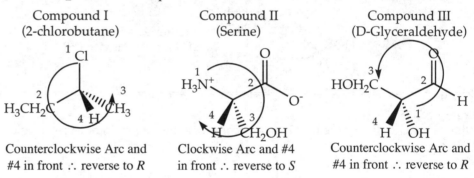

Compound I 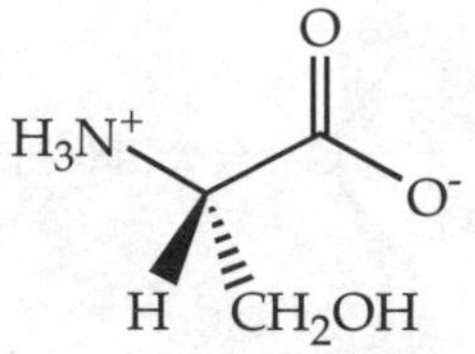   Compound II 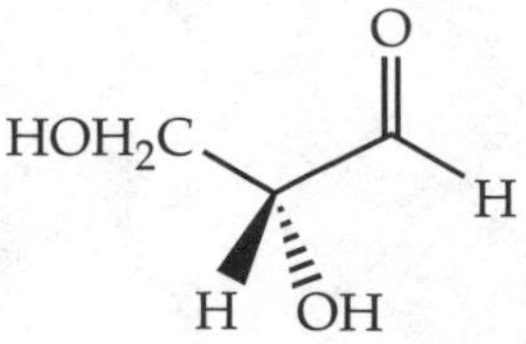   Compound III

A. Compound I only
B. Compound II only
C. Compound III only
D. Compounds I and III only

Solution
Hydrogen points out in each of the compounds. Whichever arc is seen from this view must be reversed to get the arc that would be seen from the correct view. The priorities in Compound I are: $Cl > CH_2CH_3 > CH_3 > H$. Compound I has an *R* chiral center. The priorities in Compound II are: $NH_3^+ > CO_2^- > CH_2OH > H$. Compound II has an *S* chiral center. The priorities in Compound III are: $OH > CHO > CH_2OH > H$. Compound III has an *R* chiral center. Choice **D** is best.

Compound I	Compound II	Compound III
(2-chlorobutane)	(Serine)	(D-Glyceraldehyde)

Counterclockwise Arc and #4 in front ∴ reverse to *R*	Clockwise Arc and #4 in front ∴ reverse to *S*	Counterclockwise Arc and #4 in front ∴ reverse to *R*

Example 3.5
What is the stereochemical orientation of the following molecule?

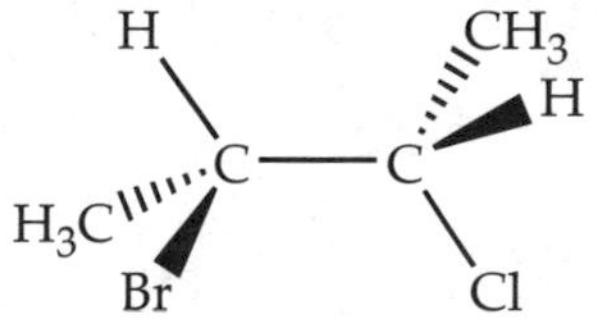

A. 2*R*,3*R*
B. 2*R*,3*S*
C. 2*S*,3*R*
D. 2*S*,3*S*

Solution
For the first chiral center (carbon 2), the fourth priority (hydrogen) is in the plane close to the group in back (a reversing position). An arc from priority one to two and on to priority three is counterclockwise. However, because H is in a reverse position, the chirality is *R*. The second chiral center (carbon 3) has H in front of the plane, so it is in a reversing position too. An arc from priority one to two and on to priority three is clockwise. However, because H is in a reverse position, the chirality is *S*. The best answer is thus 2*R*,3*S* which makes choice **B** correct.

Figure 3-8 shows a summary of the tricks presented in Figure 3-7 and applied in Examples 3.2 through 3.5.

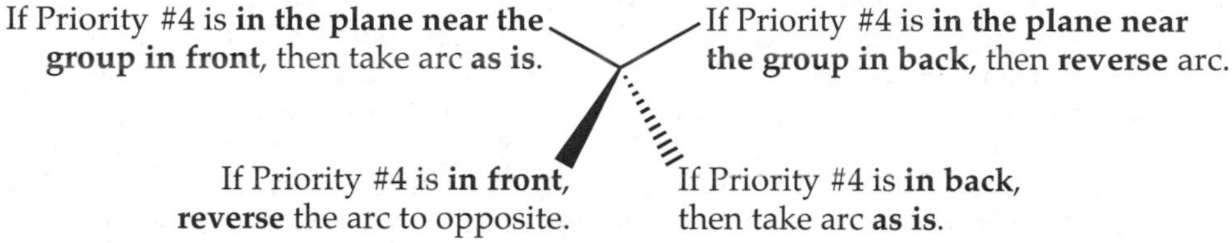

If Priority #4 is **in the plane near the group in front**, then take arc **as is.**
If Priority #4 is **in the plane near the group in back**, then **reverse** arc.
If Priority #4 is **in front**, **reverse** the arc to opposite.
If Priority #4 is **in back**, then take arc **as is.**

Figure 3-8

One last short cut for determining the configuration of a stereocenter involves interchanging substituents to generate an easier stereocenter to evaluate, and then assigning the opposite chirality to the original stereocenter. This method is based on the idea that it is easiest to solve for chirality when the fourth priority substituent is in back and that when two substituents are interchanged, the stereochemistry is inverted. Figure 3-9 shows the application of this method.

HOH2C 2
3 CH3
4 H
1 OH
Priority #4 not in back ∴
Interchange #4 and group in back
HOH2C 2
3 CH3
1 HO
H 4
Priority #4 now in back of plane ∴
New structure has a clockwise arc, so it is *R*
The original compound must be *S*
H 4
2 CH2OH
3 H3C
1 OH
Priority #4 not in back ∴
Interchange #4 and group in back
HO 1
2 CH2OH
3 H3C
H 4
Priority #4 now in back of plane ∴
New structure has a clockwise arc, so it is *R*
The original compound must be *S*
H3C 3
4 H
2 HOH2C
1 OH
Priority #4 not in back ∴
Interchange #4 and group in back
H3C 3
1 OH
2 HOH2C
H 4
Priority #4 now in back of plane ∴
New structure has a clockwise arc, so it is *R*
The original compound must be *S*

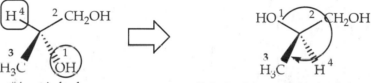

Figure 3-9

Test Tip
***R*/*S* Swithcing SubstituentsTrick**

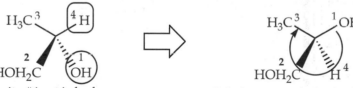

These are two-dimensional tricks that may be done on paper. There is the hand trick and the visualization method as well. No one method is more accurate than another is, so once you find the one you prefer, hone it in and use it. We will cover three dexterity-based methods in class. One involves pointing in the direction your eye should be looking, and sweeping an arc with your index finger that goes from priority 1 to 2 to 3. Another involves using your middle finger, index finger, and thumb to represent priorities #1 - #3 in the molecule. And as mentioned earlier, one method involves matching your thumb to substituent #4 and then curling your fingers with the molecule using either your right hand or your left hand.

Optical Rotation

Optical rotation is a physical measurement of the rotation of plane polarized light by a solution with a chiral molecule. A solution containing a pure compound of known concentration (dissolved into solvent) in a standardized cuvette rotates plane-polarized light the same amount each time. Consequently, the specific rotation (optical rotation under specific conditions) is a physical measurement (like melting point and boiling point) that may be used as a diagnostic test for the identity of a compound. This is common with sugars. The direction of the rotation is signified by either (+) or (-) orientation followed by the degrees of rotation. The (+) denotation describes clockwise rotation of light while the (-) denotation describes counterclockwise rotation of light by the molecule. If the R-enantiomer of a compound rotates the light in a positive direction by X°, then the S-enantiomer of the compound rotates light by X° in the negative direction.

Optical rotation is measured using a polarimeter, which is basically a sample tube sandwiched between two polarizing plates capable of rotation. The plates are rotated in a manner to allow for the greatest amount of light to pass through. If the plates are rotated 90° away from the orientation with highest intensity, then the new orientation of the plates does not allow for any light to pass through. A simple polarimeter is shown in Figure 3-10 below.

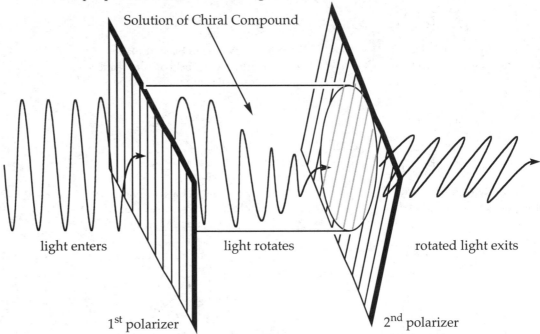

Solution of Chiral Compound

light enters   light rotates   rotated light exits

1st polarizer   2nd polarizer

Figure 3-10

Chiral molecules may be assigned a "(+)" or "(-)" preceding their name to indicate the direction that the compound will rotate plane polarized light. For instance, (+)-2-butanol rotates light in a clockwise direction while its enatiomer, (-)-2-butanol, rotates light in a counterclockwise direction. There are compounds with R-stereochemistry that rotate plane polarized light in a clockwise fashion and other compounds with R-stereochemistry that rotate plane polarized light in a counterclockwise fashion. Consequently, R stereochemistry does not necessarily correspond to either (+) or (-) rotation of plane polarized light. In biochemistry, the designation of D and L is based on threose, where (+) was originally assigned to D-threose and (-) was assigned to L-threose. However, because of the vast multitude of sugars, there is no correlation between uppercase D and uppercase L designation and (+) or (-) rotation of plane polarized light. In biology, a lowercase *d* replaces (+) and a lowercase *l* replaces (-).

Having chiral centers does not always result in the rotation of plane polarized light. Meso compounds have opposing chiral centers that cancel one another out, resulting in no net rotation of plane polarized light. Meso compounds are therefore *optically inactive*, meaning they have a specific rotation of zero.

Polarimeters measure the optical rotation of a solution. The specific rotation of a compound, $[\alpha]_D$, is calculated from the optical rotation using Equation 3.1.

$$[\alpha]_D^T = \frac{\text{observed rotation in degrees}}{(\text{length of sample in dm})(\text{concentration of sample in } \frac{\text{grams}}{\text{mL}})} \quad \textbf{(3.1)}$$

As seen in Equation 3.1, the standard cell length of a cuvette is 1 decimeter (10 centimeters), and the standard concentration is 1 gram solute per milliliter solution. The superscript T refers to temperature as measured in Celsius and the subscript D refers to monochromatic light from a sodium lamp, known as the D-band. Specific rotation is the optical rotation observed under specific conditions.

Enantiomers and Diastereomers
Often times, a molecule can be asymmetric in more than one way, as seen when there is more than one stereogenic carbon in a molecule. There are terms that describe the relationship between two stereoisomers. The relationship requires determining whether the structures are mirror images and whether they are superimposable. Configurational isomers can be classified as either *enantiomers* or *diastereomers*. Enantiomers and diastereomers have the same bonds, but a different spatial orientation of their atoms.

> *Enantiomer:* Enantiomers are configurational isomers that are nonsuperimposable mirror images (reflections that you can't overlay)

> *Diastereomer:* Diastereomers are configurational isomers that are nonsuperimposable and that are not mirror images.

Thus, to classify a pair of configurational isomers as either enantiomers or diastereomers requires evaluating whether the structures are mirror images and whether they are superimposable.

Compounds are not always drawn in a manner where it's easy to see if they are reflections of one another or superimposable. There is a wonderful short cut for determining whether two compounds are enantiomers or diastereomers based on what we know about reflections. Consider a molecule that has two chiral centers, let's say *R* and *R*. To be mirror images, all of the chiral centers must differ, because each chiral center must switch when it is reflected (just as a left hand in the mirror turns into a right hand). If you were to place an *R,R*-molecule into the mirror it would reflect an *S,S*-molecule, so the *S,S*-molecule is the enantiomer of the *R,R*-molecule. This means that to be **enantiomers, all of the chiral centers must differ** between the two configurational isomers. If no chiral centers differ, then the two structures are identical (the same molecule). If one of the two stereocenters differs, then the two compounds are neither mirror images of one another nor the same molecule. This makes them diastereomers. If only **a few, but not all chiral centers differ**, then the compounds are **diastereomers**. Listed below are the *modified* definitions of enantiomers and diastereomers.

> *Enantiomer:* Enantiomers are configurational isomers in which **all** of the chiral centers in each molecule are different from one another.

> *Diastereomer:* Diastereomers are configurational isomers in which **at least one, but not all** of the chiral centers in each molecule is different from one another.

Test Tip
Enantiomer vs. Diastereomer

These modified definitions should prove to be easier to use than the traditional definitions. Figure 3-11 shows two pairs of enantiomers where the mirror plane is not obvious and Figure 3-12 shows two pairs of diastereomers.

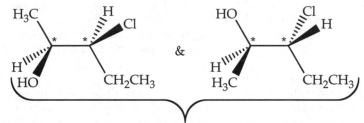

Enantiomeric pair because both of the chiral centers are different

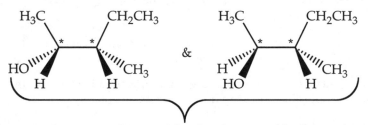

Enantiomeric pair because both of the chiral centers are different

Figure 3-11

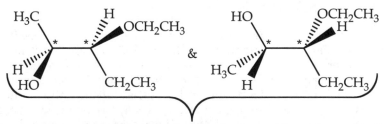

Diastereomers, because only one of the chiral centers (the left one) is different

Diastereomers, because only one of the chiral centers (the right one) is different

Figure 3-12

You should be able to just scan structures to look for interchanged substituents (chiral centers that are different.) First, look for any chiral centers (sp^3-carbons with four unique substituents). From that point, compare the comparable chiral centers in the two structures. If the structure is oriented in a similar fashion, but two substituents are in different positions, then the chiral center is different between the two compounds. If the structure is oriented in a similar fashion, but three substituents are in different positions, then the chiral center is the same between the two compounds. Finally, it is a matter of deciding if all, some, or none of the chiral centers on the two molecules are different and then determining their relationship.

Example 3.6
The following pair of compounds is best described as which of the following?

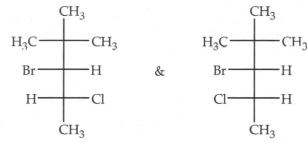

A. Diastereomers
B. Enantiomers
C. Identical achiral compounds
D. Identical chiral compounds

Solution
At first glance, the structures are not aligned to see a mirror plane between them. This means that we should determine the relationship by comparing each stereocenter. When the orientation of the bonds remains constant and three substituents change their location, this implies that the compound has been rotated about that chiral center. The left chiral center is just rotated between the two compounds, so it has the same chirality. When two substituents interchange their location, this implies that the chiral center changed. The right chiral center has changed, because the H and aldehyde group have exchanged places. This means that only one out of the two chiral centers has changed its orientation between the two structures. The two compounds are therefore **diastereomers** of one another, making choice **A** the best answer. There is no need to determine the chirality of the stereocenters (*R* or *S*) within molecules to determine whether they are enantiomers or diastereomers. Deciding whether two molecules are enantiomers or diastereomers is as easy as asking whether *all* of the stereocenters or just *some* of the stereocenters have changed their orientation between the two compounds.

Example 3.7
The following molecules are best described as:

$$CH_3$$
$$H_3C \quad \text{—} \quad CH_3$$
$$Br \quad \text{—} \quad H$$
$$H \quad \text{—} \quad Cl$$
$$CH_3$$

&

$$CH_3$$
$$H_3C \quad \text{—} \quad CH_3$$
$$Br \quad \text{—} \quad H$$
$$Cl \quad \text{—} \quad H$$
$$CH_3$$

A. diastereomers.
B. enantiomers.
C. identical achiral compounds.
D. identical chiral compounds.

Solution
Both structures are drawn as Fischer projections, which represent the top view of the all eclipsed form of the molecule. In a Fischer projection, the side groups are coming out at you in the three dimensional perspective. The two isomers have two chiral centers (the quaternary carbon is not chiral). The chiral carbon with bromine has not changed, because the substituents have not moved. Only the chiral center with the chlorine is different when comparing the two compounds. Only one out of the two chiral centers differs between the structures, so the compounds are diastereomers. This makes choice **A** the best answer.

Example 3.8
How can the relationship of the following pair of molecules be described?

A. Diastereomers
B. Enantiomers
C. Identical achiral compounds
D. Identical chiral compounds

Solution
In this example, the mirror plane between the two molecules can be seen easily as they are drawn. So there is no need to rotate the structures or to count chiral centers. Because of the mirror plane between the two structures, the two compounds can be identified as **enantiomers** of one another. Enantiomers are nonsuperimposable mirror images. Choice **B** is the best answer.

Example 3.9
The following two molecules are best described as a pair of:

A. anomers.
B. constitutional isomers.
C. diastereomers.
D. enantiomers.

Solution
The difficulty here is that the two structures are not aligned in an equivalent fashion (with their bonds in the same position) nor are they aligned to see a potential mirror plane between them. So one of the two structures must be rotated into a structure with its bonds equivalent to the other structure.

After rotating the structure, it is easier to see that both the left chiral center and the right chiral center have each had two substituents change places between the two structures. This means that both chiral centers have changed (two out of two have changed), so the compounds are **enantiomers**. With enantiomers *all* of the stereocenters change their orientation. With diastereomers just *some* of the stereocenters change their orientation.

Example 3.10
What is true of the physical properties for the following stereoisomers?

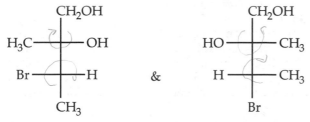

A. They have the same boiling point, but different melting points.
B. They have the same density, but different boiling points.
C. They have different boiling points and different melting points.
D. They have different densities, but the same boiling point.

Solution
The chiral center on carbon 2 is different between the two structures, because the CH_3 and OH have changed positions. The chiral center on carbon 3 is not different between the two structures, because the H, CH_3 and the Br have all changed positions. When three substituents interconvert, the chiral center is not changed. This means that one out of two chiral centers differ, so the two compounds are diastereomers. Diastereomers have different physical properties including melting point, boiling point, and density. No physical properties are the same, so choice **C** is the best answer.

Example 3.11
The following pair of isomers is best described by which of the following terms?

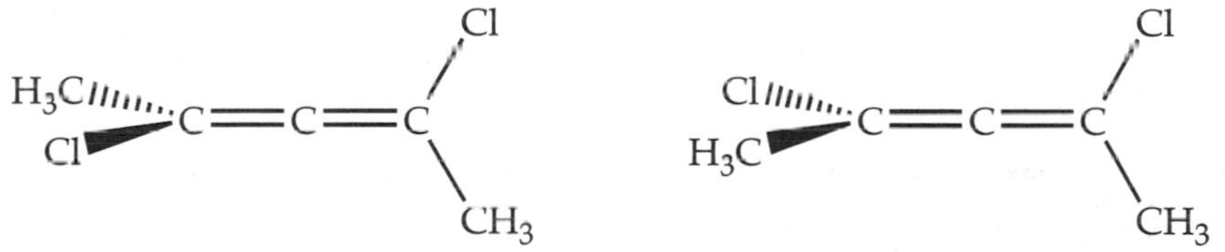

A. Anomers
B. Diastereomers
C. Enantiomers
D. Identical meso compounds

Solution
This allene example is a typical *trick* question organic chemistry teachers like to throw. We get so used to looking for stereogenic centers that contain four unique substituents that we forget the simpler definitions for stereoisomers. These two structures are not sugars in a cyclic conformation, so they cannot be anomers. Choice A is eliminated. They are not identical compounds with a mirror plane within their structure, so choice D is eliminated. It comes down to whether there is a mirror plane between the two non-superimposable structures. If you rotate either structure by 180°, you can see the mirror plane, making them enantiomers. Choice **C** is the best answer.

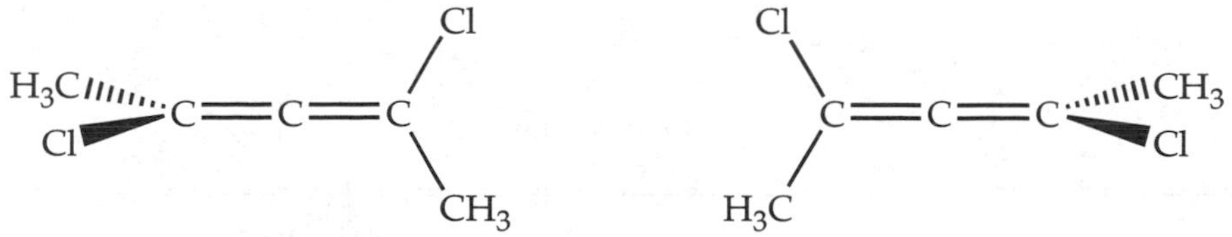

Meso Structures

Meso compounds are individual structures which contain a mirror plane slicing through the middle of the compound and an *even number* of chiral centers symmetrically displaced about the mirror plane. The net optical rotation of a meso compound is 0°. It is zero, because the opposing chiral centers on each half of the molecule cancel one another out, leaving no net rotation of plane polarized light. Meso compounds are referred to as *optically inactive*. Remember the phrase, "Me so inactive", a high-energy rap lyric that describes your physical state while studying for the MCAT. Figure 3-13 shows a meso compound (it has been rotated into a side view to see the mirror plane more easily).

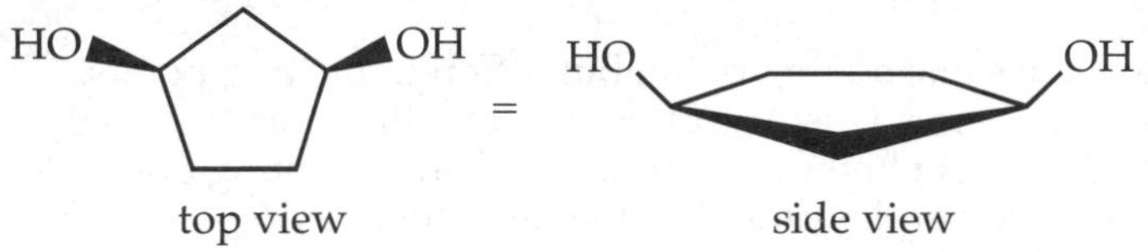

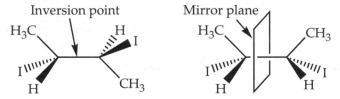

top view   =   side view

Figure 3-13

A meso compound may be identified by either an inversion center in the middle of the molecule or a mirror plane through the middle of the molecule. Figure 3-14 shows two conformational isomers of a meso compound, one in its most stable conformation (where it has an inversion point), and the other in its least stable conformation (where it has a mirror plane of symmetry.) A meso compound has the same number of R-stereocenters as S-stereocenters.

Figure 3-14

Example 3.12
The reflection of a meso compound can be classified as which of the following?

A. Identical to the original compound
B. An enantiomer of the original compound
C. A diastereomer of the original compound
D. An ameso compound from the fifth dimension where evil lurks and the socks that disappear from laundry loads in our world gather.

Solution
A meso compound when viewed in a mirror reflects the identical compound. This makes choice **A** the best choice, although choice D sounds extremely tempting. An example of a meso compound and its reflection is drawn below.

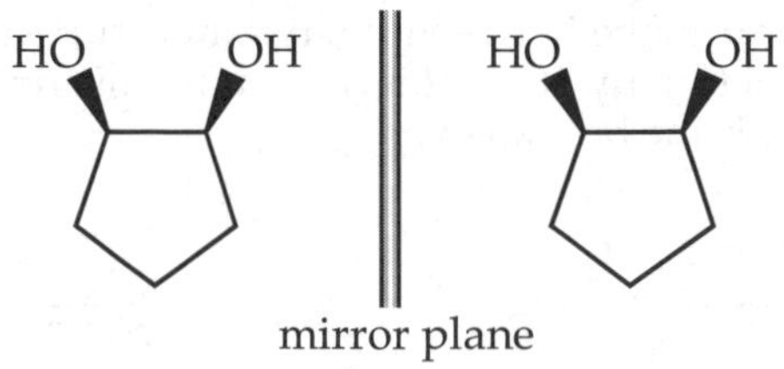

mirror plane

Stereoisomerism
When a molecule contains more than one chiral center, the maximum number of stereoisomers increases exponentially with each new chiral center according to Equation 3.2.

$$\#Stereoisomers = 2^n \tag{3.2}$$

where n is the number of chiral carbons in the molecule.

There are less than 2^n stereoisomers, if one of the possible structures is meso. If there are an odd number of chiral centers, the structure cannot be meso, so there is exactly 2^n possible stereoisomers. For example, consider the compound 3,4,5-trimethyloctane, which has three chiral centers and thus eight possible stereoisomers. 3R,4R,5R-trimethyloctane is just one of the eight possible stereoisomers. Table 3-1 shows the possible stereoisomers for compounds with a variable number of chiral centers.

Chiral Centers	Maximum Stereoisomers	Stereoisomers
1	2	R or S
2	4	RR, RS, SR, or SS
3	8	RRR, SRR, RSR, RRS, SSR, SRS, RSS, or SSS

Table 3-1

Stereoisomerism is more of an issue when a molecule contains more than one chiral center. Many macromolecules in biological sciences have multiple chiral centers (in some instances enzymes have in excess of 200 stereocenters).

Example 3.13
How many stereoisomers are possible for the following structure?

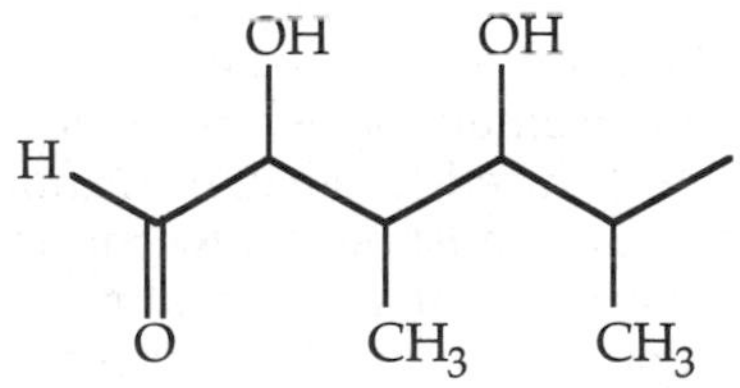

A. 4
B. 8
C. 12
D. 16

Solution
The molecule is drawn in a way to make you mistakenly see four chiral centers if you don't pay close attention, but the number of chiral centers is only three. Carbon five is not a chiral center, because there are two methyl substituents attached to it (one that is drawn as a methyl substituent and the other that is drawn as carbon six of the longest chain). By having two methyl groups attached, it does not have four unique substituents attached, thus it is not a chiral carbon. This means that only carbons two, three, and four are chiral. The maximum number of stereoisomers is derived using the equation 2^n, which is this case is 2^3. Because there is an odd number of chiral centers, the compound cannot be meso, so there are eight stereoisomers. The best answer is choice **B**.

Example 3.14

The relationship of the following pair of compounds is best described as:

A. Anomers
B. Diastereomers
C. Enantiomers
D. Structural isomers

Solution

The hydroxyl group is attached to different carbons in the two structures. In the left structure the hydroxyl group is on carbon 4 while in the right structure, the hydroxyl group is on carbon 2. This makes the two compounds structural isomers, which makes choice **D** the best answer. You may recall that if the two compounds have different IUPAC names, then they are structural isomers. By virtue of the hydroxyl being in a different position, the two compounds in question have different IUPAC names.

Example 3.15

Which of the following compounds is/are optically inactive?

I.   2R,3S-dibromopentane

II. 2S,3R-dichlorobutane

III. 1R,2R-diiodocyclopentane

A. Compound I only
B. Compound II only
C. Compound III only
D. Compounds I and III only

Solution

To be optically inactive, the compound must either be achiral or meso. All of the compounds listed have stereocenters, so achiral is not a possibility for any of the structures. The question is reduced to whether or not each structure is meso or not. To be meso, the compound must be symmetric and have an even number of chiral centers equally displaced about an internal mirror plane (i.e., R on one side and S on the other). Compound I is eliminated, because the chiral centers are not symmetric about the a plane (the mirror plane would have to slice through carbon three to break the five carbon species into halves). To be symmetric, carbons two and four would have to have the same substituents, which they do not. Compound I is chiral, so it is optically active and therefore choices A and D are eliminated. Compound III is eliminated, because it does not have opposite chiral centers (they are both R). For diiodocyclopentane to be meso, carbons one and two would have to have opposite absolute configurations, which they do not. Compound III is chiral, so it is optically active and therefore choice C eliminated. The only compound left is Compound II, which is symmetric, because it has a mirror plane that slices through the bond between carbon two and carbon three. Compound II is meso and therefore optically inactive, so the best answer is choice **B**.

Stereochemistry in Reactions

Stereoisomer Formation

When a chemical reaction involves chiral reactants, they are often selective for one stereoisomer over another, as seen with enzymatic selectivity. However, when a reaction involves achiral reactants, the formation of stereoisomers is random. The type of stereoisomers formed depends on the chirality of the starting reagents. When a symmetric nucleophile can attack a planar achiral electrophile from either side, two enantiomers are formed in equal proportion. When a nucleophile is hindered from attacking a planar species from one side more than the other (due to a chiral center in the electrophile that creates greater steric hindrance on one side than the other), there are two diastereomers formed in unequal proportions. Figure 3-15 shows an example of an electrophilic addition reaction that forms two enantiomers.

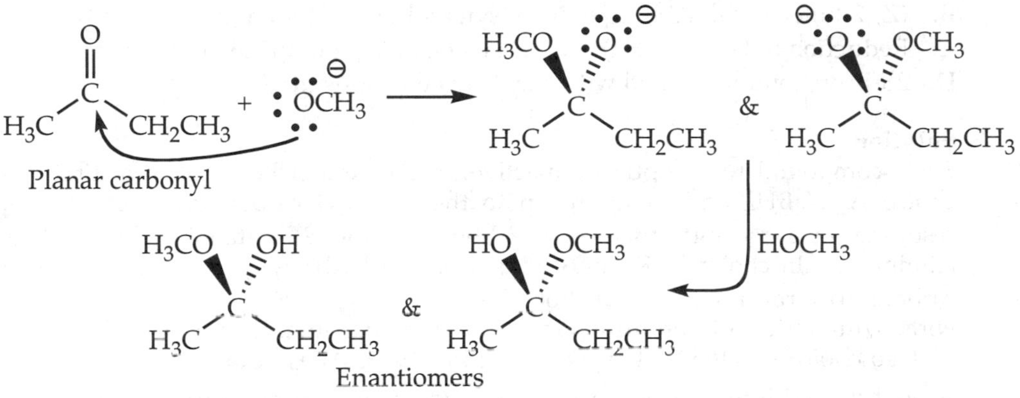

Figure 3-15

Example 3.16

The addition of alkyl magnesium bromide (RMgBr) to a carbonyl in ether adds a new alkyl substituent to the carbonyl carbon, resulting in conversion of the carbonyl into an alcohol. The addition of H_3CMgBr to R-2-methylcyclohexanone in diethyl ether yields which products?

A. One meso compound
B. Two diastereomers
C. Two enantiomers
D. Two epimers

Solution

In this reaction, the methyl group can add to either the top or bottom of the sp^2-hybridized carbon. This results in a new chiral center that can be either R or S. However, there is already a chiral center present in the reactant that is not involved in the reaction, which retains its original chirality. The chiral center present in the reactant does not change during the course of a reaction, so the products cannot be enantiomers. This eliminates choice C. The compound is not a sugar, so choice D is eliminated. It is not meso, so choice A is eliminated. One of the two chiral centers differs between the two stereoisomer products, so they are diastereomers. Choice **B** is correct. Due to steric hindrance from the ethyl group on carbon two, the product mixture of the two diastereomers is not 50/50.

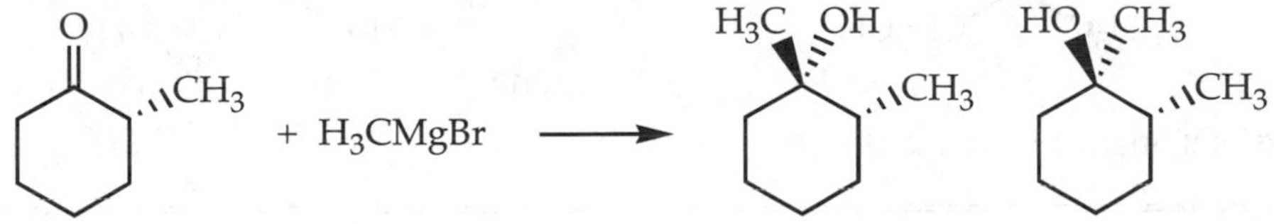

When two enantiomers are formed, they are formed in equal quantity, and the product mixture is said to be *racemic*. When the two enantiomers are equally present, there is no net rotation of plane polarized light. When two diastereomers are formed, they are formed unequally, so the product mixture has a major and a minor product. When the two diastereomers are present in unequal amounts, there can be a net rotation of plane polarized light. Enantiomers can be formed in an unequal ratio if a chiral catalyst is present. This leads to the concept of *enantiomeric excess*, used to analyze product distributions from reactions with a chiral catalyst (most often an enzyme).

Example 3.17

Which of the following reactions produces no optically active compounds?

A. 2-Butanone treated with $NaBH_4$ in ether followed by acidic workup.

B. (Z)-2-butene with $KMnO_4$ in base (syn addition of two hydroxyl groups).

C. Reduction of $HN=C(CH_3)CH_2CH_3$ using $LiAlH_4$ in thf solvent.

D. 2S-Bromobutane treated with NaCN in ether solvent.

Solution

For a compound to be optically inactive, it must either be meso or achiral. In choice A, $NaBH_4$ adds a hydrogen to the carbonyl carbon from either side, resulting in a racemic mixture of 2R-butanol and 2S-butanol. Choice A is eliminated. In choice B, $KMnO_4$ adds a pair of hydroxyl groups to the alkene carbons to form a syn vicinal diol. Because the alkene is symmetric to begin with, symmetric addition results in a symmetric product. The product is a meso diol, so choice B is the best answer. In choice C, $LiAlH_4$ adds a hydrogen to the sp^2-hybridized imine carbon from either side, resulting in a racemic mixture of 2R-aminobutane and 2S-aminobutane following workup. Choice C is eliminated. In choice D, a good nucleophile attacks a secondary alkyl halide, resulting in inversion of stereochemistry (via an S_N2-reaction). One chiral species is formed, so choice D is out.

Choice A — Racemic mixture of enantiomers

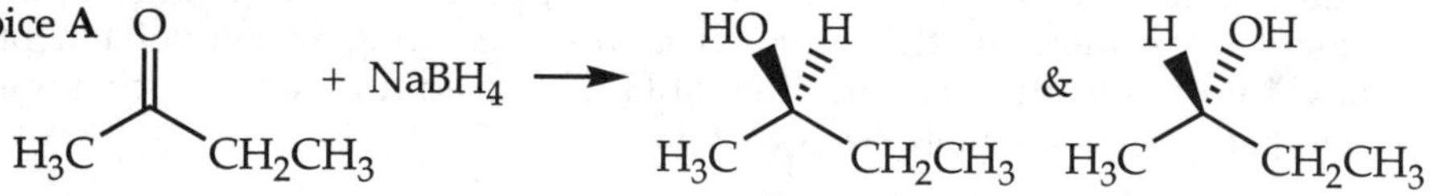

Choice B — Symmetric about plane / Symmetric addition / = Symmetric product: **meso vicinal diol**

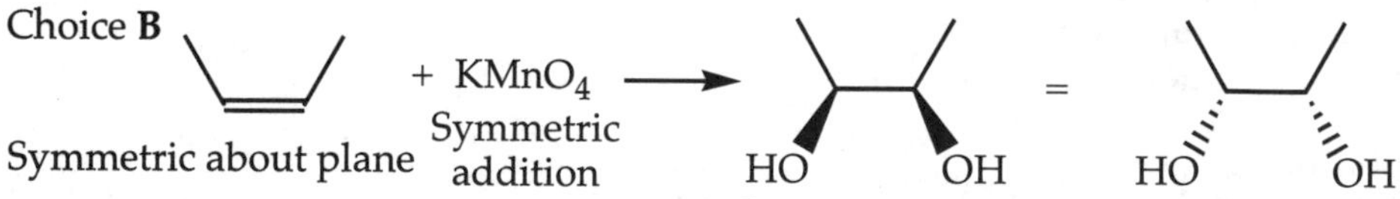

Choice C — Racemic mixture of enantiomers

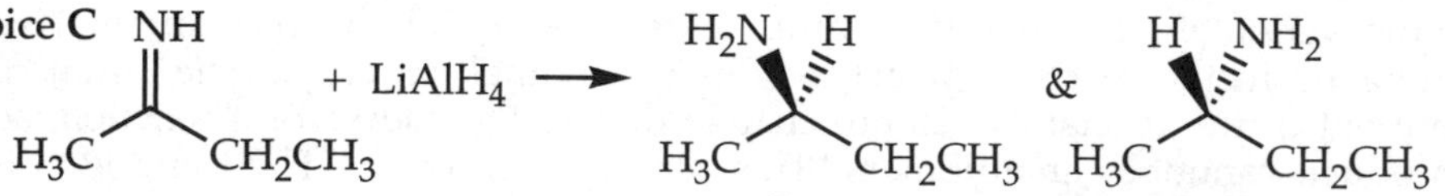

Choice D — One stereoisomer (with *R* chirality)

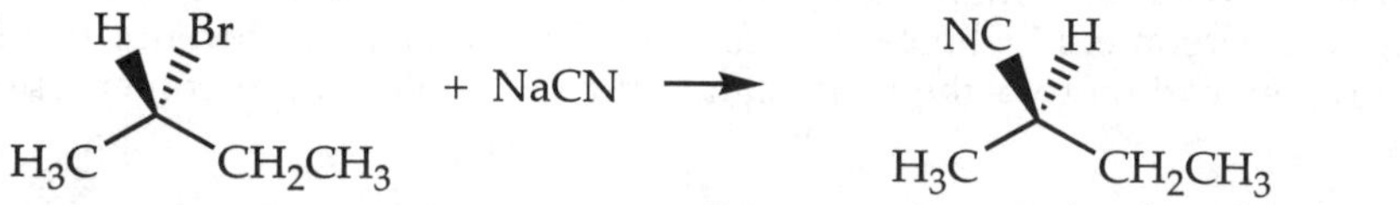

The best answer is choice **B**.

Enantiomeric Excess

Enantiomers rotate light in opposite directions of one another, but with equal magnitude. When both enantiomers are present in equal quantities in solution (a 50-50 mixture), the solution exhibits no net rotation of plane-polarized light. Based on this idea, when a mixture is not in a 50-50 ratio, then the net rotation of light by the solution is not zero. The farther the value deviates from zero, the greater the difference in concentration of the two enantiomers. From the observed rotation of the solution, the percentage of the enantiomer in excess can be derived. Equation 3.3 shows how to determine the enantiomeric excess from the observed specific rotation. The enantiomeric excess is the difference in percentage between the more abundant enantiomer and the less abundant enantiomer.

$$\%ee \text{ (enantiomeric excess)} = \frac{\text{measured specific rotation}}{\text{specific rotation of the pure enantiomer}} \times 100\% \quad \textbf{(3.3)}$$

Example 3.18

What enantiomeric distribution would account for a specific rotation of +13.6° if the pure enantiomers have specific rotations of +27.2° and -27.2° respectively?

A. (+)-enantiomer = 25% and (-)-enantiomer = 75%
B. (+)-enantiomer = 33% and (-)-enantiomer = 67%
C. (+)-enantiomer = 67% and (-)-enantiomer = 75%
D. (+)-enantiomer = 75% and (-)-enantiomer = 25%

Solution

Because the net rotation is positive, the (+)-enantiomer must be in higher concentration than the (-)-enantiomer. This eliminates choices A and B. To determine the exact quantity, Equation 3.3 can be applied.

$$\%ee = \frac{+13.6}{27.2} \times 100\% = \frac{1}{2} \times 100\% = 50\% \text{ in favor of the (+)-enantiomer}$$

The exact ratio is found using the following relationship:

$$\%(+)\text{-enantiomer} + \%(-)\text{-enantiomer} = 100\% \text{ and } (+)\text{-enantiomer} - (-)\text{-enantiomer} = 50\%$$

$$\therefore (+)\text{-enantiomer} = 75\% \text{ and } (-)\text{-enantiomer} = 25\%, \text{ choice } \textbf{D}$$

Example 3.19

What is the observed rotation for a mixture with an enantiomeric excess of +40% for enantiomers with specific rotations of -75° and +75°?

A. +60°
B. +30°
C. -30°
D. -60°

Solution

Because the percentage is positive, the (+)-enantiomer must be in higher concentration than the (-)-enantiomer. This eliminates choices C and D. To determine the exact quantity, Equation 3.3 can be manipulated to yield %ee × pure rotation = observed rotation and then applied as follows:

$$+40\% \times +75° = +30°$$

This makes choice **B** the best answer. The exact ratio in solution is:

$$70\%(+)\text{-enantiomer with } 30\%(-)\text{-enantiomer}$$

$$\therefore (70\% \times +75°) + (30\% \times -75°) = +52.5° + (-22.5°) = +30° = \text{choice } \textbf{B}$$

Nucleophilic Substitution

Nucleophilic Substitution

Nucleophilic substitution is a recurring reaction in organic chemistry and it involves the substitution of one functional group for another. It involves the attack of an electropositive carbon by a nucleophile (Lewis base) to dislodge an atom or functional group (referred to as the leaving group). Nucleophilic substitution can proceed by more than one reaction pathway. It can proceed by the two-step S_N1 mechanism, or it can proceed by the one-step S_N2 mechanism. Nucleophilic substitution reactions are based on the fundamental chemistry concept that negative charge seeks positive charge. The electron pair of the nucleophile hunts for an electron deficient carbon to attach to. Figure 3-16 shows an example of a nucleophilic substitution reaction.

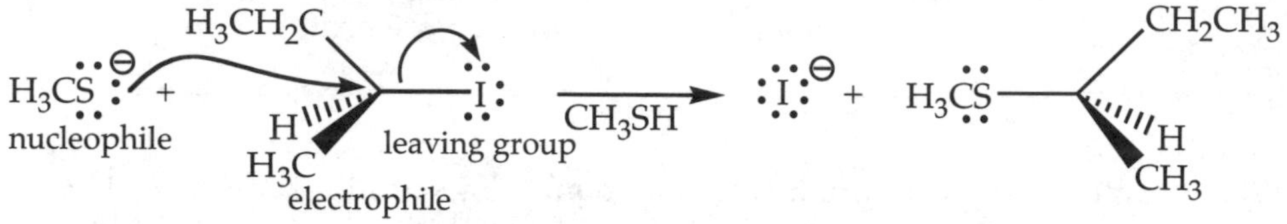

Figure 3-16

We will discuss the mechanism shortly, but for now, there are some fundamental definitions with which to be familiar. Listed below are the most important definitions. Each definition is followed by some general comments about the relative reactivity of the species and how to discern its reactive strength.

Nucleophile

The species donating an electron pair in a nucleophilic substitution reaction (Lewis base). As its name implies, it *loves* (philes) a *positive charge* (nucleo). Nucleophiles must have an available pair of electrons to share. Nucleophile strength is closely approximated by its base strength, although steric factors (nucleophile size) affect nucleophilicity. Small nucleophiles are generally better nucleophiles. This is to say that steric hindrance plays a larger role in nucleophilic substitution reactions than proton transfer reactions. The strength of the nucleophile does not perfectly correlate with base strength, but it is close enough to say that it parallels. A short list of nucleophilic strength in water solvent is as follows:

$$SH^- \geq CN^- > I^- > OR^- > OH^- > Br^- > NH_3 > C_6H_5O^- > CH_3CO_2^- \geq Cl^- > F^- > ROH > H_2O$$

It should be noted that if the base is too strong, an elimination reaction can occur (as is the case with OR^- and OH^-). The solvent also has an effect in that nucleophiles that can hydrogen bond are hindered in protic solvents, because they are solvated. The solvation by the protic solvent binds the electron pair of the nucleophile and reduces its nucleophilicity. This phenomenon explains why SH^-, CN^- and I^- are stronger nucleophiles in water than OH^- despite being weaker bases than OH^-. In aprotic solvents and the gas phase, nucleophilicity more closely parallels basicity. The big difference in nucleophilicity is that size of the anion is not as important as it is with basicity.

Electrophile

An electrophile is the species accepting an electron pair in a nucleophilic substitution reaction (Lewis acid). The electrophile holds the reactive carbon and the leaving group. The weaker the bond between the leaving group and the electrophilic carbon, the better it is an electrophile. Electrophile strength can be approximated by the stability of the leaving group once it is off of the electrophile. Electrophilic carbons typically have a partially positive charge.

Leaving group

The functional group that dissociates from the electrophile in a nucleophilic substitution reaction. The more stable the leaving group, the weaker it is as a base. This means that the strength of a leaving group can be predicted by the strength (pK_a) of its conjugate acid. The theory is that the more stable the leaving group, the less basic the leaving group, and thus the more acidic the conjugate acid of the leaving group. The strength of a leaving group increases as the pK_a of its conjugate acid decreases. This is most true in water, but can also be seen in organic solvents. Leaving group strength increases as the strength of the bond between carbon and the leaving group decreases. This is why iodine is a better leaving group than fluorine.

Racemic mixture

A racemic mixture is a product mixture that has an even distribution of enantiomers (50% of each enantiomer). A racemic mixture is the observed product when the mechanism involves an intermediate where the reactive site is an sp^2-hybridized carbon (like a carbonyl or carbocation) and the molecule is symmetric (has no other chiral centers). There is no such thing as a racemic mixture of diastereomers, because diastereomers have at least two chiral centers associated with them, and a chiral center present in the reaction hinders attack of one side of the electrophile relative to the other, causing the distribution to not be fifty-fifty.

All nucleophilic substitution reactions involve a nucleophile and an electrophile with a leaving group. Some, but not all, nucleophilic reactions generate a racemic mixture. Whether a racemic mixture is generated or not depends on the reaction pathway. The fundamental question in a nucleophilic substitution reaction is, "does the nucleophile come in first, or does the leaving group leave first?" This is the basic difference between the S_N1 and the S_N2 mechanisms. The nucleophile attacks first in an S_N2 reaction mechanism, while in the leaving group leaves first in an S_N1 reaction mechanism. We will look at these two scenarios in more detail.

Example 3.20
A favorable nucleophilic substitution reaction has all of the following EXCEPT:

A. a good leaving group.
B. a reactant with a weak bond to the leaving group.
C. a strong Lewis base as the nucleophile.
D. a weak Lewis base as the nucleophile.

Solution
A favorable nucleophilic substitution reaction is one that forms a stronger bond than the one broken. A good nucleophile is one that forms a stronger bond with carbon than the bond between carbon and the leaving group. A good leaving group is one that forms a weak bond with carbon, thus minimal energy is needed to break the bond between it and carbon. When the leaving group is strong, the reaction is said to be favorable, so choice A is a valid statement. Choice A is eliminated. A weak bond to the leaving group makes it a good leaving group, so choice B is also a valid statement. This eliminates choice B. The nucleophile should be a strong Lewis base, so choice C is a valid statement and choice **D** is an invalid statement. This eliminates choice C and makes choice **D** the best answer. You might note that to determine the favorability of a nucleophilic substitution reaction, you need to consider both the nucleophile and leaving group.

S_N2

In an S_N2 reaction, the nucleophile attacks prior to the leaving group leaving. In essence, the nucleophile comes in from the *backside* and pushes the leaving group off of the electrophile. An important factor to consider is the transition state that forms during the reaction. Transition states cannot be viewed directly (their lifetimes are too short), but evidence in the product (inversion of configuration at a chiral carbon) infers they must have occurred. Backside attack by a nucleophile causes this inversion at the chiral carbon. Certain properties in the reactants (nucleophile and electrophile) and the product (if it is chiral) indicate that the reaction proceeded by an S_N2 mechanism. Each property favors one of the two mechanisms. They can be used to distinguish an S_N2 reaction from an S_N1 reaction. Figure 3-17 shows a generic mechanism for an S_N2 reaction.

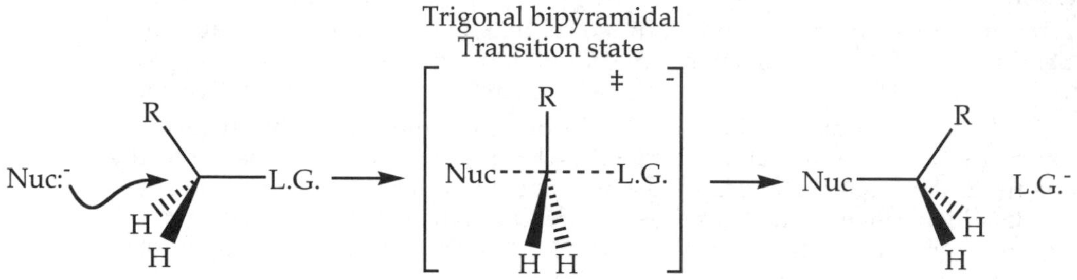

Figure 3-17

The reaction takes place in one step, so the rate of an S_N2 reaction depends on both the concentration of the nucleophile and the concentration of the electrophile. The nucleophile initiates the reaction by attacking the electrophile and forcing the bond between the carbon and the leaving group to stretch and weaken. At the same time that the nucleophile approaches the electrophilic carbon, the electron density of the nucleophile repels the substituents on the electrophilic carbon and thus they form the trigonal bipyramidal transition state. As the leaving group begins to leave, the substituents on the electrophilic carbon begin to fold in the direction of the less hindered side of the molecule (less hindered because the leaving group has left). The hybridization finishes as sp^3. Table 3-2 lists some key features associated with an S_N2 reaction, according to observation order. What is meant by observation order is that the first features (features of the reactants) are observed before the reaction begins, the second features (features of the transition state) are observed during the reaction, and the last features (features of the products) are observed after the reaction ends.

Reactant Features	Course of Reaction Features	Product Features
The reactivity preference in an S_N2 mechanism is $1° > 2° > 3°$ in terms of electrophiles	An S_N2 mechanism forms a five-ligand transition state during the middle of the reaction	A single enantiomeric product is formed (No racemic mixture)
An S_N2 mechanism is favored with a good nucleophile	The 5-ligand transition state is the highest energy state and it exists for just a split second	S_N2 reactions exhibit second order kinetics (rate = k[Nuc][Elect])
An S_N2 mechanism is favored in polar, aprotic solvents such as ethers and ketones	Steric forces destabilize the transition state by forcing bond angles to values less than 109.5°	S_N2 reactions are one-step reactions, so they have fast rates of formation

Table 3-2

The reaction in Figure 3-18 proceeds by an S_N2 mechanism, because the electrophile is primary and it has a good nucleophile. With a primary electrophile, the reaction must proceed by an S_N2 mechanism. The ether solvent is polar and aprotic, which further favors the S_N2 reaction pathway.

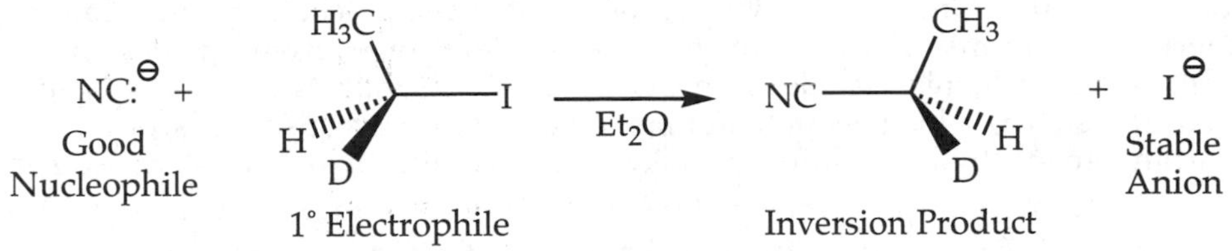

Figure 3-18

Example 3.21

All of the following are associated with an S_N2 reaction EXCEPT:

A. backside attack of the electrophile by the nucleophile.
B. inversion of configuration at the stereogenic carbon.
C. nucleophile concentration affecting the reaction rate.
D. rearrangement of alkyl groups from reactant to product.

Solution

This question focuses on the fundamentals of an S_N2 reaction. For an S_N2 reaction to proceed, the nucleophile must attack the electrophile from the opposite side as the leaving group in a collinear fashion relative to the bond to the leaving group. This is referred to as *backside attack*, so choice A is valid, and thus eliminated. Backside attack results in inversion of stereochemistry if the electrophilic carbon is a chiral carbon. This makes choice B valid, which eliminates it. Because there is just one step in an S_N2 reaction, the rate depends on all of the reactants, including the nucleophile. This makes choice C valid, and thus eliminates choice C. Rearrangement can occur when there is a carbocation present, because carbocations lack a bond. Carbocations are associated with S_N1 reactions, not S_N2 reactions, so choice **D** is invalid and thus the best answer to this question.

S_N1:

In an S_N1 reaction, the leaving group leaves before the nucleophile attacks. In essence, the nucleophile waits until the leaving group has left, allowing it more room to attack. The S_N1 reaction rate does not depend on nucleophile concentration. Once the leaving group has dissociated, a planar cationic intermediate forms. Evidence for the intermediate comes from kinetics data as well as stereochemical evidence provided by the products. The carbocation intermediate has a long enough lifetime to be detected using spectroscopy. Both rearrangement (hydride shifts and alkyl shifts) and a mixture of stereoisomers (formed from the sp^2-intermediate) are observed with S_N1 reactions. The nucleophile is free to attack from either side of the carbocation intermediate, if the carbocation is symmetric. As a result, a racemic mixture of enantiomers is formed as the product mixture. Figure 3-19 shows a generic mechanism for an S_N1 reaction.

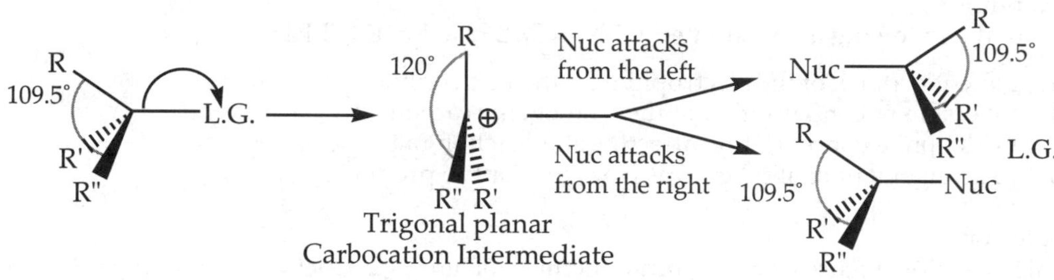

Figure 3-19

The reaction takes place in two steps, where the first step is the slowest. In the first step, the bond between the carbon and the leaving group breaks. As the leaving group begins to leave, the substituents on the carbon fold in the direction of the less hindered side of the molecule, allowing the bond angles to increase from 109.5° to 120° as the carbon re-hybridizes from sp^3 to sp^2. This results in a slight increase in stability, accounting for the intermediate being at a lower energy level than the first transition state in the energy diagram. In addition to re-hybridization, the planar cation is solvated, which also increases the stability of the intermediate. The nucleophile can attack the carbocation intermediate and displace the solvent from either side of the carbocation intermediate. This displacement of solvent and the re-hybridization from sp^2 back to sp^3 causes a decrease in stability from the intermediate to the second transition state. Finally, as the new bond is formed, the energy level decreases until it reaches the level of the products. Bond formation is an exothermic process. The hybridization of the central carbon finishes at sp^3. Table 3-3 lists features associated with the S_N1 reaction. Like in Table 3-2, the features are listed according to observation order.

Reactant Features	Course of Reaction Features	Product Features
The reactivity preference in an S_N1 mechanism is 3° > 2° > 1° in terms of electrophiles	Steric hindrance pushes the leaving group off of the electrophile	A racemic mixture forms when the electrophile has chirality
An S_N1 mechanism is favored in a protic solvent such as alcohol	The intermediate is a planar, three-ligand carbocation where the carbon has sp^2-hybridization	S_N1 reactions exhibit first order kinetics 　　　(rate = k[Elect])
An S_N1 reaction is seen with a poor nucleophile	An intermediate is observed in addition to transition states	S_N1 reactions are slow two-step reactions

Table 3-3

The S_N1 reaction can be complicated by rearrangement, because of the carbocation intermediate formed. If a secondary carbocation (R_2CH^+) is formed, it can rearrange to form a tertiary carbocation (R_3C^+), if a tertiary carbocation is possible. For alkyl carbocations, the relative stability is $3° > 2° > 1°$, the same preference that is observed with free radicals. The features in an S_N1 reaction are opposite of those in the S_N2 reaction. These features of a reaction can be used to predict whether a reaction will proceed by an S_N1 or S_N2 reaction mechanism. The reaction in Figure 3-20 proceeds by an S_N1 mechanism, because the electrophile is tertiary and it has a good leaving group.

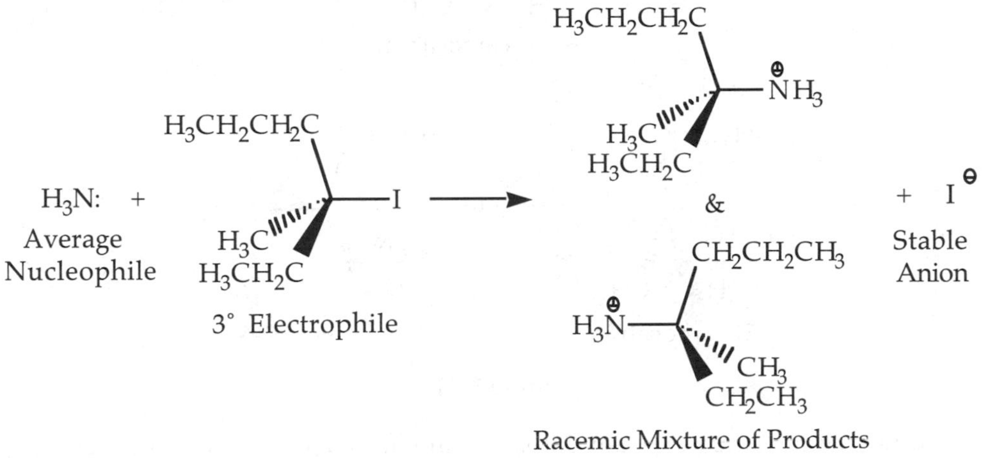

Racemic Mixture of Products

Figure 3-20

The reaction is favorable, because the leaving group is a good leaving group and the nucleophile forms a stronger bond with carbon than the leaving group.

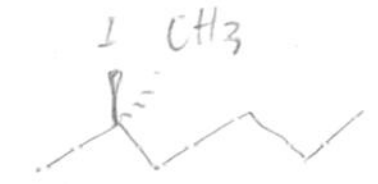

Example 3.22
The addition of ammonia to $3R$-iodo-3-methylhexane at low temperature would yield:

A. one product with R configuration exclusively (retention of stereochemistry).
B. one product with S configuration exclusively (inversion of stereochemistry).
C. two products in an enantiomer mixture.
D. two products in a diastereomeric mixture.

Solution
First, we must determine whether the reaction proceeds by an S_N1 or S_N2 mechanism. The electrophile ($3R$-iodo-3-methylhexane) is tertiary, so the reaction proceeds by an S_N1 mechanism. The chiral center is lost with the formation of the carbocation intermediate, because the intermediate is planar with symmetric sides. This results in a racemic product mixture of two enantiomers. Choice **C** is a swell answer for this question.

In Figure 3-19, the electrophile is tertiary. In cases where the reactive carbon is secondary, an S_N1 reaction can be complicated by rearrangement. This is shown in Figure 3-21.

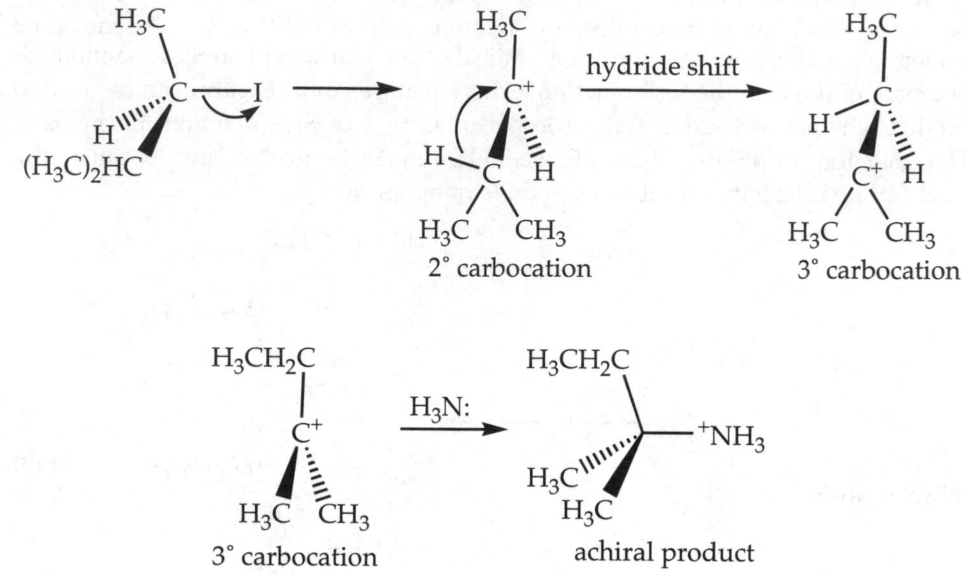

Figure 3-21

Rearrangement is rapid, because it is an intramolecular process. In the example in Figure 3-21, the secondary carbocation rearranges to form a more stable tertiary carbocation before the ammonia nucleophile attacks the carbocation intermediate. This results in a tertiary product. The halide leaving group is not basic enough to deprotonate the ammonium cation formed from the substitution reaction, so the product remains as a cation.

If the electrophile has a chiral center at a site other than the electrophilic carbon, an S_N1 reaction will form both a major and minor product. The major product results from the transition state with least steric hindrance.

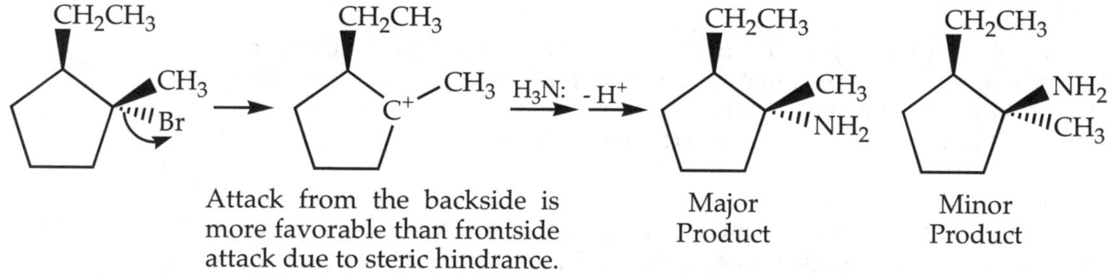

Figure 3-22

In the example in Figure 3-22, the ethyl group in front of the plane interferes with the attack by the nucleophile, which results in an uneven distribution of diastereomers as the product mixture. The major product is formed when ammonia attacks the less hindered face of the carbocation (backside attack in this example). The minor product is formed when ammonia attacks the more hindered face of the carbocation (front side attack in this example).

Distinguishing an S$_N$2 reaction from an S$_N$1 reaction

The first thing to look for when determining the mechanism by which a nucleophilic substitution reaction will proceed, is the substitution of the electrophile. Tertiary and allylic (adjacent to a π-bond) electrophiles will proceed by an S$_N$1 mechanism while methyl and primary electrophiles will proceed by an S$_N$2 mechanism. This is the first factor to view. If the electrophile is secondary, then the reaction can proceed by either mechanism. After considering the substitution of the electrophile, the next feature to consider is the nucleophilic strength. The stronger the nucleophile, the more likely the reaction will proceed by an S$_N$2 mechanism. The better the leaving group, the more likely the reaction will proceed by an S$_N$1 mechanism. Lastly, you should consider the solvent. If the solvent is protic (capable of forming hydrogen bonds), the reaction will have a tendency to proceed by an S$_N$1 mechanism. If the solvent is aprotic (not capable of forming hydrogen bonds), the reaction will have a tendency to proceed by an S$_N$2 mechanism. These factors can be applied when looking at the reactants.

If rate data are given, then the mechanism can be inferred without ambiguity. The rate law associated with an S$_N$1 mechanism is shown in Equation 3.4, while the rate law associated with an S$_N$2 mechanism is shown in Equation 3.5.

$$S_N1 \text{ Rate} = k \text{ [Electrophile]} \qquad \textbf{(3.4)}$$

$$S_N2 \text{ Rate} = k \text{ [Nucleophile][Electrophile]} \qquad \textbf{(3.5)}$$

If the rate of a reaction changes as the nucleophile concentration is varied, the reaction is proceeding by an S$_N$2 mechanism. Conversely, if the rate of a reaction does not change as the nucleophile concentration is varied, the reaction is proceeding by an S$_N$1 mechanism. Because the solvent can affect the strength of a nucleophile, solvent and nucleophile are often considered together. The rates of both reactions vary with a change in electrophile concentration.

The energy diagrams for the two mechanisms also differ. There is no intermediate associated with an S$_N$2 reaction, only a transition state. There is an intermediate and two transition states associated with an S$_N$1 reaction. Figure 3-23 shows the energy diagrams for the one-step S$_N$2 reaction (on the left) and the two-step S$_N$1 reaction (on the right).

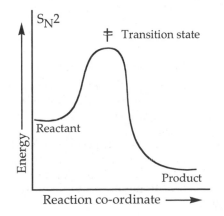 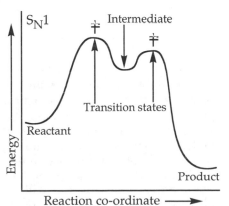

Figure 3-23

The energy level increases at the start of each energy diagram, because a bond is being broken. In the case of the S_N1 reaction, the intermediate is of lower energy than the transition state, because the carbocation can rehybridize to the less crowded sp^2-center rather than an sp^3-center and the intermediate can be solvated in a protic solvent. The increase in energy from the intermediate to the second transition state is associated with rehybridization to the more crowded sp^3-center and the intermediate losing solvation to allow the nucleophile to attack.

Example 3.23

The addition of sodium methoxide to 2S-bromohexane at low temperature would yield:

A. one product with R configuration exclusively (retention of stereochemistry).
B. one product with S configuration exclusively (inversion of stereochemistry).
C. two products in an enantiomeric mixture.
D. two products in a diastereomeric mixture.

Solution

First, we must determine whether the reaction proceeds by an S_N1 or S_N2 mechanism. The electrophile (2S-bromohexane) is secondary so the reaction can proceed by either an S_N1 or S_N2 mechanism. The nucleophile is a strong nucleophile, so we can assume the reaction will proceed via an S_N2 mechanism. This results in inversion of the chiral center and the final product having R stereochemistry, so choice **A** is the best answer. The low temperature is important, so that there is little to no elimination product formed.

Example 3.24

The following reaction shows what relationship between nucleophile concentration and reaction rate?

$$H_3CCH_2S^- + H_3CCH_2Br \longrightarrow H_3CCH_2SCH_2CH_3 + Br^-$$

A. The reaction rate increases in a linear fashion with increasing nucleophile concentration.
B. The reaction rate increases in an exponential fashion with increasing nucleophile concentration.
C. The reaction rate does not change with increasing nucleophile concentration.
D. The reaction rate decreases in a linear fashion with increasing nucleophile concentration.

Solution

The reaction has a primary electrophile and a good nucleophile, which favors an S_N2 mechanism. The rate equation associated with a reaction proceeding by an S_N2 mechanism is rate = k [Electrophile][Nucleophile]. The equation shows that the reaction rate is directly proportional to the nucleophile concentration. The rate increases in a linear fashion with increasing nucleophile concentration, as stated in choice **A**. The best answer is choice **A**. Choice B should be eliminated, because the rate of a nucleophilic substitution reaction does not depend on the concentration of any species in an exponential fashion. Choice D should also be eliminated, because the rate will not decrease with additional nucleophile. It will either increase in a linear fashion or not change.

Example 3.25
A transition state with no intermediate is associated with which of the following reactions?

A. $H_3CCH_2O^- + H_3CCH_2Br \longrightarrow H_3CCH_2OCH_2CH_3 + Br^-$

B. $H_3CCH_2OH + (H_3C)_3CBr \longrightarrow H_3CCH_2OC(CH_3)_3 + HBr$

C. $(H_3C)_3CSH + (H_3C)_2CHOH_2^+ \longrightarrow (H_3C)_3CS^+HCH(CH_3)_2 + H_2O$

D. $NH_3 + (H_3CH_2C)_3CBr \longrightarrow (H_3CCH_2)_3NH_3^+ + Br^-$

Solution
No intermediate is observed with an S_N2 mechanism, so we must find the reaction most likely to proceed by an S_N2 mechanism. The reaction most likely to proceed by an S_N2 mechanism should have a good nucleophile and ideally a primary electrophile. A low temperature is important here so that there will be little to no E_2 product formed. Choices B and D involve tertiary electrophiles, therefore they definitely will proceed by an S_N1 reaction mechanism. This eliminates both choice B and choice D. Choice C is the reaction of a secondary electrophile with a poor nucleophile, so it will likely proceed by an S_N1 reaction mechanism. This eliminates choice C. Choice **A** has a primary electrophile and a good nucleophile, which makes it the most likely to proceed by an S_N2 mechanism, and therefore makes it the best answer. The ethoxide anion is also a strong base, so elimination is possible in choice **A**. Despite the competition with the E_2 reaction, choice A is still the best answer.

Reaction Kinetics
The rate of a reaction depends on several factors. The rate depends on the available energy for the molecules to collide, orient, and break the necessary bonds. The rate depends on the likelihood of the molecules colliding. For an S_N2 reaction, the rate depends on the availability of nucleophile, while it does not depend on the nucleophile concentration in an S_N1 reaction. Consider the S_N2 reaction shown in Figure 3-24 with an ethoxide concentration, $[CH_3CH_2O^-]$, of 0.01 M, a 2-bromopropane concentration, $[CH_3CHBrCH_3]$, of 0.01 M, and a k_{rx} of 2.53×10^{-2} L·mol^{-1}·s^{-1} at 298 K.

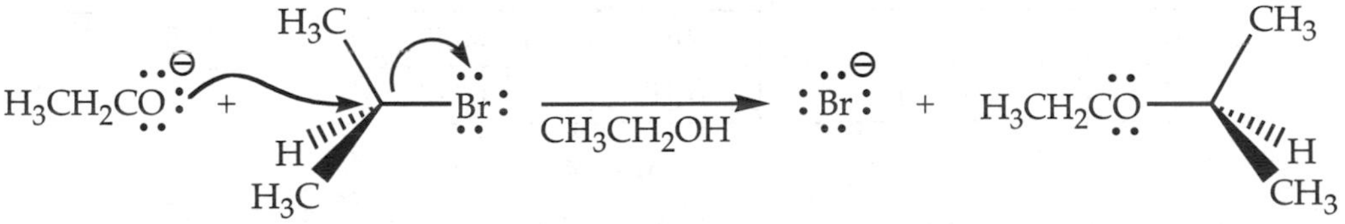

Figure 3-24

The concentrations are low, so the reaction is very slow. Plugging the values into Equation 3.5 yields a rate of 2.53×10^{-6} M per second. The reaction rate may be increased by increasing the reactant concentrations, increasing the temperature, or by adding a catalyst. A catalyst stabilizes the transition state complex and lowers E_{act}. Transition states are short-lived complexes. In the course of the reaction, reactants collide with the correct orientation (from backside attack) to form the transition state complex, when eventually splits to generate the products. Figure 3-25 represents the species of the S_N2 reaction in Figure 3-24 at different stages in chronological order over the duration of the reaction.

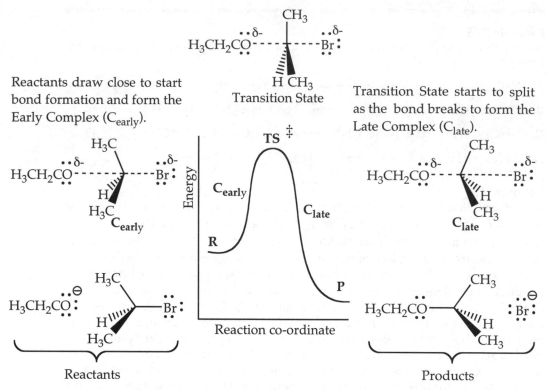

Reactants draw close to start bond formation and form the Early Complex (C_{early}).

Transition State starts to split as the bond breaks to form the Late Complex (C_{late}).

Figure 3-25

Physical Properties of Stereoisomers

Enantiomers have identical physical properties (boiling point, melting point, and density to name a few), while diastereomers have slightly different physical properties. Because they have slightly different physical properties, diastereomers are easier to separate than enantiomers. Enantiomeric mixtures are difficult to purify, because a racemic mixture often has stronger intermolecular forces than the pure enantiomer. Table 3-4 lists the physical properties of the two enantiomers and the racemic mixture of 2-butanol.

Form	Chirality	α_D	Boiling Point	Density	Index of Refraction
(+)	S	+ 13.5°	99.4°C	0.808	1.398
(-)	R	- 13.5°	99.4°C	0.808	1.398
(±)	R/S	0°	101.2°C	0.840	1.442

Table 3-4

From the data in Table 3-4, it can be seen that a racemic mixture allows the molecules to get closer together. This can be thought of when considering your hands, where a left and right hand fit together nicely. It is common that a racemic solid mixture has a higher melting point and greater density than either enantiomer alone.

Separating Stereoisomers

One of the most challenging tasks a synthetic organic chemist faces is the separation of stereoisomers. If a reaction generates a new chiral center in the product, then it will be complicated by stereoisomerism. To generate a pure stereoisomer as a product, chirality must be invoked at some point. From biochemical examples, we know that enzymes (chiral polypeptides) orient molecules in a specific fashion, allowing just one stereoisomer to form. The chirality of the enzyme helps to select for the desired product. In organic chemistry, there are compounds known as *chiral auxiliaries*, which introduce chirality to, or exaggerate existing chirality within, a reactant molecule. Chiral auxiliaries serve in a similar fashion to an enzyme. When aiming for one specific stereoisomer, it is often easiest to select for it in the reaction. If not, a mixture of stereoisomers is formed and chirally selective separation techniques must be applied.

Chirally selective separation techniques come in two types. The first involves employing an enzyme (or chirally selective molecule) to react specifically with one stereoisomer within the mixture. By reacting and therefore introducing a new functional group to only one stereoisomer, the two enantiomers now have different physical properties and can easily be separated. Once separated, the same enzyme can be employed to return the compound back to its original form. An example of such an enzyme is *porcine renal acylase*, which selectively acylates the N-terminal of L-amino acids. By acylating the L-amino acid, it is no longer a zwitterion at neutral pH, while the D-amino acid is a zwitterion. Because only one carries a net charge, They are easily separated from one another.

The second chirally selective separation technique involves invoking chirality in an existing separation technique. For instance, a column chromatography gel can be made from a pure stereoisomer. If the column is made with an *R*-alcohol for instance, then when a racemic mixture of alcohols is added, the *S*-enantiomer has a greater affinity for the column and thus has a greater elution time. This is the basic principle behind affinity chromatography in biochemistry, where an antibody is bound to the column so that it can selectively bind an antigen. Chiral columns in organic chemistry are not as specific as enzyme columns and they hinder solutes, but do not actually bind them. In theory, chirality could be invoked in any organic chemistry separation technique, including distillation, but only it is chiral columns that are commonly used.

Example 3.26
How can the main products of an S_N1 reaction with an asymmetric secondary alkyl iodide be separated from one another?

A. Using fractional distillation
B. Using extraction
C. Using chiral column chromatography
D. Using plane-polarized light and a polarimeter

Solution
An S_N1 reaction with a secondary iodide where the two R-groups are different will generate a pair of enantiomers in a 50-50 ratio. The problem with separating enantiomers from one another is that they have the same physical properties. They can't be separated using distillation (via boiling), because enantiomers have the same boiling point. Choice A is eliminated. They can't be separated by extraction, because the two enantiomers will exhibit the same solubility in any given solvent. Choice B is eliminated. Passing the product mixture through a chiral column will result in one enantiomer having a greater affinity for the column than the other, which means that chiral chromatography can separate one enantiomer from another. Choice **C** is the best answer. While enantiomers exhibit opposite rotation of plane-polarized light, it is an identification technique and not a separation technique. This eliminates choice D.

Example 3.27
How can an enantiomeric excess of 72% be explained for the product mixture formed from the reaction of methylamine with $2R$-bromopentane?

A. Some of the amine nucleophile reacted with the alkylamine product.
B. The reaction proceeded by mostly an S_N2 mechanism with a small amount of an S_N1 mechanism.
C. The reaction proceeded by mostly an S_N1 mechanism with a small amount of an S_N2 mechanism.
D. The inversion of chirality reversed its direction in the later stages of the reaction.

Solution
An enantiomeric excess implies that the reaction generated a chiral center. An S_N2 mechanism would predict 100% inversion and therefore an enantiomeric excess of 100%. An S_N1 mechanism would predict racemization and therefore an enantiomeric excess of 0%. An amine is a terrible leaving group and it is highly unlikely unless the temperature was extremely high that an amine would be forced off a carbon, even by another amine. Choice A is eliminated. Choice D is crazy talk about inversion reversing in the later stages of the reaction. Inversion depends on the reactants not the timing of the reaction, so choice D is eliminated. With a secondary electrophile that has a good leaving group and a strong nucleophile, a mixture of an S_N2 and S_N1 reaction is viable. An enantiomeric excess of 72% is much closer to 100% than 0%, so it is reasonable that it went mostly by an S_N2 mechanism, with a small percentage proceeding by an S_N1 mechanism. The best answer is choice **B**. Choice C would have resulted in a smaller enantiomeric excess.

Key Points for Stereochemistry (Section 3)

Chirality and Asymmetry

1. Chiral Molecules
   a) Have asymmetry within their structure due to atoms that are unevenly substituted
      i. Stereogenic carbons are sp^3-hybridized carbons with four unique substituents
      ii. Chiral molecules are predominant in many organic reactions
   b) Stereogenic carbons are assigned an absolute configuration of either R or S to describe their chirality
      i. Priorities are assigned according to atomic mass of the atoms attached to the stereogenic center. If two atoms are identical, then you proceed along its connectivity until there is a difference
      ii. When priority #4 is in back, a clockwise arc connects priorities #1, #2, and #3 in R-stereogenic centers. When priority #4 is in back, a counterclockwise arc connects priorities #1, #2, and #3 in S-stereogenic centers.
      iii. To determine whether a center is R or S, you can place your thumb in the direction of substituent #4 and curl your fingers from priority #1, through priority #2, and on to priority #3. Only one of your hands can do this. If it is a right hand that does this, the stereogenic carbon has R-chirality. If it is a left hand that does this, the stereogenic carbon has S-chirality.
   c) Short cuts for determining R and S involve the positioning of priority #4
      i. If priority #4 is in back, then the arc determines the chirality (clockwise for R and counterclockwise for S). If priority #4 is in front, then the arc must be reversed to determine the chirality (a clockwise arc is reversed to represent S and a counterclockwise arc is reversed to represent R). If priority #4 is drawn in the plane close to the group going back, then the arc is reversed to determine the chirality. If priority #4 is drawn in the plane far away from the group going back, then the arc as is determines the chirality.
      ii. Whenever two groups are switched, the chirality reverses

Configurational Isomers

1. Same connectivity, but different spatial arrangement of atoms
   a) Can be categorized as either optical isomers or geometrical isomers
      i. Optical isomers rotate plane-polarized light
      ii. Geometrical isomers differ about a feature in the molecule about which rotation is not possible (π-bond or ring)
      iii. Optical isomers are identified by a standard rotation value
   b) Can be categorized as enantiomers or diastereomers
      i. Enantiomers are nonsuperimposable stereoisomers that are mirror images
      ii. Diastereomers are nonsuperimposable stereoisomers that are not mirror images
      iii. Enantiomeric optical isomers are better thought of as stereoisomers where all of the chiral centers differ
      iv. Diastereomeric optical isomers are better thought of as stereoisomers where some, but not all, of the chiral centers differ

Stereochemistry in Reactions

1. Stereoisomers are formed when a nucleophile attacks an asymmetric molecule in multiple ways
   a) Racemic mixtures form when there is no preexisting chirality

    b)   Diastereomers are formed in a major/minor distribution when one of the reactants has a chiral center at a non-reactive site

        i.   Mixtures are resolved by using chiral reagents or lab techniques that invoke chirality.

        ii.   Enzymatic reactions use a chiral catalyst to cause the reaction to drastically favor the formation of one stereoisomer over all other possible stereoisomer products

        iii. When two enantiomers are present in unequal amount, there is said to be an enantiomeric excess. Enantiomeric excess is used to describe the success in a stereoselective synthesis

    c)   Enantiomers have identical physical properties as one another while diastereomers have different physical properties.

Nucleophilic Substitution

1.   Proceeds by either an S_N1-mechanism or S_N2-mechanism

    a)   In an S_N1-mechanism, the electrophile is highly substituted, the solvent is protic, and a carbocation intermediate is formed because the leaving group leaves in the first step. There is potentially rearrangement and the product mixture is often racemic. The reaction rate only depends on the electrophile.

    b)   In an S_N2-mechanism, the electrophile is minimally substituted, the solvent is polar and aprotic, and a transition state is formed because the nucleophile attacks to force the leaving group off in the only step. There is inversion of chirality so the product mixture is often the opposite chirality of the reactant and the reaction is fast. The reaction rate depends on both the nucleophile and the electrophile.

"Better living through chemistry!"

25 Stereochemistry Review Questions

The main purpose of this 25-question set is to serve as a review of the material presented in the chapter. Do not worry about the timing for these questions. Focus on learning. Once you complete these questions, grade them using the answer key. For any question you missed, repeat it and write down your thought process. Then grade the questions you repeated and thoroughly read the answer explanation. Compare your thought process to the answer explanation and assess whether you missed the question because of a careless error (such as misreading the question), because of an error in reasoning, or because you were lacking information. Your goal is to fill in any informational gaps and solidify your reasoning before you begin your practice exam for this section. Preparing for the MCAT is best done in stages. This first stage is meant to help you evaluate how well you know this subject matter.

Nucleophilic substitution is the process by which functional groups bonded to an sp^3-hybridized carbon can be exchanged for a different functional group. It is commonly viewed as a reaction that can proceed by one of two pathways. The first of the pathways is named S_N1 for its rate dependence on one reactant. The second pathway is referred to as S_N2 for its rate dependence on two reactants.

Two different experiments involving two different electrophiles (one primary and the other tertiary) were carried out where the nucleophile was varied from trial to trial. The reactions were monitored using UV spectroscopy where the magnitude of the rate of disappearance for the peak corresponding to the electrophile varies directly with the reaction rate. Tables 1 and 2 list the initial reaction rate observed in each trial.

Nucleophile	Reaction rate w/ $CH_3CH_2CH_2Cl$
H_3CNH_2	4.7×10^{-2} M/sec
NH_3	4.2×10^{-2} M/sec
H_3CSH	2.1×10^{-2} M/sec
H_3COH	8.2×10^{-3} M/sec

Table 1 Reactions with n-Propylchloride

Nucleophile	Reaction rate w/ $(H_3C)_3CCl$
H_3CNH_2	3.3×10^{-4} M/sec
NH_3	3.6×10^{-4} M/sec
H_3CSH	3.3×10^{-4} M/sec
H_3COH	3.5×10^{-4} M/sec

Table 2 Reactions with t-Butylchloride

All other variables that can affect the reaction rate besides the nucleophile, such as temperature and reactant concentration, were held constant across all of the trials.

1. Which of the following electrophiles is the best choice to react with $NaOCH_3$ to yield the following ether?

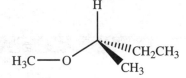

    A. $2R$-chlorobutane
    B. $2S$-chlorobutane
    C. $2R$-aminobutane
    D. $2S$-aminobutane

2. A nucleophilic substitution reaction proceeds MOST rapidly with the leaving group on what type of carbon?

    A. 1°
    B. 2°
    C. 3°
    D. The reaction rate is independent of the degree of substitution.

3. Reaction of ($2R,3S$) 2-bromo-3-methylpentane with ammonia yields which of the following products?

    A. ($2S,3S$) 2-amino-3-methylpentane
    B. ($2R,3S$) 2-amino-3-methylpentane
    C. ($2S,3R$) 2-amino-3-methylpentane
    D. A mixture of ($2S,3S$) 2-amino-3-methylpentane and ($2S,3R$) 2-amino-3-methylpentane in a 50:50 ratio.

4. A reaction in which the specific rotation of the starting material is + 32° and the product (which still contains a chiral center) is 0° is which of the following?

    A. S_N1
    B. S_N2
    C. S_NE1
    D. S_NE2

5. Which of the following graphs BEST represents the Cl^- concentration as a function of time for the reaction of ammonia with 1-chloropropane?

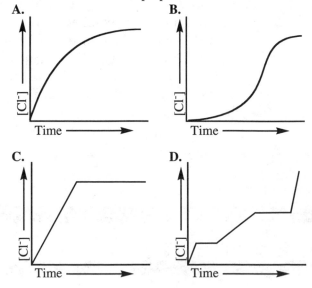

6. Based on the data presented in Tables 1 and 2, which of the following is the best nucleophile?

A. H_3CNH_2

B. NH_3

C. H_3CSH

D. H_3COH

7. Monitoring the following reaction by optical rotation would yield which of the following graphs?

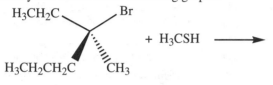

A.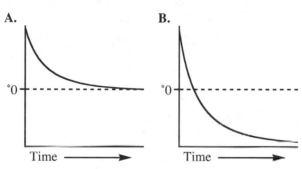

B.

C.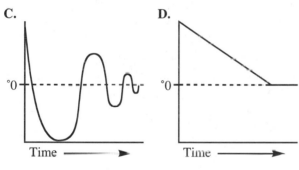

D.

Passage II (Questions 8 - 14)

Stereogenic carbons, *stereocenters*, are important features in chiral organic compounds. Stereocenters are responsible for physical properties, chemical reactivity, and biological function. Variations in stereochemistry impact the physical properties of a compound. An example of the correlation between physical properties and chirality is shown with the stereoisomers of tartaric acid. Drawn in Figure 1 is the generic structure of tartaric acid. and a data table of the physical properties of the stereoisomers:

Figure 1 Tartaric Acid

Table 1 shows the physical properties of the three stereoisomers of tartaric acid and the physical properties of the enantiomeric mixture.

Form	m.p.	α_D	Density	H_2O sol. @ 20°C
(+)	168-170	+ 12°	1.7598	139 g/100mL
(-)	168-170	- 12°	1.7598	139 g/100mL
meso	146-148	0°	1.5996	125 g/100mL
(±)	205-207	0°	1.7880	21 g/100mL

Table 1

The differences in density and melting point can be attributed to lattice formation in the solid phase. The compound can pack most tightly when the mixture is symmetric. This can be seen in the density and the melting point of each stereoisomer.

Examples of stereochemical influences in biological reactivity are numerous. A common example involves the digestion of D-sugars. Our body can metabolize D-glucose yet it cannot metabolize L-glucose (the enantiomer of D-glucose), because our enzymes are selective for one enantiomer over the other. A recent example involves the compound L-Dopa. L-Dopa is used as an anti-Parkinson drug while D-Dopa has no effect and can in fact be toxic in large enough doses. L-Dopa is drawn in Figure 2 below.

Figure 2 L-Dopa

8. How can a compound with an optical rotation of +233.0° be discerned from a compound with an optical rotation of -127.0°?

- **A.** The intensity of the light is greater with the positive optical rotation.
- **B.** The sample with +233.0° optical rotation when diluted to half of its original concentration would show an optical rotation of +116.5°.
- **C.** The larger the absolute value of the optical rotation, the greater the density of the compound.
- **D.** It is not possible to distinguish the two compounds from one another.

9. Given that the specific rotation of D-Glucose is +52.6°, what can be said about the specific rotation of D-mannose (the C-2 epimer of glucose)? Note: An epimer is a diastereomer that varies at only one stereocenter.

D-Glucose

- **A.** It cannot be +52.6°, -52.6°, or 0°.
- **B.** It must be either +52.6°, -52.6°, or 0°.
- **C.** It is 0°.
- **D.** It is -52.6°.

10. How many stereoisomers are possible for penicillin V?

- **A.** 1
- **B.** 2
- **C.** 4
- **D.** 8

11. Which of the following physical properties would have the same value for morphine and a diastereomer of morphine?

- **A.** Melting point.
- **B.** Density.
- **C.** Molecular mass.
- **D.** Specific rotation.

12. What can be concluded about the packing of molecules in the crystal lattice of the stereoisomers of tartaric acid?

- **A.** The meso compound packs most tightly while the (+) enantiomer and (-) enantiomer pack the same.
- **B.** The meso compound packs least tightly while the (+) enantiomer and (-) enantiomer pack the same.
- **C.** The meso compound packs most tightly of all of the stereoisomers. The (+) enantiomer packs more tightly than the (-) enantiomer.
- **D.** The meso compound packs most tightly of all of the stereoisomers. The (+) enantiomer packs less tightly than the (-) enantiomer.

13. How many stereocenters are present in the molecule camphor which shows an optical rotation of +44.3°?

- **A.** 0
- **B.** 1
- **C.** 2
- **D.** 3

14. Which of the following statements best explains why an R/S enantiomeric mixture has a higher melting point than pure samples of either the R-enantiomer or the S-enantiomer?

- **A.** It requires more energy to break the hydrogen bonds within a pure compound than within a mixture of compounds.
- **B.** Enantiomers readily form covalent bonds with one another.
- **C.** The covalent bonds are weaker when the material is one pure stereoisomer then when it is a mixture of two or more stereoisomers.
- **D.** The R-stereoisomer packs more tightly with its enantiomer than it does with itself.

220   **GO ON TO THE NEXT PAGE**

The Diels-Alder reaction of isoprene upon itself at 100°C yields two enantiomers of limonene in a fifty-fifty ratio as the major product. In the reaction, the diene of one isoprene molecule reacts with the less hindered double bond of another isoprene molecule to form the product. Because isoprene is a planar molecule, there is an equal chance for the reaction to occur on the top face as the bottom face of isoprene. The Diels-Alder reaction that synthesizes limonene is shown in Figure 1 below.

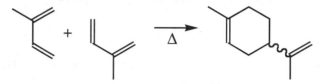

Figure 1 Diels-Alder Condensation Reaction of Isoprene

The two enantiomers that are formed have similar physical properties, but have different applications in the flavoring agent industry. One enantiomer has a lemon scent while the other has an orange scent. The two enantiomers of limonene are shown in Figure 2 below.

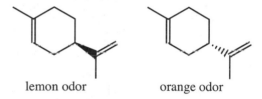

lemon odor   orange odor

Figure 2 Enantiomers of Limonene

The percentage of each enantiomer in the product mixture can be altered only with the addition of another chiral reagent involved in the transition state. To isolate either the lemon flavoring or the orange flavoring, the chosen enantiomer must be separated from the product mixture by one of several possible laboratory techniques that involve chirality, such as the use of a column with a chiral adsorbent in column chromatography.

15. The lemon flavored isomer has what stereochemistry associated with it?

A. One chiral center with R stereochemistry
B. One chiral center with S stereochemistry
C. Two chiral centers with R,R stereochemistry
D. Two chiral centers with S,S stereochemistry

16. Which of the following physical properties is MOST likely different for the two enantiomers?

A. Boiling point
B. Density
C. Alcohol solubility
D. Optical Rotation

17. Which of the following techniques does NOT work to isolate one enantiomer from the presence of an enantiomeric mixture?

A. Adding the mixture to a chiral gel in a column chromatography.
B. Distillation of the product mixture.
C. Crystallization of the mixture with the addition of an enantiomerically pure compound.
D. Filtering through an enzymatic membrane.

18. Which of the following will lead to a product mixture composed of more than fifty percent of one of the enantiomers (the product mixture not being racemic)?

A. Carrying the reaction out with a chiral solvent.
B. Carrying the reaction out with a chiral catalyst.
C. Carrying the reaction out at a lower temperature.
D. Carrying the reaction out at a higher concentration.

19. How does the following minor side product of the reaction in Figure 1 relate to the major product with lemon odor?

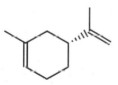

A. It is a structural isomer.
B. It is a diastereomer.
C. It is an anomer.
D. It is an enantiomer.

20. What can be concluded about the olfactory receptors?

A. They are symmetric (achiral) because they can distinguish between enantiomers.
B. They are asymmetric (chiral) because they can distinguish between enantiomers.
C. They are symmetric (achiral) because they cannot distinguish between enantiomers.
D. They are asymmetric (chiral) because they cannot distinguish between enantiomers.

                                       GO ON TO THE NEXT PAGE

21. If the following molecule were the reactant in the reaction shown in Figure 1, rather than isoprene, how would the results differ?

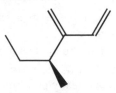

A. The product mixture would no longer be racemic.
B. The product mixture would still be racemic.
C. The products would be achiral.
D. The products would have four stereocenters each.

Questions 22 through 25 are **NOT** based on a descriptive passage.

22. The amino acid glycine has an H as its side chain. What would you predict for the optical rotation for naturally occurring glycine?

A. (+) 32°
B. (-) 32°
C. 0°
D. More information is needed. (Never choose this!)

23. What BEST describes the transition state of $NaSCH_3$ with 2-bromobutane at 50°C in diethyl ether?

A.

B.

C.

D.

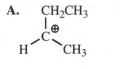

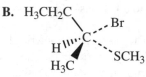

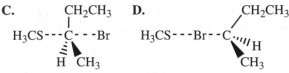

24. A nucleophile can also be classified as which of the following?

A. A Lewis acid
B. A Lewis base
C. An oxidizing agent
D. A reducing agent

25. What is the observed optical rotation for a solution with an enantiomeric excess of +60% for a pair enantiomers which have specific rotations of +50° and -50°?

A. +30°
B. +15°
C. +7.5°
D. +300°

1. A	2. A	3. A	4. A	5. A
6. A	7. A	8. B	9. A	10. D
11. C	12. B	13. C	14. D	15. A
16. D	17. B	18. B	19. A	20. B
21. A	22. C	23. C	24. B	25. A

PACK IT IN, BECAUSE YOU ARE FIN.

Answers to 25-Question Stereochemistry Review

1. **Choice A is the best answer.** The ether product has S stereochemistry as drawn and was formed by a substitution reaction using $NaOCH_3$ as the nucleophile. Sodium methoxide ($NaOCH_3$) is a strong base, and thus can act as a nucleophile when it does not deprotonate a hydrogen. Because the nucleophile is good, the reaction must have proceeded by an S_N2 mechanism, which tells us that the product resulted from inversion of stereochemistry. Because the final product has S stereochemistry, the starting material (electrophile) must have had R stereochemistry to form the S product from inversion. This eliminates choices B and D. For the substitution reaction to proceed, the electrophile must have had a good leaving group. Ammonia is not a leaving group, therefore the chlorine leaving group is the better choice. This eliminates choice C and makes choice **A** the best answer.

2. **Choice A is the best answer.** From the data in the tables, faster reactions are observed with primary electrophiles than with tertiary electrophiles, so choices C and D are eliminated. It is a reasonable assumption that the reaction with the primary alkyl halide proceeds more rapidly than it would with a secondary alkyl halide, because of steric hindrance, so choice B is eliminated. Choice **A** is the best answer (as well as the only one left).

3. **Choice A is the best answer.** The reaction can proceed by either an S_N1 or S_N2 mechanism with a secondary alkyl halide as the electrophile. Carbon 2 is the reactive carbon, so the stereochemistry at carbon 2 is our focus. If the reaction were to proceed by an S_N2 mechanism, then the product would be the $2S,3S$ stereoisomer. Only the stereocenter from which the bromine substituent left underwent a change in chirality (inversion), thus only that stereocenter will show a change in its absolute configuration. If the reaction were to proceed by an S_N1 mechanism, then the intermediate would undergo rearrangement, and thus the ammonia would attack the third carbon leaving an achiral product. Given the answer choices, choices B and C can't form, and there is no achiral choice, therefore the reaction must have proceeded by an S_N2 mechanism. This means that inversion of the second carbon will transpire to yield $2S,3S$. Choice **A** is the best answer.

4. **Choice A is the best answer.** To have optical activity and lose it during the course of the reaction eliminates choice B, because the S_N2 reaction proceeds with inversion (thus an optically active product is formed). The question states that the product has no optical activity, but has a chiral center. This eliminates the option for an achiral product. The product, based on the hints, must be a racemic mixture. A racemic product mixture is associated with the S_N1 reaction. Choices C and D should be throwaway answers as they don't exist. Pick **A**.

5. **Choice A is the best answer.** The reaction proceeds at the fastest rate during the first segment of the reaction because initially the concentration of 1-chloropropane (a reactant in the rate determining step) is greatest and both reactants (nucleophile and electrophile) are depleted over time. Chloride anion is the leaving group, thus its concentration will increase over time. All of the graphs show chloride increasing concentration, so that doesn't help. Over time, the concentration of 1-chloropropane gradually decreases, thus the reaction rate decreases gradually; this results in a slower production of Cl^- anion. Graph A best depicts this gradual decrease in reaction rate. Choice B is out because there is no reason to show an increasing rate at first followed by a decreasing rate. Choices C and D are not viable because of their abrupt changes. Choose **A** and be a wünder student.

6. **Choice A is the best answer.** The reactions in Table 1 proceed by way of an S_N2 mechanism, because the electrophile is a primary alkyl halide. The reactions in Table 2 proceed by way of an S_N1 mechanism, because the electrophile is a tertiary alkyl halide. Only the rate of an S_N2 reaction depends on the nucleophile, therefore to determine the best nucleophile, the data from the reaction with the primary alkyl halide (the data in Table 1) should be used. The best nucleophile is the compound that has the fastest reaction rate, which according to Table 1, is methylamine (H_3CNH_2). Choose **A** if you're a table believer.

7. **Choice A is the best answer.** Because the electrophile is a tertiary alkyl halide, the reaction is an S_N1 reaction, which proceeds with racemization. The optical rotation of the product mixture after an S_N1 reaction is 0°. This eliminates choice B. Graph C (the schizophrenic graph) shows the correct final optical rotation, but no reaction will proceed with such an erratic change in optical rotation. Choice D shows that the reaction proceeds at a constant rate until the reaction is complete. This would be seen with a zero-order reaction, not a first-order reaction. The S_N1 reaction is first-order, so answer choice D is eliminated. Graph A best depicts the gradual loss of chirality. The optical rotation will never switch to the opposite sign unless there is inversion which is not possible with an S_N1 reaction. Choose **A** and make your support group proud.

8.   **Choice B is the best answer.** When using a polarimeter, an observed optical rotation of +233.0° and -127.0° would result in the same reading (given that a full circle is 360°). To discern one optical rotation from the other, the sample should be diluted to reduce the magnitude of the observed rotation. If the actual optical rotation were in fact +233.0°, then the lower concentration would show a rotation less than +233.0° (less clockwise). If the actual optical rotation were in fact -127.0°, then the lower concentration would show a rotation of lesser magnitude than -127.0° (less counterclockwise). If the solution concentration were cut in half for instance, the observed rotation would be either +116.5° or -63.5°. The change in rotation can therefore determine the original rotation value. The only answer that indicates changing the concentration is choice **B**. The intensity of the light depends on absorption, not rotation of plane-polarized light, so choice A should have been eliminated. The magnitude of the rotation does not depend on the solution density or compound density, so choice C should have been eliminated.

9.   **Choice A is the best answer.** If D-glucose has an optical rotation of +52.6°, then the enantiomer of D-glucose (L-glucose) must have an optical rotation of -52.6°. Mannose, the C-2 epimer of glucose (the diastereomer of glucose that only differs at carbon two) is neither of these two structures (L-glucose or D-glucose), thus it will not show an optical rotation of either + 52.6° or -52.6°. This eliminates choices B and D. Mannose is chiral and not meso, so it cannot have an optical rotation of 0°. This eliminates choice C and makes choice **A** the best answer.

10.   **Choice D is the best answer.** The number of stereoisomers (assuming that there is not a meso structure), can be determined by raising 2 to the power of the number of stereogenic carbons (stereocenters). There are three stereocenters associated with penicillin V, thus there will be eight (2^3) stereoisomers for the structure of penicillin V. The 2^n formula determines the maximum number of stereoisomers. For every meso structure, you would subtract one from the maximum total, but that's not the case here. Choice **D** is the best answer.

11.   **Choice C is the best answer.** As indicated in Table 1 in the passage, diastereomers show different physical properties. The melting points of diastereomers are different, because the molecules pack into their respective lattice structures differently. This eliminates choice A. Density is different for diastereomers, because the two diastereomers have different conformations that also pack into their respective lattice structures differently. This eliminates choice B. The specific rotation of diastereomers must be different given the fact that they are identified by their specific rotation. This eliminates choice D. Because diastereomers are isomers, and they have the same molecular formula, thus they have the same molecular mass. The best answer is therefore choice **C**.

12.   **Choice B is the best answer.** The greater the density of a compound, the more tightly packed the compound is in its crystal lattice. This question is a read-the-chart-to-find-the-density question. The meso compound is less dense than the other compounds according to the data in the table, thus it must pack least tightly of all of the choices. Knowing that enantiomers have the same physical properties supports the notion that they pack the same, but that information was not essential to finding the best answer. The best answer is choice **B**.

13.   **Choice C is the best answer.** Stereocenters can be identified quickly as sp^3-hybridized carbons with four different substituents attached. In camphor, there are two carbons that fit this description. The correct choice is answer **C**. Drawn below is camphor with the two chiral carbons (stereocenters) labeled:

14.   **Choice D is the best answer.** If the hydrogen bonds in a pure compound were stronger than the hydrogen bonds in an enantiomer mixture, then the melting point for the pure compound would be greater than it is for the mixture. This is the opposite of the premise. Choice A is an untrue statement, and thus it is eliminated. Physical properties, such as melting point, result from intermolecular forces, not covalent bonds. Enantiomers are no more likely to form covalent bonds with one another than diastereomers. Choice B is an untrue statement that does not explain the observed melting points. Choice B is eliminated. Covalent bonds are not affected when a compound melts, so choice C should be eliminated. The best explanation is choice **D**, because when the molecules pack more tightly, they exert stronger forces on each other. Because the enantiomeric mixture (*R* with *S*) has a higher melting point than the pure enantiomer (R with itself), the forces are in fact stronger in the enantiomeric mixture than the pure compound. This makes choice **D** the best answer.

15. **Choice A is the best answer.** Both enantiomers have only one stereocenter, therefore choices C and D are eliminated. The lemon flavored extract is the structure on the left, which has its lone stereogenic center in R configuration. This eliminates choice B and makes choice **A** the correct answer.

16. **Choice D is the best answer.** The one physical property that definitely changes with the chiral center is the optical rotation. The specific rotation of a product mixture measures its enantiomeric purity (percentage of each enantiomer). The boiling point, density, and solubility in a given solvent do not vary between enantiomers. These physical properties can vary between diastereomers, but enantiomers are identical in their packing and intermolecular forces, unless the alcohol solvent is chiral and optically pure. The best answer is choice **D**.

17. **Choice B is the best answer.** To separate enantiomers from one another, the separation technique employed must be able to bind one enantiomer more than the other. This will require the use of a chiral molecule in the separation technique. The best method is the use of chiral gel in column chromatography. The two enantiomers exhibit different migration rates down the column, because the two adhere to the column to a different extent. Choice A is a valid method. Enantiomers have the same boiling points, so distillation will *not* separate the two enantiomers. No chirality preference has been incorporated into the distillation process, so choice **B** is the best answer. The mixture can be selectively crystallized with a pure R-compound or a pure S-compound. This is often carried out with tartaric acid. Choice C is a valid separation technique for enantiomers. Enzymes are chiral, so chiral compounds will pass through an enzyme filter at different rates. This makes choice D valid.

18. **Choice B is the best answer.** To prevent an enantiomeric product mixture from being racemic, chirality must be present in the transition state of the reaction pathway. A change in temperature does not affect the chirality of the products, so choice C is eliminated. The concentration does not affect the alignment of the molecules in the transition state, only the frequency with which the reactants collide to form the transition state. This eliminates choice D. The presence of a chiral center in the solvent does not affect the chirality of the transition state unless the solvent is involved in the transition state. Choice A cannot be eliminated yet, but it is not a likely choice. The only change that will definitely affect the distribution of enantiomers is the addition of a chiral catalyst, which affects the transition state. This is the whole idea behind the activity and specificity of enzymes (chiral catalysts) in biological reactions. The best answer is therefore choice **B**.

19. **Choice A is the best answer.** It's really easy to get caught up on the stereochemistry on this question and not notice that the structures in question have nonequivalent substitution. The lemon odor molecule has alkyl substituents on carbons 1 and 4 of the six-membered ring while the molecule in the question has alkyl substituents on carbons 1 and 3 of the six-membered ring. This makes the two compounds structural isomers and not any type of stereoisomer such as diastereomers, anomers, or enantiomers. The best answer is choice **A**.

Lemon odor molecule   Structure in question

20. **Choice B is the best answer.** The two enantiomers have a different flavor (and thus a different smell as well), so they must bind the olfactory receptors differently. Olfactory receptors can distinguish between the two enantiomers, so choices C and D are eliminated. Because olfactory receptors recognize the difference between the two enantiomers, they too must be asymmetric (and thus chiral). The best answer is choice **B**.

21. **Choice A is the best answer.** The isoprene molecule has no chiral centers, so the products are formed in a racemic mixture. The molecule listed in the question as an alternative reactant to isoprene has a chiral center present that will influence the orientation in the transition state. Because each react starts with a stereocenter and a third one is formed from the reaction, the products would contain three chiral centers not four. This eliminates choices C and D. The stereoisomer products would be a mixture of diastereomers and not enantiomers, because two of the three chiral centers are the same when comparing the product stereoisomers. Diastereomers cannot be present in a racemic mixture, therefore the product mixture could not be racemic for the new reaction. This eliminates choice B. The best answer is choice **A**.

Major stereoisomer product   Minor stereoisomer product

1 out of 3 stereocenters differ
∴ they are diastereomers

22. **Choice C is the best answer.** With H as the side chain, carbon two of glycine (the alpha carbon) has two hydrogens attached, thus there is no chiral center present on glycine. Neither of the two carbons in glycine have four different substituents attached. The absence of a chiral center in glycine results in an optical rotation of 0°. Choose **C** and be happy.

23. **Choice C is the best answer.** The electrophile is secondary, so the nucleophilic substitution reaction could proceed by either an S_N1 mechanism or an S_N2 mechanism. The solvent is aprotic and the nucleophile is a very good one, so the reaction is likely proceeding via an S_N2 mechanism. Choice A is eliminated, because it is a carbocation, which is an intermediate, not a transition state. On top of that, S_N2 reactions do not have carbocation intermediates. The transition state of an S_N2 reaction results from the backside attack of the electrophile by the nucleophile, with respect to the leaving group. The leaving group and nucleophile should be collinear with the reactive carbon. Choice B does not show collinear alignment, so it is eliminated. Choice D shows collinear alignment, but it is not the result of the nucleophile attacking the electrophilic carbon, so choice D is eliminated. Collinear alignment with the nucleophile attacking the electrophilic carbon while the leaving group is leaving is shown in answer choice **C**, so choice **C** is the best answer.

24. **Choice B is the best answer.** By definition, a nucleophile is a lone pair donor, which by yet another definition is a Lewis base. This makes this question a freebie and the best answer is choice **B**. A Lewis acid is an electron pair acceptor, which describes an electrophile, not a nucleophile. Choice A is eliminated. On occasions, such as with the Grignard reaction, the nucleophile can cause the breaking of a carbon-oxygen pi-bond and in doing so cause reduction, but that is not always the case with a nucleophile. So while a nucleophile can act as a reducing agent when it undergoes attack and addition to a carbonyl compound, choice **B** is a better answer than choice D.

25. **Choice A is the best answer.** If the solution contains 100% of the (+)-enantiomer, then the observed optical rotation would be 50°. The observed rotation of a mixture of two enantiomers must therefore fall between -50° and +50°, which eliminates choice D. All of the choices are + rotations, so the mixture must be richer in the (+)-enantiomer than the (-)-enantiomer. The observed rotation is found by multiplying the maximum rotation by the enantiomeric excess. In this case, $60\% \times (+50°) = +30°$, which makes choice **A** the best answer.

52-Question Stereochemistry Practice Exam

Stereochemistry Exam Scoring Scale

Raw Score	MCAT Score
44 - 52	13 - 15
35 - 43	10 - 12
24 - 34	7 - 9
17 - 23	4 - 6
1 - 16	1 - 3

Natural products are molecules that are synthesized by plants. In many naturally occurring synthesis pathways, the products of the reaction are stereochemically pure. Because the enzymes that carry out the synthesis are asymmetric, the products that are formed are asymmetric. This is known as the *induction of chirality*. Figure 1 shows two examples of natural products that can be extracted from plants:

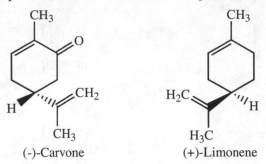

(-)-Carvone   (+)-Limonene

Figure 1

Carvone is present in both spearmint oil and caraway oil. The *R*-enantiomer is found in spearmint oil. Limonene is found in the rind of citrus fruits such as the grapefruit, the lemon, and the orange. The two enantiomers of limonene have a different fragrance, which implies that the human olfactory lobes are chirally sensitive.

Carvone and limonene are part of the diterpene family. Terpenes are synthesized in plants from isoprene units of five carbons. Two isoprene units can combine by way of a Diels-Alder reaction to form the basic ring structure of both carvone and limonene. Figure 2 shows an isoprene subunit.

H3C

H2C   CH2

Figure 2. Isoprene Subunit

1. Given that (-)-carvone has $\alpha_D = -61.2°$, what can be said about (+)-carvone and (+)-limonene?

   A. (+)-carvone $\alpha_D = +30.6°$, (+)-limonene $\alpha_D = +124°$
   B. (+)-carvone $\alpha_D = +30.6°$, (+)-limonene $\alpha_D = -124°$
   C. (+)-carvone $\alpha_D = +61.2°$, (+)-limonene $\alpha_D = +124°$
   D. (+)-carvone $\alpha_D = +61.2°$, (+)-limonene $\alpha_D = -124°$

2. Which of the following statement(s) is/are valid for the isomers of carvone and limonene?

   I. Both limonene and carvone have four possible stereoisomers each.

   II. (+)-Limonene has *R* stereochemistry.

   III. (-)-Carvone has *S* stereochemistry.

   A. II only
   B. III only
   C. I and II only
   D. II and III only

3. How many chiral centers are present in (+)-carvone?

   A. 0
   B. 1
   C. 2
   D. 3

4. Which carbons in (-)-carvone can carry a positive charge, if carvone is treated with strong acid?

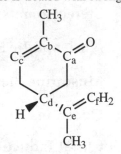

   A. Carbons a, b, and c
   B. Carbons a, c, and e
   C. Carbons b, c, and f
   D. Carbons a, b, c, e, and f

5. Which of the following compounds has the same molecular formula as (-)-carvone, but does not show an IR peak between 1680 and 1740 cm^{-1}?

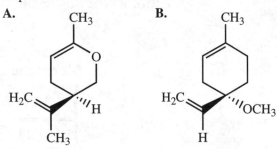

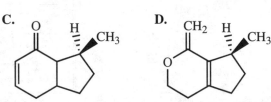

6. How do (+)-limonene and (-)-limonene relate to one another?

   A. Anomers
   B. Diastereomers
   C. Enantiomers
   D. Epimers

228   **GO ON TO THE NEXT PAGE**

Passage II (Questions 7 - 12)

Nucleophilic substitution involves the exchange of a nucleophile for a leaving group on an electrophilic carbon. When dealing with sp^3-hybridized carbons, there are two common mechanisms for nucleophilic substitution reactions, named for their kinetic behavior. The mechanisms are S_N1 and S_N2. For the following reaction, four unique nucleophiles are observed at different temperatures in different solvents. The results are listed in the tables below:

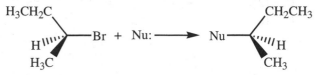

Figure 1. Experimental Nucleophilic Substitution Reaction

Trial 1

Solvent: Et_2O	Temperature 35°C	
Nucleophile	Reaction Rate	α_D
0.5 M NaCN	5.18×10^{-3} M/s	+31.2°
0.5 M NaSCH$_3$	4.92×10^{-3} M/s	+26.4°
0.5 M NaF	4.11×10^{-3} M/s	+28.6°
0.5 M NH(CH$_3$)$_2$	2.55×10^{-3} M/s	+30.9°

Trial 2

Solvent: Et_2O	Temperature 50°C	
Nucleophile	Reaction Rate	α_D
0.5 M NaCN	1.16×10^{-2} M/s	+30.6°
0.5 M NaSCH$_3$	1.10×10^{-2} M/s	+26.0°
0.5 M NaF	8.83×10^{-3} M/s	+28.1°
0.5 M NH(CH$_3$)$_2$	5.65×10^{-3} M/s	+30.1°

Trial 3

Solvent: EtOH	Temperature 35°C	
Nucleophile	Reaction Rate	α_D
0.5 M NaCN	1.45×10^{-4} M/s	+10.2°
0.5 M NaSCH$_3$	1.39×10^{-4} M/s	+08.1°
0.5 M NaF	1.26×10^{-4} M/s	+10.0°
0.5 M NH(CH$_3$)$_2$	1.29×10^{-4} M/s	+09.8°

Trial 4

Solvent: EtOH	Temperature 50°C	
Nucleophile	Reaction Rate	α_D
0.5 M NaCN	3.77×10^{-4} M/s	+7.2°
0.5 M NaSCH$_3$	3.63×10^{-4} M/s	+3.1°
0.5 M NaI	3.72×10^{-4} M/s	+2.6°
0.5 M NH(CH$_3$)$_2$	3.52×10^{-4} M/s	+4.8°

7. Which of the following reactions is the fastest?

A. NaF + a primary alkyl halide in a protic solvent

B. NaF + a tertiary alkyl halide in a protic solvent

C. NaF + a primary alkyl halide in an aprotic solvent

D. NaF + a tertiary alkyl halide in an aprotic solvent

8. What reaction rate is expected for the reaction of 0.5 M NaCN with (R)-2-bromobutane at 40.0°C in ether?

A. 3.33×10^{-3} M/s

B. 6.59×10^{-3} M/s

C. 1.07×10^{-2} M/s

D. 1.72×10^{-2} M/s

9. What is the effect of a protic solvent on nucleophilicity?

A. Nucleophiles that form H-bonds are hindered; non-hydrogen bonding nucleophiles show no effect.

B. Nucleophiles that form H-bonds are enhanced; non-hydrogen bonding nucleophiles show no effect.

C. Nucleophiles that form H-bonds are hindered; non-hydrogen bonding nucleophiles are enhanced.

D. Nucleophiles that form H-bonds are enhanced; non-hydrogen bonding nucleophiles are hindered.

10. What is the effect of temperature on reaction rate?

A. As temperature increases, nucleophiles can migrate through the solvent more rapidly.

B. As temperature increases, solvents get more viscous.

C. As temperature increases, molecules have more energy available to break bonds.

D. As temperature increases, solvents form a less stable interaction with intermediates.

11. The reactions can be monitored by observing the:

A. disappearance of the IR peak at 1712 cm^{-1}.

B. change in ppm value for the 3H doublet observed in ^{1}H NMR spectroscopy.

C. the change over time in the index of refraction.

D. disappearance of the UV peak at 242 nm.

12. What CANNOT be concluded from the experiment?

A. Secondary alkyl bromides react with sodium cyanide in ether solvent via the S_N2 mechanism.

B. Sodium methyl sulfide is a better nucleophile than dimethyl amine.

C. Chirality is retained more significantly in protic solvent than in aprotic solvent.

D. The nucleophilicity of halides varies with solvent.

Passage III (Questions 13 - 17)

Many age old recipes call for the addition of mushrooms, not for flavor (as mushrooms have none) but simply out of the perceived need to add another ingredient. A genuine concern of the European aristocracy at the turn of the eighteenth century was the addition of toxic mushrooms to soup broth in lieu of standard ingredients. The toxic component in "bitter mushrooms" is muscarine, which in later times was extracted, isolated, and used in combination with strychnine as a rat poison. The structure of muscarine is shown below:

Figure 1. Muscarine

Studies have shown that if any one of the chiral centers of muscarine is inverted, the compound is no longer toxic, implying that the molecule is site-specific in cytotoxic activity. This means that enantiomers and diastereomers of muscarine are non-toxic. One plausible conclusion from this is that biochemistry is a stereospecific science.

13. If a compound has chirality *2R,3S,4S* with an α_D equal to + 42°, what can be said of the diastereomer with chirality of *2S,3R,4S*?

    A. The diastereomer has α_D = - 42°.

    B. The diastereomer has α_D = + 42°.

    C. The diastereomer has the same melting point as the original compound.

    D. The diastereomer could have α_D = - 13°.

14. The chirality of muscarine is BEST described as:

    A. *2S,4R,5S*

    B. *2S,4S,5S*

    C. *2S,4S,5R*

    D. *2R,4R,5S*

15. What constitutes a racemic mixture?

    A. 50% of a compound with its diastereomer

    B. 50% of a compound with its enantiomer

    C. 25% of a compound with one enantiomer and two diastereomers

    D. 25% of a compound with three enantiomers

16. How many stereoisomers are possible for the following structure?

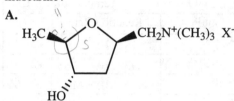

    A. 6

    B. 8

    C. 12

    D. 16

17. Which of the following structures is the enantiomer of muscarine?

    A.

    B.

    C.

    D.

GO ON TO THE NEXT PAGE

Questions 18 through 21 are **NOT** based on a descriptive passage.

18. The following molecule has which of the following stereochemical orientations?

CH₃
H — — OCH₃
R
H — — OH
CH₃

A. *2R,3R*

B. *2R,3S*

C. *2S,3R*

D. *2S,3S*

19. How many stereoisomers are possible for the molecule 1,2,3-trifluoropentane?

A. 2

B. 4

C. 6

D. 8

20. When synthesized from an achiral molecule, only twenty-five percent of synthesized isoleucine can be used biologically.

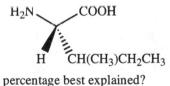

How is this percentage best explained?

A. Only 25% exists as a zwitterion in the body.

B. 75% of synthetic isoleucine does not have the correct side chain.

C. In synthesizing isoleucine, the two chiral centers result in four stereoisomers being formed. Only one of the four is biologically correct.

D. In synthesizing isoleucine, the two chiral centers result in eight stereoisomers being formed. Only one of the eight is biologically correct.

21. Which of the following is the MOST stable leaving group?

A. HCN

B. CN⁻

C. $H_3CCH_2S^-$

D. H_3CCH_2SH

Specific chirality can be induced into a product by the stereochemistry of the reactants. This chiral induction is what allows enzymes to generate nearly 100% formation of the desired stereoisomer. A common practice in organic synthesis involves the use of a chiral auxiliary. Like a protecting group, an auxiliary is added early in the synthesis and removed later, so it is ultimately not a part of the overall transformation. It serves to orient a transition state in one of the intermediate steps of a synthesis, so as to generate a product mixture rich in the desired stereoisomer. Figure 1 shows such a synthesis.

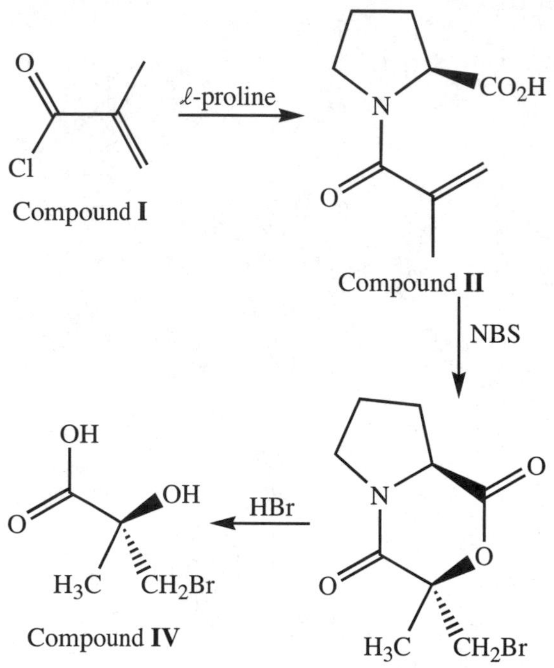

Figure 1 Stepwise synthesis of chiral-specific bromo-alcohol

Under the ideal conditions, the reaction is capable of generating an enantiomeric excess of nearly 90%. Enantiomeric excess is determined from the ratio of the optical rotation of the product mixture to the optical rotation of a pure sample of the predominant enantiomer.

22. How can the stereochemical preference in step 2 of the synthesis in Figure 1 be explained?

   A. Resonance favors the attack by NBS taking place on the side of the ring opposite of where the COOH group sits.

   B. Steric hindrance favors the attack by NBS taking place on the side of the ring opposite of where the COOH group sits.

   C. Electrostatics favors the attack by NBS taking place on the side of the ring where the COOH group sits.

   D. The inductive effect favors the attack by NBS taking place on the side of the ring where the COOH group sits.

23. What would be expected from the synthesis if *d*-proline were used instead of *l*-proline?

   A. Compound IV would still be formed
   B. The enantiomer of Compound IV
   C. A diastereomer of Compound IV
   D. An epimer of Compound IV

24. Compound III has:

   A. one stereogenic center which has *R* configuration.
   B. two stereogenic centers, both of which have *R* configuration.
   C. two stereogenic centers, both of which have *S* configuration.
   D. three stereogenic centers, all of which have *S* configuration.

25. In the synthesis in Figure 1, proline is serving as a:

   A. chiral auxiliary.
   B. catalyst.
   C. protecting group.
   D. solvent.

26. The reaction with NBS adds:

   A. a CH_3 group and a Br to Compound II.
   B. an OH group and a Br to Compound II.
   C. an H and a Br to Compound II.
   D. a Br to and removes an H from Compound II.

27. Which of the following statements accurately describes the enantiomeric excess associated with syntheses that invoke the use of a chiral auxiliary?

   I. As the effectiveness of the auxiliary increases, the enantiomeric excess increases.

   II. For a product mixture exhibiting an optical rotation of 20° with enantiomers exhibiting optical rotations of 40° and -40°, the enantiomeric excess is 50%.

   III. Racemic mixtures exhibit an enantiomeric excess of 50%.

   A. I only
   B. I and II only
   C. I and III only
   D. II and III only

Isoleucine is one of eight *essential* amino acids. The term essential is applied to amino acids that humans cannot produce, and therefore must take in through diet. Isoleucine exists as a zwitterion in aqueous solution. The natural form of isoleucine has the same chirality as other naturally occurring amino acids at carbon number two. Isoleucine is found naturally in the L form. Naturally occurring amino acids have an *S* chiral center on carbon two (except cysteine).

Isoleucine has a second chiral center in addition to the one at carbon two. Seventeen of the amino acids we code for have exactly one chiral center, with glycine (which has no chiral center) and threonine (which has two chiral centers) being the other exceptions. The second chiral center of L-isoleucine has fixed chirality, so a diastereomer of isoleucine varying at the side chain is not a biological substitute for L-isoleucine. Figure 1 shows the zwitterion form of L-isoleucine.

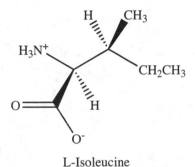

L-Isoleucine

Figure 1 Zwitterion form of L-Isoleucine

The only other amino acid coded for by human beings that has a chiral side chain attached is threonine. The threonine side chain contains an alcohol functionality. Like isoleucine, the side chain chiral center must be specific for the amino acid to be biologically incorporated. Threonine is also an essential amino acid. The diastereomer of threonine that varies at the side chain is known as "allo-threonine."

28. What is the stereoconfiguration for isoleucine?

A. 2R,3R

B. 2R,3S

C. 2S,3R

D. 2S,3S

29. If the side chain chiral center were changed, the new structure would be which of the following?

A. An enantiomer of isoleucine.

B. A diastereomer of isoleucine.

C. An anomer of isoleucine.

D. Identical to isoleucine.

30. Most naturally occurring amino acids have which stereochemical orientation?

A. R

B. S

C. E

D. Z

31. If L-isoleucine were found to have an optical rotation of -62° from plane-polarized light studies, what would you predict for the optical rotation of its enantiomer?

A. -62°

B. +62°

C. -31°

D. +31°

32. Only twenty-five percent of synthesized isoleucine can be used biologically. This is best explained by which of the following explanations?

A. Only 25% exists as a zwitterion in the body.

B. 75% of synthetic isoleucine does not have the correct side chain.

C. In synthesizing isoleucine, the two chiral centers result in four stereoisomers being formed. Only one of the four is biologically usable.

D. In synthesizing isoleucine, the two chiral centers result in eight stereoisomers being formed. Only two of the eight are biologically usable.

Questions 33 through 36 are **NOT** based on a descriptive passage.

33. What are the absolute configurations for the stereocenters of the compound shown below?

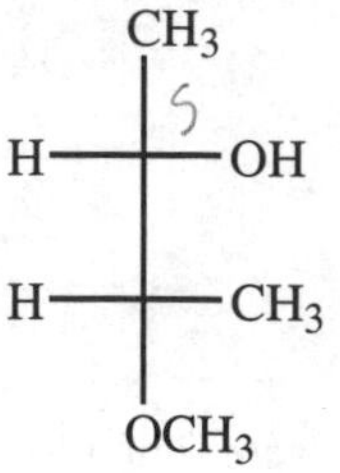

A. 2R,3R
B. 2R,3S
C. 2S,3R
D. 2S,3S

34. Which of the following compounds is optically active?

A. 2R,3S-dibromobutane
B. 2R,4S-dibromopentane
C. 2R,4S-dibromohexane
D. cis-1,3-dichlorocyclohexane

35. How can the following two compounds be separated from one another most effectively?

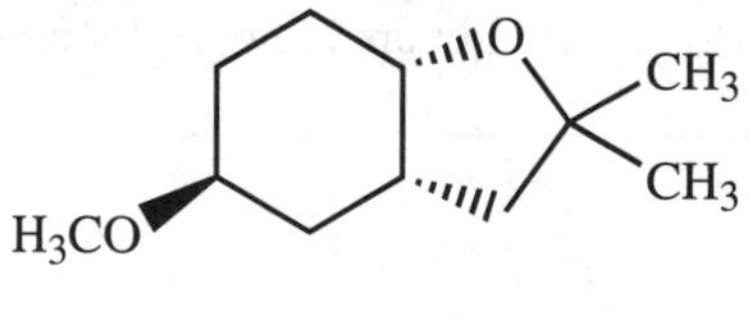

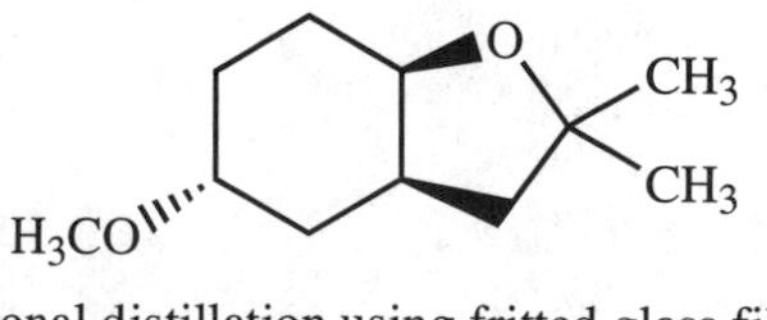

A. Fractional distillation using fritted glass filling
B. Acid-base extraction at 37°C with ether
C. Recrystallization from thf with 10% acetate
D. Column chromatography through a column with an adsorbent of R-hydroxypolystyrene

36. Which of the following compounds does NOT show any optical rotation of planar light?

A. 2R,3R-dibromobutane
B. 2R,3S-dibromobutane
C. 2R,3R-dibromohexane
D. 2R,3S-dibromohexane

In two controversial laboratory studies, Compound P, shown in Figure 1 below, has been determined to reduce constipation in the Southern European Red-Eared Jumping Lizard during mating season. The effects are less significant during courting periods and do not occur at all during the first three days following a Blue Moon. The two studies compared the effects of this particular compound with both stereoisomers and structural isomers of Compound P. The dosages used were the same for each trial. The disagreement between researchers came in determining the binding activity of each stereoisomer and its subsequent reactivity.

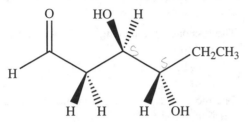

Figure 1 Compound P

The exact mechanism for the constipation reducing behavior is not known, but it is speculated to work in conjunction with natural sex hormones to induce muscle relaxation. In another study, the compound was applied to the abdomen of the Saskatchewan Green-Nosed Squatting Frog to test for similar effects. To date, no solid conclusions have been formed as to the constipation reducing effect of Compound P in other organisms. Being such an important chemical to the bowel process of reptiles and amphibians everywhere, much research is sure to be done. Researchers have continued to develop other structural isomers that will hopefully show similar effects in creatures such as the very rare Yellow-Tongued Sabertooth Barking Spider.

37. If treated with PBr3, the OH groups of an alcohol can be converted into Br groups through a reaction which proceeds by an S_N2 mechanism. What chirality would be observed for the dibromo product formed from Compound P with excess PBr3?

A. 3S,4S

B. 3R,4S

C. 3S,4R

D. 3R,4R

38. Enzymatic active sites can be described as all of the following EXCEPT:

A. chiral specific.

B. size specific.

C. functional group specific.

D. isotope specific.

39. For a branched diol, a researcher found the following boiling points for three of the stereoisomers:

Isomer	C2	C3	C4	b.p. (°C)
I	R	S	R	142
II	S	S	R	146
III	S	S	S	151

Which of the following relationships accurately correlates the boiling points for the stereoisomers?

A. 2R,3S,4R > 2S,3S,4R > 2R,3R,4R

B. 2R,3R,4S > 2S,3R,4S > 2S,3S,4S

C. 2R,3R,4R > 2R,3R,4S > 2R,3S,4R

D. 2S,3S,4S > 2S,3S,4R > 2R,3R,4S

40. The following structure relates in what way to Compound P, the Southern European Red-Eared Jumping Lizard's constipation medication?

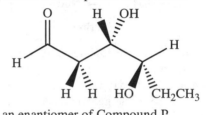

A. It is an enantiomer of Compound P

B. It is a diastereomer of Compound P

C. It is identical to Compound P

D. It is a meso structural isomer of Compound P

41. What is the absolute configuration at carbons 1 and 2 in the following compound?

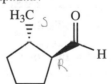

A. 1S,2S

B. 1R,2S

C. 1S,2R

D. 1R,2R

42. The enantiomer of Compound P has:

A. the same boiling point as Compound P

B. a higher melting point than Compound P.

C. A lower density than Compound P.

D. The same specific rotation as Compound P.

The strength of a leaving group can be determined from the reaction rate of a nucleophilic substitution reaction. The rate shows a linear dependence on the concentration of the electrophile. An electrophile with a better leaving group undergoes nucleophilic substitution at a faster rate than an electrophile with a worse leaving group. A chemist designed a study that varied the leaving group on an electrophile while keeping all other factors that influence the rate constant, such as temperature, solvent, and nucleophile concentration.

A difficulty that can arise with this experiment is competition between substitution reactions and elimination reactions. To alleviate the problem of the competing elimination reaction, a one-carbon electrophile is chosen. When the electrophile has only one carbon, the substitution reaction must proceed via an S_N2 mechanism. Reaction 1 shown below is a generic reaction representing each of the sixteen trial runs.

$$Nuc + CH_3-X \rightarrow Nuc-CH_3 + X$$

Reaction 1

There were four nucleophiles and four leaving groups used in the experiment to account for sixteen combinations. Table 1 is a matrix showing the four nucleophiles and four leaving groups used in the generic reaction. The value listed in each box in the table is the log of the reaction rate.

Nuc \ X	OSO_3CH_3	I	Cl	OCH_3
H_3N	-3.82	-3.37	-4.11	No Rx
CN^-	-1.39	-1.17	-1.92	No Rx
H_3CS^-	-2.16	-1.92	-2.42	No Rx
H_3COH	-5.21	-4.80	-5.70	No Rx

Table 1

The pK_a values for the conjugate acids of the leaving groups can be used to estimate reactivity. The relative pK_as are $pK_{a(H_3COCH_3)} > pK_{a(HCl)} > pK_{a(HOSO_3CH_3)} > pK_{a(HI)}$.

The rate for the reaction is measured in molar per second, therefore the less negative the log value of the initial reaction rate, the faster the reaction. Because the rate of an S_N2 reaction depends on both the nucleophile and the electrophile, this experiment can be used to determine the strength of both nucleophiles and leaving groups.

43. The relative strength of the nucleophiles is best described by which of the following relationships?

   A. $CN^- > CH_3S^- > NH_3 > HOCH_3$

   B. $CN^- > CH_3S^- > HOCH_3 > NH_3$

   C. $CH_3S^- > CN^- > NH_3 > HOCH_3$

   D. $CH_3S^- > CN^- > HOCH_3 > NH_3$

44. What difficulty arises if Reaction 1 is carried out using a secondary propyl electrophile instead of the methyl electrophile?

   A. The electrophile exhibits more steric hindrance.

   B. The electrophile exhibits less steric hindrance.

   C. There is the chance of an elimination side reaction.

   D. The chance for an elimination side reaction is reduced.

45. Generally, nucleophilicity and basicity run parallel to one another. What can be said about the correlation between the leaving group's basicity and the strength of the leaving group?

   A. The less basic the leaving group, the better it is as a leaving group.

   B. The less basic the leaving group, the worse it is as a leaving group.

   C. The more basic the leaving group, the better it is as a leaving group.

   D. There is no observable correlation between basicity and leaving group strength.

46. Which of the following does NOT directly affect the strength of the nucleophile?

   A. The nature of the solvent.

   B. The basicity of the nucleophile.

   C. The steric bulkiness of the nucleophile.

   D. The quality of the leaving group on the electrophile.

47. Which of the following could NOT be determined from a similar experiment carried out with an S_N1 reaction instead of the S_N2 reaction?

   A. The strength of the leaving group.

   B. The strength of the nucleophile.

   C. The effect of temperature.

   D. The effect of varying solvent.

48. The best explanation for the lack of any observed reaction when NH_3 was added to H_3COCH_3 is that:

   A. NH_3 is a poor nucleophile.

   B. NH_3 is a poor leaving group.

   C. $^-OCH_3$ is a poor nucleophile.

   D. $^-OCH_3$ is a poor leaving group.

Questions 49 through 52 are **NOT** based on a descriptive passage.

49. Which of the following compounds CANNOT be optically active?

A. 2-chlorocyclopentanol

B. 2-chlorocyclohexanol

C. 3-chlorocyclohexanol

D. 4-chlorocyclohexanol

50. The following pair of molecules can best be described as which of the following?

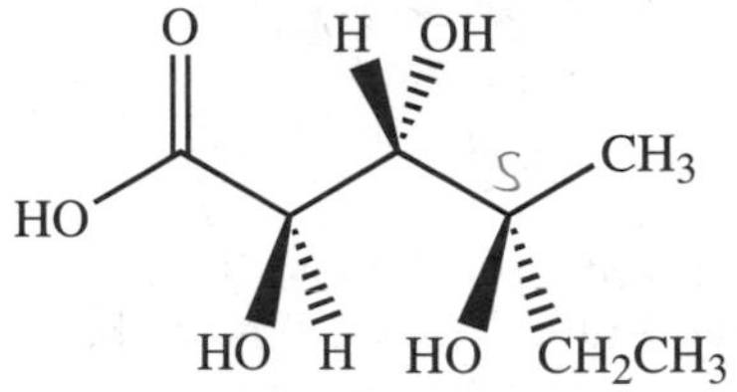

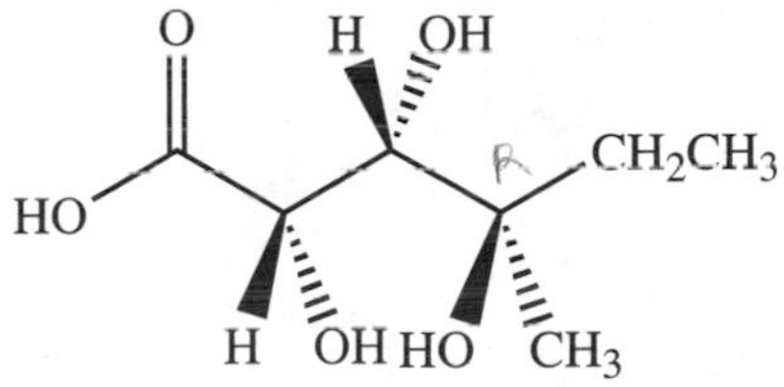

A. Diastereomers

B. Enantiomers

C. Epimers

D. Anomers

51. Addition of $KMnO_4(aq)$ at pH = 10 generates a vicinal diol with syn stereoselectivity. What does the addition of $KMnO_4(aq)$ at pH = 10 to E-2-butene would yield which of the following?

A. Two enantiomers

B. Two diastereomers

C. Two meso compounds (not identical)

D. One meso compound

52. Which compound can form diastereomers?

A. A 1,2-vicinal diol

B. A 2,3-vicinal diol

C. A geminal diol

D. Glycerol

1. C	2. A	3. B	4. B	5. D	6. C
7. C	8. B	9. A	10. C	11. D	12. C
13. D	14. A	15. B	16. B	17. A	18. A
19. B	20. C	21. D	22. B	23. B	24. C
25. A	26. D	27. B	28. D	29. B	30. B
31. B	32. C	33. D	34. C	35. D	36. B
37. C	38. D	39. C	40. B	41. A	42. A
43. A	44. C	45. A	46. D	47. B	48. D
49. D	50. A	51. A	52. B		

YOU ARE DONE.

Answers to 52-Question Stereochemistry Practice Exam

1. **Choice C is the best answer.** The (+) that precedes the name refers to the direction of rotation of plane-polarized light as it passes through a solution of the compound. This eliminates choices B and D, because the rotation of light cannot be negative, given the (+) preceding the names. If (-)-carvone has an optical rotation of -61.2°, then the enantiomer ((+)-carvone) has +61.2°. The best answer is thus choice **C**.

2. **Choice A is the best answer.** Both carvone and limonene have one chiral center, so they will each have two possible stereoisomers (enantiomers). This makes statement I invalid. The chirality of both (-)-carvone and (+)-limonene are R, according to conventional rules. This makes statement II valid and statement III invalid. The best answer is therefore choice **A**. The chirality for both (-)-carvone and (+)-limonene are drawn below:

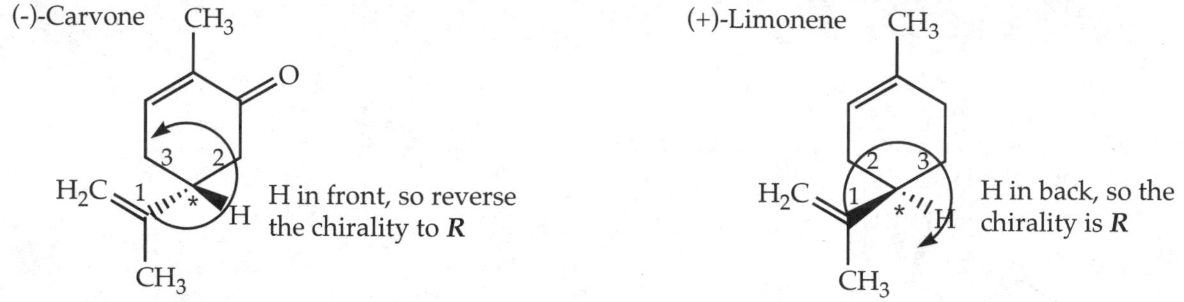

3. **Choice B is the best answer.** A chiral center has four unique substituents attached to it. Only one carbon in carvone has four unique substituents attached, so there is only one stereocenter. Choice **B** is the best answer.

4. **Choice B is the best answer.** The carbons that support a positive charge when carvone is treated with an acid are drawn below:

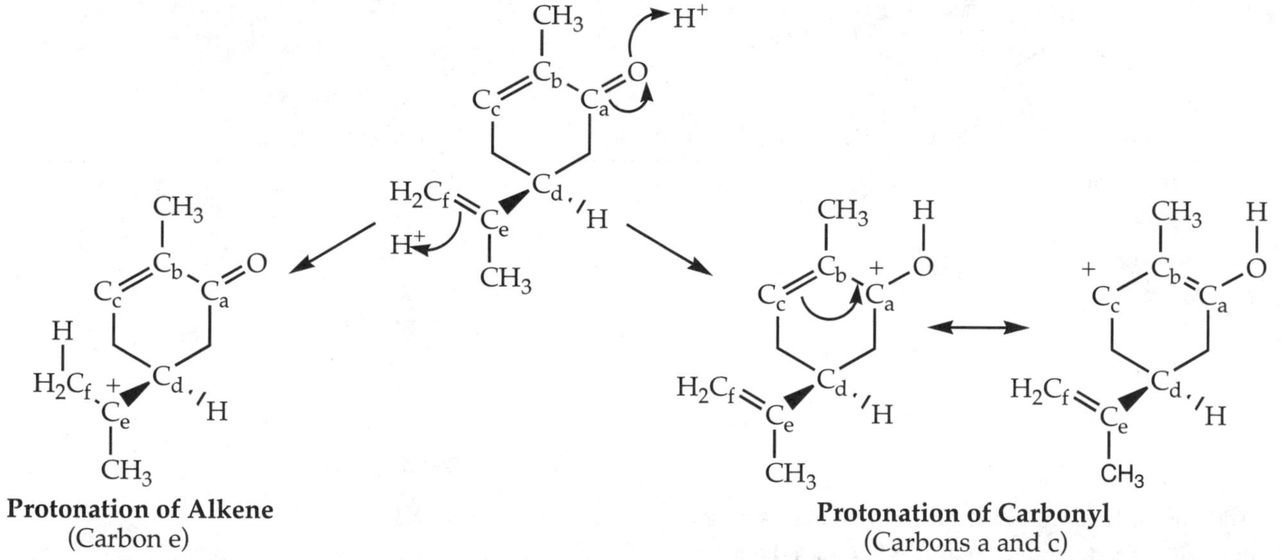

    Protonation of Alkene   **Protonation of Carbonyl**
    (Carbon e)   (Carbons a and c)

    Because Carbons a, c, and e support the positive charge, the best answer is choice **B**.

5. **Choice D is the best answer.** Carvone has four units of unsaturation (three for the π-bonds and one for the ring). Choices A and B can be eliminated, because they both have only three units of unsaturation. Choice C can be eliminated, because the carbonyl would show an IR peak between 1680 and 1740 cm^{-1}, and the compound does not show such a peak. Choice **D** is therefore correct, because it has four units of unsaturation (two rings and two π-bonds), and no carbonyl group. Pick **D** and be a stellar nova.

6. **Choice C is the best answer.** Anomer and epimer refer to carbohydrates, and limonene is not a sugar, so choices A and D should be eliminated right away. Limonene has only one stereocenter in its structure, so (+)-limonene and (-)-limonene vary at their one stereogenic center. This makes the two structures enantiomers of one another. In order to be diastereomers, the molecules must have at least two stereogenic carbons. This eliminates choice B and makes choice **C** the best answer.

7. **Choice C is the best answer.** The nucleophile is the same in each case, so the rate varies with the solvent and the electrophile at comparable temperatures. According to the data in the tables, reactions are faster in aprotic solvents than in protic solvents, eliminating choices A and B. The optical rotation of the product mixture tells us that the reactions proceeded by an S_N2 mechanism in aprotic solvent. Had it been by an S_N1 mechanism, there would have been no observed optical rotation because of the racemic product mixture. Because S_N2 reactions are typically faster than S_N1 reactions, the fastest reaction occurs under S_N2 conditions. This means that the fastest reaction is observed in the primary electrophile. Choice **C** is the best answer.

8. **Choice B is the best answer.** This question requires using the tables to establish a window of reasonable values. Because the reaction is done in ether, the best two tables to compare are from Trial 1 and Trial 2. From Table 1, we see that at 35°C, the reaction rate is 5.18×10^{-3} M/s. From Table 2, we see that at 50°C, the reaction rate is 1.16×10^{-2} M/s. The optical rotation of the product mixture has not changed drastically, so the predominant reaction in both cases is by the S_N2 mechanism. This means that the value at 40°C should be greater than 5.18×10^{-3} M/s, but less than 1.16×10^{-2} M/s, which eliminates choices A and D. Because 40°C is closer to 35°C than to 50°C, and rates generally relate to temperature in an exponential (rather than linear) fashion, the best answer is the value closer to 5.18×10^{-3} M/s than to 1.16×10^{-2} M/s, which is 6.59×10^{-3} M/s, choice **B**.

9. **Choice A is the best answer.** Trials 1 and 2 occur in an aprotic solvent, while Trials 3 and 4 are conducted in a protic solvent. This question requires comparing Trial 1 to Trial 3, and Trial 2 to Trial 4. NaF and $NH(CH_3)_2$ can form hydrogen bonds, and both show a slower rate in protic solvent. The slowest rate in the aprotic solvent occurs with $NH(CH_3)_2$ and NaI, so nothing can be concluded from the data. Based on the data for NaF, the tendency is to say that NaF is hindered in the protic solvent, where it may undergo hydrogen bonding. The amine is not as conclusive. The question does not state "Based on the data...," so we can invoke outside knowledge. If the solvent cage surrounds the nucleophile, it is slowed by the solvent and thus reacts slower. This eliminates choices B and D. Nucleophiles that do not form hydrogen bonds are unaffected, as opposed to being enhanced, so choice **A** is a better answer than choice C.

10. **Choice C is the best answer.** As the temperature increases, the reaction rates are increasing, so temperature has a direct effect on the rate. Temperature increases generally make a solvent less viscous, allowing nucleophiles to migrate more easily, but this factor is not significant enough to account for the drastic rate increase seen with 15°C changes. The first statement is a true statement, but it does not explain the large increase in rate. Choice A should be eliminated. Choice B is incorrect, and it is eliminated. As temperature increases, the solvation of intermediates may or may not change. If the intermediate is less stable, the rate may not be affected, because rates depend on the transition state. Choice D is an irrelevant answer. It is definitely true that as temperature is increased, there is more energy in the system, so the bonds can break more easily. The best answer is choice **C**.

11. **Choice D is the best answer.** Neither the reactant nor the product exhibits an IR peak at 1712 cm^{-1} (indicative of a carbonyl), because both compounds lack a carbonyl. Choice A is eliminated. The shift value of the 3H doublet changes as the reaction proceeds, so the product can be identified by the NMR signal. The problem is that we are interested in the reaction rate, and the NMR time scale is not useful for most reaction rates at room temperature. To use NMR in rate studies, the solution temperature must be lowered for simple reactions. Choice B is not the best choice. The index of refraction is not useful in observing the rate, mostly because the solution is predominantly solvent. Thus, as the reaction proceeds, the index of refraction for the solution does not change much. Choice C is eliminated. Ultraviolet spectroscopy is ideal for observing the rate, because the concentration in solution is directly proportional to the absorbance of light in the UV range. Ultravioloet-visible spectroscopy is often employed in rate studied. The best answer is choice **D**.

12. **Choice C is the best answer.** Because there is optical rotation observed in all of the reactions in Table 1 and Table 2, it can be concluded that these reactions went predominantly by the S_N2 mechanism. Because these reactions are in ether, it can be concluded that the S_N2 mechanism is observed with secondary alkyl bromides in ether solvent. Choice A is a valid statement, so it is eliminated. In every trial, sodium methyl sulfide ($NaSCH_3$) reacted faster than dimethyl amine ($NH(CH_3)_2$). Therefore, the methyl sulfide anion can be called a better nucleophile than dimethyl amine. Choice B is a valid statement, so it is also eliminated. In ether solvent, there are greater observed optical rotation values for the product mixture than in alcohol. This means that chirality is retained more in the aprotic solvent than in the protic solvent. Choice **C** is an invalid statement, making it the correct answer choice. Only two halides (iodide and fluoride) are observed in the experiment. In protic solvent, the iodide reacts faster, while in aprotic solvent the fluoride reacts faster. This means that the nucleophilicity of halides does vary with solvent. Choice D is a valid statement and is eliminated. The correct answer is choice **C**.

13. Choice D is the best answer. If a compound has a specific rotation of + 42°, then the **enantiomer** of that compound has a specific rotation of - 42°. A diastereomer differs by at least one stereocenter, so it cannot have the same specific rotation. This eliminates choice B. The diastereomer cannot have the same chirality as the enantiomer, so the optical rotation of the diastereomer cannot be - 42°. This eliminates choice A. The diastereomer is packed differently into its lattice structure, so the forces holding the solid together are different. The difference in intermolecular forces results in a difference in melting points. This eliminates choice C. The only other possible choice is answer choice **D**. This is not necessarily true, but it is the only choice that is not necessarily wrong. Questions like this can be tricky, because there is no reason that you should know that the specific rotation is - 13°. You must therefore prove that the other choices are incorrect. It is often better to eliminate three wrong answers than it is to try to identify the one best answer.

14. Choice A is the best answer. The Haworth projection of Muscarine used in the passage does not allow for easy analysis of the stereochemistry. It is best to start by translating that structure into an easier to view version, as shown below.

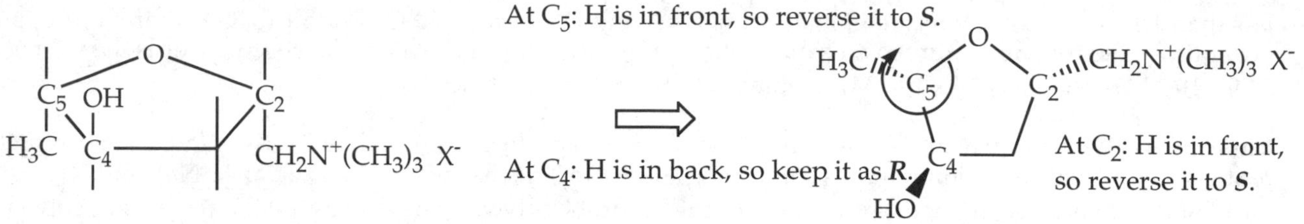

At C5: H is in front, so reverse it to S.
At C4: H is in back, so keep it as R.
At C2: H is in front, so reverse it to S.
C5 OH
H3C
C4
C2
CH2N+(CH3)3 X-
O
HO

The chirality is *2S,4R,5S*, making choice **A** the correct answer.

15. Choice B is the best answer. A racemic mixture by definition is a mixture of stereoisomers that has no net optical rotation, most often achieved by mixing 50% each of two enantiomers. This makes choice **B** the best answer. Choice A is wrong, and choice D is not possible. If the two diastereomers of the compound mentioned in choice C are enantiomers of one another, then technically choice C could be correct. But choice C is not as good as choice **B**.

16. Choice B is the best answer. This question requires counting the chiral centers. There are three chiral carbons, so the maximum number of stereoisomers is 2^3, which equals 8. The compound cannot be meso, so the best answer is 8 possible stereoisomers, making choice **B** the best. Choices A and C are eliminated because they are not exponential products of two. Choice D is too big.

17. Choice A is the best answer. The enantiomer of muscarine has all (three) chiral centers inverted. Muscarine has substituents down at carbons 2 and 5 and up at carbon 4, so the enantiomer of muscarine must have substituents up at carbons 2 and 5 and down at carbon 4. This is seen in choice **A**, so pick choice **A** to feel the tingly sensation of correctness. Choices B and C are diastereomers and choice D is muscarine itself.

A.

H3C
O
CH2N+(CH3)3 X-
HO

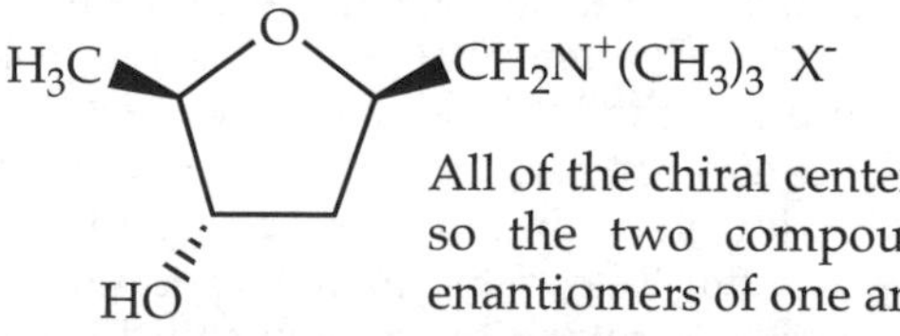

All of the chiral centers differ, so the two compounds are enantiomers of one another.

D.

H3C
O
CH2N+(CH3)3 X-
HO

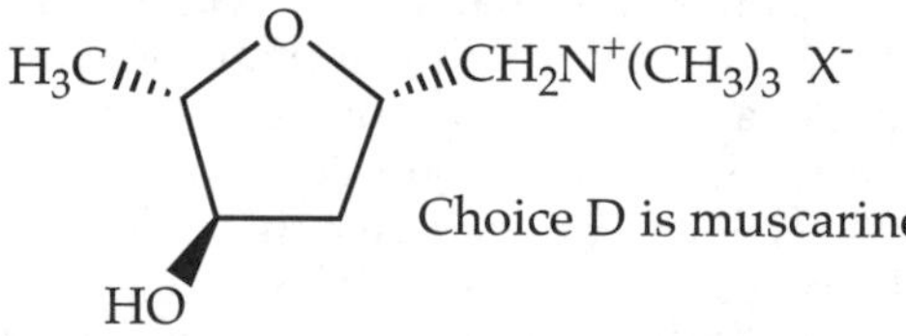

Choice D is muscarine.

Questions 18 - 21 Not Based on a Descriptive Passage

18. Choice A is the best answer. If you are well versed in using the thumb technique, then you can place your thumb in the direction of the C—H bond and curl your fingers from priorities 1-2-3 using a right hand for both stereocenters. This makes both centers R. For some, it may be easier to rotate the molecule to the side view rather than using the Newman projection to determine the chirality. From the side perspective, it is much easier to see the three dimensional orientation of the molecule. As shown in the determination below, the molecule has *2R,3R* stereochemistry. Choose **A**; be a chem star.

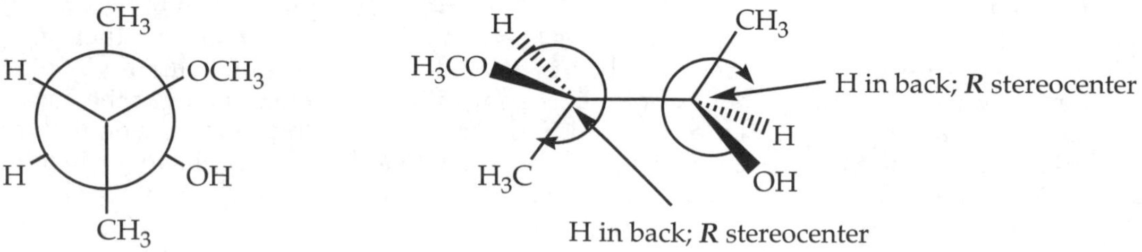

CH3
H
OCH3
H
OH
CH3
H
H3CO
H3C
CH3
H in back; R stereocenter
H
OH
H in back; R stereocenter

19. **Choice B is the best answer.** To determine the number In the molecule, carbons two and three are chiral centers. However, carbon one is not a chiral center, because it contains two equivalent hydrogen atoms. The maximum number of stereoisomers is equal to 2^n where n is the number of chiral centers in the molecule, which in this case is 2. This yields a total of four (2^2) stereoisomers. Be stellar and choose **B**.

20. **Choice C is the best answer.** Isoleucine contains two chiral centers, one for the alpha carbon and one in the side chain. Plugging into the stereoisomer equation 2^n, where n represents the number of chiral centers, there are four possible stereoisomers for the isoleucine structure. Because isoleucine contains two chiral centers that must have specific orientation, only one of the four stereoisomers has the correct chirality to be biologically useful. Choose **C** to be a successful point collector.

21. **Choice D is the best answer.** A leaving group, once it has left an electrophile, must have at least one lone pair (as a result of the heterolytic bond cleaving). This stipulation eliminates choice A, because the carbon of the cyanic acid has no lone pair, and the nitrogen does not interact with a carbon to be a leaving group. The most stable leaving group is the weakest base. Of the three choices left, CH_3CH_2SH has the strongest conjugate acid ($CH_3CH_2SH_2^+$ is a stronger acid than CH_3CH_2SH and HCN), thus CH_3CH_2SH is a weaker base than $CH_3CH_2S^-$ and CN^-. CH_3CH_2SH is the weakest base of the choices remaining, therefore it is the best leaving group. Choose **D** to score a point in this contest of point collecting.

Passage IV (Questions 22 - 27)	Chiral Induction

22. **Choice B is the best answer.** Rather than consider the preferred side of attack, let's first consider the reason why one side would be more preferable for attack than the other. There is no resonance associated with the transition state, so choice A can be eliminated. The inductive effect does not impact one side of the structure more than the other, so choice D is not a likely candidate for the answer. Stereoselectivity is often attributed to steric hindrance. The bulky carboxylic acid group lies above the ring as drawn, which makes the bottom plane of the double bond less hindered than the top. The result is that NBS attacks from the less hindered side of the molecule. Electrostatics can explain the behavior if one side is more electron rich than the other, which although may be true in this case, is not as significant as steric hindrance. Choice **B** is the best answer.

23. **Choice B is the best answer.** Proline has one stereogenic center, which means that d-proline is the enantiomer of ℓ-proline. If d-proline were used in lieu of ℓ-proline, then the crowdedness of the transition state would be on the opposite side. The result would be the formation of the opposite stereocenter. Given that Compound IV has only one stereocenter, if it changes, then the enantiomer results. Choice **B** is the best answer. Choice A should have been eliminated, because the chirality changes. Choice C should have been eliminated, because Compound IV has only one stereocenter, and in order for two stereoisomers to be diastereomers, there must be at least two stereocenters. Choice D should have been eliminated, because the term *epimer* refers to monosaccharides. Compound IV is not a sugar, so only choice **B** is possible.

24. **Choice C is the best answer.** Compound III has two stereogenic centers, so choices A and D are eliminated. It is easier to determine the configuration of the upper stereocenter than the lower stereocenter, because the #4 priority is in back at the upper stereocenter. The priorities are the N, followed by the carbonyl C, and then followed by the ring carbon. The arc from 1-to-2-to-3 is counterclockwise and H (priority #4) is in back, so the configuration is S. This eliminates choice B and makes choice **C** the best answer. Both stereocenters are shown below.

25. **Choice A is the best answer.** Proline is added in an early step and then removed in a later step, so it is not a solvent. This eliminates choice D. Proline is part of the intermediate products, so it is not a catalyst. Catalysts are involved in transition states, but not as part of products that are isolated. This eliminates choice B. Both protecting groups and chiral auxiliaries are added early in a synthetic pathway and then removed in the end, so we need to evaluate the purpose of proline in terms of the compound. There is no functional group being preserved from reactant to product, but there is the influencing of the stereogenic center. This means that proline is acting as a chiral auxiliary and not as a protecting group. Choice **A** is the best answer.

26. **Choice D is the best answer.** This question entails comparing the product of Step 2 to the reactant of Step 2. The molecule gains a bromine at the terminal carbon of the π-bond, but that doesn't help us to answer the question given that each answer mentions the gain of bromine. The other carbon of the π-bond forms a new bond to the hydroxyl oxygen of the carboxylic acid group. Before forming that bond, the acid group loses a proton. This means that an H is lost, so choice **D** is the best answer.

27. **Choice B is the best answer.** A chiral auxiliary is employed to favor the formation of one stereogenic configuration over another. The better the auxiliary, the greater the percentage of the desired stereoisomer in the product mixture. This makes Statement I valid, because enantiomeric excess increases as the preference increases. This eliminates choice D. The enantiomeric excess is the ratio of the observed rotation to the maximum rotation (rotation if the solution were purely one enantiomer). The ratio of 20° to 40° is 1 : 2, so the enantiomeric excess is 50%. This means that the solution has 75% 40°-enantiomer and 25% -40°-enantiomer. Statement II is valid, which eliminates choices A and C. That also makes choice **B** the best answer. Racemic mixtures are 50-50 mixtures of two enantiomers that exhibit no net optical rotation. The enantiomeric excess for a racemic mixture is 0, because neither enantiomer is present in excess. Statement III is invalid, confirming choice **B** as the best answer.

28. **Choice D is the best answer.** Using the Cahn-Ingold-Prelog rules for substituent priority and drawing the appropriate arcs, the configurations for the two stereogenic carbons of isoleucine are determined as follows:

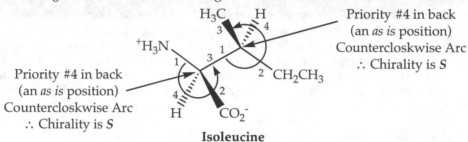

Isoleucine

Both of the chiral carbons have S chirality, which makes the compound $2S,3S$. It would be swell of you to choose **D**. The stereogenic center on carbon two of an amino acid must be S according to the rules discussed in the passage, so choices A and B could have been eliminated early. Regardless, the chiral center on the side chain of the amino acid must be solved for. Determining R and S is actually rather simple when you get the hang of it. The key is to find a method that works for you and hone it in by repeated use.

29. **Choice B is the best answer.** If the side chain (carbon three of isoleucine) were to change its absolute configuration while carbon 2 retained the orientation of its stereocenter, then only one of the two chiral centers would differ between the two compounds. The two stereoisomers (isoleucine and the other compound) would be classified as diastereomers. To be enantiomers, all of the chiral centers would need to be different. They would not be anomers of one another, as there is no new chiral center formed by cyclization. They are not identical structures, because they vary at one stereocenter. The best answer is choice **B**.

30. **Choice B is the best answer.** This question can be solved from straight memorization, which you likely had to do in a few of your biology classes. Naturally occurring amino acids are "L" as in life and natural. It is also stated in the passage that naturally occurring amino acids have S stereoconfiguration at the alpha carbon and that S stereochemistry is associated with L-amino acids (with the exception of cysteine, where R stereochemistry correlates with L-cysteine). The best answer is choice **B**.

31. **Choice B is the best answer.** Enantiomers are nonsuperimposable mirror images, thus all of the chiral centers must be different between the two structures. If all of the chiral centers are reversed, then the specific rotation should be completely reversed, which would lead to a value of +62° rather than -62°. It would be terrific if you were to select answer choice **B** as your answer selection. Enantiomers always have the same absolute value for the specific rotation, only the sign (direction of rotation) differs.

32. **Choice C is the best answer.** Isoleucine contains two stereogenic centers, one for the alpha carbon and one on the side chain. Plugging into the equation for the maximum number of stereoisomers (max # = 2^n where n is the number of chiral centers), there are four possible stereoisomers for the isoleucine structure. Because isoleucine contains two stereogenic centers that must have specific orientation, only one of the four stereoisomers will have the correct chirality to be biologically usable. This is stated in the passage in two fragments. The best answer is choice **C**.

33. **Choice D is the best answer.** With Fischer projections, you must remember that when an H is drawn on the side, it represents an H coming out at you in a three dimensional perspective. Hence, whatever arc you determine from the Fischer projection must subsequently be reversed to get the chirality of the stereocenter. In this example, both chiral centers generate clockwise circles in a two-dimensional perspective. But after reversing the clockwise circles to counterclockwise because of the hydrogen atoms are in front, both centers have *S* chirality. Choose **D** and be a scholar.

CH₃
Clockwise arc with H in front; *S*-stereocenter
H—OH
H—CH₃
Clockwise arc with H in front; *S*-stereocenter
OCH₃

34. **Choice C is the best answer.** If a compound has stereocenters but is not optically active, this implies that the compound must be meso. To be meso, a compound must have a mirror plane in the molecule about which the stereocenters are evenly displaced. This mirror plane slices the molecule into two equivalent halves. *2R,3S*-dibromobutane and *2R,4S*-dibromopentane each have equivalent mirror halves (thus mirror symmetry) so they are both meso compounds. This eliminates choices A and B. Cis-1,3-dichlorocyclohexane has equivalent halves as well as a mirror slicing through carbon 2, so it is a meso compound. This eliminates choice D. Only *2R,4S*-dibromohexane does not have two equivalent halves, which means it is not meso and is therefore optically active. The best answer is thus choice **C**.

35. **Choice D is the best answer.** The two structures shown in the question have identical bonds and they differ at all three of their stereocenters. This makes them enantiomers of one another, because enantiomers are mirror images of one another and thus must differ at all stereogenic carbons. Enantiomers have the same physical properties, such as boiling point and melting point, so they are difficult to separate using traditional organic chemistry methods. Fractional distillation can separate compounds with relatively close boiling point, but not with the same boiling point. Choice A is eliminated. Acid-base extraction takes advantage of differences in pKₐ values, which in the case of enantiomers there are none. Acid-base extraction, no matter what organic solvent is used in conjunction with water, will not work to separate enantiomers. Choice B is eliminated. Enantiomers have the same solubility properties, so they cannot be separated using recrystallization methods, unless the solvent is chiral or a chiral molecule is added that selectively binds one of the two enantiomers. Choice C is eliminated. Sending enantiomers down a column that has chiral centers will result in the preferential affinity to the column of one enantiomer over the other, so using a chiral chromatography column will work to separate enantiomers. Choice **D** is the best answer.

36. **Choice B is the best answer.** For a compound with chiral centers to be optically inactive, it must be meso. and thus contain an internal mirror plane of symmetry. The molecule must have *R,S* chirality to be meso. This eliminates choices A and C. The mirror plane must be through the C_2-C_3 bond according to the chiral centers in the answer choices. This mirror plane is possible only with butane, so the correct answer must be choice **B**.

37. **Choice C is the best answer.** PBr₃ converts the OH group of an alcohol into a Br group through an S_N2 reaction. Because the reaction is by way of an S_N2 mechanism, the stereocenters must undergo inversion. If you recall, stereogenic centers invert in S_N2 reactions, but not in S_N1 reactions. This means the product shows the opposite stereochemistry of Compound P. The stereochemistry of Compound P is *3R,4S*, so the stereochemistry of the dibromo product should be *3S,4R*. Select choice **C** for the sensation of correctness and satisfaction.

O HO H Priority #4 in back
                 Clockwise = R
H   3   2   CH₂CH₃
              2   3
H   H   H   OH Priority #4 in front
                 Clockwise = S

O H   Br Priority #4 in front
                 Clockwise = S
H   3   2   CH₂CH₃
              2   3
H   H   Br   H Priority #4 in back
                 Clockwise = R

38. **Choice D is the best answer.** The active site of an enzyme carries out a highly specific function (reaction), so they must be highly selective in terms of reactivity. As implied by the passage, active sites are highly specific in terms of chirality. This eliminates choice A. Although it is not stated in the passage, you should know that the active site has specific dimensions, so it is size specific. This eliminates choice B. Active sites are highly specific for the functional groups involved in a chemical reaction, so choice C is eliminated. Because isotopes show the same chemical reactivity, enzymes are unable to distinguish isotopes. This means that enzyme active sites are *not* isotope specific, making choice **D** the best answer.

39. **Choice C is the best answer.** There are two concepts being tested here. The first is that all of the stereocenters differ between enantiomers and the second is that enantiomers have the same physical properties, in this case boiling point being of interest. They tell us that 2R,3S,4R has a boiling point of 142°C, so that means that 2S,3R,4S also has a boiling point of 142°C. They tell us that 2S,3S,4R has a boiling point of 146°C, so that means that 2R,3R,4S also has a boiling point of 146°C. Finally, they tell us that 2S,3S,4S has a boiling point of 151°C, so that means that 2R,3R,4R also has a boiling point of 151°C. Choices A and B can be eliminated immediately, because they show 2R,3R,4R and 2S,3S,4S having the lowest boiling points in their set of three. Choice D can be eliminated, because it shows two enantiomers (2S,3S,4R and 2R,3R,4S) as having different boiling points, which is not possible. This leaves only choice **C** as possible. Let's consider the boiling points to verify the relationship. 2R,3R,4R has a boiling point of 151°C, 2R,3R,4S has a boiling point of 146°C, and 2R,3S,4R has a boiling point of 142°C, so the relationship 2R,3R,4R > 2R,3R,4S > 2R,3S,4R is valid. Select choice **C** for optimal correctness and the satisfaction that goes with it.

40. **Choice B is the best answer.** On the third carbon, the OH and H groups have interchanged, so that chiral center has changed. On the fourth carbon, the ethyl group, hydrogen and hydroxyl group have interchanged, so that chiral center has not changed. When only one out of two (some, not all) chiral centers change, it is not a mirror image, nor identical (superimposable), making the two compounds diastereomers. Pick answer **B**.

Compound P   Mystery Compound

41. **Choice A is the best answer.** Using the rules of priorities, the following is determined.

H in front, so reverse chirality from R to S

Carbon 1
H in back, so chirality is S as shown

Carbon 2

This makes the compound 1S,2S. Luckily, there was the same chirality at carbon 1 as carbon 2, so we didn't need to decide which carbon was which. Choose **A** for the good feeling you get when pick correct answers.

42. **Choice A is the best answer.** Enantiomers have the exact same physical properties, such as boiling point, melting point, and density. This makes choice **A** correct and eliminates choices B and C. Enantiomers have the same magnitude for specific rotation, but with the opposite sign (in the opposite direction). This makes choice D an incorrect answer, and leave choice **A** as the best choice in a sea of many choices (well maybe not many, but four.)

Passage VII (Questions 43 - 48)   **Reaction Rates of Nucleophilic Substitution**

43. **Choice A is the best answer.** The strength of a nucleophile can be measured by its reaction rate in a second-order nucleophilic substitution reaction (an S_N2 reaction). The nucleophiles are listed in the first column of Table 1. Any other column can be used to determine the relative strength of the nucleophiles, because all other factors in the reaction are constant. The less negative the value in the table, the faster the reaction, and therefore the better the nucleophile. The CN^- has the lowest value in all three columns, so the best nucleophile is CN^-. This eliminates choices C and D. The question now is to determine whether the ammonia (NH_3) or methanol ($HOCH_3$) is the better nucleophile. The stronger nucleophile is ammonia, because in each column, the less negative value is associated with ammonia. The best answer is choice **A**, $CN^- > CH_3S^- > NH_3 > HOCH_3$.

44. **Choice C is the best answer.** As mentioned in the passage, the methyl electrophile is chosen to avoid the complication of the competing elimination reaction. It is not possible to form a double bond with only one carbon in the reactant (at least two carbons are required for the formation of a double bond). This makes choice **C** the best answer. Steric hindrance increases when using the isopropyl electrophile in lieu of the methyl electrophile, but that is not necessarily a difficulty. The effect should be uniform across the reaction chart, so choices A and B can be eliminated.

45. **Choice A is the best answer.** The best leaving group is the functional group that takes electrons from carbon and retains them to the greatest extent. Retaining electrons can also be viewed as not sharing electrons. By not sharing electrons, an ion or molecule can be viewed as being a weak base. The strength of a leaving group is generally correlated (in a linear fashion) to the strength of the conjugate acid of the leaving group. As an acid becomes stronger, the conjugate base becomes weaker. This implies that it is valid to compare the strength of the leaving group in a linear fashion with weakening base strength. This makes choice **A**, "The less basic the leaving group, the better it is as a leaving group," the best answer. Choices B and C are essentially the same answer, therefore they should both be eliminated.

46. **Choice D is the best answer.** The strength of a nucleophile can vary with many reaction features. Depending on its nature, a solvent hinders a nucleophile to a varying degree. For instance, if a solvent is capable of forming hydrogen bonds, then it will hinder the attack of nucleophiles that are capable of forming hydrogen bonds. This can be seen in the differing nucleophilic strength of halides as they are observed in aprotic and protic solvents. The fluoride is the strongest nucleophile of the halides in aprotic solvents while it is the weakest nucleophile of the halides in protic solvents. This eliminates choice A. The nucleophilicity of a compound can be correlated to its basicity in terms of a Lewis base. Generally, for a nucleophile that is more basic than another, it is the better nucleophile of the two, with steric hindrance responsible for most deviations from that pattern. This eliminates choice B. The strength of a nucleophile reduces with increasing bulk. This implies that nucleophilicity can vary with steric hindrance, which eliminates choice C. The only answer choice left is choice **D**. The leaving group is independent of the nucleophile in nucleophilic substitution reactions. This makes choice **D** the best answer.

47. **Choice B is the best answer.** Because the rate of an S_N1 reaction depends only on the leaving group breaking free from the electrophile in the rate-determining step, the nucleophile is irrelevant to the reaction rate for an S_N1 reaction. The strength of a nucleophile cannot be determined by a rate study in which the nucleophile does not influence the rate. The rate can vary with changes in the leaving group strength (which can be viewed as changes in the electrophile), the temperature (temperature always affects the rate of a reaction), and solvent. It is only the strength of the nucleophile that cannot be determined from the reaction rate data of an S_N1 reaction. Choose **B** for yet another chance to flash a happy "*I just got another one right*" smile.

48. **Choice D is the best answer.** Choice B can be eliminated immediately, because NH_3 is the nucleophile and not the leaving group. Choice C can be eliminated immediately, because $^-OCH_3$ is the leaving group (if it were to react) and not the nucleophile. The data in Table 1 shows that no reaction was observed each time that the electrophile was dimethyl ether (CH_3OCH_3). On the other hand, the data in Table 1 shows that ammonia (NH_3) is a reactive nucleophile with the other three electrophiles used in the experiment ($CH_3OSO_3CH_3$, CH_3I, and CH_3Cl). This implies that the lack of reactivity can be attributed to the electrophile rather than the nucleophile. The leaving group in the cases where dimethyl ether is the electrophile is a methoxide anion ($^-OCH_3$). Pick **D** to prosper and score... well score at least.

Questions 49 - 52   **Not Based on a Descriptive Passage**

49. **Choice D is the best answer.** 4-chlorocyclohexanol contains no stereocenters (chiral carbons), therefore it cannot rotate plane-polarized light. The result is that 4-chlorocyclohexanol is not optically active. Choose wisely by choosing **D**. The other three compounds have two chiral carbons and are not meso, therefore they are all optically active. It is possible for the compound (4-chlorocyclohexanol) to exhibit isomerism in the form of geometrical isomers (cis and trans), but geometrical isomers do not rotate plane-polarized light.

50. **Choice A is the best answer.** On the second carbon, the OH and H groups have interchanged, so that chiral center differs between the two stereoisomers. On the third carbon, the OH and H groups have not interchanged, so that chiral center is identical in the two stereoisomers. On the fourth carbon, the ethyl and methyl groups have interchanged, so that chiral center differs between the two stereoisomers. When two out of three (i.e., some, but not all) of the chiral centers differ, the two stereoisomers are neither superimposable, nor are they mirror images of one another, which defines diastereomers. Pick **A** and be jovial.

---

51. **Choice A is the best answer.** Alkene chemistry is not tested on the MCAT, so in the event a question like this were to appear on your exam, you should note right away that they are focusing on some other topic, in this case stereochemistry. Syn addition of equivalent substituents to a trans double bond in an alkene results in the formation of two enantiomers (specifically the *R,R* and *S,S* enantiomers) as shown below. Choose **A** for best results. A meso compound can be obtained from syn addition of equivalent substituents to a cis alkene, where the alkyl groups on the alkene are identical.

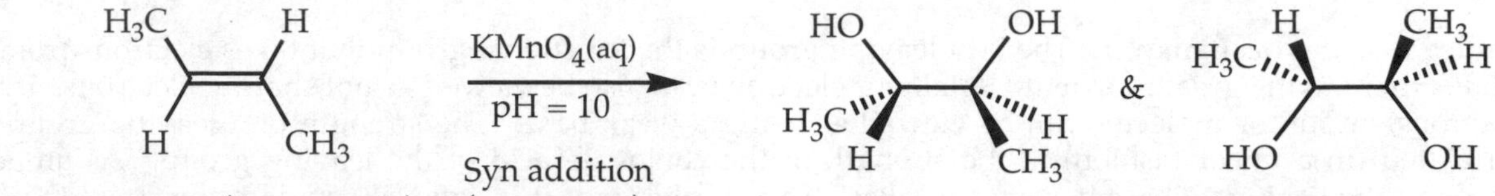

Trans reactant (asymmetric)   Syn addition (symmetric)   Asymmetric products

52. **Choice B is the best answer.** In order to be diastereomers, the two stereoisomers must have at least one stereocenter different, but not all of the stereocenters can be different. In order for this to be possible, the structure must contain two or more stereocenters. Choice A is eliminated, because carbon one is not a stereocenter (primary carbons with two Hs attached are not stereocenters), so it at most has only one stereocenter in the molecule. Choice C is eliminated, because a geminal diol has two equivalent OH groups on the same carbon, so there may not be any stereocenters on a geminal diol. Choice D is eliminated, because carbons 1 and 3 both contain 2 Hs and thus are not chiral centers, and carbon 2 has two identical CH_2OH groups attached. Glycerol does not have two stereocenters, so it cannot form diastereomers. Only is choice **B** is it possible for there to be two stereocenters, because carbons 2 and 3 each contain an H, an OH, and alkyl group, and an R-group with a hydroxyl group.

Phase III Homework for Stereochemistry

Stereochemistry Phase III Scoring Scale

Raw Score	MCAT Score
29 - 32	13 - 15
23 - 28	10 - 12
17 - 22	7 - 9
12 - 16	4 - 6
1 - 11	1 - 3

A chemist sets out to perform a multistep synthesis. The first step, Reaction 1, is a standard Diels Alder reaction.

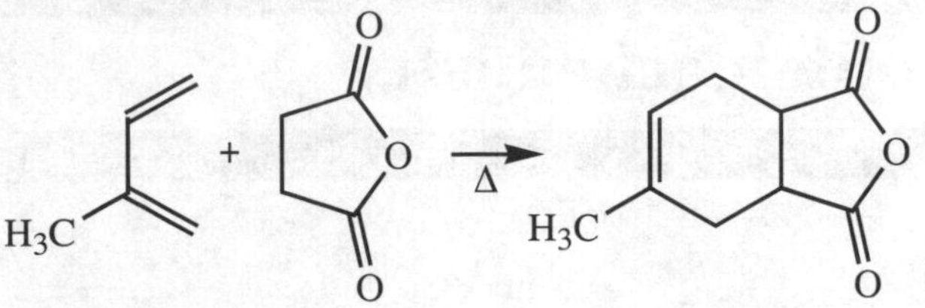

Compound 1   Compound 2   Compound 3

Reaction 1

Compound 3 represents a mixture of enantiomers. The mixture undergoes a chirally specific laboratory technique to isolate Compound 3a, shown below, from Compound 3b.

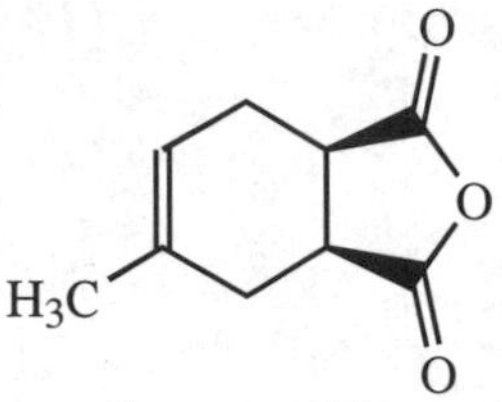

Compound 3a

In the second step, Reaction 2, Compound 3a is treated with meta-chloro peroxybenzoic acid, mcpba, in ether to form Compound 4.

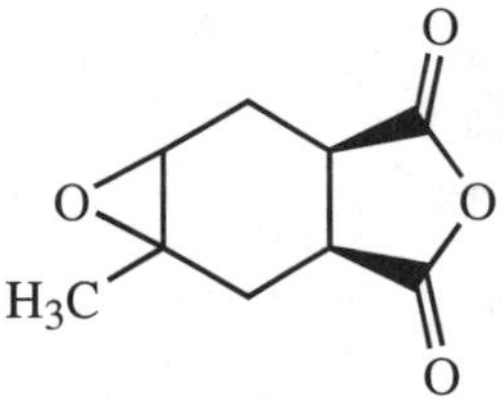

Compound 4

Compound 4 then undergoes Reaction 3 to form Compound 5.

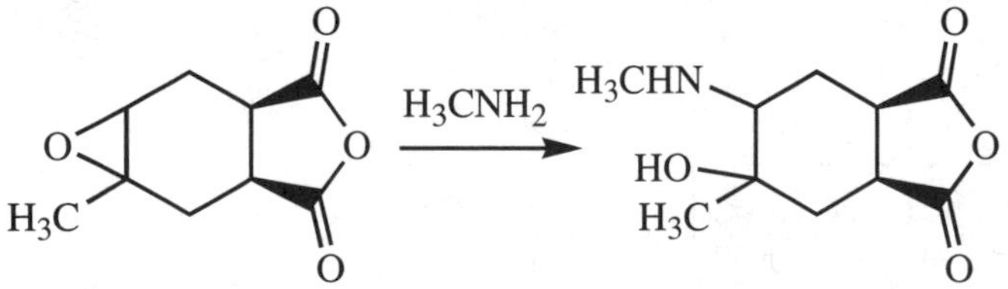

H₃CNH₂

Compound 4   Compound 5

Reaction 3

In Reaction 4, Compound 5 is hydrolyzed using water at 90°C to form Compound 6.

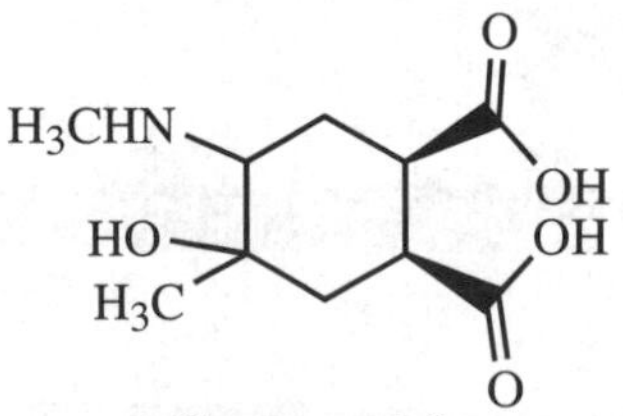

Compound 6

1. Which of the following is Compound 3b?

A.   B.

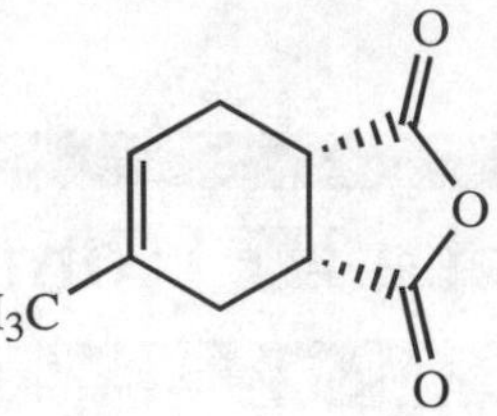

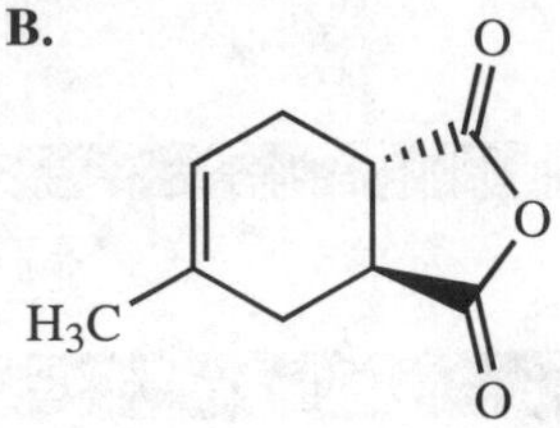

C. 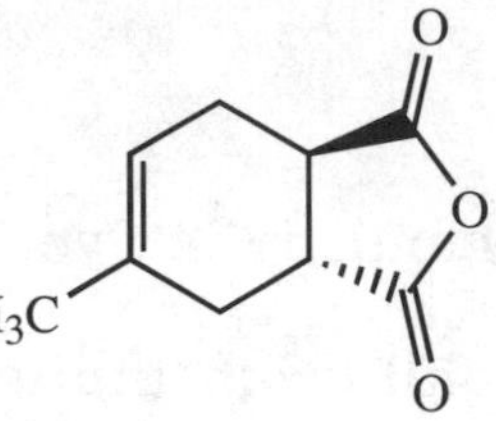   D.

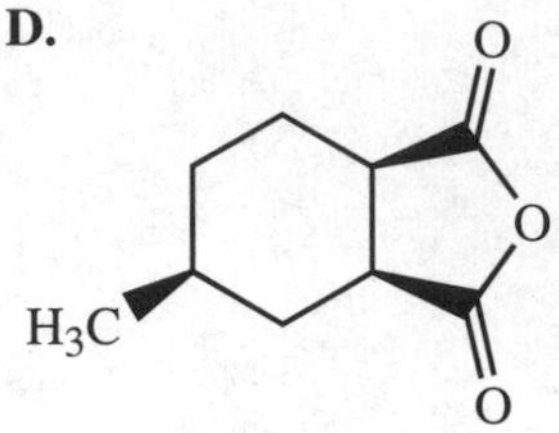

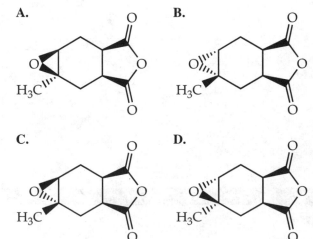

2. What laboratory technique would be MOST effective in obtaining a pure enantiomer from a racemic mixture?

A. Adding the mixture to a chromatography column filled with a gel with both enantiomers bound to it.

B. Adding the mixture to a chromatography column filled with a gel with just one of the enantiomers bound to it.

C. Distilling the mixture using a vertical column filled with beads that contained both enantiomers bound to their surface.

D. Using a chirally pure carrier gas in a gas chromatography experiment.

3. What is the major product (i.e., the most abundant stereoisomer) formed in Reaction 2?

A.   B.

C.   D.

4. All of the steps in the overall synthesis shown in the passage generate an optically active product mixture EXCEPT:

- **A.** Reaction 1
- **B.** Reaction 2
- **C.** Reaction 3
- **D.** Reaction 4

5. What is a likely side product of Reaction 3, if excess amine is used?

A.

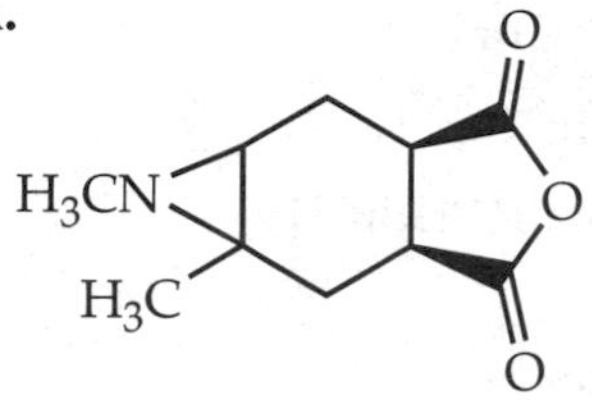

B.

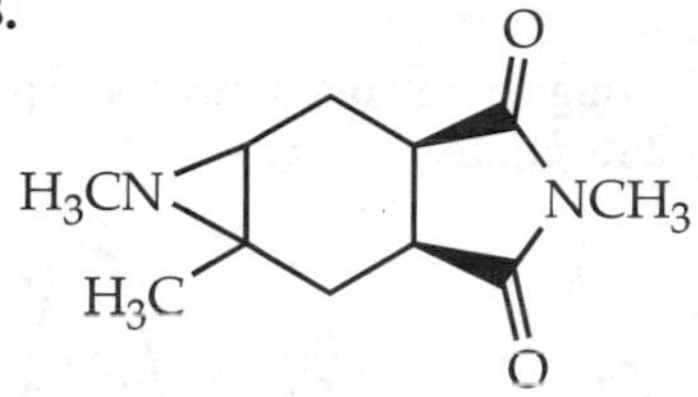

C.

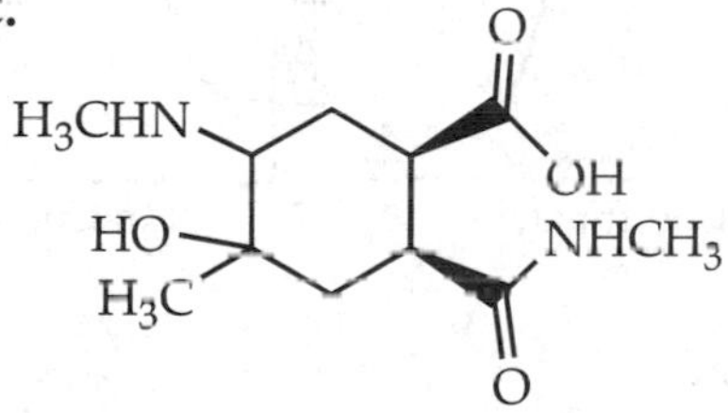

D.

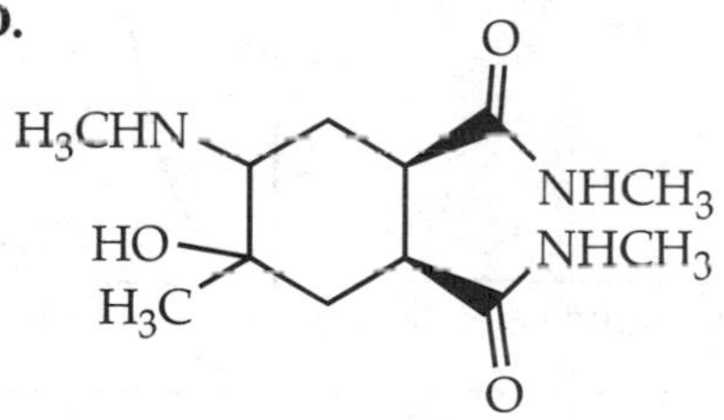

6. The final product mixture following Reaction 4 can best be described as:

- **A.** an enantiomeric mixture with $\alpha_D = 0°$.
- **B.** a diastereomeric mixture with $\alpha_D = 0°$.
- **C.** a diastereomeric mixture with $\alpha_D \neq 0°$.
- **D.** a meso mixture with $\alpha_D \neq 0°$.

Passage II (Questions 7 - 13)

It is possible to exchange one functional group on a substituted alkane for another by performing a nucleophilic substitution reaction. There are two versions of nucleophilic substitution, known as S_N1 and S_N2. The number in each reaction describes the rate dependence. The rate of an S_N1 reaction depends only on the electrophile concentration and not on the nucleophile concentration. The rate of an S_N2 reaction depends on both the concentration of nucleophile and the concentration of electrophile.

The difference between the two mechanisms boils down to the sequence and timing of the bond formation and bond breaking aspects of the reaction. In S_N1 reactions, a leaving group first leaves followed by nucleophilic attack of the carbocation intermediate. In S_N2 reactions, the nucleophile attacks the electrophilic carbon, simultaneously forcing the leaving group off of the molecule. In a mechanistic study, a secondary alkyl chloride was treated with two different nucleophiles to get the same ether product, and rate data were collected for each.

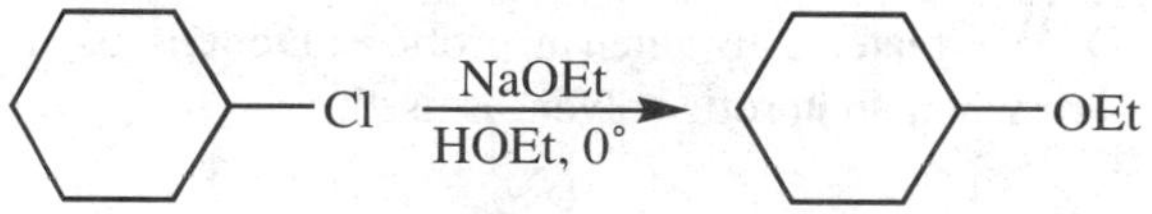

Reaction 1

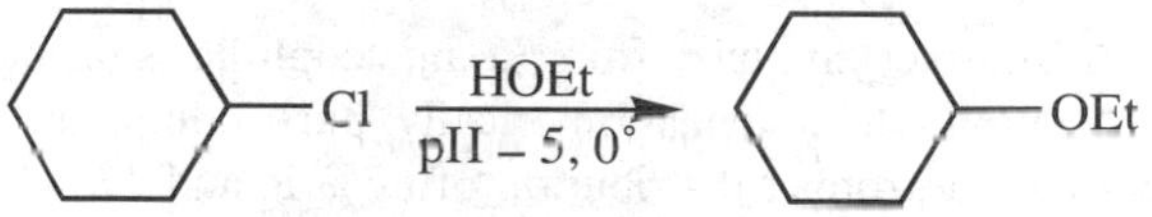

Reaction 2

Tables 1 and 2 show the initial rate data for three separate trials for each of the two reactions.

Reaction 1		
Rate (M/s)	**[CH₃CH₂ONa]**	**[C₆H₁₁Cl]**
1.32×10^{-2}	0.05 M	0.05 M
2.63×10^{-2}	0.10 M	0.05 M
5.25×10^{-2}	0.10 M	0.10 M

Table 1 Initial Rates for Reaction 1

Reaction 2		
Rate (M/s)	**[CH₃CH₂OH]**	**[C₆H₁₁Cl]**
1.93×10^{-3}	0.20 M	0.05 M
1.95×10^{-3}	0.40 M	0.05 M
3.83×10^{-3}	0.40 M	0.10 M

Table 2 Initial Rates for Reaction 2

Based on the data presented, the nature of the mechanism (whether it follows S_N1 or S_N2 kinetics) can be determined. The key to the analysis is to observe the change in rate as the nucleophile concentration changes. As a rule, S_N2 reactions are faster than S_N1 reactions.

7. Reaction 1 and Reaction 2 are best described as what type of reactions?

A. Reaction 1 is an S_N1; Reaction 2 is an S_N2

B. Reaction 1 is an S_N2; Reaction 2 is an S_N1

C. Reaction 1 is an E1; Reaction 2 is an S_N2

D. Reaction 1 is an S_N1; Reaction 2 is an E2

8. All of the following are associated with Reaction 2 EXCEPT:

A. inversion of the chiral center.

B. a carbocation intermediate.

C. the rate depending on the electrophile.

D. a greater rate when a protic solvent is used than when an aprotic solvent is used.

9. A product mixture from a nucleophilic substitution reaction on an enantiomerically pure compound that yields a product distribution of 87% R and 13% S can best be explained by which of the following?

A. The reaction goes purely by an S_N2 mechanism.

B. The reaction goes mostly by an S_N2 mechanism with some S_N1 mechanism transpiring.

C. The reaction goes mostly by an S_N1 mechanism with some S_N2 mechanism transpiring.

D. The reaction goes purely by an S_N1 mechanism.

10. If bromine were used as the leaving group from the cyclohexane in lieu of chlorine, what effect would you expect on the rate? (Note that a C-Cl bond is stronger than a C-Br bond)

A. Both the S_N1 and S_N2 rates would increase.

B. The S_N1 rate would increase, while the S_N2 rate would decrease.

C. The S_N1 rate would decrease, while the S_N2 rate would increase.

D. Both the S_N1 and S_N2 rates would decrease.

11. Which of the following is the BEST nucleophile?

A. H_3CO^-

B. H_3COH

C. Cl^-

D. HCl

12. Which of the following reactions is most likely to proceed by an S_N2 mechanism?

A. $CN^- + (H_3C)_3CBr \rightarrow$

B. $H_3COH + (H_3C)_3CBr \rightarrow$

C. $CN^- + (H_3C)_2CHCHBrCH_3 \rightarrow$

D. $H_3COH + (H_3C)_2CHCHBrCH_3 \rightarrow$

13. Which of the following energy diagrams corresponds to an exothermic S_N2 reaction?

A.
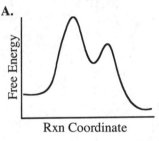

B.
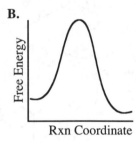

C.
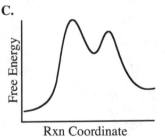

D.
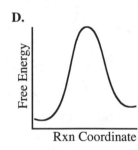

     GO ON TO THE NEXT PAGE

Not all stereocenters are chemically reactive. A good example is a tertiary carbon with a hydrogen where all three alkyl substituents are nonequivalent. When a reaction is carried out on a molecule with an unreactive stereocenter present, there exists the possibility that diastereomers will be formed in unequal quantities, due to the asymmetry in the molecule. This influence is referred to as *stereochemical control*. Reaction 1, drawn below, demonstrates this principle.

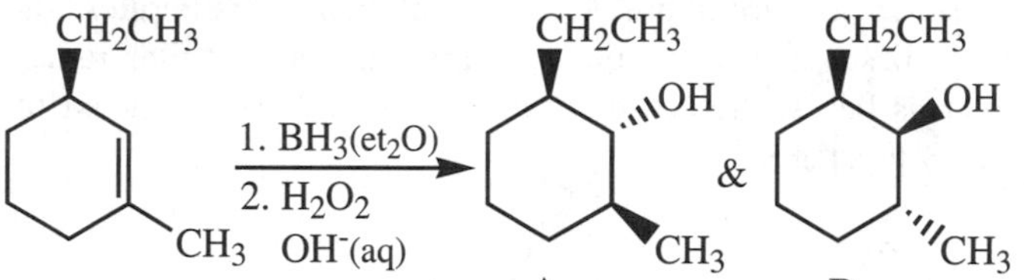

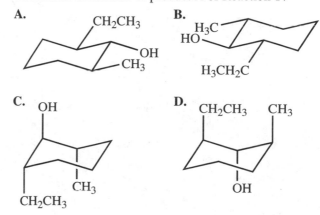

Reaction 1

The two products, Compound A and Compound B, are nonsuperimposable and they are not mirror images. In first step (hydroboration), the hydroxyl group prefers to add to the less hindered carbon of the π-bond and the less hindered face of the molecule, which means that the two products are present in unequal amounts. Their percentages can be found from the observed specific rotation using Equation 1 below. The percentages determined using this equation can be referenced against the quantitative values obtained using GC analysis.

$$\alpha_{obs} = x_a\alpha_a + (1 - x_a)\alpha_b$$

Equation 1

α_{obs} is the observed optical rotation for the mixture and x_a is the mole fraction of component a in the mixture.

This same diastereomeric preference phenomenon can be observed any time a nucleophile is attacking an sp^2-hybridized carbon of an asymmetric molecule. This means that unequal amounts of diastereomers may be observed with S_N1 reactions, electrophilic addition reactions, and carbonyl addition reactions. Reaction 2, shown below, is an S_N1 reaction that results in the formation of two stereosiomers in unequal portions.

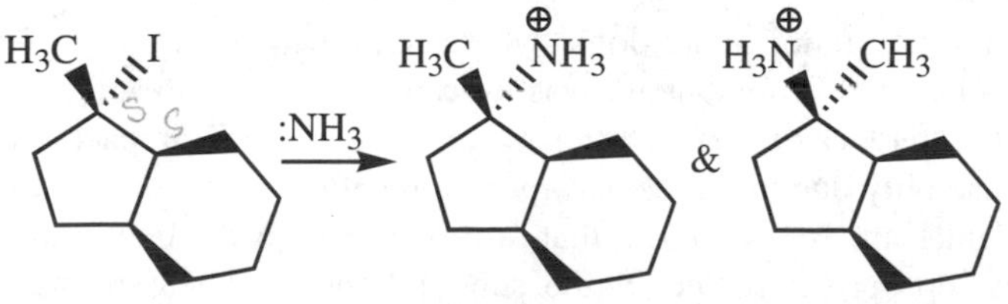

Reaction 2

14. For Reaction 2, what is the observed specific rotation for the product mixture?
    A. Greater than 62°
    B. Between 46° and 62°
    C. Between 30° and 46°
    D. Less than 30°

15. What would be the specific rotation for Reaction 1 if Compound A is 80% of the diastereomeric mixture?
    A. 48°
    B. 42°
    C. 33°
    D. 18°

16. The two products in Reaction 2 are best described as:
    A. enantiomers.
    B. epimers.
    C. diastereomers.
    D. anomers.

17. The products of Reaction 1 can be distinguished from one another by all of the following methods EXCEPT:
    A. specific rotation.
    B. melting point.
    C. retention time on a GC.
    D. IR spectroscopy.

18. Which of the following structures best represents the most stable conformer of product A of Reaction 1?

19. What are the orientations of the three chiral centers in the reactant in Reaction 2, starting with the chiral center on which the iodine is attached and moving clockwise around the cyclopentane?

A. S,R,S

B. R,R,S

C. S,S,S

D. R,S,S

20. How many stereogenic centers (chiral carbons) are present in the alkene reactant in Reaction 1?

A. 0

B. 1

C. 2

D. 3

Passage IV (Questions 21 - 27)

For certain reactant combinations in a given solvent, it is possible to convert a reaction that yields nearly 100% substitution product (a substituted alkane) into a reaction that yields nearly 100% elimination product (an alkene) by varying only the temperature. Studies have shown that favorable conditions for an elimination reaction involve higher temperatures (elimination is endothermic and has a higher activation energy than the competing substitution reaction). Elimination by an E_2 mechanism requires the presence of a strong bulky base in solution. This implies that weak bases at low temperature react as nucleophiles rather than as bases. Reaction 1, drawn below, was designed to verify this theory.

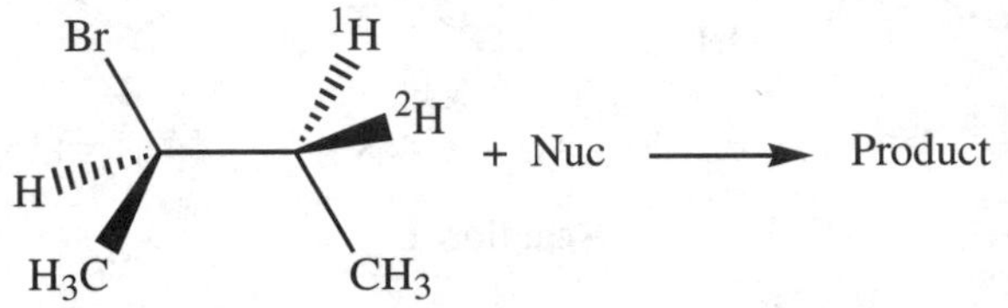

Reaction 1

A chemist monitored the reaction over time by observing the optical rotation of plane polarized-light by the solution. When undergoing an S_N2 reaction, the solution remains optically active, although the exact value of the specific rotation ($[\alpha]_D$) is not always predictable. Table 1 shows the initial and final specific rotations for six unique trials of Reaction 1, where either the nucleophile or the temperature was varied from trial to trial.

Trial	Temperature	Nucleophile	Init $[\alpha]_D$	Final $[\alpha]_D$
Trial I	10°C	NH_3	+24°	-36°
Trial II	60°C	NH_3	+24°	-28°
Trial III	10°C	NaOH	+23°	-38°
Trial IV	60°C	NaOH	+24°	0°
Trial V	10°C	$NaNH_2$	+23°	0°
Trial VI	60°C	$NaNH_2$	+24°	0°

Table 1

The two competing reactions when a good nucleophile is present in solution, in the absence of an acid, are the E_2 and S_N2 reactions. The internal alkene is the predominant product under conditions where elimination is favored. Deuterated bromobutane was used in Reaction 1 to monitor the stereochemistry, at the expense of a small impact on reactivity due to the *deuterium isotope effect*. It is found that deuterium is less acidic than a proton due to the deuterium isotope effect rooted in the shorter bond length associated with the deuterium-carbon bond. An E_1 reaction can compete with a substitution reaction if the leaving group is a good leaving group and it is situated on a tertiary carbon.

21. An elimination product Reaction 1 would result in what optical rotation?

   A. +24°

   B. 0°

   C. -24°

   D. -42°

22. Which of the following BEST describes the stereochemistry of the reactant in Reaction 1?

   A. *2R*

   B. *2S*

   C. *2R,3R*

   D. *2R,3S*

23. Which of the following statements is true regarding the interchanging of stereoisomers for the reactant?

   A. When the enantiomer of the reactant is used, the same geometrical isomers are formed, so either the reactant or its enantiomer may be used.

   B. When the enantiomer of the reactant is used, different geometrical isomers are formed, so an enantiomer cannot be substituted for the reactant.

   C. When a diastereomer of the reactant is used, the same geometrical isomers are formed, so either the reactant or its diastereomer may be used.

   D. When a diastereomer of the reactant is used, different geometrical isomers are formed, so a diastereomer may be substituted for the reactant.

24. Which of the following explanations can BEST explain the -28° optical rotation for the product mixture observed in Trial II?

   A. The reaction goes purely by an S_N2 mechanism.

   B. The reaction goes purely by an E_2 mechanism.

   C. The reaction is an S_N1 reaction with some competing elimination reaction side product present.

   D. The reaction is an S_N2 reaction with some competing elimination reaction side product present.

25. Based on the data listed in Table 1, Trial I is predominantly what type of reaction?

   A. S_N1

   B. S_N2

   C. E_1

   D. E_2

26. How can the loss of optical activity be explained when a secondary alkyl chloride is treated with sodium methoxide at 65°C?

   A. An S_N1 reaction was the predominant reaction.

   B. An S_N2 reaction was the predominant reaction.

   C. An E_1 reaction was the predominant reaction.

   D. An E_2 reaction was the predominant reaction.

27. To support the theory that an E_2 reaction mechanism is taking place, it would be best to use chiral centers on which carbons of a deuterated 2-bromobutane?

   A. Carbon 2 only

   B. Carbon 3 only

   C. Both carbon 2 and carbon 3

   D. Carbons 1, 2 and 3

In nucleophilic substitution reactions, the reactivity of an electrophile dictates the reaction order (whether the reaction is first-order or second-order). The reactivity of an electrophile is correlated to the strength of the leaving group. An electrophile with the better leaving group is the more reactive electrophile, and thus reacts faster and undergoes the more favorable nucleophilic substitution reaction. A good leaving group is stable once it has left the electrophile, so a stable leaving group does not readily donate its electron pair. This implies that a good leaving group is a weak base. The weaker the compound is as a base, the stronger its conjugate acid is. As acid strength increases, the pK_a of the acid decreases. This ultimately means that the lower the pK_a of the conjugate acid of the leaving group, the more reactive the electrophile.

Based on the pK_a values, it is possible to predict the relative reactivity of various electrophiles. The favorability of a nucleophilic substitution reaction can be approximated by comparing the pK_a value of the conjugate acid of the nucleophile with the pK_a value of the conjugate acid of the leaving group. Equation 1 can be employed to approximate a reactivity constant, C, for the reaction:

$$C = 10^{[pK_a(\text{H-Nucleophile}) - pK_a(\text{H-Leaving group})]}$$

Equation 1

A reaction can be classified anywhere from very favorable to very unfavorable. The C value can be used as follows to approximate the favorability of a reaction:

If $C > 10^3$, then the reaction is very favorable

If $10^3 > C > 1$, then the reaction is slightly favorable

If $1 > C > 10^{-3}$, then the reaction is slightly unfavorable

If $10^{-3} > C$, then the reaction is very unfavorable

Table 1 lists pK_a values for the conjugate acids of some common leaving groups.

Acid	pKa	Acid	pK$_a$
HI	-10.5	HCN	9.1
HBr	-8.5	C$_6$H$_5$OH	10.0
HCl	-7.0	H$_3$CCH$_2$SH	10.5
HF	3.3	H$_2$O	15.7

Table 1

The pK_a data given in Table 1 can be used to predict the favorability of a nucleophilic substitution reaction. The accuracy is within experimental error for substitution studies. Equation 1 does not hold well in protic solvents due to variations in nucleophile strength from hydrogen bonding. In general though, the better a group is at leaving from a protic H, the better it will be at leaving from a C.

28. Which of the following compounds is the BEST electrophile?

A. $(CH_3)_3CI$

B. $(CH_3)_3CBr$

C. $(CH_3)_3CCl$

D. $(CH_3)_3CF$

29. Which of the following compounds is the MOST reactive when treated with cyanide nucleophile?

A. CH_3CH_2F

B. $CH_3CH_2OC_6H_5$

C. $CH_3CH_2SCH_3$

D. CH_3CH_2Br

30. The best explanation of why $NaSCH_3$ is a better nucleophile than $NaSCH(CH_3)_2$ is which of the following?

A. Inductive effect of methyl is weaker than isopropyl

B. Resonance affects only three carbon fragments

C. Hybridization of carbon varies with substitution

D. Steric hindrance is less with the methyl group

31. The reaction of methylthiol (CH_3SH) with R-2-butanol is which of the following?

A. Very favorable

B. Slightly favorable

C. Slightly unfavorable

D. Very unfavorable

32. How can it be explained that fluoride, F^-, is a better nucleophile than iodide, I^-, in ether solvent but a worse nucleophile in alcohol solvent?

A. In a protic solvent such as alcohol, F^- is hindered by hydrogen bonding, and cannot migrate as well.

B. In an aprotic solvent such as ether, F^- is hindered by hydrogen bonding, and cannot migrate as well.

C. In a protic solvent such as alcohol, F^- exhibits no hydrogen bonding, so it cannot migrate as well.

D. In an aprotic solvent such as ether, F^- exhibits no hydrogen bonding, so it cannot migrate as well.

Answers to Stereochemistry Phase III Homework

1.	A	2.	B	3.	B	4.	A	5.	C	6.	C	7.	B	8.	A	9.	B	10.	A
11.	A	12.	C	13.	B	14.	B	15.	B	16.	C	17.	D	18.	A	19.	C	20.	B
21.	B	22.	D	23.	A	24.	D	25.	B	26.	D	27.	C	28.	A	29.	D	30.	D
31.	D	32.	A																

1. **Choice A is the best answer.** It is stated in the passage that Compound 3 represents a mixture of enantiomers, so Compound 3b is the enantiomer of Compound 3a. Enantiomers are stereoisomers that are mirror images of one another, therefore all of their chiral centers differ between the two enantiomers. There are two stereogenic carbons in Compound 3, so Compound 3b must have the opposite configuration of Compound 3a at these two stereocenters. This is true in choice **A**, so choice **A** is the best answer.

2. **Choice B is the best answer.** To separate a compound from its enantiomer, the technique must select for one of the two enantiomers. This requires that there is chirality (asymmetry) involved in the lab technique. If the mixture travels through a column with one enantiomer attached, the other enantiomer is likely to adhere to the column as it travels. This means that one enantiomer will migrate quickly while the other travels slowly. This makes choice **B** a strong answer. If the adsorbent of the column has both enantiomers bound to it, then both of the free enantiomers in the solution will be hindered by the column, slowing them equally. This does not result in separation. Choice A is eliminated. The same logic can be used to eliminate choice C. If the distilling column has beads with both enantiomers, then both of the free enantiomers in solution will exhibit the same affinity for the beads, and will not separate as well. Choice C is eliminated. The compounds do not interact with the carrier gas in gas chromatography to any notable extent. This means that choice D will do nothing to help separate the enantiomers. Choice D is eliminated.

3. **Choice B is the best answer.** Reaction 2 converts Compound 3a into Compound 4, using a peroxyacid (a strong oxidizing agent that inserts oxygen into π-bonds). The epoxide ring can form from either side of the π-bond. However, because of the steric hindrance above the ring with the alkene (caused by the adjacent six-membered ring), it is preferential to form the epoxide on the back side. Both bonds to oxygen in the epoxide must be on the same side, so choices C and D are eliminated. Because of steric hindrance, choice **B** is a better structure than choice A. The best answer is choice **B**.

4. **Choice A is the best answer.** It is stated in the passage that Reaction 1 generates a mixture of enantiomers. When enantiomers are formed, they are formed in a racemic mixture. The result is that the optical activity of the product mixture is zero, because the rotation of plane-polarized light by the two isomers cancels one another out. This means that Reaction 1 generates an optically inactive product mixture. Once the enantiomer mixture is separated, isolating Compound 3a, the subsequent reactions all start with an optically active starting material, resulting in optical activity in the end. Reactions 2 and 3 form diastereomers and Reaction 4 cleaves the anhydride to retain the same chirality as the starting material. Because the material is optically pure at the start, the product of reaction 4 is also optically pure. The best answer is choice **A**.

5. **Choice C is the best answer.** Methyl amine, like all small amines, is a very good nucleophile. The first equivalent reacts with the most reactive electrophile, which in this case is the epoxide ring (the three-membered ring is extremely strained and therefore extremely reactive). However, an anhydride is also highly reactive. In the event excess amine is added, it can easily add to the carbonyl, cleaving the anhydride and generating a carboxylic acid and amide. Choices A and B can be eliminated immediately, because the three-membered ring is highly unstable and will not reform once it has been broken. The OH group is a poor leaving group, so it is not likely that an amine will substitute for the hydroxyl group, once the anhydride is cleaved, so choice D is eliminated. The result is that choice **C** is the best answer.

6. **Choice C is the best answer.** In Reaction 2, a mixture of stereoisomers is formed that is never resolved. As a result, the reactant in Reaction 4, Compound 5, represents a mixture of stereoisomers. Two of the chiral centers are the same in all of the stereoisomers, so they cannot be enantiomers (stereoisomers where all of the chiral centers differ). This eliminates choice A. The product is not a meso compound, given that it does not have an internal mirror plane, so choice D is eliminated. Because the mixture starts with optical activity, and Reaction 4 does nothing to affect the chirality, the product mixture in Reaction 4, Compound 6, must be optically active. This makes choice **C** the best answer.

7. **Choice B is the best answer.** The ether product shown in both Reaction 1 and 2 is the result of a substitution reaction, not an elimination reaction, so choices C and D are eliminated. To determine the type of substitution reaction that takes place, we need to consider the rate data. The data listed in Table 1 correlates to Reaction 1. Because the rate of the reaction varies directly with both the concentration of the nucleophile and the concentration of the electrophile, Reaction 1 must be an S_N2 reaction. S_N2 reactions show a rate dependence on both the nucleophile and the electrophile. The data listed in Table 2 correlates to Reaction 2. Because the rate of the reaction varies directly with the concentration of the electrophile, but does not vary with the concentration of the nucleophile, the reaction must be an S_N1 reaction. The rate of an S_N1 reaction only depends on the concentration of the electrophile, and does not vary with the concentration of the nucleophile. This means that you must choose **B** to live up to your potential.

8. **Choice A is the best answer.** Because the rate of Reaction 2 varies directly with the concentration of the electrophile, but does not vary with the concentration of the nucleophile, Reaction 2 must be an S_N1 reaction. An S_N1 reaction can undergo racemization if the leaving group is on a stereogenic carbon, but it cannot undergo inversion, so choice **A** cannot apply to Reaction 2. In addition, Reaction 2 has no chirality, so choice **A** is invalid. The best answer is choice **A**. A carbocation intermediate corresponds with an S_N1 reaction, so choice B is a valid statement and thus eliminated. All nucleophilic substitution reactions, whether it is an S_N1 or S_N2 mechanism, have a rate that depends on the electrophile. Choice C is a valid statement, and thus eliminated. A protic solvent helps to stabilize the carbocation intermediate and the leaving group, so a protic solvent increases the rate of an S_N1 reaction. This makes choice D a valid statement, and thus eliminates it. Choice **A** is in fact the top dog of the choices.

9. **Choice B is the best answer.** The key here is that the reaction starts with one single stereoisomer, so the resulting chirality of the product can tell us about the mechanism. If the reaction were to proceed purely by an S_N2 mechanism, the product would be 100% of one stereoisomer (in this question it happens to have *R* configuration), because the reactant is enantiomerically pure and the S_N2 reaction results in complete inversion. This eliminates choice A. If the reaction were to proceed purely by an S_N1 mechanism, the product mixture would be 50% *R* and 50% *S*, because the reaction goes through a planar carbocation intermediate resulting in a racemic mixture. This eliminates choice D. The mixture is 87% *R* and 13% *S*, so both mechanisms must have occurred simultaneously. The product distribution is closer to the products of an S_N2 mechanism than the products of an S_N1 mechanism, so the reaction can be thought of as an S_N2 reaction with some S_N1 side reaction. It is not a pure reaction so choice **B** is the best answer.

10. **Choice A is the best answer.** Because the carbon-bromine bond is weaker than the carbon-chlorine bond, it is more easily broken. This makes the bromine a better leaving group than a chlorine. An alkyl bromide is therefore a more reactive electrophile than an alkyl chloride. With a better electrophile, the reaction is faster for both the S_N1 and the S_N2 mechanisms, because they both depend on the electrophile. This makes choice **A** correct.

11. **Choice A is the best answer.** The strongest nucleophile is most willing to donate its lone pair to carbon. The answer choices include two conjugate pairs. The conjugate base is the better nucleophile of the pair, so choices B and D are eliminated. HCl is a strong acid while methanol is a weak acid, so methoxide is a stronger base than chloride. This means that methoxide is more willing to donate electrons than chloride, and therefore methoxide is the better nucleophile. Pick **A** and see your score improve.

12. **Choice C is the best answer.** An S_N2 reaction favors a primary electrophile over a secondary or tertiary electrophile, and a good nucleophile is required. Choices A and B can both be eliminated, because the electrophiles are tertiary (and tertiary electrophiles proceed via the S_N1 mechanism). Choice **C** is a better choice than choice D, because cyanide is a better nucleophile than methanol, and a better nucleophile will tend to react by an S_N2 mechanism rather than an S_N1 mechanism. Pick **C** for optimal results.

13. **Choice B is the best answer.** An S_N2 reaction proceeds by way of a one-step mechanism, which eliminates choices A and C (both of which show an intermediate and two steps). An exothermic reaction has the products at a lower energy level than the reactants, which eliminates choice D and leaves choice **B** as the correct answer. The apex of the graph represents the transition state, and the absence of a valley on the graph implies that there is no intermediate for the reaction. Choice A is an exothermic S_N1 reaction, choice C is an endothermic S_N1 reaction, and choice D is an endothermic S_N2 reaction.

14. **Choice B is the best answer.** Because the electrophile is a tertiary alkyl halide, Reaction 2 proceeds by way of an S_N1 mechanism. The two products have specific rotations of +62° and +30° respectively as written. A fifty/fifty mixture of the two products would yield an observed specific rotation of +46° (the average of the values for the two diastereomers). Because of steric hindrance from the bonds to the six membered ring, the nucleophile (NH_3) prefers to attack from the backside of the molecule. This makes the major product Compound A, the first product in Reaction 1. The major product has a specific rotation of +62°, thus the specific rotation of the mixture is closer to +62° than +30°. The specific rotation is between 46° and 62°, which makes choice **B** the best answer.

15. **Choice B is the best answer.** The specific rotation for the mixture is found by taking a weighted average of the specific rotations for the components in the mixture, which is essentially what Equation 1 does. Because there is more of the component with an α = +48° than the component with an α = +18°, the averaged value should be closer to +48° than +18°. However, because it is not purely one component, the specific rotation for the mixture must be less than +48° (within the range of +33° to +48°). The best answer is therefore +42°, choice **B**. The exact value can be determined mathematically as follows:

$$\alpha_{obs} = 80\% \ (+48°) + 20\% \ (+18°) = 38.4 + 3.6 = 42°$$

16. **Choice C is the best answer.** The two products formed in Reaction 2 both have identical bonds to one another and three chiral centers each. In comparing the two structures, only one of the three chiral centers differs, making the two structures diastereomers. If some, but not all, of the chiral centers differ between two stereoisomers, they are not superimposable nor are they mirror images. This, by definition, makes them diastereomers. The best answer is choice **C**. The term epimers describes diastereomers that differ at one chiral center, but it applies specifically to the backbones of sugars.

17. **Choice D is the best answer.** The two products for Reaction 1 are diastereomers of one another so they have different specific rotations. This means that they can be distinguished by their different specific rotation values. This eliminates choice A. Because they have different geometry (asymmetry), they pack differently into their respective solid lattices and thus they exhibit different melting points. This eliminates choice B. Because of their varying asymmetry, they bind a gas chromatography column differently (due to a difference in steric hindrance) and thus they show different retention times on the gas chromatographer (GC). It can be inferred from the last sentence in paragraph two of the passage that the two products have different retention times on the gas chromatographer (GC), since the concentration values can be determined (and thus verified in this example) using the GC. This eliminates choice C. Infrared spectroscopy measures the type of bonds in the molecules, therefore it is difficult, if not impossible, to distinguish the two diastereomers by infrared spectroscopy. Diastereomers have identical bonds as one another. The best answer is choice **D** even if you have no idea what infrared spectroscopy does.

18. **Choice A is the best answer.** The first product has the methyl and ethyl groups both up and the hydroxyl group down. To retain the chiral integrity shown in Figure 1, the chair conformations must have ethyl and methyl up with the hydroxyl down. This eliminates choices B and C, which have the exact opposite geometry (ethyl and methyl are down and the hydroxyl group is up). The most stable conformer has the least steric repulsion, which ideally occurs if the three substituents are in equatorial orientation rather than having the three substituents in axial orientation. Because the substituents are on adjacent carbons, they alternate up/down/up, which allows all the substituents to be equatorial. This makes the best answer choice **A**.

19. **Choice C is the best answer.** The three chiral centers are determined as follows:

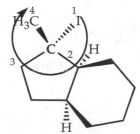 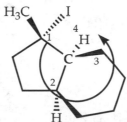 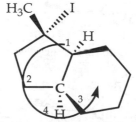

Substituent number four is in front, so the arc must be reversed from clockwise to counterclockwise. This makes the chiral center *S*.

Substituent number four is in back, so the arc is correct as drawn. The counterclockwise arc makes the chiral center *S*.

Substituent number four is in back, so the arc is correct as drawn. The counterclockwise arc makes the chiral center *S*.

The correct answer is *S,S,S*, which makes choice **C** the best answer.

20. **Choice B is the best answer.** In the alkene reactant in Reaction 1, only one carbon has sp^3-hybridization and four different substituents attached, therefore only one carbon in the compound is chiral. This makes choice **B** the best answer. As drawn, the chirality is specified in the reactant for the ring carbon with the ethyl substituent attached, so choice A should have been eliminated immediately.

Passage IV (Questions 21 - 27)   **Elimination versus Substitution Experiment**

21. **Choice B is the best answer.** The reactant has two stereogenic carbons, so it starts optically active. The elimination product would be optically inactive, because it loses both stereocenters (chiral carbons) when it forms the alkene product. This means that the specific rotation of the alkene product is zero making choice **B** the best answer. This can be inferred from the results of Trials IV, V, and VI in Table 1, where the combination of a strong base and heat resulted in an elimination reaction.

22. **Choice D is the best answer.** Because deuterium isotope and standard hydrogen isotope are not equivalent, carbon 3 has four unique substituents. There are two chiral centers in the reactant, located at carbons two and three. This eliminates choices A and B. The number four priority is hydrogen on both chiral centers and conveniently it is in the back in both cases. The first chiral center (carbon two) has priorities bromine > deutero ethyl > methyl which form a clockwise arc. The first chiral center is thus *R*. This didn't help much, given that both of the remaining answer choices show this. The second chiral center (carbon three) has priorities ethylbromide > methyl > deuterium which form a counterclockwise arc. The second chiral center is thus *S*. The solution is drawn below:

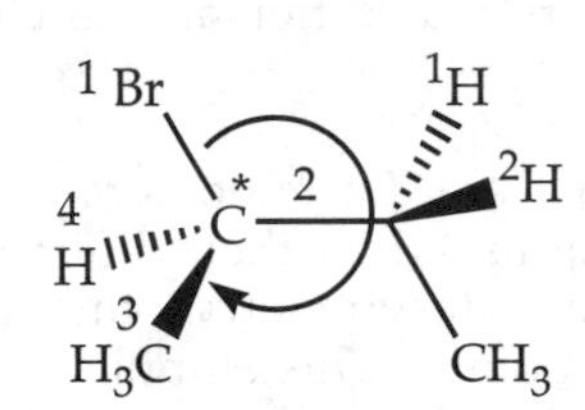

Carbon 2 = *R* 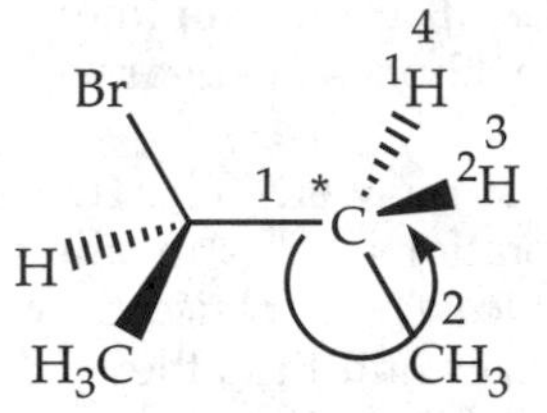   Carbon 3 = *S*

The best answer is *2R,3S*, which makes choice **D** correct.

23. **Choice A is the best answer.** Because the enantiomer is a mirror image of the reactant, it forms a transition state when it is eliminating that is a mirror image of the reactant's transition state. This means that the products are also mirror images, but without stereogenic centers, they can be rotated to match as identical compounds. This symmetry presents itself in the product as an identical geometric isomer. Because a diastereomer varies at only one chiral center, it is not a mirror image of the reactant when it is eliminating. This asymmetry presents itself in the product as different geometric isomers. This may not make sense in words so the drawing below shows the products.

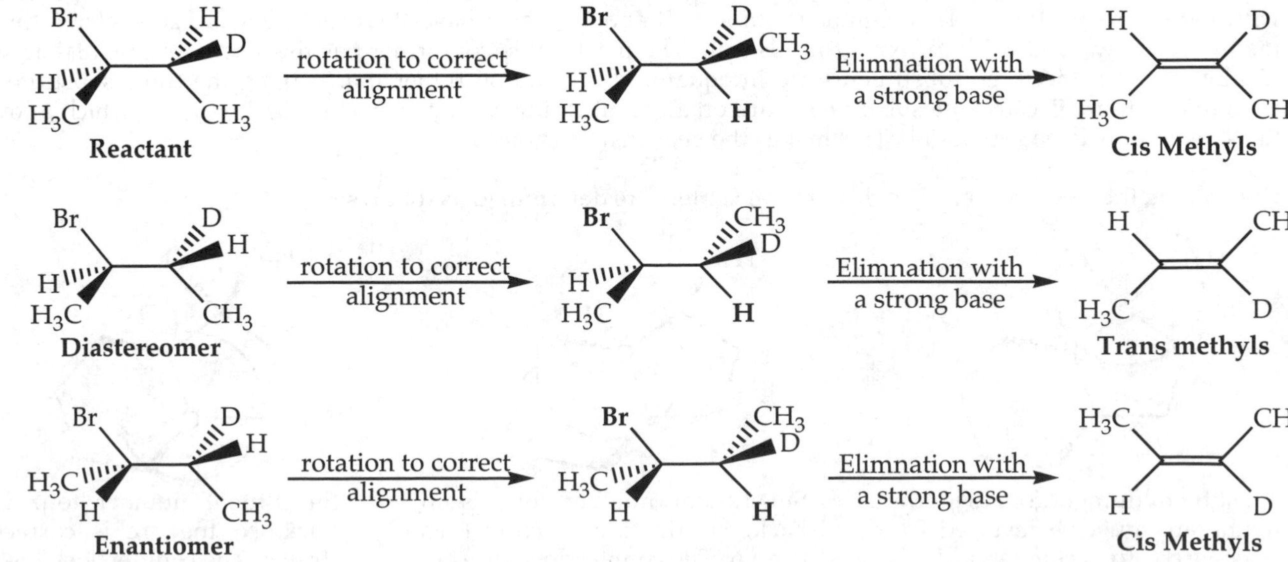

The enantiomer forms the same products while a diastereomer forms geometric isomers, making the best answer choice **A**.

24. **Choice D is the best answer.** If the reaction proceeded purely by an S_N2 mechanism, then the optical rotation would be the same as was observed for Trial I (-36°), a purely S_N2 reaction. This eliminates choice A. An elimination reaction would yield an optically inactive product so the optical rotation observed for an elimination reaction would be zero. This eliminates choice B. The optical activity observed in Trial II (very close to the -36° observed in the pure S_N2 reaction of Trial I) implies that an S_N2 reaction must have been occurring to some degree. The reduction in optical activity must be attributed to the presence of some stereoisomer impurities or an achiral side product (from some side reaction). The best answer is choice **D**.

25. **Choice B is the best answer.** From the low temperature of the reaction and the retention of optical activity in the product, it can be inferred that the reaction proceeds by way of an S_N2 mechanism. Elimination and S_N1 reactions produce products that lose their optical activity. Choices C and D can be eliminated because the alkene products would show no optical rotation given that they lose both stereocenters in the formation of the alkene. The products from a reaction proceeding by an S_N1 mechanism in this case would be a mixture of diastereomers (not enantiomers), which would lead to an optical rotation close to zero (the exact value is not easily predicted with diastereomer mixtures, because they are formed in major-minor distributions and not 50-50). Enantiomers are obtained if the reactant is symmetric. The best (although not perfect) answer is choice **B**. Part of doing well on the MCAT is learning to pick a best answer even when there is some ambiguity.

26. **Choice D is the best answer.** As observed from the data in Table 1, at high temperature, the predominant reaction is elimination. This eliminates choices A and B. Because a strong base ($NaOCH_3$) was used, the mechanism must have been an E_2 rather than an E_1 mechanism. The best answer is choice **D**. This can be verified by looking at Trial IV in Table 1, which show nearly identical reaction conditions as the reaction in the question. The loss of optical rotation in the product implies that the reaction was an elimination reaction. A substitution reaction would yield some sort of optical activity. You have to know that base infers that the mechanism is E_2.

27. **Choice C is the best answer.** An E_2 mechanism involves the removal of a proton alpha to the leaving group which then shifts the electrons into a π-bond forcing the leaving group off. The mechanism is concerted, implying that both events occur simultaneously. This results in very predictable geometry with respect to the product alkene. To support the operation of the E_2 mechanism, both carbons that become involved in the π-bond should be chirally labeled to trace the reaction. If the mechanism is specific, then the final product is a specific geometrical isomer. This is why the reactant is deutero labeled at carbon three. Therefore, the best answer is choice **C**.

Passage V   (Questions 28 - 32)   **Leaving Group Strength**

28. **Choice A is the best answer.** The best electrophile is the compound with the best leaving group. The best leaving group is the leaving group with the strongest conjugate acid. In this case, iodide is the best leaving group, because HI (hydroiodic acid) is the strongest conjugate acid of the choices listed. This makes choice **A** the best answer.

29. **Choice D is the best answer.** This question requires that you identify the best electrophile. Again, the best electrophile is the compound with the best leaving group. The best leaving group has the strongest conjugate acid, which in this question is the bromide leaving group. The ranking of the conjugate acids for the leaving groups are: $HBr > HF > HOC_6H_5 > HSCH_3$. It is in your best interest to choose **D**.

30. **Choice D is the best answer.** The difference between the two molecules is the alkyl group. According to the question, the smaller molecule is the better nucleophile. The inductive effect would predict that the electron donating methyl groups would make the larger alkyl group more electron donating and thus more nucleophilic. This is the opposite of what is observed, so choice A is eliminated. Resonance is not a factor, because there is no π-system. Choice B is eliminated. The hybridization is sp^3 in both cases, so the difference in nucleophilicity cannot be attributed to hybridization. This eliminates choice C. Steric hindrance predicts that the smaller nucleophile has less interference in the transition state, thus it is a better nucleophile. In this case, steric hindrance plays a larger role than the inductive effect in the reactivity of the nucleophile. The correct answer is choice **D**.

31. **Choice D is the best answer.** Hydroxyl groups are terrible leaving groups. Thiols are average to poor nucleophiles. The reaction between a poor nucleophile and an electrophile with a poor leaving group should be very unfavorable by intuition. The difference between their pK_a values is -5.2, which implies that the K_{eq} for this reaction is near $10^{-5.2} = 6 \times 10^{-6}$. This defines a reaction that stays predominantly as reactant, which supports the evaluation that the reaction is very unfavorable. Choose **D**.

32. Choice A is the best answer. In protic solvents, there is hydrogen bonding, so choice C is eliminated. Equally, in an aprotic solvent, there is no hydrogen bonding, so choice B is eliminated. Hydrogen bonding affects fluoride and not iodide, so the fact that fluoride is a worse nucleophile than iodide in alcohol implies that hydrogen bonding reduces the nucleophilicity of fluoride. This can be attributed to hindrance to migration caused by hydrogen bonding. The best answer is choice **A**. Choice D can be eliminated, because if it were true, then the opposite relative nucleophilicity would be observed for fluoride and iodide.

Hydrocarbons

Organic Chemistry Chapter 4

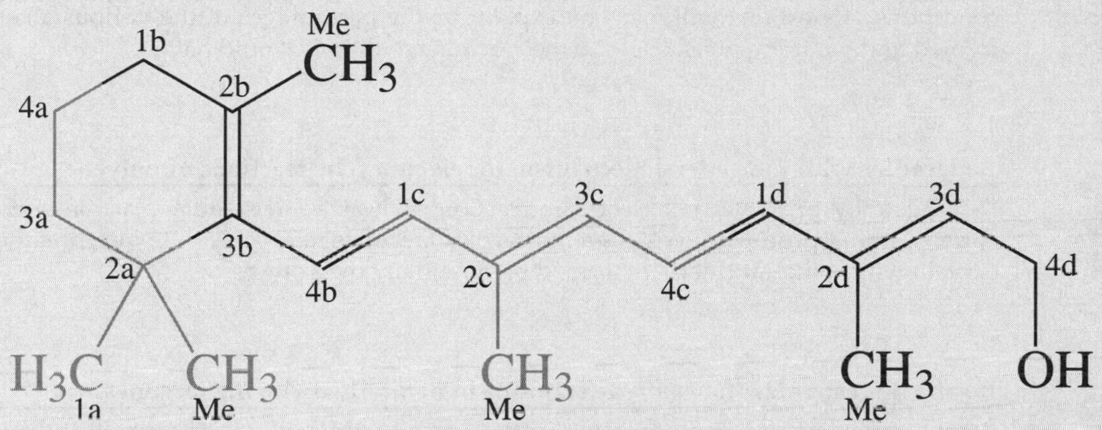

Vitamin A$_1$

(Diterpene = 20 carbon terpene)

by Todd Bennett of

the Berkeley Review

Hydrocarbons

Key objectives of this section

Know the general mechanism for free-radical reactions of alkanes and biological molecules.

Passages may present a free radical reaction or a biological molecule that engages in free radical chemistry followed by questions that asked you for details about the stability of a free radical or the steps in a pathway involving free radicals.

Know the mechanisms for elimination reactions, in particular Hofmann Elimination.

Passages may present an elimination reaction and the product distribution with varying reaction conditions. Questions will focus on explaining the percentages of the various alkenes that are formed and what impact changes to the reaction conditions would have.

Be familiar with the general mechanism for electrocyclic reactions of polyenes.

Passages may present an electrocyclic reaction such as a Diels-Alder reaction and a table of corresponding product distribution numbers. Questions may ask you to interpret the data and explain why some products are formed preferentially over others.

Be able to recognize the isoprene subunits in naturally occurring terpenes.

Passages may present some terpenes isolated from various plants or animals and tell you about their utility to the plant or animal from which they were extracted. Questions may ask about the skeletal makeup of a given terpene in terms of 5-carbon isoprene units or terpene properties.

Be aware of biological hydrocarbons and their physical properties *in vivo*.

Passages could present a biologically significant hydrocarbon and information on its pathway of activity. Questions may focus on what would result if the molecule were treated with a given chemical reagent or if its environment was altered in some way.

Hydrocarbons

The crux of organic chemistry centers on reactivity. In organic chemistry there are many classes of reactions. They are organized according to mechanistic features. The MCAT doesn't test you on all of the reaction types you learned in your organic chemistry course, which should make your review a little less arduous. We have covered acid-base reactions in section 1 and nucleophilic substitution reactions in section 3. In this chapter, we shall cover free radical reactions (halogenation of an alkane), elimination, and electrocyclic reactions. There are other types of reactions we shall address in future sections, most of which we shall address by functional group. However, in this section, we shall address the reactions of alkanes and substituted alkanes.

Free radical reactions follow three basic mechanistic steps: *initiation*, *propagation*, and *termination*. Whether we consider free radical halogenation of an alkane or free radical polymerization of an alkene, the first step of the process is initiation. Initiation entails the homolytic cleavage of a weak sigma bond in only a small portion of the molecules present in the reaction mixture. In halogenation reactions, the halogen-to-halogen bond is cleaved to initiate the reaction. In free radical polymerization, the oxygen-to-oxygen bond of a peroxide initiator is cleaved to generate a low concentration of free radical compounds. The product of a free radical halogenation reaction is an alkyl halide. An alkyl halide can undergo nucleophilic substitution reactions (as we saw in the stereochemistry section) and elimination reactions. Elimination reactions result in the formation of a π-bond. Starting with an alkane, most any compound can be synthesized.

Although the MCAT test writers do not require that you know the reactions of alkenes, as they have required in the past, π-bonds can be part of a diene, triene, or any other conjugated system of multiple π-bonds. We shall consider the Diels Alder reaction, an electrocyclic reaction involving the addition of an alkene to a conjugated diene to form a cyclohexene moiety. There are other electrocyclic reactions as well, but it is more important to know the big picture and be able to extract critical information from a passage centered on the reaction than it is to memorize the details of the reaction.

From this section on, we shall focus on the reactivity of organic compounds. To best prepare for the MCAT, your goal should not be to memorize every reaction, but instead, learn a few simple, common mechanisms and have a conceptual picture of how they work. Reaction details will be provided in the passage, so from this point on, know the general reaction and work on your information extraction skills by reading graphs, tables, and data charts.

Alkanes

Alkane Structure

Alkanes contain only carbon and hydrogen atoms, and all of the carbons have sp^3-hybridization. All of the hydrogens in alkanes use s-orbitals to form bonds. Alkanes are held together exclusively by σ-bonds. In any alkane, there are only two types of bonds present: C—C bonds (which are $\sigma_{sp^3-sp^3}$) and C—H bonds (which are σ_{sp^3-s}). Both types of bonds present in alkanes are shown in Figure 4-1 as molecular orbitals.

$\sigma_{sp^3-sp^3}$ σ_{s-sp^3}

Figure 4-1

Alkanes can be classified as either *aliphatic* (straight chain form) or *cyclic* (containing a ring in its structure). Aliphatic alkanes have a molecular formula of C_nH_{2n+2} while cycloalkanes with one ring have a molecular formula of C_nH_{2n}. For each additional ring in a cyclic alkane, the molecule has two less hydrogen atoms. Table 4-1 lists some common linear alkanes up to ten carbons and cyclic alkanes. It should be noted that at least three carbons are needed to form a ring.

C_nH_{2n+2} for linear alkanes (no rings)			
Methane	CH_4	Hexane	C_6H_{14}
Ethane	C_2H_6	Heptane	C_7H_{16}
Propane	C_3H_8	Octane	C_8H_{18}
Butane	C_4H_{10}	Nonane	C_9H_{20}
Pentane	C_5H_{12}	Decane	$C_{10}H_{22}$
C_nH_{2n} for cycloalkanes (with one ring)			
Cyclopropane	C_3H_6	Cyclopentane	C_5H_{10}
Cyclobutane	C_4H_8	Cyclohexane	C_6H_{12}

Table 4-1

Alkane Properties

Alkanes are hydrophobic, nonpolar molecules. They can also be defined as *lipophilic*, which implies that they are highly soluble in oils such as the lipid membrane of a cell. The physical properties of concern associated with an alkane are its solubility features, its density, its melting point, and its boiling point. As with all compounds, their physical properties vary with mass and branching. As the molecular mass increases, both the boiling point and melting points increase. As the branching increases, the boiling point generally decreases. Table 4-2 shows the physical properties of several aliphatic alkanes. From the data in Table 4-2, the effects of mass and branching on the physical properties can be observed and extrapolated.

Isomer	Name	Boiling Point	Melting Point	Density (g/mL)	Mass (g/mole)
CH_4	Methane	-162°C	-183°C		16.043
H_3CCH_3	Ethane	-89°C	-183°C		30.070
$H_3CCH_2CH_3$	Propane	-42°C	-187°C		44.097
$H_3C(CH_2)_2CH_3$	Butane	0°C	-138°C		58.124
$H_3C(CH_2)_3CH_3$	Pentane	36°C	-130°C	0.557	72.151
$H_3C(CH_2)_4CH_3$	n-Hexane	69°C	-95.3°C	0.659	86.178
$(H_3C)_2CH(CH_2)_2CH_3$	2-Methylpentane	60°C	-154°C	0.654	86.178
$H_3CCH_2CH(CH_3)CH_2CH_3$	3-Methylpentane	63°C	-118°C	0.676	86.178
$(H_3C)_3CCH_2CH_3$	2,2-Dimethylbutane	50°C	-98°C	0.649	86.178
$(H_3C)_2CHCH(CH_3)_2$	2,3-Dimethylbutane	58°C	-129°C	0.668	86.178
$H_3C(CH_2)_5CH_3$	n-Heptane	98°C	-90.5°C	0.684	100.205
$H_3C(CH_2)_6CH_3$	n-Octane	126°C	-57°C	0.703	114.232
$H_3C(CH_2)_7CH_3$	n-Nonane	151°C	-54°C	0.718	128.259
$H_3C(CH_2)_8CH_3$	n-Decane	174°C	-30°C	0.7362	142.286

Table 4-2

Example 4.1

What is the molecular weight of 2,2-dimethyl-4-propyl-5-cyclopentylnonane?

A. 228.21 grams/mole
B. 266.51 grams/mole
C. 268.51 grams/mole
D. 280.54 grams/mole

Solution

First, we must determine the number of carbon atoms and then the number of hydrogen atoms. Dimethyl accounts for two carbons, propyl accounts for another three, pentyl accounts for another five, and nonane accounts for nine. The compound contains 19 carbon atoms total. Because of the "cyclo" in the name, there is one unit of unsaturation. The one unit of unsaturation implies that there are 38 hydrogens (two less then the 40 that would be present in an aliphatic, linear alkane). The molecular mass is approximately 19(12) + 38 = 266. The answer closest to 266 g/mole is choice **B**.

Alkane Reactivity

Alkanes undergo a minimal number of reactions, and the few they do undergo involve free radical chemistry. The two reactions of concern are free radical halogenation (more specifically bromination, using Br_2, and chlorination, using Cl_2) and combustion. Reaction 4.1 is the free radical chlorination of methane.

$$CH_4(g) + Cl_2(g) \xrightarrow{h\nu} CH_3Cl(g) + CH_2Cl_2(l) + CHCl_3(l) + CCl_4(l) + C_2Cl_6(l)$$

85%   12%   minor   minor   minor

Reaction 4.1

Free Radical Halogenation of Alkanes

A free radical halogenation reaction starts with the addition of activation energy to cleave a halogen-halogen bond (the weakest bond in the reactants) to form two free radical halogen atoms. A free radical is an atom, such as a halogen or carbon, with one unpaired electron. Free radicals lack a full octet, so they are highly reactive. Figure 4-2 shows a 3-D perspective of four alkyl free radicals with the p-orbital filled with one electron according to relative stability. Tertiary free radicals are more stable than secondary free radicals, which in turn are more stable than primary free radicals. The three substituents are drawn slightly below the carbon atom, because the free radical molecule is slightly trigonal planar due the electrostatic repulsion from the single electron. Because the electron can exist in either lobe of the p-orbital, the substituents can be angled up or down, so the average of the two trigonal pyramidal forms is planar.

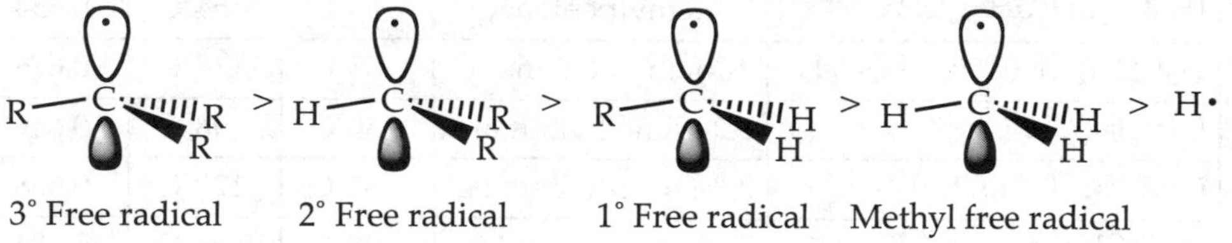

3° Free radical   2° Free radical   1° Free radical   Methyl free radical

Figure 4-2

Once a free radical halogenation reaction has been initiated by the addition of light (activation energy), a free radical halogen atom then attacks an alkane and abstracts a hydrogen from the alkane to leave behind an alkyl free radical. The halogen free radical abstracts the first hydrogen it encounters, but because alkyl free radicals can react with other alkanes to generate new alkanes and alkyl free radicals, over time the distribution favors the formation of the more stable tertiary free radicals. The conversion from a primary free radical into a tertiary free radical is shown in Figure 4-3 below.

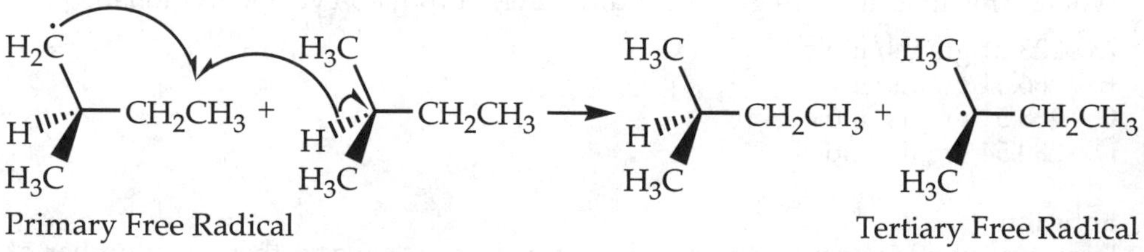

Primary Free Radical   Tertiary Free Radical

Figure 4-3

The reaction in Figure 4-3 heavily favors the formation of product, because the tertiary free radical is substantially more stable than the primary free radical.

Free Radical Mechanism

The mechanism for a free radical halogenation is a chain reaction process involving an initiation reaction, followed by propagation reactions, and ultimately a termination reaction. An initiation reaction breaks a halogen-halogen covalent bond in a homolytic fashion to form two free radicals, so an initiation reaction goes from no free radicals to two free radicals. Homolytic cleavage is different from heterolytic cleavage in that each atom gets a single electron (resulting in free radicals) as opposed to the more electronegative atom getting both bonding electrons (resulting in a cation and an anion). Propagation steps involve the abstraction of an atom from a neutral molecule by a free radical to form a new free radical. Propagation reactions include the consumption and formation of a free radical, so a propagation reaction goes from one free radical to one free radical. In free radical halogenation, there are two propagation steps. Termination occurs when two free radicals combine to form a neutral, stable molecule. Termination steps involve the consumption of two free radicals, so a termination reaction goes from two free radicals to no free radicals. There are several possible termination reactions in a free radical halogenation reaction, most of which form minor side products. The steps for a generic halogenation of an alkane are shown below as Reactions 4.2, 4.3, and 4.4.

Initiation: $X-X \longrightarrow X\cdot + \cdot X$

Reaction 4.2

Propagation: $R-H + \cdot X \longrightarrow R\cdot + H-X$

Reaction 4.3a

$R\cdot + X-X \longrightarrow R-X + \cdot X$

Reaction 4.3b

Termination: $R\cdot + \cdot R \longrightarrow R-R$

Reaction 4.4a

$R\cdot + \cdot X \longrightarrow R-X$

Reaction 4.4b

$X\cdot + \cdot X \longrightarrow X-X$

Reaction 4.4c

Overall Reaction: $R-H + X-X \longrightarrow R-X + H-X$

Reaction 4.5

The sum of the propagation steps for a free radical halogenation reaction gives the overall reaction, Reaction 4.5. The initiation step is brief, for just a split second at the start of a free radical reaction. However, the propagation steps continue until the reaction is quenched or the free radicals are completely consumed in termination reactions. There are always multiple termination steps possible. One of the possible termination steps is the reverse of the initiation reaction. A termination step is any reaction that combines two free radicals to generate a stable compound. Termination steps are responsible for several minor side products.

Example 4.2
Which of the following reactions represents an initiation step?

A. $H_3CCH_2CH_2\cdot$ + $Br\cdot$ → $H_3CCH_2CH_2Br$
B. $H_3CCH_2CH_2\cdot$ + $H_3CCH_2CH_3$ → $H_3CCH_2CH_3$ + $(H_3C)_2CH\cdot$
C. $(H_3C)_2CH\cdot$ + Br_2 → $H_3CCHBrCH_3$ + $Br\cdot$
D. $HOBr$ → $HO\cdot$ + $Br\cdot$

Solution
In an initiation reaction, free radicals are generated, so the product side of the equation has more radicals than the reactant side of the equation. Choice A is eliminated, because there are no radicals on the product side, making it a termination reaction. In choices B and C, there is the same number of radicals on both sides of the reaction, so they are propagation reactions. This eliminates choices B and C. In choice **D**, the reaction goes from zero free radicals on the reactant side to two free radicals on the product side, so it is an initiation reaction. Choice **D** is the only initiation step of the choices.

Example 4.3
In the free radical chlorination of ethane, butane is a minor side product. How can this best be explained?

A. An ethane molecule attacked an ethyl chloride in a nucleophilic substitution reaction to form butane.
B. An ethyl free radical removed a hydrogen from an ethane molecule.
C. Two ethyl free radicals combined to form a new sigma bond.
D. The carbon-carbon bond of ethane was cleaved during initiation to form methyl free radicals, which rapidly combine to form long-chain alkanes.

Solution
An ethane molecule has neither a lone pair of electrons nor an available pair of bonding electrons to share (like a π-bond), so it is definitely not going to act as a nucleophile. This eliminates choice A. An ethyl free radical can definitely remove a hydrogen from an ethane molecule. However, that does not result in the formation of butane, it simply regenerates the same molecules (as shown below).

$$H_3CCH_2\cdot \ + \ H_3CCH_3 \ \rightarrow \ H_3CCH_3 \ + \ H_3CCH_2\cdot$$

Choice B is eliminated. When two ethyl free radicals combine, they form a new sigma bond between the two free radical carbons. Combining the two two-carbon fragments results in the formation of a four-carbon fragment. The result is that butane is formed from the termination reaction of two ethyl free radicals. The best answer is choice **C**. Choice D is unlikely because carbon-carbon bonds are not easily cleaved, so the activation energy added in the initiation step is not high enough to cleave a carbon-carbon bond. Even if it could cleave the carbon-carbon bond to form methyl free radicals, there is no chance that four CH_3 groups would combine to form C_4H_{10}. The loss of two hydrogen atoms would not occur.

Free Radical Halogenation Energetics

With each reaction, we consider how much product is formed (thermodynamics) and how fast the reaction proceeds (kinetics). ΔH and ΔG values determine how much is formed while the activation energy (E_{act}) dictates the speed. For the chlorination of methane, Reaction 4.1, the following enthalpy values apply:

$$Cl—Cl \quad \rightarrow \quad Cl\cdot + \cdot Cl \qquad \Delta H_{initiation} = 58 \text{ kcal}$$

$$H_3C—H + \cdot Cl \quad \rightarrow \quad H_3C\cdot + H—Cl \qquad \Delta H_1 = 1 \text{ kcal}$$

$$H_3C\cdot + Cl—Cl \quad \rightarrow \quad H_3C—Cl + \cdot Cl \qquad \Delta H_2 = -26 \text{ kcal}$$

Figure 4-4 shows the energy diagram associated with propagation steps in Reaction 4.1.

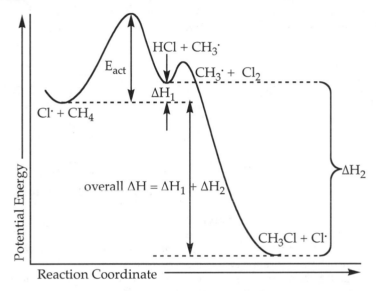

Figure 4-4

The energetics of free radical halogenation reaction varies with the halogen. For instance, bromine has a smaller bond dissociation energy than chlorine, so bromination requires less activation energy than chlorination. This is why chlorination requires light for initiation, while either light or heat can initiate a bromination reaction. However, this does not mean that bromination proceeds faster than chlorination. The reaction rate is determined from the activation energy of the rate-determining propagation step. Table 4-3 lists the energies for the halogenation of methane. From Table 4-3, you can determine which reaction generates the greatest amount of heat energy. The data shows that free radical iodination of methane is unfavorable and free radical fluorination of methane is too favorable, generating enough energy to explode.

ΔH values ($^{Kcal}/_{mole}$)				
Halogenation Reaction	X = F	X = Cl	X = Br	X = I
Initiation: $X_2 \rightarrow 2 X\cdot$	38	58	46	36
$X\cdot + CH_4 \rightarrow HX + H_3C\cdot$	-32	+1	+16	+33
$H_3C\cdot + X_2 \rightarrow H_3CX + X\cdot$	-70	-26	-24	-20
$CH_4 + X_2 \rightarrow H_3CX + HX$	-102	-25	-8	+13

Table 4-3

Free Radical Halogenation Selectivity
Because tertiary free radicals are more stable than other free radicals, halogenation occurs preferentially at tertiary carbons. When there is more than one unique carbon in the alkane reactant, the product distribution is a result of the relative free radical intermediate stability, the relative abundance of equivalent hydrogens, and the rate of the reaction. For the chlorination reaction, the relative reactivity of 3° : 2° : 1° carbons is 5 : 3.8 : 1 at room temperature. At temperatures around 100°C, chlorination selects for tertiary over secondary over primary by a ratio of roughly 4 : 2.5 : 1. As the temperature increases, the reaction proceeds faster, and is therefore less selective. For the bromination reaction, the relative reactivity of 3° : 2° : 1° carbons is 1600 : 62 : 1 at room temperature. This means that the product of free radical bromination is almost exclusively tertiary, while the free radical chlorination reaction gives a more balanced product mixture. Figure 4-5 shows the product distribution for comparable chlorination and bromination reactions at room temperature.

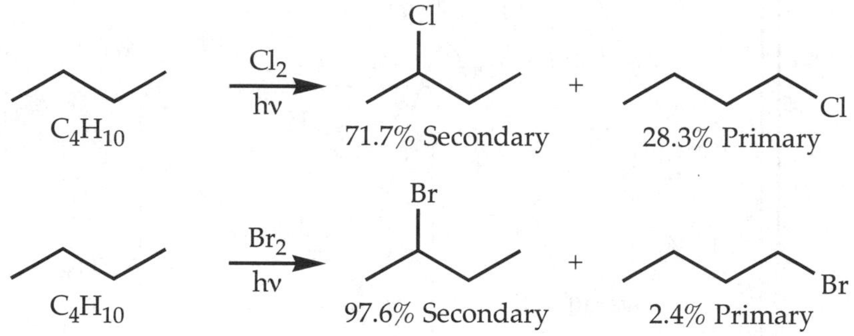

Figure 4-5

As a general rule, slower reactions are more selective than faster reactions, because reactants have more time to select the best site for reacting. Chlorination reactions are faster than bromination reactions, so bromination is more selective than chlorination. In the slower bromination reaction, if a primary free radical is formed, it has time to abstract a hydrogen from another alkane and form a new, possibly more stable free radical. If the new free radical is tertiary, it is likely to only react with a dihalogen molecule. Consider Reaction 4.6 and the data in Table 4-4 corresponding to the distribution of mono-halogenated products.

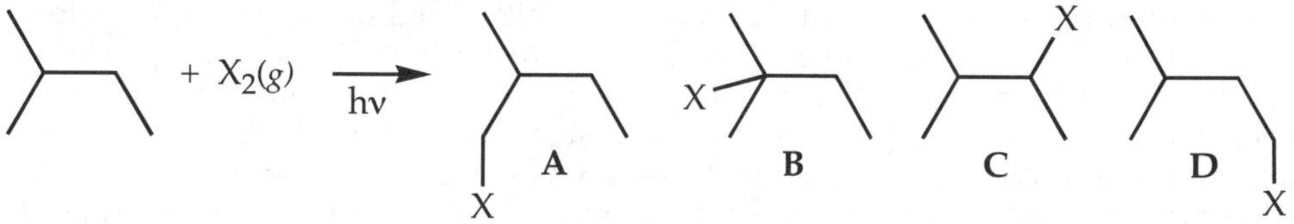

Reaction 4.6

Trial	Halogen	Temp (K)	Product A	Product B	Product C	Product D
I	Br_2	298	0.3%	89.4%	10.1%	0.2%
II	Cl_2	298	29.1%	24.3%	32.0%	14.6%
III	Br_2	373	0.4%	88.3%	11.1%	0.2%
IV	Cl_2	373	33.3%	22.2%	27.8%	16.7%
V	I_2	373	No Rxn	No Rxn	No Rxn	No Rxn

Table 4-4

The data in Table 4-4 confirms that bromination is more selective than chlorination for tertiary over secondary over primary. Bromination is slower than chlorination, but it should also be noted that bromination is more reversible than chlorination, so it is more likely undergo a reverse reaction from an unstable product to ultimately form the most stable product. The data in Table 4-4 also shows that temperature has an effect on the reaction rate and therefore on the selectivity. As the reaction temperature is increased, the reaction proceeds at a faster rate, resulting in the formation of products based more on random probability rather than selection for the most stable intermediate. In addition, Boltzmann's law states that as energy is added to a system, the distribution of compounds is shifted to the less stable compounds, to absorb the energy. Actually, who really knows if Boltzmann said it, or if it's even a law. The key thing is that as energy is added, less stable compounds are formed.

Example 4.4

Why in Trial II of Table 4-4 is Product A formed to a greater extent than product B?

A. Product A results from the more stable free radical, thus it is selected for.
B. Product B rearranges to form product A.
C. Product B is more stable, but there are more hydrogens that lead to Product A, so overall less Product B is formed.
D. Product A is more stable, but there are more hydrogens that lead to Product B, so overall less Product B is formed.

Solution

Product A results from a reaction at a primary carbon, so it proceeds via a primary free radical. Product B results from reaction at a tertiary carbon, so it proceeds via a tertiary free radical. This means that Product B is more selected for than Product A, which eliminates choice A. Rearrangement is seen with carbocations, but not with free radicals or carbanions, so choice B is eliminated. The best answer is choice C. It is often possible to answer a question without full analysis. The reason for the substantial amount of Product A is because there are six hydrogens that lead to Product A while there is only one hydrogen that leads to Product B. Although tertiary reactivity with chlorination is roughly four to five times greater than primary reactivity, the six-to-one abundance ratio outweighs the four or five-to-one reactivity preference, making the probability of forming Product A greater than the probability of forming Product B. This is makes choice C the best answer. Choice D can be eliminated, because there are more hydrogens available to form Product A than Product B.

Example 4.5
Why is no reaction observed when iodine is used?

A. Iodine cannot form a free radical.
B. The iodine-iodine bond is too strong to cleave.
C. Free-radical iodination of an alkane is too reactive.
D. Free-radical iodination of an alkane is unfavorable.

Solution
Because chlorine and bromine form free radicals, we can be assume that another halogens, such as iodine, can also form a free radical. This eliminates choice A. Iodine is lower in the periodic table than chlorine and bromine, so the iodine-iodine bond is weaker than the chlorine-chlorine bond and the bromine-bromine bond. Because Cl_2 and Br_2 are cleaved, it is safe to assume that I_2 is even easier to cleave. This eliminates choice B. Iodine forms weak bonds to carbon and hydrogen (which explains why HI is the strongest haloacid and why I is the best leaving group of the halides), so the products are less stable than the reactants. Because the products of free radical iodination are less stable than the reactants, the reaction is unfavorable, so there is no reaction observed with iodine. This makes choice **D** the best answer and eliminates choice C. Fluorine is not used for completely opposite reasons. Fluorine forms strong bonds to carbon and hydrogen, and the fluorine-fluorine bond is weak. The products are so much more stable than the reactants that the free radical fluorination reaction is explosive.

Example 4.6
Why are minimal di-halogenated products formed in the free-radical chlorination of an alkane?

A. The addition of the halogen makes the alkyl halide less acidic than the alkane, so it is less reactive to subsequent halogenation reactions.
B. The addition of the halogen makes the alkyl halide more acidic than the alkane, so it is more reactive to subsequent halogenation reactions.
C. After the first halogen is added to the alkane, the carbon-hydrogen bonds grow weaker and thus more reactive.
D. After the first halogen is added to the alkane, the weakest bond is a carbon-halogen bond and not the carbon-hydrogen bond. As a result, it is easier to remove the halogen rather than the hydrogen from the mono-substituted alkyl halide.

Solution
Halogens are electron-withdrawing, so their presence on a molecule increases its acidity. This eliminates choice A. Choice B is invalid, because an increase in reactivity would imply that more poly-halogenated products would form, not less. Choice C can be eliminated for almost the same reason. If the carbon-hydrogen bond is weaker, and thus more reactive, then it would be easier to add a second halogen than the first, making poly-halogenation preferable. Once an alkane is halogenated, the weakest bond is the carbon-halogen bond, not a carbon-hydrogen bond. If a second halogen free radical reacts with an alkyl halide (rather than an alkane), it preferentially removes the halogen (breaking the weakest bond), forming a non-halogenated alkyl free radical. This is because the reverse halogenation reaction (in propagation) is more favorable than the removal of a hydrogen and subsequent additional halogenation reaction. Choice **D** is the best answer.

Example 4.7
To synthesize a primary alkyl halide from an alkane in the highest yield, what should be done?

A. Bromination at 25°C
B. Chlorination at 25°C
C. Bromination at 100°C
D. Chlorination at 100°C

Solution
A primary alkyl halide is a less favorable product than a secondary alkyl halide or tertiary alkyl halide, so the best free radical halogenation reaction in this case is the one with lowest selectivity. According to the data in Table 4-4, chlorination is less selective than bromination, so choices A and C are eliminated. Selectivity is reduced at higher temperatures, so choice **D** is a better answer than choice B. Choice **D**, chlorination at the highest listed temperature, is the best answer.

Example 4.8
Using the data listed in Table 4-4, what percent of the mono-halogenated products is 2-bromo-2-methylbutane following the free-radical bromination of 2-methylbutane at 75°C?

A. 88.1%
B. 88.7%
C. 89.1%
D. 89.7%

Solution
In Trials I and III of Table 4-4, Product B is 2-bromo-2-methylbutane. Therefore, we need to estimate how much Product B would be formed at 75°C. At 25°C (Trial I), there is 89.4% of Product B formed, while at 100°C (Trial III) there is 88.3% of Product B formed. This means that the amount of Product B formed at 75°C should be between 88.3% and 89.4%, which eliminates choices A and D. The amount formed at 75°C should be closer to 88.3% than 89.4%, because 75°C is closers to 100°C than 25°C, so choice **B** is the best answer.

Example 4.9
How many mono-chlorinated structural isomer products are possible when 2,5-dimethylhexane undergoes free radical chlorination?

A. 3
B. 5
C. 6
D. 8

Solution
This question is asking for how many structural isomers there are for chloro-2,5-dimethylhexane. Because of the mirror plane through the carbon 3-to-carbon 4, bond, there are three unique carbons on 2,5-dimethylhexane. This means that there are just three carbons that can be chlorinated, so there are only three mono-chlorinated structural isomers. If stereoisomers were included, there would be four, given that carbon 3 could be a stereocenter. The best answer is choice **A**.

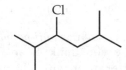

1-chloro-2,5-dimethylhexane   2-chloro-2,5-dimethylhexane   3-chloro-2,5-dimethylhexane

Hydrocarbon Reactions

Elimination Reactions

The reaction that forms an alkene from a substituted alkane is elimination. It is named from the fact that a functional group and a hydrogen on adjacent carbons are eliminated in order to form a new π-bond. The reaction requires elevated temperatures to help overcome the activation energy and to push the reaction in the forward direction. Like the nucleophilic substitution reactions, there are two reaction mechanisms, appropriately named E_1 and E_2. As with nucleophilic substitution, the two versions are named also for their reaction orders (kinetic rate dependence). E_1 is similar to S_N1 and E_2 is similar to S_N2, except that the product is an alkene. In an E_1 elimination, the leaving group first leaves and there is a carbocation formed. The empty *p*-orbital of the carbocation eventually becomes one of the two *p*-orbitals in the new π-bond. In an E_2 elimination, a base removes an alpha-hydrogen to force the leaving group off of the neighboring carbon. Elimination converts a functionalized alkyl group into an alkene.

While elimination is not tested directly as you learned it in organic chemistry, it can appear on the MCAT in Hofmann elimination or in a bio-organic fashion in dehydration reactions to form alkenes and α,ß-unsaturated alkenes.

E_2 Reaction (Carried out Under Basic Conditions at High Temperature)

The E_2 reaction is concerted (one-step) like the S_N2 reaction, with one major exception being that the E_2 reaction occurs at higher temperatures (temperatures above ambient temperature) than the S_N2 reaction. An E_2 reaction also requires that the base be bulky. Because of the steric hindrance associated with a bulky base, it is less apt to act as a nucleophile and thereby minimize the competing S_N2 reaction. An important feature of the E_2 reaction is that the substituents being eliminated must be *anti* to one another (have a dihedral angle of 180°). The mechanism for an E_2 reaction is shown in Figure 4-6.

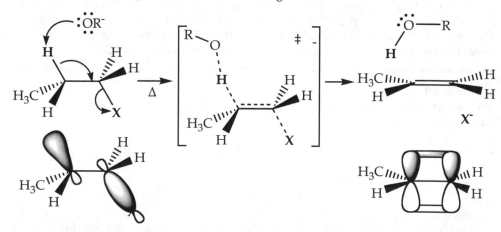

Figure 4-6

In an E_2 reaction, the compound may have to rotate to proper conformation with the leaving group oriented anti to the hydrogen being eliminated before the base attacks the proton to start the reaction. Whenever there are two alpha hydrogens that can be eliminated from the starting reagent, there are two possible products.

Terms such as *anti-periplanar orientation* should sound familiar and immediately make you think of an E_2 reaction. Any time you see a strong bulky base, a hydrocarbon with a leaving group, and high temperature, you should think of an E_2 reaction.

E₁ Reaction (Carried out Under Acidic Conditions at High Temperature)
The E₁ reaction also yields an alkene, but it goes through a different mechanism than the E₂ reaction. The mechanism for the E₁ reaction is quite similar to that of the S_N1 reaction. In both the E₁ and S_N1 reactions, there is (1) a carbocation intermediate formed after the leaving group leaves in the rate determining step of the reaction and (2) the possibility of rearrangement with the carbocation intermediate. A schematic for a typical E₁ reaction is shown in Figure 4-7.

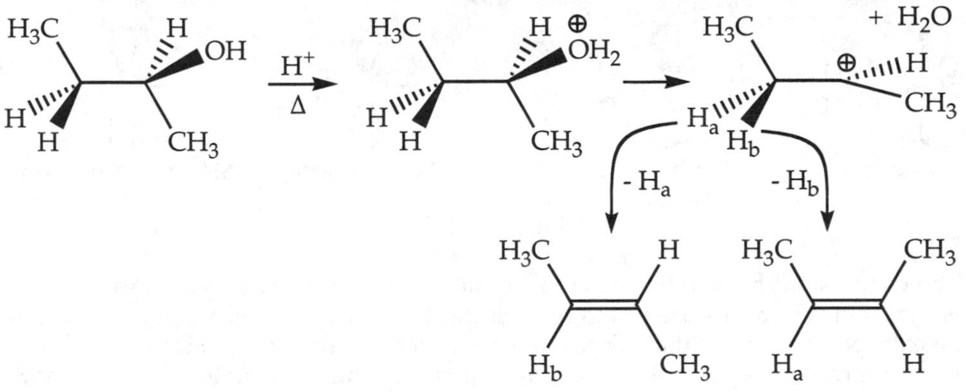

Figure 4-7

E₁ reactions are best carried out under acidic conditions unlike E₂ reactions, which require basic conditions. Both reactions proceed under thermal conditions (elevated temperature) and yield the most substituted alkene as the major product. There may be some of the less substituted alkene as a side product.

Example 4.10
What is the major product when 2-methylcyclopentanol is treated with concentrated sulfuric acid at 50°C?

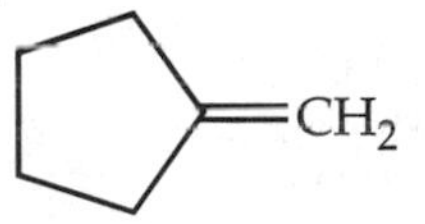

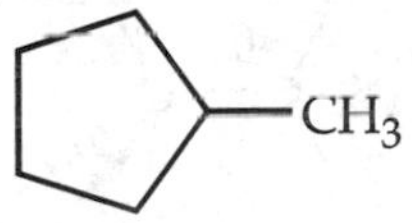

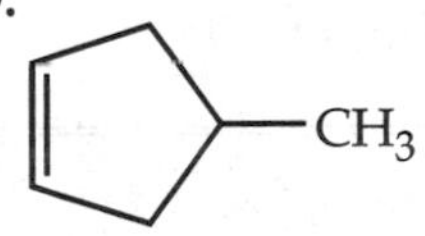

Solution
At an elevated temperature in the presence of a strong acid, the reaction proceeds by an E₁ mechanism, so the product is a highly substituted alkene. Choice A is eliminated, because it is a terminal alkene. Choice B is eliminated, because it is an alkane and not an alkene. Choice D is eliminated, because it is not the most substituted alkene and it formed via a secondary carbocation, a less stable intermediate than the tertiary carbocation. The best answer is choice **C**, because the π-bond is highly substituted and it includes the tertiary carbon, implying that it was formed via a tertiary carbon intermediate.

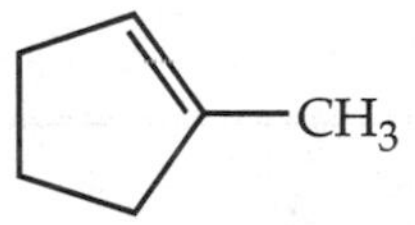

Rearrangement can occur with carbocation intermediates, so E₁ reactions are susceptible to rearrangement. Hydride and alkyl shifts are rapid, intramolecular processes that occur before the loss of the neighboring proton to form an alkene.

Carbocation Stability
The relative stability of alkyl carbocations is 3° > 2° > 1° > Methyl. For carbocations conjugated to a π-bond, vinylic and benzylic carbocations, there is additional stability due to resonance. Carbocations can undergo rearrangement by having hydrides or alkyl groups shift. For instance, a secondary carbocation (R_2CH^+) can rearrange to form a tertiary carbocation $(R_2R'C^+)$, if the tertiary carbocation is possible. Figure 4-8 shows the relative stability of the four alkyl carbocations.

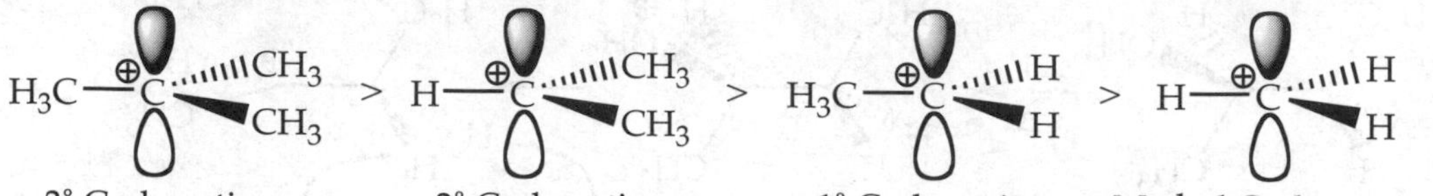

3° Carbocation   2° Carbocation   1° Carbocation   Methyl Carbocation

Figure 4-8

The conclusion that can be drawn from the relative stability of alkyl carbocations is that methyl groups are electron donating to electron poor carbons, which can be extrapolated to say that alkyl groups are electron donating. Figure 4-9 shows three rearrangements where a less stable carbocation is converted into a more stable carbocation via a hydride shift. The third example forms an allylic carbocation, which is more stable than alkyl carbocations, because of resonance.

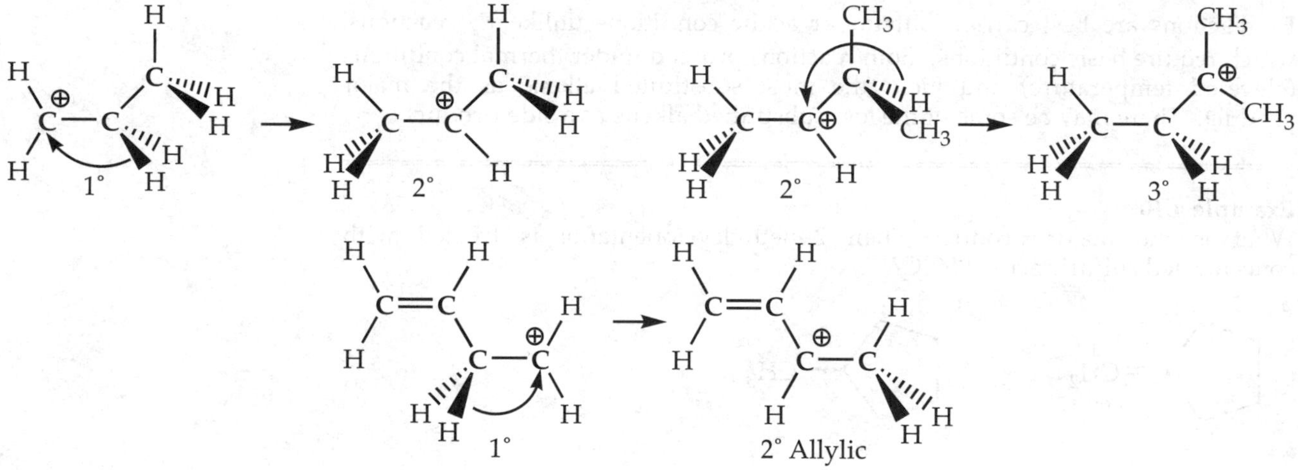

Figure 4-9

Example 4.11
Which of the following carbocations is apt to undergo rearrangement?

A. $(H_3C)_3C^+$

B. $(H_3C)_2CH^+$

C. $H_3CH_2C^+$

D. $(H_3C)_2CHCH_2^+$

Solution
Choice A is already a tertiary carbocation, so it has no reason to rearrange, least of all to a primary carbocation. Choice A is eliminated. Choice B is a secondary carbocation, but can only rearrange to form a primary carbocation, so it is eliminated. Choice C is a primary carbocation that only has primary carbons, so it is eliminated. In choice **D**, a hydride shift can covert a primary carbocation into a tertiary carbocation, making choice **D** the best answer.

Hofmann Elimination

The mechanism for the Hofmann elimination reaction is a straightforward E_2 mechanism. The Hofmann elimination reaction involves forming a cationic quaternary amine (nitrogen with four alkyl groups attached). When the quaternary amine is anti to a ß-hydrogen (hydrogen on the carbon adjacent to the carbon bonded to the quaternary amine), it can be eliminated with strong base. Ag_2O, when hydrated by water, yields two hydroxide anions (OH^-) and two silver cations (Ag^+), so it is a strong base. The silver cation can bind the iodide anion and precipitate out of solution while the hydroxide anion deprotonates the ß-hydrogen resulting in elimination. The E_2 reaction does not have rearrangement associated with it, therefore the product is the least substituted alkene. This is one of few ways to synthesize a terminal alkene. Figure 4-10 shows the orientation of a generic molecule in a Hofmann elimination reaction.

The beta hydrogen and the quaternary amine are anti to one another for E_2 reaction.

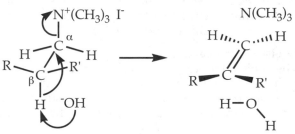

Figure 4-10

It is important that the compound have ß-hydrogens relative to the quaternary amine, otherwise there can be no elimination product. Be particularly aware of this when dealing with cyclic amines. Figure 4-11 shows Hofmann elimination of a cyclic amine.

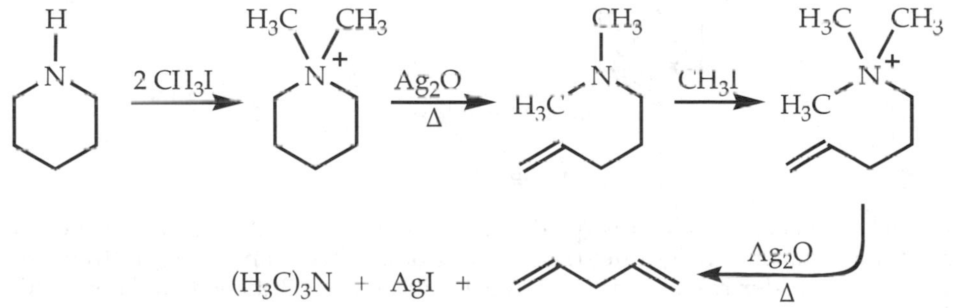

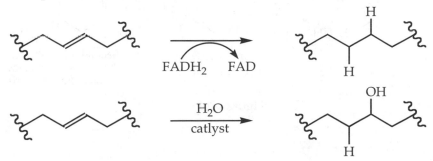

Figure 4-11

Biochemical Alkene Reactions

Although reactions of alkene are not listed as an MCAT topic in organic chemistry, they are still a possibility in biochemistry. You should be familiar with hydration, dehydration, hydrogenation, and dehydrogenation. Figure 4-12 shows simple biochemical reactions of alkenes.

Figure 4-12

Pericyclic Reactions

Pericyclic reactions involve the repositioning of both sigma-bonds and pi-bonds through a cyclic transition state. These reactions are believed to be concerted, meaning that the formation and breaking of all bonds occur simultaneously. Pericyclic reactions include *cycloaddition reactions*, which most notably include the Diels-Alder reaction, *sigmatropic rearrangement*, and e*lectrocyclic reactions*. We will address only cycloadditions and sigmatropic rearrangement. The significant difference between a cycloaddition reaction and sigmatropic rearrangement involves the number of molecules. In cycloaddition, two separate compounds come together, resulting in a single new compound. In sigmatropic rearrangement reactions, it is an intramolecular rearrangement that takes place.

Paramount to understanding these reactions is having a good idea about orbital overlap in both sigma-bonds and pi-bonds. In everything we'll address in terms of the MCAT, we shall only consider the positioning of the atoms and not the spin of the electrons within the molecular orbitals. The first reaction we shall consider is the Diels-Alder reaction.

Diels-Alder Reaction

The Diels-Alder reaction, an electrocyclic addition reaction, involves the addition of a conjugated diene (4 π-electrons) to an alkene (2 π-electrons) to from a six membered cyclohexene ring. The transition state for a Diels-Alder reaction is similar to the resonance of benzene, as shown in Figure 4-13.

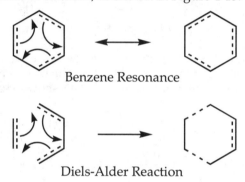

Benzene Resonance

Diels-Alder Reaction

Figure 4-13

Six π-electrons in a cyclic π-network make benzene aromatic, so we refer to the transition state of a Diels-Alder reaction as aromatic (containing 6 π-electrons in a ring). Diels-Alder reactions involve the addition of a 1,3-diene to a dieneophile. The diene must have cis orientation about the central sigma bond to undergo a Diels-Alder reaction. A sample Diels-Alder reaction is drawn in Figure 4-14.

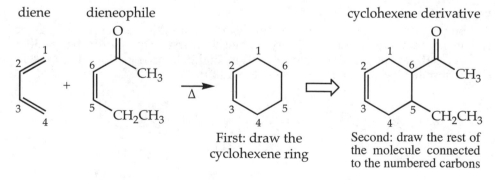

Figure 4-14

The six membered ring that is formed is cyclohexene. The carbons are numbered to help identify the product, which will make large, polycyclic products easier to evaluate. Figure 4-15 shows a more complex Diels-Alder reaction. Because both the diene and dienophile have substituents, there is a chance that stereoisomers can form. The stereoselectivity is driven by orbital overlap in the transition state. The two stereoisomers products, diastereomers, are drawn for the reaction.

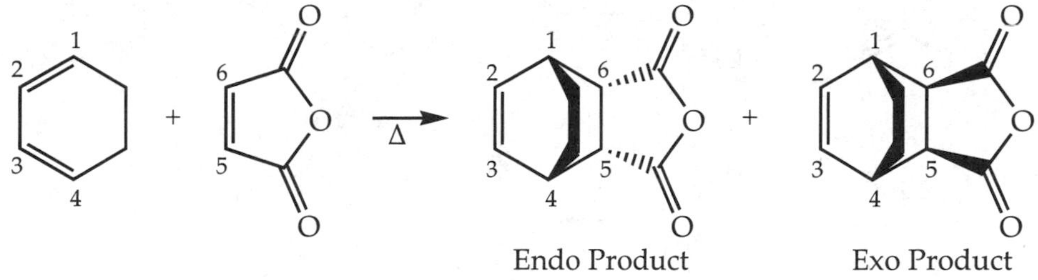

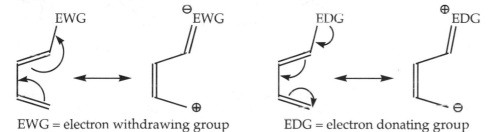

Endo Product   **Exo Product**

Figure 4-15

The last thing for us to consider is regioselectivity. When the diene and dienophile have substituents, there exists the potential for different structural isomers. Regioselectivity can be predicted using resonance, where the most electron rich terminal carbon of the diene attacks the electron poor carbon of the dienophile. The reaction is optimized when the dienophile has electron-withdrawing groups. Figure 4-16 shows the effect of electron-donating and electron-withdrawing groups on the diene through resonance.

EWG $^{\ominus}$EWG   EDG $^{\oplus}$EDG

EWG = electron withdrawing group   EDG = electron donating group

Figure 4-16

When it comes to predicting regiochemistry, it's as simple as plus attracts minus. Figure 4-17 shows a Diels-Alder reaction where regioselectivity is an issue.

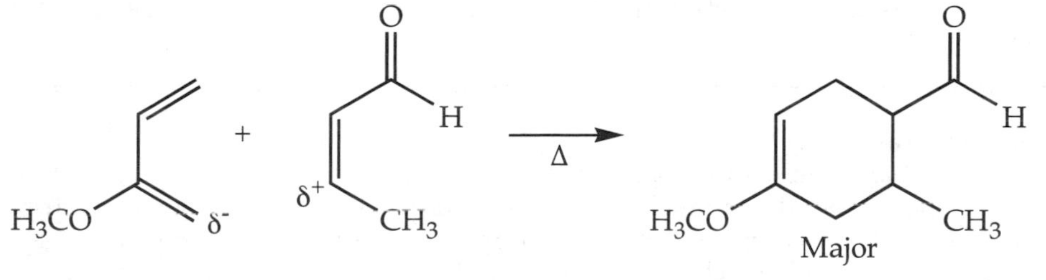

H_3CO δ^- δ^+ CH_3 → Δ H_3CO Major CH_3

Figure 4-17

Example 4.12

Which of the following Diels-Alder reactions is fastest?

A.

B.

C.

D.

Solution

The rate of a Diels-Alder reaction is increased by the presence of an electron donating group on the diene and an electron withdrawing group on the dienophile. The rate of a Diels-Alder reaction is decreased by the presence of bulky groups in the transition state. Choices C and D are eliminated because of the two methyl groups on the dienophile. No matter how the molecule aligns entering the transition state, one of the methyl groups will be in the way. In choice **B**, there is a methoxy group on the diene, while in choice A is just a methyl group. Methoxy groups donate electron density through resonance, so choice **B** has the more electron rich diene, resulting in a faster reaction than choice A.

Cope Rearrangement

The Cope rearrangement is a sigmatropic rearrangement involving two pi-bonds and one sigma-bond. Figure 4-18 shows a simple Cope rearrangement carried out on a 1,5-diene. In more complex examples, stereochemistry may be an issue, because stereocenters can be both formed and lost as hybridization changes.

Figure 4-18

The Cope rearrangement involves two pi-bonds and one sigma-bond aligned in such a way that the terminal *p*-orbitals of the two pi-bonds are close enough to overlap. The reaction requires energy to overcome the activation barrier. The structure of the product is dictated by the orbital overlap in the transition state.

Claisen Rearrangement

The Claisen rearrangement is similar to Cope rearrangement, except that in a Claisen rearrangement, the reactant is a vinylic allyl ether. The rearrangement involves two pi-bonds and one sigma-bond and has a transition state that is similar to the one observed with the Cope rearrangement. The difference is the presence of an oxygen. Figure 4-19 shows a Claisen rearrangement.

Figure 4-19

When the ether is benzylic instead of vinylic, the cyclic ketone can quickly tautomerize to form a phenol. The preference of a phenol over the cyclic ketone is due to the aromaticity of the benzene ring.

Example 4.13

Which statement is valid in terms of the sigmatropic rearrangement reactions?

A. Aldehydes are formed from a Claisen rearrangement of a vinylic allyl ether when the allylic ether carbon is unsubstituted.
B. Aldehydes are formed from a Claisen rearrangement of a vinylic allyl ether when the vinylic ether carbon is unsubstituted.
C. Aldehydes are formed from a Cope rearrangement of a vinylic allyl ether when the allylic ether carbon is unsubstituted.
D. Aldehydes are formed from a Cope rearrangement of a vinylic allyl ether when the vinylic ether carbon is unsubstituted.

Solution

Choices C and D are eliminated immediately, because Cope rearrangement results in the conversion of one 1,5-diene into another 1,5-diene, not an aldehyde. The question is reduced to determining which carbon in the reactant forms the carbonyl group following Claisen rearrangement. The reaction is shown below.

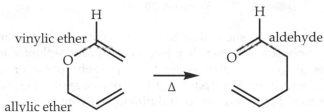

It is the vinylic ether carbon that becomes the carbonyl carbon, not the allylic ether carbon. This means that the vinylic ether carbon must only have a hydrogen, and not an alkyl group attached, in order to form an aldehyde and not a ketone. The best answer is choice **B**.

Terpenes

Classification

Terpenes and *terpenoids*, biological molecules derived from terpenes, are natural hydrocarbons found in plants and animals that are made from 5-carbon isoprene (2-methyl-1,3-butadiene) units. The five-carbon skeleton of isoprene can be found in terpenes. Terpenes are classified by their number of carbon atoms. Monoterpenes have ten carbon atoms, sesquiterpenes have fifteen carbons, diterpenes have twenty carbons, sesterterpenes have twenty-five carbons and so on. The *in vitro*

synthesis of terpenes and terpenoids is called *natural product synthesis*. Some naturally occurring monoterpenes are shown in Figure 4-20.

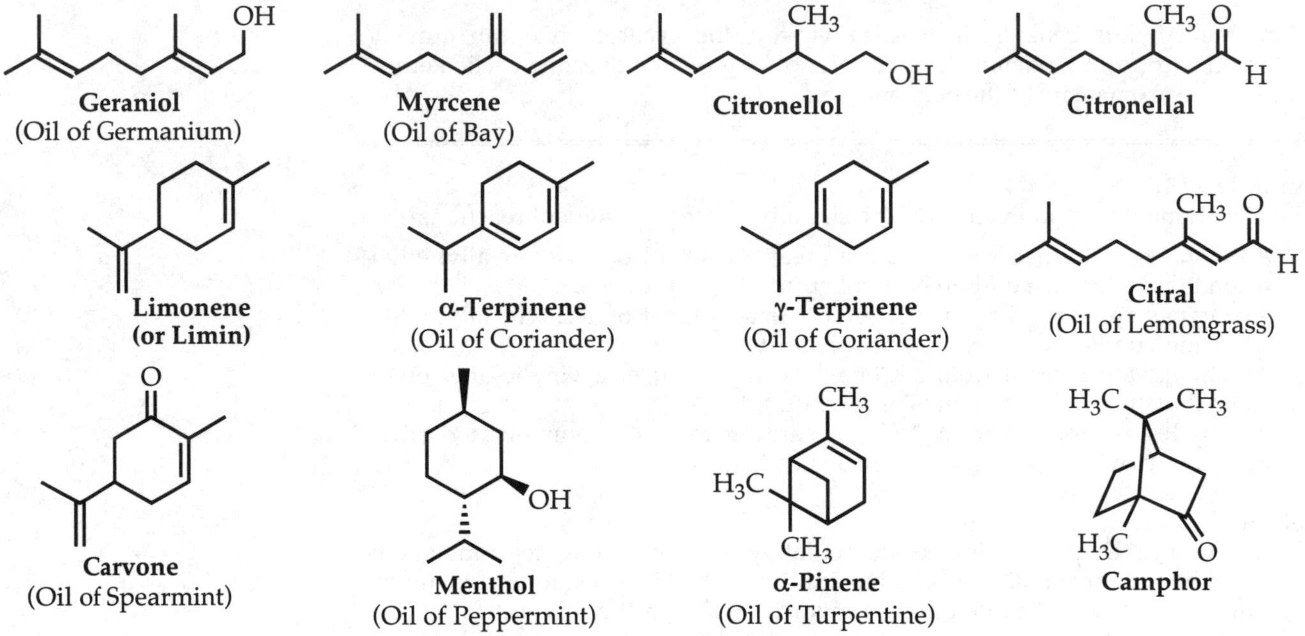

Geraniol
(Oil of Germanium)

Myrcene
(Oil of Bay)

Citronellol

Citronellal

Limonene
(or Limin)

α-Terpinene
(Oil of Coriander)

γ-Terpinene
(Oil of Coriander)

Citral
(Oil of Lemongrass)

Carvone
(Oil of Spearmint)

Menthol
(Oil of Peppermint)

α-Pinene
(Oil of Turpentine)

Camphor

Figure 4-20

Studies in biogenesis show that the large terpenes are synthesized using isopentenyl pyrophosphate rather than isoprene. Pyrophosphate adds across the diene of isoprene to form either isopentenyl pyrophosphate or dimethylallyl pyrophosphate, which are interconverted by isomerization. Figure 4-21 shows isoprene, isopentenyl pyrophosphate, and dimethylallyl pyrophosphate.

Isoprene

Isopentyl pyrophosphate

Dimethylallyl pyrophosphate

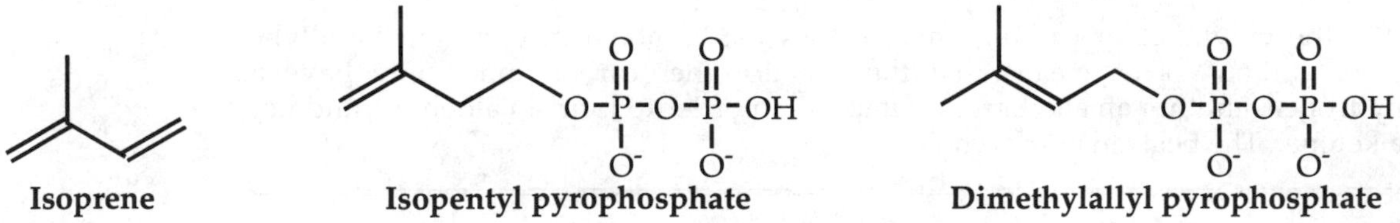

Figure 4-21

These molecules add to one another in a way where the π-bond of isopentyl pyrophosphate is the nucleophile and pyrophosphate of another molecule is the leaving group. A proton is lost from the nucleophilic moiety to regenerate a π-bond. The reaction involves head-to-tail addition. When cyclizing, the bond that is formed to complete the ring is rarely connected head-to-tail. Figure 4-22 shows the reaction of isopentenyl pyrophosphate and dimethylallyl pyrophosphate.

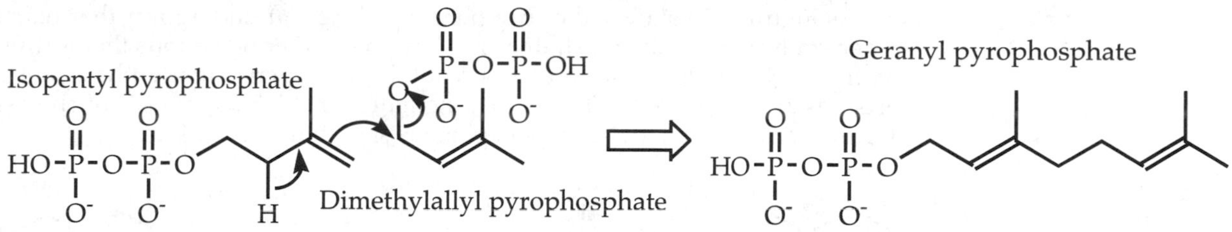

Figure 4-22

Both plants and animals synthesize terpenes. Larger terpenes are built from multiple additions of isoprene units, including both isopentenyl pyrophosphate and dimethylallyl pyrophosphate. Geranyl pyrophosphate (a C-10 terpene derived from the head-to-tail connection of two isopentenyl pyrophosphate molecules) is the first monoterpene in many natural synthetic pathways. Another isoprene unit can be added to geranyl pyrophosphate to form farnesyl pyrophosphate (a C-15 terpene). These molecules can undergo further addition, dimerization, or modification into other terpenes and terpenoids. Figure 4-23 shows a generic pathway for the biosynthesis of larger terpenes.

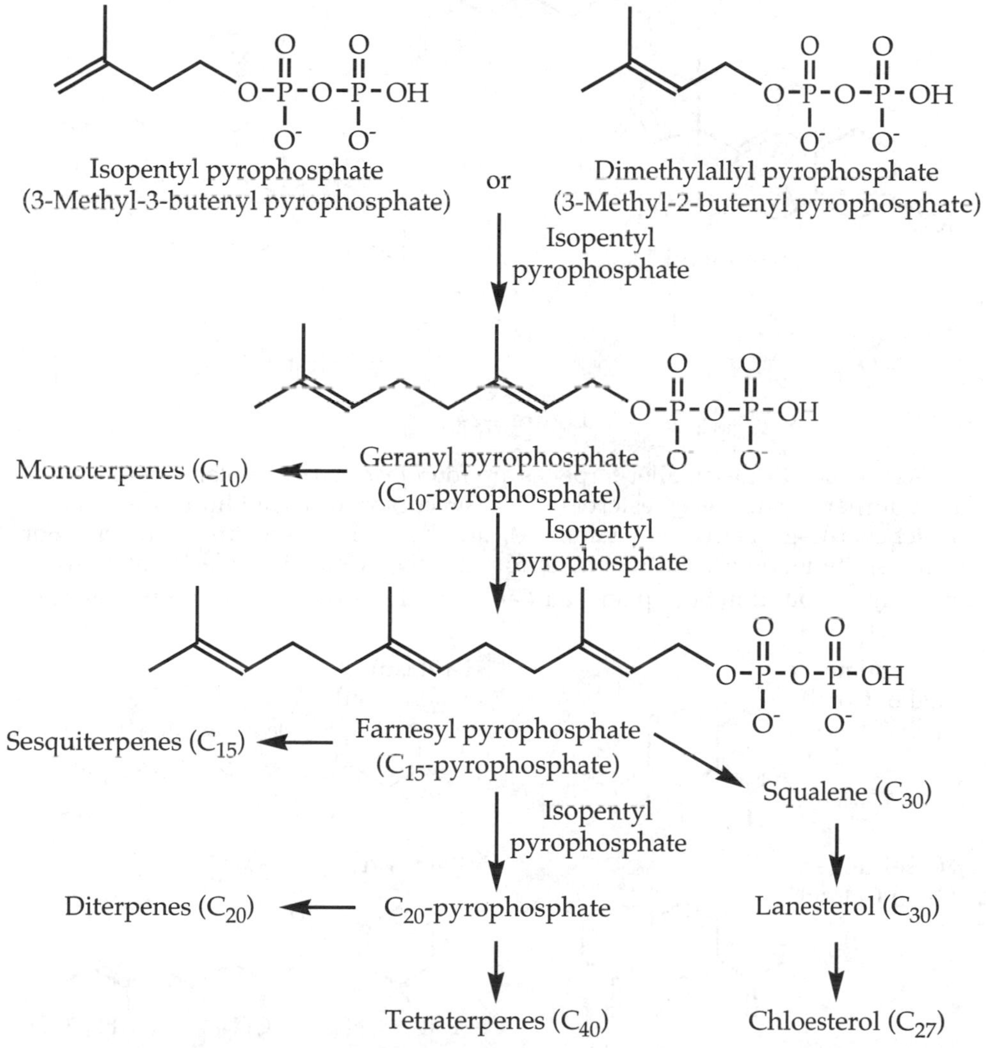

Figure 4-23

As Figure 4-23 shows, the triterpene squalene can undergo further reactivity to generate cholesterol, which does not have a number of carbons that is divisible by five. So while cholesterol may not be a terpene, its synthesis involves terpenes and terpenoids. The basic schematic for the biosynthesis of cholesterol starting from isopentenyl pyrophosphate is shown in Figure 4-24.

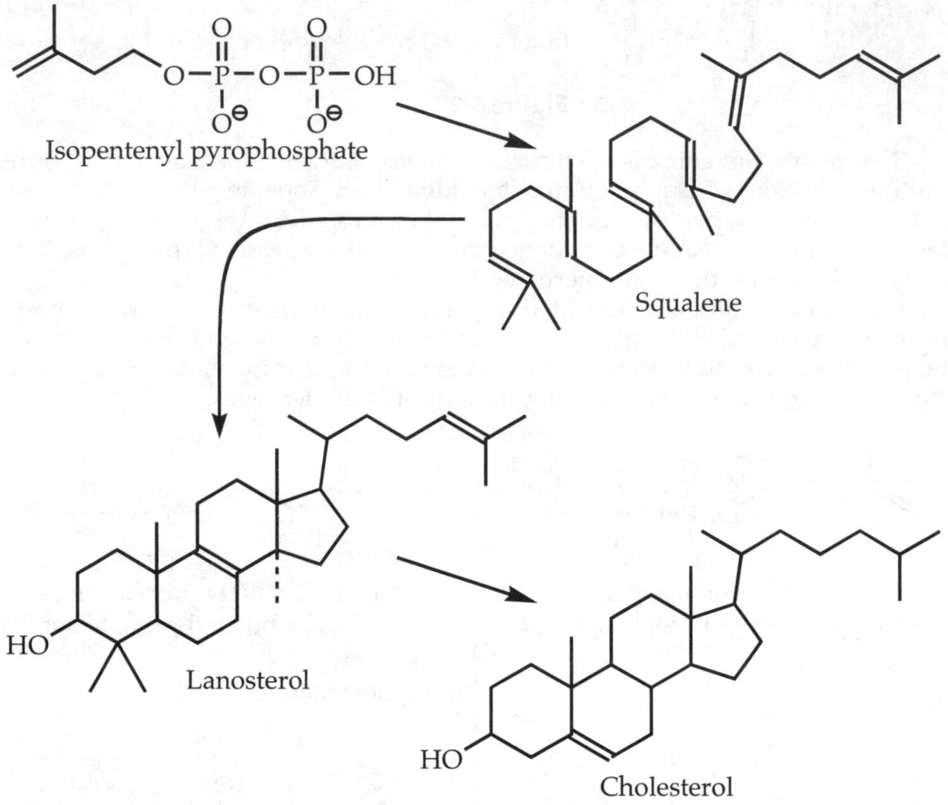

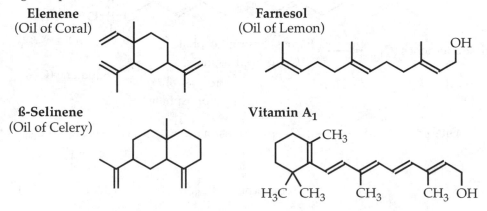

Isopentenyl pyrophosphate

Squalene

Lanosterol

Cholesterol

Figure 4-24

As a general rule, smaller terpenes are found primarily in plants, while some larger terpenes, such as lanesterol (a C-30 precursor to steroid hormones) and ß-carotene (a C-40 source of vitamin A), are found in plants and animals. For instance, the monoterpene pinene is found only in plants while Vitamin A_1, a diterpene, is found in both plants and animals. Figure 4-25 shows some selected larger terpenes.

Elemene
(Oil of Coral)

Farnesol
(Oil of Lemon)

ß-Selinene
(Oil of Celery)

Vitamin A_1

Figure 4-25

One of the skills that you must develop to do well on terpene related questions on the MCAT is to recognize terpenes and be able to identify the isoprene subunits in the carbon skeleton. Figure 4-26 shows the analysis of some terpenes for the isoprene units in the skeletal fragments.

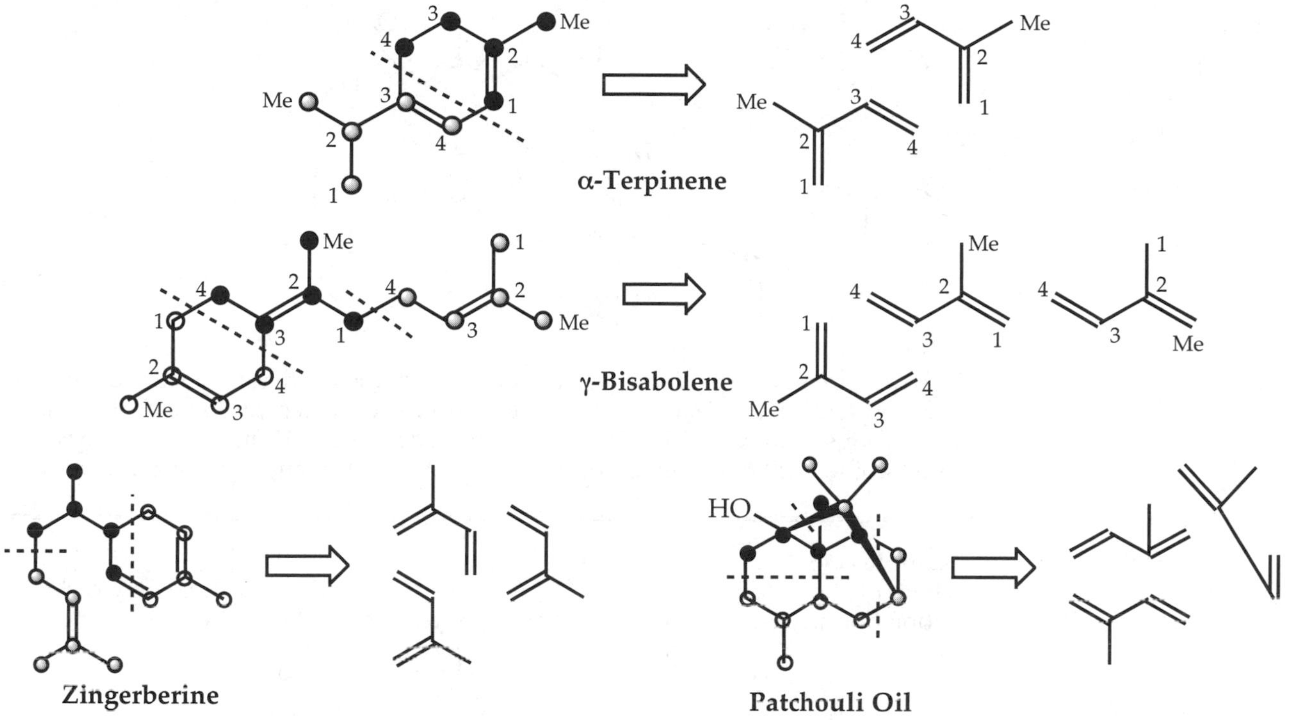

α-Terpinene

γ-Bisabolene

Zingerberine   **Patchouli Oil**

Figure 4-26

A common lab technique employed to isolate terpenes is steam distillation, where the pulp of a natural material is placed into water and boiled so that the natural oils are distilled from the pulp. This allows the essential oils to vaporize at a temperature lower than their boiling point, so they do not degrade. The distillate is a mixture of water and terpenes, which are easily separated using extraction techniques. Terpenes can also be extracted from pulp. When isolating terpenes, it is a mixture of geometrical isomers that is collected. The different geometrical isomers of a terpene are given the prefixes α-, ß-, γ- and so on. The different geometrical isomers have similar physical properties, but because of differences in conjugation, they exhibit differences in the absorption of photons in the ultraviolet (UV) and visible range of the EM spectrum.

Terpenes are UV active, because of their π-bonds. An isolated alkene has a UV absorbance around 180 nm. A conjugated diene has a UV absorbance around 225 nm, which is significantly more intense than the absorbance of an isolated alkene. As the conjugation of a π-network increases, the wavelength of maximum absorbance, λ_{max}, and the intensity of absorbance, ε, increase. Some terpenes contain oxygen, which is added in a way that does not alter the carbon skeleton. Carbonyls exhibit absorbances of greater wavelength than alkenes of the same conjugation. For instance, carvone (shown in Figure 4-26) is evident by a carbonyl absorption at 1744 cm^{-1} in its IR spectrum and a strong UV ($\varepsilon >$ 10,000) absorption at λ_{max} = 242 nm. Terpenes are often isolated in educational laboratory experiments. Because of their biological significance and the fact they are isolated in lab experiments, they are highly represented on the MCAT. If you have a fundamental understanding of terpenes, then you should be fine.

Example 4.14
Which of the following compounds is NOT a terpene or terpenoid?

A.

B.

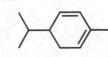

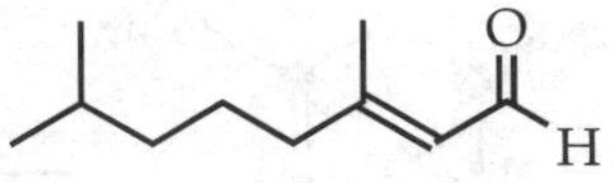

C.

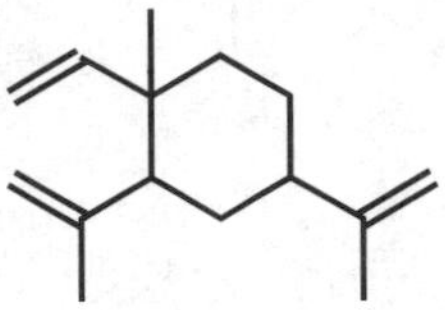

D.

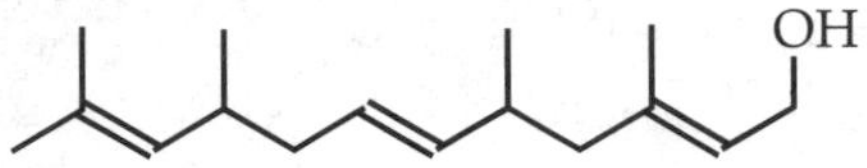

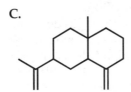

Solution
Terpenes are built from 5-carbon subunits, which means that they should contain a carbon total that is a multiple of five. Choice A has ten carbons, choice B has ten carbons, choice C has fifteen carbons, and choice **D** has sixteen carbons. Because choice **D** has sixteen carbons, it cannot be a terpene or terpenoid.

Example 4.15
Which of the following compounds requires the formation of three new carbon-carbon bonds when synthesized from isopentenyl pyrophosphate?

A. H_3C CH_3

H_3C O

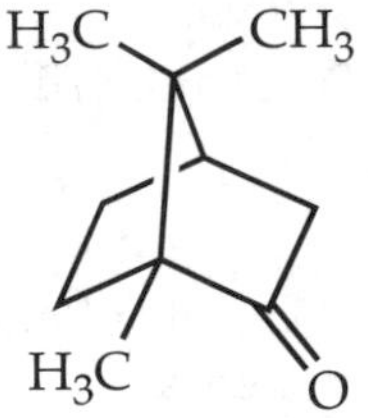

B.

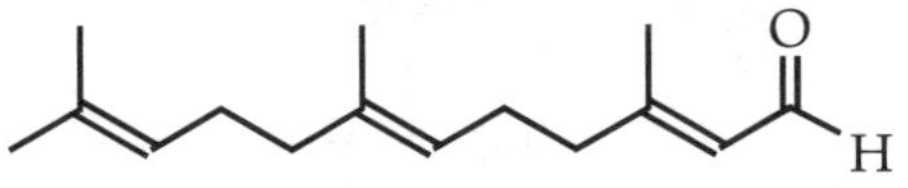

O
H

C.

D. CH_3

H_3C CH_3 CH_3 CH_3 OH

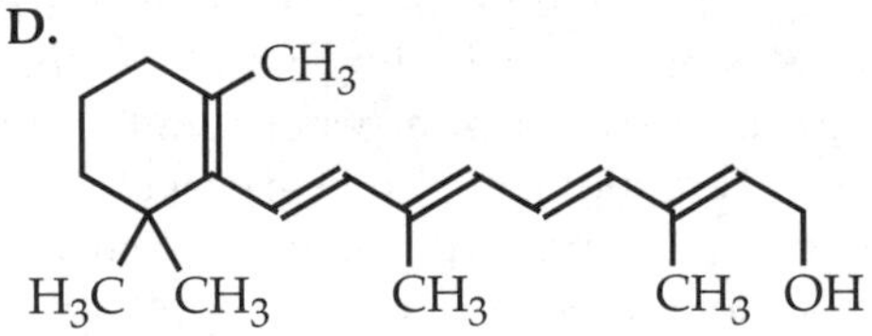

Solution
A new carbon-carbon bond results in the lengthening of the carbon chain or a the formation of a ring. We need to systematically analyze each choice for the carbon count and ring total. In choice A, there are ten carbons and two rings. One new carbon-carbon bond is necessary to make a ten-carbon species and two more new carbon-carbon bonds are required to form the bicyclic system, so choice **A** requires three carbon-carbon bonds when formed from 5-carbon isoprene derivatives. In choice B there are fifteen carbons and no rings, so two new carbon-carbon bonds were formed in its synthesis from isoprene derivatives. Choice B is eliminated. In choice C there are fifteen carbons and two rings, so four new carbon-carbon bonds were formed in its synthesis from isoprene derivatives (two to increase the carbon count to 15 and two more for the rings). Choice C is eliminated. In choice D there are twenty carbons and one ring, so four new carbon-carbon bonds were formed in its synthesis from isoprene derivatives (three to increase the carbon count to 20 and one more for the ring). Choice D is eliminated.

Key Points for Hydrocarbons (Section 4)

Alkanes

1. Hydrocarbon compounds with only carbons, hydrogens, and sigma bonds

    a) Only contain C—C and C—H single bonds

        i.   Can be aliphatic (straight chain) or cyclic
        ii. Low water solubility, low boiling point, and low melting point
        iii. Relatively inert compounds that are used as solvents

    b) Undergo free radical halogenation reactions with chlorine and bromine

        i.   Involves initiation, propagation, and termination in that order
        ii. Bromination is more selective than chlorination
        iii. The relative stability for alkyl free radicals is: $3° > 2° > 1° >$ methyl

Hydrocarbon Reactions (Reactions involving π-bonds)

1. Elimination

    a) Loss of an H and a leaving group to form a π-bond

        i.   Requires high temperature
        ii. Competes with nucleophilic substitution reactions
        iii. Goes by way of one of two mechanisms: E_1 or E_2

    b) E_1 reactions are similar to S_N1 reactions

        i.   Requires a strong acid (Brønsted-Lowry or Lewis)
        ii. Forms carbocation intermediate so rearrangement is possible
        iii. Forms most substituted and least sterically hindered alkene

    c) E_2 reactions are similar to S_N2 reactions

        i.   Concerted reaction that requires a strong, bulky base
        ii. Proton to be lost and the leaving group must be anti to one another
        iii. No intermediate formed, only a transition state

    d) Hofmann Elimination (E_2 reaction with a bulky leaving group)

        i.   Quaternary amine forms a bulky leaving group
        ii. Forms the non-Zaitsev (less substituted) alkene product
        iii. Requires heat and a strong base, like the E_2 reaction

2. Diels-Alder Reaction

    a) Reaction of a diene and a dienophile (alkene)

        i.   An electrocyclic reaction carried out with either light or heat
        ii. Forms a cyclohexene product
        iii. Stereoselectivity: Endo product is preferred over exo product
        iv. Regioselectivity: Depends on the resonance nature of the groups on the reactants

3. Sigmatropic Rearrangement (Cope and Claisen Rearrangements)

    a) Both sigma-bonds and pi-bonds are broken and formed via a cyclic transition state

        i.   Cope rearrangement converts a γ,δ-unsaturated alkene into another γ,δ-unsaturated alkene via a realignment of molecular orbitals
        ii. Claisen rearrangement converts a vinylic allyl ether into another γ,δ-unsaturated carbonyl via a realignment of molecular orbitals
        iii. Sigmatropic rearrangement requires heat

Terpenes

1. Natural products derived from the connecting of five-carbon units

    a) Derived via biosynthesis involving either isopentyl pyrophosphate or dimethylallyl pyrophosphate

    b) Can be cleaved into isoprene subunits

        i. Terpenes are named for their carbon count: 10 C = monoterpene, etc.

        ii. Isolated by steam distillation or extraction as natural oils

        iii. Presence of π-bonds results in UV absorbances. As conjugation increases, intensity and λ_{max} both increase.

"3.14? Phooey, π is not a number, it's a nucleophile"

25 Hydrocarbon Review Questions

The main purpose of this 25-question set is to serve as a review of the material presented in the chapter. Do not worry about the timing for these questions. Focus on learning. Once you complete these questions, grade them using the answer key. For any question you missed, repeat it and write down your thought process. Then grade the questions you repeated and thoroughly read the answer explanation. Compare your thought process to the answer explanation and assess whether you missed the question because of a careless error (such as misreading the question), because of an error in reasoning, or because you were lacking information. Your goal is to fill in any informational gaps and solidify your reasoning before you begin your practice exam for this section. Preparing for the MCAT is best done in stages. This first stage is meant to help you evaluate how well you know this subject matter.

A halide can be substituted onto an alkane by way of a free radical mechanism. Halogenation of an alkane is initiated by the homolytic cleavage of a diatomic halogen molecule into highly reactive free radical halogen atoms. During subsequent steps in the reaction, an alkane reacts with the halogen free radicals to form an alkyl halide. The reaction requires some source of activation energy to cleave the halogen-halogen bond. Depending on the halogen-halogen bond strength, the activation energy varies from thermal energy to ultraviolet radiation for the initiation step.

The mechanism is a sequence broken down into steps that fit into one of three categories: initiation, propagation, and termination, in that order. The initiation step involves homolytic cleavage of a halogen-halogen bond to form two free radicals. The second phase of the reaction sequence is propagation where the free radical is transferred through a set of abstraction reactions. The last phase of the sequence is the termination step where two free radicals combine to form a sigma bond. The reaction involves two transition states, in which the second is of higher energy than the first. Table 1 shows the bond energies of the halogens and the reaction enthalpies for the various halogenation reactions:

Compound	B.D.E.	ΔH_{rx}
F_2	$154 \frac{kJ}{mole}$	$-483 \frac{kJ}{mole}$
Cl_2	$239 \frac{kJ}{mole}$	$-114 \frac{kJ}{mole}$
Br_2	$193 \frac{kJ}{mole}$	$-33 \frac{kJ}{mole}$
I_2	$149 \frac{kJ}{mole}$	$+27 \frac{kJ}{mole}$

Table 1

The enthalpy of a chemical reaction can be found by using Equation 1.

$$\Delta H_{rxn} = \Sigma \text{ Energy}_{bonds broken} - \text{Energy}_{bonds formed}$$

Equation 1

The average bond dissociation energy for a sigma bond between an sp^3-hybridized carbon and a hydrogen is 413 kJ per mole. A hydrogen free radical cannot be formed in this reaction mechanism.

1. The MOST stable type of carbon free radical formed in the monobromination of (R)-3-methylhexane is best described as:

   A. primary.
   B. secondary.
   C. tertiary.
   D. quaternary.

2. Which of the following energy diagrams corresponds to reaction of I_2 with an alkane?

   A.
   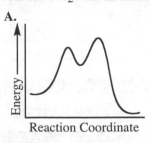
   B.
   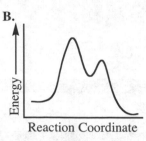
   C.
   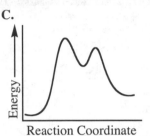
   D.
   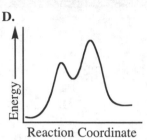

3. The first propagation step in a free radical reaction is which of the following?

   A. $X_2 + R\cdot \rightarrow RX + X\cdot$
   B. $RH + X\cdot \rightarrow HX + R\cdot$
   C. $X_2 \rightarrow 2\,X\cdot$
   D. $X\cdot + R\cdot \rightarrow RX$

4. The strongest halogen-halogen bond corresponds to which of the following?

   A. The shortest halogen-halogen bond.
   B. The second shortest halogen-halogen bond.
   C. The longest halogen-halogen bond.
   D. The second longest halogen-halogen bond.

5. Which of the following steps is NOT found in a free radical halogenation reaction?

   A. $RH + X\cdot \rightarrow RX + H\cdot$
   B. $X_2 + R\cdot \rightarrow RX + X\cdot$
   C. $RH + X\cdot \rightarrow HX + R\cdot$
   D. $X\cdot + R\cdot \rightarrow RX$

6. Which of the following conclusions can be inferred from the observation that usually only one halide reacts with the alkane and minimal multiple halogenated products are isolated from the product mixture?

I. Halogens do not help to stabilize free radical intermediates.

II. Halogens, once on an alkane, increase the C-H bond strength.

III. Halogens, once on an alkane, decrease the C-H bond strength.

A. II only
B. III only
C. I and II only
D. I and III only

7. Given that a C-F bond energy is 462 kJ per mole and a H-F bond energy is 588 kJ per mole, what is the heat of reaction associated with fluorination of an alkane?

A. $- 483 \dfrac{kJ}{mole}$

B. $- 116 \dfrac{kJ}{molc}$

C. $+ 116 \dfrac{kJ}{mole}$

D. $+ 483 \dfrac{kJ}{molc}$

Passage II (Questions 8 - 14)

Pheromones are chemicals secreted by animals (most commonly insects) that elicit a specific behavioral reaction in other members of their same species. They are effective in low concentration in sending signals between members of the same species for such things as reproduction, danger warnings, and aggregation (in the case of a food supply.) Many pheromones are simple hydrocarbons. For instance, when in danger, ants secrete undecane ($C_{11}H_{24}$) or tridecane ($C_{13}H_{28}$) to inform other ants of the trouble. Many of the traps and sprays we use to capture and kill insects take advantage of sex attractants. The structures of four sex pheromones are shown in Figure 1.

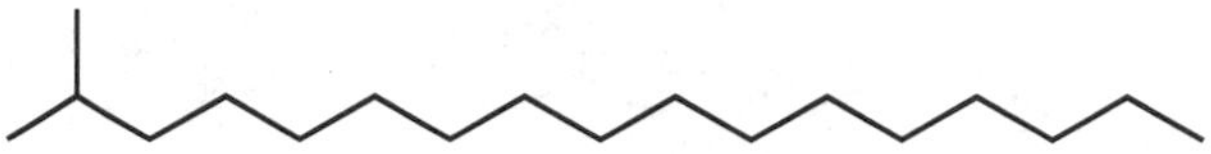

Tiger Moth sex attractant
(2-Methylheptadecane)

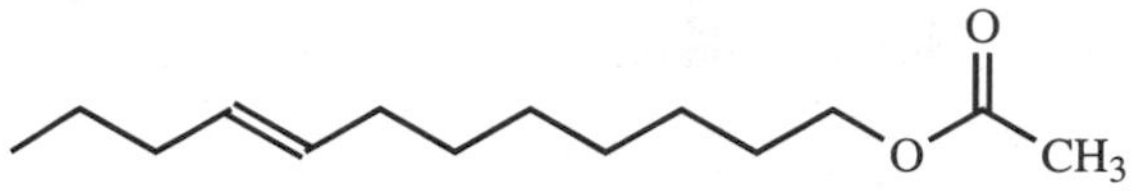

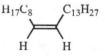

Oriental Fruit Moth sex attractant
[(E)-8-Dodecen-1-yl acetate]

House Fly sex attractant
(Muscalure [(9Z)-Tricosene])

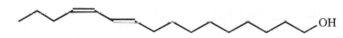

Silkworm Moth sex attractant
(Bombykol)

Figure 1 Four natural pheromones

Pheromones are specific to each species, because receptor proteins are highly selective in what they bind. In one of the rare cases where two geometrical isomers both elicit the same response, the Oriental Fruit Moth responds to both the E-isomer, shown in Figure 1, and the Z-isomer. There are cases where two similar species to a pheromone that is similar in structure, but not exactly the same. For instance, the Grape Berry Moth uses (Z)-9-dodecen-1-yl acetate as a sex attractant in roughly the same concentration that the Oriental Fruit Moth uses (Z)-8-dodecen-1-yl acetate.

8. The Silkworm Moth sex pheromone has all of the following structural features EXCEPT:

A. one stereogenic center.
B. one cis double bond.
C. no tertiary carbons.
D. conjugation.

9. Which of the pheromones in Figure 1 has the greatest number of primary carbons?

   A. The Tiger Moth sex pheromone
   B. The House Fly sex pheromone
   C. The Oriental Fruit Moth sex pheromone
   D. The Silkworm Moth sex pheromone

10. Relative to the Oriental Fruit Moth sex pheromone shown in Figure 1, the following compound is:

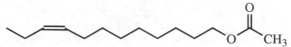

   A. a conformational isomer.
   B. a geometrical isomer.
   C. an optical isomer.
   D. a structural isomer.

11. Which of the following statements accurately relates the four structures shown in Figure 1?

   I. Muscalure has a shorter wavelength of maximum absorbance in UV-visible spectroscopy bombykol.
   II. The Tiger Moth sex pheromone has the more units of unsaturation than undecane.
   III. The Oriental Fruit Moth sex pheromone can be classified as a terpene.

   A. I only
   B. III only
   C. I and II only
   D. I and III only

12. What physical property is NOT expected for muscalure?

   A. Low miscibility in water
   B. A boiling point above room temperature
   C. High lipid solubility
   D. The ability to rotate plane-polarized light

13. The Green Peach Aphid defense pheromone is shown below.

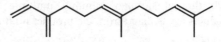

What is NOT true of the structure?

   A. It can be synthesized from isoprene units.
   B. It has more sp^2-hybridized carbons than sp^3-hybridized carbons.
   C. It can potentially undergo 1,4-addition.
   D. It is highly flexible.

14. Which spectroscopic observation does NOT correlate with the corresponding compound?

   A. The Oriental Fruit Moth sex pheromone: an IR absorbance at 1741 cm^{-1}
   B. Bombykol: a UV-visible absorbance at 227 nm
   C. Muscalure: two signals around 5.00 ppm in its ^{1}H NMR
   D. The Tiger Moth sex pheromone: 14 signals in its ^{13}C NMR spectrum

Many processed foods contain partially hydrogenated vegetable oil. Partial hydrogenation serves to reduce some of the π-bonds found in natural oils, which results in an increase in their melting point, and can convert a naturally occurring liquid into a solid. Naturally occurring fatty acids often have long carbon chains. They can be hydrogenated to convert the alkyl chain, which may contain multiple double bonds, into to an aliphatic R group. Fatty acids in nature are often found as part of a fatty acid triglyceride or cell membrane. Figure 1 shows the enzymatically-controlled conversion of a fatty acid triglyceride into glycerol and three fatty acids.

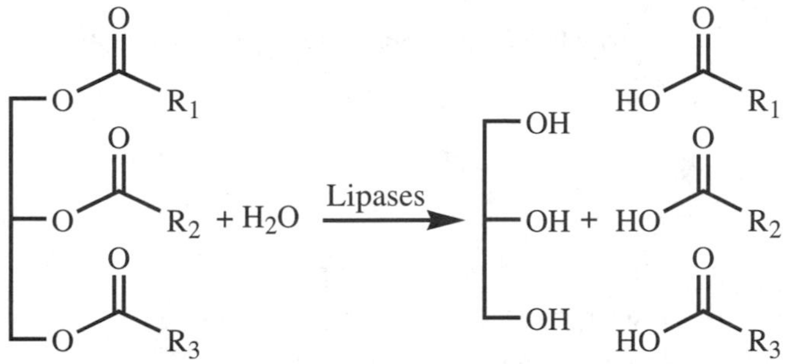

Figure 1 Enzymatic Hydrolysis of a Triglyceride

Three carboxylic acids are isolated when a fatty acid triglyceride is hydrolyzed. In naturally occurring fatty acids, the R represents an alkyl chain with an odd number of carbons. This is because naturally occurring fatty acids have an even number of carbons. An even number of carbons is attributed to the fact that fatty acid biosynthesis occurs two carbons at a time, via acetyl coenzyme A. Natural fats can be distinguished from synthetic fats by their carbon chain length. Table 1 lists some common fatty acids that are naturally found in animals:

Acid	Formula	π
Arachidic	$CH_3(CH_2)_{18}CO_2H$	0
Arachidonic	$CH_3(CH_2)_4(CH=CHCH_2)_4(CH_2)_2CO_2H$	4
Behenic	$CH_3(CH_2)_{20}CO_2H$	0
Lauric	$CH_3(CH_2)_{10}CO_2H$	0
Lignocaric	$CH_3(CH_2)_{22}CO_2H$	0
Linoleic	$CH_3(CH_2)_4(CH=CHCH_2)_2(CH_2)_6CO_2H$	2
Linolenic	$CH_3CH_2(CH=CHCH_2)_3(CH_2)_6CO_2H$	3
Myristic	$CH_3(CH_2)_{12}CO_2H$	0
Oleic	$CH_3(CH_2)_7CH=CH(CH_2)_7CO_2H$	1
Palmitic	$CH_3(CH_2)_{14}CO_2H$	0
Palmitoleic	$CH_3(CH_2)_5CH=CH(CH_2)_7CO_2H$	1
Stearic	$CH_3(CH_2)_{16}CO_2H$	0

Table 1 Common Natural Fatty Acids

Vegetable oils generally have more unsaturation than animal fats. For instance, corn oil is 63% linoleic acid and 26% oleic acid, with the rest being made of other saturated fatty acids. Safflower oil is 75% linoleic acid, 14% oleic acid, and 4% linolenic acid with the rest being made of other saturated fatty acids. As the amount of unsaturation increases, the melting point of the fatty acid decreases, assuming that the number of carbons remains constant. For this reason, many animal fats are solids while many vegetable oils are liquids at room temperature. Fatty acids often play one of three roles in biological systems. (1) They are found as the building blocks of cell membranes as phospholipids and glycolipids. (2) Fatty acids are synthetic building blocks for hormones. (3) Fatty acids are used for fuel through fatty acid metabolism.

15. The π-bond of a fatty acid can be reduced via hydrogenation when treated with hydrogen gas and a catalytic metal or by $FADH_2$. Treatment of linoleic acid with $FADH_2$ yields a product:

    A. with lower molecular mass and a lower melting point than linoleic acid.
    B. with higher molecular mass but a lower melting point than linoleic acid.
    C. with a lower molecular mass but a higher melting point than linoleic acid.
    D. with a higher molecular mass and a higher melting point than linoleic acid.

16. What is the structure for the MOST abundant fatty acid found in corn oil?

    A.

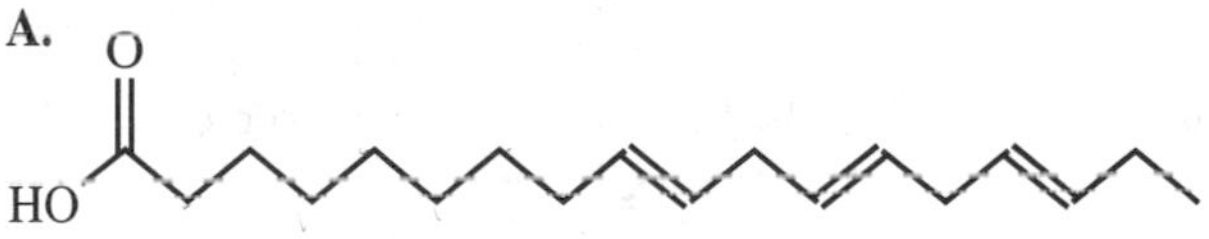

    B.

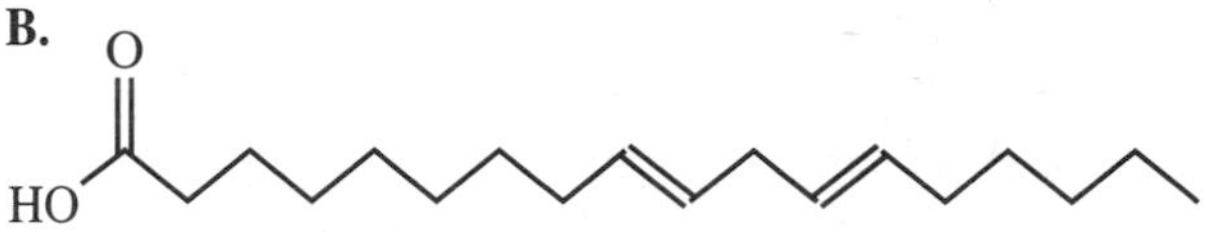

    C.

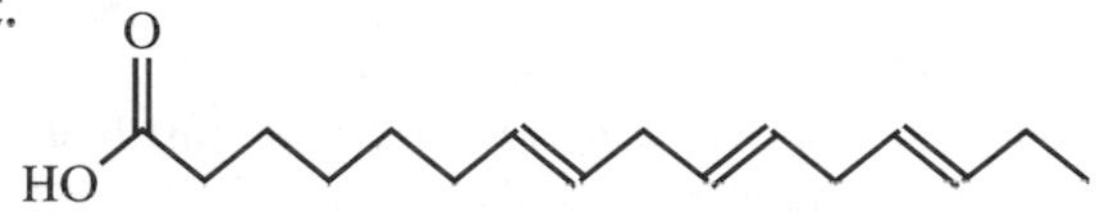

    D.

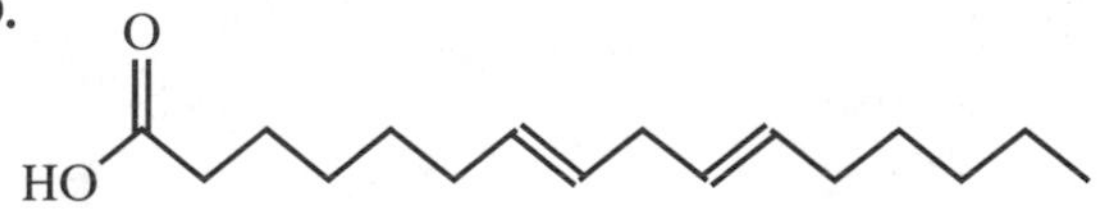

17. Addition of D_2 with Pd catalyst reduces π-bonds by adding deuterium to each π-bond carbon. Treatment of oleic acid with D_2 and palladium yields a compound with how many chiral centers?

A. Zero
B. One
C. Two
D. Four

18. The presence of which fatty acid in a cell membrane would most reduced the membrane's fluidity?

A. Arachidic
B. Arachidonic
C. Lauric
D. Linolenic

19. Bromine liquid is used as a quantitative test reagent to determine the amount of π-bonds per molecule of a compound. Which of the following acids consumes the MOST Br_2 per molecule?

A. Lauric
B. Arachidonic
C. Palmitoleic
D. Linolenic

20. Complete hydrogenation of palmitoleic acid yields which of the following acids?

A. Myristic
B. Palmitic
C. Stearic
D. Arachidic

21. Which of the following fatty acids is most likely found in the cell membranes of Artic salmon?

A. Lauric
B. Linoleic
C. Myristic
D. Oleic

Questions 22 through 25 are **NOT** based on a descriptive passage.

22. The chlorination of methylcyclopentane would yield how many different structural isomers?

A. 2
B. 3
C. 4
D. 5

23. The terpene (±)-ß-trans-Bergamontene shown below:

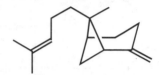

A. is generated from three isoprene units.
B. is a terpenoid and not a terpene.
C. has three units of unsaturation.
D. has sixteen possible stereoisomers.

24. Which of the following molecules have dipoles NOT equal to zero?

I. E-butene

II. C_2H_4

III. Z-butene

A. I only
B. II only
C. III only
D. I and III only

25. Terpenes have all of the following properties EXCEPT:

A. high volatility.
B. distinct odor.
C. fluidity at room temperature.
D. high water solubility.

1. C	2. D	3. B	4. B	5. A
6. C	7. A	8. A	9. A	10. D
11. A	12. D	13. D	14. D	15. D
16. B	17. C	18. A	19. B	20. B
21. B	22. C	23. A	24. C	25. D

Answers to 25-Question Hydrocarbons Review

1. **Choice C is the best answer.** The stability of the carbon free radical is attributed to the donation of electron density from the alkyl substituents through hyperconjugation. Because hydrogens cannot donate electron density through hyperconjugation, the stability of a free radical depends on the number of alkyl substituents attached. As a result, the stability of free radicals is tertiary > secondary > primary ($3° > 2° > 1°$). Quaternary free radicals cannot exist, because the presence of four bonds and a free electron on carbon would exceed the octet rule for carbon. The best answer is therefore choice **C**.

2. **Choice D is the best answer.** According to Table 1, the enthalpy change is positive for the reaction of iodine with an alkene, so it is an endothermic reaction. This means that the products are in a higher energy state than the reactants, which eliminates choices A and B. In the next to the last sentence of the first paragraph, it is stated that the second transition state is of higher energy than the first transition state, so the best answer is choice **D**. If you find yourself asking "do they really expect me to know this?", it's probably in the passage... find it!

3. **Choice B is the best answer.** Initiation forms the halogen free radical (X·), so the first propagation step involves the halogen free radical as a reactant. This eliminates choices A and C. In propagation step 1, the free radical abstracts a hydrogen from an alkane, which is choice **B**. Eliminate choice D, because it is a termination step.

4. **Choice B is the best answer.** According to the data in Table 1, the strongest halogen-halogen bond is formed between two chlorine atoms. Chlorine is the second halogen from the top in the column VII of the periodic table. Atomic radius increases as you descend a column of the periodic table, so chlorine is the second smallest halogen. Therefore, the strongest halogen-halogen bond is formed between the second smallest halogen. The fluorine-fluorine bond is an exception to the shorter bond equals stronger bond rule, because of inter-nuclear repulsion and the odd fact that the single bond is actually a pi-bond, rather than a sigma-bond. The best answer is choice **B**.

5. **Choice A is the best answer.** Hydrogen free radical is unstable, and thus it cannot be formed in the reaction mechanism. Choice **A** produces a hydrogen free radical, therefore the best answer is choice **A**.

6. **Choice C is the best answer.** If the halogen were to stabilize the free radical when attached, it would lower the transition state and make the reaction pathway for adding a second halogen more favorable. The halogen will not stabilize the free radical, because halogens are electron withdrawing by the inductive effect. Halogens therefore do not help stabilize the free radical intermediate so statement **I** is true. Because a second halide does not add to an alkyl halide, but a halide does add to an alkane, we assume that the alkane is more reactive. The difference is either in the bond broken or the bond formed. It is safe to assume that the reaction will choose a pathway of lowest energy so by breaking the C-H bond of the alkane preferentially over the C-H of the alkyl halide, it can be concluded that the bond broken is of lower energy. This makes statement **II** true. If statement **II** is true, then statement **III** cannot be true. The best answer is therefore choice **C**. As a note, an R-H bond is stronger than an R-X bond, so if a halogen free radical (X·) were to react with an alkyl halide, it would abstract the halide, not a hydrogen. This is the more logical explanation for the absence of multiple substitution products with free radical halogenation.

7. **Choice A is the best answer.** The enthalpy of reaction for a reaction between an alkane and fluorine is listed in Table 1. By simply reading the chart, it can be seen that best answer is choice **A**. Sometimes answers are this easy to get, so don't be fooled into thinking every question on the MCAT will be difficult.

8. **Choice A is the best answer.** The Silkworm Moth sex pheromone has two double bonds, one that is cis substituted and the other that is trans substituted. This eliminates choice B. All of the carbons are part of a straight chain with no branching, so it has two terminal carbons that are primary and all the internal carbons are secondary. There are no tertiary carbons, so choice C is eliminated. Only one single bond separates the two double bonds, so they are in fact conjugated. This eliminates choice D. All of the carbons have at least two identical substituents or they have sp^2-hybridization, so there are no stereogenic centers. This makes choice **A** the best answer.

9. **Choice A is the best answer.** All of the compounds in Figure 1 have straight chains (no rings), so each has at least two primary carbons. Only 2-methylheptadecane has branching, so it has an extra primary carbon. No other structure in Figure 1 has any branching, so 2-methylheptadecane, the Tiger Moth sex pheromone, has the most primary carbons. Choice **A** is the best answer.

10. **Choice D is the best answer.** The Oriental Fruit Moth sex pheromone differs from the structure in the question at the position of the double bond. The structure in the question has cis geometry, while the pheromone in Figure 1 has trans geometry. This can be misleading and tempt you to pick choice B. But, the connectivity is not the same, so the structures are structural isomers. The π-bond is between carbons 8 and 9 in the Oriental Fruit Moth sex pheromone, but it is between carbons 9 and 10 in the compound that is shown. This makes choice **D** the best answer. The two structures are not interchangeable by a rotation about a bond, so they are not conformational isomers. This eliminates choice A. There is no stereogenic carbon, so the two structures cannot be optical isomers. This eliminates choice C. The two structures are structural isomers, making choice **D** the best answer.

11. **Choice A is the best answer.** UV-visible spectroscopy is used to detect π-bonds. Bombykol has conjugated π-bonds, while muscalure just one π-bond. Conjugation reduces the transition energy, so the wavelength of maximum absorbance increases with conjugation. This means that bombykol has a greater λ_{max} than muscalure, making Statement I a valid statement. Choice B is eliminated. The Tiger Moth sex hormone is an aliphatic alkane, so it has no units of unsaturation. Undecane is an 11-carbon aliphatic hydrocarbon, so it too has no units of unsaturation. The two compounds have the same units of unsaturation, zero, so Statement II is invalid. This eliminates choice C. Terpenes and terpenoids contain a number of carbons that is divisible by five and a predictable connectivity that can be partitioned into isoprene subunits. The Oriental Fruit Moth sex pheromone has twelve carbons in its chain and two more for the acetate group. Fourteen is not divisible by five nor is the structure one that can be broken into isoprene subunits. This makes statement III invalid and makes the choice **A** the best answer.

12. **Choice D is the best answer.** Muscalure is a cis alkene made of 23 carbons and 46 hydrogens. It is a long chain hydrocarbon, so it has low water miscibility. Choice A is a valid statement, and thereby eliminated. It is excreted, so it must be a liquid under ambient conditions. This makes choice B a valid statement, which eliminates it. Because it is a long chain hydrocarbon, lipids can dissolve into it. It has high lipid solubility, making choice C a valid statement, thereby eliminating it. There are no stereogenic centers on muscalure, so it will not rotate plane-polarized light. This makes choice **D** an invalid statement, so choice **D** is the best answer.

13. **Choice D is the best answer.** The Green Peach Aphid defense pheromone has 15 carbons connected in such a way that it can be partitioned into three isoprene subunits. Choice A is a valid statement, so it is eliminated. The Green Peach Aphid defense pheromone has four double bonds, so it has eight sp^2-hybridized carbons. With fifteen carbons total, more than half of the carbons are sp^2-hybridized. Choice B is a valid statement, so it is eliminated. The Green Peach Aphid defense pheromone has a conjugated diene, so it can undergo 1,4-addition of an electrophile. Choice C is a valid statement, which eliminates it. Because of all of the π-bonds in the Green Peach Aphid defense pheromone, it is not very flexible. Choice **D** is an invalid statement, which makes it the best answer.

14. **Choice D is the best answer.** The Oriental Fruit Moth sex pheromone has an ester group. A carbonyl has an IR absorbance above 1700 cm^{-1}, so an ester accounts for the IR absorbance at 1741 cm^{-1}. Choice A is a valid correlation of structure to spectroscopic observation, so it is eliminated. Bombykol has two π-bonds in a conjugated network. The presence of π-bonds in a structure results in an absorbance in the ultraviolet-visible range of the EM spectrum, so an absorbance of 227 nm seems viable for a conjugated diene. Choice B is a valid correlation of structure to spectroscopic observation, so it is eliminated. Muscalure has two carbons involved in double bonds, each of which has a hydrogen attached. This means that the hydrogens on those carbons will be found downfield, resulting in two signals with values around 5.00 ppm in ^{1}H NMR. Choice C is a valid correlation of structure to spectroscopic observation, so it is eliminated. The Tiger Moth sex pheromone has eighteen carbons and no plane of symmetry. There are two equivalent methyl groups, so there are seventeen unique carbons. The ^{13}C NMR would show 17 signals if it were of high enough resolution. The reality is that many of the signals would overlap, so it would likely show less. It will not show fourteen signals in its ^{13}C NMR spectrum, so choice **D** is an invalid correlation of structure to spectroscopic observation, making it the best answer.

Passage III (Questions 15 - 21)   **Fatty Acids and Oils**

15. **Choice D is the best answer.** Linoleic acid contains two π-bonds, both with cis geometry. When linoleic acid is treated with FADH$_2$, the result is hydrogenation of the diene and the formation of the aliphatic carboxylic acid (of eighteen carbons) stearic acid. The gain of four hydrogen atoms increases the molecular mass of the acid (by four), and the loss of unsaturation results in more molecular flexibility, which results in a higher melting point. Unsaturated fats, with less flexibility and therefore less ability to engage in intermolecular interactions, have lower melting points than saturated fats of comparable mass. This is common organic chemistry knowledge that you should have addressed when comparing vegetable and animal fats. The correct answer is choice **D**.

16. **Choice B is the best answer.** It is stated in the passage that corn oil is 63% linoleic acid. Looking at the information in Table 1 shows that linoleic acid consists of eighteen carbons and has two π-bonds. Choices C and D are eliminated, because they only have sixteen carbons. Choice A is eliminated, because it has three π-bonds. The best answer is choice **B**. You can try to match the exact location of each π-bond from the formula in Table 1 to the drawing in the answer choices, but doing so is not time efficient. Once you have isolated an answer using process of elimination, try not to waste too much time verifying that answer by a second pathway no matter how much a part of you yearns to do it.

17. **Choice C is the best answer.** Oleic acid is an eighteen-carbon acid with one π-bond between the eighth and ninth carbons. The π-bond in oleic acid has cis orientation. Treating oleic acid with deuterium (D_2) and a catalytic metal like palladium adds a deuterium atom to each of the carbons in the π-bond of the alkene molecule. The two deuterium atoms add in a syn fashion relative to one another at carbons eight and nine. The result is the formation of two new chiral centers. There are no chiral centers to begin with, so the product has two chiral centers. The best answer is choice **C**.

18. **Choice A is the best answer.** Cell fluidity depends on the packing of the alkyl groups in the cell membrane. Saturated alkyl groups pack best, as evident by the higher melting points of saturated alkanes relative to unsaturated alkanes of the same size. Cell fluidity is more reduced by a long alkyl chain than a short alkyl chain. Arachidic acid is twenty carbons in length and contains no π-bonds, so it will reduce cell fluidity more than arachadonic acid (which has four π-bonds), lauric acid (which only has twelve carbons), and linioleic acid (which has three π-bonds). Choice **A** is the best answer.

19. **Choice B is the best answer.** The *most* bromine per molecule is consumed by the fatty acid with the greatest number of π-bonds present in its structure. For every π-bond present, one molecule of bromine liquid will be consumed. Arachidonic acid contains four π-bonds total, while arachidic acid has no π-bonds present in its structure, lauric acid has no π-bonds present in its structure, and linolenic acid has three π-bonds present in its structure. Arachidonic acid is the most unsaturated of the four choices. The best answer is thus choice **B**.

20. **Choice B is the best answer.** Palmitoleic acid is a sixteen-carbon chain that contains one π-bond. When palmitoleic acid is fully hydrogenated, it forms the aliphatic acid of sixteen carbons (which is listed in Table 1 as palmitic acid). The best answer choice is **B**.

21. **Choice B is the best answer.** Artic salmon swim in water at or close to 0°C, so the low temperature of their environment will naturally reduce their cell fluidity. To compensate for the reduced fluidity caused by the surrounding cold, they have more unsaturated fats in their cell membranes to raise cell fluidity (counteracting the effects of the cold water). Of the four answer choices, linoleic is the most unsaturated with two π-bonds. Oleic has only one π-bond and both lauric acid and myristic acid have no π-bonds at all. Linoleic acid, choice **B**, is the best answer.

Questions 22 - 25   **Not Based on a Descriptive Passage**

22. **Choice C is the best answer.** By symmetry, there are four unique carbons on methylcyclopentane, therefore chlorination can occur at a total of four different sites (four different carbons). This yields a total of four structural isomers. The correct answer is choice **C**.

23. **Choice A is the best answer.** Bergamontene contains fifteen carbons, so it is likely made from three 5-carbon isoprene units. We can't be sure without analyzing the structure to find the isoprene fragments, but that is not time efficient. Choice **A** is the best answer so far, and shall remain our choice until a better one comes. Bergamontene is a hydrocarbon with no heteroatoms, so it is a terpene and not a terpenoid. This eliminates choice B. Bergamontene has two π-bonds and a cyclohexane ring, so at first look choice C is tempting. But the molecule is bicyclic, meaning it has a second ring, the four-membered ring connected to the cyclohexane ring. Bergamontene has four units of unsaturation, not three. This eliminates choice C. To verify this, bergamontene has 24 hydrogens and therefore a formula of $C_{15}H_{24}$. The units of unsaturation are $(2(15) + 2 - 24)/2 = 4$, so choice C is eliminated. There are three chiral centers on bergamontene, so 8 (2^3) is the maximum number of stereoisomers, not 16. This eliminates choice D and secures choice **A** as the best answer.

24. **Choice C is the best answer.** To have a dipole *not* equal to zero is a convoluted was of saying that the molecule has a dipole. We are looking for polar compounds. Cis compounds have dipoles because of their symmetry so Compound III has a dipole. Ethylene is perfectly symmetric, so choice Compound II is nonpolar. This eliminates choices A and B. The question comes down to: "Is Compound I polar or not?" Compound I is not polar, because the methyl groups on the alkene cancel one another and sum to a resultant vector of 0. Only Compound III is polar, so you must choose choice **C** for optimal results of correctness.

25. **Choice D is the best answer.** Plants and animals use terpenes to either attract or repel a target, so a terpene needs to be volatile and have an odor that nearby prey or mates can detect. Choices A and B are both properties of terpenes, so they are eliminated. Terpenes are generally liquids, so choice C is a valid statement. Choice C is eliminated. Terpenes are hydrophobic and thus not water soluble, so choice **D** is an invalid statement. Choice **D** is the best answer.

52-Question Hydrocarbon Practice Exam

Hydrocarbon Exam Scoring Scale

Raw Score	MCAT Score
45 - 52	13 - 15
36 - 44	10 - 12
25 - 35	7 - 9
17 - 24	4 - 6
1 - 16	1 - 3

A researcher treats an unknown alkane with chlorine gas (Cl_2) in the presence of low-end ultraviolet light at 25°C. After three minutes of 80W exposure, the light is removed, and the system is maintained at 25°C. After an hour, the system is vented to remove hydrochloric acid side product and the atmosphere is replaced with nitrogen gas. Once the system is thoroughly vented, unreacted alkane is removed under reduced atmospheric pressure via distillation. The remaining product mixture is analyzed using gas chromatography and mass spectroscopy. The results show that there are three structural isomers formed in measurable quantities. Each of the three structural isomers has a molecular mass of 132.5 grams per mole.

Elemental analysis of all three isomers shows that each contains 63.2% carbon by mass. This leads the researcher to conclude that each of the structural isomers is the result of monochlorination of the original alkane. Further analysis using rate studies and spectroscopy shows that the chlorination reaction proceeded by way of a free-radical mechanism involving initiation, two sequential propagation steps, and termination. Free-radical chlorination reaction is not highly selective, so all three isomers are present in detectable quantities. Free-radical bromination under similar conditions is found to yield a tertiary alkyl bromide as the predominant isomer in the product mixture.

1. In purifying the crude product mixture, which of the following accurately describes how the corresponding impurity could be removed from solution?

   A. HCl can be sublimed out of solution.
   B. Cl_2 can be separated using gravity filtration.
   C. The chlorohydrocarbon products can be distilled from one another.
   D. The HCl can be precipitated from solution by gradually decreasing the pH of the solution.

2. Based on the results of the experiment, which of the following statements are valid?

   I: A $C-C$ single bond has a greater bond dissociation energy than a $C-H$ bond.
   II: Alkanes are more susceptible to free radical chlorination than monochlorinated alkylchlorides.
   III: Primary free radicals are more stable than tertiary free radicals.

   A. I only
   B. I and II only
   C. I and III only
   D. I, II, and III are all valid

3. Which of the following IUPAC names is NOT possible for one of the structural isomers formed in the reaction?

   A. 1-chloro-1,1-dimethylcyclopentane
   B. 2-chloro-1,1-dimethylcyclopentane
   C. 3-chloro-1,1-dimethylcyclopentane
   D. 1-chloromethyl-1-methylcyclopentane

4. How can the distribution of structural isomers formed in the reaction be explained?

   A. There are three unique carbons in the alkane reactant.
   B. There are three unique hydrogens in the alkane reactant.
   C. There is unequal attack of the alkane reactant with respect to the top side and bottom side of the molecule.
   D. There were three different isotopes of chlorine present in the Cl_2 reactant.

5. Which of the following steps is (are) a propagation step in the chlorination mechanism?

   I: $Cl_2 + R \cdot \rightarrow R\text{-}Cl + Cl \cdot$
   II: $Cl \cdot + R \cdot \rightarrow R\text{-}Cl$
   III: $R\text{-}H + Cl \cdot \rightarrow H\text{-}Cl + R \cdot$

   A. I only
   B. II only
   C. I and II only
   D. I and III only

6. Tert-butyl bromide would result from the free-radical bromination of which of the following alkane reactants?

   A. *n*-Butane
   B. 2-Methylpropane
   C. 2-Methylbutane
   D. *sec*-Butane

Terpenes are hydrocarbons that are built from isoprene (2-methyl-1,3-butadiene). In nature, they form from activated isoprene that contains a pyrophosphate group at carbon 4. Activated isoprene is built from acetyl CoA. Many organic chemists have developed synthetic pathways to obtain rare terpenes in higher abundance than they can be obtained using steam distillation or extraction of natural materials.

The term comes from *turpentine*, a viscous, natural extract from the resin of pine trees. Turpentine was found to contain hydrocarbons that were multiples of C_5H_8. Terpenes are responsible for the smell, flavor, and in some instance pharmacological effects of many natural substances such as flowers and fruits. Figure 1 below shows four terpenoids (derivatives of terpenes which contain oxygen).

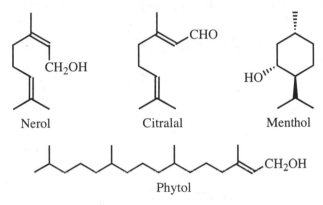

Nerol   Citralal   Menthol

Phytol

Figure 1. Examples of Terpenoids

Terpenes are generically named for their carbon content. All have multiples of five carbons and are given prefixes of *hemi-* (C_5), *mono* (C_{10}), *sesqui-* (C_{15}), *di-* (C_{20}), *sester-* (C_{25}), *tri-* (C_{30}), and so on.

7. Which of the following structures is NOT a terpene?

A.

B.

C.

D.

8. What terpene requires three new carbon-carbon bonds to form when synthesized from isoprene?

A. A linear sesquiterpene

B. A cyclic sesquiterpene

C. A linear sesterterpene

D. A cyclic diterpene

9. In the biosynthesis from isopenyenyl-pyrophosphate (activated isoprene) to nerol, what is true?

A. One unit of unsaturation is lost

B. Pyrophosphate acts as a leaving group

C. Two new carbon-carbon bonds are formed

D. NADPH and H^+ are required

10. Which of the following is/are TRUE regarding terpenes?

I. Biological isoprene is derived from 3 acetyl CoA molecules and requires a decarboxylation reaction.

II. Terpenes are often insoluble in water.

III. Linear monoterpenes are highly chiral.

A. I only

B. II only

C. I and II only

D. I and III only

11. Terpenes are best described as:

A. Acetal polymers

B. Lipids

C. Polyamides

D. Starches

12. Which of the following terpenes would exhibit the highest lambda max for absorption in the UV-visible range?

A.   B.

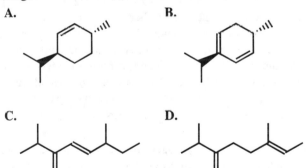

C.   D.

13. What is NOT true for the terpenoids shown in Figure 1?

A. Of the monoterpenes, menthol has the highest molecular mass.

B. Phytol can be classified as diterpene.

C. Formation of menthol requires two new carbon-carbons when synthesized from isoprene.

D. Nerol results from head-to-tail connectivity of two isoprene units while citralal does not.

Prostaglandins are similar to hormones with a notable exception that they are produced at the cellular level. They are said to be derivatives of prostanoic acid, but are in fact synthesized from a linear twenty-carbon tetraunsaturated all-*cis* fatty acid (arachidonic acid). Prostaglandins are classified according to the functional groups on their five-membered ring and numbered according to the number of π-bonds in their structure. Figure 1 shows some types of prostaglandins and their common precursor, PGH$_2$.

Figure 1 Selected Prostaglandins derived from PGH$_2$

Thromboxanes are derived from PGH$_2$, and they have a six-membered oxane ring rather than a cyclopentane ring. Biosyntheis of prostaglandins is triggered by a signal received by the cell membrane. Arachidonic acid is released from the phospholipid (second carbon of glycerol) by a phospholipase A2 reaction. Arachidonic acid is first converted into PGG$_2$ via the cyclooxygenase pathway before PGG$_2$ is converted into the target prostaglandin.

14. PGG$_2$ has a hydrogen peroxyl group at carbon-15 where PGH$_2$ a hydroxyl group. How can PGG$_2$ be converted into PGH$_2$?

   A. By using an oxidizing agent.
   B. By using an reducing agent.
   C. By using an epoxidizing agent.
   D. By using a protonating agent.

15. PGD$_2$ is best described as being:

   A. a conformational isomer of PGE$_2$.
   B. a diastereomer of PGE$_2$.
   C. an enantiomer of PGE$_2$.
   D. a structural isomer of PGE$_2$.

16. Which of the following statements accurately reflect the structures shown in Figure 1?

   I. PGB$_2$ has a longer wavelength absorbance in UV-visible spectroscopy than PGD$_2$.

   II. Conversion from PGH$_2$ to PGD$_2$ involves a chiral-specific oxidation of carbon.

   III. Thormboxane has two fewer stereogenic carbons than PGH$_2$.

   A. I only
   B. III only
   C. I and II only
   D. I and III only

17. Which of the following compounds is arachidonic acid?

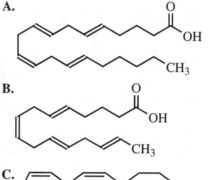

18. What type of reaction had to transpire in the synthesis of PGB$_2$?

   A. An elimination between C-8 and C-12.
   B. An elimination between C-9 and C-10.
   C. An electrocyclic ring closure.
   D. An electrocyclic ring opening.

19. Which observation does NOT correlate with the corresponding compound?

   A. PGB$_2$ has two stereocenters with R configuration.
   B. PGD$_2$ has an IR absorbance at 1717 cm^{-1}.
   C. PGE$_2$ has a strong UV-visible absorbance between 200 nm and 400 nm.
   D. PGH$_2$ has two broad signals in its ^{1}H NMR.

Questions 20 through 23 are **NOT** based on a descriptive passage.

20. What is the most abundant product in the bromination of 2-methylbutane?

A. 1-bromo-2-methylbutane
B. 2-bromo-2-methylbutane
C. 2-bromo-3-methylbutane
D. 1-bromo-3-methylbutane

21. Leukotriene A4, LTA4, is derived from arachadonic acid. Its structure is shown below:

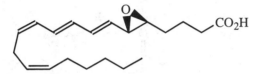

What is NOT true of LTA4?

A. LTA4 has six units of unsaturation.
B. LTA4 has six π-electrons in a conjugated system.
C. LTA4 is capable of undergoing 1,2-, 1,4-, 1,6-, or 1,8-addition when treated with an electrophile and nucleophile.
D. LTA4 has more sp^2-hybridized carbons than it has sp^3-hybridized carbons.

22. A conjugated diene is necessary in which of the following reactions?

A. Claisen rearrangement
B. Clemmensen reduction
C. Cope rearrangement
D. Diels-Alder cycloaddition

23. Which of the following carbocations is the most stable structure possible for the indicated cation?

A.

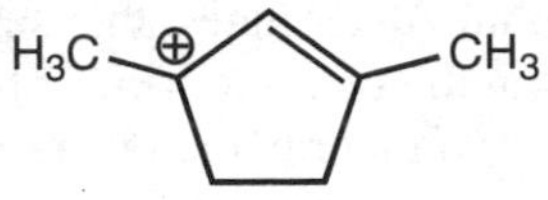

B.

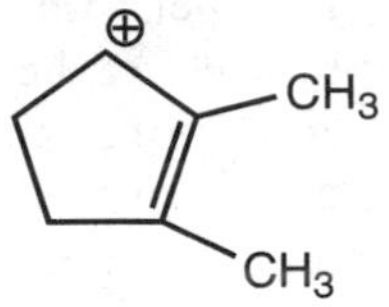

C.

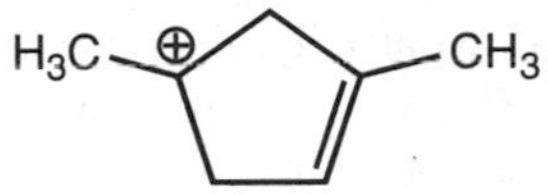

D.

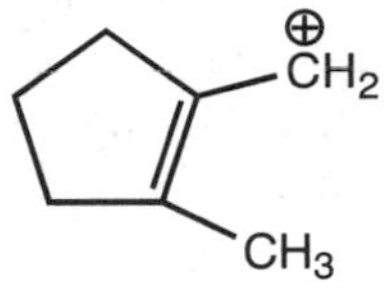

In a Diels-Alder reaction, the alignment of the diene with respect to the dieneophile determines the structural orientation of the substituents in the final product. If both the diene and the dieneophile are asymmetric, then there are two different orientations that the two reactants can assume in the transition state. The preferred alignment can be predicted using resonance theory, where the reactants align such that a partially positive site attacks a partially negative site. A generic Diels-Alder reaction of an asymmetric diene with an asymmetric dieneophile is shown in Figure 1.

Compound A   **Compound B**

Figure 1 Asymmetric Diels-Alder reaction

If the reactants are asymmetric, the product distribution of Product A to Product B is never 50-to-50. When X is electron donating and Y is electron donating, Product A is the major product. When X is electron withdrawing and Y is electron donating, Product B is the major product. Table 1 lists the product distributions for a series of reactions where the X and Y groups are varied. In both Product A and Product B, the Y group is always cis to the carbonyl group.

X	Y	A	B
OCH$_3$	NHCH$_3$	94%	6%
OCH$_3$	CH$_3$	88%	12%
CH$_3$	NHCH$_3$	87%	13%
CH$_3$	CH$_3$	63%	37%
COCH$_3$	NHCH$_3$	18%	82%
COCH$_3$	CH$_3$	31%	69%

Table 1

The product distribution in Table 1 supports the prediction about the electron donating and withdrawing effects based on resonance theory. A methyl substituent is considered to be mildly electron donating.

24. If the Y-substituent is a second carbonyl functional group (—CR=O), making the alkene reactant symmetric, what would be predicted for the distribution between Product A and Product B?

    A. > 50% Product A; < 50% Product B
    B. < 50% Product A; > 50% Product B
    C. 50% Product A; 50% Product B
    D. Product A and Product B are the same compound

25. Which of the following conclusions can be drawn from the data in Table 1?

    A. OCH$_3$ is more electron donating than CH$_3$ because OCH$_3$ in the X position yields more product A.
    B. OCH$_3$ is more electron donating than CH$_3$ because OCH$_3$ in the X position yields more product B.
    C. CH$_3$ is more electron donating than OCH$_3$ because CH$_3$ in the X position yields more product A.
    D. CH$_3$ is more electron donating than OCH$_3$ because CH$_3$ in the X position yields more product B.

26. Predict the major product for the following reaction:

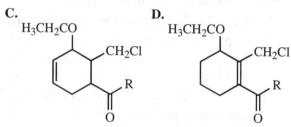

    A.   B.

    C.   D.

27. Two structural isomers are formed from Diels-Alder reactions that involve:

    A. a symmetric diene with a symmetric dieneophile.
    B. an asymmetric diene with symmetric dieneophile.
    C. a symmetric diene with asymmetric dieneophile.
    D. an asymmetric diene with asymmetric dieneophile.

28. Counting stereoisomers, how many possible products can be formed from the following reaction?

    A. 2
    B. 4
    C. 6
    D. 12

GO ON TO THE NEXT PAGE

Hofmann elimination generates a less-substituted alkene than standard elimination reactions. It is similar to an E_2-reaction, but with Hofmann elimination, the leaving group is a bulky trimethyl amine moiety. Because of the bulk of the leaving group, hydrogens on secondary and tertiary carbons are difficult to align in an anti fashion. This results in the favored transition state involving a hydrogen on a primary carbon. Hofmann elimination is shown in Figure 1 below.

Step 1

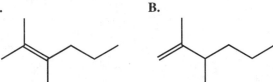

Step 2

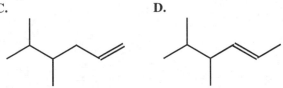

Figure 1. Hofmann Elimination

Hofmann elimination requires exhaustive methylation of an amine group to form the bulky leaving group. Because of the cationic nature of the nitrogen after exhaustive methylation, it is an excellent leaving group that will not attack the alkene that is formed.

29. Why is Ag_2O a better reagent in Step 2 than K_2O?

   A. Ag_2O is a stronger acid in organic solvents than K_2O.

   B. Ag_2O is less soluble in ether than K_2O.

   C. Ag^+ cation binds nitrogen stronger than K^+ cation binds nitrogen.

   D. Ag^+ cation binds I^-, which precipitates from solution.

30. What forms when 2-amino-2,3-dimethyl hexane is treated with excess methyl iodide followed by treatment with silver oxide in water?

   A.

   B.

   C.

   D.

31. In Hofmann elimination, the amine acts as:

   A. both a nucleophile and a base.

   B. a nucleophile only.

   C. both an electrophile and a base.

   D. an electrophile only.

32. All of the following statements about Hofmann elimination are valid EXCEPT that it:

   A. results in the formation of the non-Zaitsev alkene product.

   B. takes advantage of steric hindrance in its transition state.

   C. results in the rearrangement of the alkene pi-bond.

   D. requires a strong base to remove the proton from a carbon.

33. Hofmann elimination would be a necessary step in which of the following syntheses (where an alkene is converted into a vicinal diol in the final step)?

   A.

   B.

   C.

   D.

Questions 34 through 37 are **NOT** based on a descriptive passage.

34. What is the major organic product of the reaction below?

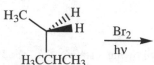

H3C
H
H
H3CCHCH3
Br2
hν

A.

BrH2C
H
H
H3CCHCH3

B.

H3C
Br
H
H3CCHCH3

C.

H3C
H
Br
H3CCHCH3

D.

H3C
H
H
H3CCBrCH3

35. All of the following observations are associated with an E_2 reaction EXCEPT:

A. the base must be bulky and strong.

B. whether the major product has cis or trans geometry depends on the stereochemistry of the reactant.

C. that rearrangement is observed.

D. heat is required to drive the reaction.

36. When the following reaction is carried out, why does the optical activity disappear?

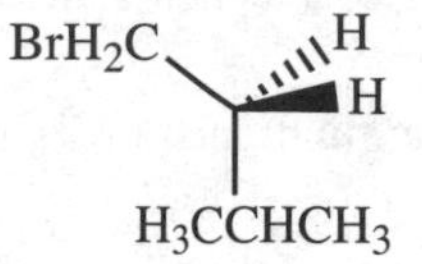

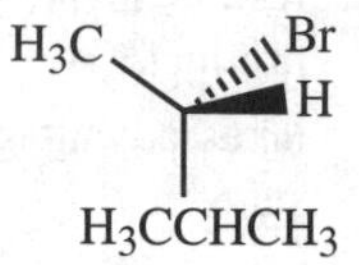

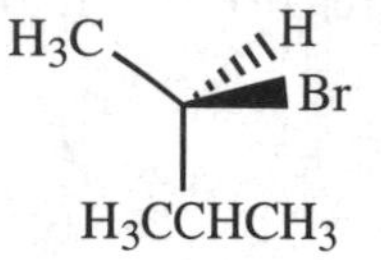

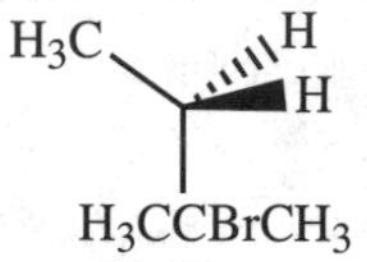

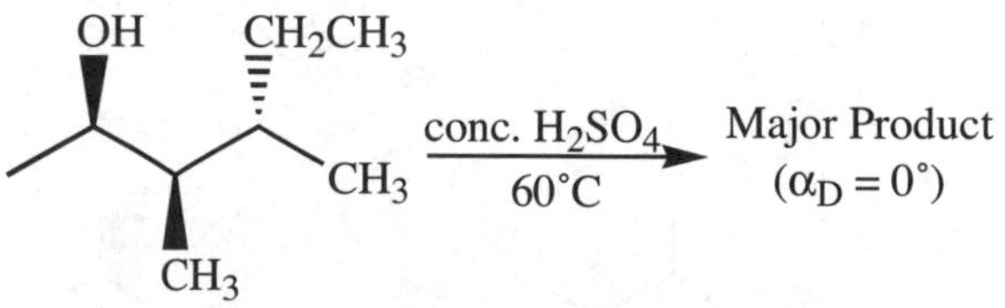

OH
CH2CH3
CH3
CH3
conc. H2SO4
60°C
Major Product
(αD = 0°)

A. After the sulfate group substitutes for the hydroxyl group, the chiral centers cancel one another.

B. The product is meso.

C. The major product is an achiral alkene, resulting from rearrangement.

D. The product is an achiral alcohol.

37. How many units of unsaturation are present in the product of chlorocyclohexane and strong base and heat?

A. 0

B. 1

C. 2

D. 3

Passage VI (Questions 38 - 43)

Terpenes and terpenoids are natural compounds found in plants and animals that are built from 5-carbon reactants. Figure 1 shows the sesquiterpenoid (±)-occidentalol.

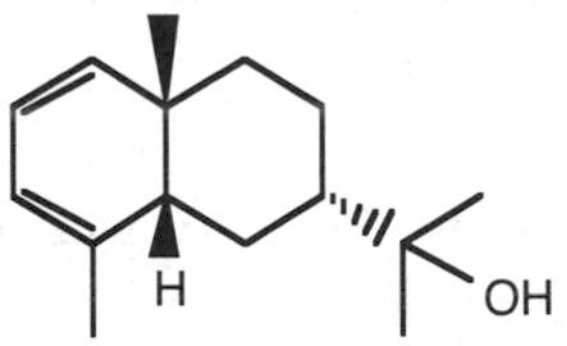

Figure 1 (±)-Occidentalol

A multistep synthesis leading to occidentalol begins with the conversion of Compound 1 into Compound 6, which can further react to form occidentalol. Figure 2 shows the synthesis of Compound 6.

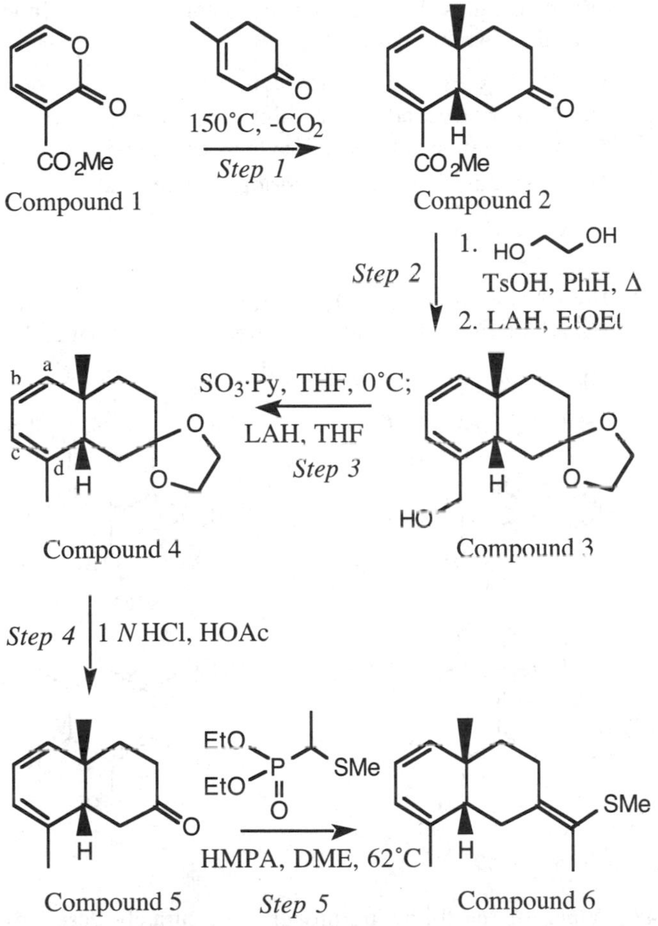

Figure 2 Synthesis of Compound 6

Step 1 involves a Diels-Alder cycloaddition followed by decarboxylation of the polycyclic system. Step 2 involves the conversion of the ketone group of Compound 2 into a ketal followed by the reduction of the ester into a primary alcohol. Further reduction of the vinylic alcohol group in Compound 3 forms a methyl group in Compound 4. The protecting group is removed in Step 4 to reform the ketone. Compound 5 undergoes a variation on the Wittig reaction to form an alkene in Compound 6.

38. How many chiral centers are present in occidentalol?

- A. 1
- B. 2
- C. 3
- D. 4

39. Terpenes containing fifteen carbons are best described as:

- A. monoterpenes.
- B. diterpenes.
- C. triterpenes.
- D. sesquiterpenes.

40. Which compound has the longest maximum wavelength of absorbance, λ_{max}, in ultraviolet spectroscopy?

- A. Compound 1
- B. Compound 2
- C. Compound 3
- D. Compound 4

41. What intermediate compound forms in Step 1 before the decarboxylation takes place?

- A. A cyclohexadiene
- B. A cyclohexene
- C. An α,β-unsaturated ketone
- D. A lactam

42. To synthesize occidentalol, Compound 6 is first converted into a methyl ketone, which is then treated with MeLi in Et_2O at $-70°C$. What is the role of MeLi?

- A. To act as an electrophile and accept electron density form the alpha carbon.
- B. To act as a nucleophile and donate electron density to the carbonyl carbon.
- C. To act as a base and deprotonate the alpha proton.
- D. To act as an acid and protonate the carbonyl oxygen.

43. If Compound 4 were treated with strong acid, at which carbon in the π-network is it most likely to gain H^+?

- A. Carbon a
- B. Carbon b
- C. Carbon c
- D. Carbon d

307

GO ON TO THE NEXT PAGE

Oxidation reactions are crucial for life, but in excess they can be damaging to living organisms. In the presence of O_2, oxidation is common, so humans must employ a series of antioxidants to maintain a balance. Natural antioxidants are generally classified as either hydrophilic or lipophilic. Lipophilic antioxidants protect cell membranes from lipid peroxidation while hydrophilic antioxidants typically react with oxidants in the cell cytosol and the blood plasma.

A common water-soluble antioxidant found in humans is glutathione. Glutathione is formed from three amino acids, although the first amide bond is not a typical peptide linkage. A common lipid-soluble antioxidant is ubiquinol. Ubiquinol contains a highly substituted benzene ring and a long chain unsaturated hydrocarbon. Both compounds are shown in Figure 1 below.

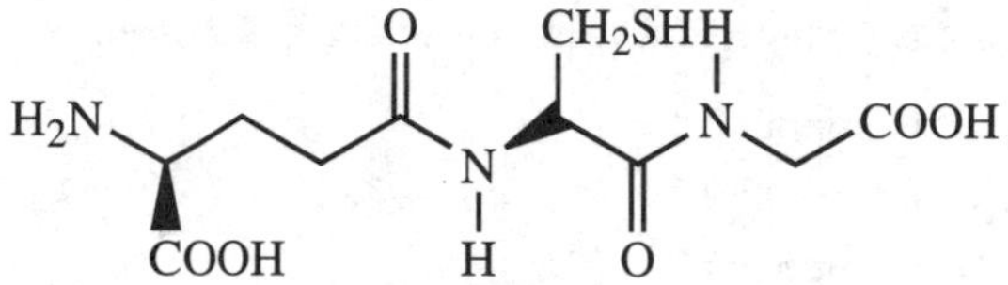

Figure 1. Glutathione and Ubiquinol

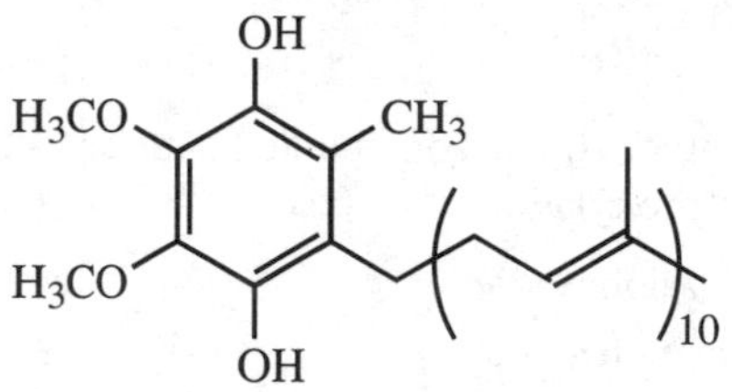

Ubiquinol serves as a free radical scavenger in the body and is known to help regenerate other antioxidants such as ascorbate (Vitamin C) and tocopherol (Vitamin E). These help to slow lipid peroxidation, shown in Figure 2,

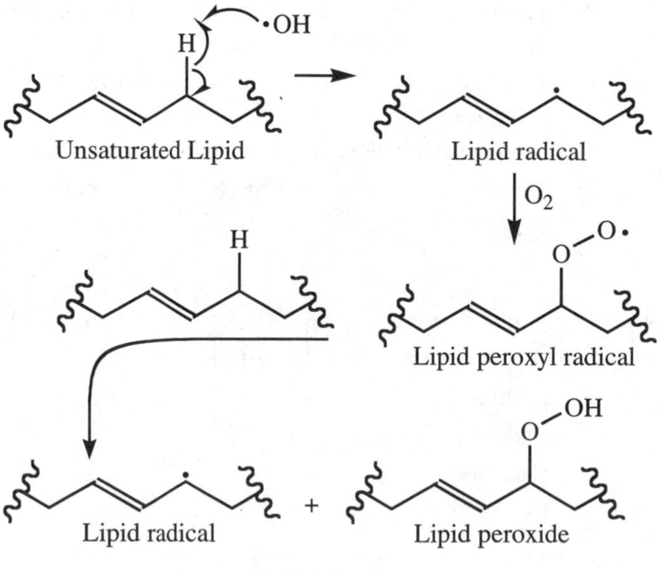

Figure 2. Lipid Peroxidation

44. Glutathione is likely an antioxidant because:

    A. the thiol group can form a semi-stable free radical.
    B. it is naturally a free radical.
    C. carboxyl acid groups are peroxides.
    D. the carbonyl groups are readily reduced by O_2.

45. The conversion of lipid peroxyl radical into lipid radical is best described as a:

    A. free radical initiation reaction.
    B. free radical termination reaction.
    C. free radical propagation reaction.
    D. nucleophilic oxidation reaction.

46. What accounts for the unusual stability of the lipid radical shown in Figure 2?

    A. Tertiary free radicals are highly stable.
    B. Primary free radicals are highly reactive.
    C. Conjugation helps stabilize the free radical.
    D. Free radicals with sp^2-hybridization are stable.

47. Which structure is NOT a resonance structure for ubiquinol after it has undergone free radical oxidation?

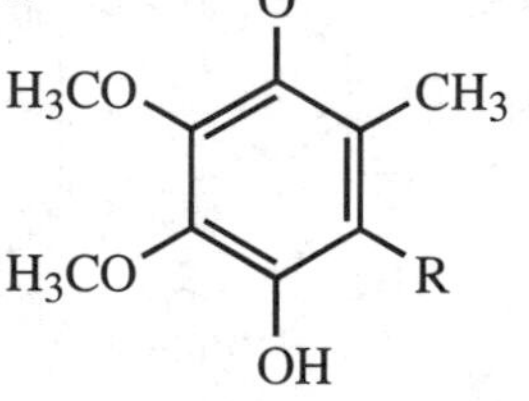

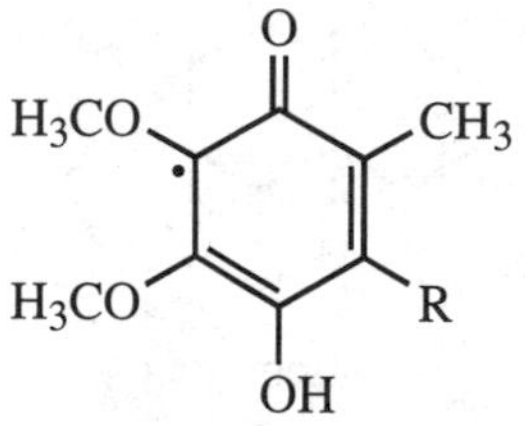

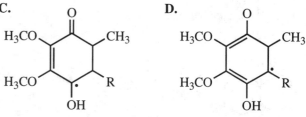

48. Which of the following properties accurately describes ubiquinol?

    I. Ubiquinol has a pK_a around 10.

    II. Ubiquinol has high hydrophilicity.

    III. Ubiquinol is readily oxidized.

    A. I only
    B. II only
    C. I and II only
    D. I and III only

     GO ON TO THE NEXT PAGE

Questions 49 through 52 are **NOT** based on a descriptive passage.

49. Which of the following reactions is a propagation reaction?

A. $H_3C\cdot + H_3CCH_2CH_3 \rightarrow 2\ H_3C\cdot + H_3CCH_2\cdot$

B. $H_3C\cdot + H_3CCH_2\cdot \rightarrow H_3CCH_2CH_3$

C. $H_3CH_2C\cdot + H_3CCH_3 \rightarrow 2\ H_3CCH_2\cdot + \frac{1}{2}\ H_2$

D. $H_3C\cdot + H_3CCH_2CH_3 \rightarrow CH_4 + (H_3C)_2CH\cdot$

50. All of the following are physical properties of a terpene EXCEPT:

A. High lipid solubility
B. High boiling point
C. Low volatility
D. High specific rotation

51. Which of the following compounds is an allylic alcohol?

A.

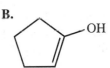

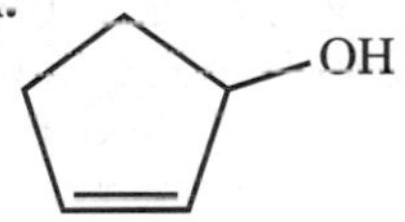

B.

C.

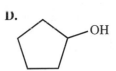

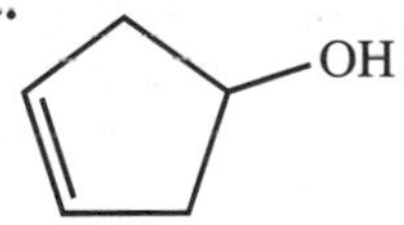

D.

52. How do the physical properties of *n*-hexane compare to those of 2,3-dimethylbutane?

A. The boiling point for *n*-hexane is lower.
B. The ambient vapor pressure for *n*-hexane is higher.
C. The melting point for *n*-hexane is higher.
D. the density of *n*-hexane liquid is greater.

1. C	2. B	3. A	4. B	5. D	6. B
7. B	8. B	9. B	10. C	11. B	12. C
13. D	14. B	15. D	16. C	17. C	18. A
19. A	20. B	21. D	22. D	23. A	24. D
25. A	26. A	27. D	28. B	29. D	30. B
31. A	32. C	33. D	34. D	35. C	36. C
37. C	38. C	39. D	40. A	41. B	42. B
43. A	44. A	45. C	46. C	47. D	48. D
49. D	50. D	51. A	52. C		

YOU ARE DONE.

Answers to 52-Question Hydrocarbons Practice Exam

1. **Choice C is the best answer.** HCl is a gas and sublimation involves solids, so choice A can be eliminated immediately. In addition, the passage told us that hydrochloric acid was vented out. Chlorine gas also escapes to the environment when the system is vented, so choice B is eliminated. HCl reacts with base so separation would require an increasing pH, not a decreasing pH. This eliminates choice D. Structural isomers have different boiling points, so the products can be separated using distillation. Choice **C** is the best answer.

2. **Choice B is the best answer.** In a free-radical reaction, a carbon-hydrogen bond is broken before forming a carbon-halogen bond. Because the weakest bond is broken, a carbon-hydrogen bond must be weaker than a carbon-carbon bond. This makes Statement I valid. No multiple halogenation products are observed to a notable extent in this experiment, so either an alkane is more reactive than an alkyl halide or a carbon-halogen bond is the weakest bond in a monohalogenated hydrocarbon and thus the Cl is removed rather than a second hydrogen. Either way, a second halogen is not added, making Statement II valid in this experiment. Tertiary free-radicals are more stable than primary free-radicals, so Statement III is invalid. Choice **B** is the best answer.

3. **Choice A is the best answer.** Choice A has five bonds to carbon 1, which is not possible. This makes choice **A** the best answer without having to analyze the reaction. The other three answer choices result from chlorination of 1,1-dimethylcyclopentane at one of the three unique carbons, so choices B, C, and D are all possible.

4. **Choice B is the best answer.** The passage tells us that three unique structural isomers are formed. Structural isomers have different connectivity (bonds), which for this reaction could only be the result of the chlorine atom being bonded to three unique carbons. However, the compound could have more than three unique carbons if there is a quaternary carbon present. A quaternary carbon could not form a bond to chlorine, so choice A, although tempting, is not the best answer. Given that hydrogen is lost to make way for the chlorine atom, there must be three unique types of hydrogen to lose in this chlorination reaction. Choice **B** explains this best. Choice C could have been eliminated because top vs. bottom attack typically results in two stereoisomers, not three structural isomers. Choice D is our throwaway answer, because isotopes do not result in the formation of isomers.

5. **Choice D is the best answer.** Propagation steps involve one free-radical on the reactant side of the equation and one free-radical on the product side of the equation. Reaction II has two free-radicals on the reactant side of the equation and no free-radicals on the product side of the equation, so it is a termination step, not a propagation step. Choices B and C are eliminated. Both Reaction I and Reaction III are propagation steps, because they each have one free-radical on each side of the reaction arrow. Choice **D** is the best answer.

6. **Choice B is the best answer.** Tert-butyl bromide is properly named 2-bromo-2-methylpropane (tert is short for tertiary). It helps to convert the name to IUPAC convention so that we know where the bromine added to the carbon skeleton. Tert-butyl bromide is formed from the bromination of the tertiary carbon of 2-methylpropane, so choice **B** is the best answer.

7. **Choice B is the best answer**. Because terpenes are built from 5-carbon isoprene subunits, they contain a number of carbons that is evenly divisible by 5. Choices A, C, and D all contain ten carbons, while choice **B** has eleven carbons. We have the best answer at this point (choice **B**), but in case you chose to look at other structural features such as head-to-tail connectivity and placement of tertiary carbons, we should consider that as well. Choices A and C have head-to-tail connectivity and two tertiary carbons, so they are standard monoterpenes. Choice D is bicyclic, so it's not as easy to see the connectivity, but it can be seen that it is built from the standard head-to-tail connection plus two more connections between the separate subunits to build the multiple ring system. Choice **B** should stand out as incorrect, because it has a quaternary carbon but is not bicyclic. Choice **B** is not a terpene by structural backbone as well as by carbon count. The best answer is choice **B**.

8. **Choice B is the best answer**. A new carbon-carbon bond must form in a head-to-tail fashion to connect isoprene units forming a linear terpene. To form a cyclic structure, an additional carbon-carbon bond must form for every ring in the structure. A sesquiterpene contains 15 carbons, so it is built from three isoprene subunits. This means that a linear sesquiterpene will require only two new carbon-carbon bonds, not three. Choice A is eliminated. A cyclic sesquiterpene, on the other hand, requires not only the two new carbon-carbon bonds to build the carbon count to fifteen, but also an additional carbon-carbon bond to complete the ring. This means that a cyclic sesquiterpene will require three new carbon-carbon bonds to form, making choice **B** the best answer. A sesterterpene contains 25 carbons, so it is built from five isoprene subunits. This means that a linear sesquiterpene will require four new carbon-carbon bonds, not three. Choice C is eliminated. A cyclic diterpene contains 20 carbons, so it is built from four isoprene subunits. A linear diterpene would require three new carbon-carbon bonds, but because the structure is cyclic, it requires one additional carbon-carbon bond for four total. Choice D is eliminated. The best answer is choice **B**.

9. **Choice B is the best answer**. This question requires some background knowledge that the average student likely doesn't have. When this is the case, you need to either extract it from the passage, or do the best you can at eliminating choices based on what you do know. Nerol is a linear monoterpene, so it requires one new carbon-carbon bond to form head-to-tail between two isoprene subunits. Because only one new carbon-carbon bond forms, choice C is eliminated. Because you start with two isoprene subunits (activated isoprenes in this case), the total number of units of unsaturation must be an even number. Nerol has two units of unsaturation, so if any units of unsaturation are lost it must be an even number, and therefore can't be one. Choice A is eliminated. As it were, activated isoprene has one unit of unsaturation (as shown below). We now have two choices remaining, one that says the coupling reaction involves substitution (choice **B**) and the other that says it involves reduction (choice D). The coupling reaction involves substitution, where pyrophosphate (OPP) is the leaving group. Choice **B** is the best answer.

Geranylpyrophoshpate   Nerol

10. **Choice C is the best answer**. Statement I requires either background information or the counting of carbons and some trust. Acetyl CoA contains two carbons in the acetyl group, so coupling three would yield a six-carbon molecule. After decarboxylation, five carbons would remain, so is possible that biological isoprene forms in this fashion. Given that Statement I is in three of the four answer choices, we should lean towards Statement I being true. In the interest of building knowledge, the full reaction is shown below, confirming that Statement I is in fact true.

Biological Claisen condensation   Biological aldol reaction   ß-Hydroxy-ß-methyl-glutaryl-CoA

Isopentyl-pyrophosphate   (R)-melvanoic acid
(activated isoprene)

Terpenes are hydrocarbons, so they hydrophobic and insoluble in water. This makes Statement II a valid statement, and makes choice **C** the best answer. Linear monoterpenes, such as nerol and citralal, have mostly achiral carbons, so linear monoterpenes are relatively achiral. This makes Statement III invalid, which further supports choice **C**. Choice **C** is the best answer.

11. **Choice B is the best answer**. Terpenes are long hydrocarbons built from isoprene. They are not acetal polymers (built from carbonyls), polyamides (built from amides), or starches (built from carbohydrates). They are classified as lipids, so choice **B** is the best answer.

12. **Choice C is the best answer.** To estimate what will be expected in UV-visible spectroscopy of terpenes, we must recall that π-bonds are UV active. Carbonyls have higher values of lambda max for absorption (λ_{max}) in the UV-visible spectrum than alkenes, and conjugation increases the value of λ_{max}. Given these four choices, the greatest λ_{max} will be associated with the most conjugated species, choosing a carbonyl over an equally conjugated alkene. Choices A and D are eliminated, because neither species is conjugated. Choice **C** is a better option than choice B, because it contains a carbonyl group. Choice **C** is the best answer.

13. **Choice D is correct.** Of the three monoterpenes in Figure 1, menthol has the fewest units of unsaturation, so it therefore has the greatest number of hydrogen atoms (given that the three structures have the same number of other atoms). You are welcome to count the hydrogens if you wish, but for the sake of time you should accept that by determining the units of unsaturation, you are indirectly determining the number of hydrogens. Because menthol has the same number of oxygens and carbons as nerol and citralal, but has a greater number of hydrogens, menthol has the greatest molecular mass of the three compounds. Choice A is valid and therefore eliminated. Phytol has twenty carbons total, which makes it a diterpene. Choice B is valid and therefore eliminated. Menthol is a cyclic monoterpene, so it requires two new carbon-carbon bonds when synthesized from isoprene subunits. The first new carbon-carbon bond connects the subunits head-to-tail while the second carbon-carbon bond closes the ring. Choice C is valid and therefore eliminated. Nerol and citralal have identical carbon-skeletal structures, so they must have been connected in the same fashion. Both form from the head-to-tail connection of two isoprene subunits. Choice **D** is NOT true, so choice **D** is the best answer.

Passage III (Questions 14 - 19)   Prostaglandins

14. **Choice B is the best answer.** The conversion of a peroxyl group (-OOH) to a hydroxyl group (-OH) involves the loss of an oxygen atom. Loss of oxygen is a reductive process, so it requires a reducing agent. The best answer is choice **B**. Choice C should have been eliminated because no three-membered ring with an oxygen is involved and choice D is an alternate way of saying acid. Acid will not remove an oxygen, so choice D is not possible.

15. **Choice D is the best answer.** At first glance, it could be tempting to focus on the chiral carbons and think they are some time of stereoisomers. But the two structures have different functional groups at carbons 9 and 11 (ketone and hydroxyl group versus hydroxyl group and ketone). They are not stereoisomers, so choices A, B, and C can be eliminated. Having different functional groups on corresponding carbons makes the two compounds structural isomers. Choice **D** describes this best.

16. **Choice C is the best answer.** Ultraviolet-visible spectroscopy is used to detect π-bonds. Isolated C=C double bonds absorb UV photons around 180 nm while isolated C=O double bonds absorb around 270 nm. Conjugation raises the wavelength associated with maximum absorbance by about 45 nm. PGB_2 has an alpha-beta unsaturated ketone, PGD_2 has an isolated carbonyl group without conjugation. This means that PGB_2 has a UV-visible absorbance around 45 nm greater than PGD_2. This makes Statement I a valid statement, eliminating choice B. In converting PGH2 into PGD2, a peroxide group is converted into carbonyl group and an alcohol group. This means that the structure increased the number of bonds from carbon to oxygen, which means that carbon was oxidized. The final product has a specific chirality, so the oxidation must have been chirally specific. This makes Statement II a valid statement. This eliminates choices A and D, and leave just choice **C** as the only remaining choice. PGH_2 has four chiral centers on the ring structure plus a fifth one at carbon 15. Thormboxane also has four chiral centers on the ring structure plus a fifth one at carbon 15. This means that thormboxane has the same number of stereogenic carbons as PGH_2, which makes Statement III invalid and confirms that choice **D** is the best answer.

17. **Choice C is the best answer.** The passage tells us that arachidonic acid is a linear twenty-carbon tetraunsaturated all-*cis* fatty acid. Choice A is a twenty carbon carboxylic acid with four π-bonds, which sounds good so far. But all of the double bonds have trans orientation, so choice A is incorrect. Choice B can be eliminated immediately, because it contains only 16 carbons and the doubles bonds have trans alignment. Choice **C** has twenty carbons and four double bonds, so it's looking good so far. The double bonds are all cis, so choice **C** is the best answer. Choice D should have been eliminated immediately because it has only eighteen carbons.

18. **Choice A is the best answer.** PGB_2 has a double bond in the five-membered ring that was not present in the PGH_2 precursor. While double bonds can be formed and broken in electrocyclic reactions, such reactions also result in a change in the number of rings in the system. PGB_2 shows no difference in the number of rings present when compared to PGH_2 precursor, so the reaction cannot be an electrocyclic reaction. Choices C and D are eliminated. The formation of the double bond must result from elimination. The answer is arrived at by counting from the carboxylic acid carbon. The ring is formed from carbons 8 through 12, so the new double bond is formed between C-8 and C-12. The best answer is choice **A**.

19. **Choice A is the best answer.** PGB_2 has no stereocenters on the ring and one at carbon 15 for a total of one chiral carbon. Its one and only chiral center has S configuration, so choice **A** does not correlate with PGB_2. PGD_2 has a ketone group. A carbonyl has an IR absorbance above 1700 cm^{-1}, so a ketone likely accounts for an IR absorbance at 1717 cm^{-1}. Choice B is a valid correlation of structure to spectroscopic observation, so it is eliminated. PGE_2 has four π-bonds, including two carbonyl groups. The presence of π-bonds in a structure results in an absorbance in the ultraviolet-visible range of the EM spectrum, so an absorbance between 200 and 400 nm seems viable. Choice C is a valid correlation of structure to spectroscopic observation, so it is eliminated. PGH_2 has two hydroxyl groups (one in the carboxylic acid group and one at carbon-15). Alcohol protons are broad, which means that those two hydrogens will result in two broad signals in its proton NMR. Choice D is a valid correlation of structure to spectroscopic observation, so it is eliminated. Choice **D** is the only invalid observation, making it the best answer.

---

20. **Choice B is the best answer.** Bromination is so highly selective for tertiary carbons over secondary carbons and primary carbons that the exact quantity of each type of hydrogen need not be accounted for. The most abundant product from a free-radical bromination reaction results from the bromination of a tertiary carbon. In the hydrocarbon reactant, only carbon number two is tertiary, so the most abundant product from the free-radical bromination reaction is 2-bromo-2-methylbutane. This makes choice **B** the best answer. Pick choice **B**, and be a chemistry master.

21. **Choice D is the best answer.** Leukotriene A_4, LTA_4, has four alkene π-bonds, one carbonyl π-bond, and an epoxide ring. This results in a total of six units of unsaturation. Choice A is a valid statement, which eliminates it. LTA_4 has three alkene π-bonds in conjugation, resulting in six π-electrons in a conjugated system. Choice B is a valid statement, which eliminates it. Because of the extensive conjugation, there are several sites at which a nucleophile and an electrophile may add. For instance, if the epoxide oxygen were protonated, a nucleophile could attack the ring or the left carbon of any π-bond to add across the system. This means that 1,2-addition, 1,4-addition, 1,6-addition, and 1,8-addition are all possible. Choice C is a valid statement, which eliminates it. In all likelihood, answer choice C earned the coveted "huh?", meaning you can't eliminate it, because you're just not sure what it means. On a multiple choice exam, uncertainty like this is not a problem. You just need to look at choice **D** and use your testing logic. LTA_4 contains four alkene π-bonds and one carbonyl π-bond, so there are a total of nine sp^2-hybridized carbons. There are twenty carbons in LTA_4, so the remaining eleven carbons must all have sp^3-hybridization. There are more sp^3-hybridized carbons than sp^2-hybridized carbons, so choice **D** is an invalid statement, which makes it the best answer. Process of elimination is your most powerful test0taking tool on a multiple-choice exam.

22. **Choice D is the best answer.** Both the Claisen rearrangement and the Cope rearrangement require dienes, but they need not be conjugated. The two π-bonds must be separated by three sigma bonds, so choices A and C are eliminated. Clemmensen reduction converts a carbonyl into an alkane, so no diene of any kind is required. Choice B is eliminated. A Diels-Alder reaction involves the cyclization of a conjugated diene and a dienophile, so it must have a conjugated diene. This makes choice **D** the best answer.

23. **Choice A is the best answer.** Choice **A** is a tertiary carbocation that can resonate to form another tertiary carbocation. The two resonance structures are equal in stability, so choice **A** is the most stable resonance structure possible for that compound. Choice B is a secondary carbocation that can resonate to form a tertiary carbocation. The secondary carbocation is less stable than the tertiary carbocation, so choice B is not the most stable resonance structure for that compound. Choice B is eliminated. Choice C is a tertiary carbocation, but it has no resonance. If the carbocation undergoes rearrangement, then a more stable carbocation is possible. It is not a resonance structure, because a hydride shift involves migration of a nucleus, but the hydride shift does lead to a more stable carbocation structure. The tertiary carbocation shown is not stabilized by resonance, so choice C should be eliminated. Choice D is a primary carbocation that can resonate to form a tertiary carbocation. The primary carbocation is less stable than the tertiary carbocation, so choice D is not the most stable resonance structure. Choice D is eliminated. Of these four answer choices, the best one is choice **A**.

---

24. **Choice D is the best answer.** If the Y-group is a carbonyl group, then it is the exact same substituent as the other carbonyl group (on the adjacent carbon), making the compound symmetric and thus indistinguishable. Both Product A and Product B are the same compound, if the reactant is symmetric, so choice **D** is the best answer.

25. **Choice A is the best answer.** In the second paragraph of the passage it is stated that when X is an electron-donating group, product A is the major product. Because the reactant with the OCH_3 group yields more Product A than the reactant with the CH_3 group in comparable reactions, it can be concluded that an OCH_3 group is more electron donating than a CH_3 group. The best answer is choice **A**. Choices B and D should have been eliminated, because the major product from the reaction is Product A, not Product B.

26. **Choice A is the best answer.** By analogy to other alkoxy groups, OCH_2CH_3 (ethoxy) is an electron-donating group like OCH_3 (methoxy). The presence of the electron-donating group makes Product A the more favorable product. Product A from the generic reaction of the passage is choice **A**. Be careful not to choose B without paying attention to the location of the double bond. The double bond in choice B is on the side opposite from where it should be formed in a Diels-Alder reaction. Pick choice **A**, and you will score like the mighty MCAT whiz that you are!

27. **Choice D is the best answer.** Structural isomers have different bonds (connectivity of atoms). Product A and Product B in the sample reaction in Figure 1 are structural isomers. Structural isomers result when both reactants are asymmetric. The best answer is choice **D**.

28. **Choice B is the best answer.** For the reaction in this question, with two asymmetric reactants, there are two possible structural isomers (corresponding to Product A and Product B in the generic reaction). In both structural isomers, there are two new chiral centers that have formed. For a compound with two chiral centers that cannot be meso, there are four (2^2) possible stereoisomers, meaning that there are four possible stereoisomers for each structural isomer. The overall result is that there are eight possible isomers total, but there is not a choice of 8, so we must be missing something. In reality, not all eight isomers can be formed in a Diels-Alder reaction. The product results from the syn-alignment in the transition state, so only two stereoisomers can form for each of the structural isomer possibilities.. In a typical Diels-Alder reaction such as this, the major products are an enantiomeric pair of one of the two possible structural isomers. The less favorable structural isomer may also be formed, resulting in an enantiomeric pair, but it is generally in much lower concentration than the more favorable structural isomer. Overall there are four possible isomers formed, so choice **B** is the best answer.

Passage V (Questions 29 - 33)   ·   **Hofmann Elimination**

29. **Choice D is the best answer.** Step 2 of Hofmann elimination requires deprotonation of a hydrogen from carbon, the leaving of the bulky alkylated amine group, and the complexing of the iodide anion. This means that Ag_2O is acting like a base and not like an acid, so choice A can be eliminated. You should also recall from general chemistry that metal oxides are basic compounds. The solubility of Ag_2O and K_2O in ether is irrelevant given that the reaction is taking place in water, so choice B is eliminated. Nitrogen is not being bound by any cation in the Hofmann elimination reaction, so choice C can be eliminated. The reason for selecting Ag_2O as the base rather than K_2O is that Ag^+ is better at binding I^- to form an insoluble precipitate in water than K^+ is. The best answer is choice **D**.

30. **Choice B is the best answer.** The reaction described in the question is a Hofmann elimination, which yields the least-substituted alkene product, which is often a terminal alkene. Choice A is eliminated immediately, because it is a highly substituted alkene. The amine group is connected to the alkyl chain at carbon 2 in the reactant, so the pi-bond that forms in the alkene product must include carbon 2. Choices C and D have pi-bonds that do not include carbon 2, so they can both be eliminated, which leaves only choice **B** remaining. The best answer is choice **B**. The reaction is shown below.

31. **Choice A is the best answer.** During the exhaustive methylation step (Step 1), the amine first attacks a methyl chloride molecule to form a bond to carbon and kick out the chloride leaving group. This makes the amine a nucleophile, which eliminates choices C and D. At this point the amine carries a positive charge and must be deprotonated before it can nucleophilically attack another methyl chloride. Another amine in solution must act as a base and remove the proton from the more substituted amine, so some of the amines in solution are acting as a weak base rather than as a nucleophile. This means that overall the amine is acting as both a nucleophile and a base. The best answer is choice **A**.

32. Choice C is the best answer. Hofmann elimination forms the least substituted alkene of the possible alkene products. The Zaitsev product is the most highly substituted alkene, so Hofmann elimination does in fact form the non-Zaitsev alkene product. Choice A is a valid statement and thus eliminated. The reason for the formation of the less-hindered alkene is because the bulky quaternary ammonium group must align in a way to minimize steric hindrance in the transition state, so Hofmann elimination does in fact take advantage of steric hindrance in its transition state. Choice B is valid and thus eliminated. The alkene that results is less-substituted not because of rearrangement, but because of steric hindrance. Choice **C** is an invalid statement, and is thus the best answer. Choice D is a valid statement, because a strong base is always required to remove a proton from carbon. The best answer is choice **C**.

33. Choice D is the best answer. The question mentions that the final step involves the conversion of an alkene into a vicinal diol, so we need to consider the alkene precursor to the diol shown in each answer choice and compare it to the alkene that would be formed from Hofmann elimination of the alkyl chloride starting material. The Hofmann product and corresponding vicinal diol for each of the four choices are shown below.

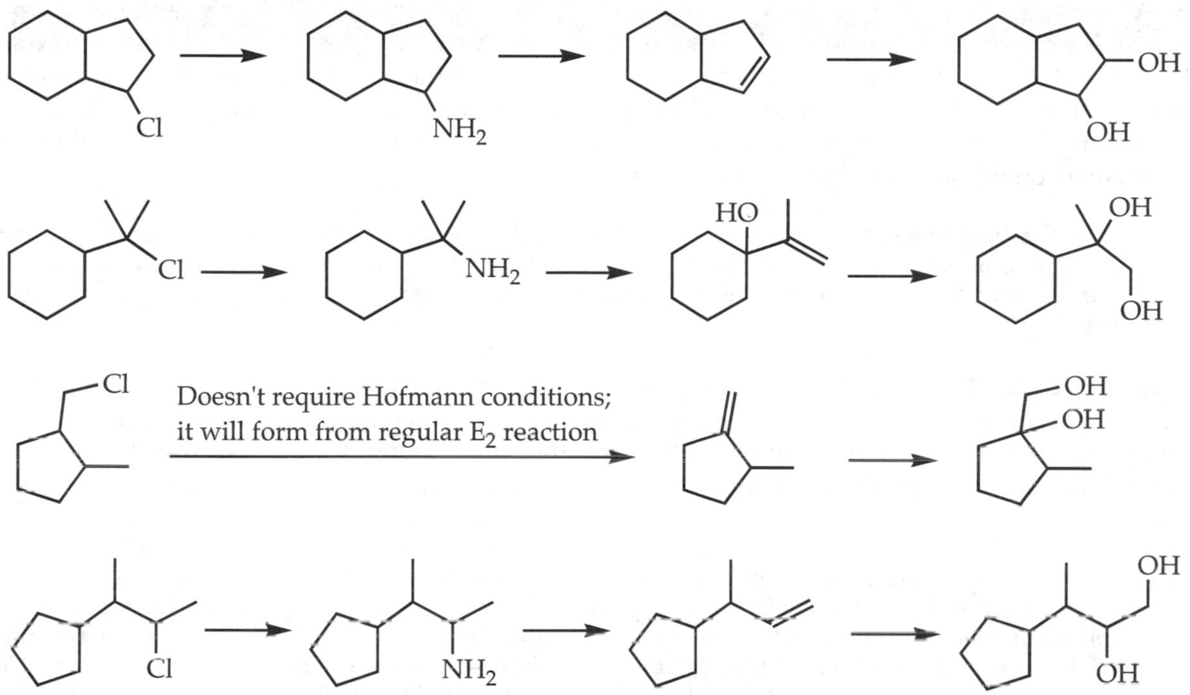

In choices A and B, the wrong vicinal diol is formed, so they are eliminated. In choice C, the alkene intermediate can form without employing Hofmann elimination, so Hofmann elimination is not required. This eliminates choice C. In choice **D**, the reaction must proceed by Hofmann elimination to get the correct alkene intermediate. The best answer is choice **D**.

Questions 34 - 37   **Not Based on a Descriptive Passage**

34. **Choice D is the best answer.** Bromine, in the presence of light, adds to the most substituted carbon of an alkane by way of a free radical mechanism. Of the four unique carbons in the structure, the most substituted carbon is tertiary. Although there is only one hydrogen on the tertiary carbon, the reactivity preference for tertiary is so great that it outweighs in difference in abundance with other carbons. The choice with bromine added to the tertiary carbon, choice **D**, is the best answer. The product shown, as well as its enantiomer, are both formed.

35. **Choice C is the best answer.** For an E_2 reaction, the base must be strong enough to remove a proton from carbon and bulky enough to not undergo substitution. This makes choice A a valid statement and thereby eliminates it. For an E_2 reaction, the leaving group and proton being lost from carbon must be positioned anti to one another, so the geometry of the product is dependent upon the alignment of the reactant. Cis versus trans results from the orientation and stereochemistry, so choice B is a valid statement and thereby eliminated. For an E_1 reaction, a leaving group first leaves, resulting in a carbocation. With carbocations, rearrangement can be observed, so it is with E_1 reactions that we see rearrangement, not E_2 reactions. Because E_2 reactions are concerted, there is no rearrangement observed, so choice **C** is an invalid statement and thereby the correct answer. Heat is required to drive both E_1 and E_2 reactions, so choice D is a valid statement. It is eliminated, leaving choice **C** as our choice.

36. **Choice C is the best answer.** The sulfate group does not substitute for the hydroxyl group, so choice A is eliminated. The reaction involves the use of concentrated strong acid at high temperature, so the reaction is apt to proceed via an E_1-mechanism. An E_1-mechanism entails the hydroxyl group being protonated to form water, after which the water leaves to produce a secondary carbocation. A hydride shift results in the conversion from a secondary carbocation into a tertiary carbocation, which is the intermediate from which deprotonation to form the alkene product occurs. All three chiral centers are lost, one through rearrangement and two through elimination. The product is neither an alcohol nor is it meso, so choices B and D are eliminated. The product is an achiral alkene that resulted from rearrangement, so choice **C** is the best answer.

37. **Choice C is the best answer.** Chlorocyclohexane when treated with a strong base undergoes an elimination reaction by way of an E_2 mechanism to yield cyclohexene. There are two units of unsaturation in cyclohexene, one unit of unsaturation for the π-bond and one unit of unsaturation for the ring. The best answer is choice **C**.

Passage VI (Questions 38 - 43)   **Occidentilol Synthesis**

38. **Choice C is the best answer.** Figure 1 shows occidentalol with three specified chiral centers, so choices A and B can be eliminated. All of the carbons in the ring structure either have sp^2-hybridization or they are methylene (CH_2) groups. The methyl group and tertiary alcohol carbon do not have stereocenters, so there are no other chiral centers on the structure. The best answer is choice **C**.

39. **Choice D is the best answer.** The first paragraph states that occidentalol is a sesquiterpenoid. Occidentalol has fifteen carbons total, so it is a reasonable conclusion that sesquiterpenes must have fifteen carbons. This makes choice **D** the best answer. Monoterpenes have ten carbons, diterpenes have twenty carbons, and triterpenes have thirty carbons.

40. **Choice A is the best answer.** The wavelength of maximum absorbance, λ_{max}, increases as the conjugation of the π-network increases. All four choices are conjugated dienes in terms of carbon-carbon pi-networks, but Compound 1 also has a carbonyl in its conjugated π-network, giving it the longest extended π-network of the answer choices. As such, the compound that has the longest λ_{max} is Compound 1, making choice **A** the best answer.

41. **Choice B is the best answer.** Step 1 involves a Diels-Alder reaction followed by decarboxylation. The intermediate compound is the Diels-Alder product. There is no nitrogen present in either reactant, so the compound cannot be a lactam (cyclic amide). This eliminates choice D. The product of a Diels-Alder reaction involving a diene and an alkene (dienophile) is cyclohexene, so choice **B** is the best answer. The diene in Compound 2 is regenerated from cyclohexene after decarboxylation, so choice A is eliminated. The reaction is shown below:

The compound is a cyclohexene with a lactone that is not conjugated to the alkene.

42. **Choice B is the best answer.** Occidentalol has one more methyl group than Compound 6, so the role of methyl lithium, MeLi, must be to add a methyl group to Compound 6. This eliminates choices C and D. Methyl lithium has an anionic carbon, so it acts as a nucleophile rather than an electrophile. This eliminates choice A and makes choice **B** the best answer. The methyl anion attacks the carbonyl carbon in the same fashion as an alkyl magnesium bromide anion attacks a carbonyl in a Grignard reaction.

43. **Choice A is the best answer.** A conjugated diene can be protonated at either terminal carbon of the π-network, because the carbocation that results is resonance stabilized. This eliminates choices B and C. Carbon a is a secondary carbon while carbon d is a tertiary carbon. It is easier to protonate the less hindered site, so carbon a is the site that is most likely to gain H^+. The best answer is choice **A**.

44.   Choice A is the best answer. The passage shows that oxidation is carried out via a free-radical mechanism, so antioxidant activity must be rooted in the ability to consume free radicals. This would imply that a good antioxidant should be a semi-stable free radical, making it stable enough to be present but reactive enough to react with other free radicals. This makes choice **A** a feasible explanation. Without knowing background information about thiols, we can keep it as a *good* choice but not our final answer yet. Thiols are not naturally free radicals, so choice B is eliminated. Carboxylic acids do not have an O—O bond, so they are not peroxides, which eliminates choice C. Oxygen gas, O_2, does not readily reduce any molecule, as it is a strong oxidizing agent. Choice D is eliminated, which leaves only choice **A** still standing. The best answer is choice **A**.

45.   Choice C is the best answer. In Figure 2, we can see that in the conversion of lipid peroxyl radical into lipid radical plus lipid peroxide, a free radical reactant results in one free radical product. In free radical initiation reactions, a non free radical reactant forms two free radicals, so choice A is eliminated. In free radical termination reactions, two free radical reactants form a non free radical product, so choice B is eliminated. In free radical propagation reactions, one free radical reactant forms one free radical product, so choice **C** is a valid description of the reaction. There is no nucleophilic oxidation transpiring, so choice D is eliminated. The best answer is choice **C**.

46.   Choice C is the best answer. The lipid free radical in Figure 2 shows very little of the molecule, with just a pi-bond and a free radical as items of interest. The free radical is secondary and conjugated, so choices A (tertiary free radical) and B (primary free radical) can be eliminated. All free radicals have the same hybridization, so hybridization can't be a rationale for explaining the stability of one free radical over another. The best explanation is that the free radical is stabilized by resonance that results from the conjugation. The best answer is choice **C**.

47.   Choice D is the best answer. When ubiquinol becomes a free radical, it does so by losing an H· from one of its hydroxyl groups. Because of steric hindrance, the upper hydroxyl group is more reactive than the lower hydroxyl group, so a free radical oxygen at the top of the ring as shown is a viable resonance structure. The other resonance structures are shown below.

Choices A, B, and C are all possible, as shown in the resonance diagram. It is not possible to relocate the free radical to the carbon containing the long alkyl chain, so choice D is not a possible resonance structure. The best answer is choice **D**.

48.   Choice D is the best answer. Ubiquinol is a phenol, and phenolic hydrogens have a pK_a around 10. This is general information you are expected to know. Statement I is valid, so choice B is eliminated. Although ubiquinol has two hydroxyl groups, the long alkyl chain makes it hydrophobic. This is confirmed by the passage which tells us that ubiquinol is a common lipid-soluble antioxidant. Statement II is invalid, which eliminates choice C. Because ubiquinol serves as an antioxidant, it must readily react with free radicals, which means it must readily be oxidized. Statement III is valid, so choice A is eliminated, and the best answer is choice **D**.

Questions 49 - 52   **Not Based on a Descriptive Passage**

49.   Choice D is the best answer. Free radical propagation reactions keep a free radical reaction going, so they have the same number of free radicals on each side of the equation. In choice A, there is one free radical on the reactant side and three free radicals on the product side, so it is not a propagation step. Choice A is eliminated. In choice B, there are two free radicals on the reactant side and no free radicals on the product side, so it is a termination step and not a propagation step. Choice B is eliminated. In choice C, there is one free radical on the reactant side and two free radicals on the product side, so it is not a propagation step. Choice C is eliminated. In choice **D**, there is one free radical on the reactant side and one free radical on the product side, so it is a propagation step. Choice **D** is the best answer. You may not recognize the reaction from the overall mechanism, but it converts a less stable free radical into a more stable free radical, which ultimately impacts the product distribution.

50. **Choice D is the best answer.** Terpenes are hydrocarbons of 10, 15, 20, etc... carbons, so they are somewhat massive lipids. Because they are hydrocarbons, they are lipid soluble, so choice A is a valid statement. Choice A is consequently eliminated. Terpenes have molecular masses of about 140 g/mole, about 210 g/mole, about 280 g/mole, etc..., so they have somewhat high boiling points. High is a relative term, so we can't be certain in eliminating choice B. However, choices B and C are the same concept, so they mutually exclude one another from consideration. It is important that you use your test taking skills. The specific rotation of a compound is dictated by its chiral centers, which a terpene may or may not have. Given that there is no general rule about the chirality of terpenes, we cannot conclude that they have high specific rotations. Choice **D** is the best answer.

51. **Choice A is the best answer.** If you recall your general nomenclature, then you should know that when a functional group, in this case the hydroxyl group, is on the carbon bonded to an alkene carbon, it is said to be allylic. Choice **A** fits this description. Choice D should have been eliminated early, because it does not contain a π-bond. Choice B is eliminated, because it is a vinylic alcohol (hydroxyl group directly bonded to the alkene carbon). Choice C has the double bond too far from the alcohol group to be allylic, so it is eliminated as well.

52. **Choice C is the best answer.** Both compounds are six-carbon alkanes, so any differences in their physical properties will stem from intermolecular interactions. A lower boiling point correlates with a higher vapor pressure, so choices A and B are the same answer. Both choices are thus eliminated. Branching hinders molecular packing, so *n*-hexane packs more tightly than 2,3 –dimethylbutane, resulting in a higher melting point. Choice **C** is the best answer. The density is hard to predict, but a more compact structure generally leads to higher density.

Phase III Homework for Hydrocarbons

Hydrocarbons Phase III Scoring Scale

Raw Score	MCAT Score
28 - 31	13 - 15
22 - 27	10 - 12
16 - 21	7 - 9
11 - 15	4 - 6
1 - 10	1 - 3

Passage I (Questions 1 - 6)

A chemist set out to synthesize a series of conjugated dienes. Starting with an allylic alcohol, generating a conjugated diene involves an acid catalyzed elimination reaction. Elimination by way of an E_1 mechanism to form a conjugated diene is shown in Reaction 1.

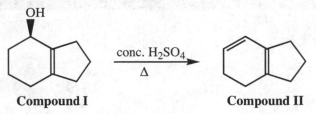

Reaction 1

Reaction 1 is monitored using UV spectroscopy. Over the course of the reaction an intense UV absorbance at 179 nm diminishes as a new peak at 222 nm appears.

When the product of Reaction 1 is treated with acidic water, two products of detectable quantity are formed. Figure 1 shows the distribution of the two hydration products at 35°C, labeled Compound 3a and Compound 3b.

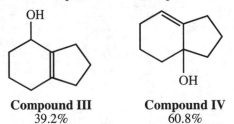

Compound III   **Compound IV**
39.2%   60.8%

Figure 1

The percentage of the secondary alcohol formed increases as the temperature of the hydration reaction increases. This is attributed to a shift from kinetic control to thermodynamic control.

It is found that if the allylic alcohol in Reaction 1 is replaced by a new compound containing both an alcohol group and a carbon-carbon π-bond, with the exception of a vinylic alcohol, a conjugated diene is formed upon treatment with concentrated strong acid at elevated temperatures.

1. Which of the following species is NOT an intermediate formed during the hydration of Compound II?

    A.
    B.
    C.
    D.

2. Which of the following statements accurately reflect Reaction 1?

    I.   Rearrangement is possible during the reaction.
    II. A vinylic carbocation is formed as an intermediate in the reaction.
    III. The first step of the reaction is the protonation of the hydroxyl oxygen.

    A. I only
    B. II only
    C. I and II only
    D. I and III only

3. Which spectroscopy technique is MOST effective in distinguishing Compound III from Compound IV?

    A. ^{1}H NMR
    B. Infrared
    C. Ultraviolet
    D. Visible

4. What reagent could carry out the reaction below?

    A. NADH + H$^+$
    B. FADH$_2$
    C. MgSO$_4$
    D. Tartrate with H$_2$SO$_4$

5. Compound IV is best described as:

    A. a single, achiral molecule
    B. a single, chiral molecule.
    C. a pair of diastereomers.
    D. a pair of enantiomers.

6. 1,2- and 1,4-addition is possible in all of the following compounds EXCEPT:

    A. 2,4-Hexadiene
    B. 2-methylcyclopentadiene
    C. 1,4-cycloheptadiene
    D. 1,3-cyclohexadiene

Passage II (Questions 7 - 12)

Terpenes are natural organic molecules found in plants and animals. They are formed from the basic subunit of isoprene, a five-carbon conjugated diene. Terpenes and *terpenoids*, biological molecules derived from terpenes, have a total carbon count that is divisible by five. Terpenes are classified according to the number of carbon atoms they contain. Monoterpenes have ten carbon atom, sesquiterpenes have fifteen carbon atoms, diterpenes have twenty carbon atoms, sesterterpene has twenty-five carbons and so on.

Because terpenes are natural products, they are common in many household items, such as flavoring agents in various foods and the active molecule in many drugs. Much of organic chemistry research involves the development of *in vitro* synthesis of terpenes and terpenoids. Some naturally occurring monoterpenes are shown in Figure 1.

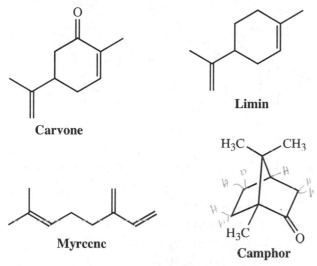

Figure 1. Four Common Monoterpenes

Some terpenes contain oxygen, which is added in a way that does not alter the carbon skeleton. Carvone is evident by a carbonyl absorption at 1750 cm^{-1} in the IR spectrum and a strong UV ($\varepsilon > 10,000$) absorption at $\lambda_{max} = 242$ nm.

7. When limin is converted into carvone, what type of reaction has to transpire?

   A. Oxidation of carbon
   B. Reduction of carbon
   C. Hydrolysis of a π-bond
   D. Nucleophilic substitution

8. How many singlets does camphor show in its proton NMR spectrum?

   A. Two
   B. Three
   C. Six
   D. Nine

9. Camphor is likely to show which of the following physical and chemical properties?

   I. High water solubility
   II. A boiling point above 298K
   III. No specific rotation of plane polarized light

   A. I only
   B. II only
   C. I and II only
   D. I and III only

10. If myrcene reacts with another isoprene unit, what kind of terpene is formed?

    A. Diterpene
    B. Monoterpene
    C. Sesquiterpene
    D. Sesterterpene

11. Does limin display a strong (log $\varepsilon > 4$) UV absorption?

    A. Yes, because the π-bonds are spaced far apart.
    B. Yes, because of the six-membered ring.
    C. No, because there is no carbonyl group.
    D. No, because the π-bonds are not conjugated.

12. Which compound is the direct product of a Diels Alder condensation of two isoprene units?

    A. Camphor
    B. Carvone
    C. Limin
    D. Myrcene

321   **GO ON TO THE NEXT PAGE**

In the recent years, many chemists around the world have shifted their focus to so called *green chemistry*. Green chemistry, also called sustainable chemistry, aims to develop chemical reactions and processes that are environmentally safe. The goal is to reduce waste generation rather than employing waste management--the "end of the pipe" solution. The most significant alteration to traditional chemistry is the recycling of solvent, or in optimal cases, the elimination of solvent. This is achieved in many ways, including doing reactions under high pressure to make the system act like a supercritical fluid.

Areas of current research in green chemistry include the use of renewable raw materials, direct oxidations using oxygen, improved separation during the course of a reaction, and all forms of catalysts. The aim is to maximize *atom-economy*, the tracking of how many atoms used in the reaction end up in the product, by not using solvents or protecting groups. Figure 1 lists three atom-economical reactions used in green synthesis.

Reaction I:

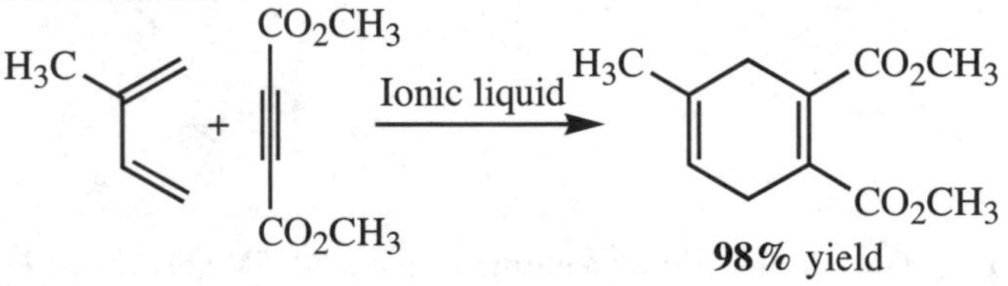

Reaction II:

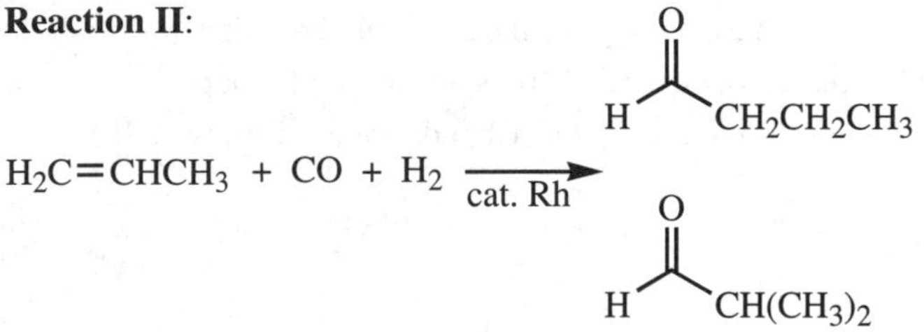

Reaction III:

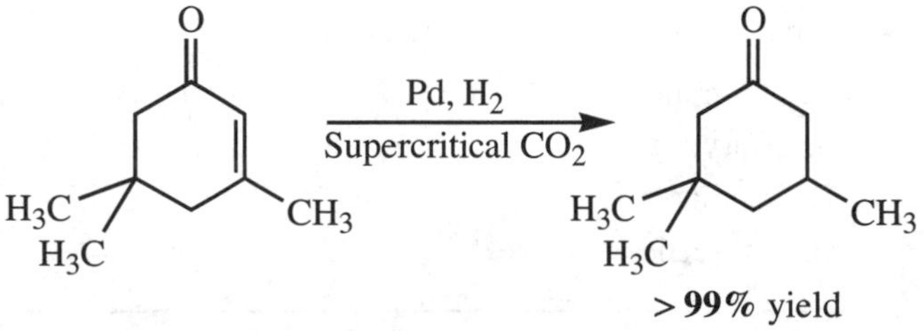

Figure 1. Three Atom-economical Green Syntheses

Reaction 1 is a Diels-Alder reaction, Reaction 2 is a hydroformylation reaction, and Reaction 3 is a hydrogenation reaction. All of the reactions in Figure 1 start with alkenes, a common starting material in the production of plastics and polymers. Green chemistry is ideal for polymerization reactions, which by design aims to minimize the material need to carry out the propagation reaction. Green synthesis techniques can be applied to any reaction.

13. In Reaction I, the alkyne is best described as:

- **A.** a dienophile.
- **B.** an electrophile.
- **C.** a nucleophile.
- **D.** an oxidant.

14. Which of the following intermediates is consistent with the two structural isomers formed in Reaction II?

A.

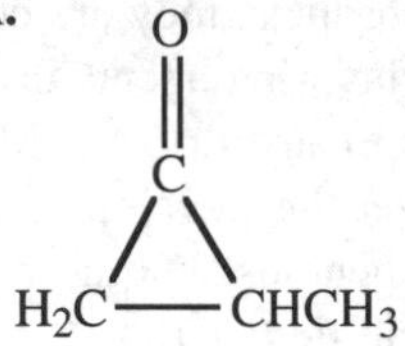

B.

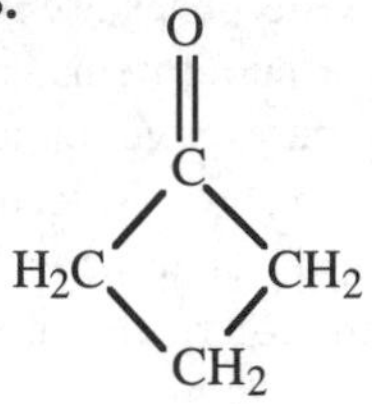

C.

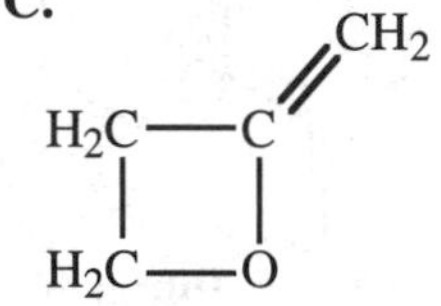

D.

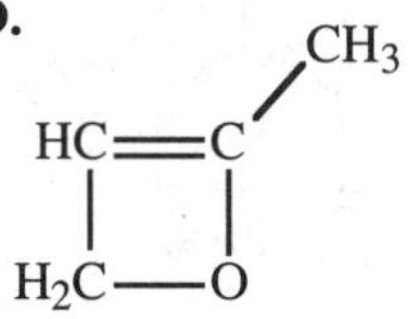

15. Which of the reactions in Figure 1 involves the formation of new stereocenters?

- **A.** Reaction III only
- **B.** Reactions I and II only
- **C.** Reactions I and III only
- **D.** Reactions II and III only

16. Which of the following changes does NOT fit with the philosophy of green chemistry?

- **A.** Using supercritical fluid as a solvent.
- **B.** Using protecting groups and not removing them until the very last step of the reaction.
- **C.** Using solid-state catalysts built into the lab equipment.
- **D.** Running a constant stream of oxygen gas through the reaction vessel for oxidation reactions.

17. Reaction III can be described by all of the following terms EXCEPT:

- **A.** reduction.
- **B.** hydrogenation.
- **C.** stereoselective.
- **D.** regioselective.

18. What is the major product of the reaction below?

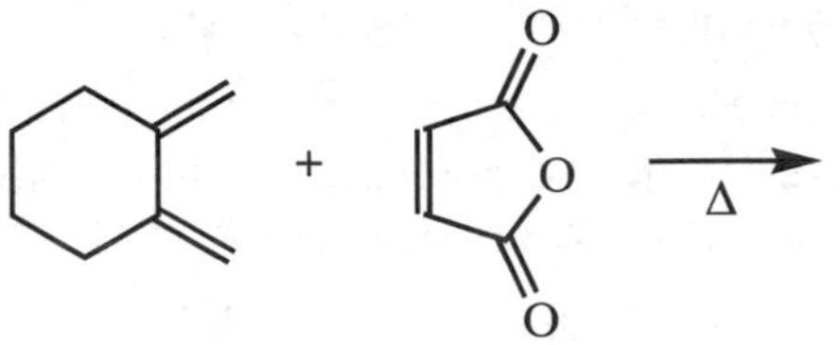

A.

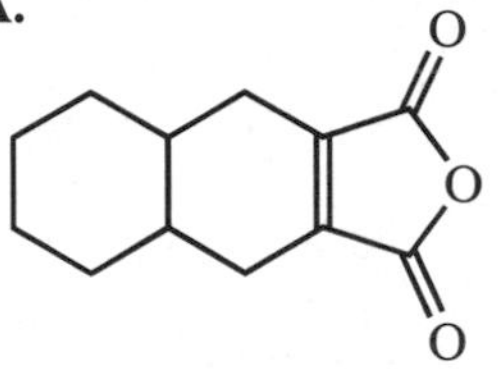

B.

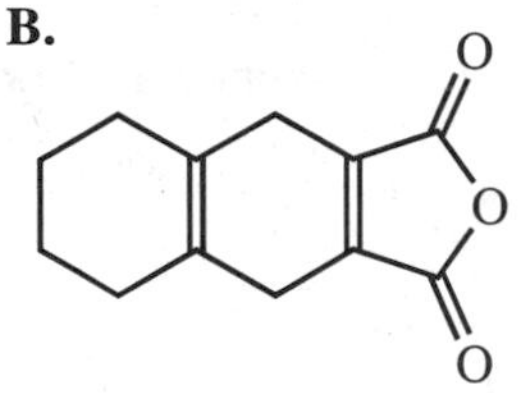

C.

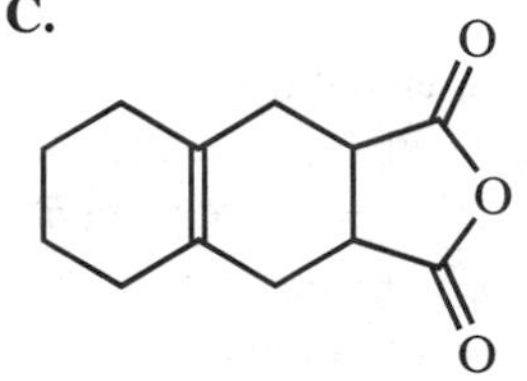

D.

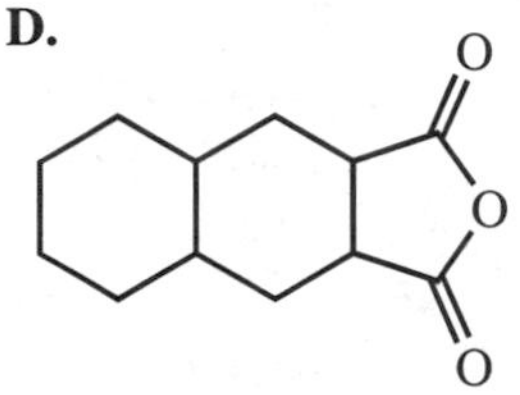

Passage IV (Questions 19 - 25)

Pericyclic reactions are single-step reactions that involve the movement of electrons through cyclic transition states that involve pi and sigma orbitals. One class of pericyclic reactions is the *sigmatropic rearrangement*, which involves the migration of a sigma-bonded group across a pi-electron system. The two most common sigmatropic rearrangements are the *Cope rearrangement* and the *Claisen rearrangement*. In the Cope rearrangement, one 1,5-hexadiene yields a new 1,5-hexadiene. In the Claisen rearrangement, an allyl vinylic ether yields an unsaturated carbonyl compound. Both reactions are shown in Figure 1 below.

Cope rearrangement

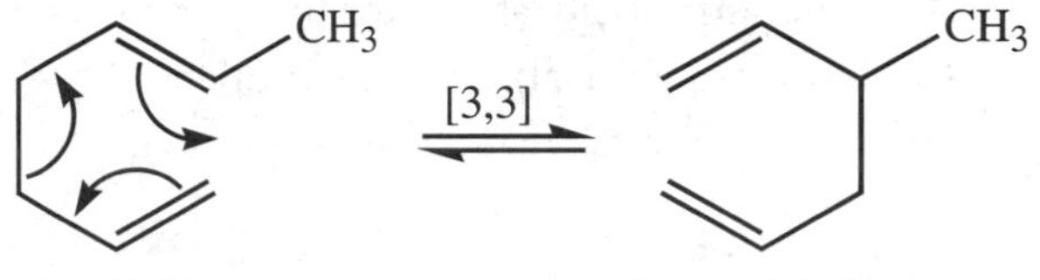

A 1,5-diene   A new 1,5-diene

Claisen rearrangement

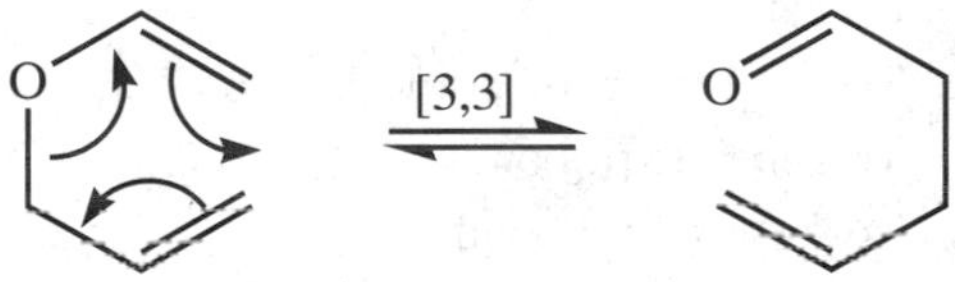

An allyl vinylic ether   A γ,δ-unsaturated carbonyl compound

Figure 1 Cope and Claisen rearrangements

When the reactant in a Claisen rearrangement includes a benzene ring, the ketone formed from the allyl phenylic ether undergoes tautomerization and converts into a phenol. The ultimate product is the one that is most stable. Figure 2 shows a synthesis pathway that involves a Claisen rearrangement, a Cope rearrangement, and tautomerization.

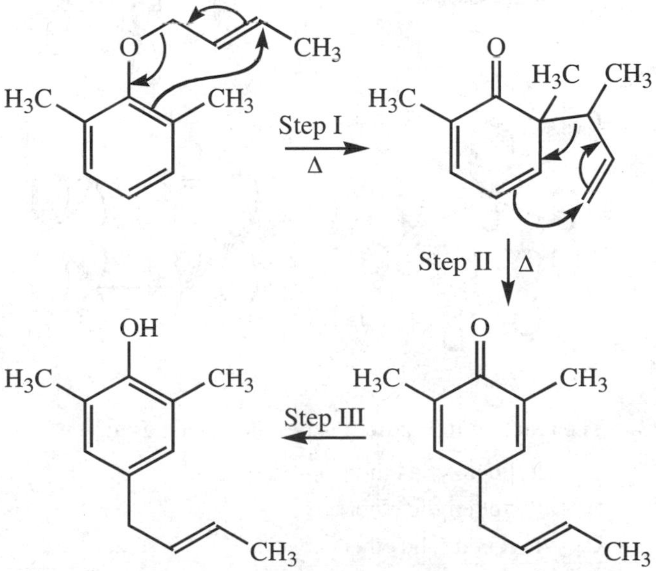

Figure 2 Synthesis using Claisen and Cope rearrangements

19. How can it be supported that the Cope rearrangement is concerted rather than a multistep process involving substitution?

    A. All of the stereocenters are retained

    B. All of the stereocenters are inverted

    C. Several cross products are formed

    D. No cross products are formed

20. Step III in the synthesis shown in Figure 2 occurs because the product:

    A. loses steric hindrance after oxidation.

    B. gains aromaticity after reduction.

    C. loses resonance after tautomerization.

    D. gains aromaticity after tautomerization.

21. Heat serves what role in the Claisen rearrangement?

    A. To provide energy to overcome the activation barrier

    B. To drive the exothermic reaction

    C. To generate pi-bonds

    D. To form sigma-bonds

22. Which of the following orbital arrangements represents the transition state of a Cope rearrangement?

    A. 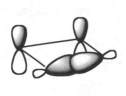   **B.**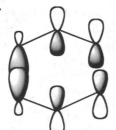

    C. 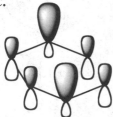   **D.**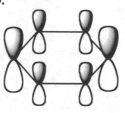

23. The reactant in Figure 2 is best described as a:

    A. allyl benzylic ether.

    B. allyl phenylic ether.

    C. vinyl benzylic ether.

    D. vinyl phenylic ether.

24. What spectroscopic evidence supports the formation of a product in a Claisen rearrangement?

    A. Appearance of a signal at 9.5 ppm in the ^{1}H NMR

    B. Appearance of a broad absorbance around 3400 cm^{-1} in infrared spectroscopy

    C. Disappearance of an absorbance around 1700 cm^{-1} in infrared spectroscopy

    D. Disappearance of two signals between 5 and 6 ppm in the ^{1}H NMR

25. What is true of the Claisen and Cope rearrangements in Figure 2?

    A. Step I is Claisen rearrangement and step II is Cope rearrangement; the units of unsaturation decrease from 5 to 4 during the Claisen rearrangement.

    B. Step I is Cope rearrangement and step II is Clasien rearrangement; the units of unsaturation decrease from 5 to 4 during the Cope rearrangement.

    C. Step I is Claisen rearrangement and step II is Cope rearrangement; the units of unsaturation remain 5 during the Claisen rearrangement.

    D. Step I is Cope rearrangement and step II is Claisen rearrangement; the units of unsaturation remain 5 during the Cope rearrangement.

         GO ON TO THE NEXT PAGE

The isoprene unit is one of nature's favorite building blocks. Isoprene (2-methyl-1,3-butadiene) reacts at carbons one and two or one and four with other isoprene molecules to form terpenes, a class of bio-organic molecules. Terpenes are found in such natural products as rubber and essential oils. Nearly all of the naturally occurring terpenes result from the head-to-tail connectivity of isoprene units. They connect by undergoing either nucleophilic substitution or electrocyclic addition, such as a Diels Alder reaction. Figure 1 shows some common terpenes.

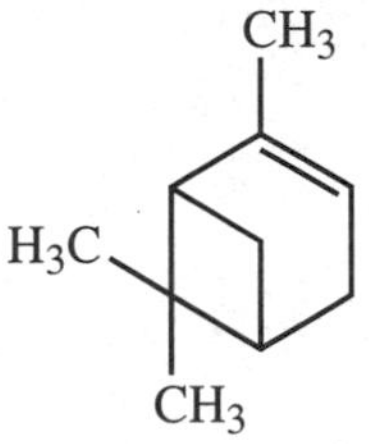

α-Pinene

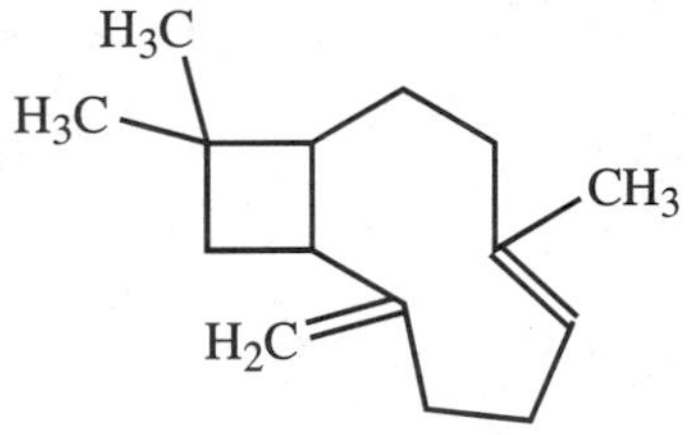

Caryophyllene

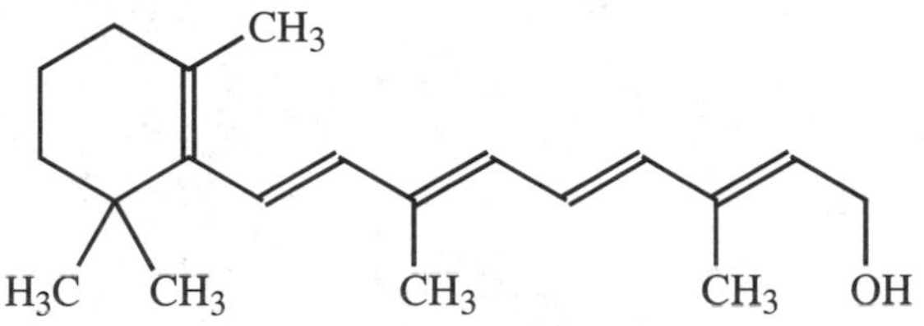

Vitamin A_1

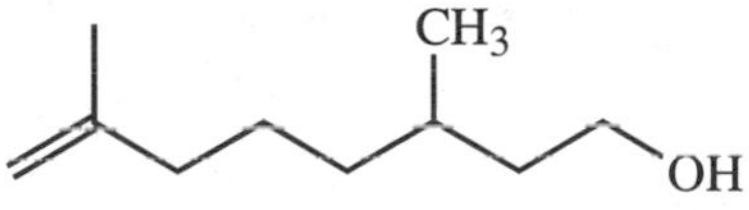

Citronellol

Figure 1. Common Terpenes

Both plants and animals synthesize terpenes. Pinene, a monoterpene, is found in plants and Vitamin A_1, a diterpene, is found in both plants and animals. Smaller terpenes are found primarily in plants, while some larger terpenes, such as lanesterol (a C-30 precursor to steroid hormones) and ß-carotene (a C-40 source of vitamin A), are found in plants and animals. Terpenes can be modified into other compounds, known as *terpenoids*.

Studies in biogenesis show that the large terpenes are synthesized starting from isopentenyl pyrophosphate. The pyrophosphate adds across the diene of isoprene to form either isopentenyl pyrophosphate or dimethylallyl pyrophosphate. These molecules then add to one another by way of nucleophilic substitution reactions, where the pyrophosphate acts as a leaving group. Geranyl pyrophosphate (a name given to C-10 terpenes) is the first monoterpene in many natural synthetic pathways. More isoprene units are added to the monoterpene to form other terpenes and terpenoids. Figure 2 shows a basic schematic for the biosynthesis of cholesterol starting from isopentenyl pyrophosphate.

Isopentenyl pyrophosphate

Squalene

Lanosterol

Cholesterol

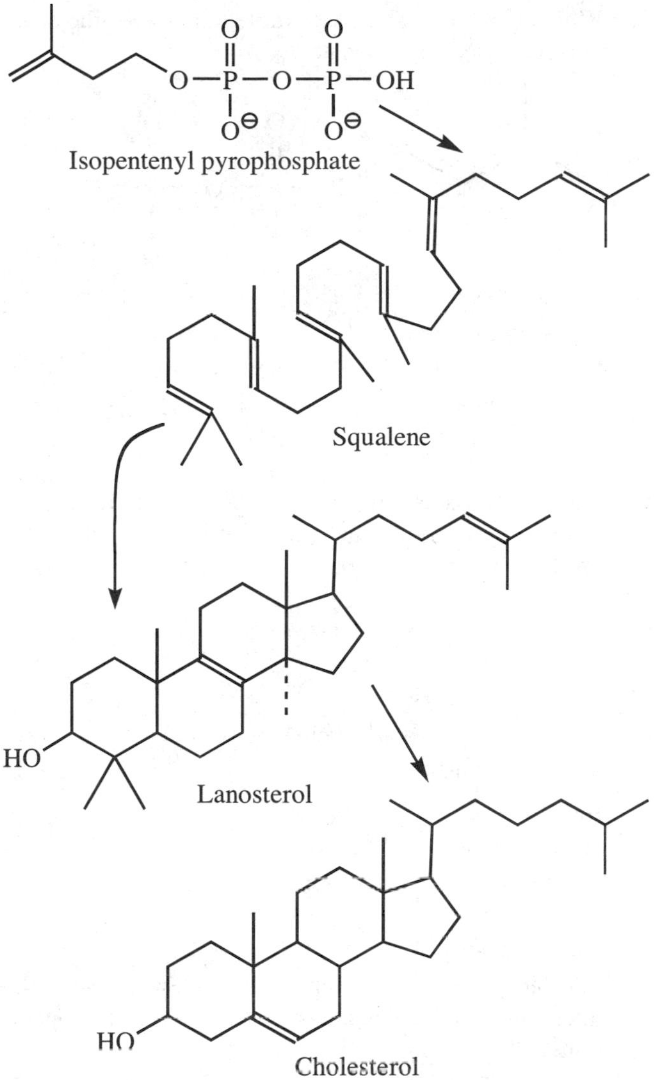

Figure 2. Biosynthesis of Cholesterol

26. Which of the following compounds is NOT a terpene?

A. Limonine ($C_{10}H_{16}$)

B. Geraniol ($C_{10}H_{18}O$)

C. Patchouli alcohol ($C_{15}H_{26}O$)

D. Stearol ($C_{18}H_{38}O$)

27. What irregularity in a sample of a sesquiterpene (15 carbon terpene) would indicate that the compound was synthesized in lab as opposed to extracted from a plant?

A. The compound is not enantiomerically pure.

B. The compound is not a racemic mixture.

C. The compound had impurities with 16 carbons.

D. The compound had impurities with 20 carbons.

28. Which carbon is most susceptible to nucleophilic attack in isopentyl pyrophosphate?

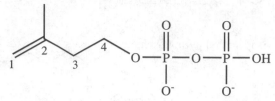

A. Carbon 1
B. Carbon 2
C. Carbon 3
D. Carbon 4

29. Isoprene units are believed to be formed from three acetyl coenzyme A molecules. What is a likely side product from the reaction?

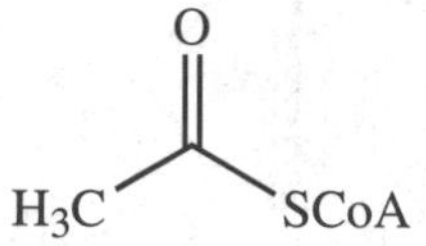

$$H_3C - C(=O) - SCoA$$
Acetyl Coenzyme A

A. Carbon dioxide gas
B. Ethanol
C. Acetic acid
D. Isopropanol

30. The biosynthesis of which of the following molecules likely involved a Diels Alder reaction with isoprene units?

A. Caryophyllene
B. Citronellol
C. α-Pinene
D. Vitamin A_1

31. Which of the labeled bonds in γ-terpinene was formed in the biological synthesis from isoprene units?

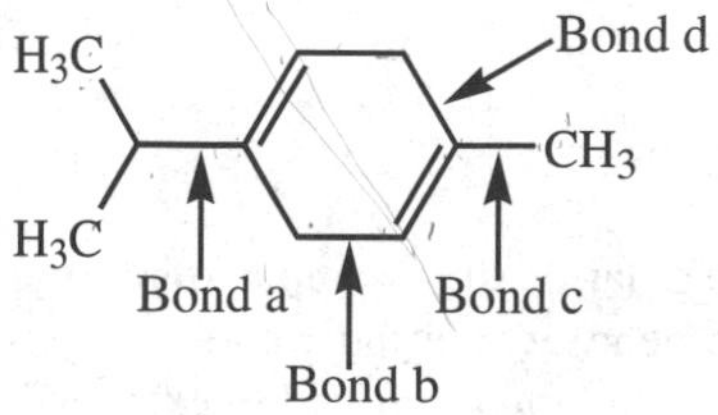

A. Bond a
B. Bond b
C. Bond c
D. Bond d

Answers to Hydrocarbons Phase III Homework

1. B	2. D	3. A	4. B	5. D	6. C	7. A	8. B	9. B	10. C
11. D	12. C	13. A	14. A	15. A	16. B	17. D	18. C	19. D	20. D
21. A	22. B	23. B	24. A	25. C	26. D	27. C	28. D	29. A	30. C
31. B									

Passage I (Questions 1 - 6)   **Allylic Alcohols**

1. **Choice B is the best answer.** The hydration of Compound II starts with the addition of a proton to the conjugated π-network. The easiest carbon to protonate, because of steric hindrance and resonance stability, is the secondary, terminal carbon of the system. This generates the structure in choice C, so choice C is eliminated. That structure can undergo resonance to generate the structure shown in choice D. This eliminates choice D. If water were to attack the structure shown in choice C, the structure in choice A, a new intermediate, forms. This eliminates choice A. By default, the best answer is choice **B**. Choice **B** is not possible, because the structure would have to gain a proton at the more sterically hindered terminal carbon of the π-system.

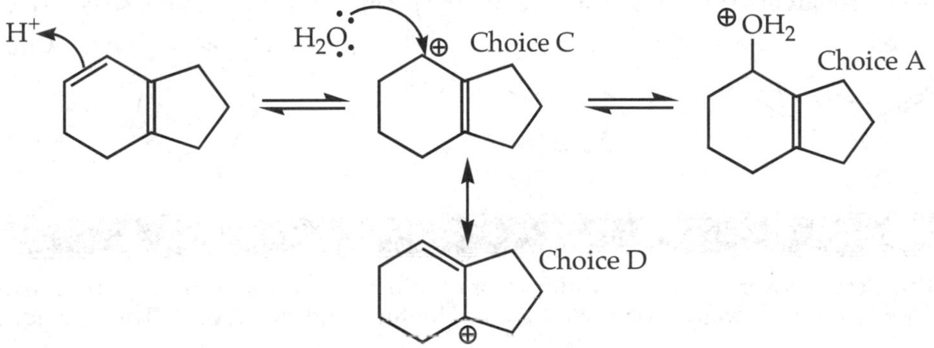

2. **Choice D is the best answer.** Reaction 1 is an elimination reaction by way of an E_1 mechanism. In an E_1 reaction, a carbocation is formed, so rearrangement is possible. Whether it is observed depends on the compound, but it is possible. Statement I is a valid statement. The intermediate is an allylic carbocation, where the cationic carbon is bonded to one of the carbons in the double bond, not a vinylic carbocation, where the cation carbon is one of the carbons in the double bond. Statement II is invalid, which eliminates choices B and C. The first step in acid catalyzed reactions is the protonation of some functional group on the reactant. In this particular case, the hydroxyl group is the most basic site, so it is protonated. This generates a good leaving group, which then leaves in the second step. Because the hydroxyl group is protonated to start the reaction, Statement III is valid. This makes choice **D** the best answer.

3. **Choice A is the best answer.** Compound III and Compound IV are structural isomers of one another. They each have a hydroxyl group and an alkene functionality, so infrared spectroscopy yields the same key absorbances. This makes infrared spectroscopy ineffective at distinguishing the two allylic alcohols, so choice B is eliminated. Ultraviolet spectroscopy is great for determining the amount of conjugation in a system. However, both compounds have the same number of π-bonds, one, so ultraviolet spectroscopy yields essentially the same spectrum for both compounds. Choice C is eliminated. Neither structure absorbs light in the visible range, given that neither structure has extensive conjugation. This can be inferred from the passage when they mention that the peak at 179 nm disappears. That peak is associated with Compound I, which happens to be one of the two enantiomers represented by Compound III. Choice D is eliminated, because 179 nm is not in the visible range of the EM spectrum. The best method is ^1H NMR, which can distinguish structural isomers by their equivalent hydrogens. Choice **A** is the best answer.

4. **Choice B is the best answer.** A π-bond has been hydrogenated in the reaction. This reaction requires a reducing agent, which in organic chemistry is often recognizable by the presence of hydrogens bonded to atoms that are less electronegative than hydrogen. We can eliminate choices C and D because they are not reducing agents. To get this question correct, you need to know from biology that NADH is responsible for reducing carbonyl compounds and $FADH_2$ is responsible for reducing (hydrogenating) π-bonds. Because a π-bond has been reduced in the reaction, the best answer is choice **B**. As a point of preparation interest, although alkene chemistry is not listed as a test topic in organic chemistry, hydrogenation and hydration of π-bonds in biochemistry is still fair game. This question serves as a reminder that alkene chemistry is also present in biology.

---

5. **Choice D is the best answer.** The tertiary carbon with the hydroxyl group has four unique substituents, so it is chiral. This eliminates choice A. There is only one chiral center, so diastereomers are not possible (there must be at least two chiral centers for diastereomers to be possible). This eliminates choice C. Because the hydroxyl group can be above the plane or below the plane, there is more than one structure possible for Compound IV. This eliminates choice B and makes choice **D** the best answer.

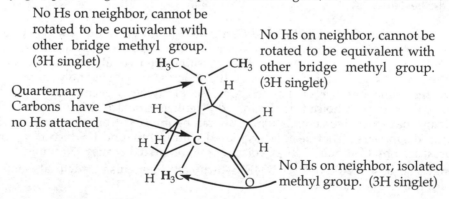

6. **Choice C is the best answer.** The option for either 1,2-addition or 1,4-addition occurs when the reactant has conjugated π-bonds. Choices A and D should be eliminated immediately, because when the two numbers describing the π-bonds differ by 2, then the π-bonds are conjugated. Cyclopentadiene has only five carbons, so one π-bond must be between carbons one and two. The second π-bond must be between carbons three and four, because in a five-carbon ring, no matter how you place two double bonds, for the ring to not be so strained it can't exist, they must be conjugated. Only in choice C are the π-bonds not conjugated, so choice **C** is the best answer.

Choice A   Choice B   Choice C   Choice D

CH₃

Passage II   (Questions 7 - 12)   **Terpenes**

7. **Choice A is the best answer.** Carvone differs from limin by a carbonyl group. To go from limin to carvone, a carbon must lose two bonds to hydrogen and gain a double bond to oxygen. This is oxidation, so choice **A** is the best answer.

8. **Choice B is the best answer.** Singlets in the proton NMR are caused by unique hydrogen atoms in an environment where the adjacent atoms have no bonds to hydrogen, and thus there are no neighboring hydrogens with which coupling can take place. In camphor, all of the methyl groups are bonded to quaternary carbons, so they all fit this description. Because the cyclic structure is incapable of rotation, like an alkene, the two methyl groups bonded to the bridge carbon are not equivalent, causing them to express different NMR signals. The result is that each of the methyl groups are represented by a singlet in the proton NMR. All of the remaining hydrogens on camphor are on carbons adjacent to neighboring carbons with hydrogens, so there are no other singlets than the ones from the methyl groups. This generates three proton NMR singlets, so the best answer is choice **B**.

No Hs on neighbor, cannot be rotated to be equivalent with other bridge methyl group. (3H singlet)

No Hs on neighbor, cannot be rotated to be equivalent with other bridge methyl group. (3H singlet)

Quarternary Carbons have no Hs attached

H₃C   CH₃
C   H
H
H
H   H
H   C
H   H₃C   O

No Hs on neighbor, isolated methyl group. (3H singlet)

9. **Choice B is the best answer.** Camphor has a carbonyl group (water soluble) and a large alkyl ring system (not water soluble). It is hard to decide based on the structure. It happens that the compound is water soluble, which you may know first hand from using camphor-containing cleaning agents for skin. The question is whether or not it is highly water soluble. Because there is some ambiguity, let's say for now that it likely not highly water soluble, and consider statement I to be invalid. Camphor is a liquid at room temperature, as you might have seen if you synthesized it in a lab experiment. Being a liquid at standard temperature, its boiling point is above 298 K. Statement II is valid. Camphor has two chiral carbons, so it rotates plane-polarized light. This makes statement III invalid. Choice **B** is the best answer, but not with one hundred percent certainty.

10. **Choice C is the best answer.** Myrcene contains ten carbon atoms, so the addition of another isoprene unit would result in a product with fifteen carbons total. According to the first paragraph of the passage, terpenes having fifteen carbons are referred to as sesquiterpene, making choice **C** the best answer.

11. **Choice D is the best answer.** It is stated in the passage that carvone has a strong UV absorbance ($\varepsilon > 10,000$). Carvone has conjugation, which causes its intense UV absorbance. On the other hand, limin has no conjugation, so its UV absorbance is not as intense as that of carvone. This means that the UV absorbance for limin has an ε less than 10,000 (therefore, $\log e < \log 10^4 = 4$). The best answer is choice **D**. This question required some background information on UV spectroscopy. The minimum you should know is that π-bonds are UV active, and with conjugation, the intensity of the absorbance increases and the energy of the absorbance decreases.

12. **Choice C is the best answer.** A Diels-Alder reaction is a cyclization reaction that involves the addition of a diene to a dienophile (alkene) to form a cyclohexene product. Both limin and carvone are cyclohexene compounds, eliminating choices A and D, but carvone has a carbonyl group and isoprene contains only Cs and Hs. The best answer is limin, choice **C**. Choose **C** for a brighter smile when scoring like you did.

Passage III (Questions 13 - 18)   **Green Synthesis**

13. **Choice A is the best answer.** Reaction I is a Diels-Alder reaction. Diels-Alder reactions involve the reaction of a conjugated diene and a dienophile. Normally we think of the dienophile as an alkene, but the only requirement is that it has a π-bond. The alkyne meets this requirement, so it is a dienophile. The best answer is choice **A**. There is no nucleophilic substitution going on, so choices B and C are eliminated. There is no change in oxidation state, so the compound is not an oxidant or reductant, eliminating choice D.

14. **Choice A is the best answer.** Each of the answer choices is lacking two hydrogens from the formula of the final product, C_4H_8O. This means that hydrogenation converts the intermediate to the final product. The final product is an aldehyde and hydrogenation cannot convert a cyclic ether into a carbonyl, so choices C and D can be eliminated. Hydrogenation adds two hydrogen atoms to neighboring carbons. Because an aldehyde is generated, we know that one of the hydrogen atoms is added to the carbonyl carbon. The ring is cleaved, so hydrogenation must break the strained ring by adding a hydrogen to the carbonyl carbon and a hydrogen to the neighboring atom. In choice **A**, the hydrogen atoms are correctly displaced on the intermediate (CH_2-CH-CH_3) to form both aldehyde products (CH_2-CH_2-CH_3 and CH_3-CH-CH_3) when a single hydrogen is added to the alkyl chain. This is not the case in choice B (CH_2-CH_2-CH_2), so it is eliminated.

15. **Choice A is the best answer.** On the product of Reaction I, all of the functional groups are bonded to sp^2-hybridized carbons, so there are no stereocenters. This eliminates choices B and C. Based on the remaining answer choices, Reaction III must have formed a new stereocenter. The new stereocenter is located on the ring carbon with the methyl substituent. Hydrogenation can occur from above or below the ring, so the methyl is above the plane in fifty percent of the product mixture and below the plane in fifty percent of the mixture. Reaction III forms a racemic mixture. In Reaction II, the products have no chiral centers, so no new stereocenters were formed during the reaction. This eliminates choice D and makes choice **A** the best answer.

16. **Choice B is the best answer.** The basic tenet of green chemistry is to minimize waste and side products and maximize atom-economy. Atom-economy aims to get every atom added to the reaction container ending up in the product. Using a supercritical fluid as a solvent makes for easy recovery and reuse of the solvent. Reaction III uses supercritical CO_2, so choice A is valid and thus eliminated. Using protecting groups adds extra atoms to the solution that are not destined to be part of the product, so it violates the principle of atom-economy. Protecting groups are difficult to recycle without spending a great deal of solvent, so they do not fit the green chemistry philosophy. Choice **B** is an exception. If catalysts are part of the lab equipment, such as catalytic beads, then they are easily recovered and reused. This makes choice C in philosophical agreement with the principles of green chemistry. This eliminates choice C. It is stated in the passage that direct oxidation using oxygen fits in the philosophy of green chemistry, so choice D is eliminated. Choose **B** and be on top of your game.

17. **Choice D is the best answer.** Reaction III is described in the passage as hydrogenation, the term applied to a reaction that adds hydrogen atoms. This eliminates choice B. The gain of bonds to hydrogen, a less electronegative atom than carbon, is defined as reduction, so choice A is eliminated. Although it is not specified in the passage, when hydrogenating with a metal catalyst, the process adds the hydrogen atoms in a syn fashion, which means that the reaction is stereoselective. This eliminates choice C. Both carbons gain a hydrogen atom, so there is no regioselectivity. This makes choice **D** the best answer. Choose **D** for the sake of correctness.

---

18. **Choice C is the best answer.** The reaction is a Diels-Alder reaction, similar to Reaction I, except an alkene is serving as the dienophile, rather than an alkyne. Diels-Alder reactions form a new six-membered ring, which is observed in all of the choices. When the reaction involves a conjugated diene and an alkene, the product is a cyclohexene ring, so choices B and D are eliminated. To form choice B, the dienophile would have needed to be an alkyne, like Reaction I. The π-bond in the product is located between the two internal carbons of the original conjugated diene, so they should be found on the left side of the central ring. This makes choice **C** the best answer.

---

19. **Choice D is the best answer.** A concerted reaction occurs in one step. Given that a sigmatropic rearrangement involves just one molecule, if it occurs in just one step, then only one product can be formed. This eliminates choice C, because there are not multiple products, let alone cross products. The stereochemistry can be lost at centers that go from sp^3-hybridization to sp^2-hybridization and it can be gained at centers that go from sp^2-hybridization to sp^3-hybridization. Carbons that do not change hybridization cannot experience a change in stereochemistry. This means that there is no set rule about the complete retention or the complete inversion of all stereocenters. This eliminates choices A and B. The only possible answer is the one that supports no cross products being formed, because the molecule only reacts one way. Choice **D** is the best answer.

20. **Choice D is the best answer.** Step III converts a cyclic ketone into a phenol, so the product has aromaticity that the reactant does not. The gain of aromaticity drives the reaction, so choices A and C are eliminated. The conversion from a ketone to phenol shifts the π-bond from the carbonyl to the benzene ring, so it is the result of tautomerization, not reduction. The best answer is choice **D**.

21. **Choice A is the best answer.** The role of heat in any pericyclic reaction is to provide energy for the reactant to realign its orbitals to achieve the transition state. The best answer is choice **A**. Choice B should have been eliminated, because exothermic reactions generate heat, so no heat must be added to drive them. Heat is released when bonds are formed, sigma or pi, so choices C and D are eliminated.

22. **Choice B is the best answer.** The Cope rearrangement involves a 1,5-diene, so there are six carbons within the molecular orbital of the transition state. Choice A is eliminated because it has only four carbons. Choice C is eliminated because the orbitals show no π-overlap between adjacent carbons. Choice D is eliminated because there is no overlap across the complete cycle. The best overlap is choice **B**, where the sigma-bond is present on the left and the terminal orbitals are aligned correctly to form a pi-bond.

23. **Choice B is the best answer.** The oxygen is directly bonded to the benzene ring in the reactant, so it is phenylic and not benzylic. This eliminates choices A and C. The oxygen is also bonded to the carbon alpha to the alkene. This makes the carbon allylic, so choice **B** is the best answer.

24. **Choice A is the best answer.** The Claisen rearrangement converts an ether into a carbonyl, so the spectroscopic evidence must depict either the loss of an ether or gain of a carbonyl group. Aldehyde protons show a signal around 9.5 ppm in the ^{1}H NMR, so the formation of an aldehyde would in fact correspond with the appearance of a signal around 9.5 ppm. Choice **A** is the best answer. Infrared absorbances around 1700 cm^{-1} indicate the presence of a carbonyl group and broad infrared absorbances around 3400 cm^{-1} indicate the presence of an alcohol group. No hydroxyl group appears in either the reactant or product, so choice B is eliminated. The reaction would be supported by the appearance of an absorbance around 1700 cm^{-1} in infrared spectroscopy, not a disappearance, so choice C is eliminated. Signals between 5 and 6 ppm in the ^{1}H NMR correspond to vinylic hydrogens bonded to alkene carbons, which are present before and after the reaction, so choice D is eliminated.

25. **Choice C is the best answer.** The first reaction in the synthesis in Figure 2, Step I, involves oxygen. The Claisen rearrangement converts an ether into a ketone, so it involves oxygen. This eliminates choices B and D. According to the remaining choices, Step II is a Cope rearrangement. To determine the best answer, we must decide if the units of unsaturation decrease by one during the Claisen rearrangement or whether they remain constant at five. In all compounds in Figure 2, there are four π-bonds and one ring, so there are always five units of unsaturation. This makes choice **C** the best answer. You could also concluded that the units of unsaturation do not change by looking at the Claisen rearrangement in Figure 1, where there are two π-bonds in both the reactant and product.

26. **Choice D is the best answer.** Terpenes are composed of isoprene subunits which are made of five carbons. To be a terpene, a molecule must have a number of carbons that is divisible by five. Stearol has eighteen carbons, so it cannot be a terpene. The correct choice is **D**.

27. **Choice C is the best answer.** If the sesquiterpene were derived from a natural source (such as extraction or distillation from a plant), then any impurities would be naturally occurring impurities. If there were two enantiomers present, that would be explained by attack at a planar site from two sides. This can occur in nature although enzymes strongly favor synthesis of one enantiomer over another. Choices A and B are eliminated, because chiral impurities can occur in nature. The dead give-away would be an impurity with sixteen carbons. Terpenes have multiples of five for their carbon values. Because sixteen carbons is not possible, choice **C** is the best choice. A twenty-carbon impurity is a terpene, thus it is naturally occurring.

28. **Choice D is the best answer.** The carbon that is most susceptible to nucleophilic attack is the carbon with a leaving group attached. Carbon four, with the pyrophosphate leaving group, is the most electrophilic. Alkene carbons do act as electrophiles on occasion, but in this compound, carbon four is more electrophilic than an alkene carbon. The best answer is choice **D**.

29. **Choice A is the best answer.** Combining three acetyl coenzyme A molecules result in six carbons total. Isoprene units have only five carbons, so one carbon must be in a side product. Carbon dioxide contains only one carbon, so choice **A** is the best choice. Ethanol and acetic acid each contain two carbons and isopropanol contains three carbons. Choices B, C, and D are all eliminated.

30. **Choice C is the best answer.** A Diels-Alder reaction forms cyclohexene, so caryophyllene and citronellol cannot have been formed from a Diels-Alder reaction. This eliminates choices A and B. Both α-pinene and Vitamin A_1 have a cyclohexene moiety, so we must look closer. Diels-Alder reactions involve a diene and dienophile, so we can look at the compounds in a retrosynthetic fashion. In Vitamin A_1, the retro Diels-Alder reaction does not generate terpene fragments, so choice D is eliminated. Choice **C** is the best answer by default.

31. **Choice B is the best answer.** Bond a can be eliminated immediately, because the fragments formed from the break are three carbons and seven carbons. Bond c can be also eliminated immediately, because the fragments formed from the break are nine carbons and one carbon. These are not multiples of five, therefore the two fragments cannot be involved in the synthesis. This eliminates choices A and C. Bond b and Bond d when broken can leave a ten carbon molecule, so neither can be eliminated. The trouble with bond d is that the fragment to the right of the break cannot form a 2-methylbutene, because it loses the tertiary carbon. Choice D is eliminated. Isoprene units must be isopentenyl, not straight chain pentenyl, thus the break is not allowed. The two possible retro synthesis pathways are shown below, and only Bond b is involved. Choice **B** is the best answer.

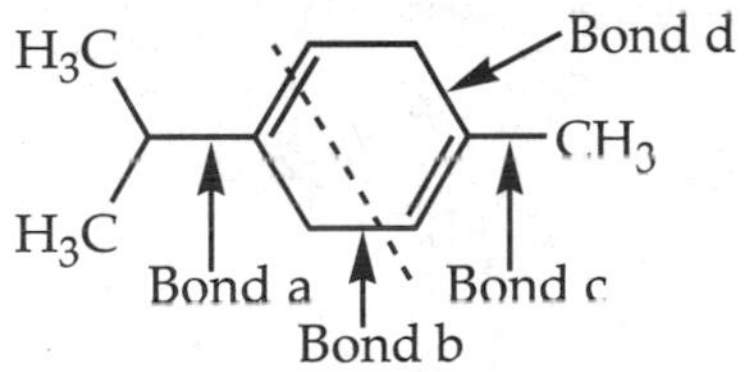

Bond b must have been formed to connect the isoprene units.

or

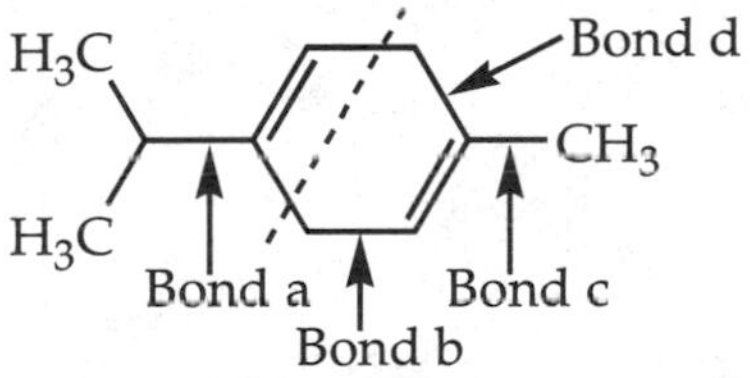

None of the labeled bonds were formed to connect the isoprene units.

Molecular Structure

Date Reviewed:	Text Questions to Repeat:

Score on Review Questions:	/25	Review Questions to Repeat:
Score on Practice Test:	/52	Practice Test Questions to Repeat:
Score on Phase III:	/33	Phase III Questions to Repeat:

Key Information for Molecular Structure Section:

Structure Elucidation

Date Reviewed:	Text Questions to Repeat:

Score on Review Questions:	/25	Review Questions to Repeat:
Score on Practice Test:	/52	Practice Test Questions to Repeat:
Score on Phase III:	/28	Phase III Questions to Repeat:

Key Information for Structure Elucidation Section:

Stereochemistry

Date Reviewed:	Text Questions to Repeat:	
Score on Review Questions:	/25	Review Questions to Repeat:
Score on Practice Test:	/52	Practice Test Questions to Repeat:
Score on Phase III:	/32	Phase III Questions to Repeat:

Key Information for Stereochemistry Section:

Hydrocarbons

Date Reviewed:	Text Questions to Repeat:	
Score on Review Questions:	/25	Review Questions to Repeat:
Score on Practice Test:	/52	Practice Test Questions to Repeat:
Score on Phase III:	/31	Phase III Questions to Repeat:

Key Information for Hydrocarbons Section:

Organic Chemistry Book 1 Index